An Introduction to XML and Web Technologies

CITY OF BRISTOL COLLEGE
COLLEGE GREEN LEARNING RESOURCE CENTRE
ST. GEORGES ROAD
BRISTOL BS1 5UA
TEL: (0117) 3122718

We work with leading authors to develop the
strongest educational materials in computer science,
bringing cutting-edge thinking and best
learning practice to a global market.

Under a range of well-known imprints, including
Addison Wesley, we craft high quality print and
electronic publications which help readers to understand
and apply their content, whether studying or at work.

To find out more about the complete range of our
publishing, please visit us on the World Wide Web at:
www.pearsoned.co.uk

An Introduction to XML and Web Technologies

Anders Møller and Michael I. Schwartzbach

ADDISON-WESLEY

Harlow, England • London • New York • Boston • San Francisco • Toronto • Sydney • Singapore • Hong Kong
Tokyo • Seoul • Taipei • New Delhi • Cape Town • Madrid • Mexico City • Amsterdam • Munich • Paris • Milan

Pearson Education Limited
Edinburgh Gate
Harlow
Essex CM20 2JE
England

and Associated Companies throughout the world

Visit us on the World Wide Web at:
www.pearsoned.co.uk

First published 2006

ISBN-13: 978-0-321-26966-9

British Library Cataloguing-in-Publication Data
A catalogue record for this book is available from the British Library

Library of Congress Cataloging-in-Publication Data

Møller, Anders.
    An introduction to XML and Web technologies / Anders Møller and Michael I. Schwartzbach.
       p. cm.
    Includes bibliographical references and index.
    ISBN 0-321-26966-7 (pbk.)
    1. XML (Document markup language) 2. World Wide Web I. Schwartzbach, Michael I.
  II. Title.
  QA76.76.H94M58 2006
  006.7′4–dc22   2005048117

10 9 8 7 6 5
15 14 13 12 11

Typeset in 10/12pt Times and Arial by 59
Printed and bound by Ashford Colour Press Ltd. Gosport, Hampshire

The publisher's policy is to use paper, manufactured from sustainable forests.

BRIEF CONTENTS

CONTENTS

FOREWORD

The Web has revolutionized the way the world accesses and shares information. Early on, the Web was a primarily passive, unidirectional platform for serving static HTML pages on demand to people. In no time, business users discovered that the Web not only enabled them to present unified views of products and services to customers around the clock, but that with some programming effort, the Web could support transactional customer-to-business interactions. Today, major corporations world wide increasingly depend on the Web for deploying widely distributed business-to-business processes both within and across the corporate boundary. These applications typically provide services that integrate data from Web and non-Web sources and coordinate interactions with existing business processes – a long way from one page-at-a-time HTML programming.

The Web's core technologies – HTML and HTTP – were strained to the limit by this rapid evolution. In response, an alphabet soup of new technologies emerged to do what HTML and HTTP could not. XML, XSLT, DTD, JSP, SOAP, WSDL, and UDDI are just a few of the myriad technologies that promise to make the Web application developer's job easier. Developers, however, sit uncomfortably between the promise and the reality of Web technologies. The XML and Web technologies at their disposal are immature. Many are just emerging from standardization, have few robust or interoperable implementations, and lack the application development environments available for more mature technologies.

In 'An Introduction to XML and Web Technologies', Anders Møller and Michael Schwartzbach expertly decipher the alphabet soup of Web technologies. They lucidly describe the technical features of each technology, compare closely related technologies, and show how to apply them in various application scenarios. In Part I, they describe XML's genesis from SGML to become the standard data format on the Web, compare various XML schema languages including DTD and XML Schema, contrast the XML query languages XPath, XSLT, and XQuery, and most importantly, explain how XML technologies can co-exist with general purpose programming languages. In Part II, they describe technologies for building stateful Web servers – Servlets and JSP – as well as the standards for defining, publishing, and connecting to Web services.

Anders and Michael hold their readers in high regard. They write in a clear and plain-spoken voice that disguises their deep understanding of their subject. Each carefully crafted example teaches several concepts at once, and when put together, the examples yield non-trivial (and entertaining!) results. Anders and Michael also describe the cutting-edge research that will effect the way we program for the Web in the future, which is invaluable to the reader who wants to develop a deep and lasting understanding of these technologies.

This book is a genuine pleasure to read – I learned a lot, and I learned it fast! I hope that Anders and Michael continue to track the Web's rapid changes and provide us with more valuable information in future editions.

Mary Fernández
AT&T Labs Research

PREFACE

XML and Web Technologies

In the early 1990s, the World Wide Web was defined by a triumvirate consisting of the HTML language for writing hypertext documents, the HTTP communication protocol, and the URL notation for addressing resources. Today, new Web technologies are being developed and deployed at amazing rates, building on top of the early foundations. This book offers a comprehensive introduction to the area.

There are two main threads of development, corresponding to the two parts of this book. *XML technologies* generalize the notion of data on the Web from hypertext documents to arbitrary data, including those that have traditionally been the realm of databases. In this book we cover the basic XML technology and the supporting technologies of XPath, DTD, XML Schema, DSD2, RELAX NG, XSLT, XQuery, DOM, JDOM, JAXB, SAX, STX, XDuce, and XACT. *Web technologies* build on top of the HTTP protocol to provide richer languages for constructing applications and services. In this book we cover the basic HTTP protocol and the increasingly abstract technologies of Servlets, JSP, JWIG, WSDL, SOAP, and UDDI.

These are, for better or worse, core technologies that will exist for many years or provide the foundation for future developments.

Aims of This Book

The topics covered by this book are, of course, all richly described in free online standards documents, totaling several thousand pages, but those are wholly unsuited for a self-contained course. This book is unique in providing a coherent overview of the most important XML and Web technologies. It goes into great detail but still aims for conciseness, thereby enabling the reader to see the big picture and yet obtain practical experience with the technologies and supporting tools.

The book also contains critical analyses and discussions of the technologies, in contrast to standards documents and technical manuals, which mainly present and exemplify features. It also provides a uniform terminology that is familiar to readers with a standard computer science background.

The book describes the newest technologies, including XML 1.1, XPath 2.0, XSLT 2.0, XQuery 1.0, JDOM 1.0, SAX2, JAXB 1.0, STX 1.0, HTTP/1.1, Java Servlet 2.4, JSP 2.0, JSTL 1.1, SOAP 1.2, WSDL 2.0, and UDDI 3.0. It focuses on concepts and technologies, rather than on vendor-specific tools. Moreover, the book presents selected research projects – DSD2, RELAX NG, STX, XDuce, XACT, and JWIG – that may influence future technologies.

How to Use This Book

The intended audience of this book includes computer science students, computer professionals, and researchers that want an overview of the area. Preliminary versions of this book have been used several times for undergraduate courses at the University of Aarhus and at the IT University of Copenhagen, and have been the basis for numerous industrial courses. The book can be the complete curriculum for an XML/Web course, or it may be used as a supplement for database or programming courses.

Each chapter contains carefully selected links to the essential online resources, references to further reading, and exercises that help the readers test their understanding and gain familiarity and practical experience with the most important technical specifications and tools.

Chapter 1 contains survivor's guides to HTML and CSS, and motivates the need for XML. It also covers technical issues related to Web publication, such as URLs, URNs, URIs, and Unicode. Moreover, this chapter briefly introduces the workings of the World Wide Web Consortium, which develops many of the technologies covered by the book. In Chapter 2, we explain the XML notation, its dual nature as a textual format and a tree structure, and the namespace mechanism. Chapter 3 covers the XPath language, which is used in several other languages for pointing into XML documents and much more. Chapter 4 describes the use of schema languages. It explains the languages DTD and XML Schema, and also two less widely known alternatives, DSD2 and RELAX NG, and compares the languages. Additionally, this chapter contains an introduction to the notion of regular expressions, which is commonly used in schema languages. In Chapters 5 and 6, we show how the XSLT and XQuery languages can be used to define transformations between XML languages, and we provide a thorough comparison between the two. XSLT is mainly targeted at stylesheet transformations for presenting XML data, whereas XQuery is designed primarily for database-like queries. Chapter 7 shows how to work with XML in programming languages using DOM, JDOM, JAXB, SAX, and STX. As a running example, we develop an XML-based language for recipe collections and show how the various technologies become useful.

Chapter 8 contains an introduction to the HTTP protocol and shows how to program HTTP servers and clients. Chapter 9 describes the Servlet platform, which is a convenient API that builds upon HTTP. Closely related technologies are JSP and JSTL, which are the topics of Chapter 10. Chapter 11 explains the basic technologies related to Web services that communicate XML data on the Web, in particular the WSDL, SOAP, and UDDI initiatives. Finally, Chapter 12 collects the essential knowledge from the other chapters and applies it to a larger project: development of an interactive Web service, *The Web of Jokes*, for sharing jokes on the Web.

All chapters contain numerous 'gold nuggets' showing concrete examples of how typical tasks can be solved with the technologies being described.

The chapter dependencies may be illustrated by the following diagram:

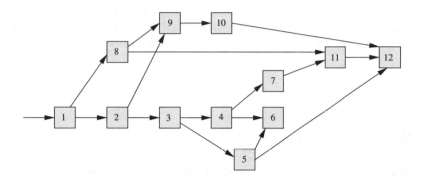

Chapters 7, 8, 9, 10, 11, and 12 assume a basic knowledge of the Java programming language. This language is natural to use when illustrating Web technologies because of its platform independence and native support for Unicode and migration of data and code, and furthermore, a majority of the freely available tools that exist for XML and Web development are based on Java. Except from this prerequisite, the book is self-contained.

Some sections of this book are intended for advanced studies and may safely be skipped by readers who only need to obtain basic familiarity with the presented technologies. These sections, marked with the symbol ★, contain further discussions and presentations of advanced features and research topics.

The Companion Web Site

The book has a companion Web site located at

```
http://www.brics.dk/ixwt/
```

This site contains additional material for teachers and students: an extensive collection of slides, examples from the book, additional projects, and multiple choice tests for each topic. Qualified instructors may obtain solutions to the exercises and the PowerPoint sources for the slides. Moreover, many exercises in the book refer to online data. We use *EX* as an abbreviation of the URL http://www.brics.dk/ixwt/exercises/.

A preliminary version of the online material has been continually updated since March 2000 and has been visited by more than 300,000 people (counted as unique IP numbers).

Acknowledgements

Thanks to Claus Brabrand, Mary Fernández, Thomas Hildebrandt, Martin Mosegaard Jensen, Lars Michael Kristensen, Henning Niss, Peter Thiemann, Phil Wadler, and the anonymous reviewers for detailed comments to the contents of this book. The participants of several XML and Web courses at the University of Aarhus and the IT University of Copenhagen have also contributed to structuring and proofreading the presented material. Thanks to the people from Pearson Education: to Sami Taalas and Kate Brewin for persuading us to enter into the project, and to Owen Knight, Mary Lince, Karen McLaren Simon Plumtree, and Simon Turner for guiding us through the process.

Anders Møller
Michael I. Schwartzbach

Publisher's Acknowledgements

Screen shots on pages 14 and 343 used with permission from Google Inc. Google™ is a trademark of Google Inc.

PART I
XML TECHNOLOGIES

1

HTML AND WEB PAGES

Objectives

In this chapter, you will learn:

- The history of HTML

- URLs and related schemes

- Survivor's guides to HTML and CSS

- Limitations of HTML

- An introduction to The World Wide Web Consortium (W3C)

- Unicode representations

1.1   Hypertext and Markup Languages

The origins of XML are intertwined with those of HTML. To fully appreciate the many decisions influencing the current design of XML, it is beneficial first to take a historical view.

HTML is an acronym for *Hyper-Text Markup Language*, and the HTML language really is a combination of the independent concepts of *hypertext* and *markup language*.

Hypertext is a concept that predates the World Wide Web by many years. It describes information as collections of documents connected by *hyperlinks*. Vannevar Bush is often credited with first inventing the hypertext mechanism in 1945 in a hypothetical system called Memex, which provided an automated desk in which documents were stored on microfilm and referenced by code numbers. Sometimes the intellectual origins of hypertext are even traced back to a philosophical treatise from 1934 by Paul Otlet. In a computer science context, the first working hypertext system, and indeed the phrase *hypertext* itself, was introduced by Ted Nelson in 1968. This has been an active and fruitful research area ever since, evolving into the broader concept of *hypermedia*, which goes beyond text documents to encompass all kinds of media files connected by general classes of links.

Markup languages provide a notation for enriching text documents with formal structure and have a similar long history. The idea is credited to Charles F. Goldfarb who in 1970 motivated the need for such notations and described a simple system called INTIME. The culmination of this line of research was the *Standard Generalized Markup Language (SGML)*, which was standardized in 1986. The SGML system introduced the now ubiquitous angle brackets for expressing structure and also the *Document Type Definition (DTD)* language for defining syntax of specific SGML languages. SGML was adopted by large organizations generating huge amounts of documents (such as the European Union and the US Department of Defense) and is now widely applied to describe documents from such diverse application domains as financial records, legal texts, movie scripts, medical records, and patent filings.

To give a flavor of SGML, consider the following simple SGML document:

```
<!DOCTYPE greeting [
  <!ELEMENT greeting (#PCDATA)>
  <!ATTLIST greeting style (big|small) "small">
  <!ENTITY hi "Hello">
]>
<greeting style="big"> &hi; world! </greeting>
```

The actual contents, which is the last line in this example, consists of a *start tag* (`<greeting style="big">`), some text, and an *end tag* (`</greeting>`). Together, this forms an *element* named `greeting`. Generally, tags provide logical structure to the textual contents in the document. The start tag contains an *attribute* named `style` with value `big`. The `DOCTYPE` part, consisting of the first five lines, is a DTD schema describing the allowed document structure. It also defines `&hi;` as a macro that expands to the text `Hello`, and the contents of the document is thus the text `Hello world` structured inside a `greeting` element. The `ELEMENT` part describes the allowed contents of a `greeting` element, which in this case is just plain text. The `ATTLIST` part tells that the `greeting` element must have a `style` attribute with possible values `big` and `small` of which the latter is the default. XML has inherited much of its terminology from SGML as we shall see in Chapter 2.

1.2 The History of HTML

The origins of the World Wide Web can be traced back to 1989 when Tim Berners-Lee proposed to organize information at the CERN physics laboratory using a simple global hypermedia system. Research projects at CERN generated huge amounts of data that were previously accessed by international participants through primitive mechanisms like file transfers using the FTP protocol. Also, the collection of data was poorly organized and extraction of information was hampered by the variety of file formats being used.

In 1990, Tim Berners-Lee developed the infrastructure for the World Wide Web. The main constituents were the HTTP protocol, the URL concept, and the HTML language,

1992	HTML 1.0	first definition
1993	HTML+	some physical layout, forms, and tables
1994	HTML 2.0	standard containing the best HTML+ features
1994	HTML 3.0	an extension of HTML+ submitted as a draft standard
1995		Netscape-specific non-standard HTML appears
1996		competing Netscape and Internet Explorer versions of HTML
1996	HTML 3.2	standard based on current practices
1997	HTML 4.0	separates structure and presentation with stylesheets
1999	HTML 4.01	slight modifications only
2000	XHTML 1.0	XML version of HTML 4.01
2001	XHTML 1.1	modularization to allow different subsets
2002	XHTML 2.0	simplifying and generalizing several tags

Figure 1.1 Different versions of HTML.

implemented through the first Web server and browser. HTTP is a high-level protocol for transmitting documents on the Internet, and the URL concept provides means for locating such documents as files on specific servers. HTML was designed as a combination of the well-known concepts of hypertext and markup languages, being an SGML language for defining hypertext documents with simple text formatting and links to other documents and files.

HTML 1.0 was published in 1992 (see the overview in Figure 1.1). Compared to the later versions, it is very simple and has an almost purist design. The markup tags are meant to describe the *logical* structure of documents, and browsers are free to interpret those tags as they please, depending on, for example, their graphical capabilities. In fact, the essential information in a document should still be available even if the browser chooses to ignore the markup completely. For example, the `title` tag describes the document title but offers no opinion about the color, font, or size in which it should be displayed. Similarly, the `ul` and `li` tags describe lists of items, but leave the choice of bullets and indentations undefined. With this language design, a browser with true color and high-resolution capabilities will be able to render documents in high quality, whereas a browser that operates on a black-and-white low-resolution screen can still make them intelligible.

Thus, the text formatting capabilities of early HTML were not very advanced but offered other advantages. In particular, the markup emphasized the separation between logical structure and physical layout of documents, while traditional document formats allowed the author precisely to control the layout of the resulting documents, requiring all details like font descriptions to be stored with the contents. In comparison, HTML documents are slim because such details are not part of the representation. This can be illustrated by creating various documents containing only the text 'Hello World' and comparing the sizes of the resulting files:

Postscript	11,274 bytes
PDF	4,915 bytes
MS Word	19,456 bytes
HTML	28 bytes

This is, of course, an extreme example, but generally HTML documents are seen to be significantly smaller than other document formats. The compactness lowers network traffic and saves space on servers, two issues that were, of course, more pressing in 1992 than today. Another advantage is that HTML documents are more robust and independent of particular versions of proprietary tools; they may, in fact, be written and modified with any raw-text editor.

The World Wide Web was an immediate success at CERN and quickly Web servers were installed at unrelated institutions as well, and numerous alternative implementations of browsers and servers cropped up. As the base of users grew exponentially, the purist ideas behind HTML came under pressure because of the limited layout control that was offered. Authors were not satisfied with the h2 tag to indicate that a text should appear as a header at level two, but wanted to express that the text should be centered and written in Times Roman font in 28pt.

This issue came to a point when marketing departments in companies started making early homepages that were little more than brochures on the Web. They naturally wanted strict control of the layout and when HTML failed to provide this, they resorted to publishing GIF images containing all the contents. Considering succinctness and flexibility, this is probably the worst document format imaginable. The HTML designers quickly responded by adding some tags for controlling the physical layout, such as b for bold style and i for italics style. In comparison, the existing em tag indicates that the text should be emphasized by *some* means to be decided by the browser.

Other major influences of HTML came about as the CERN-based programmers of the early Mosaic browser ventured to California and started the Netscape Corporation developing a commercial Web implementation. As a company, Netscape was, of course, very attentive to the wishes of customers and rapidly their version of HTML diverged from the standard. Things became even more heated when Microsoft entered the market with their Internet Explorer browser, leading to a period where the two companies developed competing non-standard versions of HTML. This made it difficult for developers to produce HTML documents that worked with all major browsers.

Fortunately, common sense prevailed and in 1996 HTML 3.2 was defined by W3C as a new standard based on the best of current practices. In a process of mutual disarmament, Netscape traded its infamous blink tag for Internet Explorer's gaudy marquee tag, neither of which became a part of HTML even though they are both still supported by the respective browsers.

HTML 3.2 was rife with physical layout tags and, in particular, the font tag gave complete control over colors, fonts, and sizes. When large Web sites with hundreds or thousands of documents were to be maintained with a uniform layout, it quickly became apparent that this was an impractical technology. If an organization defined a common look for all its Web documents, then every author had to follow a set of font guidelines that were only informally documented. Even if such a level of consistency could be obtained, then it would almost be inevitable that a decision would materialize to change this common look, requiring tedious editing of all document files.

These scenarios motivated the invention of Cascading Style Sheets (CSS), a language that allows the physical layout of an HTML document to be described in a separate file. This separation of concerns solves the above problems, since all Web documents may use the same stylesheet, which can then be updated with immediate and universal effect. We describe CSS in Section 1.5.

Stylesheets were first used with HTML 4.0, which was standardized in 1997, and HTML 4.01 from 1999 introduced only slight modifications. The only real development since then is the migration in 2000 to the XML version, called XHTML 1.0, which we describe in the next chapter.

1.3   URLs, URIs, URNs, and IRIs

HTML documents and other Web resources are denoted by *Uniform Resource Locators (URLs)*, which typically have a familiar structure:

```
http://www.w3.org/TR/html4/
```

This URL consists of a *scheme* (`http`, which identifies the HTTP communication protocol), a *server* (`www.w3.org`, the machine where the resource is located), and a *path* (`TR/html4/`, typically corresponding to a file on the server). The HTTP protocol and the format of HTTP URLs will be covered in detail in Chapter 8.

However, URLs are just a subset of the more general concept of *Uniform Resource Identifiers (URIs)*, which are meant to describe all points in the information space, even those that do not have a physical presence. The actual syntax of URIs is very permissive and includes many other schemes besides `http`, such as `ftp`, `file`, `mailto`, `imap`, or `https` (some of which are mentioned further in Chapter 8). The official register of schemes is maintained by The Internet Assigned Numbers Authority (IANA).

In fact, a general URI essentially has the form

```
scheme:scheme-specific-part
```

so everything following the first colon depends entirely on the choice of the scheme. However, all schemes satisfy certain informal rules: the slash character (`/`) always implies a hierarchical structure (as in directory paths on operating systems), a question mark (`?`) separates *query strings* from queryable resources, as described in Chapter 8, and the hash character (`#`) is reserved as a delimiter separating a URI from a *fragment identifier* (described below). Special symbols are escaped using the notation `%NN` with character codes written in hexadecimal; and only US-ASCII characters are permitted.

The concept of a *relative* URI is used to specify a URI that should be resolved relatively to a *base* URI. For example, in an HTML document with URI

```
http://www.w3.org/TR/html4/
```

the relative URI

```
sgml/dtd.html
```

is resolved to mean the absolute URI

```
http://www.w3.org/TR/html4/sgml/dtd.html
```

For HTML documents, the `base` tag can be used to specify a base URI different from the document URI.

A fragment of a resource can be identified by appending a # character and a fragment identifier to a URI:

```
http://www.w3.org/TR/html4/#minitoc
```

This reference identifies the fragment named `minitoc` in the resource located at `http://www.w3.org/TR/html4/`.

A special class of URIs, called *Uniform Resource Names (URNs)*, is defined by the `urn` scheme. A URN is a pointer to a resource, but without a reference to a particular location. As an example, the URN

```
urn:isbn:0-471-94128-X
```

denotes a particular book title identified by an ISBN number, which is clearly a specific piece of information that does not have a physical location on the Web. In contrast, a URL specifies the location of a resource.

There has been great confusion about the terms URL, URI, and URN. One reason for this is that URNs are not widely used, and 'URI' and 'URL' are often used interchangeably. In the description above, we apply what is called the *contemporary* view on this issue.

As mentioned above, the syntax for URIs is restricted to use US-ASCII characters, which precludes the use of international characters. To remedy this shortcoming, the concept of *Internationalized Resource Identifiers (IRIs)* is being developed. An IRI is defined to be a string that maps to a URI when subjected to a specific encoding function. Unfortunately, this function is rather complicated, since different encoding schemes currently are used for domain names and other parts of the URI string. For example, the IRI

```
http://www.blåbærgrød.dk/blåbærgrød.html
```

corresponds to the following URI:

```
http://www.xn--blbrgrd-fxak7p.dk/bl%E5b%E6rgr%F8d.html
```

The intention is that tools perform this encoding behind the scenes and then work with the encoded URIs. Since the encoding scheme allows arbitrary subsets of characters to be encoded, there are now combinatorially many IRIs that are displayed the same by complying browsers, which is a potential security problem since clients can no longer be sure which server their browser will contact.

1.4   Survivor's Guide to HTML

HTML is a large language, but it is easy to provide a small survivor's guide covering the essential elements used in this book. The overall structure of an HTML document is as follows:

```
<html>
  <head>
    <title>The Title of the Document</title>
  </head>
  <body bgcolor="white">
    ...
  </body>
</html>
```

In this example, html, head, title, and body are tag *names*, which occur in *start tags* like <head> and *end tags* like </head>. Also, bgcolor is an *attribute name*, whose corresponding *attribute value* is white.

The title text is the one that appears in the browser window frame. The body part contains the contents of the document, which is plain text adorned with various text formatting markup tags.

Simple Formatting

HTML has two basic content models: *inline* describes character level elements and text strings, while *block* describes contents like paragraphs, lists, and forms. These models impose various restrictions in how the HTML tags may be mixed among each other: for example, a b tag may not contain a form tag. In the following, we do not describe these restrictions but refer the reader to the HTML specification.

Headers at different levels can be specified using the tags h1 through to h6. Note that it is specific to the given browser exactly how a header is distinguished typographically from the plain text.

Text styles can be chosen using the b tag for boldface, the i tag for italics style, and the tt tag for fixed-width font. Line breaks are indicated by the br tag and new paragraphs by the p tag. More specialized text styles can be chosen using the general font tag. As an example, consider the following tiny HTML document:

```
<html>
  <head>
    <title>Good Advice</title>
  </head>
  <body>
    <h1>Good Advice for Everyday Life</h1>
    <h2>For UNIX programmers</h2>
    <b>Never</b> type: <p><tt>rm -rf /*</tt><p> on your computer.
    <h2>For Nuclear Scientists</h2>
    <b>Never</b> press the
    <i>Big <font color="red">Red</font> Button</i>.
  </body>
</html>
```

This document is rendered in the Mozilla browser as follows:

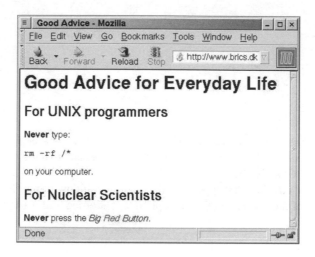

The hr tag draws a horizontal line across the rendered page. Preformatted text, like program listings where whitespace is significant, may be presented using the pre tag. Unordered lists are indicated by the ul tag, where each item is initiated by the li tag; numbered lists are similarly indicated by the ol tag. An example illustrating these possibilities:

```
<html>
  <head>
    <title>Things To Do</title>
  </head>
  <body>
    <ol>
      <li>Feed the cat.
      <li>Try out the shell command:
      <pre>foreach x ( ls )
  cat $x | tr "aeiouy" "x" > $x
end</pre>
      <li>Buy ticket for Timbuktu.
    </ol>
  </body>
</html>
```

Note that the contents of the pre tag are not indented, since the extra whitespace would appear in the output. It is generally a source of confusion whether whitespace in a markup document is part of the intended output or simply a visual formatting of the document itself (see Section 2.4). This document is rendered as follows:

```
1. Feed the cat.
2. Try out the shell command:

   foreach x ( `ls` )
     cat $x | tr "aeiouy" "x" > $x
   end

3. Buy ticket for Timbuktu.
```

Hyperlinks

Hyperlinks that shall appear as clickable links are inserted using the a tag, in which the href attribute indicates the URL of the target file. Images are inserted using the img tag, in which the src attribute indicates the URL of the target image. Note that images are in most browsers automatically inlined into the rendered page, whereas the links to other documents must be explicitly clicked in order to be activated. When a link is activated, the browser content is replaced by the rendering of the new document. It is possible to request the browser to scroll down into the new document if the link contains a suffix of the form #foo (a fragment identifier, as explained earlier) and the new document contains a corresponding anchor of the form <a name="foo">...</a>. Thus, the source document

```
<html>
  <head>
    <title>Source Document</title>
  </head>
  <body>
    <a href="target.html#danger">Better look here</a>.
  </body>
</html>
```

and the corresponding target document

```
<html>
  <head>
    <title>Target Document</title>
  </head>
  <body>
    ...
    <a name="danger"></a>
    <h2>Chapter 17: Dangerous Shell Commands</h2>
    Never execute a shell command that inadvertently changes
    all vowels to the character 'x'.
    ...
  </body>
</html>
```

are rendered as follows:

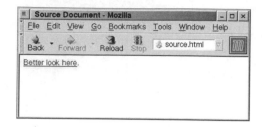 

Tables

A simple table can be made as follows:

```
<table border="1">
  <tr>
    <td>PostScript</td>
    <td align="right">11,274 bytes</td>
  </tr>
  <tr>
    <td>PDF</td>
    <td align="right">4,915 bytes</td>
  </tr>
  <tr>
    <td>MS Word</td>
    <td align="right">19,456 bytes</td>
  </tr>
  <tr>
    <td>HTML</td>
    <td align="right">28 bytes</td>
  </tr>
</table>
```

The `table` tags surround a sequence of `tr` rows, each of which contains `td` table data, and the author may specify attributes like `border`, `width`, `align`, and `valign` for tuning the layout. The above table is rendered as follows:

PostScript	11,274 bytes
PDF	4,915 bytes
MS Word	19,456 bytes
HTML	28 bytes

Another use for tables is to position parts of the document on the resulting page. An example is the following HTML fragment specifying four navigation arrows built from hyperlinks that surround images:

```
<table width="100%">
  <tr>
    <td align="left">
      <a href="index.html"><img src="home.gif" border="0"></a>
      <a href="info.html"><img src="info.gif" border="0"></a>
    </td>
    <td align="right">
      <a href="hyperlinks.html"><img src="left.gif" border="0"></a>
      <a href="htmlsurvivor.html"><img src="right.gif" border="0"></a>
    </td>
  </tr>
</table>
<h1>Using Tables</h1>
...
```

The `align` attributes are used to position the two pairs of buttons at the sides of the page:

Forms

A final important feature of HTML is the ability to invoke remote services using *fill-out forms*. This is a very simple mechanism, in which the browser accepts user input that is then sent to some server, which in turn runs a program that responds with a new HTML document. As a simple example, the following HTML fragment accesses the Google search engine:

```
<form method="get" action="http://www.google.com/search">
  <input type="text" name="q">
  <input type="submit" name="btnG" value="Google Search">
</form>
```

This HTML form was constructed by viewing the source of the front page of the Google site (go to `http://www.google.com/` and click 'View Source' in the 'View' menu of the browser) and observing the URL of the search service (in this case `http://www.google.`

com/search) and the name of the search string that must be supplied (which is q). The btnG field is always sent with the value Google Search, which tells the Google program which button the client has pressed. The resulting Google interface is rendered as follows:

The details of the underlying HTTP protocol will be presented in Chapter 8.

There are several different GUI tags that collect user input. Common to them all is that they always produce pairs of names and values, both of which are strings. The following HTML fragment shows all the different versions:

```html
<input name="foo" type="text" size="20">
<hr>
<input name="bar" type="radio" value="s">Small
<input name="bar" type="radio" value="m">Medium
<input name="bar" type="radio" value="l">Large
<hr>
<input name="baz" type="checkbox" value="c">Cheese
<input name="baz" type="checkbox" value="p">Pepperoni
<input name="baz" type="checkbox" value="a">Anchovies
<hr>
<select name="bar">
  <option value="s">Small
  <option value="m">Medium
  <option value="l">Large
</select>
<hr>
<select name="baz" multiple>
  <option value="c">Cheese
  <option value="p">Pepperoni
  <option value="a">Anchovies
</select>
<hr>
<textarea name="foo" rows="5" cols="20">
Write something here...
</textarea>
<hr>
<input name="foo" type="password" value="tomato">
<hr>
<input name="foo" type="file">
<hr>
<input name="foo" type="hidden" value="you can't see this">
<hr>
<input name="qux" type="image" src="Denmark.gif">
<hr>
<input type="submit" value="Submit this form">
<hr>
<input type="reset" value="Reset this form">
```

(If you have never before encountered the terms foo, bar, and baz, then you should read the memo at `http://www.ietf.org/rfc/rfc3092.txt`.) The `input` tag of type `text` accepts a single text string, which is named `foo`. The `input` tags of type `radio` allow a choice between three predefined values (`s`, `m`, `l`), and the chosen value is named `bar`. The `input` tags of type `checkbox` allows the choice of a subset of the specified values (`c`, `p`, `a`), and all the chosen values are named `baz`. The `select` tag is similar to the radio buttons, since it also allows a choice between three values. The `select` variant with a `multiple` attribute is similar to the `checkbox` buttons, since it allows a choice of up to three values. The `textarea` tag is similar to the `input` tag of type `text`, except that the text may run over several lines. The `input` tags of type `password` is similar to that of type `text`, except that the text being entered is masked. The `input` tag of type `file` allows the contents of a file to be uploaded to the server. The `input` tag of type `hidden` cannot be changed by the client, and is used to retain information between interactions (see Section 8.2). The `input` tag of type `image` expects the given image to be clicked by the client, and sends the chosen coordinates as two values named `qux.x` and `qux.y`. The `input` tag of type `submit` is a button that initiates the invocation of the remote server, and the `input` tag of type `reset` renders the form from scratch. This collection of GUI tags is rendered as follows:

The name–value pairs are collected in the order of occurrence in the HTML document as explained in full detail in Section 8.1.1. Multiple pairs with the same name are possible.

1.5   Survivor's Guide to CSS

An HTML page has both *logical structure* and *physical layout*. Consider the following example of an HTML page showing some phone numbers:

Here, the logical structure includes the following information:

- the page starts with a header;

- the entries are written in a list; and

- numbers are emphasized.

The physical layout can be described as follows:

- headers are centered, huge and gray;

- lists have square bullets; and

- emphasis is rendered in boldface italics.

CSS separates logical structure from *physical layout*.

Cascading Style Sheets (CSS) allow us to specify these two aspects in separate documents: the markup in the HTML document describes only logical structure, and the physical layout is described using CSS.

The essential concepts in CSS are *selectors* and *properties*, which have also influenced later XML technologies.

Properties describe the physical layout of specific HTML tags. There are in all 51 properties whose values may be defined, even though only some properties will be relevant for a particular tag. Examples of properties and possible values are shown in Figure 1.2.

A CSS stylesheet associates the chosen property values to specific HTML tags. A simple case looks like this:

```
b {color: red; font-size: 12pt}
i {color: green}
```

color	red, yellow, rgb(212,120,20)
font-style	normal, italics, oblique
font-size	12pt, larger, 150%, 1.5em
text-align	left, right, center, justify
line-height	normal, 1.2em, 120%
display	block, inline, list-item, none

Figure 1.2 Examples of CSS properties and values.

This specifies that b tags are rendered in red and in 12pt, whereas i tags are rendered in green. The standard rendering of HTML documents simply corresponds to a browser-specific default stylesheet, where b tags are rendered in boldface and i tags in italics.

It is possible to associate different property values to an HTML tag depending on its *context*, which consists of the HTML tags that surround it in the document. Thus, the following more advanced stylesheet specifies that b tags inside table tags (perhaps deeply nested) are red, whereas b tags inside form tags are yellow:

```
table b {color: red; font-size: 12pt}
form b {color: yellow; font-size: 12pt}
i {color: green}
```

The table and form tags could appear at any level around the b tag, they are not required to immediately surround it. The context may be arbitrarily long, thus the following stylesheet specifies a very particular condition for coloring the text orange:

```
html body table tr td form b {color: orange}
```

The whole sequence in front of the defined property values is known as a *selector*.

If the plain context is not sufficiently advanced, then the HTML tags may be annotated with class attributes, which pick out specific selectors in the stylesheet. Thus, the stylesheet:

```
b.huge {font-size: 36pt}
```

applies to tags of the form <b class="huge">. For the a tag, it is possible to use four *pseudo-classes* named

```
a:link
a:hover
a:active
a:visited
```

which correspond to different states of an HTML link.

In general, several selectors may apply to a given HTML tag, which raises the question of which set of property values will then be chosen. CSS solves this problem by introducing a complicated notion of *specificity*, defining an order on all selectors. It can be informally summarized as 'the most complicated selector wins'.

To illustrate how stylesheets work in full generality, we consider this HTML document with an inlined stylesheet:

```
<html>
  <head>
    <style type="text/css">
      b {color: red;}
      b b {color: blue;}
      b.foo {color: green;}
      b b.foo {color: yellow;}
      b.bar {color: maroon;}
    </style>
    <title>CSS Test</title>
  </head>
  <body>
    <b class=foo>Hey!</b>
    <b>Wow!
      <b>Amazing!</b>
      <b class=foo>Impressive!</b>
      <b class=bar>k00l!</b>
      <i>Fantastic!</i>
    </b>
  </body>
</html>
```

With which colors will the different words be rendered? The word Hey! is clearly green, since its surrounding start and end tag directly match the selector b.foo and there is no better match. The word Wow! is red, since its tag matches only the simplest selector. The word Amazing! is blue, since the selector b b applies. The word Impressive! is yellow, since the selector b b.foo is a more specific match than b.foo. The word k00l! is maroon, since b.bar is the only match.

Finally, the word Fantastic! is red, which requires some more explanation. As suggested by their name, stylesheets work in a *cascading* manner. This means that once the value of a property has been defined for an occurrence of a tag, that value will hold for all the tags that it surrounds unless they themselves define a new value. Thus, the i tag inherits the color red from its surrounding b tag, since the default stylesheet does not specify colors for i tags.

The stylesheet shown above could also be placed in a separate file:

```
b {color: red;}
b b {color: blue;}
b.foo {color: green;}
b b.foo {color: yellow;}
b.bar {color: maroon;}
```

Assuming this stylesheet file is located at the URI `bolds.css`, the HTML document could specify the connection using a link:

```
<head>
  <link href="bolds.css" rel="stylesheet" type="text/css">
  <title>CSS Test</title>
</head>
```

The CSS properties are powerful enough to change the presentation of any HTML tag into virtually any other. In particular, a stylesheet author may invent new tags. This is done by exploiting the HTML tags `div` and `span`, which have no layout properties of their own except that `div` breaks paragraphs. Also, `span` tags are allowed in the inline content model, while `div` is allowed in the block content model. If an author dreams up a new HTML tag `redcenter` which centers text and colors it red, then that can for all practical purposes be obtained by the stylesheet definition

```
div.redcenter {color:red; display:block; text-align:center;}
```

and invoked as `<div class="redcenter">`. We will later see that XML provides a more general solution to this.

Returning to the example of phone numbers, we can define the physical layout in a file called `style.css` with the contents

```
h1 { color: #888; font: 50px/50px "Impact"; text-align: center; }
ul { list-style-type: square; }
em { font-style: italic; font-weight: bold; }
```

and apply this to our logical layout:

```
<html>
  <head>
    <title>Phone Numbers</title>
    <link href="style.css" rel="stylesheet" type="text/css">
  </head>
  <body>
    <h1>Phone Numbers</h1>
    <ul>
      <li>John Doe, <em>(202) 555-1414</em>
      <li>Jane Dow, <em>(202) 555-9132</em>
      <li>Jack Doe, <em>(212) 555-1742</em>
    </ul>
  </body>
</html>
```

Clearly, the same stylesheet may be applied to many documents, and their common layout may then be changed simultaneously by editing that single CSS file.

1.6   Syntax and Validation

Many HTML authors struggle with Web pages that appear differently in various browsers. This is typically blamed on inconsistencies in implementations, but often the blame rests with the author.

There are indeed many different browsers, even though a few obviously dominate. The current observed market shares show Internet Explorer at around 67%, the Netscape, Mozilla, and Firefox family at around 25%, Opera clocking in at 2%, and more than 200 lesser known browsers sharing the rest. However, the Internet Explorer figure actually covers more than 100 different programs, when combinations of different releases and platforms are considered.

Well-written Web pages should work well on all reasonably new browsers, but authors still experience problems. Even professional authors sometimes make the mistake of only testing their pages on the single browser that is installed on their computer. When customers complain about problems with rendering a page in other browsers, a cowardly response is to display warnings like 'this page is optimized for the . . . browser' or 'this page is best viewed in 1024×768', which, of course, in reality means 'I only tested this page on the . . . browser' and 'my screen has resolution 1024×768'.

Most HTML documents are really **invalid**, but the Web still works.

A large portion of these problems could be avoided if documents were *valid*. Being an SGML language, HTML has a formal syntax that is defined in around 800 lines of the DTD notation, and a valid HTML document is one that conforms to all these requirements. Validity can be automatically checked and errors reported in a style similar to those of syntax errors reported by compilers. For example, the alleged HTML document

```
<html>
  <body>
    <table><b>123</i></table>
  </body>
</html>
```

produces the following error messages when submitted to the official W3C validator (see the Online Resources for this chapter):

```
Line 3, column 7: document type does not allow element "BODY" here.
    <body>
       ^
Line 4, column 13: document type does not allow element "B" here;
    assuming missing "CAPTION" start-tag
    <table><b>123</i></table>
         ^
Line 4, column 20: end tag for element "I" which is not open.
    <table><b>123</i></table>
                  ^
Line 4, column 28: end tag for "B" omitted, but its declaration
    does not permit this.
    <table><b>123</i></table>
                          ^
```

```
Line 4, column 11: start tag was here.
    <table><b>123</i></table>
            ^

Line 4, column 28: end tag for "CAPTION" omitted, but its
    declaration does not permit this.
    <table><b>123</i></table>
                             ^

Line 4, column 11: start tag was here.
    <table><b>123</i></table>
            ^

Line 4, column 28: end tag for "TABLE" which is not finished.
    <table><b>123</i></table>
                            ^

Line 6, column 6: end tag for "HTML" which is not finished.
    </html>
          ^
```

Disappointingly, most HTML documents on the Web are not valid. Even technically savvy companies have scores of validity errors on the front pages of their Web sites:

`www.microsoft.com`	123 errors
`www.cnn.com`	58 errors
`www.ibm.com`	30 errors
`www.google.com`	27 errors
`www.sun.com`	19 errors

There are several reasons why validity is often ignored. First, many authors are unaware of the requirements contained in the DTD for HTML, or even of its existence. Second, many HTML pages are generated automatically by authoring tools, which unfortunately frequently generate invalid output containing both vendor-specific non-standard extensions and plain bugs. For example, saving the simplest possible Word document containing just the text 'Hello World' in HTML format generates a document with 24 validation errors when using Microsoft Word XP. Third, there are seemingly no substantial advantages in generating valid HTML, since browsers never report validation errors but instead try to make the best of invalid input.

The forgiving nature of browsers can be illustrated by the following example of horribly invalid HTML:

```
<h2>Lousy HTML</h1>
<li><a>This is not very</b> good.
<li><i>In fact, it is quite bad</em>
</ul>
But the browser does <a naem="goof">something.
```

Figure 1.3 An icon that is often placed in valid HTML documents.

The Mozilla browser obligingly renders this as follows:

> # Lousy HTML
>
> - This is not very good.
> - *In fact, it is quite bad*

The only tangible benefit from producing valid HTML is the boy scout's badge (shown in Figure 1.3) with which authors of valid documents are often encouraged to adorn their pages (and not many of those are seen during everyday Web surfing).

This situation is in sharp contrast to the attitude of compilers for programming languages, which mercilessly reject any program with a syntax error. Of course, that a compiler should try to resolve such errors by guessing what the programmer meant is a fairly chilling prospect. Conversely, a browser that only reported syntax errors when encountering invalid HTML documents would make for a rather boring surfing experience.

However, there is a much more insipid problem caused by invalid HTML. Recall, that Web documents are rendered by several different browsers, each of which is supported by numerous implementations. Each of those hundreds of programs will conscientiously try to follow the HTML specification and render the documents correctly. However, the specifications naturally mention only the behavior of valid documents. Assigning a sensible behavior to invalid documents requires each of the hundreds of individual programmers to figure out what to code in the rendering program. Since there is no standard for *invalid* HTML, chances are that they will make different and incompatible choices. Thus, invalid HTML documents are not likely to look the same in different browsers. The fact that browsers accept invalid HTML has effectively undermined the HTML standard.

The creator of the later HTML versions has tried to remedy this unfortunate situation by, in effect, introducing a standard for invalid HTML. He has created the tool HTML Tidy, which transforms an invalid HTML document into a corresponding valid one. This implementation will, of course, also make many arbitrary guesses and assumptions, but if all authors or browsers were to agree on using this tool, then documents could again be rendered consistently in different browsers. The HTML Tidy tool transforms the lousy document above into the following almost valid version:

```
<html>
<head>
<title></title>
</head>
```

```
<body>
<h2>Lousy HTML</h2>
<ul class="noindent">
<li><a>This is not very good.</a></li>
<li><i>In fact, it is quite bad</i></li>
</ul>
But the browser does <a naem="goof">something.</a>
</body>
</html>
```

This indeed seems to capture the author's muddled intentions reasonably well, except that the misspelled `naem` attribute is not corrected. But still, this is not the ideal solution to the problem, since the guesses do not always coincide with the HTML author's intentions.

1.7   Limitations of HTML

We now describe a more fundamental problem with HTML. Recall that HTML is designed to represent hypertext documents with simple text formatting. However, it is often stretched beyond its design. Consider, for example, a Web site publishing recipes as Web pages. If the browser is to present the recipes, then they must necessarily be written in HTML. However, the recipe publisher also needs the recipes to be consistent with respect to their structure. Thus, they will quickly agree on a standard layout for recipes, which could look like this:

```
<h1>Rhubarb Cobbler</h1>
<h2>Wed, 4 Jun 95</h2>
This recipe is suggested by Jane Dow.
Rhubarb Cobbler made with bananas as the main sweetener.
It was delicious.

  <table>
  <tr><td> 2 1/2 cups <td> diced rhubarb
  <tr><td> 2 tablespoons <td> sugar
  <tr><td> 2 <td> fairly ripe bananas
  <tr><td> 1/4 teaspoon <td> cinnamon
  <tr><td> dash of <td> nutmeg
  </table>

<i>Combine all and use as cobbler, pie, or crisp.</i>
<p>
This recipe has 170 calories, 28% from fat,
58% from carbohydrates, and 14% from protein.
<p>
Related recipes: <a href="#GardenQuiche">Garden Quiche</a>
is also yummy.
```

This could be rendered as follows:

Rhubarb Cobbler

Wed, 4 Jun 95

This recipe is suggested by Jane Dow. Rhubarb Cobbler made with bananas as the main sweetener. It was delicious.

2 1/2 cups	diced rhubarb
2 tablespoons	sugar
2	fairly ripe bananas
1/4 teaspoon	cinnamon
dash of	nutmeg

Combine all and use as cobbler, pie, or crisp.

This recipe has 170 calories, 28% from fat, 58% from carbohydrates, and 14% from protein.

Related recipes: Garden Quiche is also yummy.

HTML is a shaky foundation for publishing general data on the Web.

The adopted standard can easily be inferred from this single example: the title of the dish is written in an `h1` tag, the date it was created is then in an `h2` tag, a description follows as plain text, the ingredients are listed in a two-column table, the preparation guide follows in an `i` tag, the nutritional contents is described following a `p` tag, and finally, links to related recipes appear after another `p` tag. The typical way to document this format is using yellow notes attached to the edge of the publisher's screen.

The general problem is that HTML was never designed to be used like this. HTML is a domain-specific language targeted at hypertext, into which we are now trying to squeeze the domain of recipes. This gives rise to all sorts of inconveniences. First, HTML validity by itself does not imply any guarantees about the document conforming to our recipe design. Thus we have no way of automatically checking if a recipe has been written correctly according to the conventions. Second, we are unable to change the layout of our recipes beyond the meager capabilities of CSS stylesheets, since the structure of recipes is coupled with specific HTML tags; for example, we are unable to reorder the information and list related recipes at the top. Third, it is difficult to perform computations on the recipe data, since the corresponding programs would have to accept HTML as input and perform the cumbersome task of extracting the essential recipe data from the enmeshing markup tags.

To summarize, HTML is powerful for hypertext, but it is a shaky foundation for many Web development projects. The language is by design hardwired to describe hypertext, as there is a fixed collection of tags with a fixed semantics, but much information fundamentally just is not hypertext. Also, the syntax and semantics are mixed together, since the structuring of data dictates its presentation in browsers and stylesheets only provide a weak solution to separating contents and presentation. Finally, the HTML standard has been undermined since most HTML documents are invalid and the browsers define sloppy ad hoc standards.

1.8 Unicode

HTML files and many other data formats are represented as text files, which conceptually are sequences of *characters*. Physically, however, a text file is a sequence of *bytes*. The mapping from bytes to characters has not been generally agreed upon and may vary between platforms, operating systems, and individual applications. Well-known mappings are ASCII and EBCDIC, which cover the most essential Western European characters.

Web publications should cater for the needs of all cultures and must be universally available. This requires a more comprehensive solution, which is provided by the *Unicode* system that aims to cover all characters in all past or present written languages. This ambitious project introduces a stratified model with several conceptual views of characters.

A *character* is a symbol that may appear as part of a text. Characters include the usual alphabet symbols, but also more abstract pictograms (such as a copyright sign), and modifiers (such as accents). Unicode characters are abstract entities that are described by names such as the following four:

```
LATIN CAPITAL LETTER A
LATIN CAPITAL LETTER A WITH RING ABOVE
HIRAGANA LETTER SA
RUNIC LETTER THURISAZ THURS THORN
```

By themselves, these letters have neither graphical presentations nor byte representations.

A *glyph* is a graphical presentation of a part of a text. A typical example is Å which is a glyph representing the second character written above. Several letters may be represented by the same glyph; for example, the character

```
ANGSTROM SIGN
```

(a unit of physics) also has the glyph Å. Furthermore, some sequences of characters may be represented by a single glyph. The sequence of two characters

```
LATIN CAPITAL LETTER A
COMBINING RING ABOVE
```

will yet again result in the single glyph Å. There are also examples where a single character results in several glyphs. Consequently, there is no one-to-one mapping between characters and glyphs. The Unicode standard defines several notions of *normalization* of sequences of characters, which may be used if unique character representations of glyphs are required.

A *code point* is a unique number assigned to every character. The Unicode standard allows for code points between 0 and 1,114,112, but currently only around 100,000 code points have been assigned to characters (most of which are Chinese). For example, the HIRAGANA LETTER SA character is assigned the code point 12,373. The code points from 0 through 127 have been chosen to coincide with the ASCII characters. For technical reasons explained below, some code points will never be assigned to characters.

The **Unicode** character set contains essentially all characters in past or present written languages.

A *character encoding* interprets a sequence of bytes as a sequence of code points, and consequently as a sequence of characters. The sequence of bytes is first parsed as a sequence of *code units* each consisting of a number of bytes. A code unit may in itself correspond to a code point, or it may have a value indicating that more code units must be read in order to determine the next code point. Unicode supports three main character encodings, which we describe in the following. This part is invariably quite technical, but it provides a good background for later chapters.

In UTF-8, a code unit is a single byte. Each code point is represented by between one and four code units. The code points between 0 and 127 are represented in a single code unit as themselves. If a code unit matches the bits 110XXXXX, the code point is encoded in two code units, if it matches 1110XXXX in three code units, and if it matches 11110XXX in four code units. The additional code units must match the bits 10XXXXXX, which ensures that byte-wise substring matching is possible in UTF-8 encoded text. As noted above, UTF-8 is also compatible with the 7-bit version of ASCII. As an example, consider the following UTF-8 sequence:

```
11100011 10000001 10010101
```

Some of the bits are used to indicate the structure, as explained above:

```
11100011 10000001 10010101
```

The remaining bits form the binary number 11000001010101 which corresponds to the code point 12,373 (HIRAGANA LETTER SA).

In UTF-16, a code unit consists of two bytes. Code points below 65,536 are represented as a single code unit. Higher code points are represented as pairs of code units, respectively matching the bits 110110XXXXXXXXXX and 110111XXXXXXXXXX. This only makes sense since Unicode has been designed not to assign any code points in the interval between the binary numbers 1101100000000000 (55,296) and 1101111111111111 (57,343).

When reading several bytes at once, the byte order of the given architecture becomes significant. To handle this problem, a UTF-16 encoded text must begin with the special *byte order mark* code point with bit value 1111111011111111 (65,279), called a *zero-width non-breaking space*, which will reveal the byte order since the dual code point 1111111111111110 (65,534) is never assigned. As an example, consider the following UTF-16 sequence:

```
11111110 11111111 00110000 01010101
```

Again, some of the bits are used to indicate the structure:

```
11111110 11111111 00110000 01010101
```

The remaining bits correspond to the code point 12,373. If this use of byte order marks is considered wasteful, the variant UTF-16LE may be used if the architecture is known to be *little-endian* and dually UTF-16BE if it is known to be *big-endian*.

In UTF-32, a code unit consists of four bytes whose corresponding integer value immediately corresponds to a Unicode code point. Note that a code point will never actually occupy more than 21 bits. As for UTF-16, an encoded text must begin with four bytes containing the byte order mark. Now, consider the following UTF-32 sequence:

```
00000000 00000000 11111110 11111111
00000000 00000000 00110000 01010101
```

Some of the bits are used to indicate the structure:

00000000 00000000 11111110 11111111
00000000 00000000 00110000 01010101

and the remaining bits once again yield the code point 12,373. The variants UTF-32LE and UTF-32BE also exist.

The most common choices are UTF-8 and UTF-16. In terms of file size, UTF-8 is more compact if the text contains mainly ASCII characters, while UTF-16 is more efficient at representing higher code points.

The Java language represents characters as sequences of UTF-16 code units – not as sequences of code points. This is a pragmatic choice that allows `char` values to be represented in 16 bits. This difference will never be noticed, unless exotic characters which need two code units in UTF-16 are used, and these are likely to remain exceedingly rare. However, it is possible in Java to construct strings that correspond to illegal UTF-16 encodings, and moreover the `length` function on strings returns the number of code units rather than the number of code points.

Besides Unicode, other encodings are in use. An example is ISO-8859-1, also known as Latin-1, which is a popular encoding with 256 code points and correspondingly code units of size one byte. As for Unicode, the code points from 0 to 127 coincide with ASCII. However, note that general Unicode documents cannot be represented in ISO-8859-1. In all, hundreds of different character encodings exist, many supporting regional character sets. Ideally, they will eventually be replaced by Unicode.

An HTML document may be written in many different character encodings. The client application should, of course, find out what this encoding is, in order to interpret the document correctly. A Web server producing an HTML document may use an HTTP response header for this information (see Section 8.1.2), or the document may contain a declaration such as the following:

```
<meta http-equiv="Content-Type"
      content="text/html; charset=ISO-8859-1">
```

The meta approach, of course, only makes sense if the character encoding coincides with ASCII to enable this declaration to be parsed correctly. Regardless of the chosen encoding, an HTML document may represent arbitrary Unicode characters using *character references* of the form

```
&#12373;
```

for the Unicode character with code point 12,373.

1.9 The World Wide Web Consortium (W3C)

The future development of HTML, CSS, and most other Web technology resides with the *The World Wide Web Consortium (W3C)* which was founded in 1994. W3C also handles broader issues like accessibility and internationalization. At the time of writing, this organization consists of around 380 companies and organizations and is directed by Tim Berners-Lee, the main creator of the World Wide Web.

Most basic Web technologies are developed as open standards by **W3C**.

The W3C employs several technical staff members, who are located at MIT, INRIA, and Keio University. Companies and organizations become *members* of W3C by paying a yearly fee of $50,000 (reduced to $5,000 for small players) and contributing manpower to the activities. All the well-known hi-tech companies are members of W3C, which enables the organization to react quickly and interact with business initiatives. There is also an elected *Advisory Board* dealing with high-level strategy and a *Technical Architecture Group*, which aims to build consensus around the principles of the Web architecture. The W3C also organizes events like workshops, symposia, and the annual *International World Wide Web Conference*.

The technical activities of the W3C are mainly carried out by *working groups*, which produce specifications and occasionally also prototypes. The members of a group typically consist of technical professionals from relevant companies. Their progress is documented through *technical reports*, which are the real source of information. Reports on a future technical specification may be at various stages. A *working draft* simply reports on the current status and lists remaining problems to be solved. A *candidate recommendation* is a stable working draft that is almost ready to be submitted for review. A *proposed recommendation* is currently under review by the W3C staff. Finally, a *recommendation* is a standard sponsored by the W3C and will often quickly be adopted by industry. It is important to note the exact status of such documents, since for instance working drafts are likely to change dramatically.

There are other kinds of W3C publications, such as *working group notes* which document discussions and decisions, but are not on the recommendation track. A *member submission* is written by members, typically in a small group, and proposes a new technology. They are subsequently acknowledged by an official *W3C staff comment*. Similarly, *team submissions* contain proposals from the W3C team.

W3C recommendations aim at consensus among its members, which generally succeeds even though some technologies may be hotly contested for a long time. A very positive aspect is that intellectual property rights by the members are severely limited, which ensures wide availability and dissemination of the developed technologies. Also, all technical reports are freely available on the Web, which is markedly different from organizations like ISO that charge exorbitant fees for the same service.

Most W3C sponsored technologies have been successful and represent solid work. However, design by committee does not necessarily produce the best solutions, and in this book we will take care to point out shortcomings of the presented technologies whenever appropriate.

1.10   Chapter Summary

In this chapter we have studied HTML from its origins in a concrete hypertext project carried out by Tim Berners-Lee to its present standing as a foundation for the Web.

HTML has during its development become more sophisticated with richer facilities for controlling layout and presentation. In particular, the introduction of CSS has allowed a clean separation of content and logical structure on one side and presentation on the other.

We have presented small survivor's guides for using HTML and CSS, sufficient to understand the concepts and examples that we use in the remainder of this book. Full details of these languages are best picked up from the online resources and technical manuals listed below.

We have identified the widespread use of invalid HTML documents as an Achilles heel of Web publication, making it difficult to obtain a consistent behavior in different browsers. Also, HTML has been seen to be unsuited for representing more general data that cannot be viewed naturally as hypertext.

We have briefly presented technical issues related to Web publication, such as URLs, URNs, URIs, and Unicode.

Finally, we have seen a brief description of the W3C, which is responsible for developing standards for basic Web technologies.

1.11   Further Reading

HTML 4.01 is a W3C recommendation [72], and CSS 2.1 is currently a candidate recommendation [11]. There are countless books providing detailed presentations of HTML and CSS, but these technologies are also amply documented through online resources. The history of the Web is best described in the book by Tim Berners-Lee [6]. Information about the W3C is best obtained at their Web site. The Unicode standard is described in the book [78].

1.12   Online Resources

http://www.w3.org/
  The World Wide Web Consortium.

http://www.w3.org/TR/html4/
  The official HTML 4.01 specification is still the best place to find out about the details of HTML.

http://www.w3.org/Addressing/
  Specifications of and discussions about URIs, URLs, and URNs.

```
http://www.unicode.org/
```
The Unicode consortium. Contains character code charts and technical reports defining the various encodings.

```
http://www.w3.org/Style/CSS/
```
The W3C homepage for CSS, with links to specifications, authoring tools, and news.

```
http://www.zvon.org/xxl/css1Reference/Output/
```
A handy tool that allows you to browse through the different CSS properties and inspect their possible values.

```
http://validator.w3.org/
```
The official interactive HTML validator tool.

```
http://www.w3.org/People/Raggett/tidy/
```
The HTML Tidy tool for fixing invalid HTML.

1.13 Exercises

The main lessons to be learned from these exercises are:

- familiarity with HTML and CSS concepts; and
- the notion of HTML validity.

Exercise 1.1 Look at the HTML source behind the front pages of Web sites such as www.microsoft.com, www.google.com, and www.w3.org. How many tags do you recognize?

Exercise 1.2 Write an HTML document (like a simple home page). Use a simple text editor, not a graphical authoring tool.

Exercise 1.3 Experiment with the GUI tags for HTML forms. Use the URL

```
http://www.brics.dk/ixwt/echo
```

as the value of the `action` attribute in the `form` element, as this will display all the pairs of names and values that are received.

Exercise 1.4 The HTML page *EX*/physical.html makes heavy use of physical markup (such as <i>, <tt>, and <font color="blue">. Convert it to using only logical markup (such as <em>, <code>, and <h2>) and add a CSS stylesheet to obtain the original looks.

Exercise 1.5 Use the W3C validator to check whether the front pages of Web sites such as www.microsoft.com, www.google.com, and www.w3.org are valid. If they are not, then describe some common errors.

TIP

To run the W3C validator on a page without a DOCTYPE and encoding, try using HTML 4.01 Transitional and iso-8859-1.

Exercise 1.6 Use the W3C validator to check whether the HTML page you construct in Exercise 1.4 is valid. If not, try to use the HTML Tidy tool to fix it.

Exercise 1.7 Find the code point for the Unicode character

```
MUSICAL SYMBOL QUINDICESIMA ALTA
```

and represent it in UTF-8, UTF-16, and UTF-32.

XML DOCUMENTS

Objectives

In this chapter, you will learn:

- What is XML, in particular in relation to HTML
- The XML data model and its textual representation
- The XML Namespace mechanism

2.1   Introduction

XML, *Extensible Markup Language*, is a framework for defining markup languages. In contrast to HTML, there is no fixed collection of markup tags in XML. Instead, XML lets us define our own tags, tailored for the kind of information that we wish to represent. Each XML language is targeted at a particular application domain, but the languages will share many features: they all use the same basic markup syntax, and they all benefit from a common set of generic tools for processing documents.

The name 'extensible markup language' is, in fact, quite misleading. XML is not a single markup language that can be extended for other uses, but rather it is a common notation that markup languages can build upon. XML is not an extension of HTML, nor is it a replacement for HTML, which ideally should be just another XML language. However, because of a number of minor syntactical differences, HTML does not directly fit into the XML framework. As a remedy, the W3C has designed XHTML as an XML variant of HTML, which we shall return to later in this chapter.

XML has been designed with some simple but powerful principles in mind. It allows tailor-made markup for any imaginable application domain. By itself, XML is merely a standard notation for markup languages. The XML specification says nothing about the semantics of the markup tags – this is left to the specifications of the individual XML languages. For example, a Web browser can do very little with an XML document from our own homemade

XML language. One way to make use of such a document is to specify a stylesheet that defines a meaning of the markup tags in terms of instructions for rendering the document on the screen. Later in this chapter we shall discuss the language design process of constructing suitable markup for a given domain.

As an additional benefit, XML is inherently internationalized and platform independent. All XML documents are written in the Unicode alphabet (see Section 1.8). Annoyances with other textual formats, such as encoding of line breaks, that often depend on the operating system being used, are also addressed.

In general, XML is intended to be the future of all structured information. This even includes information stored in relational databases, which has motivated the development of the powerful query language XQuery that we describe in Chapter 6.

The development of XML began in the mid-90s, and in November 1996, the initial XML draft was produced as a pure subset of SGML. In February 1998, XML 1.0 became a W3C recommendation. At the time of writing, the latest version is the third edition from February 2004, which has incorporated a large number of minor changes from the first edition errata. Also in February 2004, XML 1.1 became a W3C recommendation. The main new features in this new version are support for recent and future changes in the Unicode standard, and a notion of normalization of character encodings. (Unfortunately, XML 1.1 is technically not fully compatible with XML 1.0, so many prefer to stick with 1.0.) With the exception of technical details, the standard has been remarkably stable since the very first version. We will later see that the standard perhaps could or should have been made even simpler, but considering the enormous number of XML languages, tools, and applications that exist today it would presumably not be feasible to make notable improvements of the core notation.

XML was designed to bring the power of SGML to the Web.

2.2   Recipes in XML

Let us reconsider the HTML recipe collection from Chapter 1. We have seen the problems that arise when using HTML for structuring non-hypertext information, such as our recipes. With XML, we can instead define our own 'recipe markup language', *RecipeML*, where the markup tags directly correspond to concepts in the world of recipes. This process is reminiscent of an object-oriented analysis in which the application domain is analyzed and the central concepts are identified. In our case, the concepts include 'recipe', 'ingredient', 'amount', and so on. The example recipe could then be written as follows in our newly invented RecipeML:

```
<collection>
  <description>Recipes suggested by Jane Dow</description>

  <recipe id="r117">
    <title>Rhubarb Cobbler</title>
    <date>Wed, 14 Jun 95</date>

    <ingredient name="diced rhubarb" amount="2.5" unit="cup"/>
    <ingredient name="sugar" amount="2" unit="tablespoon"/>
```

```
<ingredient name="fairly ripe banana" amount="2"/>
<ingredient name="cinnamon" amount="0.25" unit="teaspoon"/>
<ingredient name="nutmeg" amount="1" unit="dash"/>

<preparation>
  <step>
    Combine all and use as cobbler, pie, or crisp.
  </step>
</preparation>
<comment>
  Rhubarb Cobbler made with bananas as the main sweetener.
  It was delicious.
</comment>

<nutrition calories="170" fat="28%"
           carbohydrates="58%" protein="14%"/>
<related ref="42">Garden Quiche is also yummy</related>
  </recipe>
</collection>
```

The process of developing an XML representation for a class of data is often called *XML-ification*. Notice that we have chosen markup tags purely for specifying the logical structure of the underlying information. Conceptually, we choose to view a 'recipe' as consisting of a 'title', the 'date' it was entered, a number of 'ingredients', steps for 'preparation', and so on, and these choices are directly reflected by the possible contents of the `recipe` tag. Also, we have chosen to add an `id` attribute to the `recipe` tag, anticipating that we might need a simple way of referring to a single recipe in a large collection. In a sense, the essential information in the recipe document is in the text between the tags and in attribute values, while the rest represents *meta-information* about the various fragments of text.

This example illustrates only one possible choice of markup design. Depending on the applications we might have in mind, we could for example choose to add further markup to the date information, such as `day` or `month`, around the constituents. (This observation is related to the view of XML as a notation for *semi-structured data* – we can use markup to impose structure on some parts of the data while leaving other parts as unstructured text.) We could choose to write the ingredient and nutrition information with more elements and fewer attributes. Also, we could choose to write the recipe ID information in an `id` tag instead of using an attribute. Such choices are mostly a matter of taste, although there are in some occasions technical reasons for choosing one design over another, as we will see later when describing the languages (for example DTD) that build upon the core XML notation.

In later chapters we will continue the RecipeML example. When designing a new XML-based language, we clearly need to define precisely which XML documents we regard as conforming to this language before we can start building tools that operate on our data. That is, we need to specify which tags are allowed and what may appear inside each tag, for example, that a `preparation` tag always contains only `step` tags, which themselves must contain only text. In Chapter 4, we will use the schema language XML Schema formally to define the syntax of RecipeML.

A major benefit of using XML is the availability of **generic tools and technologies** that surround the core XML notation.

So far, we have not defined any *semantics* of our homegrown language. We might have chosen some informative tag names (for example, `preparation` instead of `tag117`), but what they actually mean has not been specified anywhere. Typical browsers, such as, Internet Explorer or Mozilla, of course, know nothing about the semantics of RecipeML, so they will not be able to present our recipe documents to the users in any reasonable way without extra help. In Chapter 5, we will use the transformation language XSLT to define a transformation from RecipeML to XHTML, which the browsers understand. In this way, we define the semantics of our language in terms of another language that certain tools understand.

Imagine that we have produced thousands of recipes written in RecipeML. We may now want to be able to search through our collection in various ways or extract information, such as, a list of ingredients used by a given set of recipes. When viewing the XML data as a database, the query language XQuery, which we describe in Chapter 6, becomes important.

Finally, for more specialized applications it is often necessary to resort to a general-purpose programming language, such as Java. If we want to write a Web-based recipe editor where our users can contribute to our recipe collection, we will need to master yet other technologies, for example, Servlets and JSP, which we return to in Chapters 7–10.

2.3   XML Trees

Conceptually, an XML document is a hierarchical structure called an *XML tree*, which consists of nodes of various kinds arranged as a tree. Unfortunately, there is no consensus on the terminology used to describe such trees. The *XML information set* does provide a consistent set of definitions for referring to the information in an XML document. However, its terminology can be difficult to learn and is not widely used, so we will focus on an alternative description, the prevailing *XPath data model*.

We describe the conceptual data model of an XML document before showing its concrete textual representation to emphasize the view of XML as tree-structured information.

Figure 2.1 shows an example of a tree. Nodes are here drawn as circles. The topmost node is called the *root*. (Trees are upside-down in our world.) The edges show the parent–child relationship between the nodes, for example, *B* is a *child* of *A*, and *A* is the *parent* of *B*. The *content* of a node is the sequence of its child nodes. For the node *A*, the content is the sequence (*B*, *C*, *D*). The nodes in a tree may have different numbers of children. Nodes with no children are called *leaves*; in the example, *E*, *F*, *C*, and *D* are leaves. An XML tree is

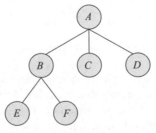

Figure 2.1 A tree.

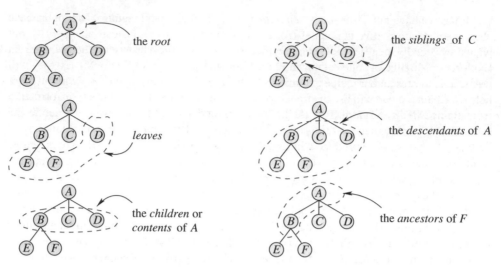

Figure 2.2 The essential tree terminology.

ordered meaning that the ordering of children of a node generally is significant. The *siblings* of a node are the other children of the parent of the node. The *ancestors* of a node consist of its parent, the parent of the parent, and so on, including the root node; for example, the ancestors of *F* are *B* and *A*. The *descendants* of a node is the set consisting of its children, the children of the children, and so on. For example, the descendants of the root node is the set of all nodes in the tree, except the root itself. These concepts are illustrated in Figure 2.2.

As an analogy, think of a file system where files are arranged in directories, which also form a tree structure, although an unordered one. The root of the file system is the root node, files appear as leaf nodes, and directories correspond to nodes whose children constitute their contents:

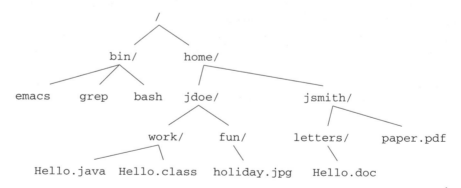

In this example, the root contains two directories, `bin` and `home`, where the former contains three files, and the latter contains two sub-directories. The file `paper.pdf` thus appears in the `jsmith` sub-directory of the `home` directory. This analogy between XML trees and file systems also becomes useful when in Chapter 3 we describe the XPath language for navigating around XML trees.

In the XPath data model, an XML tree is a special kind of ordered tree whose nodes can be of the following kinds:

text nodes A text node corresponds to a fragment of the actual information being represented by the XML document. Every text node is labeled with a nonempty text string containing this information, for example, the string 'fairly ripe bananas'. Text nodes have no children, that is, they are leaves in the tree. Also, two text nodes cannot occur as siblings of each other, except if another kind of node appears in between.

element nodes An element node defines a logical grouping of the information represented by its descendants. Every element node has a *name*, a word that describes the grouping. One example could be an element named recipe, encompassing the entire description of one recipe. We often use the shorter term 'element' instead of 'element node', and similarly for the other kinds of nodes.

attribute nodes An attribute node is associated with an element node, that is, its parent is always an element. Attributes typically act as refinements of the element's name, describing further properties of the grouping that the element node defines. An attribute is a pair of a *name* and a *value*, where the name is a word describing the property, and the value is some text string. Every element can have at most one attribute of a given name. An example of an attribute is the id attribute of recipe elements, where the value of the attribute is interpreted as a unique identification of the recipe.

comment nodes A comment node is a special leaf node labeled with a text string. One should think of comment nodes as comments in programming languages: they contain informal meta-information that most tools simply ignore. A comment could, for example, contain the string 'author's note: this recipe needs more garlic'.

processing instruction nodes A processing instruction node has a *target* and a *value*, and can be used to convey specialized meta-information to various XML processing tools. The target is a word that specifies the kind of processing tool that the processing instruction is directed toward; all other tools can ignore it. The value is a text string containing the relevant meta-information to the tool. For instance, the target could be xml-stylesheet, which is recognized by XSLT processors, and the value a URI reference to an XSLT stylesheet used by such a processor. Processing instructions never have child nodes.

root nodes Every XML tree starts with a single *root* node, which represents the entire document. The children of the root node consist of any number of comment and processing instruction nodes together with exactly one element node, which is called the *root element*. (A common mistake is to confuse the root *node* with the root *element* of a document.)

The XPath data model has a few potentially confusing subtleties regarding attribute nodes. The parent of such a node is always an element node, but when we talk about the children of this element node, the attribute nodes are not included. In other words, the parent–child relationship is not symmetric. Also, we generally say that the ordering of nodes in an XML tree is significant, but this does not include attribute nodes. In other words, the *children*

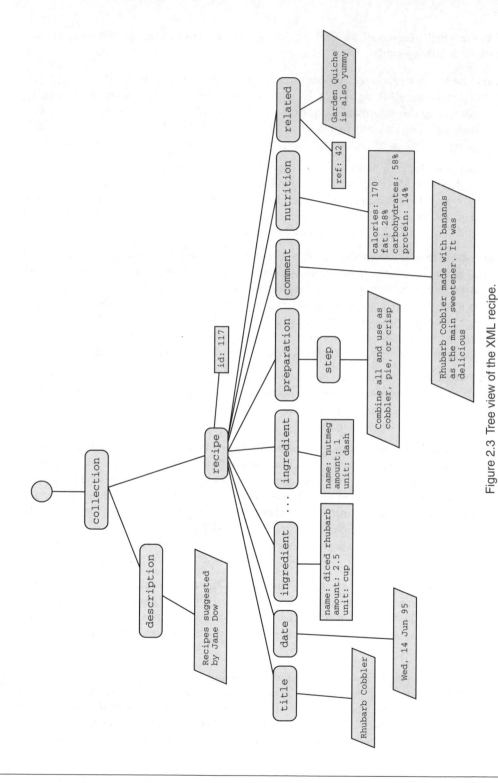

Figure 2.3 Tree view of the XML recipe.

of an element is an ordered sequence containing text, elements, comments, and processing instructions; in addition, the element is associated with a *set* of attributes nodes.

Some of the later XML technologies that we shall look at rely on the *document ordering* of nodes in an XML tree. According to this ordering, a node *x* is *before* a node *y* if *x* appears before *y* in a left-to-right preorder traversal of the tree (that is, a parent comes before its children, and children are ordered left-to-right), however, no ordering is defined for two attribute nodes that have the same parent element. In particular, the root node will always be the first node of an XML tree, and element nodes occur before their children.

A tree view of the XML recipe from the previous section is shown in Figure 2.3. The root node is drawn as a circle; element nodes are rounded boxes, text nodes are parallelograms; and attributes are written as 'name: value' in boxes. Compared to the textual representation, a few simplifications have been made to improve readability: some of the `ingredient` nodes are here written with '...' for brevity. All text nodes containing pure whitespace (spaces, newlines, and tabs) are omitted from this drawing. Also, whitespace in the remaining character data has been changed for readability.

The tree structure of an XML document can be examined, for example, in the Internet Explorer and Mozilla browsers, although that does not reveal the full structure since extra line breaks and indentation is added to the text. Assuming that the document contains no XSLT stylesheet reference, one can simply enter the URL of the document to obtain this view. As an example, Mozilla renders our raw XML recipe as shown in Figure 2.4.

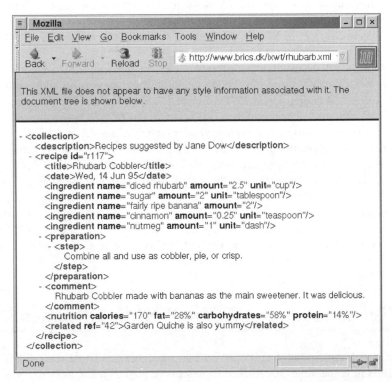

Figure 2.4 Mozilla rendering of an XML document without XSLT references.

Note that two fragments of an XML tree can have the same values without being 'identical':

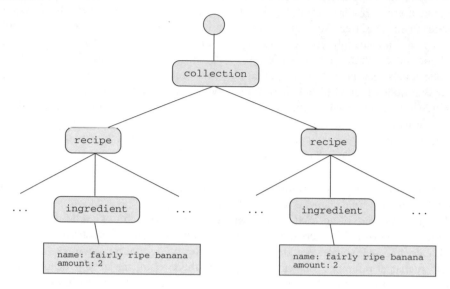

This fragment contains two `ingredient` elements that both have a `name="fairly ripe banana"` attribute and an `amount="2"` attribute, but the elements correspond to two distinct element nodes in the tree. In XPath (see Chapter 3), this distinction between equality and identity becomes particularly important.

Other data models have slightly different views on what an XML document is. For example, in both the DOM and the JDOM model, a tree can contain additional kinds of nodes: *document type* nodes contain DTD information, *entity reference* nodes are references to named XML fragments defined in the DTD schema, and *CDATA* nodes are another flavor of text nodes. These constructs are explained later (see Sections 2.4 and 4.3.4).

In this conceptual description of XML, we use text nodes to contain the actual information, whereas elements and their attributes are used to convey the logical structure of the information. The dividing line between the actual information and the meta-information is not always obvious when designing an XML language. In many XML languages, elements have a more prominent role; in some cases, text nodes do not appear at all. This is all a design issue when making particular XML languages, such as our RecipeML. XML by itself permits arbitrary decisions about how much meta-information is needed, whether attributes should be used in favor of child elements, and so on.

2.4 Textual Representation of XML Documents

No matter which conceptual data model we use, the concrete textual representation of an XML document is the same. An XML document is written as a Unicode text with markup tags and other meta-information representing the elements, attributes, and other nodes.

Text nodes are simply written as the text they represent. This text is also called *character data*. Element nodes are denoted by markup tags:

```
<related ref="42">Garden Quiche is also yummy</related>
```

Here, `<related ref="42">` is an element *start tag* with name `related`, and `</related>` is a matching *end tag*. The text in between, which generally also may contain markup, is the *content* of the element, corresponding to the descendants of the element node if we view the document as a tree. Attributes are written inside the element start tag. In this case, the element has a single attribute named `ref` with value `42`. Within a start tag, the ordering of attributes and all whitespace surrounding them are always insignificant. Attribute values are enclosed by `'` or `"`. Elements without contents are called *empty*, and such elements may be written with a short-hand notation `<pineapple/>` as an alternative to `<pineapple></pineapple>`.

An XML document in its textual form must be *well-formed*. This essentially means that it defines a tree structure, corresponding to the conceptual model presented earlier. To be well-formed, start and end tags must match and nest properly. (Note that this requirement is different in SGML languages, such as HTML, which permits certain tags to be omitted, in particular many end tags.) The following two XML fragments are *not* well-formed:

```
<banana></orange>
```

```
<banana><orange></banana></orange>
```

In the first, the start and end tags do not match; in the second, the `banana` and `orange` tags do not nest properly. In contrast to HTML, XML is case sensitive. For example,

```
<related rcf="42">Garden Quiche is also yummy</ReLAtED>
```

is *not* well-formed since the start and end tags differ in casing. A well-formed document must have exactly one root element. In addition, there is a range of more subtle syntactical requirements for an XML document to be well-formed, most of which are related to the DTD information that we describe later. Since a non-well-formed XML document has no meaning, we always implicitly mean 'well-formed XML document' when we say 'XML document', unless otherwise stated.

An XML document usually begins with an *XML declaration*

```
<?xml version="1.0" encoding="UTF-8"?>
```

which is followed by the representation of the children of the root node. The `version` part indicates the version of XML being used, here 1.0. The `encoding` part is the *encoding declaration* that states in which encoding the document is written. All XML parsers are required to understand the Unicode encodings `UTF-8` and `UTF-16`. Many XML parsers will support other encodings, such as `ISO-8859-1`, and must then be able to convert from this encoding to Unicode code points (see Section 1.8). If some exotic encoding is used, it

Symbol	Entity reference
<	`&lt;` *(less than)*
>	`&gt;` *(greater than)*
&	`&amp;` *(ampersand)*
'	`&apos;` *(apostrophe)*
"	`&quot;` *(quotation mark)*

Figure 2.5 Predefined entities in XML.

might be necessary to convert the documents to one of the Unicode encodings to obtain full interoperability.

In character data and attribute values, characters that have a special meaning, such as <, need to be written using Unicode *character references*. The syntax `&#N;` denotes the single character whose Unicode code point is N in decimal notation. Hexadecimal notation can be used with the syntax `&#xN;`. The characters < and & must be escaped in this way in both character data and attribute values. Additionally, in attribute values that are enclosed by ", this character must also be escaped, and similarly for the ' character. Character references can also be used to express Unicode characters that are not directly available on the keyboard. As an example, to express the string さけ (the word 'sake' in hiragana) in character data, one can write

```
&#x3055;&#x3051;
```

For a complete list of available Unicode characters, consult the Unicode consortium Web site. A few symbols also have predefined symbolic names that are easier to remember than their respective Unicode code points, as shown in Figure 2.5. One can use *CDATA sections* (corresponding to the CDATA nodes mentioned earlier) as an alternative to escaping many characters. For example,

```
<![CDATA[a<b & b>c]]>
```

is, for most purposes, equivalent with

```
a&lt;b &amp; b&gt;c
```

The strange syntax for CDATA sections originates from SGML. Comments are written as known from HTML:

```
<!-- this is a comment -->
```

Processing instructions are written as, for example,

```
<?xml-stylesheet type="text/xsl" href="mystyle.xsl"?>
```

where `xml-stylesheet` is the target, and the entire string `type="text/xsl" href="mystyle.xsl"` is its single value, even though it looks like two name–value pairs. Finally,

DTD information (corresponding to the document type nodes mentioned earlier) is written as follows:

```
<!DOCTYPE ... >
```

The DTD formalism is described in Chapter 4.

The following small but complete XML document uses all the constructs we have described, except namespaces:

```
<?xml version="1.1" encoding="ISO-8859-1"?>
<!DOCTYPE features SYSTEM "example.dtd">
<features a="b">
  <?mytool here is some information specific to mytool?>
  El señor está bien, garçon!
  Copyright &#169; 2005
  <![CDATA[ <this is not a tag> ]]>
  <!-- always remember to specify the right character encoding -->
</features>
```

It contains a single element having a single attribute and whose content consists of a processing instruction, some character data, and a comment. Notice the whitespace between, for example, the comment and the end tag, which by itself corresponds to one character data node in the tree model. As a technical detail, whitespace that appears outside the root element is always considered insignificant and is never represented as character data nodes. However, no whitespace is permitted before the XML declaration.

When we use a textual format for describing the structure of text as in XML, we inevitably have problems with whitespace (spaces, newlines, and tabs). To make an XML document readable, it is convenient to allow extra newlines and indentation. However, there is no *a priori* way of determining when whitespace is part of the actual contents and when it is used only to break up the text into readable lines. The core XML notation provides only little help here: a special attribute `xml:space="preserve"` can be used to indicate that whitespace is significant in the contents of the element. The alternative value `default` (which is, not surprisingly, the default value) may be used to indicate that it is left to the application to determine how to handle whitespace. If the `xml:space` attribute is absent in an element, the specified behavior is inherited from the nearest ancestor where one is present. This attribute is rarely used, though. Typically, this problem is handled at a higher level, depending on the specific XML language. For example, in some XML languages (including XHTML), character data consisting of whitespace only is considered significant or insignificant depending on the names of the ancestor element.

Another special attribute is `xml:lang`, which can be used to describe the natural language in which text inside the element is written, for example, using the code `es` for Spanish:

```
<p xml:lang="es">¿Quién se cree que he cazado una salchicha?</p>
```

However, some XML language designs use other conventions for describing such properties of the text, like the situation with whitespace.

An XML document can be considered both in its **textual representation** and as a **tree structure**.

One may argue that verbose markup in XML documents causes a tremendous waste of space when working with large data sets, compared to using relational databases with highly tuned data formats, for example. Often, this leads to misguided advice, for example 'when designing XML languages, you should favor attributes over sub-elements to save space' or 'always use short names for elements and attributes'. The main problem with such advice is that it tends to lead to inflexible and incomprehensible language designs. Instead, it is usually preferable to disregard such implementation issues during the language design phase and then later rely on data compression to save space. In fact, standard compression techniques are most often very efficient on XML data. Furthermore, specialized compression algorithms, such as XMill, have been developed for exploiting the special structure of well-formed XML documents to achieve even better compression ratios.

Since an XML document is just a text file, any text editor can be used for editing XML documents (provided it supports the chosen character encoding). This is different from, say, the native format of Word files, which requires tools from a particular vendor if one wants to make sure all details are interpreted correctly. (Acknowledging the benefits of XML, even Word now also supports an XML format, called WordML.)

An *XML parser* is a tool that is able to construct a tree representation of a textual XML document. The details of the representation depend on the programming language and the data model being used. An *XML serializer* is a tool that performs the inverse translation from trees to documents. We return to these issues in Chapter 7.

One may question whether all these kinds of nodes and syntactical constructs that appear in XML documents are really necessary. Much of the complexity is a legacy from SGML, which contains even more peculiar language features. From a highly simplistic point of view, text and element nodes are all that is really needed to describe structured information. XML is neither the simplest nor the first notation that fits this purpose. The notion of S-expressions from the programming language Lisp dating back to 1958 is perhaps the simplest alternative. As an example, the recipe example could be coded as the following S-expression (abbreviated with '...'):

```
(collection
  (recipe
    (title "Rhubarb Cobbler") (date "Wed, 14 Jun 95")
    ...
  )
)
```

This clearly contains the same information as the XML version. There have been various suggestions for simplifying the core XML standard along these lines, but the present XML specification has become the *de facto* standard that everybody uses. The simple fact that people agree on the XML notation is a major reason for its success.

2.5 Applications of XML

We have now seen that XML is a notation that everyone can use to build their own markup languages. There are already thousands of serious applications of XML. Generally, XML languages can be classified roughly into four groups:

data-oriented languages These languages are used for describing information that would traditionally be stored in a database system. A typical example is information about the inventory and customers of a company. Typically, the XML documents from these languages have a rather flat but wide tree structure since they often represent a large number of records that each have a similar and relatively simple structure. We shall look more into the connection between XML and databases in Chapter 6.

document-oriented languages A typical example of a language in this group is XHTML, but many others exist for structuring non-hypertext documents. These are best described as natural language text that is marked up to describe its logical structure. Usually, these languages are more loosely structured than data-oriented languages; for example, it is common that a given element may contain an arbitrary mixture of character data and some set of elements (this is also called *mixed content*). Instances of document-oriented languages usually make sense even if some of the markup tags are not understood – unlike for data-oriented languages.

protocols and programming languages This group contains, for example, the languages XML Schema, XSLT, and WSDL that are covered later in this book. It also contains more specialized languages, such as various configuration languages. This group tends to exhibit the most complex syntactical structures, which can be difficult to capture with schema languages.

hybrids Some languages are a mixture of, in particular, the data-oriented and the document-oriented styles. A typical example is a patient record that involves both highly structured information, such as billing information, and more loosely structured information, such as notes from doctors. Another example is an article collection that contains both data-oriented catalog information, such as ISBN numbers, titles, and author names, and abstracts which are document-oriented. We have designed our RecipeML language in a hybrid style, perhaps leaning towards the data-oriented style with only little use of markup in the descriptions of recipe preparation, for example.

Of course, not all applications fit directly into one of these groups, but it can be useful to be aware of the different uses of XML since many tools focus on, for example, the data-oriented languages and exploit their characteristics. In the following, we show a few examples of XML languages to demonstrate the variety of possible applications.

2.5.1 XHTML

XHTML 1.0 is W3C's XMLification of HTML 4.01. An example XHTML document:

```
<?xml version="1.0" encoding="UTF-8"?>
<html xmlns="http://www.w3.org/1999/xhtml">
  <head><title>Hello world!</title></head>
```

```
<body>
  <h1>This is a heading</h1>
  This is some text.
</body>
</html>
```

This certainly looks like an HTML document. (The xmlns attribute is a namespace declaration, which we explain later.) There are only minor syntactical differences between the two languages, all of which stem from the stronger requirement for being well-formed in XML compared to SGML. The most notable differences are the following:

- HTML allows certain elements to omit the end tag, which is forbidden in XML – in return, XHTML permits the short form of empty elements (such as <br/>);

- XHTML element and attribute names must be in lower case; and

- attribute values in XML must be present and they must be surrounded by quotes (for example, the HTML attribute checked is written as checked="checked" in XHTML);

Because of the close resemblance with HTML, even old browsers are often able to interpret XHTML documents reasonably well. The HTML Tidy tool can also be used for converting HTML documents to XHTML.

XHTML 1.0 comes in three variants: *Strict* is for clean markup where all layout is specified using CSS; *Transitional* additionally permits the explicit layout markup, such as the bgcolor attribute for specifying background color and the font element for controlling the text font; and *Frameset* is for documents that use frames, which permit multiple views to be presented within the same browser window.

Motivated by an increasing need for variants and fragments of XHTML to be used in other XML languages, *XHTML Modularization* has been developed as a decomposition of XHTML 1.0 into a collection of abstract modules. Each module provides a specific type of functionality: *structure* (include the html, head, and body tags), *text* (has tags for basic markup of text), *hypertext* (containing the a tag), *list* (with ul, ol, dl, . . .), *forms* (form, input, . . .), and a number of others. Each module is described using the DTD language, which we explore in a later chapter. If we are designing a new XML language and need some functionality for basic markup for text, links, and lists, for example, we can then reuse the sublanguages that correspond to this functionality. XHTML 1.1 is a reformulation of the entire XHTML language based upon this elegant modular framework.

2.5.2   CML

Chemical Markup Language (CML) is an XML-based data-oriented language for representation of molecules and chemical reactions. It was among the very first applications of XML and has had a close relationship with the XML developer community. The following XML fragment is a CML description of a methanol molecule (abbreviated with '...'):

```
<molecule id="METHANOL">
  <atomArray>
     <stringArray builtin="id">a1 a2 a3 a4 a5 a6</stringArray>
     <stringArray builtin="elementType">C O H H H H</stringArray>
     <floatArray builtin="x3" units="pm">-0.748 0.558 ...</floatArray>
     <floatArray builtin="y3" units="pm">-0.015 0.420 ...</floatArray>
     <floatArray builtin="z3" units="pm">0.024 -0.278 ...</floatArray>
  </atomArray>
</molecule>
```

CML is accompanied by a wide range of tools, such as specialized browsers and editors.

2.5.3 WML

Mobile devices, in particular mobile phones, usually have small displays, limited user input facilities, and low bandwidth, which makes XHTML (and HTML) less suitable than for ordinary browsers. The Wireless Application Protocol (WAP) has been developed by a consortium of mobile phone companies and others to support these different characteristics. A core ingredient of the WAP standard is Wireless Markup Language (WML), an XML-based document-oriented language that acts as a replacement for HTML for such devices. (For WAP 2.0, WML has been replaced with XHTML Mobile Profile, a strict subset of XHTML.)

WML uses a metaphor of *decks of cards*. A single interaction between a user agent and a user is described by a card, and a set of cards can be grouped together in a WML document forming a deck. In this way, multiple screens can be downloaded in a single file. The description of each card resembles XHTML, but WML provides less control over the layout. Notions of tasks, events, and variables allow the cards to be tied together and define reactions to user input.

The following WML document describes two cards: one where the user selects a name from a list of options, and one where a password is entered in an input text field.

```
<wml>
  <card id="Login" title="Login">
    <do type="accept" label="Password">
      <go href="#Password"/>
    </do>
    <p>
      Please select your name:
      <select name="user" title="Name:">
        <option value="jdoe">John Doe</option>
        <option value="jsmith">Joe Smith</option>
      </select>
    </p>
  </card>
```

```
<card id="Password" title="Password">
  <do type="accept" label="Results">
    <go href="submit?u=$(user:e)&amp;p=$(pwd:e)"/>
  </do>
  <p>
    Please enter your password:
    <input type="text" name="pwd"/>
  </p>
</card>
</wml>
```

When both pieces of information have been entered, a program on the server is activated.

2.5.4   ebXML

The Electronic Business XML Initiative (ebXML) is a worldwide initiative aiming to utilize XML for exchange of electronic business data. The project has delivered comprehensive XML standards for business processes, core data components, collaboration protocol agreements, messaging, registries and repositories.

The following tiny example shows the ebXML specification of a 'multiparty collaboration' involving three business partners:

```
<MultiPartyCollaboration name="DropShip">
  <BusinessPartnerRole name="Customer">
    <Performs
      initiatingRole='//binaryCollaboration[@name="Firm Order"]/
                      InitiatingRole[@name="buyer"]' />
  </BusinessPartnerRole>
  <BusinessPartnerRole name="Retailer">
    <Performs
      respondingRole='//binaryCollaboration[@name="Firm Order"]/
                      RespondingRole[@name="seller"]' />
    <Performs
      initiatingRole='//binaryCollaboration
                         [@name="Product Fulfillment"]/
                      InitiatingRole[@name="buyer"]' />
  </BusinessPartnerRole>
  <BusinessPartnerRole name="DropShip Vendor">
    <Performs
      respondingRole='//binaryCollaboration
                         [@name="Product Fulfillment"]/
                      RespondingRole[@name="seller"]' />
  </BusinessPartnerRole>
</MultiPartyCollaboration>
```

The complex attribute values, which we will not explain the meaning of here, contain expressions written in the XPath language that we describe in Chapter 3. As the example indicates, this language has a very complex structure and can best be categorized as belonging to the 'protocols and programming languages' group. Many major software companies provide industry solutions based on ebXML.

2.5.5 ThML

Theological Markup Language (ThML) is an XML-based markup language for theological texts. It is designed as a superset of XHTML with special support for scripture references, annotations, glossaries, and markup of verse and hymns. The following snippet shows some of the various kinds of markup used in ThML (and makes it clear that theologians love to add footnotes):

```
<h3 class="s05" id="One.2.p0.2">Having a Humble Opinion of Self</h3>
<p class="First" id="One.2.p0.3">
  EVERY man naturally desires knowledge
  <note place="foot" id="One.2.p0.4">
   <p class="Footnote" id="One.2.p0.5"><added id="One.2.p0.6">
     <name id="One.2.p0.7">Aristotle</name>, Metaphysics, i. 1.
   </added></p>
  </note>;
  but what good is knowledge without fear of God? Indeed a humble
  rustic who serves God is better than a proud intellectual who
  neglects his soul to study the course of the stars.
  <added id="One.2.p0.8"><note place="foot" id="One.2.p0.9">
    <p class="Footnote" id="One.2.p0.10">
    Augustine, Confessions V. 4.
    </p>
  </note></added>
</p>
```

The h3 and p tags are known from XHTML, whereas note, added, and name are some of the extensions that are specific to the ThML language.

2.6 XML Namespaces

The XML notation provides a solid foundation for building markup languages, however, there is one particular addition that most applications rely on: the *namespace* mechanism.

This mechanism is motivated by a specific problem. Consider an XML language *WidgetML*, an imaginary language for describing widgets. In addition to describing technical properties of the widgets, explanatory messages can be written using XHTML. In other words, WidgetML uses XHTML as a sublanguage. The following XML document describes a particular widget, called a *gadget*, which has a medium-size head and a big gizmo subwidget:

```
<widget type="gadget">
  <head size="medium"/>
  <big><subwidget ref="gizmo"/></big>
  <info>
    <head>
      <title>Description of gadget</title>
    </head>
    <body>
      <h1>Gadget</h1>
      A gadget contains a big gizmo
    </body>
  </info>
</widget>
```

The XHTML message is contained within the `info` element.

Now, the problem is that the meaning of each tag suddenly depends on their context. For example, the tags `head` and `big` are used both in XHTML and in the non-XHTML part of WidgetML. This name clash complicates things for tools that use WidgetML, and it might even cause ambiguities unless the language is designed carefully, for example, by ensuring that all XHTML is enclosed by a recognizable element as the `info` element here.

One may argue that the fault is in the design of WidgetML and that the designers should have chosen tag names that were not occupied. However, the problem appears not just when building languages on top of preexisting languages as in WidgetML, but also when combining existing languages.

Programming languages address the problem of clashing names from different modules by using different name spaces and qualified names. In XML, we use URIs to identify different name spaces. The Web infrastructure already provides control over the domain names used in the URIs, so by qualifying tag names by URIs we can obtain distinct name spaces for sublanguages that logically are distinct. The XHTML languages is developed within the W3C, so the W3C assigns a name space `http://www.w3.org/1999/xhtml` to this language. The WidgetML language is developed by an imaginary organization that owns the (imaginary) domain `www.widget.inc` and chooses `http://www.widget.inc` as name space URI for the WidgetML language. Assuming that language developers choose name space URIs from domains they are in control of and that they have some internal rules for assigning URIs from those domains to their new languages, we can ensure that each language gets a unique name space URI. (From now on, we write *namespace*, in one word, following the XML specifications.)

Instead of writing the ambiguous tag name `head`, we might now write

```
{http://www.w3.org/1999/xhtml}head
```

to elucidate that we mean the `head` tag from the XHTML language, not the one from the WidgetML language. This is the basic idea of XML namespaces, however, prefixing every name in an XML document with a long URI would seriously damage readability. The actual solution is less verbose but slightly more complicated: a namespace can be given a shorter name using a *namespace declaration*:

```
<... xmlns:foo="http://www.w3.org/TR/xhtml1">
  ...
  <foo:head>...</foo:head>
  ...
</...>
```

Here, the special attribute named `xmlns:foo` *declares* a namespace named `http://www.w3.org/TR/xhtml1` and gives it a *prefix* `foo`. The `head` element is now qualified by this namespace by prefixing the name with `foo:`. The prefix merely acts as a proxy for the URI and has no other meaning. The part of the element name that follows the colon is called the *local part* of the name.

Namespace declarations have lexical scope: each declaration covers the element containing the declaration and all its descendants. In case a qualified name `foo:bar` is covered by more than one declaration of `foo`, the nearest one has effect.

The predefined prefix `xmlns` is reserved for namespace declarations. All other prefixes beginning with the three-letter sequence x, m, l, in any case combination, are reserved for use by future XML specifications, but any other prefix may be used by authors of XML documents.

Do not be confused by the use of URIs for namespaces; they are not supposed to point at anything, but using URIs is simply the cheapest way of getting unique names in the same way that URLs are used in package names in Java programs. As a technical note, the most recent namespace specification uses IRIs instead of URIs to permit characters beyond the US-ASCII alphabet.

For backward compatibility and simplicity, unprefixed element names are assigned a *default* namespace. This can be overridden using a special namespace declaration of the form `xmlns="URI"`. The default behavior corresponds to the declaration `xmlns=""`. A *QName*, short for *qualified name*, is a name that may or may not begin with a namespace prefix and a colon. An *NCName*, short for *no-colon name*, is a name that does not contain a colon. For example, a namespace prefix must be an NCName. We shall use the terms QName and NCName throughout the book.

With namespaces, the example WidgetML document could be written unambiguously as follows (XHTML parts emphasized):

```
<widget type="gadget" xmlns="http://www.widget.inc">
  <head size="medium"/>
  <big><subwidget ref="gizmo"/></big>
  <info xmlns:xhtml="http://www.w3.org/TR/xhtml1">
    <xhtml:head>
      <xhtml:title>Description of gadget</xhtml:title>
    </xhtml:head>
```

The XML namespace mechanism supports **coexistence of sublanguages**.

```
        <xhtml:body>
          <xhtml:h1>Gadget</xhtml:h1>
          A gadget contains a big gizmo
        </xhtml:body>
      </info>
    </widget>
```

This document contains two namespace declarations: in the `widget` element, the empty prefix is set to the WidgetML namespace, and in the `info` element, the prefix `xhtml` is set to the XHTML namespace. The effect is that we can directly identify to which sublanguage an element name belongs. This example illustrates just one possible placement of the namespace declarations. One alternative could be to use an explicit prefix for the WidgetML names, and the XHTML namespace declaration could have been placed at the root element instead of at the `info` element.

Also attribute names can be qualified with namespaces. For example, the designers of WidgetML might choose to apply the XLink language for making references between widget parts:

```
<subwidget xmlns:xlink="http://www.w3.org/1999/xlink"
           xlink:href="gizmo" xlink:type="simple" xlink:show="embed"/>
```

The XLink language, which we briefly explain in Chapter 3, is intended as a sublanguage of other XML languages and is identified by the namespace `http://www.w3.org/1999/xlink`. Here, the attributes `href`, `type`, and `show` belong to this namespace.

The default namespace does *not* apply to unprefixed attribute names – such attributes are always interpreted as 'belonging to' the containing element (but they are not inheriting its namespace). As an example, consider the following elements with attributes:

```
<w:gadget size="42" xmlns:w="http://www.widget.inc"/>

<gadget size="42" xmlns="http://www.widget.inc"/>

<w:gadget w:size="42" xmlns:w="http://www.widget.inc"/>
```

Here, the first and the second are generally equivalent, but the first and the third are not.

In the XPath data model, namespace declarations are *not* regarded as attributes. Instead, the associated namespace information may be accessed through special functions (see Section 3.5.11).

This namespace mechanism is admittedly quite simple, but it nevertheless contains some problematic issues. A namespace is identified by a URI. How should a relative URI be interpreted? There are several options: (1) relative to the URI of the containing document; (2) relative to the base URI, which may involve the *XML Base* mechanism (see the reference in Section 2.8); or (3) just as a string. When this question was raised, it appeared that different implementors of tools had chosen different interpretations. This innocent question spawned a controversy within the W3C that resulted in leaving the matter undefined by deprecating such namespaces. This means: although relative URIs are technically possible in namespaces, do not use them!

Another source of confusion is related to the prefixes. Does the choice of prefix matter, or can we be certain that `<a:foo xmlns:a="http://www.widget.inc"/>` always means the same as `<b:foo xmlns:b="http://www.widget.inc"/>` (in the same way that the ordering of attributes within a start tag is always insignificant)? The specification does not give a clear answer to this question. Ideally, the prefix is just a proxy for the namespace URI, as previously mentioned, so one may argue that the answer is that the choice of prefix is insignificant. However, several other XML technologies (for example, XSLT, XML Schema, and WSDL) use an extended variant of the namespace mechanism where also certain attribute *values* exploit the mapping from prefixes to URIs (see, for example, Section 4.4.5), so generally, the prefixes can have meaning outside what the basic namespace mechanism prescribes. Also, the XQuery language uses namespaces in a non-XML syntax.

Despite the technical controversies, we have seen one of the strengths of XML: when people discover that many applications have a need for a particular feature, such as namespaces, then an extra layer is built on top of the core XML specification in a generic fashion, such that everybody can benefit from it. Typically, the extensions are accompanied by tools, which are often Open Source implementations. In the case of namespaces, the essential accompanying tools are namespace compliant parsers that are able to construct namespace maps for nodes. The namespace mechanism is such a widely used extension that, usually, when people talk about XML they really mean 'XML with namespaces'.

2.7   Running Example: More Recipes

In the remainder of this book, we will use the recipe collection as a running example on which we apply the various XML technologies being presented.

We start by giving an informal description of the RecipeML language. We introduce an explicit namespace `http://www.brics.dk/ixwt/recipes`, and in example documents we typically use the corresponding namespace prefix `rcp`. The root element is `collection`, which contains an informal description in a `description` element and a sequence of `recipe` elements.

Each `recipe` element contains a `title` element, a `date` element, a sequence of `ingredient` elements, a `preparation` element, a `nutrition` element, and possibly a sequence of `related` elements. Additionally, every `recipe` element may optionally contain one `comment` element anywhere among its contents. A `preparation` element contains a sequence of `step` elements that describe the individual steps involved in the recipe. All `description`, `title`, `date`, `step`, `comment`, and `related` elements contain only character data.

A `nutrition` element contains the mandatory attributes `calories`, `fat`, `carbohydrates`, and `protein`, as well as the optional attribute `alcohol`, which is used for those rare dishes that obtain a measurable amount of calories from their contents of alcohol (such as Zuppa Inglese, which is basically an alternative way of drinking liqueur).

The most complicated element is `ingredient`, which comes in two flavors: *simple* and *composite*. Both kinds have a `name` attribute, which identifies the ingredient.

A simple ingredient is one that is readily available from the cupboard or refrigerator. It is described by an `amount` attribute, which may be of three different kinds: First, an amount may be a *dimensionless* number, such as the number 2 in '2 apples'. Second, if a unit is used, as in '2 cups of sugar', then this unit is described by the optional `unit` attribute. Third, some recipes may use annoying terms, such as 'a suitable amount' or 'some', which are modeled in our language by giving the `amount` attribute the value '*'. Thus, the following are examples of simple ingredients:

```
<ingredient name="apple" amount="2"/>

<ingredient name="sugar" amount="2" unit="cup"/>

<ingredient name="parsley" amount="*"/>
```

A composite ingredient is one that requires its own preparation, such as dough for pizza or stock for sauce. The corresponding element is characterized by *not* having an `amount` element and instead containing its own nested `ingredient` and `preparation` elements.

Each `recipe` element may contain an attribute named `id` whose value must uniquely identify that recipe in the recipe collection document. Each `related` element contains a `ref` attribute whose value must match the value of some `id` attribute. The meaning is that the designated recipe is somehow related to the one containing the `related` element.

The XML recipe introduced in Section 2.2 fits into the language that we have just described. As additional example data, we use a collection of the following five recipes:

- Beef Parmesan with Garlic Angel Hair Pasta
- Ricotta Pie
- Linguine Pescadoro
- Zuppa Inglese
- Cailles en Sarcophages

The last one in particular is chosen due to its complicated nature, with ingredient nesting depth four (most often seen in such French recipes). The XML document containing these recipes is available online at this URL:

```
http://www.brics.dk/ixwt/examples/recipes.xml
```

Note that we have presented just one possible design of an XML language for recipes. We do not claim that this design is particularly ingenious, but it is nevertheless a reasonably realistic one and it suffices to illustrate the central points about XML and the related technologies.

2.8   Chapter Summary

XML is a hot technology that supports the development of markup languages for any imaginable domain of information. Still, XML is by itself just a notation for hierarchically structured text, and not even a particularly clever one. The real force of XML is that people agree on it and that it is surrounded by a swarm of generic languages and tools. This means that by building on XML, one gets a massive infrastructure for free. XML has an advantageous tradition of openness, which is reflected by the immediate availability of specifications and free or Open Source tools.

In this chapter, we have seen the conceptual view of XML as a tree model and the concrete textual representation, and in addition, the namespace mechanism that most other XML technologies rely on. A central concept is that of *well-formedness* which ties together the two views of XML.

In the following chapters, we will see that the XML vision offers *schemas* for describing classes of documents, *transformations* for converting from one document class to another, *querying* for extraction of information from XML documents, and *programming APIs* for manipulating XML data from general-purpose programming languages. Other related technologies, which are not covered by this book, include techniques for encryption and digital signatures for XML documents, and also the development of the *semantic Web* using, in particular, the *Resource Description Framework* (RDF). More information about these activities can be found from the online resources for this chapter.

2.9   Further Reading

The XML 1.0 and 1.1 specifications are published by W3C [14, 15]; see also the online resources below. Details about the XML Namespace mechanism can be found in the specification [13]. The XHTML language is explained in the specifications [68, 1, 2]. The technical differences between SGML and XML are explained in a W3C note [21]. The W3C recommendations [58] and [26] describe the XML Base mechanism for resolving relative URIs and the XML Information Set.

The XMill compression tool is presented in the paper [56]. For more information about CML, see the paper [65]. The specification for the WML language and the related standards can be found on the Open Mobile Alliance Web site [86]. More information about ebXML can be found at the project Web site [81]. A long list of other XML applications is available from the XML Cover Pages (see below).

2.10   Online Resources

http://www.w3.org/XML/
> W3C's XML home page. Contains an overview of the W3C's XML activities and specifications.

http://www.w3.org/TR/xml11/
> The XML 1.1 W3C recommendation – this is where to look for the gory technical details of the XML notation.

```
http://www.w3.org/TR/xml-names11
```
Namespaces in XML 1.1, a W3C recommendation.

```
http://www.w3.org/TR/xpath-datamodel/
```
The definition of the data model for XPath 2.0 and XQuery 1.0.

```
http://www.xmlhack.com/
```
`<?xmlhack?>`, a site with concise news from the XML community.

```
http://xml.coverpages.org/
```
The Cover Pages. A comprehensive and cumulative reference collection of XML language standards and their applications.

```
http://www.xml.org/
```
OASIS's portal to XML resources.

```
http://www.ibiblio.org/xml/
```
Cafe con Leche, yet another useful site with XML news.

```
http://www.xmlsoftware.com/
```
A comprehensive list of tools for XML.

```
http://www.xmlspy.com/
```
XML Spy, one of many alternatives to Notepad and Emacs for editing XML documents at the tree level instead of the textual level.

```
http://xml.apache.org/
```
The Apache XML project, with popular and high quality Open Source tools for XML.

```
http://msdn.microsoft.com/xml/
```
Microsoft's XML Developer Center, with lots of XML information specific to Microsoft products.

```
http://www.xml.org/xml/xmldev.shtml
```
XML-DEV. A popular mail list dedicated to XML implementation and development discussions.

2.11   Exercises

The main lessons to be learned from these exercises are:

- XMLification of data, and editing XML documents with a raw text editor; and
- the notion of well-formedness and relevant tools.

Exercise 2.1 Explain briefly the relations between SGML, XML, HTML, and XHTML.

Exercise 2.2 Design an XML language to represent *driving directions*. For an example of a driving direction, see *EX*/driving.txt. There are countless different solutions, but try to make a fine-grained model. Convert *EX*/driving.txt to fit into your new XML language.

Exercise 2.3

    (a)   Draw the tree representation of the XML document *EX*/tree1.xml.

    (b)   Write the textual representation of the XML tree shown at *EX*/tree2.gif.

Exercise 2.4 Identify all the constituents (elements, attributes, character data, processing instructions, and so on) of the XML document *EX*/moose.xml.

Exercise 2.5 Which of the documents *EX*/doc1.xml, *EX*/doc2.xml, ..., *EX*/doc5.xml consist of well-formed XML? (Try first without using a tool.)

TIP

A simple way of checking that a document is well-formed XML is to view it in a (reasonably new) browser. If the XML tree structure is shown (as in Figure 2.4) without error messages, the document is well-formed. (This requires the file extension to be '.xml' and that there are no stylesheet references in the file.)

You can also use the sample program CheckWellformed shown in Section 7.3.3.

Exercise 2.6 Add the ravioli recipe at *EX*/ravioli.txt to the recipe collection XML file. Make sure the result is well-formed XML.

Exercise 2.7 Convert the HTML document *EX*/cows.html to XHTML. Try first manually, then using HTML Tidy.

Exercise 2.8 Consider the document *EX*/namespaces.xml.

    (a)   Which namespaces do the elements foo, bar, and baz belong to?

    (b)   Which namespaces do the attributes qux, quux, and corge belong to?

Exercise 2.9 Answer the following questions by studying the specifications of XML 1.1 and namespaces:

    (a)   Which element names and attribute names are allowed? (That is, what exactly is a legal QName?)

    (b)   Which Unicode code points are allowed in character data and attribute values?

    (c)   Which strings are allowed in XML comments?

Exercise 2.10 In XML documents that have an XML declaration, no whitespace or comments are permitted before this XML declaration. Is there a good reason for this requirement?

Exercise 2.11 Research the technical differences between XML 1.0 and 1.1 and find the motivation for the changes.

NAVIGATING XML TREES WITH XPATH

3

Objectives

In this chapter, you will learn:

- Location steps and paths for navigating around XML documents

- Abbreviations

- General expressions

3.1   Pointing into XML Documents

The development of several different XML technologies has identified a common need for a flexible notation for pointing into and navigating around XML documents. This has resulted in the XPath language, which is used for uniqueness and scope descriptions in XML Schema, for pattern matching and selection in XSLT, for selection and iteration in XQuery, and as a key component of XLink and XPointer. A part of XPath is also able to express computations on data values, which is exploited in XSLT and XQuery.

A typical example of XPath applied to our recipe collection is the following expression, which selects the names of those ingredients of which half a cup is used:

```
//rcp:ingredient[@amount='0.5' and @unit='cup']/@name
```

This particular expression uses an abbreviated notation and exploits several tacit conventions. However, we will start by learning the general structure of unabbreviated XPath expressions.

XPath started out as a relatively simple language, known as XPath 1.0. Through its interaction with the development of the XQuery language, it has evolved into a much larger language, XPath 2.0. The following presentation will start by presenting the XPath 1.0

features (which form a subset of XPath 2.0) and then dive into the more advanced features which are mostly used in connection with XQuery, the topic of Chapter 6. Some important differences between the two different XPath versions will be explained en route.

3.2 Location Steps and Paths

An XPath *location path* evaluates to a *sequence* of nodes in a given XML tree (as defined in Section 2.3). The resulting sequence will always be sorted in document order and will never contain duplicates of identical nodes. The location path itself is built as a sequence of *location steps* (separated by a / character), each of which consists of an *axis*, a *node test*, and zero or more *predicates* (which are XPath expressions):

```
axis :: nodetest [ exp₁ ] [ exp₂ ] ...
```

An example of a location path is

```
child::rcp:recipe[attribute::id='117'] /
child::rcp:ingredient /
attribute::amount
```

which in a recipe collection selects all the `amount` attributes in `ingredient` nodes below the `recipe` nodes in which the `id` attribute has value `117`. The location path consists of three location steps:

```
child::rcp:recipe[attribute::id='117']
```

```
child::rcp:ingredient
```

```
attribute::amount
```

In the first of these, `child` is the axis, `rcp:recipe` is the node test, and the condition `attribute::id='117'` is a predicate.

The axis, node test, and predicates may be viewed as increasingly detailed descriptions of the sequence of nodes to which the step should lead. A reasonable analogy is that of driving directions: as a first approximation we are told to drive north (the axis), later on we are told to look for a house (the name test), and finally we are told to stop at a particular street and number (the predicates).

A location step starts at a *context node* and evaluates to a sequence of nodes. This behavior may be generalized to a transformation from a sequence of nodes into a sequence of nodes by replacing each node in the input sequence with the result of evaluating the location step with that node as context node. With this view of a location step it is easy to define the

> A **location path** consists of **steps**, each composed of an **axis**, a **node test**, and some **predicates**. It is evaluated relatively to a **context**.

behavior of a location path as the composition of the behaviors of the steps. This definition can be illustrated by considering the following abstract XML tree:

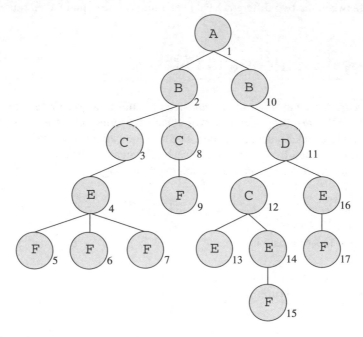

The nodes have been annotated with indices (corresponding to the document order) to allow identification of different nodes with the same element name. Evaluating the location path

```
descendant::C/child::E/child::F
```

starting at the A_1 node happens in three steps. First, the location step `descendant::C` is evaluated, which results in the sequence of nodes

$$C_3 \quad C_8 \quad C_{12}$$

corresponding to all C nodes that are descendants of the initial node. The next step `child::E` selects all child nodes named E from each of these nodes, resulting in the concatenated sequence

$$E_4 \quad E_{13} \quad E_{14}$$

Finally, the step `child::F` selects from these nodes the child nodes named F, resulting in the following sequence:

$$F_5 \quad F_6 \quad F_7 \quad F_{15}$$

Notice that the nodes C_8 and E_{13} do not contribute to the final result.

The analogy to file systems introduced in Chaper 2 is relevant again, since location paths have been inspired by Unix file paths. Consider again the directory structure:

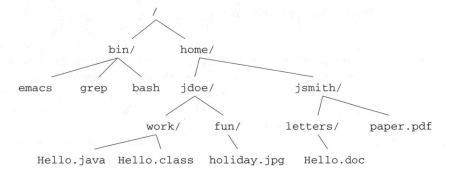

Assuming we start from the root, the Unix file path

```
home/*/*/Hello.*
```

selects all the files named `Hello` (with an arbitrary extension) two levels below the `home` directory, resulting in the files `Hello.java`, `Hello.class`, and `Hello.doc`. This file *path* may be viewed as consisting of four individual file *steps*, each of which moves from a node to a set of nodes. The step `home` selects any child node with that name, the two * steps select all child nodes, and the `Hello.*` step selects any child node with name `Hello` regardless of file extension. The composite behavior of these steps is obtained in just the same manner as for XPath location steps. Indeed, the XPath language is heavily inspired by Unix file path syntax but is much more general and expressive.

3.2.1   Contexts

The *context* of an XPath expression evaluation contains:

- a context *node* (a node in an XML tree);

- a context *position* and *size* (two non-negative integers, the meaning of which is explained below);

- a set of *variable bindings* (mapping variable names to values);

- a *function library* (providing useful functionality); and

- a set of *namespace declarations* (mapping prefixes to namespace URIs).

The initial context is determined by the application that invokes the XPath evaluation. When a location path starts with the character '/' the initial context node is forced to be the root node (*not* to be confused with the root element) of the XML tree and the initial position and size are both 1. The XPath specification guarantees that a core collection of functions is supported by all implementations. In the examples below, we assume that the context binds the namespace

```
http://www.brics.dk/ixwt/recipes
```

to the namespace prefix `rcp`.

During evaluation of multiple location steps, the context node, position, and size change. Assume that an intermediate result sequence of length n has been obtained. The next step is now evaluated for each of the contained nodes, and for the i'th one the context node is the node itself, the context position is i and the context size is n. The context position and size are used in connection with predicates as explained below.

As an example, consider again the example tree from above. The evaluation of the location path

```
descendant::E/child::F
```

contains two steps. Assume that the first step is evaluated with the document root as context node and context size and position both have value 1. The result of the first step is then this sequence:

$$\text{Ⓔ}_4 \quad \text{Ⓔ}_{13} \quad \text{Ⓔ}_{14} \quad \text{Ⓔ}_{16}$$

The second step is now evaluated with each of these four nodes as context node. In each case the context size is 4, and the context position is in turn 1, 2, 3, and 4. The results of these four evaluations are in turn $\text{Ⓕ}_5 \text{ Ⓕ}_6 \text{ Ⓕ}_7$, the empty sequence, Ⓕ_{15}, and Ⓕ_{17}, the concatenation of which forms the final result of the location path evaluation:

$$\text{Ⓕ}_5 \quad \text{Ⓕ}_6 \quad \text{Ⓕ}_7 \quad \text{Ⓕ}_{15} \quad \text{Ⓕ}_{17}$$

3.2.2   Axes

An *axis* is a sequence of nodes located relative to the context node. It is a first approximation to the sequence that we wish to obtain as the result of a location step. XPath supports 12 different axes:

`child`: the children of the context node (which do not include attribute nodes).

`descendant`: the descendants of the context node (again, not including attribute nodes).

`parent`: the unique parent node of the context node, but the empty sequence if the context node is the root node.

`ancestor`: all ancestors of the context node, from the parent to the root.

`following-sibling`: the right-hand siblings of the context node, but the empty sequence for attribute nodes.

`preceding-sibling`: the left-hand siblings of the context node, but the empty sequence for attribute nodes.

`following`: all nodes appearing strictly later in the document than the context node, but excluding descendants.

`preceding`: all nodes appearing strictly earlier in the document than the context node, but excluding ancestors.

`attribute`: all attribute nodes of the context node.

`self`: the context node itself (this axis is mainly included for completeness, but it is also useful in connection with the abbreviations explained in Section 3.4).

`descendant-or-self`: the concatenation of the `self` and `descendant` sequences.

`ancestor-or-self`: the concatenation of the `self` and `ancestor` sequences.

The main axes are illustrated in Figure 3.1. Each axis has a *direction*, which determines the order in which the nodes are assigned positions in the sequence. A *forward* axis list the nodes in document order, whereas a *backward* axis uses the reverse order. The forward axes are `child`, `descendant`, `following-sibling`, `following`, `self`, and `descendant-or-self`, and the backward axes are `parent`, `ancestor`, `preceding-sibling`, and `preceding`. For the `attribute` axis, the order unfortunately depends on the implementation but it is required to be *stable*, meaning that the implementation must always choose the same order for a given input. Note that the axes `self`, `ancestor`, `descendant`, `preceding`, and `following` for any given context node constitute a disjoint partition of the nodes in any XML tree.

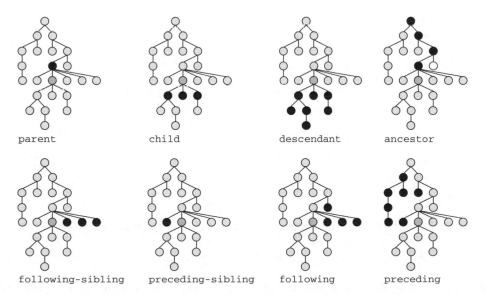

| parent | child | descendant | ancestor |
| following-sibling | preceding-sibling | following | preceding |

Figure 3.1 Some axes (black) for a context node (gray).

3.2.3 Node Tests

The second part of a location step is the *node test*, which roughly filters the kinds of nodes in the specified axis. There are several different kinds of node tests:

`text()` selects only the character data nodes.

`comment()` selects only the comment nodes.

`processing-instruction()` selects only the processing instruction nodes.

`node()` selects all nodes.

`*` selects all nodes of a certain kind depending on the axis in front of the node test: for the `attribute` axis, `*` selects all attribute nodes, and for any other axis, `*` selects all element nodes.

name selects the nodes with the given name (a QName; see Section 2.6).

`*:`*localname* selects the nodes with the given name in any namespace.

prefix`:*` selects nodes as `*` but only those in the given namespace.

The namespace prefixes are resolved using the namespace declarations in the current context. Frustratingly, the XPath 1.0 specification requires a missing namespace prefix to be interpreted as the empty URI rather than as the default namespace which would seem to be a more reasonable choice. This design bug has since been fixed in the XPath 2.0 specification, but as most tools implement XPath 1.0, this is an annoying practical problem. Consider, for example, the following XML document:

```
<widget type="gadget" xmlns="http://www.widget.inc">
  <head size="medium"/>
  <big><subwidget ref="gizmo"/></big>
  <info xmlns:xhtml="http://www.w3.org/TR/xhtml1">
    <xhtml:head>
      <xhtml:title>Description of gadget</xhtml:title>
    </xhtml:head>
    <xhtml:body>
      <xhtml:h1>Gadget</xhtml:h1>
      A gadget contains a big gizmo
    </xhtml:body>
  </info>
</widget>
```

To select attribute nodes in this document, we could try an expression like

```
/child::widget/child::big/child::subwidget/attribute::ref
```

but unfortunately, the node tests all fail, since the missing namespace prefix is interpreted as denoting the empty namespace string. In fact, no XPath 1.0 expression will work correctly.

To make this example work with both the old and the new XPath versions, we must introduce an explicit namespace prefix

```
<wdg:widget type="gadget" xmlns:wdg="http://www.widget.inc">
  <wdg:head size="medium"/>
  <wdg:big><wdg:subwidget ref="gizmo"/></wdg:big>
  <wdg:info xmlns:xhtml="http://www.w3.org/TR/xhtml1">
    <xhtml:head>
      <xhtml:title>Description of gadget</xhtml:title>
    </xhtml:head>
    <xhtml:body>
      <xhtml:h1>Gadget</xhtml:h1>
      A gadget contains a big gizmo
    </xhtml:body>
  </wdg:info>
</wdg:widget>
```

and change the XPath expression correspondingly:

```
/child::wdg:widget/child::wdg:big/child::wdg:subwidget/attribute::ref
```

3.2.4 Predicates

The final part of a location step consists of zero or more *predicates* written in [...]. These are just XPath expressions of various types that are evaluated as boolean conditions. General XPath expressions, presented later in this chapter, are as rich as expressions in, for example, Java and may produce values of many different types, including numbers, booleans, strings, and sequences. When used as predicates, these values are *coerced* into booleans as follows:

- a *number* corresponds to *true* when its value equals the current context position;
- a *string* corresponds to *true* when it has non-zero length; and
- a *sequence* corresponds to *true* when it has non-zero length.

This coercion is explained further in Section 3.5.8. Expressions of all types may be combined as booleans using the operators and and or, and the function not for which the arguments are coerced as described in Section 3.5.10. Variables from the context are referenced using the syntax $foo, where foo is the name of the variable, as described in Section 3.5.4. The usual arithmetic and comparison operators are also available, as described in Sections 3.5.5 and 3.5.9.

Note that it is very useful to use location paths as predicates, since that allows for testing properties of surrounding nodes without actually moving there. Such nested location paths are evaluated using the current node as context node. As an example, consider the expression

```
/descendant::rcp:recipe
    [descendant::rcp:ingredient[attribute::name='sugar']]
```

which selects those recipes that contain sugar as an ingredient. In contrast, the expression

```
/descendant::rcp:recipe/
descendant::rcp:ingredient[attribute::name='sugar']
```

selects those ingredients whose name is sugar.

Note that the order of predicates, in general, does not commute. Consider the position function which returns the current context position. Using this function, the location path

```
/descendant::rcp:ingredient[position()=3][position()=1]
```

returns the third ingredient, while

```
/descendant::rcp:ingredient[position()=1][position()=3]
```

returns an empty sequence. Similarly, two predicates cannot be replaced by a conjunction as again

```
/descendant::rcp:ingredient[position()=3][position()=1]
```

returns the third ingredient, while

```
/descendant::rcp:ingredient[position()=3 and position()=1]
```

returns the empty sequence.

3.3   Typical Location Paths

The full XPath language is very large, but a little goes a long way. A few patterns seem to be used repeatedly and are worth mentioning specifically.

The child, descendant, and attribute axes are by far the most common. The node test is most frequently *, text(), or *QName*, as illustrated by these examples:

```
/descendant::rcp:recipe/child::rcp:title
```

which selects the title of each recipe,

```
/descendant::rcp:recipe/descendant::rcp:ingredient/attribute::name
```

which selects the name of each ingredient, and

```
/descendant::rcp:*/child::text()
```

which selects all character data in the collection.

Predicates are more varied, but the following examples cover most cases. Testing existence of an attribute:

```
[attribute::amount]
```

Testing equality of an attribute value:

```
[attribute::name='flour']
```

Testing inequality of an attribute value:

```
[attribute::name!='flour']
```

Testing two things at once:

```
[attribute::amount<0.5 and attribute::unit='cup']
```

Testing position of the context node:

```
[position()=2]
```

Probing the subtree below (for existence of an ingredient):

```
[descendant::rcp:ingredient]
```

Finally, note that XPath expressions often appear as attribute values of other XML languages, such as XML Schema and XSLT. In those cases it is necessary to escape special characters, such that one writes

```
<xsl:apply-templates
    select="descendant::rcp:ingredient[attribute::amount&lt;0.5]"/>
```

instead of

```
<xsl:apply-templates
    select="descendant::rcp:ingredient[attribute::amount<0.5]"/>
```

simply because of the escaping rules explained in Section 2.4 that generally apply to XML documents.

3.4   Abbreviations

Inspired by Unix file path expressions, XPath allows a number of abbreviations that make location paths easier to write (but also makes XPath more difficult to learn). First, if no axis is specified, then the `child` axis is used as default. Thus, the location path

```
/child::rcp:collection/child::rcp:recipe/child::rcp:ingredient
```

may instead be written as

```
/rcp:collection/rcp:recipe/rcp:ingredient
```

Similarly, the `attribute::` axis specification may be replaced by the @ character, so that now

```
/child::rcp:collection/child::rcp:recipe/child::rcp:ingredient/
attribute::amount
```

may instead be written as

```
/rcp:collection/rcp:recipe/rcp:ingredient/@amount
```

The entire location path fragment

```
/descendant-or-self::node()/
```

may be written as `//` instead, which leads to all nodes in the current subtree. To select all `ingredient` nodes in a given recipe, we may thus write

```
//rcp:recipe[rcp:title='Ricotta Pie']//rcp:ingredient
```

Finally, the character `.` abbreviates the location step `self::node()` and `..` abbreviates the location step `parent::node()`, which correspond closely to the syntax for Unix file paths. Thus, the location path

```
//rcp:nutrition[@calories=349]/../rcp:title/text()
```

finds the titles of recipes containing 349 calories. The unabbreviated version of this location path is more daunting:

```
/descendant-or-self::node()/
child::rcp:nutrition[attribute::calories=349]/
parent::node()/child::rcp:title/child::text()
```

XPath with abbreviations suffers from some syntactic subtleties that may cause confusion. We might expect that the location path

```
//rcp:recipe/rcp:ingredient[//rcp:ingredient]
```

selects all the *composite* ingredients, but instead it selects *all* ingredients. The error comes from the fact that any XPath expression starting with the character / is evaluated with the document root as context node. Thus, the nested location path //rcp:ingredient is not evaluated relatively to the current node as we expected. The workaround is to change the location path to the seemingly equivalent syntax:

```
//rcp:recipe/rcp:ingredient[.//rcp:ingredient]
```

simply to avoid the initial / character. Another common point of confusion is that the location path

```
//rcp:ingredient[1]
```

selects *many* ingredients, namely all of those that are first among their siblings, whereas the location path

```
/descendant::rcp:ingredient[1]
```

selects only a single ingredient, namely the one that is first in the document order. The difference is, of course, that the first version really expands to

```
/descendant-or-self::node()/rcp:ingredient[1]
```

and thus performs two steps of which the predicate applies to the second.

3.5   General Expressions

XPath started out as a relatively small language corresponding to the above descriptions. However, more and more computational tasks have been included in its design, culminating with the XPath 2.0 language, which has many advanced features that are motivated mainly by its use in the XQuery 1.0 language. The following describes the features of XPath 2.0. A brief overview of keywords and operators is presented in Figure 3.2.

XPath has grown into a large language for expressing computations on **sequences**.

```
$ , to | union intersect except .
+ - * div idiv mod and or
= != > >= < <=
eq ne lt le gt ge
is << >>
for in if then else some every satisfies
```

Figure 3.2 Keywords and operators in XPath 2.0.

3.5.1 Values and Atomization

Every expression evaluates to a possibly empty *sequence* of *items*, which are either *atomic values* or *nodes*. The atomic values may be of the following kinds:

- numbers which are either *integers*, *decimals*, *floats*, or *doubles*, as described in Section 4.4.2;

- *booleans*;

- *strings* of Unicode characters;

- *datatypes* defined in XML Schema, as described in Chapter 4.

In the following, we disregard the latter possibility and only consider the simple atomic values.

Note that values are always sequences, thus atomic values and nodes are not permitted by themselves. As a convenience, XPath allows expressions denoting such values automatically to be interpreted as singleton sequences.

A node identifies a particular node in a given input tree. Thus, it has a node *identity* as explained in Section 2.3. Also, a node unambiguously corresponds to the subtree that it roots.

A sequence may be *atomized*, which results in a sequence of atomic values. This sequence is obtained by replacing every node with its *string value*, corresponding to these rules:

text nodes: the string value is the contents of the text node.

element nodes: the string value is the concatenation in document order of the string values of all descendant text nodes.

attribute nodes: the string value is the attribute value.

comment nodes: the string value is the comment text.

processing instruction nodes: the string value is the processing instruction value.

root nodes: the string value is the concatenation in document order of the string values of all descendant text nodes.

3.5.2 Literal Expressions

A literal expression denotes a constant atomic value, or more precisely, a singleton sequence containing that value. The various kinds of numbers are written in the expected manner such that

```
42
```

denotes an integer,

```
3.1415
```

denotes a decimal number, and

```
6.022E23
```

denotes a float or a double. Strings are denoted enclosed in single or double quotes, for example:

```
'XPath is a lot of fun'
"XPath is a lot of fun"
```

Note that XPath expressions often appear as attribute values of XML document, in which case it is important to distinguish between

```
... select="'recipe'"...
```

which denotes an XPath expression that is a string literal, and

```
... select="recipe"...
```

which is an XPath expression that denotes a location step. Quoting always raises the question of how to write string literals that themselves contain quotes. In XPath the solution is to use alternating or double occurrences such that

```
'The cat said "Meow!"'
"The cat said ""Meow!"""
```

both denote the following string:

```
The cat said "Meow!"
```

Note that there is no XPath syntax for denoting other special characters in strings, like tabs, newlines, or general Unicode characters. The file containing the XPath expression is assumed to be a Unicode file in which such characters can occur directly in string constants. Thus, string constants may also contain newline characters, such as

```
"XPath is
    just
     so
    much
    fun!"
```

which certainly looks funny, but is just a sequence of Unicode characters enclosed by quotes. When XPath expressions occur inside XML files, as is the case for XSLT and XML Schema, then Unicode characters may as always be denoted using the character references explained in Section 2.4.

There are no literal expressions for denoting boolean values. Instead, the constant functions `true()` and `false()` may be used (see Section 3.5.11). The rationale is that an occurrence of an identifier as an expression should always be interpreted as abbreviated syntax for location steps, as explained in Section 3.5.7.

3.5.3   Comments

Comments are allowed throughout XPath expressions, using the following syntax:

```
(: this is a comment :)
```

Nesting of comments is allowed.

3.5.4   Variable References

Variable references are written as

```
$foo
```

where `foo` is then a variable bound either in the context of the XPath expression or created through bindings in `for` expressions (see Section 3.5.12) or quantified expressions (see Section 3.5.14). Variables may, of course, contain arbitrary values. Legal variable names correspond to the class QName defined in Chapter 2; in particular, variables may belong to namespaces:

```
$bar:foo
```

3.5.5   Arithmetic Expressions

XPath supports the usual arithmetic operators with the standard operator precedences. Specifically, all four kinds of numbers allow addition (+), subtraction (-), multiplication (*), and division (`div`). Integers furthermore allow integer division (`idiv`) and modulo (`mod`). Finally, unary minus (-) is allowed for all four kinds of numbers.

The arguments are, of course, required to be of the expected types. However, since all expressions result in sequences, the following rules must be applied:

- if any argument is an empty sequence, then the result is an empty sequence;
- if all arguments are singleton sequences containing numbers of the expected kinds, then the corresponding operation is performed;
- otherwise, a runtime error occurs.

There is yet another syntactic confusion to be concerned about. Since variables names are QNames, they may contain digits and the – character. Thus, the expression

```
$foo-17
```

is a reference to a variable whose name is supposed to be `foo-17`, a perfectly legal QName. To express the intended subtraction computation, we can instead write one of the following

```
($foo)-17
```

```
$foo -17
```

```
$foo+-17
```

or any other variation separating the minus sign from the variable name.

3.5.6   Sequence Expressions

If each exp_i is an expression, then

$$exp_1, \ exp_2, \ \ldots, \ exp_n$$

constructs a new sequence obtained by concatenation of the sequences denoted by each of the expressions. If $n = 0$ then the expression denotes the empty sequence. Note that since concatenation is always performed, it is impossible to construct nested sequences. Thus, the expression

```
(1, (2, 3, 4), ((5)), (), (((6,7),8),9))
```

evaluates to the same result as

```
1, 2, 3, 4, 5, 6, 7, 8, 9
```

The expression

$$exp_1 \ \textbf{to} \ exp_2$$

requires that exp_1 and exp_2 evaluate to (singleton sequences containing) integers and produces the sequence of integers in the given range. Thus, the above integer sequence can also be expressed as

```
1 to 9
```

Sequences containing only nodes can be combined using the infix operators `union` (or `|`), `intersect`, and `except` (meaning set difference). All these operations perform the corresponding set operation on the nodes contained in the argument sequences and return the result in a sequence in which duplicates of identical nodes are eliminated and the resulting nodes are arranged in document order. Note that the sequence generated by the expression *exp* can be sorted in document order by the expression

```
exp | ()
```

since the empty union evaluation has that side-effect.

3.5.7 Path Expressions

The location paths presented in Section 3.2 are directly XPath expressions, also when written in abbreviated syntax. As usual, a location path is evaluated in a number of steps, starting with the context node.

However, it is also possible to evaluate location steps starting from arbitrary node sequence expressions. Thus, the resulting sequence is obtained by evaluating the location path with each of the initial sequence elements as context node, with context position equal to the position in the sequence, and context size equal to the length of the sequence. The result is, as usual, the concatenation of each of these resulting sequences, sorted in document order. An example is the expression

```
(fn:doc("veggie.xml"), fn:doc("bbq.xml"))//rcp:title
```

which selects the titles of recipes from two different collections. The `fn:doc` function returns the document root node of the given document (as explained in Section 3.5.11). For multiple document, as in the above example, the document order between nodes from different trees depends on the implementation but is required to be stable.

3.5.8 Filter Expressions

The predicates from location paths are generalized to arbitrary sequences containing mixtures of atomic values and nodes. The syntax is as usual

```
exp₁ [ exp₂ ]
```

which allows filtering by an arbitrary expression that is coerced into boolean. This coercion is normally done by converting the resulting value to its effective boolean value, as described in Section 3.5.10, but if the resulting value is an integer, then it is instead compared to the value of the context position.

Inside the filter expression, the current sequence item may be referred by the *context item expression*, whose syntax is simply a dot (`.`). Do not confuse this use of `.` with the one explained in Section 3.4. Similarly, the context position is defined to be the position of the item in the sequence, and the context size is the size of the sequence. The definitions seamlessly generalize those for location step predicates as described in Section 3.2.4. As an example, the expression

```
(30 to 60)[. mod 5 = 0 and position()>20]
```

has the same result as the expression

```
50, 55, 60
```

Note that the expression

```
//rcp:ingredient[8]
```

is syntactically ambiguous, since [8] could either be a predicate or a filter expression, but fortunately the semantics of the two interpretations coincide.

3.5.9 Comparison Expressions

There are three different kinds of comparison operators, corresponding to different interpretations of the values to be compared. This choice is a potential cause of much confusion for XPath programmers.

Value Comparisons

The *value comparison* operators eq, ne, lt, le, gt, and ge are used to compare atomic values. When applied to two arbitrary values, the following steps are performed:

- the two values are atomized (see Section 3.5.1);
- if either resulting sequence is empty, the result is the empty sequence;
- if either resulting sequence has length greater than one, the result is false;
- if the two atomic values are incomparable (such as, 7 and "abc"), a runtime error occurs;
- otherwise, the result is obtained by comparing the two atomic values.

For example, the following comparisons all yield the value true:

```
8 eq 4+4

//rcp:description/text() eq "Some recipes used in the XML tutorial."

(//rcp:ingredient)[1]/@name eq "beef cube steak"
```

General Comparisons

The *general comparison* operators =, !=, <, <=, >, and >= are used to compare all values. When applied to two arbitrary values, the following steps are performed:

- the two values are atomized (see Section 3.5.1);

- if there exists a pair of atomic values, one from each argument, whose corresponding comparison holds, the result is true;

- otherwise, the result is false.

For example, the following comparisons all yield the value true:

```
8 = 4+4

(1,2) = (2,4)

//rcp:ingredient/@name = "salt"
```

Node Comparisons

The *node comparison* operators is, <<, and >> are used to compare nodes on identity and document order. When applied to two arbitrary values, the following steps are performed:

- if either sequence is empty, the result is the empty sequence;

- if both sequences are singletons containing nodes, the boolean result is obtained by comparing the two nodes;

- otherwise, a runtime error occurs.

For example, the following comparisons all yield the value true:

```
(//rcp:recipe)[2] is //rcp:recipe[rcp:title/text() eq "Ricotta Pie"]

/rcp:collection << (//rcp:recipe)[4]

(//rcp:recipe)[4] >> (//rcp:recipe[3])
```

Comparison Confusions

The three kinds of comparisons often yield different results and it must be considered carefully which one to use in a given situation. Consider again the recipe collection. In document order, ingredients number 40 and 53 are both `salt` but with different amounts. Under these assumptions, the comparison

```
(((//rcp:ingredient)[40]/@name, (//rcp:ingredient)[40]/@amount) eq
(((//rcp:ingredient)[53]/@name, (//rcp:ingredient)[53]/@amount)
```

yields the value false, since the two arguments are not singleton lists. The comparison

```
(((//rcp:ingredient)[40]/@name, (//rcp:ingredient)[40]/@amount) =
(((//rcp:ingredient)[53]/@name, (//rcp:ingredient)[53]/@amount)
```

yields the value true, since the two names are found to be equal. Finally, the comparison

```
(((//rcp:ingredient)[40]/@name, (//rcp:ingredient)[40]/@amount) is
(((//rcp:ingredient)[53]/@name, (//rcp:ingredient)[53]/@amount)
```

yields a runtime error, since the arguments are not singletons.

Yet another kind of equality test is available as the `fn:deep-equal` function, which tests for *structural* equivalence of the arguments as explained in Section 3.5.11.

The comparison operators may seem to be designed by ad hoc pragmatic considerations, however, backwards compatibility with XPath 1.0 has been a major consideration. The resulting semantics is not intuitive to most programmers. In ordinary mathematical thinking, equality operators obey the following logical axioms:

reflexivity	$x = x$
symmetry	$x = y \Rightarrow y = x$
transitivity	$x = y \wedge y = z \Rightarrow x = z$
	$x < y \wedge y < z \Rightarrow x < z$
anti-symmetry	$x \leq y \wedge y \leq x \Rightarrow x = y$
negation	$x \neq y \Leftrightarrow \neg\, x = y$

Unfortunately, the XPath comparison operators violate several of these axioms:

- reflexivity does not hold, since `()=()` yields false, and also `() is ()` yields `()`;

- transitivity of equality does not hold since `(1,2)=(2,3)` yields true and `(2,3)=(3,4)` yields true, but `(1,2)=(3,4)` yields false;

- anti-symmetry does not hold, since `(1,4)<=(2,3)` yields true and `(2,3)<=(1,4)` yields true, but `(1,4)=(2,3)` yields false;

- negation does not hold, since both `(1)!=()` and `(1)=()` yield false.

The consequence is that programmers sadly cannot rely on ordinary mathematical logic, but must think carefully about the many special cases. However, when restricted to singleton sequences, value comparisons adhere to mathematical intuition.

3.5.10 Boolean Expressions

XPath supports the usual boolean operators `and` and `or`. They both accept arbitrary values as argument, which are then coerced to *effective boolean values*. This coercion yields true for the following values:

- the boolean value true;
- a non-empty string;
- a number different from 0; or
- a non-empty sequence whose first item is a node.

The coercion yields false if the value is

- the boolean value false;
- the empty string;
- the number 0; or
- the empty sequence.

In cases not covered here, the result is undefined or an error. Boolean constants may be constructed using the functions `false()` and `true()`, and negation is computed by the unary function `not(exp)`. Notice that the only difference between this kind of coercion and the one used for predicate expressions (see Section 3.2.4) is the treatment of numbers.

3.5.11 Functions

XPath offers a lot of functionality through function libraries. The context defines function namespaces and signatures of the corresponding functions. One such namespace must correspond to the URI

```
http://www.w3.org/2005/04/xpath-functions
```

which traditionally has namespace prefix `fn` and is also chosen as the default namespace. This namespace contains 106 signatures of functions that any XPath 2.0 implementation must provide. Additionally, the namespace

```
http://www.w3.org/2001/XMLSchema
```

which traditionally has namespace prefix `xs`, provides several important functions for coercing and constructing data values (see Chapter 4).

In this section we will only look at some of the most important ones. The remaining functions and the full documentation for those presented here is available at the URL

```
http://www.w3.org/TR/xpath-functions/
```

Functions are called with the usual syntax, and the order of evaluation of arguments is defined to be dependent on the implementation. There is yet another syntactic quirk concerning function calls. The fn:avg function takes a single argument which is a sequence of numbers and computes their average value. However, the call

```
fn:avg(1,2,3,4)
```

fails, since the sequence constant is parsed as four arguments. Instead, the function must be called as

```
fn:avg((1,2,3,4))
```

In general, be careful about the somewhat brittle XPath syntax.

We now present the most important functions available in XPath (see also Figure 3.3). First, the abs, ceiling, floor, and round functions perform the usual arithmetic operations:

```
fn:abs(-23.4) = 23.4
fn:ceiling(23.4) = 24
fn:floor(23.4) = 23
fn:round(23.4) = 23
fn:round(23.5) = 24
```

fn:abs	fn:ceiling	fn:floor
fn:round	fn:concat	fn:string-join
fn:substring	fn:string-length	fn:upper-case
fn:lower-case	fn:contains	fn:matches
fn:replace	fn:true	fn:false
fn:not	fn:empty	fn:exists
fn:count	fn:distinct-values	fn:insert-before
fn:remove	fn:reverse	fn:subsequence
fn:deep-equal	fn:avg	fn:max
fn:min	fn:sum	fn:doc
fn:position	fn:last	xs:integer
xs:decimal	xs:float	xs:double
xs:boolean	xs:string	fn:in-scope-prefixes
fn:namespace-uri-for-prefix		

Figure 3.3 Important functions in XPath 2.0.

The `true` and `false` functions generate the boolean constants, and the `not` function performs negation of the effective boolean value of its argument:

```
fn:not(0) = fn:true()
fn:not(fn:true()) = fn:false()
fn:not("") = fn:true()
fn:not((1)) = fn:false()
```

The functions `concat`, `string-join`, `substring`, `string-length`, `upper-case`, and `lower-case` perform simple standard manipulation on strings:

```
fn:concat("X","ML") = "XML"
fn:concat("X","ML"," ","book") = "XML book"
fn:string-join(("XML","book")," ") = "XML book"
fn:string-join(("1","2","3"),"+") = "1+2+3"
fn:substring("XML book",5) = "book"
fn:substring("XML book",2,4) = "ML b"
fn:string-length("XML book") = 8
fn:upper-case("XML book") = "XML BOOK"
fn:lower-case("XML book") = "xml book"
```

The function `contains` checks if the second argument is a substring of the first argument. The functions `matches` and `replace` perform regular pattern matching on strings, using the notion of regular expressions that we explain in Section 4.4.2:

```
fn:contains("XML book","XML") = fn:true()
fn:matches("XML book","XM..[a-z]*") = fn:true()
fn:matches("XML book",".*Z.*") = fn:false()
fn:replace("XML book","XML","Web") = "Web book"
fn:replace("XML book","[a-z]","8") = "XML 8888"
```

The functions `fn:empty`, `fn:exists`, and `fn:count` decide cardinality of general sequences (`fn:empty` and `fn:exists` are just negations of each other):

```
fn:exists(()) = fn:false()
fn:exists((1,2,3,4)) = fn:true()
fn:empty(()) = fn:true()
fn:empty((1,2,3,4)) = fn:false()
fn:count((1,2,3,4)) = 4
fn:count(//rcp:recipe) = 5
```

The functions `fn:distinct-values`, `fn:insert-before`, `fn:remove`, `fn:reverse`, and `fn:subsequence` perform computations on general sequences:

```
fn:distinct-values((1, 2, 3, 4, 3, 2)) = (1, 2, 3, 4)
fn:insert-before((2, 4, 6, 8), 2, (3, 5)) = (2, 3, 5, 4, 6, 8)
```

```
fn:remove((2, 4, 6, 8), 3) = (2, 4, 8)
fn:reverse((2, 4, 6, 8)) = (8, 6, 4, 2)
fn:subsequence((2, 4, 6, 8, 10), 2) = (4, 6, 8, 10)
fn:subsequence((2, 4, 6, 8, 10), 2, 3) = (4, 6, 8)
```

The `fn:distinct-values` removes duplicates by comparing atomic values using the `eq` operator and nodes using the `is` operator. The order of the resulting sequence is defined to be dependent on the implementation.

The `fn:deep-equal` function compares two sequences as abstract trees, that is, recursively checks that they have the same structure with respect to node, attributes, and atomic values. This check is, of course, a potentially expensive operation, but sometimes it expresses the desired comparison when the `is` operator is too specific.

The `fn:avg`, `fn:max`, `fn:min`, and `fn:sum` aggregate functions operate on sequences of numbers:

```
fn:avg((2, 3, 4, 5, 6, 7)) = 4.5
fn:max((2, 3, 4, 5, 6, 7)) = 7
fn:min((2, 3, 4, 5, 6, 7)) = 2
fn:sum((2, 3, 4, 5, 6, 7)) = 27
```

The `doc` function reads in an XML document from a given URI and returns the document root node, such that

```
fn:doc("http://www.brics.dk/ixwt/examples/recipes.xml")//rcp:recipe
```

yields the sequence of five `recipe` nodes from our running example. Documents are cached, so that if the same URI is read again, the initially constructed root node is returned. This caching is important for testing node identity using the `is` operator. Thus, the expression

```
fn:doc("http://www.brics.dk/ixwt/examples/recipes.xml") is
fn:doc("http://www.brics.dk/ixwt/examples/recipes.xml")
```

evaluates to true.

The `fn:position` and `fn:last` functions simply access the current context position and context size.

The `fn:in-scope-prefixes` function returns for a given node the sequence of namespace prefixes that are declared for that node. The `fn:namespace-uri-for-prefix` returns for a given prefix and node the corresponding namespace URI.

The `xs:integer`, `xs:decimal`, `xs:float`, `xs:double`, `xs:boolean`, and `xs:string` functions perform casts into the given types. Examples of their results are seen in the following:

```
xs:integer("5") = 5
xs:integer(7.0) = 7
xs:decimal(5) = 5.0
```

```
xs:decimal("4.3") = 4.3
xs:decimal("4") = 4.0
xs:float(2) = 2.0E0
xs:double(14.3) = 1.43E1
xs:boolean(0) = fn:false()
xs:boolean("true") = fn:true()
xs:string(17) = "17"
xs:string(1.43E1) = "14.3"
xs:string(fn:true()) = "true"
```

As mentioned earlier, the full documentation for all XPath 2.0 functions is available online at

```
http://www.w3.org/2005/04/xpath-functions
```

3.5.12   For Expressions

The `for` expression computes a value by computing a subexpression for each item in a sequence and concatenating the results:

for $name **in** exp_1 **return** exp_2

The scope of the bound variable is the `return` expression. As an example, consider the expression

```
for $r in //rcp:recipe
   return fn:count($r//rcp:ingredient[fn:not(rcp:ingredient)])
```

It returns the value

```
11, 12, 15, 8, 30
```

corresponding to the number of simple ingredients in the five recipes. It is also possible to have nested loops:

```
for $i in (1 to 5)
   for $j in (1 to $i)
      return $j
```

This expression returns the value

```
1, 1, 2, 1, 2, 3, 1, 2, 3, 4, 1, 2, 3, 4, 5
```

Note that $i is available in the scope of the expression defining $j.

3.5.13 Conditional Expressions

XPath contains an `if` expression which chooses between two branches based on a condition. The syntax is:

if (*exp₁* **) then** *exp₂* **else** *exp₃*

The condition is evaluated and coerced to its effective boolean value, based on which the corresponding branch is chosen. The other branch is not evaluated. An example:

```
fn:avg(
  for $r in //rcp:ingredient return
    if ( $r/@unit = "cup" ) then xs:double($r/@amount) * 237
    else if ( $r/@unit = "teaspoon" )
    then xs:double($r/@amount) * 5
    else if ( $r/@unit = "tablespoon" )
    then xs:double($r/@amount) * 15
    else ()
)
```

This expression computes the average amount in milliliters of those ingredients that are measured in liquid units. Note that the test

```
$r/@unit = "cup"
```

works correctly even for composite ingredients without `unit` attributes, since the comparison

```
() = "cup"
```

yields false by definition.

3.5.14 Quantified Expressions

There are two kinds of quantified expressions:

some *$name* **in** *exp₁* **satisfies** *exp₂*

and

every *$name* **in** *exp₁* **satisfies** *exp₂*

These expressions, returning booleans, test if some item or every item of a sequence satisfies a given condition. An example is

```
some $r in //rcp:ingredient satisfies $r/@name eq "sugar"
```

which decides if sugar is an ingredient.

Quantified expressions are just syntactic sugar, in the sense that they do not add to the expressive power of the language. Using a general template, the above expression can be rewritten as

```
fn:exists(
  for $r in //rcp:ingredient return
    if ($r/@name eq "sugar") then fn:true() else ()
)
```

using just existing language features. A similar rewriting is possible for the every variant:

```
fn:empty(
  for $r in //rcp:ingredient return
    if ($r/@name eq "sugar") then () else fn:false()
)
```

3.5.15   Types

So far we have presented the *untyped* version of XPath 2.0. However, it is possible to exploit type information about XML documents, in the form of XML Schema validity, which we describe in Section 4.4.

An important aspect of type information is that atomization (see Section 3.5.1) can use the schema information to convert attribute values and character data to more specific types than strings. For example, the amount attributes of recipes can be converted to doubles, if they are so described in the schema specification. Also, the set of atomic types is extended to include all the datatypes that are defined in the relevant schemas. Finally, it is possible to perform runtime type tests to guide computations.

These considerations are postponed until Chapter 6 where we describe the XQuery 1.0 language as an extension of XPath 2.0.

3.5.16   XPath 1.0 Restrictions

Many implementations still only support XPath 1.0, which places several restrictions on programmers. A severe problem is the incorrect handling of default namespaces mentioned in Section 3.2.3. Another annoyance is that the function library in XPath 1.0 is smaller. Among the ones we mention above, only the ceiling, floor, round, concat, substring, string-length, upper-case, lower-case, true, false, not, count, sum, position, and last functions are available, and they are invoked without the namespace prefix.

The main incompatibility is that XPath 1.0 performs a multitude of implicit casts of values when they are presented as arguments to various functions and operators. This superficial convenience causes untold confusion, and fortunately this practice has been discontinued in XPath 2.0. This revision means that some expressions have changed semantics; for example, the expression

```
"4" < "4.0"
```

yields false in XPath 1.0 (which performs the comparison on numbers) but true in XPath 2.0 (which performs the comparison on strings using a lexicographical order). The behavior of some operations has also been changed.

To summarize, XPath 2.0 is more elegant and complete than XPath 1.0, but simple applications have approximately the same syntax in both languages.

3.6   XPointer and XLink ★

In Chapter 1 we noticed that the hyperlinks enabled by HTML correspond to the simplest possible hypertext model.

Naturally, a Web based on XML should allow for richer structures. For this purpose, the languages XPointer and XLink have been designed; however, they have not been very successful as little development has taken place during the last few years and no implementations are widespread. Since XLink still addresses an obvious need, we choose to provide a brief description. Also, XLink has gained considerable interest by its use in the language XBRL (eXtensible Business Reporting Language).

XPointer and **XLink** provide **hyperlinks** in general XML documents.

The XPointer language generalizes the ability to point at specific places in documents. In Chapter 1 we saw that HTML supports fragment identifiers in URLs, such that the link in the following document

```
<html>
  <head>
    <title>Source Document</title>
  </head>
  <body>
    <a href="target.html#danger">Better look here</a>.
  </body>
</html>
```

when activated will jump to the appropriate part of the target document:

```
<html>
  <head>
    <title>Target Document</title>
  </head>
  <body>
    ...
    <a name="danger"/>
    <h2>Chapter 17: Dangerous Shell Commands</h2>
    Never execute a shell command that inadvertently changes
    all vowels to the character 'x'.
    ...
  </body>
</html>
```

However, this technique only works when the author of the source document has write access to the target document in order to place the `<a name="danger"/>` at the right location.

XPointer is based on XPath and thus has the ability to point at several different places in an XML document *without* write access. An example for the recipe collection is the following XPointer URL which points to the fourth recipe in the collection:

```
http://www.brics.dk/ixwt/examples/recipes.xml#xpointer(//recipe[4])
```

The following (abbreviated) XPointer URL points to all ingredient nodes, showing that it is possible to point at several places at once:

```
...#xpointer(//rcp:ingredient)
```

Depending on the XPath expression, an XPointer URL may be more or less robust. The above example

```
...#xpointer(//recipe[4])
```

will always point to the fourth recipe, if one such exists, whereas the XPointer URL

```
...#xpointer(//rcp:recipe[./rcp:title/text()='Zuppa Inglese'])
```

will point to that same recipe, even if the collection is extended or reordered. XPointer allows for other pointing schemes as well; for example, the XPointer URL

```
...#element(/1/5)
```

uses (not very robust) absolute positions of nodes to again point to the recipe for Zuppa Inglese as the fifth child of the first child of the document root, as an alternative to using XPath. Finally, the notation

```
...#r104
```

is yet another way to point at that recipe, given that its `id` attribute has value `r104`. This syntax only makes sense because the `id` attributes in recipe collections are required to have unique values throughout the document. Such uniqueness requirements are explained further in Section 4.4.10. Note that for XHTML documents, this syntax may also be used to point at anchor elements.

XLink provides a radical generalization of the hyperlinks known from HTML. First of all, links in HTML documents are identified by particular tag names, such as `a` and `img`. This approach is, of course, unsuited for general XML languages which will typically not include those exact tags. Instead, XLink hyperlinks are identified by a particular namespace, which allows XLink aware processors to recognize the definitions of links:

```
http://www.w3.org/1999/xlink
```

Second, the links that are enabled through XLink are more expressive than those supported by HTML. An HTML hyperlink always has a single source and a single target, and the definition of the link is embedded in the source document. The richer XLink model allows links with *multiple* sources and targets, and *third-party* links that are defined externally to the source and the target. An example of a link specified by the XLink notation is the following:

```
<mylink xmlns:xlink="http://www.w3.org/1999/xlink"
        xlink:type="extended">
  <myresource xlink:type="locator"
              xlink:href="students.xml#Carl" xlink:label="student"/>
  <myresource xlink:type="locator"
              xlink:href="students.xml#Fred" xlink:label="student"/>
  <myresource xlink:type="locator"
              xlink:href="teachers.xml#Joe" xlink:label="teacher"/>
  <myarc xlink:type="arc"
         xlink:from="student" xlink:to="teacher"/>
</mylink>
```

Note that only attributes belong to the XLink namespace (and, as usual, the exact choice of namespace prefix is not significant). Thus, the designer of the concrete language is free to choose the element names. The `xlink:type` attribute defines the role of its corresponding element. The value `extended` means that this element surrounds the different components of a link definition. The value `locator` means that the element identifies a *resource* that is part of the link. A resource is a collection of nodes in XML documents specified through an XPointer URI that is the value of the `xlink:href` attribute. If the `xlink:type` attribute has value `resource`, then the resource is taken to be the surrounding node in the document containing the link (a *local* resource). Each resource is also assigned a `label`, which may be an arbitrary string. The actual link is now specified by those elements whose value of `xlink:type` is `arc`, which define a potentially many-to-many relation between resources with different labels. In our example, we specify a single link from the two students `Carl` and `Fred` to the teacher `Joe`:

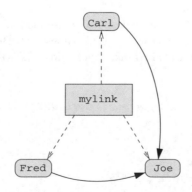

Note that this link definition may be separate from both the source and target documents. This separation enables collections of links to be stored in *link databases* and downloaded or exchanged through the Web.

It is not clear how an XLink aware browser would display a link such as the above. Such generalized links will probably only be used for more domain-specific processing, while browsers will use simpler links. There are two extra XLink attributes that partly specify how a link should be interpreted. The `xlink:show` attribute specifies what happens when a link is activated, and the possible values are `embed` (like images in HTML), `new` (open a new window), `replace` (like normal HTML links), `other`, and `none`. The `xlink:actuate` attribute specifies when the link is activated, and the possible values are `onLoad` (like HTML images), `onRequest` (like normal HTML links), `other`, and `none`. These options are not very inspired, since they only reflect existing features in HTML and make little sense for general XML languages.

XLink allows a special syntax for simpler links. The notation

```
<mylink xlink:type="simple" xlink:href="..." xlink:show="..." .../>
```

is syntactic sugar for the following extended link:

```
<mylink xlink:type="extended">
  <myresource xlink:type="resource"
              xlink:label="local"/>
  <myresource xlink:type="locator"
              xlink:label="remote" xlink:href="..."/>
  <myarc xlink:type="arc"
         xlink:from="local" xlink:to="remote" xlink:show="..." .../>
</mylink>
```

Thus, the semantics of normal HTML links are captured as follows:

```
<a xlink:type="simple"
   xlink:href="..."
   xlink:show="replace"
   xlink:actuate="onRequest"/>
```

Conceivably, XHTML could have been designed to use the XLink language in this manner, but that was rejected to avoid the intrusive XLink namespace. This lead to the proposal of an alternative linking language, called HLink, which allows HTML links to retain their usual syntax:

```
<hlink namespace="http://www.w3.org/1999/xhtml"
       element="a"
       locator="@href"
       effect="replace"
       actuate="onRequest"
       replacement="@target"/>
```

This HLink element uses namespaces and XPath to identify the parts of the host language that contain the different components of the link specification. However, HLink has been rejected by W3C as a replacement for XLink.

In all, XLink has little following, no major implementations, and no important applications. So, not all XML technologies turn out to be successful.

3.7   Chapter Summary

In this chapter we have seen that pointing at nodes in XML trees is a task that is useful in many XML tools and that has been factored out into the XPath language. An XPath location path moves in steps from sequences to sequences of nodes, inspired by Unix file paths. To understand location paths, it is necessary to master the three concepts of axes, node tests, and predicates. Abbreviations permit location paths to be written more succinctly, but add some unfortunate syntactic complications.

XPath contains a large and general expression language that is also used in other languages, particularly in XQuery and XSLT. XPath expressions evaluate to sequences of nodes and atomic values and that can be computed using a wealth of language features.

XPath has been used in XPointer and XLink to enrich the hyperlink model of HTML, but these technologies have not been generally accepted or applied.

3.8   Further Reading

XPath 2.0 is published through W3C [4]. Several books on XPath have been published, but consider first the online resources. Be warned, however, that most descriptions only cover XPath 1.0.

There are numerous research papers that investigate theoretical properties of XPath, such as, formal semantics [84, 38], expressiveness [3], and checking satisfiability or containment [60, 44, 67], but also practical issues of efficient processing [39].

3.9   Online Resources

http://www.w3.org/TR/xpath/
   The XPath 1.0 recommendation, which is the one implemented by current browsers and most tools.

http://www.w3.org/TR/xpath20/
   The XPath 2.0 working draft, describing the future standard to be generally implemented.

```
http://www.w3.org/TR/xlink/
```
The XLink 1.0 recommendation.

```
http://www.w3.org/TR/xptr-framework/
```
The XPointer 1.0 recommendation.

```
http://www.vbxml.com/xpathvisualizer/
```
A nice free tool which allows for visual debugging and analysis of XPath 1.0 expressions.

```
http://www.galaxquery.org/
```
A free up-to-date implementation of XPath 2.0 and XQuery 1.0.

3.10   Exercises

The main lessons to be learned from these exercises are:

- the concepts of axis, node test, and predicate; and
- familiarity with general XPath expressions.

Exercise 3.1 Consider the XML tree corresponding to the document *EX*/axes.xml. Assuming the element named foo is the current node, which nodes do then belong to the various axes?

Exercise 3.2 Write the unabbreviated versions of the following location paths:

(a) `.//@foo`
(b) `/foo/bar/../baz[7]`

Exercise 3.3 Write an XPath expression that for each recipe that also uses milk, finds the number of eggs being used (the result is a sequence of numbers).

Exercise 3.4 Write an XPath expression that finds the total number of eggs being used in all recipes (the result is a single number).

Exercise 3.5 Consider your solution to Exercise 2.11. Write location paths that select nodes in this document. Try to use as many axes as possible.

Exercise 3.6 Which of the following comparison expressions are true?

(a) `//rcp:ingredient[40] eq //rcp:ingredient[53]`
(b) `//rcp:ingredient[40] = //rcp:ingredient[53]`
(c) `//rcp:ingredient[40] is //rcp:ingredient[53]`

Exercise 3.7 Assume that $x contains a sequence of strings and that $y contains a single string. Use the function library to write expression that compute the following results:

(a) Whether or not $y equals one of the strings in $x.
(b) The length of the largest string occurring in $x.
(c) Whether or not the concatenation of strings in $x forms a palindrome.
(d) How many of the strings occurring in $x appear as attribute values in the document whose URL is $y.

TIP

An XPath 2.0 expression `foo` may be evaluated using an XSLT 2.0 processor, such as Saxon (see Chapter 5), by means of the following stylesheet:

```
<xsl:stylesheet xmlns:xsl="http://www.w3.org/1999/XSL/Transform"
                version="2.0">
  <xsl:template match="/">
    <xsl:value-of select="foo"/>
  </xsl:template>
</xsl:stylesheet>
```

Here, the document root is the current node. Make sure that the `stylesheet` element contains all the required namespace declarations.

SCHEMA LANGUAGES

Objectives

In this chapter, you will learn:

- The purpose of using schemas
- The schema languages DTD, XML Schema, DSD2, and RELAX NG
- Regular expressions – a commonly used formalism in schema languages

4.1 XML Languages and Validation

As we have seen in the previous chapters, XML is by itself merely a standard notation for markup languages. Every XML document uses this notation and must be well-formed to be meaningful. An XML language, for example RecipeML, is a particular family of XML documents. Such a language is defined by (1) its *syntax*, which describes the vocabulary of markup tags that this language uses and constraints on their use, and (2) its *semantics*, which gives some sort of meaning to the constituents of each syntactically correct document. In this chapter, we focus on syntax.

Valid: syntactically correct with respect to a given schema.

A *schema* is a formal definition of the syntax of an XML-based language, that is, it defines a family of XML documents. A *schema language* is a formal language for expressing schemas. There exists a variety of schema languages, as we shall see later. Each schema language is implemented in the form of *schema processors*: these are tools that as input take an XML document X, called the *instance document*, and a schema S, which is written in that particular schema language, and then checks whether or not X is syntactically correct according to S. If this is the case, then we say that X is *valid* with respect to S. If X is invalid, then most schema processors produce useful diagnostic error messages.

As a side-effect, if the schema processor determines that X does in fact conform to S, then it may *normalize X* according to rules specified in S, as indicated in Figure 4.1. Depending

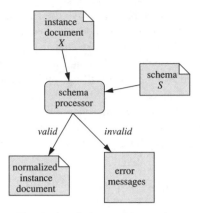

Figure 4.1 Schema processing.

on the choice of schema language, normalization may involve insertion of default attributes and elements, removal of insignificant whitespace, and addition of parsing information.

Schemas are in many ways similar to grammars for programming languages. For example, the syntax of Java is formally described by a context-free grammar using a so-called BNF notation. In order for a text to be a meaningful Java program, it must at the very least be syntactically correct with respect to this grammar. The BNF notation has for many years been successful for describing the syntax for programming languages. However, it turns out that BNF, or similar variants of context-free grammars, are not expressive enough for XML, which has led to the development of special grammar formalisms for XML. The term 'schema' comes from the database community. As we shall see in Chapter 6, there is a close connection between schemas in XML and schemas in relational databases. For readers that are familiar with grammars in programming languages, it is appropriate to think of schemas as grammars for XML languages. One final note about the term 'schema': in this book, we use 'schema' generally to denote a document from some schema language, not necessarily from the particular schema language named XML Schema. It has caused quite a lot of confusion that W3C chose the name 'XML Schema' for their particular XML schema language proposal.

In Section 2.7, we informally described the syntax of RecipeML. Why should one bother formalizing the syntax with a schema? There are a number of good reasons for this:

> **Schema**: a formal definition of the syntax of an XML-based language. **XML Schema**: a particular language for expressing schemas.

1. A formal definition can provide a precise but human-readable reference, which is a significant advantage when others are to read and write documents in our language. In contrast, informal definitions tend to be ambiguous, incomplete, or too verbose.

2. Each schema language comes with existing, often Open Source, implementations of schema processors. This means that once we have written a schema for our XML language, for example RecipeML, we can easily check validity whenever we write new RecipeML instance documents or edit existing ones.

3. Often, new XML languages are accompanied by specialized tools; for example, we could envision a tailor-made recipe editor with a nice graphical user interface for

RecipeML. Such tools always need to parse their input, and to be meaningful, the input must be valid. If the tool is presented with invalid data (for example, a required attribute is missing) it is not satisfactory that it produces null pointer exceptions or exhibits some arbitrary behavior. Instead, the tool should in this case abort with a useful error message. Rather than writing, by hand, some code in your favorite programming language checking validity of the input, a straightforward solution is to pipe the input through a preexisting schema processor such that syntax errors are caught before the data enters our tool. As an additional benefit, the schema processor will take care of normalizing the input for us.

A schema language must satisfy three criteria to be useful. First, it must provide sufficient *expressiveness* such that most syntactic requirements can be formalized in the language. Second, it must be possible to implement *efficient* schema processors. The time and space requirements for checking validity of a document should ideally be linear in the size of the document. Third, the language must be *comprehensible* by non-experts. It is fair enough that the schema authors need to master the schema language being used, but if others should be able to write valid instance documents, then they need to be able to understand the schema.

In the remainder of this chapter, we focus our attention on the two schema languages DTD and XML Schema, both originating from the W3C. However, we shall also investigate other proposals, which have emerged due to a number of problematic issues with the W3C proposals, especially pertaining to expressiveness and comprehensibility.

4.2   Regular Expressions

The notion of *regular expressions* is an important formalism that is used – in variants – in most schema languages to describe sequences of elements or characters. For example, one may wish to constrain certain attributes named `date` such that their values are dates of the form *dd-mm-yyyy*, that is, two digits for the day of month, followed by the number of the month and then the year, all separated by '-'. Or, one may wish to specify that the content of a `number` element must be an integer. As yet another example, in XHTML, the contents of a `table` element must be a sequence consisting of optionally one `caption` element followed by either a number of `col` or `colgroup` elements, which are optionally followed by a `thead` and then a `tfoot` element, and finally at least one either `tbody` or `tr` element.

Let Σ be an *alphabet* consisting of some set of atoms, which are typically Unicode characters or element names. A *regular expression* over Σ is an expression built from the following rules:

- each atom in Σ is by itself a regular expression; and

- if α and β are regular expressions, then the following are also regular expressions: $\alpha\,?, \alpha*, \alpha+, \alpha\,\beta, \alpha\,|\,\beta$, and (α).

The operators ?, *, and + have higher precedence than concatenation (the empty operator, or juxtapositioning), which in turn has higher precedence than |. The parentheses can be used to override precedence by grouping subexpressions explicitly. For example, the expression ab*|c, where the alphabet contains a, b, and c, is interpreted as (a(b*))|c and *not* as a(b*|c) *nor* as (ab)*|c.

A finite string of atoms from Σ may or may not *match* a given regular expression α:

- an atom σ from Σ matches just the single atom σ;

- α? matches α optionally, that is, either the empty string or whatever α matches;

- α* matches zero or more repetitions of what α matches;

- α+ matches one or more repetitions of what α matches;

- $\alpha\,\beta$ matches what α matches followed by what β matches;

- $\alpha|\beta$ matches the union of what α and β match; and

- (α) matches the same as α.

The regular expression (a(b*))|c thus matches all strings which either consist of one a followed by zero or more b's or consist of a single c. A *regular language* is a set of strings that are matched by some regular expression. Besides their use in XML, regular languages are utilized in many other areas of computer science, ranging from text processing to formal verification of hardware and natural language processing.

As an example, we may define a regular expression named d (for 'digit') by

0|1|2|3|4|5|6|7|8|9

where our alphabet, for example, consists of all Unicode characters. From this definition, we can choose to define another regular expression *date* by the expression *dd-dd-dddd*. Of course, this expression matches strings, such as 87-13-2005, that do not describe real dates, but with a slightly more complicated expression, it is, in fact, possible to capture the desired set of strings. (Even if we handle leap years properly this set is a regular language, but then the corresponding regular expression becomes quite complicated!)

As another example, the following regular expression describes integers (using an alphabet that contains 0, 1, ..., 9 and -):

0|-?(1|2|3|4|5|6|7|8|9)(0|1|2|3|4|5|6|7|8|9)*

According to this definition, -42, 0, and 117 are permissible, but 000, -0, and 3.14 are not.

To capture the constraint on the contents of table elements described above, let Σ denote the alphabet of element names in XHTML. The constraint now corresponds to the regular expression

caption? (col | colgroup)* thead? tfoot? (tbody | tr)+

There exist many variants of regular expressions, most of which simply add syntactic sugar on top of the basic notation presented here. One common extension is *character ranges*: for example, the character range [0-9] is a convenient abbreviation for the basic regular expression $0|1|2|\ldots|9$. Similarly, $\alpha\{n,m\}$, where n and m are non-negative integers, often denotes from n to m repetitions of α. In the following, we will explain such variations whenever they arise.

4.3   DTD – Document Type Definition

XML has since the first working draft contained a built-in schema language: *Document Type Definition (DTD)*. Just as the XML notation itself is designed as a subset of SGML, the DTD part of XML is designed as a subset of the DTD part of SGML. When we refer to 'DTD', it will be the XML variant. Also, to avoid confusion, we will use the term 'DTD schema' for referring to a particular schema written in the DTD language. (Elsewhere, 'DTD' is often used as a noun referring to a particular DTD schema.)

DTD is a reasonably simple schema language with a rather restricted expressive power. From a language design point of view, it is not particularly elegant, but there exist thousands of DTD schemas so it is useful to know the DTD language. Also, it has provided the starting point for the development of newer and more expressive schema languages. In the following, note that DTD is *not* itself written in the XML notation (which is somewhat peculiar, since XML was designed to be suitable for all kinds of structured information). Another thing to note is that DTD does not support namespaces – this is not surprising since the DTD language was introduced before the namespace mechanism.

4.3.1   Document Type Declarations

An XML document may contain a *document type declaration*, which is essentially a reference to a DTD schema. By inserting such a declaration, the author states that the XML document is intended to be valid relative to that schema. In this way, documents become *self-describing*, which makes it easy for tools to determine what kind of input they receive. (Be aware of the difference between a document type *declaration* and document type *definition*.)

A document type declaration typically has the form

```
<!DOCTYPE root SYSTEM "URI">
```

where `root` is an element name, and `URI`, called the *system identifier*, is a URI of the DTD schema. The document type declaration appears between the XML declaration (`<?xml ...?>`), if present, and the root element in the instance document. The instance document is *valid* if the name of its root element is `root` and the document satisfies all constraints specified in the DTD schema as described below.

Assume that we have written a DTD schema for RecipeML and made it available at the URL `http://www.brics.dk/ixwt/recipes.dtd`. Our recipe collection could then look as follows (where the content of the root element is shown as '...'):

```
<?xml version="1.1"?>
<!DOCTYPE collection
    SYSTEM "http://www.brics.dk/ixwt/recipes.dtd">
<collection>
  ...
</collection>
```

As a supplement to the system identifier, a document type declaration may contain a *public identifier*, which is an alternative way of specifying the DTD schema. For example, XHTML documents often contain the following declaration:

```
<!DOCTYPE html
    PUBLIC "-//W3C//DTD XHTML 1.0 Transitional//EN"
    "http://www.w3.org/TR/xhtml1/DTD/xhtml1-transitional.dtd">
```

Here, the string following PUBLIC is the public identifier, and the string on the next line is the system identifier. This specific public identifier is technically an unregistered identifier (that is, not centrally assigned, which is specified by the leading '-'), it is owned by the W3C, it refers to a DTD for the 'XHTML 1.0 Transitional' language, and it is written in English. The notion of public identifiers is a relic from SGML; usually, public identifiers are simply ignored. However, they do come in handy in situations where the DTD schema may exist at many different locations. For example, W3C's HTML/XHTML validator reads the public identifier to determine the version of HTML or XHTML being used; it cannot determine the version from the system identifier since it is not required that the schema resides at a fixed location. The URN mechanism (see Section 1.3) provides a more general solution to the issue of naming resources without specific locations, and some systems allow URNs as system identifiers.

One might encounter document type declarations of the form

```
<!DOCTYPE root [ ... ]>
```

where '...' consists of declarations of elements, attributes, and so on, as described below. Such *internal* declarations that appear within the instance document have exactly the same meaning as if they were moved to a separate file being referred to with a system identifier. The document type declarations may even contain a mix of internal and external declarations. However, most often it is a much better idea to keep the DTD schema separately from the instance documents, such that many instance documents can share the same schema.

DTD schemas may contain comments using the same notation as in XML:

```
<!-- this is a comment -->
```

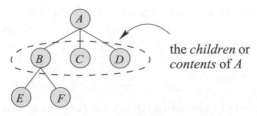

Figure 4.2 The *contents* of an element.

As usual, comments have no formal meaning, but they are often used in DTD schemas to explain extra restrictions that DTD is unable to express formally. For example, in the DTD schema for XHTML, one may find a comment like this:

```
<!-- anchors shouldn't be nested -->
```

Likewise, DTD schemas may contain processing instructions.

4.3.2 Element Declarations

A DTD schema consists of declarations of elements, attributes, and various other constructs, as explained in the following. An *element declaration* looks as follows:

```
<!ELEMENT element-name content-model>
```

where `element-name` is an element name, such as `table` or `ingredient`, and `content-model` is a description of a *content model*, which defines the validity requirements of the contents of all elements of the given name. (Recall that the *contents* of an element node is the sequence of its child nodes, which does not include nodes further down the tree; see Figure 4.2.) Every element name that occurs in the instance document must correspond to one element declaration in order for the document to be valid. Moreover, the contents of the element must match the associated content model as defined below.

Content models come in four different flavors:

empty: If the content model of an element is EMPTY, then the element must be empty. As previously explained, being empty means that it has no contents, but this says nothing about attributes.

any: The content model ANY means that the contents of the element can consist of any sequence of character data and elements. Still, each of these elements must be declared by corresponding element declarations (so using ANY is not a solution for describing open content models). The ANY content model is mostly used during development of DTD schemas for elements that have not been described yet – it is rarely used in the final schemas.

mixed content: A content model of the form

```
(#PCDATA | e₁ | e₂ | ... | eₙ)*
```

where each e_i is an element name, means that the contents may contain arbitrary character data, interspersed with any number of elements of the specified names (n may be zero in which case the '*' is optional and only character data is permitted).

element content: To specify constraints on the order and number of occurrences of child elements, a content model can be written using the following variation of the regular expression notation presented in Section 4.2:

- the alphabet consists of all element names;
- concatenation is written with comma (,) instead of using juxtaposition of the operands (but the remaining operators, ?, *, +, and |, and also parentheses behave as explained earlier); and
- only a restricted form of regular expressions called *deterministic regular expressions* is permitted, which makes it easier to check whether or not a sequence of element names matches an expression. (We will not tire the reader with technicalities here and refer to the XML specification for details.)

For the contents of an element with such a content model to be valid, it must match the regular expression.

The various constructs are summarized in Figure 4.3. So far, we have not mentioned comments and processing instructions. Implicitly, comments and processing instructions may occur anywhere in the instance document; their use cannot be constrained, except with EMPTY since 'empty contents' means 'no elements, character data, comments, or processing instructions whatsoever'. (The fact that comments and processing instructions may appear in the DTD schema has nothing to do with this.)

Element declarations associate content models with element names.

At this point, we might wonder about the design of the DTD language. First, either arbitrary character data is permitted in the contents or no character data is permitted. Why are we not allowed to impose constraints on character data, for example, such that only

Construct	Meaning
EMPTY	empty contents
ANY	any contents
#PCDATA	character data
element name	an element
,	concatenation
|	union
?	optional
*	zero or more repetitions
+	one or more repetitions

Figure 4.3 Constructs used in content model descriptions in DTD.

whitespace and digits are allowed in the contents of certain elements? Second, if character data is to be permitted in the contents, then we have no choice but using the mixed content model, which cannot constrain the order and number of occurrences of the child elements. Why is it not possible to use character data together with the element content model? This question is related to a tradition of roughly classifying SGML and XML languages as either *document oriented* or *data oriented* depending on whether they use the mixed content model or not (as discussed in Section 2.5), but such an artificial classification should not be necessary. Third, why do we need the restriction to deterministic content models? After all, it has been known for more than thirty years how to perform efficient pattern matching on general regular expressions. Clearly, these limitations become practical problems in the real world. The simple answer to these questions is that a design goal was that XML (and hence also DTD) should be a subset of the SGML language, which has these unfortunate properties. From another point of view, the identification of these limitations, together with others that we mention later, has motivated the design of alternative schema languages.

Let us see some examples of element declarations. First, the declaration of `table` elements in the DTD for XHTML:

```
<!ELEMENT table
        (caption?, (col|colgroup)*, thead?, tfoot?, (tbody|tr)+) >
```

This declaration corresponds to the informal description given in Section 4.2. The following snippet is valid XHTML:

```
<table>
  <caption><em>Great Cities of the World</em></caption>
  <thead>
    <tr><td>City</td><td>Country</td></tr>
  </thead>
  <tbody>
    <tr><td>Aarhus</td><td>Denmark</td></tr>
    <tr><td>San Francisco</td><td>USA</td></tr>
    <tr><td>Paris</td><td>France</td></tr>
  </tbody>
</table>
```

whercas this one is not (although it is well-formed):

```
<table>
  <thead>
    <tr><td>City</td><td>Country</td></tr>
  </thead>
  <thead>
    <tr><td>City</td><td>Country</td></tr>
  </thead>
  <tBodY>
    <tr><td>Aarhus</td><td>Denmark</td></tr>
```

```
    <tr><td>San Francisco</td><td>USA</td></tr>
    <tr><td>Paris</td><td>France</td></tr>
  </tBodY>
  <caption><em>Great Cities of the World</em></caption>
</table>
```

because the `caption` element appears in the wrong place, there are two `thead` elements, and `tbody` is misspelled in the contents of `table`.

One more example: In Section 2.7, we informally stated that `comment` elements in RecipeML should contain just character data. This requirement can be formalized as follows:

```
<!ELEMENT comment (#PCDATA)>
```

This `comment` element is then valid:

```
<comment>
  Rhubarb Cobbler made with bananas as the main sweetener.
  It was delicious.
</comment>
```

but the following is invalid:

```
<comment><title>Rhubarb Cobbler</title> is delicious.</comment>
```

As mentioned, DTD does not support namespaces. Still, many XML languages that do use namespaces also have DTD descriptions, for example XHTML. How is this possible? Since DTD is not aware of the meaning of prefixes and namespace declarations, the DTD schema for XHTML simply assumes the empty prefix for all elements and declares that the `html` element must have an attribute named `xmlns` with the value `http://www.w3.org/1999/xhtml`. (Note that after the introduction of namespaces, this will technically not be an *attribute* but a *namespace declaration*.) The effect is that an XHTML instance document validates with respect to the DTD schema only if the document does not use the namespace mechanism beyond this, for example, by using an explicit namespace prefix. These issues with namespaces are, of course, something that newer schema languages have amended.

4.3.3   Attribute-List Declarations

An *attribute-list declaration* has the following form:

```
<!ATTLIST element-name attribute-definitions>
```

where `element-name` is an element name and `attribute-definitions` is a list of attribute definitions, each having three constituents:

```
attribute-name attribute-type default-declaration
```

The *attribute-name* is an attribute name, and *attribute-type* and *default-declaration* are an *attribute type* and a *default declaration*, respectively, as explained below. An attribute list declaration specifies a list of attributes that are permitted (or required) in elements of the given name. As for elements and element declarations, the instance document is invalid if it contains attributes that are not declared or do not satisfy their declarations.

As a simple example, the `align` attribute of p elements in XHTML is declared by

```
<!ATTLIST p align (left|center|right|justify) #IMPLIED>
```

Here, the attribute type specifies that the possible values of such attributes are `left`, `center`, `right`, and `justify`, and the default declaration `#IMPLIED` means that the attribute is optional and no default value is provided.

The most important categories of attribute types are the following:

string type: The attribute type CDATA (for *character data*) means that the attribute can have any value.

enumeration: An attribute type of the form

$$(\ s_1 \ | \ s_2 \ | \ \ldots \ | \ s_n \ )$$

where each s_i is some string, means that the value of the attribute must be among the strings $s_1, s_2, \ldots, s_n$.

name tokens: The attribute type NMTOKEN means that the attribute value must be a *name token*. In XML 1.1, almost all characters are permitted in name tokens, except those which are delimiters (for example, whitespace characters and commas); however, hyphens, underscores, colons, and periods are explicitly permitted. (This definition was more restrictive in XML 1.0.) The variant NMTOKENS denotes a whitespace separated nonempty list of name tokens.

identity/reference type: The attribute type ID means that the value of the attribute uniquely identifies the element containing the attribute. That is, no two attributes of type ID can have the same value in an XML document. Only one attribute of type ID is permitted per element.

The attribute type IDREF is used for references to elements with an ID attribute. The value of an attribute of type IDREF must match the value of some attribute of type ID in the same document. The attribute type IDREFS is like IDREF but permits multiple references (whitespace separated lists of names) as attribute values.

For all attribute types other than CDATA, the attribute value is – before the actual validation takes place – normalized by discarding any leading and trailing whitespace and replacing sequences of whitespace by a single space character. (The motivation for this whitespace normalization feature is not obvious; even the original designers of XML call it a design mistake.)

We have already seen an application of the enumeration type for the `align` attribute in XHTML. The CDATA type is, for example, used for both the `maxlength` and the `tabindex` attribute in `input` elements in XHTML:

```
<!ATTLIST input maxlength CDATA #IMPLIED
                tabindex  CDATA #IMPLIED>
```

These attributes are used to specify the maximal number of characters in a text input field and the field position in tabbing order, respectively. In both cases, only numbers make sense, but DTD does not have the ability to capture that requirement: the attribute type that comes closest permits any value. This is a typical example where a DTD schema 'permits too much' because a desired constraint is not expressible. Interestingly, the authors of the DTD schema for XHTML have inserted the informal comment

Attribute-list declarations describe the attributes, and their types and default behavior.

```
<!-- one or more digits -->
```

at that place in the schema as an attempt to make it clear to the human reader that not all values make sense. This example shows that an XML document may be valid XHTML with respect to the DTD schema without being syntactically correct in a strict sense; similar situations occur in most other XML languages.

The NMTOKEN type is, for example, used for certain `name` attributes in XHTML:

```
<!ATTLIST form name NMTOKEN #IMPLIED ...>
```

This declaration shows that `name="my.form"`, `name="87"`, and `name=" 87 "` are all valid in `form` elements (the latter because of the pruning of whitespace in non-CDATA attributes), whereas `name="my form"` and `name=""` are invalid.

The ID and IDREF(S) types can be used as a intra-document reference mechanism, for denoting keys when XML documents are used as databases, and for specifying anchors for easy addressing into documents. In each case, ID and IDREF(S) provide only very primitive support, however. Other technologies, such as XML Schema and XPath, are usually much better suited for these purposes. Nevertheless, we will use these types in our DTD description of RecipeML: the `id` attribute of `recipe` elements has type ID, and the `ref` attribute of `related` elements has type IDREF:

```
<!ATTLIST recipe id ID #IMPLIED>
<!ATTLIST related ref IDREF #REQUIRED>
```

The following RecipeML document is then valid (abbreviated with '...'):

```
<collection>
  <description>My Valid Recipe Collection</description>

  <recipe id="r101">
    <title>Beef Parmesan with Garlic Angel Hair Pasta</title>
```

```
      . . .
      <related ref="r103">
          this goes well with Linguine Pescadoro
      </related>
    </recipe>

    <recipe id="r102">
      <title>Ricotta Pie</title>
      . . .
    </recipe>

    <recipe id="r103">
      <title>Linguine Pescadoro</title>
      . . .
    </recipe>
  </collection>
```

whereas the following is invalid because it contains two ID attributes with the value r101 (both are named id) and also an IDREF attribute (named ref) whose value r12345 does not match that of an ID attribute:

```
<collection>
  <description>My Invalid Recipe Collection</description>

  <recipe id="r101">
    <title>Beef Parmesan with Garlic Angel Hair Pasta</title>
    . . .
    <related ref="r12345">Spiced Beef Stew is also great</related>
  </recipe>

  <recipe id="r101">
    <title>Ricotta Pie</title>
    . . .
  </recipe>

  <recipe id="r113">
    <title>Linguine Pescadoro</title>
    . . .
  </recipe>
</collection>
```

One may think of this mechanism as going beyond purely tree-structured data: an IDREF attribute may be thought of as a special pointer from its containing element to the element with the corresponding ID attribute.

In addition to the main attribute types described above, the DTD language contains three rather obscure types: ENTITY, ENTITIES, and NOTATION. These are used in conjunction with *entity declarations* and *notation declarations* as described in the next section.

Construct	Meaning
#REQUIRED	required
#IMPLIED	optional, no default
"*value*"	optional, *value* is default value
#FIXED "*value*"	as the previous, but only this value is permitted

Figure 4.4 Default declarations for attributes in DTD.

The third constituent of an attribute declaration – the default declaration – specifies whether the attribute is required or optional and potentially also a default value. (It is misleading that this constituent is called a default declaration since it might not specify a default.) The following kinds are possible:

required: #REQUIRED means that the attribute must be present. (If the attribute is absent, then no default is provided and the document is invalid.)

optional: #IMPLIED means that the attribute is optional. No default is provided if the attribute is absent.

optional, but default provided: "*value*", where *value* is a legal attribute value, means that the attribute is optional, but if it is absent, this value is used as a default.

fixed: #FIXED "*value*" means that the attribute is optional; if it is absent, then this value is used as a default, but if it is present, then it must have this specific value.

These variants are summarized in Figure 4.4. The following declaration from the DTD schema for XHTML illustrates the first three variants:

```
<!ATTLIST form
    action      CDATA           #REQUIRED
    onsubmit    CDATA           #IMPLIED
    method      (get|post)      "get"
    enctype     CDATA           "application/x-www-form-urlencoded">
```

This declaration shows that the action attribute in form elements is required, and the onsubmit attribute is optional. The method attribute is also optional, but if it is omitted, the default value get is inserted by the DTD processor, and similarly for the enctype attribute. (The actual attribute-list declaration for form contains other attributes, which we ignore here.) A DTD processor will then validate the following part of an instance document (we here concentrate on the attributes and ignore the contents of the element):

```
<form action="http://www.brics.dk/ixwt/examples/hello.jsp">
   ...
</form>
```

and normalize it as follows:

```
<form action="http://www.brics.dk/ixwt/examples/hello.jsp"
      method="get"
      enctype="application/x-www-form-urlencoded">
  ...
</form>
```

As usual, the ordering of attributes and whitespace between them are insignificant.

The 'fixed' variant seems strange. It certainly conveys little information to say that a certain attribute after normalization must have one specific value. A typical use of #FIXED is to fake namespace declarations, as in the DTD schema for XHTML:

```
<!ATTLIST html xmlns CDATA #FIXED "http://www.w3.org/1999/xhtml">
```

In Chapter 2, we mentioned how the special attribute named xml:space can be used to indicate significance of whitespace. When this attribute is used, it is often declared in the schema using #FIXED so that the instance document author does not have to worry about it:

```
<!ATTLIST pre xml:space (preserve) #FIXED "preserve">
```

However, irrespective of this attribute, the DTD processor never throws away any whitespace – this is left to the application.

When more than one attribute-list declaration is provided for a given element name, the declarations are merged. If an attribute of a given name is specified more than once for an element, then the first one takes effect, but friendly XML parsers issue a warning if this situation occurs.

4.3.4 Conditional Sections, Entity, and Notation Declarations

The features described in this section are not essential to the workings of XML and DTD, so you might skip this section in a first reading. In existing DTD schemas, you might encounter applications of them, but they are rarely indispensable when developing new schemas.

First, *internal entity declarations* constitute a poor man's macro mechanism. If our DTD schema contains

```
<!ENTITY copyrightnotice "Copyright &#169; 2005 Widgets'R'Us.">
```

then the DTD processor may convert the following fragment of an instance document

```
A gadget has a medium size head and a big gizmo subwidget.
&copyrightnotice;
```

into

```
A gadget has a medium size head and a big gizmo subwidget.
Copyright &#169; 2005 Widgets'R'Us.
```

If the copyright notice appears often, this mechanism allows us to save some space (which was a big concern when SGML was developed). The contents of such a declaration may consist of any well-formed XML data, including markup. The construct &*entity*;, where *entity* is the name of a previously declared entity, is called an *entity reference*. Some XML parsers that support validation with DTD actually perform the expansion of entity references, whereas others instead maintain special *entity reference nodes* in the XML tree representing the entity references together with pointers to their declarations.

The predefined entities mentioned in Section 2.4 are implicitly defined using internal entity declarations. We may also add another declaration:

```
<!ENTITY copy "&#169;">
```

so that we can write

```
&copy;
```

which is easier to remember than © whenever we want a © symbol.

An *internal parameter entity declaration* is a macro definition that is only applicable within the DTD schema, and not in the instance document. For example, as in XHTML, we may define

```
<!ENTITY % Shape "(rect|circle|poly|default)">
```

(notice the % symbol) and then, within the schema, use references such as in

```
<!ATTLIST area shape %Shape; "rect">
```

which is then equivalent to

```
<!ATTLIST area shape (rect|circle|poly|default) "rect">
```

The % symbol in the declaration and the reference indicates a parameter entity, whereas & is used for normal entity references.

An *external entity declaration* is a reference to another resource, which consists of XML or non-XML data. A reference to another XML file may be declared by, for example:

```
<!ENTITY widgets SYSTEM "http://www.brics.dk/ixwt/widgets.xml">
```

(A public identifier, as described earlier, may also be used.) Occurrences of the entity reference &widgets; will then result in the designated XML data being inserted in place of the entity reference, perhaps via an entity reference node as explained above.

A reference to a non-XML resource, called an *unparsed entity*, can be declared as in

```
<!ENTITY widget-image
         SYSTEM "http://www.brics.dk/ixwt/widget.gif"
         NDATA gif>
```

Here, the NDATA part refers to a *notation*, which describes the format of an unparsed entity, for example by the declaration

```
<!NOTATION gif
    SYSTEM "http://www.iana.org/assignments/media-types/image/gif">
```

which could be used as a description of GIF images. Notation declarations may also be used for description of processing instruction targets.

Of course, it does not make sense for an instance document to contain entity references to unparsed entities. Instead, these entities are used in conjunction with the special attribute types ENTITY and ENTITIES: the value of an attribute of type ENTITY must match the name of an unparsed entity, and ENTITIES must match a whitespace separated nonempty list of such names. When an XML parser that performs validation with DTD encounters such attributes in the instance document, it informs the application of the associated SYSTEM/PUBLIC identifiers and notation names.

Notations may also be used directly in attributes: the value of an attribute of type NOTATION must match the name of a notation declaration. This can be used to describe formats of non-XML data.

Finally, *conditional sections* allow parts of the schema to be included or excluded via a switch. Although it is not indispensable, the typical use of this mechanism is to let an external DTD schema contain a number of declarations and then select only some of them for use in the instance document. Conditional sections are typically combined with the parameter entity mechanism. For example, an external DTD schema may contain

```
<![%person.simple; [
  <!ELEMENT person (firstname,lastname)>
]]>
<![%person.full; [
  <!ELEMENT person (firstname,lastname,email+,phone?)>
  <!ELEMENT email (#PCDATA)>
  <!ELEMENT phone (#PCDATA)>
]]>
<!ELEMENT firstname (#PCDATA)>
<!ELEMENT lastname (#PCDATA)>
```

In the internal DTD schema, we can then define either

```
<!ENTITY % person.simple "INCLUDE" >
<!ENTITY % person.full   "IGNORE" >
```

to select the simple version of the `person` element, or

```
<!ENTITY % person.simple "IGNORE">
<!ENTITY % person.full   "INCLUDE">
```

to get the full version. The parameter entity references expand to the keywords IGNORE and INCLUDE, which result in, respectively, disabling and enabling the contents of the blocks. The conditional section mechanism is used extensively in the XHTML modularization framework that we described in Section 2.5.

We have deliberately left out a number of annoying technical details of the DTD language in this section. Most users of XML fortunately never need to know about them, but if you for some reason are forced in that direction, then look in the XML specification (its URL is provided among the online resources at the end of the chapter).

4.3.5 Checking Validity with DTD

A DTD processor (also called a *validating XML parser*) works by first parsing the instance document, that is, constructing its XML tree representation, and the DTD schema, including all external schema subsets. Parsing succeeds if the document is well-formed. Note that since the DTD language does not itself use an XML notation, a different parsing technique (typically based on a BNF-like grammar) is needed for parsing the DTD schema.

Then, the DTD processor checks that the name of the root element of the instance document is correct. In the next phase, most of the actual validation work is performed in a simple traversal of the XML document: for each element node, the processor looks up the associated element declaration and attribute-list declarations and (1) checks that the content of the element node matches the content model of the element declaration, (2) normalizes the attributes according to the declarations, which consists of insertion of default attributes and pruning of whitespace where applicable, (3) checks that all required attributes are present, and (4) checks that the values of the attributes match the associated attribute types. Entity references are either expanded during the traversal or kept in the tree as entity reference nodes – in either case, the validation treats them as if they were expanded. In the same traversal, all ID attributes are collected and checked for uniqueness.

After this phase, the only thing that remains is the check for IDREF and IDREFS attributes. For each of these, the processor checks that each reference corresponds to some ID attribute.

Finally, if no validation errors were detected, the processor outputs the normalized instance document, either in its textual form or in its tree representation to the application. Naturally, a DTD processor is not required to follow this exact sequence of phases as long as it has the same resulting behavior.

As a final note, instance documents that do refer to external DTD declarations but do not rely on attribute defaults and entity declarations from these external parts may contain a *standalone declaration* in the XML declaration:

```
<?xml version="1.1" standalone="yes"?>
```

This declaration tells the XML processors that if they are only interested in parsing the document but not in checking validity, then the external DTD declarations can safely be ignored.

4.3.6   Recipe Collections with DTD

We are now in a position to formalize the syntax for RecipeML using DTD, based on the informal description given in Section 2.7:

```
<!ELEMENT collection (description,recipe*)>

<!ELEMENT description (#PCDATA)>

<!ELEMENT recipe
      (title,date,ingredient*,preparation,comment?,
                            nutrition,related*)>
<!ATTLIST recipe id ID #IMPLIED>

<!ELEMENT title (#PCDATA)>

<!ELEMENT date (#PCDATA)>

<!ELEMENT ingredient (ingredient*,preparation)?>
<!ATTLIST ingredient name CDATA #REQUIRED
                     amount CDATA #IMPLIED
                     unit CDATA #IMPLIED>

<!ELEMENT preparation (step*)>

<!ELEMENT step (#PCDATA)>

<!ELEMENT comment (#PCDATA)>

<!ELEMENT nutrition EMPTY>
<!ATTLIST nutrition calories CDATA #REQUIRED
                    carbohydrates CDATA #REQUIRED
                    fat CDATA #REQUIRED
                    protein CDATA #REQUIRED
                    alcohol CDATA #IMPLIED>

<!ELEMENT related (#PCDATA)>
<!ATTLIST related ref IDREF #REQUIRED>
```

This DTD schema simply uses the ELEMENT and ATTLIST constructs to describe the RecipeML vocabulary of elements and attributes. A collection element has no attributes but contains a description element followed by zero or more recipe elements, and so on. The schema captures most of the requirements that were informally expressed earlier; however, there are some notable exceptions: even a simple XML language as RecipeML reveals practical limitations of the expressiveness of DTD. The schema presented above inevitably has obvious shortcomings:

DTD cannot express all details of the syntax of our small XML language for recipe collections.

- we cannot express that the `calories` attribute must contain a non-negative number and, for example, `protein` must contain a value on the form N% where N is between 0 and 100;

- the `unit` attribute should only be allowed in an element when `amount` is present; and

- nested `ingredient` elements should only be allowed when `amount` is absent.

As previously discussed, the effect is that the schema allows too much, so our applications that operate on the recipe collections need to perform some extra checking of the input to make sure that it is meaningful.

Moreover, we would have liked the `comment` element to be allowed to appear anywhere in the contents of a `recipe` element, not just between `preparation` and `nutrition`. This property is, in fact, expressible, but only with a long-winded content model expression that unions all the possible places where `comment` should be permitted (and the requirement that the expression must be deterministic makes this extra tricky). As a result, the schema in this case is too restrictive compared to our informal description.

Assume that we store this DTD schema in a file and make it available at the URL

```
http://www.brics.dk/ixwt/recipes.dtd
```

By inserting

```
<!DOCTYPE collection SYSTEM "http://www.brics.dk/ixwt/recipes.dtd">
```

in the headers of our recipe collection instance documents, we state that they are intended to conform to the designated DTD schema.

As described earlier, we can insert a fake namespace declaration in the schema:

```
<!ATTLIST collection
          xmlns CDATA #FIXED "http://www.brics.dk/ixwt/recipes">
```

Notice that in this simple example, we use only the fundamental features of DTD: element and attribute-list declarations. We have no need for parameter entities, notations, or the other murky legacies from SGML.

If we run a DTD schema processor on an invalid document, for example omitting the `description` element, we will get an error message that helps us locate the problem:

```
[Error] recipes.xml:366:14: The content of element type "collection"
must match "(description,recipe*)".
```

Here, `366:14` refers to the line and column of the end tag of the surrounding `collection` element. (This particular output is generated by the Xerces parser.)

If we accidentally had made a syntax error in the DTD schema, for instance, forgetting the parentheses around `#PCDATA`, then the schema processor might report the following:

```
[Fatal Error] recipes.dtd:5:23: A '(' character or an element type is
required in the declaration of element type "title".
```

It then aborts without performing any validation of the instance document. An easy way of checking that your newly written DTD schemas are syntactically correct according to the formal syntax of DTD is to run a DTD processor with a dummy instance document.

4.3.7   Limitations of DTD

DTD has a number of problems that limit its practical use:

1. DTD cannot constrain character data. In the contents of a particular element, either any character data is permitted or none at all. Obviously, we would like more control here, as mentioned earlier. What we need is a more powerful *datatype* mechanism for describing character data.

2. By the same token, the attribute types are too limited. DTD cannot specify that the value of a particular attribute must be, for example, an integer, a URI, a date, or whatever datatypes we might use.

3. Element and attribute declarations are entirely context insensitive. That is, descriptions cannot depend on attributes or element context, as we saw with `unit` attributes and `ingredient` elements in the DTD description of RecipeML. However, it is very common in the design of XML languages that certain declarations depend on whether or not a certain attribute exists and has a particular value or the current element has a particular ancestor element.

4. Character data cannot be combined with the regular expression content model. This means that if we need to permit character data in the contents, then we cannot control the order of elements or their number of occurrences.

5. The content models lack an 'interleaving' operator, as we just saw with the `comment` element in RecipeML.

6. DTD provides very limited support for modularity, reuse, and evolution of schemas. The entity and conditional section mechanisms are low-level and difficult to apply elegantly. This makes it hard to write, maintain, and read large DTD schemas and to define families of related schemas.

7. The normalization features in DTD are limited. Although there is a default mechanism for attributes, there is none for element contents. Also, using the special `xml:space`

attribute does not cause any removal of insignificant whitespace in character data by the DTD processor – it only indicates the intended meaning to the application.

8. DTD does not permit embedded structured self-documentation. Comments are allowed, but they cannot contain markup.

9. The ID/IDREF mechanism is too simple. Often, it is desirable to be able to specify a more restricted scope of uniqueness for ID attributes than the entire instance document. It is also inconvenient that only individual attribute values can be used as keys. It would be more useful if the key could consist of multiple attribute values or even character data.

10. DTD does not itself use an XML notation. A practical consequence of this design is that it is not possible to write a DTD description of the DTD language itself, which otherwise would have been handy for checking that a DTD schema is indeed a syntactically correct DTD schema. Instead, we need yet another formalism (Extended BNF) for describing the syntax of the DTD language. It also means that we cannot use standard XML tools to manipulate DTD schemas.

11. DTD does not support namespaces.

As an additional annoyance, the specification of DTD is mixed into the specification of the XML notation, which makes it difficult to separate the two.

Nevertheless, DTD is still widely used, sometimes for expressing rough approximations of available elements, attributes, and the constraints of their use, perhaps as supplements to schemas written in a more complicated schema language, such as XML Schema.

4.4 XML Schema

Shortly after XML 1.0 (and thereby also DTD) was approved as a W3C recommendation, the W3C initiated the development of the next generation schema language to attack the problems with DTD. In 1999, a note *'XML Schema Requirements'* was published by the XML Schema Working Group, outlining the goals of the project. This note lists some judicious guiding *design principles*, some of which are that the language should be

- more expressive than XML DTD (this goal is clearly rather vague, but it indicates the overall direction);

- expressed in XML (we saw above the problems that resulted from DTD not being an XML language);

- self-describing (meaning that it should be possible to describe the syntax of XML Schema in the XML Schema language itself); and

- simple enough to implement with modest design and runtime resources (which sets a limit to the first goal listed above).

In addition, the working group proclaimed that the specification of XML Schema should be prepared quickly (otherwise competing schema languages might gain a foothold) and be precise, concise, human-readable, and illustrated with examples. Some of the more technical requirements were that the language should

- contain a mechanism for constraining the use of namespaces;

- allow creation of user-defined *datatypes* for describing character data and attribute values;

- enable inheritance for element, attribute, and datatype definitions;

- support evolution of schemas; and

- permit embedded documentation within the schemas.

In 2001, the working group published the XML Schema W3C recommendation. The specification comprises two parts: Part 1, *Structures*, describes the core of XML Schema including declaration of elements and attributes; Part 2, *Datatypes*, describes the built-in datatypes and their various facets.

Unfortunately, the resulting language does not fulfill all the original requirements: although the language does provide good support for namespaces and datatypes, which are two of the most pressing issues with DTD, it is not simple (Part 1 alone is more than 130 dense pages, and even XML experts do not find it human-readable), and it is not fully self-describing (there is a schema for XML Schema, but it does not capture all syntactical aspects of the language). Furthermore, as we shall see later, despite its complexity this ambitious schema language still cannot express the full syntax of our little RecipeML language.

4.4.1 Overview

Before delving into the details of the language, let us begin with a birds-eye view. To facilitate reuse of descriptions and improve the structure of schemas, XML Schema contains a sophisticated type system inspired by those known from programming languages, in particular object-oriented languages. The following four constructs are the most central ones in XML Schema, and they all hinge on the notion of types:

- A *simple type definition* defines a family of Unicode text strings.

- A *complex type definition* defines a collection of requirements for attributes, sub-elements, and character data in the elements that are assigned that type.

- An *element declaration* associates an element name with either a simple type or a complex type. For an element in the instance document to be valid, it must satisfy all requirements defined by the type that is associated with the name of the element. If all elements in the instance document are valid, then the entire document is valid.

- An *attribute declaration* associates an attribute name with a simple type. (Since attribute values always contain unstructured text, only simple types make sense here.)

Intuitively, a *simple* type describes text without markup (in character data and attribute values), whereas a *complex* type describes text that may contain markup (that is, elements, attributes, and character data).

Two types or two elements cannot be defined with the same name within one schema, but an element or attribute declaration and a type definition may use the same name. An element or attribute declaration with no type description permits any value. We will later see how to develop advanced type definitions.

The following tiny but complete schema shows one element declaration named `student`, two attribute declarations named `id` and `score`, one complex type definition named `StudentType`, and one simple type definition named `Score`:

```
<xsd:schema xmlns:xsd="http://www.w3.org/2001/XMLSchema"
            xmlns:s="http://www.brics.dk/ixwt/students"
            targetNamespace="http://www.brics.dk/ixwt/students">

  <xsd:element name="student" type="s:StudentType"/>

  <xsd:attribute name="id" type="xsd:string"/>
  <xsd:attribute name="score" type="s:Score"/>

  <xsd:complexType name="StudentType">
    <xsd:attribute ref="s:id" use="required"/>
    <xsd:attribute ref="s:score" use="required"/>
  </xsd:complexType>

  <xsd:simpleType name="Score">
    <xsd:restriction base="xsd:integer">
      <xsd:minInclusive value="0"/>
      <xsd:maxInclusive value="100"/>
    </xsd:restriction>
  </xsd:simpleType>

</xsd:schema>
```

XML Schema elements are identified by the namespace `http://www.w3.org/2001/XMLSchema`. In this example, we use the namespace prefix `xsd`, but, as usual, the choice of prefix is insignificant. As the example shows, the root element of an XML Schema document is named `schema`, and it (usually) contains a `targetNamespace` attribute that indicates the namespace being described by the schema, in this case `http://www.brics.dk/ixwt/students`. We also declare this namespace by a normal namespace declaration, here using the prefix `s`, so that we are able to refer to our own definitions in the schema.

The declarations and definitions in the schema then *populate* the target namespace: the `element` construct declares the element name `student` and associates to it the type

In XML Schema, **definitions** create new types, and **declarations** describe constituents of the instance documents.

StudentType (from our own namespace); the following two `attribute` constructs declare two attributes named `id` and `score`; the `complexType` construct defines the type StudentType as two attribute references; and the `simpleType` construct defines a type Score, which is used to describe that the legal values of the `score` attribute are integers between 0 and 100. Both `student`, `id`, `score`, `StudentType`, and `Score` then belong to the target namespace. Notice that some of the attribute values in the schema use namespace prefixes to locate the right definitions: since `StudentType` is one of our own types, we refer to it using the `s` prefix, whereas `string` and `integer` are built-in types, so for those we use the `xsd` prefix. Definition names are never prefixed – they always belong to the target namespace. The details of the attribute declarations and the simple type definition will be explained later.

Notice the syntax for element and attribute declarations:

```
<element name="name" type="type"/>
```

and

```
<attribute name="name" type="type"/>
```

The former associates a simple or complex type to an element name; the latter associates a simple type to an attribute name.

The following instance document consisting of a single element is valid according to the schema shown above:

```
<?xml version="1.0" encoding="UTF-8"?>
<stu:student xmlns:stu="http://www.brics.dk/ixwt/students"
             stu:id="19970233"
             stu:score="97"/>
```

The `student` element here resides in the namespace that was declared as the target namespace in the schema, and the element fulfills all requirements defined in the schema for elements of that name. Notice that also the two attributes are explicitly qualified using the `stu` prefix. Typically we do not want prefixes in attribute names; we shall see in Sections 4.4.4 and 4.4.5 how to avoid them.

The presentation of XML Schema in this chapter is reasonably complete. The essential language constructs are explained in sufficient detail for most schema authors. However, to keep the presentation concise, lots of technical details of this very complex language inevitably have to be omitted.

Example: Business Cards

We now consider a slightly more complicated example that we will also build on later in the book. Assume we want to create an XML-based language for *business cards* where each card consists of a name, a title, an email address, an optional phone number, and an optional link to a logo image. An example document could be following, which we store in a file `john_doe.xml`:

```
<b:card xmlns:b="http://businesscard.org">
  <b:name>John Doe</b:name>
  <b:title>CEO, Widget Inc.</b:title>
  <b:email>john.doe@widget.inc</b:email>
  <b:phone>(202) 555-1414</b:phone>
  <b:logo b:uri="widget.gif"/>
</b:card>
```

We here assume that we own the domain `businesscard.org` such that we can be certain that no one else uses the namespace `http://businesscard.org`. Again, a more common design would not use a prefix in the `uri` attribute; we fix this in Sections 4.4.4 and 4.4.5.

To describe the syntax of our new language, we write a schema, `business_card.xsd`:

```
<schema xmlns="http://www.w3.org/2001/XMLSchema"
        xmlns:b="http://businesscard.org"
        targetNamespace="http://businesscard.org">

  <element name="card" type="b:card_type"/>
  <element name="name" type="string"/>
  <element name="title" type="string"/>
  <element name="email" type="string"/>
  <element name="phone" type="string"/>
  <element name="logo" type="b:logo_type"/>

  <attribute name="uri" type="anyURI"/>

  <complexType name="card_type">
    <sequence>
      <element ref="b:name"/>
      <element ref="b:title"/>
      <element ref="b:email"/>
      <element ref="b:phone" minOccurs="0"/>
      <element ref="b:logo" minOccurs="0"/>
    </sequence>
  </complexType>

  <complexType name="logo_type">
    <attribute ref="b:uri" use="required"/>
  </complexType>

</schema>
```

From here on, we use the empty namespace prefix for XML Schema elements in the examples to make the documents more readable.

This schema contains six element declarations followed by one attribute declaration and two complex type definitions. The one named `card_type` contains the constraints of `card` elements, and the one named `logo_type` is for the `logo` elements. The `card_type` definition resembles a DTD content model. It states that for an element to match this type, its content must be a sequence of a `name` element followed by a `title` and an `email` element and then optional `phone` and `logo` elements. The `logo_type` definition corresponds to a simple attribute-list declaration in DTD. It states that for an element to match this type, it must have an attribute named `uri` whose value is a URI. The type `anyURI` is one of the built-in simple types in XML Schema.

As in DTD, only contents and attributes that are explicitly declared are permitted. For example, a `card` element is not allowed to have any attributes, and a `logo` element is not allowed to have any contents. However, there are a few exceptions to this rule, as explained later.

Connecting Instance Documents and Schemas

An instance document may refer to a schema with the `schemaLocation` attribute from the namespace `http://www.w3.org/2001/XMLSchema-instance`:

```
<b:card xmlns:b="http://businesscard.org"
        xmlns:xsi="http://www.w3.org/2001/XMLSchema-instance"
        xsi:schemaLocation="http://businesscard.org
                            business_card.xsd">
  <b:name>John Doe</b:name>
  <b:title>CEO, Widget Inc.</b:title>
  <b:email>john.doe@widget.inc</b:email>
  <b:phone>(202) 555-1414</b:phone>
  <b:logo b:uri="widget.gif"/>
</b:card>
```

The value of the `schemaLocation` attribute consists of two parts that are separated by whitespace: a namespace URI, which must match the target namespace of the schema, and a URI that locates the schema document. (It is not particularly pretty to use attributes in this way – it would probably have been more natural to use two attributes or sub-elements instead.) By inserting this attribute, the author asserts that the instance document is intended to be valid with respect to the schema. This mechanism is reminiscent of the DOCTYPE declarations in DTD, however, there are some important differences: First, XML Schema exploits the standard namespace mechanism to make the connection between instance document and schema rather than introducing some new specialized syntax. Second, `schemaLocation` attributes may appear in any elements in the instance document, whereas DOCTYPE is restricted to the root. Most often, `schemaLocation` attributes appear in the root elements, but they may also appear further down the tree if they only apply to subtrees. This gives the instance document author the ability to combine XML languages in an ad hoc manner. Each `schemaLocation` attribute may, in fact, contain *multiple* pairs of namespace URIs and schema URIs; the effect is then that all the schemas apply independently of each other.

All attributes from the `http://www.w3.org/2001/XMLSchema-instance` namespace are implicitly always declared for all elements in the instance documents, so our schemas do not have to declare that, for example, the `schemaLocation` attribute is permitted.

The `schemaLocation` references are merely hints to the XML processors. It is not required that such references are inserted, neither are applications forced to take them into account. The main purpose of the schema references is to make the instance documents *self-describing* in the same way that most XML documents begin with an XML declaration that states the XML version and character encoding being used and also contain namespace declarations that identify the particular XML language being used. Typically, applications require their input to be valid relative to particular schemas that the application writer decides rather than to schemas that the instance document authors decide. Other schema languages use different approaches for connecting schemas and instance documents: we have seen that DTD uses the special `DOCTYPE` construct (see Section 4.3.1); the DSD2 language (see Section 4.5) instead uses a specific processing instruction; and RELAX NG (see Section 4.6) has no mechanism for specifying the association.

XML Schema contains no direct mechanism for enforcing a particular root element in the instance documents (however, there is a hack that we describe in Section 4.4.4). This means that, for example, an XML Schema description of XHTML cannot express the requirement that the root element must be an `html` element. The rationale behind this design choice is that the application that reads the instance document should be free to decide what may or may not be a root element. In practice, however, this just means that applications must check the name of the root element manually in addition to performing XML Schema validation.

4.4.2 Simple Types

A *simple type*, also called a *datatype*, is a set of Unicode strings together with a semantic interpretation of the strings. For example, `decimal` (from the XML Schema namespace) is a built-in simple type whose value space consists of all strings that represent decimal numbers, such as `3.1415`. Since the interpretation for this type is that the values represent decimal numbers, the two strings `3.1415` and `03.141500` are *equal*, and the values of the type are *ordered*, for example, `42` is *less than* `117`. Other simple types have different interpretations, and not all are ordered. These interpretations are, for example, used when atomizing values in XQuery (see Chapter 6).

A **simple type** describes text without markup; a **complex type** describes text that may contain markup.

XML Schema contains a number of *primitive* simple types, whose meanings are predefined, and various mechanisms for *deriving* new types from existing ones. The primitive simple types are listed in Figure 4.5. Some derived simple types that were expected to be commonly used have been included in the XML Schema specification; these are listed in Figure 4.6.

An element declaration can assign a simple type to an element name:

```
<element name="serialnumber" type="nonNegativeInteger"/>
```

Type	Typical values
string	*any Unicode string*
boolean	true, false, 1, 0
decimal	3.1415
float	6.02214199E23
double	42E970
duration	P1Y2M3DT10H30M (1 year, 2 months, 3 days, 10 hours, and 30 minutes)
dateTime	2004-09-26T16:29:00-05:00,2004-09-26T21:29:00Z
time	16:29:00-05:00, 21:29:00Z
date	2004-09-26, 2004-09-26-05:00
gYearMonth	2004-09, 2004-09-05:00
gYear	2004, 2004-05:00
gMonthDay	--09-26, --09-26-05:00
gDay	--26, --26-05:00
gMonth	--09, --09-05:00
hexBinary	48656c6c6f0a
base64Binary	SGVsbG8K
anyURI	http://www.brics.dk/ixwt/
QName	rcp:recipe, recipe
NOTATION	*depends on notations declared in the current schema*

Figure 4.5 Primitive simple types.

This particular element declaration assigns the built-in simple type nonNegativeInteger to elements named serialnumber. The effect is that the contents of such an element must consist of character data that matches nonNegativeInteger (perhaps with surrounding whitespace, see Section 4.4.9), and it cannot contain attributes or child elements.

New simple types can be derived from existing ones in three different ways:

- A restriction of an existing type, called a *base type*, defines a new type by restricting the set of possible values of the original one. This restriction can be performed on various *facets* of the type, as shown in Figure 4.7.

  The following defines a type for non-negative decimals with the built-in decimal type as base:

  ```
  <simpleType name="nonNegativeDecimal">
    <restriction base="decimal">
      <minInclusive value="0"/>
    </restriction>
  </simpleType>
  ```

  The next example illustrates that a single restriction may involve multiple constraining facets:

  ```
  <simpleType name="score_from_0_to_100">
    <restriction base="integer">
      <minInclusive value="0"/>
  ```

Type	Typical values
normalizedString	*as* string *but whitespace facet is* replace
token	*as* string *but whitespace facet is* collapse
language	en, da, en-US
NMTOKEN	42, my.form, r103
NMTOKENS	42 my.form r103
Name	my.form, r103, rcp:recipe
NCName	my.form, r103
ID	*as* NCName
IDREF	*as* NCName
IDREFS	my.form r103
ENTITY	*as* NCName
ENTITIES	my.form r103
integer	42, -87, +42, 0
nonPositiveInteger	-87, 0
negativeInteger	-87
nonNegativeInteger	42, 0
unsignedLong	18446744073709551615
unsignedInt	4294967295
unsignedShort	65535
unsignedByte	255
positiveInteger	42
long	-9223372036854775808, 9223372036854775807
int	-2147483648, 2147483647
short	-32768, 32767
byte	-128, 127

Figure 4.6 Built-in derived simple types.

Facet	Constraining
length	length of string or number of list items
minLength	minimal length
maxLength	maximal length
pattern	regular expression constraint
enumeration	enumeration value
whiteSpace	controls white space normalization (Section 4.4.9)
maxInclusive	inclusive upper bound (for ordered types)
maxExclusive	exclusive upper bound
minInclusive	inclusive lower bound
minExclusive	exclusive lower bound
totalDigits	maximum number of digits (for numeric types)
fractionDigits	maximum number of fractional digits

Figure 4.7 Constraining facets of simple types.

```
    <maxInclusive value="100"/>
  </restriction>
</simpleType>
```

An enumeration restricts values to a finite set of possibilities:

```
<simpleType name="language">
  <restriction base="string">
    <enumeration value="EN"/>
    <enumeration value="DA"/>
    <enumeration value="FR"/>
  </restriction>
</simpleType>
```

Note that these facet restrictions operate on the semantic level, not the syntactic level. For example, restricting the totalDigits facet to 3 for the decimal type means that the values 123, 0123, and 0123.0 are all permitted, but 1234 and 120.05 are not.

The pattern constraining facet is a powerful mechanism for constraining values to regular expressions – the formalism that we generally introduced in Section 4.2. The actual syntax used in patterns is, in fact, a slight extension of the one presented in that section. The additions include character ranges (such as [a-z]) and repetitions (such as x{3,7}), which were also briefly mentioned earlier.

As an example, we can define a simple type for integers in the range 0 to 100 that are followed by a percentage character and where superfluous leading zeros are not allowed:

```
<simpleType name="percentage">
  <restriction base="string">
    <pattern value="([0-9]|[1-9][0-9]|100)%"/>
  </restriction>
</simpleType>
```

The first branch ([0-9]) describes a single digit, the second branch ([1-9][0-9]) describes two digits where the first is nonzero, and the third branch describes the value 100. The entire branch structure is then followed by a percentage character.

Special symbols in patterns (such as *, (, and |) can be escaped by prefixing with a backslash (as in *). Unicode character categories and blocks can be expressed conveniently with names, such as \p{Sc} for all currency symbols or \p{IsHiragana} for all hiragana characters.

For most facets, restrictions may be changed in further derivations unless the attribute fixed="true" is added to the constraining facet.

- A list of a type defines a whitespace separated sequence of values of that type:

```
<simpleType name="integerList">
  <list itemType="integer"/>
</simpleType>
```

- A `union` of a number of types denotes the union of their values:

```
<simpleType name="boolean_or_decimal">
  <union>
    <simpleType>
      <restriction base="boolean"/>
    </simpleType>
    <simpleType>
      <restriction base="decimal"/>
    </simpleType>
  </union>
</simpleType>
```

Notice that we here use two 'dummy' restrictions inside the `union` – this is the only way to refer to an existing simple type inside a `union`.

Altogether, XML Schema provides useful mechanisms for describing datatypes. There are a few problematic issues nevertheless. First, one may argue that the `list` construct can easily be misused. If, during the design of a new XML language, one needs to describe a list of things, say integers, one could easily use the `list` construct to describe values such as the following:

```
<integerlist> 7 42 87 </integerlist>
```

However, one thereby loses some of the benefits of XML since additional parsing is necessary to split the character data into the integer constituents. Usually, a better solution is to add more markup to make the structure explicit:

```
<integerlist>
  <int>7</int>
  <int>42</int>
  <int>87</int>
</integerlist>
```

With this style, a standard XML parser suffices for determining the structure – at the price of more verbose markup.

A second problematic issue is that existing simple types cannot be used within regular expression patterns. For example, assume that a *product ID* is a string, such as `2005-09-26#0542`, consisting of a valid date followed by a # character and a four-digit integer. We can elegantly define simple types representing the date and the integer, but we cannot combine these with a concatenation operation as a regular expression – even though all constituents are regular languages.

Third, many other realistic examples show that the derivation mechanisms for simple types are often not sufficiently flexible. For example, the various hardwired types for date and time formats seem to be chosen more or less randomly as there exist other international standards for this kind of data that one might have preferred.

Simple types can be **derived** by restricting or combining existing types.

Finally, the type system of XML Schema is, in fact, much more involved than what we have seen so far. We come back to this issue in later sections.

Emulating DTD Features with Special Simple Types

Some of the built-in simple types have the same value spaces (see Figure 4.6) but different interpretations, for example, NCName, ID, and ENTITY. The types ID, IDREF, and others with names that are familiar from DTD are included for compatibility. The ID, IDREF, and IDREFS types provide the well-known functionality from DTD: attributes of type ID must have unique values, and every attribute of type IDREF must match the value of some ID attribute. An alternative and more powerful mechanism is more commonly used as explained in Section 4.4.10.

The NOTATION mechanism from DTD (see Section 4.3.4) can be expressed as notation declarations in XML Schema:

```
<notation name="gif" public="image/gif"
    system="http://www.iana.org/assignments/media-types/image/gif"/>
```

The values of attributes (or character data) of the type NOTATION must match such declarations. The usefulness of this feature is debatable.

Similarly, the values of type ENTITY or ENTITIES (or types derived from one of these) must match the names of unparsed entities as in DTD. However, XML Schema contains no mechanism for declaring unparsed entities; instead it relies on the presence of DTD declarations. Since XML Schema also contains no mechanism for declaring parsed entities, it is customary to utilize the one available in DTD. No other parts of the otherwise optional DTD schema are used when processing XML Schema schemas.

These DTD-like features are mostly used for emulating the special DTD mechanisms and are rarely used when developing new XML languages. The notion of conditional sections has no immediate counterpart in XML Schema, but the modularization features, which we describe in Section 4.4.7, are much more powerful.

4.4.3   Complex Types

In the previous section, we explained the meaning of assigning a simple type to an element name. An element declaration may alternatively assign a complex type to an element name, as in the schema for XML business cards:

```
<element name="card" type="b:card_type"/>
```

The meaning of such a declaration is that elements of that name must fulfill all requirements specified by the type. For complex types, these requirements may involve both attributes and contents, including child elements and character data.

A complex type can be defined using the XML Schema element `complexType` that has a `name` attribute, whose value is the name of the new type. The content of `complexType` can be of two kinds, *complex* and *simple*, as described below.

Constructing Complex Types with Elements and Attributes

The complex model can describe both elements and attributes. The elements are described through a variant of the regular expression formalism explained in Section 4.2. The alphabet then consists of all possible elements, and the various operators are written using the following XML syntax:

- An *element reference* is typically of the form

  ```
  <element ref="name"/>
  ```

  where `name` is the name of an element that has been declared elsewhere. Such a reference matches a single element of the given name. (Notice the difference between an element named `element` with a `name` attribute and one with a `ref` attribute – the former is a declaration and the latter is a reference to a declaration.)

- Concatenation is expressed using a `sequence` element. The schema for business cards on page 117 shows an example.

- Union corresponds to a `choice` element. As an example, we might have defined the complex type `card_type` differently:

  ```
  <complexType name="alternative_card_type">
    <sequence>
      <element ref="b:name"/>
      <element ref="b:title"/>
      <choice>
        <element ref="b:email"/>
        <element ref="b:phone" minOccurs="0"/>
      </choice>
      <element ref="b:logo" minOccurs="0"/>
    </sequence>
  </complexType>
  ```

  Compared to the definition on page 117, we now permit either an `email` element or a number of `phone` elements, but not both.

- The `all` construct is an additional operator for describing unordered contents. A content sequence matches an `all` expression if each constituent of the expression is matched somewhere in the content sequence, and conversely, all elements in the content sequence are matched by some constituent of the expression. One may think of this construct as a variant of `sequence` where the content order is irrelevant.

As an example, the following variant of `card_type` uses `all` instead of `sequence` to avoid restricting the ordering of the elements:

```
<complexType name="another_alternative_card_type">
  <all>
    <element ref="b:name"/>
    <element ref="b:title"/>
    <element ref="b:email"/>
    <element ref="b:phone" minOccurs="0"/>
    <element ref="b:logo" minOccurs="0"/>
  </all>
</complexType>
```

Unfortunately, the `all` construct is restricted in various ways (see pages 127 and 128).

- The `any` construct is a wildcard that matches any element. If the attribute `namespace` is present, only elements from specific namespaces are matched: its value is a whitespace separated list of namespace URIs; the special value `##targetNamespace` means the target namespace, and `##local` means the default namespace (the empty URI). Two other values are possible: `##any` (the default) means 'any namespace' and `##other` means 'any namespace except the target namespace'.

  This construct is particularly useful for defining *open* schemas where there is room for extension as in the following alternative definition of the type `card_type`:

```
<complexType name="yet_another_alternative_card_type">
  <sequence>
    <element ref="b:name"/>
    <element ref="b:title"/>
    <element ref="b:email"/>
    <element ref="b:phone" minOccurs="0"/>
    <element ref="b:logo" minOccurs="0"/>
    <any namespace="##other"
         minOccurs="0" maxOccurs="unbounded"
         processContents="skip"/>
  </sequence>
</complexType>
```

Here we explicitly permit elements from other namespaces than the target namespace to appear after the explicitly described elements. The `processContents="skip"` attribute instructs the schema processor to skip checking validity of these extra elements and their descendants. Other possible values are `strict` (the default), which means that checking must be performed, and `lax`, which means checking must be performed only on those elements where a schema description is available.

Another common use of `any` is for connecting sublanguages loosely. For example, we may in a schema for WidgetML (see Section 2.6) declare the `info` element, which may contain XHTML data, using the following type:

```
<complexType name="info_type">
  <sequence>
    <any namespace="http://www.w3.org/1999/xhtml"
        minOccurs="1" maxOccurs="unbounded"/>
  </sequence>
</complexType>
```

To match this type, the contents must consist of one or more element from the XHTML namespace, but we do not in this schema specify which elements are permitted in that namespace. A more tight integration of sublanguages is possible with the `import` mechanism described in Section 4.4.7.

Additionally, the contents of `complexType` can be empty, which simply corresponds to the empty `sequence` of elements. The various constructs are summarized in Figure 4.8 (which also mentions a `group` construct that we explain later; see page 132).

A few restrictions apply to the `all` construct: `all` may only contain `element` references (not `sequence`, `choice`, or `all`), no element may be described more than once within a given `all` operator, and `sequence` and `choice` cannot contain `all` operators. Additionally, a complete expression cannot consist of one `element` or `any` declaration alone (just wrap it into a `sequence` or `choice` if you need to express a single element reference, as in the `info_type` example above). Also, all expressions must be *deterministic* as in DTD (see Section 4.3.2). The rationale behind these peculiar and often annoying restrictions is in most cases that XML Schema processors should be easier to implement.

A `complexType` may optionally also contain a number of *attribute references* that typically have the form

```
<attribute ref="name"/>
```

where *name* is the name of the attribute that has been declared elsewhere. Such a declaration states that elements that are assigned the complex type containing this declaration may

Construct	Meaning
element	element reference
sequence	concatenation
choice	union
all	unordered sequence
any	any element
group	named subexpression

Figure 4.8 Constructs used in complex content model descriptions.

have an attribute of the given name and with a value that matches the given type. Attribute references must be placed *after* the content model description.

Every attribute reference can have an attribute named use whose value can be optional (the default) or required with the obvious meaning.

Similarly, for the content model part, each element, sequence, choice, all, and any element (and also group, which we describe later) occurring in a type definition may have attributes named minOccurs and maxOccurs that define *cardinalities* of the declarations. The values can be non-negative integers, and the special value unbounded is also permitted for maxOccurs. By default, both attributes have the value 1. For example, the expression

```
<element ref="r:recipe" minOccurs="0" maxOccurs="unbounded"/>
```

matches any sequence of zero or more recipe elements (assuming that the prefix r is properly declared), and

```
<choice maxOccurs="unbounded">
  <element ref="xhtml:th"/>
  <element ref="xhtml:td"/>
</choice>
```

matches any sequence of one or more elements, each named th or td (from the right namespace). For the all construct, minOccurs must be 0 or 1, and maxOccurs must be 1 – and similarly for element constructs inside all.

We are now in a position to fully understand the complex type definitions in the business card example we saw earlier:

```
<complexType name="card_type">
  <sequence>
    <element ref="b:name"/>
    <element ref="b:title"/>
    <element ref="b:email"/>
    <element ref="b:phone" minOccurs="0"/>
    <element ref="b:logo" minOccurs="0"/>
  </sequence>
</complexType>

<complexType name="logo_type">
  <attribute ref="b:uri" use="required"/>
</complexType>
```

The first type definition describes a sequence of elements where the first three are required (since minOccurs and maxOccurs are both 1 by default) and the last two are optional (because of the minOccurs="0" attributes). The second type definition describes a single attribute, which is required in elements that are assigned that type.

With the complex content model, the `complexType` element may optionally contain an attribute `mixed="true"`, which means that, in addition to the elements that have been declared in the contents, also arbitrary character data is permitted anywhere in the contents. This resembles the mixed content model in DTD, except that we now have control of the order and number of occurrences of the elements in the contents. Without `mixed="true"`, only whitespace is permitted. If we wish to constrain the character data according to some simple type, we have to use the simple content model, which we describe later. However, it is not possible with XML Schema to constrain the character data if we want to permit both character data and elements in a content sequence.

The following example shows a complex type describing both mixed contents and an attribute (we assume that the `n` prefix identifies the target namespace):

```
<element name="order" type="n:order_type"/>
<attribute name="id" type="unsignedInt"/>

<complexType name="order_type" mixed="true">
  <choice>
    <element ref="n:address"/>
    <sequence>
      <element ref="n:email" minOccurs="0" maxOccurs="unbounded"/>
      <element ref="n:phone"/>
    </sequence>
  </choice>
  <attribute ref="n:id" use="required"/>
</complexType>
```

In this definition, an `order` element must contain elements according to the regular expression (`<choice>...</choice>`), together with arbitrary character data and a mandatory attribute named `id`.

As a counterpart to `any` for attributes, the attribute declarations in a complex type definition may be followed by an `anyAttribute` declaration. This declaration uses `namespace` and `processContents` attributes in the same way as `any`, as described earlier.

Type Derivation

In the following, we look into the mechanisms for deriving new complex types from existing types. These features facilitate reuse and comprehensibility and are directly inspired by the type systems found in object-oriented programming languages.

Constructing Complex Types with Simple Content

A complex type that describes attributes, but whose contents consist of character data only and no elements, can be described using a `simpleContent` construction that contains an `extension` of a simple type where some attribute declarations are added. For example, we can build a complex type from a simple type (`integer`) and an attribute (named `class`, declared elsewhere):

```
<complexType name="category">
  <simpleContent>
    <extension base="integer">
      <attribute ref="n:class"/>
    </extension>
  </simpleContent>
</complexType>
```

An element matches this type if its contents constitute an integer and the element has no attributes, except an optional one named `class`. In this way, we effectively construct a complex type from simple types.

A complex type with *simple content* can also be constructed from an existing complex type, provided that it has simple content (as the `category` type shown above does, for example):

```
<complexType name="extended_category">
  <simpleContent>
    <extension base="n:category">
      <attribute ref="n:kind"/>
    </extension>
  </simpleContent>
</complexType>

<complexType name="restricted_category">
  <simpleContent>
    <restriction base="n:category">
      <totalDigits value="3"/>
      <attribute ref="n:class" use="required"/>
    </restriction>
  </simpleContent>
</complexType>
```

The type named `extended_category` extends the `category` type with an extra attribute declaration named `kind` (assumed to be declared elsewhere). Such an extension inherits the content type and attribute declarations from the base type. The type named `restricted_category` matches the same values as `category`, except that it only permits integers with at most three digits (see the discussion of the semantic versus the syntactic level of simple types in Section 4.4.2) and that the `class` attribute is no longer optional. Such a restriction also inherits the properties of the base type, but it may contain overriding restricting declarations. Note that a restriction always matches a subset of the values matched by the base type. The converse is *not* true for extensions since these may add extra tree components that are mandatory in all values of the derived type.

One combination of these constructs is not permitted: it is not possible to define a complex type with `simpleContent` as a `restriction` of a simple type, but in that case one could just use a simple type definition instead.

Derivation of Complex Types with Complex Content

We have so far seen two ways of constructing complex types: the complex model for describing XML structures with elements, and the simple model for controlling character data contents. As a third possibility, new complex types can be derived from existing ones having complex content models. (The complex type mechanism is indeed complicated!)

Assume that we have a description of 'basic' business cards containing just a `name` element:

```
<complexType name="basic_card_type">
  <sequence>
    <element ref="b:name"/>
  </sequence>
</complexType>
```

We might want to produce various extended versions of this description, all sharing a common base. That can be achieved using the `extension` mechanism for complex content types:

```
<complexType name="an_extended_card_type">
  <complexContent>
    <extension base="b:basic_card_type">
      <sequence>
        <element ref="b:title"/>
        <element ref="b:email" minOccurs="0"/>
      </sequence>
    </extension>
  </complexContent>
</complexType>
```

The effect of this definition is that the original content model and the extension are concatenated, that is, an element matches `an_extended_card_type` if its contents are a `name` element followed by a `title` and an optional `email` element. It is not possible to extend content models by other means than concatenation. Also, it is not possible to define a complex type with complex content (that is, using `complexContent`) as an extension of a type with simple content (that is, either a simple type or a complex type defined with `simple-Content`). Generally for complex type derivations, the contents of `extension` can consist of `sequence`, `choice`, `all`, `group`, `attribute`, `attributeGroup`, and `anyAttribute` elements. For declaring mixed contents, a `mixed="true"` attribute can be placed in either the `complexType` or the `complexContent` element.

Complex types can be derived by **extending** or **restricting** existing types.

Complex types can also be derived by `restriction`:

```
<complexType name="a_further_derived_card_type">
  <complexContent>
    <restriction base="b:an_extended_card_type">
      <sequence>
        <element ref="b:name"/>
        <element ref="b:title"/>
        <element ref="b:email"/>
      </sequence>
    </restriction>
  </complexContent>
</complexType>
```

Here, we construct a further derivation of `an_extended_card_type` where the `email` element is mandatory (recall that `minOccurs="1"` is the default). A type derived by restriction must repeat all the constituents of the content model of the base type, except that it is permitted to match fewer values. Attribute declarations need not be repeated, but, as in restrictions of complex types with simple contents, attribute declarations may be overridden by more restrictive ones.

Again, we see that type derivation by extension adds constituents to the valid documents, whereas type derivation by restriction confines the set of valid documents.

Generally, the type derivation mechanisms promote a well-structured reuse of descriptions, much like inheritance in object-oriented programming languages. Using the extension mechanism is reminiscent of defining subclasses in object-oriented languages by adding new fields. We shall see in Section 4.4.8 that the notion of subsumption known from object-oriented languages is also present in XML Schema.

Groups

Expressions used in complex types can be reused via the `group` construct. The following snippet is taken from an XML Schema description of XHTML:

```
<group name="heading">
  <choice>
    <element ref="xhtml:h1"/>
    <element ref="xhtml:h2"/>
    <element ref="xhtml:h3"/>
    <element ref="xhtml:h4"/>
    <element ref="xhtml:h5"/>
    <element ref="xhtml:h6"/>
  </choice>
</group>

<group name="block">
```

```
    <choice>
      <element ref="xhtml:p"/>
      <group ref="xhtml:heading"/>
      <element ref="xhtml:div"/>
      <group ref="xhtml:lists"/>
      <group ref="xhtml:blocktext"/>
      <element ref="xhtml:isindex"/>
      <element ref="xhtml:fieldset"/>
      <element ref="xhtml:table"/>
    </choice>
  </group>

  <complexType name="button.content" mixed="true">
    <choice minOccurs="0" maxOccurs="unbounded">
      <element ref="xhtml:p"/>
      <group ref="xhtml:heading"/>
      ...
    </choice>
  </complexType>
```

In this example, a `heading` group is defined as the union of six element references, and this group is then subsequently used in another group definition named `block` and also in a complex type definition named `button.content`. The effect is as if the `choice` construction containing the six element references were inserted in place of the two group references.

Similarly, a collection of attribute declarations may be defined and reused multiple times using `attributeGroup`:

```
  <attributeGroup name="Focus">
    <attribute ref="xhtml:accesskey"/>
    <attribute ref="xhtml:tabindex"/>
    <attribute ref="xhtml:onfocus"/>
    <attribute ref="xhtml:onblur"/>
  </attributeGroup>

  <complexType name="SelectType" mixed="true">
    <choice maxOccurs="unbounded">
      <element ref="xhtml:optgroup"/>
      <element ref="xhtml:option"/>
    </choice>
    <attributeGroup ref="xhtml:Focus"/>
    ...
  </complexType>

  <complexType name="TextAreaType" mixed="true">
    ...
    <attributeGroup ref="xhtml:Focus"/>
  </complexType>
```

Four attribute declarations that are logically related are here collected into an attribute group called `Focus`, which is then used in two (abbreviated) complex type definitions. (As we have seen in earlier examples involving attribute declarations, this one also requires the attributes to have namespace prefixes in the instance documents; to avoid that, see Sections 4.4.4 and 4.4.5.)

Nil Values in Elements

When modeling databases, it is occasionally useful to be able to describe 'missing contents'. An element can be declared as *nillable*:

```
<element name="recipe" type="r:recipe_type" nillable="true"/>
```

This declaration means that the content of a `recipe` element in the instance document may be empty – even if its type `recipe_type` requires certain elements – provided that the `recipe` element contains a special `nil="true"` attribute from the XML Schema instance namespace:

```
<recipe xmlns:xsi="http://www.w3.org/2001/XMLSchema-instance"
        xsi:nil="true"/>
```

The attribute declarations are unaffected by this mechanism.

This mechanism provides a very simple form of conditional constraints: If a certain attribute is present and has a certain value (`xsi:nil="true"`), then one content model is applicable (the empty one), otherwise another content model is applicable (the one specified in the type). It would certainly be useful to have a more general form of such dependencies, as we discuss elsewhere in this chapter. Moreover, in many XML applications, nil values are often represented by absent elements instead of using `xsi:nil`.

4.4.4 Global versus Local Descriptions

In the schema examples we have seen so far, all element and attribute declarations and all type definitions appear at the top-level of the schema, that is, with the `schema` element as parent. Such descriptions are also called *global*. An alternative style is to use inlined, or *local*, descriptions. As an example, the following descriptions from our business card language use a purely global style:

```
<element name="card" type="b:card_type"/>
<element name="name" type="string"/>

<complexType name="card_type">
  <sequence>
    <element ref="b:name"/>
    <element ref="b:title"/>
```

```
      <element ref="b:email" maxOccurs="unbounded"/>
      <element ref="b:phone" minOccurs="0"/>
      <element ref="b:background" minOccurs="0"/>
    </sequence>
  </complexType>
```

Notice that the complex type named `card_type` is only used once, namely in the declaration of `card` elements, and `name` elements only appear as children of `card` elements. The alternative declaration below has the same meaning but uses local descriptions for the complex type named `card_type` and the `name` child element:

```
<element name="card">
  <complexType>
    <sequence>
      <element name="name" type="string"/>
      <element ref="b:title"/>
      <element ref="b:email" maxOccurs="unbounded"/>
      <element ref="b:phone" minOccurs="0"/>
      <element ref="b:background" minOccurs="0"/>
    </sequence>
  </complexType>
</element>
```

Notice how the `card_type` definition and the `name` element declaration have been inlined where they were used in the global style version.

Choosing between these two styles is largely a matter of personal preference of the schema author, however, there are some important technical differences:

- local type definitions are anonymous (as in the second `complexType` above), so they cannot be referred to for reuse – but on the other hand, we do not have to invent names for them;

- local element declarations can be *overloaded*, that is, two elements with the same name (and namespace) can have different types if one or both declarations are local – and similarly for attribute declarations;

- only globally declared elements can be starting points for validation (that is, root elements in the instance documents, if validating complete documents); and

- as we discuss in the next section on namespaces, local and global descriptions behave differently with respect to namespaces (in particular, local attribute declarations can describe non-prefixed attributes).

The schema author may exploit the third item listed above to express that only certain elements may occur as roots, but that implies a writing style where every reference to a non-root element name must repeat the associated type even if overloading is not used.

Local
descriptions
permit
overloading of
element and
attribute
declarations.

One concrete benefit of the purely global style is that it is always straightforward to find the description of elements with a given name. A benefit of applying the local style whenever possible is that descriptions more often appear directly where they are used, so this style tends to make the schemas more compact.

As an example of overloading, assume that we extend the business card language such that one XML document can contain a list of business cards, not just a single one. This list is expressed with a `cardlist` root element that contains a list of `card` elements. We also permit a `title` child element of `cardlist` for an XHTML description of the card list. The following instance document is then valid for this modified language:

```
<cardlist xmlns="http://businesscard.org"
          xmlns:xhtml="http://www.w3.org/1999/xhtml">
  <title>
    <xhtml:h1>My Collection of Business Cards</xhtml:h1>
    containing people from <xhtml:em>Widget Inc.</xhtml:em>
  </title>
  <card>
    <name>John Doe</name>
    <title>CEO, Widget Inc.</title>
    <email>john.doe@widget.inc</email>
    <phone>(202) 555-1414</phone>
  </card>
  <card>
    <name>Joe Smith</name>
    <title>Assistant</title>
    <email>thrall@widget.inc</email>
  </card>
</cardlist>
```

Notice now that a `title` element appearing as a child of `cardlist` can contain arbitrary XHTML whereas a `title` element appearing as a child of `card` can contain only character data as before. With local descriptions of the `title` elements this design can be expressed as follows:

```
<schema xmlns="http://www.w3.org/2001/XMLSchema"
        xmlns:b="http://businesscard.org"
        targetNamespace="http://businesscard.org"
        elementFormDefault="qualified">

  <element name="cardlist" type="b:cardlist_type"/>
  <element name="card" type="b:card_type"/>
  <element name="name" type="string"/>
  <element name="email" type="string"/>
  <element name="phone" type="string"/>
  <element name="logo" type="b:logo_type"/>

  <attribute name="uri" type="anyURI"/>
```

```xml
<complexType name="cardlist_type">
  <sequence>
    <element name="title" type="b:cardlist_title_type"
            minOccurs="0"/>
    <element ref="b:card" minOccurs="0" maxOccurs="unbounded"/>
  </sequence>
</complexType>

<complexType name="cardlist_title_type" mixed="true">
  <sequence>
    <any namespace="http://www.w3.org/1999/xhtml"
        minOccurs="0" maxOccurs="unbounded"
        processContents="lax"/>
  </sequence>
</complexType>

<complexType name="card_type">
  <sequence>
    <element ref="b:name"/>
    <element name="title" type="string"/>
    <element ref="b:email"/>
    <element ref="b:phone" minOccurs="0"/>
    <element ref="b:logo" minOccurs="0"/>
  </sequence>
</complexType>

<complexType name="logo_type">
  <attribute ref="b:uri" use="required"/>
</complexType>

</schema>
```

Compared to the original schema (page 117), we have here inlined the declaration of `title` elements. We use the `any` construct to establish the connection to the XHTML language, as explained earlier. The attribute named `elementFormDefault` is explained in the next section.

Overloading is particularly relevant for attributes. It is typical in XML languages that a given attribute name is used with different types in different elements. For example, the type for an `align` attribute in an `hr` element in XHTML is different from one in an `img` or `p` element.

Continuing the business card list example, we could apply local descriptions even further than the previous schema indicates, as the following variant shows:

```xml
<schema xmlns="http://www.w3.org/2001/XMLSchema"
        xmlns:b="http://businesscard.org"
        targetNamespace="http://businesscard.org"
        elementFormDefault="qualified"
        attributeFormDefault="qualified">
```

```
<element name="cardlist">
  <complexType>
    <sequence>
      <element name="title" minOccurs="0">
        <complexType mixed="true">
          <sequence>
            <any namespace="http://www.w3.org/1999/xhtml"
                 minOccurs="0" maxOccurs="unbounded"
                 processContents="lax"/>
          </sequence>
        </complexType>
      </element>
      <element name="card" minOccurs="0" maxOccurs="unbounded">
        <complexType>
          <sequence>
            <element name="name" type="string"/>
            <element name="title" type="string"/>
            <element name="email" type="string"/>
            <element name="phone" type="string" minOccurs="0"/>
            <element name="logo" minOccurs="0">
              <complexType>
                <attribute name="uri" type="anyURI"
                           use="required"/>
              </complexType>
            </element>
          </sequence>
        </complexType>
      </element>
    </sequence>
  </complexType>
</element>

</schema>
```

(The attribute named `attributeFormDefault` is explained in the next section.) Compared to the previous variant, we have here inlined all descriptions that were only used once. The resulting schema contains only a single global element declaration which has a high nesting depth.

The overloading mechanism is limited in an important way: two element declarations that have the same name and appear in the same complex type must have identical types. As an example, the following type is illegal:

```
<complexType name="illegal_type">
  <sequence>
    <element name="foo" type="some_type"/>
    <element name="foo" type="another_type"/>
  </sequence>
</complexType>
```

This limitation significantly reduces the theoretical expressiveness of XML Schema, but on the positive side, it greatly simplifies implementation of efficient XML Schema processors.

4.4.5 Namespaces

We have already encountered the influence of namespaces for XML Schema. Being an XML language itself, this schema language uses namespaces to identify the schema instructions. It also associates target namespaces (using the `targetNamespace` attribute) to the XML languages we are describing.

XML Schema does support XML languages without namespaces by omitting the `targetNamespace` attribute. Technically, the descriptions in the schema then populate the default (empty URI) namespace, and such a schema may be referred to using a `noNamespaceSchemaLocation` attribute in place of `schemaLocation` (see page 118).

So far, this is rather uncontroversial, but XML Schema also introduces some unconventional uses of namespaces that one should be aware of:

- First, XML Schema (as well as other XML languages, for example XSLT) uses namespace prefixes in certain attribute values. The namespace standard, as we discussed in Section 2.6, only describes prefixes on element names and attribute names. The meaning of prefixes in attribute values in XML Schema is not surprising though, as we have seen in the example schemas.

- A second, and more frustrating feature is that of *qualified* and *unqualified locals*, which is related to the discussion of global and local descriptions in the previous section.

  If 'unqualified locals' is enabled, then the name of a locally declared element or attribute must have *no* namespace prefix in the instance document; such an attribute or element is interpreted as belonging to the element declared in the surrounding global definition. For non-prefixed attributes, this is just the expected behavior (according to the usual interpretation of the namespace mechanism, as described in Section 2.6); however, this is not the case for elements: a non-prefixed element name is normally resolved by looking up the relevant default namespace declaration, as explained in Section 2.6.

  If 'qualified locals' is enabled, then the name of a locally declared attribute must have a namespace prefix, just like we have seen for globally declared attributes. For elements, however, it means that the namespace mechanism behaves just like we would expect from Section 2.6.

  These mechanisms may be controlled separately for elements and attributes, and both globally for the entire schema by `elementFormDefault` and `attributeFormDefault` attributes in the `schema` element and locally for each local declaration by a `form` attribute. The values of these special attributes are either `unqualified` or `qualified` corresponding to the two modes of operation. The value `unqualified` is the default for both elements and attributes. As explained above, for attributes, `unqualified` corresponds to the expected behavior of non-prefixed names, but this is not the case for elements. So, in order to obtain a sane interpretation of namespace prefixes in XML Schema, one should always use

```
<schema ...
        elementFormDefault="qualified"/>
  ...
</schema>
```

Of course, this declaration is only relevant if using local element declarations. To get rid of the prefixes on uri attributes in our business card example (see page 117), we simply change the attribute declaration from being global to local (and select unqualified local attributes by default):

```
<schema xmlns="http://www.w3.org/2001/XMLSchema"
        xmlns:b="http://businesscard.org"
        targetNamespace="http://businesscard.org">

  <element name="card" type="b:card_type"/>
  <element name="name" type="string"/>
  <element name="title" type="string"/>
  <element name="email" type="string"/>
  <element name="phone" type="string"/>
  <element name="logo" type="b:logo_type"/>

  <complexType name="card_type">
    <sequence>
      <element ref="b:name"/>
      <element ref="b:title"/>
      <element ref="b:email"/>
      <element ref="b:phone" minOccurs="0"/>
      <element ref="b:logo" minOccurs="0"/>
    </sequence>
  </complexType>

  <complexType name="logo_type">
    <attribute name="uri" type="anyURI" use="required"/>
  </complexType>

</schema>
```

For the remainder of the book, we use this version of the business card language. In short, unqualified local elements are bad practice: do not use them! For attributes, however, the situation is different: since the vast majority of attributes in existing XML languages are non-prefixed, most attribute declarations are local.

Qualified attributes, on the other hand, are certainly useful (although unqualified ones are more common). For example, the XLink language (see Section 3.6) can be incorporated into other languages using attributes that are qualified by the XLink namespace:

```
<schema xmlns="http://www.w3.org/2001/XMLSchema"
        xmlns:xlink="http://www.w3.org/1999/xlink"
        targetNamespace="http://www.w3.org/1999/xlink"
        attributeFormDefault="qualified">

  <attribute name="href" type="anyURI"/>
  <attribute name="show" type="xlink:showType"/>
  <attribute name="actuate" type="xlink:actuateType"/>

  <attributeGroup name="simpleLink">
    <attribute name="type" type="string" fixed="simple"/>
    <attribute ref="xlink:href"/>
    <attribute ref="xlink:show"/>
    <attribute ref="xlink:actuate"/>
    ...
  </attributeGroup>
  ...

</schema>
```

(Here, `attributeFormDefault` applies only to the `type` attribute since that is the only locally declared attribute. The `fixed` attribute is explained in Section 4.4.9.) Such a schema can then be imported into the host language (see Section 4.4.7), using, for example, the `simpleLink` attribute group in element declarations to describe simple links.

4.4.6   Annotations

Schemas can be annotated with human or machine readable documentation and other information:

```
<element name="card">
  <annotation>
    <documentation xmlns:xhtml="http://www.w3.org/1999/xhtml">
      The 'card' element represents one business card.
      See <xhtml:a href="manual.html">the manual</xhtml:a> for
      more information.
    </documentation>
    <appinfo xmlns:p="http://printers-r-us.com">
      <p:paper type="117"/>
    </appinfo>
```

```
    </annotation>
    <complexType>
      <sequence>
        <element name="name" type="string"/>
        <element name="title" type="string"/>
        <element name="email" type="string"/>
        <element name="phone" type="string" minOccurs="0"/>
        <element name="logo" type="logo_type" minOccurs="0"/>
      </sequence>
    </complexType>
  </element>
```

Such `annotation` elements may appear in the beginning of the contents of most schema constructs. The `documentation` sub-element is intended for human readable information, whereas `appinfo` is for applications. The actual contents are ignored by the schema processor. Information may also be specified externally via `source` attributes in the `documentation` and `appinfo` elements.

Note that annotations can be structured, as opposed to simple `<!-- ... -->` XML or DTD comments. For example, the `documentation` annotation in this example contains XHTML markup.

4.4.7   Modularization

Modularization is crucial for real world schemas. Schemas for realistic XML languages can become colossal due to large numbers of elements and attributes that need to be described. Also, such XML languages rarely exist in isolation but are developed in families of related languages and evolve from existing ones. As an example, the Danish OIOXML initiative for public administration is built of around 2500 interconnected XML Schema definitions. This calls for mechanisms for *modularization* of descriptions.

To support structuring, reuse, and evolution, schemas can be expressed as modules of manageable sizes that can be combined to describe complete XML languages. XML Schema provides three constructs for combining schemas in the form of instructions that may appear initially in the `schema` element:

`<include schemaLocation="URI"/>` – composes with the designated schema having the *same* target namespace as this schema. The effect is as if the `include` instruction was replaced by the contents of the included schema.

`<import namespace="NS" schemaLocation="URI"/>` – composes with the designated schema having a *different* target namespace *NS*. The `schemaLocation` attribute is optional; if omitted, the imported schema must be located by other means.

`<redefine schemaLocation="URI"> ... </redefine>` – as include, but permits redefinitions, that is, definitions of types and groups (appearing as the contents of the `redefine` element) that then take precedence of the definitions of the same names in the included schema. A type redefinition must be either an extension or a restriction of the original type, and similarly, a group redefinition must describe either a superset or a subset of the original definition (for some obscure reason).

The schema for business cards already has a quite manageable size, but as an example, let us nevertheless split it into two modules, one containing the description of the `logo` elements, and the other containing the rest. First, `business_card_logo.xsd`:

```
<schema xmlns="http://www.w3.org/2001/XMLSchema"
        xmlns:b="http://businesscard.org"
        targetNamespace="http://businesscard.org">

  <element name="logo" type="b:logo_type"/>

  <complexType name="logo_type">
    <attribute name="uri" type="anyURI" use="required"/>
  </complexType>

</schema>
```

The second module, `business_card_misc.xsd`:

```
<schema xmlns="http://www.w3.org/2001/XMLSchema"
        xmlns:b="http://businesscard.org"
        targetNamespace="http://businesscard.org">

  <element name="card" type="b:card_type"/>
  <element name="name" type="string"/>
  <element name="title" type="string"/>
  <element name="email" type="string"/>
  <element name="phone" type="string"/>

  <complexType name="card_type">
    <sequence>
      <element ref="b:name"/>
      <element ref="b:title"/>
      <element ref="b:email"/>
      <element ref="b:phone" minOccurs="0"/>
      <element ref="b:logo" minOccurs="0"/>
    </sequence>
  </complexType>

</schema>
```

These two modules can then be combined as in the following schema:

```
<schema xmlns="http://www.w3.org/2001/XMLSchema"
        targetNamespace="http://businesscard.org">
```

```
<include schemaLocation="business_card_misc.xsd"/>
<include schemaLocation="business_card_logo.xsd"/>

</schema>
```

This schema then has the same meaning as the original one presented on page 117.

Now, because of this modularization, we know that all `logo` related information is located in the file `business_card_logo.xsd`. Assume that we want to define a variant of our XML language where the `logo` element also has a `contenttype` attribute (with any value), but otherwise is exactly as before. This design can be obtained using `redefine`:

```
<schema xmlns="http://www.w3.org/2001/XMLSchema"
        xmlns:b="http://businesscard.org"
        targetNamespace="http://businesscard.org">

  <include schemaLocation="business_card_misc.xsd"/>

  <redefine schemaLocation="business_card_logo.xsd">
    <complexType name="logo_type">
      <complexContent>
        <extension base="b:logo_type">
          <attribute name="contenttype" type="string"/>
        </extension>
      </complexContent>
    </complexType>
  </redefine>

</schema>
```

Notice how the new definition refers to the original one as base for extension. Except from this apparent self-reference, a redefinition of some name has effect for every use of that name, including ones that appear in the schema module containing the original definition. The redefinition mechanism should be used with caution, as excessive use tends to make the schemas incomprehensible.

Since all descriptions within one schema file populate the same target namespace, using the `import` mechanism is the only way an XML language consisting of multiple namespaces can be described.

We saw on pages 127 and 136 how XHTML could be integrated with our XML language for lists of business cards using the `any` construct. With `import`, we can now specify a more tight connection, assuming that we have an XML Schema description for XHTML:

```
<schema xmlns="http://www.w3.org/2001/XMLSchema"
        xmlns:b="http://businesscard.org"
        xmlns:xhtml="http://www.w3.org/1999/xhtml"
```

```
            targetNamespace="http://businesscard.org"
            elementFormDefault="qualified">

  <import namespace="http://www.w3.org/1999/xhtml"
            schemaLocation="xhtml.xsd"/>

  <element name="cardlist">
    <complexType>
      <sequence>
        <element name="title">
          <complexType mixed="true">
            <sequence>
              <group ref="xhtml:Block.mix"/>
            </sequence>
          </complexType>
        </element>
        <element ref="b:card" minOccurs="0" maxOccurs="unbounded"/>
      </sequence>
    </complexType>
  </element>

  ...
</schema>
```

The '. . .' abbreviates the remaining descriptions, which are as before. We here import the schema for XHTML and refer to the `Block.mix` group definition in that schema when describing the valid contents of those `title` elements that occur as child of `cardlist`. The difference between this approach and the one using `any` is that we can now control exactly which contents are allowed. This example is inspired by W3C's modularization of XHTML, as briefly described in Section 2.5, where `Block.mix` is the name of the description of the valid contents of XHTML `body` elements.

4.4.8 Subsumption and Substitution Groups

We have seen how to derive existing types by extension or restriction. An XML value that matches a given type that has been defined as a restriction of some base type is guaranteed to also match the base type. In other words, an application that expects certain attributes and contents of an element of some type would not be surprised by values of a restriction of that type. The converse is *not* true for type extensions since these may add new mandatory elements or attributes. Nevertheless, both kinds of type derivation permit *subsumption*: If the schema at some point in the instance document requires an element to match a certain type B, then it is acceptable that the element instead matches any type D that, in some number of steps, is derived from B by restriction or extension. This property is trivial for type restrictions. However, for type extensions, it requires that the element has a special attribute from the XML Schema instance namespace identifying the actual type. Consider again the following schema declarations and definitions:

```
<element name="card" type="b:basic_card_type"/>
<element name="name" type="string"/>
<element name="title" type="string"/>
<element name="email" type="string"/>

<complexType name="basic_card_type">
  <sequence>
    <element ref="b:name"/>
  </sequence>
</complexType>

<complexType name="an_extended_card_type">
  <complexContent>
    <extension base="b:basic_card_type">
      <sequence>
        <element ref="b:title"/>
        <element ref="b:email" minOccurs="0"/>
      </sequence>
    </extension>
  </complexContent>
</complexType>
```

and an instance document:

```
<card xmlns="http://businesscard.org"
      xmlns:xsi="http://www.w3.org/2001/XMLSchema-instance"
      xsi:type="an_extended_card_type">
  <name>John Doe</name>
  <title>CEO, Widget Inc.</title>
  <email>john.doe@widget.inc</email>
</card>
```

This instance document is valid relative to the schema. The declaration of `card` elements mentions only a `name` child. The instance document does not satisfy that directly, but it does match a derived type and the `card` element contains a special `xsi:type` attribute that specifies the actual type.

This mechanism is typically used together with the modularization mechanisms: basic types are defined in core modules, and derived types are placed in other modules that extend the core in different directions.

The built-in type `anyType` is a complex type that directly or indirectly is a basis for all other types, that is, every type is derived in some number of steps from `anyType`. An element which is assigned this type may contain arbitrary contents and attributes. (This type resembles the `Object` class in Java, for example.) Similarly, the built-in type `anySimpleType` is a basis for all simple types, and is naturally a derivation of `anyType` as all other types. The main difference between `string` and `anySimpleType` is that the latter has no constraining facts, but both match all Unicode strings. The type `anyType` is the default for element declarations, and `anySimpleType` is the default for attribute declarations.

Technically, the form of type definitions described earlier where a `complexType` directly contains content model and attribute descriptions (as the definition of `basic_card_type` above, for example) is, in fact, a shorthand for a `complexType` with a `complexContent` containing a `restriction` of `anyType`.

Independently from the `xsi:type` attribute mechanism, XML Schema contains a mechanism called *substitution groups*, which provides somewhat similar possibilities. An element declaration *D* can be placed in the substitution group of another element declaration *B*, provided that both are global and the type of *D* is in one or more steps derived from the type of *B*. The effect is that whenever a *B* element is required, a *D* element may be used instead – without using the `xsi:type` attribute in the element. The following schema fragments illustrate this effect:

```
<element name="cardlist">
  <complexType>
    <sequence>
      <element ref="b:basic-card" minOccurs="0"
                                  maxOccurs="unbounded"/>
    </sequence>
  </complexType>
</element>

<element name="basic-card" type="b:basic_card_type"/>
<element name="extended-card" type="b:a_derived_card_type"
        substitutionGroup="b:basic-card"/>

<complexType name="basic_card_type">
  <sequence>
    <element name="name" type="string"/>
  </sequence>
</complexType>

<complexType name="a_derived_card_type">
  <complexContent>
    <extension base="b:basic_card_type">
      <sequence>
        <element name="title" type="string"/>
        <element name="email" type="string" minOccurs="0"/>
      </sequence>
    </extension>
  </complexContent>
</complexType>
```

A `cardlist` here contains a list of `basic-card` elements, but `extended-card` is declared as substitutable for `basic-card` elements. The following instance document is thus valid:

```
<cardlist xmlns="http://businesscard.org">
  <extended-card>
```

```
      <name>John Doe</name>
      <title>CEO, Widget Inc.</title>
      <email>john.doe@widget.inc</email>
   </extended-card>
   <basic-card>
      <name>Joe Smith</name>
   </basic-card>
</cardlist>
```

Compared to using the xsi:type attribute mechanism, we here do not rely on types from the schema in the instance document. Instead, the intended meaning is expressed by the element names.

In addition to all this, there are various mechanisms for controlling the use of derivation and substitution groups:

- If an element or type is declared to be *abstract* with abstract="true", it cannot be used directly in instance documents. However, substitutable elements and derived types are still permitted.

- A complex type defined with the attribute final="#all" cannot be base for a derivation. The values restriction or extension prohibits only derivation by restriction or extension, respectively. For simple types, the values list and union can also be specified with a similar meaning. The schema element may contain an attribute finalDefault with a default value for the final attributes.

- The block attribute in a complex type definition can be used to constrain the use of type extensions, restrictions, and substitution groups. The possible values include #all, restriction, and extension, as above. For example, block="extension" means that types derived by extension of this complex type cannot be used in place of this type with the xsi:type attribute in the instance document. An element declaration may also contain block="substitution", which prohibits substitution of another element where one matching this declaration is expected. As with final, a default value can be specified with a blockDefault attribute in the schema element.

- We have in Section 4.4.2 seen the use of the fixed="true" attribute in restrictions of simple types to prevent further changes of simple type facets. (Note that this is very different from the use of fixed in element and attribute declarations that we describe in Section 4.4.9.)

Clearly, these mechanisms are inspired by the type systems in object-oriented programming languages, and they serve similar purposes. However, things are made overly complicated by the derivation and substitution mechanisms.

The xsi:type attribute required in the instance documents when exploiting the subsumption mechanism serves to reduce the cost of checking validity and to determine the desired type among a potentially large set of possibilities. The substitution group mechanism can be seen as an alternative way of achieving similar goals.

4.4.9 Defaults and Whitespace Normalization

XML Schema provides a few normalization mechanisms as side-effects of the validation. As in DTD, defaults can be specified for attribute declarations:

```
<attribute name="uri" type="anyURI" default="anonymous.jpg"/>
```

If this declaration applies to a given element that does not have a `uri` attribute, the default `uri="anonymous.jpg"` is added.

A similar mechanism applies to elements:

```
<element ref="b:email" default="no email address available"/>
```

In the business card instance document, if an `email` element is empty, then the specified content is inserted by the schema processor. With this and the previous modification of the schema for business cards, processing the instance document

```
<card xmlns="http://businesscard.org">
  <name>John Doe</name>
  <title>CEO, Widget Inc.</title>
  <email/>
  <phone>(202) 555-1414</phone>
  <logo/>
</card>
```

yields the following output:

```
<card xmlns="http://businesscard.org">
  <name>John Doe</name>
  <title>CEO, Widget Inc.</title>
  <email>no email address available</email>
  <phone>(202) 555-1414</phone>
  <logo uri="anonymous.jpg"/>
</card>
```

Also, whitespace in attribute values and simple-typed element contents can be modified using the `whiteSpace` facet of simple type definitions:

```
<simpleType name="name_type">
  <restriction base="string">
    <whiteSpace value="collapse"/>
  </restriction>
</simpleType>
```

The value `replace` causes all tab, line feed, and carriage return characters in values that are assigned this type to be replaced by space characters; `collapse` behaves as `replace` but also collapses contiguous sequences of whitespace into single space characters and removes leading and trailing whitespace; and `preserve` (the default value of this facet) means that no whitespace normalization should be performed. Regarding the built-in simple types, most of them have whitespace type `collapse`, except `string` which is of type `preserve`, and `normalizedString` which is of type `replace`.

Notice how these normalization mechanisms slightly generalize the corresponding mechanisms from DTD (see Section 4.3.3). In particular, normalization of element contents is now also possible; although, unfortunately, that only applies to elements that contain pure character data and no markup. As in DTD, the normalization takes place early in the process, before the actual validation.

The XML Schema counterpart to `#FIXED` from DTD is the `fixed` attribute, which can be used in place of `default` in both attribute and element declarations. The meaning is as in DTD, but now it also applies to elements: the attribute or element content is optional in the input instance document; if present, it must have the value specified by `fixed`; and if omitted, the value of `fixed` is used as a default.

In addition to the normalization features presented here, a schema processor may also contribute to the *post-schema-validation infoset* (PSVI). This slick name denotes pieces of information about the validation process that are made available to the application. For example, this information describes for each validated element which element declaration in the schema it matches and which types are assigned to attribute values. One use of this information is in XQuery (see Chapter 6) where values have types and control flow can be guided by type tests.

4.4.10 Uniqueness, Keys, and References

Recall that DTD can describe uniqueness and referential constraints using the `ID` and `IDREF` attribute types, and that XML Schema contains a compatibility feature for emulating this mechanism. XML Schema also contains a powerful alternative. First, recall some limitations with the DTD features: (1) they only apply to individual attributes, not combinations of attributes or element contents, and (2) the scope is always the entire XML document. XML Schema overcomes these limitations using XPath expressions for selecting fields and confining the scope.

The counterpart to `ID` is the `key` definition:

```
<element name="widget">
  <complexType>
    ...
  </complexType>

  <key name="my_widget_key">
    <selector xpath="w:components/w:part"/>
    <field xpath="@manufacturer"/>
    <field xpath="w:info/@productid"/>
  </key>
</element>
```

XML Schema
relies on a
subset of
XPath for
expressing
keys and
references.

Notice how the `key` definition is specified separately from the type definition, in contrast to DTD where the `ID` attribute type also dictates the valid values. For each `widget` element, called the *current* element, the following steps are performed as a result of this particular `key` definition. The `selector` expression selects the set of `part` elements that have a `components` parent appearing in the contents of the current element. For each node in this set, two fields are produced as the values of the `manufacturer` attribute and the `productid` attribute below the `info` element, respectively. (We here assume that the selected `part` elements do, in fact, have such attributes – this must be declared elsewhere in the schema.) The `selector` expression is evaluated with the current element as context node and must result in a set of element nodes; the `field` expressions are evaluated with each selected element as context node, each one resulting in, at most, one attribute or simple-typed element node. In general, this results in an ordered list of field values for each selected node. Now, the document is only valid if there for each `widget` element are no two selected nodes having equal lists of field values. The notion of equality used here is the one defined for simple types (see Section 4.4.2).

Additionally, the `key` definition causes an *identity-constraint table* to be constructed for the current element. This table is used to resolve `keyref` definitions, which intuitively correspond to the `IDREF` attribute types from DTD. The table contains for each `key` name the corresponding selected elements and their associated lists of field values. Assume that the `widget` element declaration also contains a `keyref` definition:

```
<keyref name="annotation_references" refer="w:my_widget_key">
  <selector xpath=".//w:annotation"/>
  <field xpath="@manu"/>
  <field xpath="@prod"/>
</keyref>
```

The `selector` and `field` parts are evaluated as before, but now, to be valid, each field value list being produced must instead match a corresponding field value list in the identity-constraint table with the name of the `refer` attribute. Intuitively, the selected `annotation` element is then a *reference* to the corresponding selected `part` element. The following instance document satisfies these `key` and `keyref` requirements:

```
<inventory xmlns="http://www.widget.inc">

  <widget>
    <components>
      <part manufacturer="Things'R'Us"><info productid="X1000"/></part>
      <part manufacturer="Gadgets4Ever"><info productid="A-42"/></part>
    </components>
  </widget>

  <widget>
    <components>
      <part manufacturer="Things'R'Us"><info productid="X800"/></part>
```

```
      <part manufacturer="Things'R'Us">
        <info productid="X1000"/>
      </part>
    </components>
    <annotation manu="Things'R'Us" prod="X800">
      Warning: The X800 model is really slippery when wet
    </annotation>
  </widget>

</inventory>
```

One identity-constraint table is constructed for each `widget` element; however, these tables are inherited upward in the instance document tree, so in some schemas the `keyref` definition does not always occur in the same element declaration as the corresponding `key` definition.

The next instance document is *invalid*:

```
<inventory xmlns="http://www.widget.inc">

  <widget>
    <components>
      <part manufacturer="Things'R'Us"><info productid="X1000"/></part>
      <part manufacturer="Gadgets4Ever"><info productid="A-42"/></part>
      <part manufacturer="Things'R'Us"><info productid="X1000"/></part>
    </components>
    <annotation manu="Things'R'Us" prod="X802">
      The X802 model is a vast improvement of the X800
    </annotation>
  </widget>

</inventory>
```

Here, the `key` requirement is violated by the two equal `part` constituents within the same `widget`, and the `keyref` selects a node that has no corresponding field list in the identity-constraint table.

For the XPath expressions in the `xpath` attributes, only a subset of the XPath 1.0 language is permitted in order to make implementation of XML Schema processors easier. The main restrictions are that only the `child`, `attribute`, and `descendant-or-self` axcs can be used – the latter only in the abbreviated form (`//`), and that location step predicates are not allowed. One consequence is that the field nodes must be descendants of the element being validated.

XML Schema has a variant of `key` called `unique`. The main difference is that the designated fields are required to be present for `key`, whereas, for `unique`, a selected node is skipped if a designated field is absent. Note that `keyref` definitions can also match `unique` definitions.

At long last, this concludes our tour through the XML Schema language.

4.4.11   Recipe Collections with XML Schema

Having been introduced to the features of XML Schema, we are now in a position to make
an XML Schema formalization of our RecipeML language. For comparison, we informally
introduced the syntax of RecipeML in Section 2.7 and saw a DTD description in Section 4.3.6.

An XML Schema description of our recipe collections, `recipes.xsd`:

```
<schema xmlns="http://www.w3.org/2001/XMLSchema"
        xmlns:r="http://www.brics.dk/ixwt/recipes"
        targetNamespace="http://www.brics.dk/ixwt/recipes"
        elementFormDefault="qualified">

  <element name="collection">
    <complexType>
      <sequence>
        <element name="description" type="string"/>
        <element ref="r:recipe" minOccurs="0"
                                maxOccurs="unbounded"/>
      </sequence>
    </complexType>
    <unique name="recipe-id-uniqueness">
      <selector xpath=".//r:recipe"/>
      <field xpath="@id"/>
    </unique>
    <keyref name="recipe-references"
            refer="r:recipe-id-uniqueness">
      <selector xpath=".//r:related"/>
      <field xpath="@ref"/>
    </keyref>
  </element>

  <element name="recipe">
    <complexType>
      <sequence>
        <element name="title" type="string"/>
        <element name="date" type="string"/>
        <element ref="r:ingredient"
                 minOccurs="0" maxOccurs="unbounded"/>
        <element ref="r:preparation"/>
        <element name="comment" type="string" minOccurs="0"/>
        <element ref="r:nutrition"/>
        <element ref="r:related" minOccurs="0"
                                 maxOccurs="unbounded"/>
      </sequence>
      <attribute name="id" type="NMTOKEN"/>
    </complexType>
  </element>
```

```xml
<element name="ingredient">
  <complexType>
    <sequence minOccurs="0">
      <element ref="r:ingredient"
               minOccurs="0" maxOccurs="unbounded"/>
      <element ref="r:preparation"/>
    </sequence>
    <attribute name="name" use="required"/>
    <attribute name="amount" use="optional">
      <simpleType>
        <union>
          <simpleType>
            <restriction base="r:nonNegativeDecimal"/>
          </simpleType>
          <simpleType>
            <restriction base="string">
              <enumeration value="*"/>
            </restriction>
          </simpleType>
        </union>
      </simpleType>
    </attribute>
    <attribute name="unit" use="optional"/>
  </complexType>
</element>

<element name="preparation">
  <complexType>
    <sequence>
      <element name="step" type="string"
               minOccurs="0" maxOccurs="unbounded"/>
    </sequence>
  </complexType>
</element>

<element name="nutrition">
  <complexType>
    <attribute name="calories" type="r:nonNegativeDecimal"
               use="required"/>
    <attribute name="protein" type="r:percentage" use="required"/>
    <attribute name="carbohydrates" type="r:percentage"
               use="required"/>
    <attribute name="fat" type="r:percentage" use="required"/>
    <attribute name="alcohol" type="r:percentage" use="optional"/>
  </complexType>
</element>

<element name="related">
  <complexType mixed="true">
```

```
          <attribute name="ref" type="NMTOKEN" use="required"/>
      </complexType>
   </element>

   <simpleType name="nonNegativeDecimal">
     <restriction base="decimal">
        <minInclusive value="0"/>
     </restriction>
   </simpleType>

   <simpleType name="percentage">
     <restriction base="string">
        <pattern value="([0-9]|[1-9][0-9]|100)%"/>
     </restriction>
   </simpleType>

</schema>
```

Some noteworthy comments to this schema:

- The schema is significantly wordier than the DTD version, but that is mostly due to the XML-based syntax.

- We remember to set `elementFormDefault="qualified"` to get the standard namespace semantics.

- We choose a mix of global and local descriptions where the element declarations with non-trivial types and the definitions that are used more than once are global and the remaining ones are local.

- We use `unique`, not `key`, to express the uniqueness constraint on the `id` attributes since these are optional in the `recipe` elements.

- The simple type definitions were not possible to express in DTD – the DTD version used CDATA types as an approximation. However, some of the simple type definitions in this example are rather clumsy, for example, it would have been convenient if we had a simpler construct for defining the type containing just the string '*' or if we could build unions of simple types without explicitly using the restriction/extension mechanism.

- Despite using this much more complicated schema language, we still cannot express that the `unit` attribute should only be allowed when `amount` is present, or that nested `ingredient` elements should only be allowed when `amount` is absent. Furthermore, we still cannot easily express that a `comment` element should be permitted anywhere within the other contents of a `recipe` element: at first, the `all` construct seems to be what we need, but `all` may not contain `sequence` (see page 127). (As with the DTD version, we could capture this requirement precisely with a long-winded content model that unions all the possible places where `comment` should be permitted.)

By inserting the following schema reference into the root element in our recipe collection, `recipes.xml`, we state that the document is intended to be valid according to `recipes.xsd`:

```
<collection xmlns:xsi="http://www.w3.org/2001/XMLSchema-instance"
            xsi:schemaLocation="http://www.brics.dk/ixwt/recipes
                                recipes.xsd"
     ... >
  ...
</collection>
```

In summary, we have now improved our description of RecipeML compared to the DTD version by formalizing the use of namespaces and providing more precise datatypes for the attribute values.

4.4.12 Limitations of XML Schema

Among the main benefits of XML Schema is support for **namespaces**, **modularization**, **datatypes**, and **type derivation**

We have earlier argued that the expressiveness of DTD for a number of reasons is insufficient. Unfortunately, it appears that XML Schema is not the ultimate solution to those problems, but let us now carefully examine the design of this language with a critical view as we did for DTD.

First of all, XML Schema certainly does improve on DTD in a number of ways, in particular regarding namespaces, modularization, and datatypes; however, there are still problems with both expressiveness and comprehensibility of the language:

1. XML Schema is generally too complicated and hard to use by non-experts. This is a problem since many non-experts need to be able to read schemas to write valid instance documents. Also, the complicated design necessitates an incomprehensible specification style, as the following randomly selected quote from the specification indicates: *'If the item cannot be ·strictly assessed·, because neither clause 1.1 nor clause 1.2 above are satisfied, [Definition:] an element information item's schema validity may be laxly assessed if its ·context-determined declaration· is not skip by ·validating· with respect to the ·ur-type definition· as per Element Locally Valid (Type) (§3.3.4).'* Obviously, only a few people will manage to read more than 100 pages of such text, but it is sadly necessary if one needs to understand the gory details of the language.

    One important factor of the complexity of the language is the type mechanism. Even without type derivations and substitution groups, this notion of types adds an extra layer of complexity: an element in the instance document has a *name*, some element declaration in the schema then assigns a *type* to this element name, and finally, some type definition then gives us the *constraints* that must be satisfied for the given element. In DTD, an element name instead directly identifies the associated constraints. (Adding to the confusion, the XML specification uses the term 'element type' for what we call the element name.)

The dual presence of the `xsi:type` attribute subsumption mechanism and the substitution group mechanism seems to reflect conflicting design approaches in the working group resulting in an unnecessarily complex specification.

2. As in DTD, element and attribute declarations are context insensitive (see Section 4.3.7). As an example, see the comments to the schema for RecipeML in Section 4.4.11. Such dependencies are quite common in XML languages, though. In fact, XML Schema itself contains numerous such dependencies. A few examples (all about element descriptions): '`default` and `fixed` must not both be present'; 'one of `ref` or `name` must be present, but not both'; 'if `ref` is present, then all of <complexType>, <simpleType>, <key>, <keyref>, <unique>, `nillable`, `default`, `fixed`, `form`, `block` and `type` must be absent'.

3. Although XML Schema itself uses an XML syntax, there is no complete schema for XML Schema (although there is an incomplete one). One reason why XML Schema is not completely self-describing is the context insensitivity mentioned in the previous point. This is, in a sense, an admission of failure: the working group has produced an XML-based language for describing syntax of XML-based languages, but it cannot describe its own syntax.

4. When describing mixed content, the character data in the contents cannot be constrained in any way. (Compare this with Problem 4 in Section 4.3.7.)

5. The notion of *unqualified local elements* is damaging to the namespace mechanism, as previously discussed.

6. A schema cannot enforce a particular root element in the instance documents (unless the schema has only one global element declaration, but that style of writing schemas is not always recommendable).

7. Element defaults cannot contain markup, only character data.

8. The use of the `xsi:type` attribute in instance documents (see Section 4.4.8) implies an unfortunate coupling between the instance document and one particular schema. It adds to the complexity of the instance documents, and also, it does not work well with multiple schemas describing different aspects of the same instance documents.

9. In Section 4.4.2, we discussed issues related to the limited flexibility of simple type definitions.

10. As mentioned on pages 127 and 128, the `all` construct is restricted in various ways, which limits its usefulness.

11. Although the overloading feature explained in Section 4.4.4 is often useful, it is restricted in two ways: first, it only works together with local definitions; second, two element declarations that have the same name and appear in the same complex type must have identical types.

Rumors are that XML Schema version 1.1 will contain some sort of conditional constraints, which might solve the problems with context insensitivity, but, presumably, new versions will not become less complicated than the current one.

4.4.13 Best Practices

One common approach to overcome the problems with XML Schema is to adhere to a set of guidelines on how the many features of XML Schema should or should not be used. Often, XML Schema allows a task to be solved in many different ways, each having different pros and cons. Of course, there are no definitive rules, but many companies and organizations define local rules that fit their particular needs.

One typical example is the collection of guidelines developed by the XML committee of the Danish Ministry of Science, Technology and Innovation, in cooperation with various other public authorities and also private companies. Some of their guidelines are:

- Always employ namespaces (using `targetNamespace`, see Section 4.4.1) when developing new XML languages.

- Never use `redefine` (see Section 4.4.7); it makes it too difficult to locate the definitions in force.

- Only use global definitions; local definitions do not promote reuse.

- Reuse existing definitions whenever possible.

- Never use `final`, `block`, `finalDefault`, and `blockDefault` since these constructs limit reuse.

- Don't use the `list` construct in simple type definitions (as we discussed in Section 4.4.2).

- Never derive complex types by restriction (see Section 4.4.3). Such derivations counter the object-oriented principle that subtypes are specializations of supertypes.

- Avoid substitution groups (see Section 4.4.8) since they tend to complicate the schema structure.

- Don't use `notation` (Section 4.4.2) or `appinfo` (Section 4.4.6); schemas should not make application specific bindings.

- Never use unqualified local elements, as we also argued in Section 4.4.5.

In addition, the guidelines contain naming conventions, similar to those available for programming languages, such as Java. More information about this project is available (in Danish) at `http://www.oio.dk/XML`. Another example of a collection of guidelines is developed by the United Kingdom e-Government Unit, having occasionally different points of view – see `http://e-government.cabinetoffice.gov.uk/Resources/Guidelines/`.

One lesson to learn from the widespread use of such guidelines is that even advanced applications can actually be developed using only a subset of the many features available in XML Schema.

4.4.14 Other Schema Languages

Unlike for many other XML technologies, it has proved difficult to reach a consensus about how a really good schema language for XML should look. There are several reasons for this situation: it appears to be an inherently difficult problem to design a schema language that is at the same time simple and highly expressive. People have different needs from a schema language. Some have a strong need for an object-oriented type system or for advanced normalization features, others have more modest requirements. Also, the official (W3C) proposals are not very good – we have seen the many problems with DTD and XML Schema.

Between DTD and XML Schema, four other schema language proposals were published as W3C notes, the experience of which were a starting point for the design of XML Schema: XML-Data, DCD (Document Content Description), DDML (Document Definition Markup Language), and SOX (Schema for Object-Oriented XML). Outside the W3C, numerous other schema languages have been developed. In the next sections, we will briefly look at two of these – DSD2 and RELAX NG.

4.5 DSD2 ★

The DSD2 (Document Structure Description 2.0) language is a successor to the DSD 1.0 language developed in cooperation by the University of Aarhus and AT&T Labs Research. The main design goals have been that this language should

- contain few and simple language constructs based on familiar concepts, such as boolean logic and regular expressions;
- be easy to understand, also by non-XML-experts; and
- have more expressive power than other schema languages for most practical purposes.

Compared to XML Schema, DSD2 is small (the specification is only 15 pages, excluding examples), and it is 100% self-describing (so there is a *complete* DSD2 schema for DSD2; see http://www.brics.dk/DSD/dsd2.dsd).

The central ideas in DSD2 can be summarized as follows:

- A schema consists of a list of *rules*. For every element in the instance document, all rules are processed. Rules can conditionally depend on the name, attributes, and context of the current element.
- Rules contain *declare* and *require* sections. A *declare* section specifies which contents (sub-elements and character data) and attributes that are allowed for the current

element. A *require* section specifies extra restrictions on contents, attributes, and context.

- Attribute values and element contents are described by regular expressions.

- Rule conditions and extra restrictions are described by boolean logic.

4.5.1 Recipe Collections with DSD2

With DSD2, the syntax of our recipe collection language can be expressed as follows.

```
<dsd xmlns="http://www.brics.dk/DSD/2.0"
    xmlns:r="http://www.brics.dk/ixwt/recipes"
    xmlns:c="http://www.brics.dk/DSD/character-classes"
    root="r:collection">

  <import href="http://www.brics.dk/DSD/character-classes.dsd"/>

  <if><element name="r:collection"/>
    <declare><contents>
      <sequence>
        <element name="r:description"/>
        <repeat><element name="r:recipe"/></repeat>
      </sequence>
    </contents></declare>
    <unique>
      <and><element name="r:recipe"/><attribute name="id"/></and>
      <attributefield name="id"/>
    </unique>
  </if>

  <if><element name="r:recipe"/>
    <declare>
      <attribute name="id"><stringtype ref="r:NMTOKEN"/></attribute>
      <contents>
        <sequence>
          <element name="r:title"/>
          <element name="r:date"/>
          <repeat><element name="r:ingredient"/></repeat>
          <element name="r:preparation"/>
          <element name="r:nutrition"/>
          <repeat><element name="r:related"/></repeat>
        </sequence>
        <optional><element name="r:comment"/></optional>
      </contents>
    </declare>
  </if>
```

```
<if><element name="r:ingredient"/>
  <declare>
    <required><attribute name="name"/></required>
    <attribute name="amount">
      <union>
        <string value="*"/>
        <stringtype ref="r:NUMBER"/>
      </union>
    </attribute>
    <attribute name="unit"/>
  </declare>
  <if><not><attribute name="amount"/></not>
    <require><not><attribute name="unit"/></not></require>
    <declare><contents>
      <repeat><element name="r:ingredient"/></repeat>
      <element name="r:preparation"/>
    </contents></declare>
  </if>
</if>

<if><element name="r:preparation"/>
  <declare><contents>
    <repeat><element name="r:step"/></repeat>
  </contents></declare>
</if>

<if>
  <or>
    <element name="r:step"/>
    <element name="r:comment"/>
    <element name="r:title"/>
    <element name="r:description"/>
    <element name="r:date"/>
  </or>
  <declare><contents>
    <string/>
  </contents></declare>
</if>

<if><element name="r:nutrition"/>
  <declare>
    <required>
      <attribute name="calories">
        <stringtype ref="r:NUMBER"/>
      </attribute>
      <attribute name="protein">
        <stringtype ref="r:PERCENTAGE"/>
      </attribute>
      <attribute name="carbohydrates">
```

```
              <stringtype ref="r:PERCENTAGE"/>
          </attribute>
          <attribute name="fat">
              <stringtype ref="r:PERCENTAGE"/>
          </attribute>
      </required>
      <attribute name="alcohol">
          <stringtype ref="r:PERCENTAGE"/>
      </attribute>
  </declare>
</if>

<if><element name="r:related"/>
  <declare>
    <contents><string/></contents>
    <required>
      <attribute name="ref"><stringtype ref="r:NMTOKEN"/></attribute>
    </required>
  </declare>
  <pointer><attributefield name="ref"/></pointer>
</if>

<stringtype id="r:NMTOKEN">
  <sequence>
    <repeat min="1"><stringtype ref="c:NAMECHAR"/></repeat>
  </sequence>
</stringtype>

<stringtype id="r:PERCENTAGE">
  <sequence>
    <union>
      <char min="0" max="9"/>
      <sequence>
        <char min="1" max="9"/>
        <char min="0" max="9"/>
      </sequence>
      <string value="100"/>
    </union>
    <string value="%"/>
  </sequence>
</stringtype>

<stringtype id="r:NUMBER">
  <sequence>
    <repeat min="1"><char min="0" max="9"/></repeat>
    <optional>
      <sequence>
        <string value="."/>
        <repeat min="1"><char min="0" max-"9"/></repeat>
```

```
        </sequence>
      </optional>
    </sequence>
  </stringtype>

</dsd>
```

This schema contains a number of conditional rules (the `if` elements) and some string type definitions (the `stringtype` elements). The conditional rules typically check just the name of the current element, but more complex tests can be made. The string type definitions contain commonly used regular expressions. The `import` construct is used to import a preexisting definition of the `NAMECHAR` type. All constructs are explained briefly in the following.

Notice that we use a particular namespace, `http://www.brics.dk/DSD/2.0`, to identify DSD2 elements. Annotations, such as human readable documentation, can be added using the namespace `http://www.brics.dk/DSD/2.0/meta`; such elements and attributes are ignored by the schema processor but can have meaning for other tools.

An instance document can refer to a DSD2 schema using a processing instruction before the root element:

```
<?dsd href="URI"?>
```

As in other schema languages, such a reference means that the instance document is intended to be valid relative to the given schema.

For the recipe collection example, the expressiveness of DSD2 permits us to eliminate *all* the shortcomings that we discussed for the DTD and XML Schema variants in Sections 4.3.6 and 4.4.11.

DSD2 has strong support for **conditional constraints** where declarations rely on attributes and other context.

4.5.2 Rules

A *rule* defines constraints that must be satisfied for every element in the instance document for the document to be valid. Rules come in different forms:

- A *conditional* rule is an `if` element containing a boolean expression followed by a number of sub-rules. If the boolean expression evaluates to true for the current element, then the sub-rules apply.

- A *declare* rule contains declarations of attributes and contents. All attributes and contents of the current element must be declared by some rule, and conversely, all declarations must match the attributes and contents of the current element. Attributes are optional, unless declared within a `required` element.

- A *require* rule contains a boolean expression that must evaluate to true for the current element.

- *Unique* and *pointer* rules correspond to keys and references in XML Schema and are explained later.

Additionally, rules can be defined with a name and then reused multiple times, using `rule` elements with `id` and `ref` attributes.

As an example of a rule, consider the one for `recipe` elements:

```
<if><element name="r:recipe"/>
  <declare>
    <attribute name="id"><stringtype ref="r:NMTOKEN"/></attribute>
    <contents>
      <sequence>
        <element name="r:title"/>
        <element name="r:date"/>
        <repeat><element name="r:ingredient"/></repeat>
        <element name="r:preparation"/>
        <element name="r:nutrition"/>
        <repeat><element name="r:related"/></repeat>
      </sequence>
      <optional><element name="r:comment"/></optional>
    </contents>
  </declare>
</if>
```

This is a conditional rule containing a `declare` sub-rule that applies to elements named `recipe` from the recipe collection namespace. The `declare` rule contains (1) a declaration of the optional attribute `id` and specifies that the valid values are defined by the string type `NMTOKEN`, and (2) a `contents` declaration with two constituents, which are both regular expressions. The first constituent declares that the contents must consist of a sequence of a `title` element, a `date` element, any number of `ingredient` elements, and so on. (We explain the regular expression notation in a moment.) The second constituent declares that an optional `comment` element is also allowed. Whitespace between the elements is implicitly declared to be permitted (because neither regular expression mentions character data; this is explained later).

The rule-based foundation of DSD2 supports **extensibility** and **reuse** of descriptions.

The meaning of a content declaration with multiple regular expressions, such as the one above, is that each of them must match the parts of the actual contents that are mentioned in the expression. For example, the first constituent here does not mention `comment` elements, so all `comment` elements that might appear in the actual contents are ignored when considering this expression. The second constituent does mention `comment` elements, but no other elements or character data, so when considering this expression, only the `comment` elements in the actual contents are considered. And, as mentioned above, all contents must be matched by some constituent of a `contents` declaration. Another way to explain this behavior is that all applicable content declaration expressions are merged into one regular language.

This mechanism makes it straightforward to describe combinations of ordered and unordered content models: the optional `comment` element is permitted anywhere in the other contents, which are ordered. Additionally, content model descriptions can be extended simply by adding new rules to the schema, rather than being forced to modify existing ones or introducing a complicated type system into the language.

Construct	Meaning
and	conjunction
or	disjunction
not	negation
imply	implication
equiv	equivalence
one	exactly one subexpression is true
parent	subexpression true for the parent (false if at the root)
ancestor	subexpression true for some ancestor
child	subexpression true for some child
descendant	subexpression true for some descendant
this	used for uniqueness and pointer rules (explained later)
element	checks the name of the current element
attribute	checks the presence or value of an attribute in the current element
contents	pattern matching on the contents of the current element

Figure 4.9 Boolean expression constructs in DSD2.

4.5.3 Boolean Expressions

Boolean expressions consist of tests of element names, attribute presence and values, and content pattern matches that can be combined by the usual boolean operators, such as `and`, `or`, and `not`, as listed in Figure 4.9. Such expressions are always evaluated relative to a current element and result in either *true* or *false*. In addition, there are operators for moving to the parent, a child, ancestor, or descendant. As with most other syntactical categories, boolean expressions can be named and reused (with `boolexp` elements having `id` or `ref` attributes).

In the example schema, we particularly exploit conditional rules and boolean expressions in the description of `ingredient` elements:

```
<if><element name="r:ingredient"/>
  <declare>
    ...
  </declare>
  <if><not><attribute name="amount"/></not>
    <require><not><attribute name="unit"/></not></require>
    <declare><contents>
      ...
    </contents></declare>
  </if>
</if>
```

This construction allows us to distinguish between simple and composite ingredients based on the presence of the `amount` attribute.

Construct	Meaning
sequence	concatenation
optional	zero or one occurrence
complement	complement
union	union
intersection	intersection
minus	set difference
repeat	a number of occurrences (bounded or unbounded)
string	a specific or arbitrary string
char	a single character (in some interval)

Figure 4.10 Regular expression constructs in DSD2.

4.5.4 Regular Expressions

Regular expressions are used in DSD2 to express valid attribute values (string types) and content sequences (content types). In the former case, the alphabet consists of the Unicode characters, and in the latter case, all elements of the instance document are also included. Content of an element is here viewed as a sequence of elements and individual Unicode characters, rather than grouping together consecutive characters as in the normal XML tree model.

The notion of regular expressions is a generalized form of the one introduced in Section 4.2; a list of constructs is shown in Figure 4.10.

One example of a regular expression is the description of the values of amount attributes:

```
<union>
  <string value="*"/>
  <stringtype ref="r:NUMBER"/>
</union>
```

The NUMBER type is defined separately by a named string type.

Another example is the description of the contents of collection elements:

```
<sequence>
  <element name="r:description"/>
  <repeat><element name="r:recipe"/></repeat>
</sequence>
```

If character data should be permitted in this content, string or char constructs could simply be inserted in the expression.

String type expressions can be named and reused with the stringtype construct, as illustrated in the example. Similarly, content type expressions can be named and reused with the contenttype construct.

4.5.5 Normalization

DSD2 provides mechanisms for normalizing whitespace and character cases in attribute values and character data and for insertion of default attributes and contents.

Both `contents` and `attribute` declarations may contain a `normalize` directive, such as:

```
<normalize whitespace="compress" case="upper"/>
```

For the `whitespace` attribute, `compress` causes all consecutive whitespace characters to be replaced by a single space character; `trim` additionally removes leading and trailing whitespace; and `preserve` (the default) means that whitespace should be unmodified. For the `case` attribute, `upper` causes all characters to be converted to upper case, `lower` means lower case, and `preserve` means no changes.

Attribute defaults are specified within the attribute declarations:

```
<attribute name="uri">
  <default value="anonymous.jpg"/>
</attribute>
```

This declaration may be combined with the declaration of the attribute values, or specified separately.

Content defaults are similarly specified within the content declarations:

```
<contents>
  ...
  <default>no email address available</default>
</contents>
```

In contrast to XML Schema, content defaults may here contain markup, and, as with attribute defaults, the default value can be specified separately from the other aspects of the element concerned.

4.5.6 Modularization

The modularization mechanisms in DSD2 are quite simple. Schemas can be combined using `import` instructions:

```
<dsd ...>
  <import href="http://www.brics.dk/DSD/character-classes.dsd"/>
  ...
</dsd>
```

The effect is that the contents of the designated schema are inserted in place of the `import` instruction, except that repeated imports of the URI are ignored.

Together with the notion of conditional rules, this construct provides sufficient flexibility in building families of related schemas and extending basic descriptions located in other schema files. For example, one schema may import an existing one and extend the descriptions of certain elements with additional attributes or contents, simply by adding new rules in the importing schema.

4.5.7   Uniqueness and Pointers

DSD2 permits the description of uniqueness constraints and references, much in the same manner as XML Schema but without involving XPath. Instead, the boolean expression mechanism is used to select scope of uniqueness and key/reference fields. The DSD2 mechanism generalizes the corresponding features in XML Schema by not being restricted to downward axes.

This is probably the most complicated part of DSD2, so we here give just a brief introduction; for more details and examples, see the language specification.

The following uniqueness constraint appears in our schema for recipe collections in the description of `collection` elements:

```
<unique>
  <and><element name="r:recipe"/><attribute name="id"/></and>
  <attributefield name="id"/>
</unique>
```

The `unique` element contains a boolean expression followed by a number of field selectors. The effect is that whenever the DSD2 processor encounters a `collection` element in the instance document, it finds all elements in the instance document where the boolean expression evaluates to true, and then, for each of those, evaluates the field selectors with the `this` operation bound to that element to build a *key*. All keys that are built during the processing of an instance document must be unique.

The `pointer` mechanism is used in the description of `related` elements:

```
<if><element name="r:related"/>
  ...
  <pointer><attributefield name="ref"/></pointer>
</if>
```

Generally, a `pointer` element contains a optional boolean expression and a number of field selectors, essentially as `unique` rules. Each key that is produced by processing a `pointer` rule must match a key that has been produced by a `unique` rule. For the recipe example, this declaration effectively establishes references from the `related` element to the `recipe` elements.

4.6   RELAX NG ★

The RELAX NG schema language has been developed within the Organization for the Advancement of Structured Information Standards (OASIS) and is being standardized by ISO. It addresses only pure validation; RELAX NG processing has no side-effects such as normalization or post-schema-validation infoset contributions.

This language has been designed with the same fundamental goals as DSD2: simplicity and expressiveness. However, the design is quite different. DSD2 is based on a notion of *rules*, which must be satisfied for every element in the instance document; RELAX NG is based on *grammars*, which is conceptually closer to the design of DTD and XML Schema.

Validation with RELAX NG proceeds as a top-down traversal of the instance document tree. To be valid, the root element must match a *pattern*, which has been specified in the schema. Generally, a pattern may match an element, an attribute, or character data. Element patterns can contain subpatterns that describe element contents and attributes, element subpatterns can themselves contain subpatterns, and so on. The pattern matching process may involve testing multiple choices, so generally, each node in the instance document may be visited many times during the traversal.

The notion of **patterns** is central to RELAX NG.

As an introductory example, the following very simple RELAX NG schema captures the structure of our business card XML language (see Section 4.4.1):

```
<element xmlns="http://relaxng.org/ns/structure/1.0"
         datatypeLibrary=
            "http://www.w3.org/2001/XMLSchema-datatypes"
         ns="http://businesscard.org"
         name="card">
  <element name="name"><text/></element>
  <element name="title"><text/></element>
  <element name="email"><text/></element>
  <optional>
    <element name="phone"><text/></element>
  </optional>
  <optional>
    <element name="logo">
      <attribute name="uri"><data type="anyURI"/></attribute>
    </element>
  </optional>
</element>
```

The meaning of the various constructs being used here will be clear from the following tour of RELAX NG. However, one thing to note here is that the RELAX NG language is identified by the namespace

```
http://relaxng.org/ns/structure/1.0
```

A RELAX NG description of the RELAX NG language itself is available at

```
http://www.relaxng.org/relaxng.rng
```

It captures most – but not all – syntactical requirements of RELAX NG schemas.

4.6.1   Patterns and Grammars

The central kinds of patterns are the following:

`element` matches one element with a given name (or a set of possible names, as described later) and with certain contents and attributes. Example:

```
<element name="title">
  <text/>
</element>
```

This particular pattern matches a `title` element that contains character data but no attributes or child elements.

`attribute` matches one attribute:

```
<attribute name="unit">
  <text/>
</attribute>
```

This pattern matches a `unit` attribute with an arbitrary value.

`text` matches any character data or attribute value. For constraining the permitted values, see the explanation of datatypes below. The default content of `attribute` patterns is a `text` pattern (so the contents of the `attribute` pattern above could be omitted).

The contents of elements can be described with – as usual – a variant of regular expressions (see Section 4.2) with the following operators:

`group`: corresponds to concatenation.

`optional`: zero or one occurrence.

`zeroOrMore`: any number of occurrences.

`oneOrMore`: one or more occurrences.

`choice`: corresponds to union.

`empty`: the empty sequence.

`interleave`: all possible mergings of the sequences that match the subexpressions. This construct has a similar effect as specifying multiple content expressions in DSD2. The `interleave` construct is more powerful than the `all` construct in XML Schema: `interleave` permits the subexpressions to describe ordered contents, which `all` does not.

`mixed`: an abbreviation for `interleave` containing a `text` pattern in addition to whatever the `mixed` element contains. This resembles the notion of mixed content models in DTD and XML Schema.

These regular expressions can contain both `element`, `attribute`, and `text` patterns. In particular, note that attributes are described in the same expressions as the element contents. However, the actual ordering of attributes in elements in the instance document is irrelevant, as always, and no more than one attribute of a given name is permitted in any element. This means that, for example, `attribute` patterns are prohibited within `oneOrMore` patterns.

A `oneOrMore`, `zeroOrMore`, `optional`, or `mixed` pattern that has more than one subexpression is treated as one where the subexpressions are wrapped into a `group` pattern. (This also applies to `define` and `list`, which are explained later.) Note that there is no easy way of specifying, for example, exactly 7 occurrences or 3 to 5 occurrences of some element; that inevitably requires some long expressions (unlike in XML Schema and DSD2), but such constraints are not common.

Unlike DTD and XML Schema, but like DSD2, RELAX NG does not require the content expressions to be deterministic. However, heavy use of ambiguity in expressions may significantly affect performance of a RELAX NG schema processor because it then can be necessary to traverse parts of the instance document tree many times to detect whether or not there exists a right combination of choices that leads to a proof of validity.

Name Classes

As an alternative for `element` and `attribute` patterns to match elements or attributes with one specific name, the names can be described more generally with *name classes*, which occur initially in the contents of the pattern elements:

`name` specifies one specific name:

```
<element>
  <name>title</name>
  ...
</element>
```

The '...' abbreviates the description of the attributes and contents of the element.

`choice` describes a choice between several name classes, such as the following:

```
<element>
  <choice>
    <name>ol</name>
    <name>ul</name>
    <name>dl</name>
  </choice>
  ...
</element>
```

This pattern matches an element named `ol`, `ul`, or `dl`. (Note that in this context, `choice` is a name class description, not a pattern.)

`anyName` matches any name from any namespace:

```
<element>
  <anyName/>
  ...
</element>
```

`nsName` matches any name within a specific namespace:

```
<attribute>
  <nsName ns="http://www.brics.dk/ixwt/recipes"/>
  ...
</attribute>
```

Both `anyName` and `nsName` can be restricted using `except` constructions, as in this example:

```
<nsName ns="http://www.brics.dk/ixwt/recipes">
  <except>
    <choice>
      <name>collection</name>
      <name>title</name>
    </choice>
  </except>
</nsName>
```

This name class matches any name from the RecipeML namespace but `collection` and `title`.

Namespaces

Any RELAX NG element can have an `ns` attribute. This attribute is relevant for `name`, `nsName`, `element`, and `attribute` where it specifies the applicable namespace. For example,

```
<name ns="http://www.brics.dk/ixwt/recipes" name="recipe"/>
```

matches the name `recipe` in the namespace `http://www.brics.dk/ixwt/recipes` and only that name. Elements without this attribute implicitly inherit one from the nearest ancestor where one is present, or take the empty string as value if none is found – except for the `attribute` pattern where the namespace is always the empty string unless the `ns` attribute is explicitly specified. The namespace prefixes being chosen in the instance documents cannot be constrained, as usual.

Pattern Definitions and References

Definitions and references allow description of **recursive** structures.

The language constructs described so far only permit description of the instance document tree down to a bounded distance from the root element. However, typical XML languages allow recursion, that is, the descendants of some element named x may contain other elements named x. In RecipeML, for example, `ingredient` elements may contain other `ingredient` elements to an unbounded depth. The way to express this design in RELAX NG is to *define* named patterns and use recursive references to these named patterns within the definitions.

Typically, a RELAX NG schema has the following structure:

```
<grammar xmlns="http://relaxng.org/ns/structure/1.0"
         ns="...">
  <start>
    ...
  </start>

  <define name="...">
    ...
  </define>

  ...
</grammar>
```

The root element of the schema is a `grammar` element that contains (1) one `start` element containing the pattern for the root of the instance documents, and (2) a number of `define` elements that define named patterns. A `ref` element is a reference to a named pattern. Notice that this design resembles the use of global and local definitions in XML Schema, although the definition mechanism here works on all kinds of patterns and there is – fortunately – no such thing as unqualified local elements. Since every XML document must contain one root element, the `start` pattern must match exactly one element of some sort.

As an example of a typical element description, we can describe the valid contents of `recipe` elements from the RecipeML language as follows:

```
<element name="recipe">
  <interleave>
    <group>
      <element name="title"><text/></element>
      <element name="date"><text/></element>
      <zeroOrMore>
        <ref name="element-ingredient"/>
      </zeroOrMore>
      <ref name="element-preparation"/>
      <ref name="element-nutrition"/>
      <zeroOrMore>
        <ref name="element-related"/>
      </zeroOrMore>
    </group>
    <optional>
      <element name="comment"><text/></element>
    </optional>
  </interleave>
</element>
```

We show a complete RELAX NG schema for RecipeML in Section 4.6.3; this schema also contains the definitions of the named patterns that are used in the fragment shown here.

As we have seen, recursion is common. However, recursive definitions in RELAX NG are allowed only if passing through an `element` pattern. That is, the following is illegal:

```
<define name="illegal_recursion">
  <element name="foo"><empty/></element>
  <optional>
    <ref name="illegal_recursion"/>
  </optional>
</define>
```

(even though it might be mathematically well-defined, describing a sequence of `foo` elements) whereas this one is legal:

```
<define name="legal_recursion">
  <element name="foo"><empty/></element>
  <optional>
    <element name="bar">
      <ref name="legal_recursion"/>
    </element>
  </optional>
</define>
```

A similar restriction holds for definitions and references in XML Schema.

Annotations

In the schemas, elements and attributes that do *not* belong to the `http://relaxng.org/ ns/structure/1.0` are ignored by the schema processor. This can be used to incorporate annotations, such as human readable documentation, within the schemas. To annotate a group of definitions, these can be embedded into a `div` element, which has no other meaning than logically grouping its contents.

4.6.2   Datatypes

RELAX NG relies on external languages for describing datatypes that govern which attribute values and character data are valid. Usually, the datatype sublanguage of XML Schema is used (see Section 4.4.2), but others are possible depending on the implementation.

The `data` pattern describes text by some externally defined datatype. This pattern can be viewed as a refinement of the `text` pattern described earlier.

```
<element name="number">
  <data datatypeLibrary="http://www.w3.org/2001/XMLSchema-datatypes"
        type="integer"/>
</element>
```

This particular pattern describes `number` elements whose contents consist of character data that matches the built-in `integer` type from XML Schema. The `datatypeLibrary` attribute identifies the datatype vocabulary being used. If this attribute is omitted, one is inherited from the nearest ancestor having one. This means that the `datatypeLibrary` can conveniently be placed in the root element of the schema if only one library is being used. The datatype facets – in case of using XML Schema datatypes – can be constrained by a parameter mechanism:

```
<element name="interval">
  <data datatypeLibrary="http://www.w3.org/2001/XMLSchema-datatypes"
       type="integer">
    <param name="minInclusive">42</param>
    <param name="maxInclusive">87</param>
  </data>
</element>
```

This particular pattern matches `interval` elements whose content is an integer in the interval 42 to 87 (see Figure 4.7). Other datatype libraries may have different parameters for their types.

In addition to using externally defined datatypes, there are a few simple mechanisms within RELAX NG itself for defining enumeration and list types and exclusions. First, a single value can be described using the `value` pattern:

```
<attribute name="checked">
  <value>checked</value>
</attribute>
```

This pattern matches an attribute whose name and value are both `checked`.

Enumerations can be expressed by placing multiple `value` patterns within a `choice` pattern:

```
<element name="enabled">
  <choice>
    <value>true</value>
    <value>false</value>
  </choice>
</element>
```

Not surprisingly, this pattern matches an element named `enabled` whose content is either the character data `true` or `false`.

The `list` pattern defines a concatenation of datatypes where whitespace is permitted between the individual values. Example:

```
<list>
  <oneOrMore><data type="decimal"/></oneOrMore>
  <choice>
    <value>cm</value>
```

```
      <value>in</value>
    </choice>
  </list>
```

(Compare this pattern with the limitations of the list construct in XML Schema.) The string

```
-0.748 0.558 cm
```

matches this type, for instance.

Exclusion of certain values can be done with the except pattern:

```
<data type="decimal">
  <except>
    <value>0</value>
  </except>
</data>
```

This matches all strings that represent decimal numbers, except the string 0. This example raises an important point: restricting facets in XML Schema operates on the semantic level, as noted earlier, but we have not here specified the type of '0'. The effect is that this example pattern matches, for example, 000 and 0.000, which was probably not the intention. This problem is solved by adding a type qualifier:

```
<data type="decimal">
  <except>
    <value type="decimal">0</value>
  </except>
</data>
```

In contrast to the previous pattern, this one matches all strings that represent decimal numbers, except the *number* 0 which has many syntactic representations.

The datatypes string and token are built into RELAX NG and can hence be used without the XML Schema datatype library. The meanings of these two types are as in XML Schema: they both represent strings of Unicode characters, the only difference being the pruning of whitespace with the token type when performing pattern matching. The token type is the default for value patterns.

The language specification forbids using data and value in mixed content models, that is, ones where both character data and elements are allowed in a content sequence. This means that, as in DTD and XML Schema, there is no way of constraining the character data in such content models.

The ID and IDREF(S) types known from DTD are available through a special compatibility datatype library. For example, we can express that the id attributes of recipe elements must have unique values:

```
<element name="recipe">
  <optional>
    <attribute name="id">
      <data datatypeLibrary=
```

```
                "http://relaxng.org/ns/compatibility/datatypes/1.0"
          type="ID"/>
    </attribute>
  </optional>
  ...
</element>
```

4.6.3 Recipe Collections with RELAX NG

With RELAX NG, the syntax of RecipeML can be expressed as follows:

```
<grammar xmlns="http://relaxng.org/ns/structure/1.0"
         ns="http://www.brics.dk/ixwt/recipes"
         datatypeLibrary="http://www.w3.org/2001/XMLSchema-datatypes">

  <start>
    <element name="collection">
      <element name="description"><text/></element>
      <zeroOrMore>
        <ref name="element-recipe"/>
      </zeroOrMore>
    </element>
  </start>

  <define name="element-recipe">
    <element name="recipe">
      <optional>
        <attribute name="id">
          <data datatypeLibrary=
                "http://relaxng.org/ns/compatibility/datatypes/1.0"
                type="ID"/>
        </attribute>
      </optional>
      <interleave>
        <group>
          <element name="title"><text/></element>
          <element name="date"><text/></element>
          <zeroOrMore>
            <ref name="element-ingredient"/>
          </zeroOrMore>
          <ref name="element-preparation"/>
          <element name="nutrition">
            <ref name="attributes-nutrition"/>
          </element>
          <zeroOrMore>
            <ref name="element-related"/>
          </zeroOrMore>
```

```
          </group>
          <optional>
            <element name="comment"><text/></element>
          </optional>
        </interleave>
      </element>
    </define>

    <define name="element-ingredient">
      <element name="ingredient">
        <attribute name="name"/>
        <choice>
          <group>
            <attribute name="amount">
              <choice>
                <value>*</value>
                <ref name="NUMBER"/>
              </choice>
            </attribute>
            <optional>
              <attribute name="unit"/>
            </optional>
          </group>
          <group>
            <zeroOrMore>
              <ref name="element-ingredient"/>
            </zeroOrMore>
            <ref name="element-preparation"/>
          </group>
        </choice>
      </element>
    </define>

    <define name="element-preparation">
      <element name="preparation">
        <zeroOrMore>
          <element name="step"><text/></element>
        </zeroOrMore>
      </element>
    </define>

    <define name="attributes-nutrition">
      <attribute name="calories">
        <ref name="NUMBER"/>
      </attribute>
      <attribute name="protein">
        <ref name="PERCENTAGE"/>
      </attribute>
      <attribute name="carbohydrates">
```

```
      <ref name="PERCENTAGE"/>
    </attribute>
    <attribute name="fat">
      <ref name="PERCENTAGE"/>
    </attribute>
    <optional>
      <attribute name="alcohol">
        <ref name="PERCENTAGE"/>
      </attribute>
    </optional>
  </define>

  <define name="element-related">
    <element name="related">
      <text/>
      <attribute name="ref">
        <data datatypeLibrary=
              "http://relaxng.org/ns/compatibility/datatypes/1.0"
              type="IDREF"/>
      </attribute>
    </element>
  </define>

  <define name="PERCENTAGE">
    <data type="string">
      <param name="pattern">([0-9]|[1-9][0-9]|100)%</param>
    </data>
  </define>

  <define name="NUMBER">
    <data type="decimal">
      <param name="minInclusive">0</param>
    </data>
  </define>

</grammar>
```

We define a grammar with `collection` as the only possible start element. To obtain a comprehensible structure of the schema, the most complicated element patterns are placed in separate definitions and the simple ones are inlined. For the `nutrition` element, its attributes are placed in a separate definition to permit easy extensibility, as we shall see later. The last two definitions contain datatypes that are used multiple times in other patterns. The names of the definitions have been chosen to convey their meaning informally and have no formal meaning.

The language features we have seen so far are powerful enough to describe certain conditional constraints, that is, validity constraints that depend on the presence and values of other elements and attributes. The definition above named `element-ingredient` for `ingredient` elements illustrate this ability. It contains a `choice` of two `group` patterns.

The first matches if the element contains an `amount` attribute whose value is either `*` or a `NUMBER` and an optional `unit` attribute but nothing else; the second pattern matches if there are no attributes but zero or more `ingredient` elements followed by one `preparation` element. In other words, the content model depends on the presence of the attributes. Generally, arbitrarily deep dependencies can be expressed in this way. This clearly goes beyond the possibilities of XML Schema. Compared to DSD2, however, certain dependencies can be rather cumbersome to express in RELAX NG; for example, if a content model of some element depends on the presence of an attribute in a distant ancestor element, then the pattern for that ancestor has to branch into separate subpatterns to 'remember' the relevant attributes until the element is encountered.

4.6.4 Modularization

The modularization mechanisms that we describe next are among the more complicated parts of RELAX NG. First, the `externalRef` pattern allows individual patterns to be stored in separate files. For example, assuming that `date.rng` is the URI of an XML file containing some pattern, then

```
<externalRef href="date.rng"/>
```

can be inserted in other schemas to use that pattern.

An entire grammar may generally be used as a pattern: a grammar is simply equivalent to its start pattern. This means that grammars may be embedded within other grammars. The scope of definitions within a grammar is limited to that grammar, excluding any embedded grammars. A special reference, `parentRef`, behaves as `ref` but refers to a definition in the immediately enclosing grammar instead of the current one.

Using the `include` construct, grammars stored in different files can be merged such that named definitions can be reused. Assume that `some_definitions.rng` contains the following:

```
<grammar xmlns="http://relaxng.org/ns/structure/1.0"
         datatypeLibrary=
            "http://www.w3.org/2001/XMLSchema-datatypes">

  <define name="PERCENTAGE">
    <data type="string">
      <param name="pattern">([0-9]|[1-9][0-9]|100)%</param>
    </data>
  </define>

  <define name="NUMBER">
    <data type="decimal">
      <param name="minInclusive">0</param>
    </data>
  </define>

</grammar>
```

These definitions can then be included in another schema:

```
<grammar xmlns="http://relaxng.org/ns/structure/1.0">
  <include href="some_definitions.rng"/>
  ...
</grammar>
```

The effect is simply that the included definitions are available in the including schema. As in other schema languages, this mechanism makes it possible to reuse definitions and build families of related schemas from common modules.

The `include` element may itself contain `start` and `define` constructs that then override any included ones with the same names – much like `redefine` in XML Schema. As an alternative or supplement to replacing definitions entirely, the new definitions can be *combined* with the imported ones having the same names, either through a `choice` or a `interleave` operation. For example, we can make an extension of the RecipeML schema to allow an additional attribute in the `nutrition` elements by adding a second definition of `attributes-nutrition` and specifying `combine="interleave"`:

```
<grammar xmlns="http://relaxng.org/ns/structure/1.0">

  <include href="recipes.rng"/>

  <define name="attributes-nutrition" combine="interleave">
    <optional>
      <attribute name="vitamin-C">
        <ref name="NUMBER"/>
      </attribute>
    </optional>
  </define>

</grammar>
```

Both `start` and `define` may contain such a `combine` attribute, specifying how to combine with the imported definitions. Notice how this resembles the use of multiple declarations for one element in DSD2, which behaves much like combining by interleaving, except that the subexpressions of `interleave` in RELAX NG must describe disjoint sets of elements.

Finally, a special pattern `notAllowed` can be used to simulate abstract definitions that must be redefined or combined with other definitions (using `combine="choice"`) before they can be used. The `notAllowed` pattern can also be used to exclude certain choices that were declared in included grammars. This construct can be compared with the use of `require` rules in DSD2.

4.6.5 A Non-XML Syntax

An interesting aspect of RELAX NG is that it has an alternative syntax: a non-XML syntax which is more compact than the XML syntax presented above. The underlying language is exactly the same for both syntaxes, but the non-XML variant can be easier to read and write once you have learned it.

RELAX NG has a **compact non-XML syntax** as an alternative to the XML syntax.

XML syntax	Compact syntax
<group> *X* *Y* </group>	*X*, *Y*
<optional> *X* </optional>	*X*?
<zeroOrMore> *X* </zeroOrMore>	*X**
<oneOrMore> *X* </oneOrMore>	*X*+
<choice> *X* *Y* </choice>	*X* | *Y*
<interleave> *X* *Y* </interleave>	*X* & *Y*
<empty/>	empty
<mixed/>	mixed

Figure 4.11 Regular expression operators in RELAX NG.

As an example, an `element` pattern is in this syntax written

```
element name { properties }
```

where *properties* describe the attributes and contents of the element. The regular expression operators are written in a familiar notation as shown in Figure 4.11. The full specification for the entire alternative syntax can be found from the RELAX NG project home page.

The RELAX NG schema for RecipeML shown above can be expressed as follows in the alternative syntax:

```
default namespace = "http://www.brics.dk/ixwt/recipes"
datatypes d = "http://relaxng.org/ns/compatibility/datatypes/1.0"

start =
  element collection {
    element description { text },
    element-recipe*
  }

element-recipe =
  element recipe {
    attribute id { d:ID }?,
    ((element title { text },
      element date { text },
      element-ingredient*,
      element-preparation,
      element nutrition { attributes-nutrition },
      element-related*)
     & element comment { text }?)
  }

element-ingredient =
  element ingredient {
    attribute name { text },
    ((attribute amount { "*" | NUMBER },
      attribute unit { text }?)
```

```
          |  (element-ingredient*, element-preparation))
  }

element-preparation =
  element preparation {
    element step { text }*
  }

attributes-nutrition =
  attribute calories { NUMBER },
  attribute protein { PERCENTAGE },
  attribute carbohydrates { PERCENTAGE },
  attribute fat { PERCENTAGE },
  attribute alcohol { PERCENTAGE }?

element-related =
  element related {
    text,
    attribute ref { d:IDREF }
  }

PERCENTAGE = xsd:string { pattern = "([0-9]|[1-9][0-9]|100)%" }

NUMBER = xsd:decimal { minInclusive = "0" }
```

If the XML version shown in Section 4.6.3 is clear, this version should be self-explanatory. Several tools exist for converting between the XML syntax and the non-XML syntax, and for converting between RELAX NG and other schema languages.

This non-XML syntax is also used in the specification of the formal semantics of XQuery (see Chapter 6).

4.7   Chapter Summary

A schema is a formal description of the syntax of an XML language. Depending on the schema language being used, schemas may also define normalization properties, for example default insertion, and assign type information to the elements and attributes in the instance documents.

This chapter has covered four schema languages with many differences but also notable similarities, in particular, the uses of regular expressions. Choosing the right schema language is a controversial issue and there exist good arguments in favor of and against each one of them – but we will not go further into that discussion here.

The DTD language is characterized by being the first schema language for XML; it is reasonably simple but does not have sufficient expressive power for many practical situations. XML Schema, on the other hand, is vastly more complicated and provides good support for namespaces, modularization, and datatypes. Its notion of types is important for other XML technologies, such as XQuery. Essential to this type system are the distinction between simple and complex types and the derivation mechanisms: derivation by extension adds constituents to the valid documents, whereas derivation by restriction confines the set of valid documents.

The two remaining schema language alternatives that we have seen – DSD2 and RELAX NG – excel in simplicity and expressiveness but are not supported by the W3C. According to a small survey made by Oracle, two-thirds of XML programmers use XML Schema for validating XML documents, and one fourth uses DTD leaving only few percents to the alternative schema languages. Recently, however, especially RELAX NG has been gaining momentum as a significant competitor to W3C's recommendations.

4.8   Further Reading

The DTD language is defined in the XML specification [15]. The XML Schema specification is split into two parts: one describing the main structures of the language [79], and the other describing the datatypes [9]. URLs of these W3C recommendations are given below in the Online Resources section. The complexity of the XML Schema specification is demonstrated by the overwhelming errata for the first edition; we highly recommend looking for the newest revised editions. The document describing the design requirements for XML Schema is also published through the W3C [57]. The XML Schema description of XML Schema (the schema for schemas) is an appendix in Part 1 of the specification. A comparison between DTD and XML Schema is presented in the paper [8], and a formalization of idealized XML Schema appears in [74].

There exist many very general 'best practices' documents for XML Schema; however, we will not recommend any here since most of them do not recognize the versatile nature of XML and often do not substantiate their advice sufficiently. Therefore: be skeptical about such guidance! On the other hand, guidelines that are tailored towards more narrow application domains, often developed by governments and large organizations, can be quite instructive. Examples include those mentioned in Section 4.4.13.

The DSD2 specification is available from the BRICS research center [61]. Information about the first version, DSD 1.0, is presented in the article [52].

The RELAX NG specification is an OASIS Committee Specification [23] and also an ISO Draft International Standard. A book dedicated to RELAX NG is freely available online [82].

From a mathematical point of view, schema languages are known to correspond various kinds of *tree automata* [64, 66] – provided that ID and IDREF attribute types and similar features are ignored. DTD essentially corresponds to the class of *local tree grammars*. The central structure of XML Schema – including the type derivation mechanism – corresponds to the slightly more expressive notion of *single-type tree grammars* (this is closely related to the overloading feature described in Section 4.4.4). Both DSD2 and RELAX NG correspond to the even more general notion of *regular tree grammars*. Having solid mathematical foundations can make it easier to reason about the schemas and allow for more elegant and efficient implementations. The DSD2 prototype implementation exploits a classical connection between regular expressions and *finite-state automata on strings* [45]; RELAX NG is based on a notion of *hedge automata* [63], and implementations use theories of regular expression *derivatives* to obtain efficiency [22].

4.9   Online Resources

http://www.w3.org/TR/xml11/
> The XML 1.1 W3C recommendation, which defines the DTD language intertwined with the actual XML notation.

http://www.w3.org/XML/Schema
> W3C's XML Schema home page, with links to tools and examples.

http://www.w3.org/TR/xmlschema-0/
> *XML Schema Part 0: Primer* – a non-normative and incomplete introduction to XML Schema.

http://www.w3.org/TR/xmlschema-1/
> *XML Schema Part 1: Structures* – the main part of the XML Schema language specification.

http://www.w3.org/TR/xmlschema-2/
> *XML Schema Part 2: Datatypes* – describes the built-in simple types in XML Schema and the related type derivation mechanisms.

http://www.relaxng.org/
> Home page for RELAX NG, with lots of documentation and links to software and examples.

http://www.brics.dk/DSD/
> The DSD2 Web site, contains the DSD2 specification, an Open Source Java implementation, and a few example DSD2 schemas.

http://xml.apache.org/xerces2-j/
> The Apache Xerces parser for Java, with support for DTD and XML Schema.

http://www.alphaworks.ibm.com/tech/xmlsqc
> The XML Schema Quality Checker from IBM alphaWorks. A useful tool for detecting bugs and other anomalies in schemas written in XML Schema.

4.10   Exercises

The main lessons to be learned from these exercises are:

- reading and writing schemas, with a focus on DTD and XML Schema; and
- how to use schema validation tools.

Exercise 4.1 Explain the difference between *well-formed* and *valid*.

Exercise 4.2 Browse through the DTD description of XHTML 1.0 Strict (see the XHTML specification) and find the solutions to the following questions:

(a) Describe, in English, the content model of `head` elements.

(b) What are the possible attributes in h3 elements?

(c) Is it required that `input` elements only occur inside `form` elements?

(d) Can a elements be nested?

Exercise 4.3 Write for each of the following schemas a valid instance document that uses all declared elements at least once:

(a) *EX*/`store.dtd` (DTD).

(b) *EX*/`movies.xsd` (XML Schema).

(c) *EX*/`medical.dsd` (DSD2).

(d) *EX*/`family.rng` (RELAX NG).

Exercise 4.4 Validate the recipe collection against its XML Schema description. Also try validating the collection extended with the ravioli recipe from Exercise 2.6. If the extension breaks validity, modify it to become valid.

TIP

In Section 7.3.3, we shall see some small but useful Java command-line tools that perform DTD and XML Schema validation.

Exercise 4.5 Continuing Exercise 2.2, write a schema for your driving directions XML language using the following schema languages:

(a) DTD.

(b) XML Schema.

(c) DSD2.

(d) RELAX NG.

TIP

When writing schemas in XML Schema, use the XML Schema Quality Checker (see the online resources) to check that your schemas are in fact legal schemas according to the XML Schema specification.

A common way to check a DTD schema is to run a DTD processor on a dummy XML document with a document type declaration that refers to the schema. (See Section 4.3.6.)

Exercise 4.6 There exists an XML Schema description of XML Schema (see Part 1 of the XML Schema specification). Discuss how useful this schema is for detecting errors in schemas written in XML Schema. Compare this with the similar situation in other schema languages.

Exercise 4.7 Assume that we are developing an XML language for geographic information. In this language, the contents of an element named `point` must consist of elements of the following names: `address`, `latitude`, `longitude`, and `note`. In every such content sequence, the element names `address`, `latitude`, and `longitude` may each occur zero or once; `latitude` may appear if and only `longitude` appears; either `address` or `latitude` must appear, but never both; and there may be any number of `note` elements anywhere in the sequence.

Using each of the following schema languages, formalize the above description of `point` elements. Make sure that your descriptions do not impose restrictions beyond those mentioned above:

(a) DTD.
(b) XML Schema.
(c) DSD2.
(d) RELAX NG.

Exercise 4.8 Consider a toy variant of XHTML named *ToyXHTML* whose syntax may be described as follows. The root element named `doc` contains a sequence of `p` and `h1` elements. An `h1` element may contain character data but no subelements. Each `p` element contains text (character data) that may be marked up with `em` and `a` elements. Every `a` element has either a `name` attribute or an `href` attribute, and the value of the latter must be a URI.

(a) Clarify ambiguities in the above description.
(b) Formalize the syntax of ToyXHTML using your favorite schema language.

Exercise 4.9 Consider the schema at `http://www.w3.org/2005/04/schema-for-xslt20.xsd`. (As the name implies, this is a description of the XSLT 2.0 language, which is the topic of Chapter 5, but for this exercise we only study the syntax of the language.)

(a) Explain, in English, the description of `comment` elements, including the types it refers to.
(b) Explain the meaning of the simple type named `modes`.
(c) Explain the content model of `function` elements.

Exercise 4.10 Consider the schema `EX/bizarro.xsd`. Write a valid instance document. Explain (briefly) why your instance document is valid.

Exercise 4.11 Convert the DTD schema `EX/moviestudio.dtd` to the following schema languages:

(a) XML Schema.
(b) DSD2.
(c) RELAX NG.

You may find tools on the Web for solving these tasks, but try manually for this exercise.

Exercise 4.12 Convert the schema `EX/patients.xsd` written in XML Schema to DTD. Which limitations in DTD do you encounter?

Exercise 4.13 Explain how overloading of element declarations in XML Schema may be emulated in DSD2 and RELAX NG.

Exercise 4.14 Compare the following aspects of the expressiveness of the four schema languages described in this chapter:

- Namespace support.
- Description of attribute values and character data.
- Default values of attributes and elements.
- Context sensitive descriptions of elements and attributes.
- Uniqueness and referential constraints.
- Self-describability.
- Support by W3C.

Exercise 4.15 What is a *deterministic* regular expression? (Hint: see the XML specification.) Give an example of a non-deterministic regular expression that cannot be rewritten into an equivalent deterministic one.

5

TRANSFORMING XML DOCUMENTS WITH XSLT

Objectives

In this chapter, you will learn:

- How XML documents may be rendered in browsers

- How the XSLT language transforms XML documents

- How XPath is used in XSLT

- A brief introduction to XSL Formatting Objects

5.1 Transforming XML Documents

XML documents provide a general format for representing the logical structure of data. At some point, however, data must also be presented in browsers or other media, and the default tree-style representation of XML is generally not what is desired. Consider, for example, the tiny XML language for representing business cards:

```
<card xmlns="http://businesscard.org">
  <name>John Doe</name>
  <title>CEO, Widget Inc.</title>
  <email>john.doe@widget.inc</email>
  <phone>(202) 555-1414</phone>
  <logo uri="widget.gif"/>
</card>
```

When opened in the Mozilla browser, this document is rendered as follows:

```
- <card>
    <name>John Doe</name>
    <title>CEO, Widget Inc.</title>
    <email>john.doe@widget.inc</email>
    <phone>(202) 456-1414</phone>
    <logo uri="widget.gif"/>
  </card>
```

This presentation is just the tree view explained in Section 2.3 and hardly a satisfactory presentation of a business card.

In Section 1.5 we saw how CSS stylesheets could be used to guide the presentation of XHTML documents. The CSS mechanism actually does apply to XML documents as well, which is not surprising considering that XML tags could be viewed as generalized analogs of `div` and `span`.

The following CSS stylesheet is our best effort to provide a reasonable layout for a business card:

```
card   { background-color: #cccccc; border: none; width: 300;}
name   { display: block; font-size: 20pt; margin-left: 0; }
title  { display: block; margin-left: 20pt;}
email  { display: block; font-family: monospace; margin-left: 20pt;}
phone  { display: block; margin-left: 20pt;}
```

The result looks as follows in the browser:

John Doe
CEO, Widget Inc.
john.doe@widget.inc
(202) 456-1414

This presentation is clearly better, but hardly ideal; for example, the `logo` image cannot be used. In general, CSS is too limited to render XML, since

- the information cannot be rearranged: the `email` will always appear before the `phone`;

- information encoded in attributes, like the `uri`, cannot be exploited; and

- additional structure, like tables, cannot be introduced.

The solution is to introduce an entirely new language for specifying presentations of XML documents.

The *XSL (Extensible Stylesheet Language)* technology has two constituents: *XSLT (XSL Transformations)* is a declarative programming language for specifying transformations between XML languages, and *XSL-FO (XSL Formatting Objects)* is a particular target language that is suitable for specifying physical layout. We discuss XSL-FO further in Section 5.11, but the most interesting constituent is the XSLT language from a programming point of view. As for XML itself, the use of *extensible* is not really meaningful.

XSLT was originally designed as a generalized stylesheet, intended to fit into the same niche as CSS. However, it has developed into a complete programming language with many more applications. The behavior of a stylesheet may be obtained by specifying a transformation into the XHTML language, which enables rendering in a browser. But XSLT transformations may also be used to translate between other XML languages, to extract views of XML data, and to perform query-like computations.

This chapter covers XSLT 2.0, which builds upon XPath 2.0. Most implementations, however, currently support XSLT 1.0 only. We explain the main differences in Section 5.9.

XSLT transformations may be executed in standalone tools, but they are also supported by all modern browsers. Specifically, an XML document may contain a processing instruction that links to an external XSLT document. A browser will then load the XSLT file, execute the corresponding transformation and present the result, which will presumably be an XHTML document. For example, the business card document could be annotated as follows:

```
<?xml-stylesheet type="text/xsl" href="business_card.xsl"?>
<card xmlns="http://businesscard.org">
  <name>John Doe</name>
  <title>CEO, Widget Inc.</title>
  <email>john.doe@widget.inc</email>
  <phone>(202) 555-1414</phone>
  <logo uri="widget.gif"/>
</card>
```

Using this XSLT transformation, the rendering in the Mozilla browser is then just what we wanted:

The source code of the XSLT transformation we have applied looks as follows:

```
<xsl:stylesheet version="2.0"
                xmlns:xsl="http://www.w3.org/1999/XSL/Transform"
                xmlns:b="http://businesscard.org"
                xmlns="http://www.w3.org/1999/xhtml">
```

```
<xsl:template match="b:card">
  <html>
    <head>
      <title><xsl:value-of select="b:name/text()"/></title>
    </head>
    <body bgcolor="#ffffff">
      <table border="3">
        <tr>
          <td>
            <xsl:apply-templates select="b:name"/><br/>
            <xsl:apply-templates select="b:title"/><p/>
            <tt><xsl:apply-templates select="b:email"/></tt><br/>
            <xsl:if test="b:phone">
              Phone: <xsl:apply-templates select="b:phone"/><br/>
            </xsl:if>
          </td>
          <td>
            <xsl:if test="b:logo">
              <img src="{b:logo/@uri}"/>
            </xsl:if>
          </td>
        </tr>
      </table>
    </body>
  </html>
</xsl:template>

<xsl:template match="b:name|b:title|b:email|b:phone">
  <xsl:value-of select="text()"/>
</xsl:template>

</xsl:stylesheet>
```

This looks quite different from a CSS stylesheet, but some of the ideas have survived. The XSLT `stylesheet` element contains of a set of *template rules*, each denoted by a `template` element. Each rule has a *pattern*, denoted by the `match` attribute, which governs the applicability of the given template rule. However, where the body of a CSS rule merely assigns values to layout properties, the body of an XSLT template rule is clearly much more involved. It is, in fact, a program that when executed will compute a part of the target document.

The above XSLT document involves three different namespaces: the namespace with prefix `xsl` is that of the XSLT language itself; the namespace with prefix `b` is that of the source language; and the default namespace is that of the target language (but, as usual, the choice of namespace prefixes is not essential). Note that the prefix of the source namespace occurs in certain attribute values, similar to the use of target namespace prefixes in XML Schema discussed in Section 4.4.5. It is customary to use the `xsl` namespace prefix for XSLT elements to facilitate their recognition.

The processing of the business card in the above example proceeds as follows:

- The stylesheet is applied to the document root. Since no template rule matches this node, a built-in rule (see Section 5.6) proceeds by processing the `card` root element.

- The `card` element is matched by the first template rule, which means that the body of this template defines the output. The template body is clearly an XHTML document, but with some gaps that contain XSLT code in the form of *sequence constructors* (see Section 5.4).

- The `title` of the resulting XHTML document is computed by a `value-of` instruction (see Section 5.4.2) that uses an XPath expression to select the contents of the `name` node from the business card.

- The `apply-templates` instructions recursively applies the stylesheet to the selected node, which in all cases are matched by the second template rule that merely outputs the character data that they contain.

- The `if` instruction is used twice to execute only conditionally some sequence constructors.

- The occurrence of `{...}` in the `uri` attribute has the effect of computing its value using an XPath expression (see Section 5.4.1).

The resulting XHTML document looks as follows:

```
<html xmlns="http://www.w3.org/1999/xhtml">
  <head>
    <title>John Doe</title>
  </head>
  <body bgcolor="#ffffff">
    <table border="3">
      <tr>
        <td>
          John Doe<br/>
          CEO, Widget Inc.<p/>
          <tt>john.doe@widget.inc</tt><br/>
          Phone: (202) 555-1414<br/>
        </td>
        <td>
          <img src="widget.gif"/>
        </td>
      </tr>
    </table>
  </body>
</html>
```

5.2   The Processing Model

As indicated by the example in the previous section, an XSLT stylesheet is an XML document with the following structure:

```
<xsl:stylesheet version="2.0"
                xmlns:xsl="http://www.w3.org/1999/XSL/Transform" >

  <xsl:template match="...">
    ...
  </xsl:template>

  ...

</xsl:stylesheet>
```

Being an XML language, the syntax for XSLT 2.0 is defined by an XML Schema instance available at

```
http://www.w3.org/2005/02/schema-for-xslt20.xsd
```

When an XSLT processor applies a stylesheet to a target document, it finds a template rule that is appropriate for the document root and executes the corresponding template body. XSLT 2.0 uses XPath 2.0 as an expression language for four purposes:

> A **stylesheet** is a collection of **template rules**.

- specifying patterns for template rules;

- selecting nodes for processing;

- computing boolean conditions; and

- generating text contents for the output document.

Evaluation of both XSLT stylesheets and XPath expressions is performed relatively to a context, as also discussed in Section 3.2.1. The initial context of an XSLT stylesheet applied to a source document is defined as follows:

- the context item is the document root node;

- the context position and size both have value 1;

- the set of variable bindings contains only global parameters (see Section 5.5);

- the function library is the default one (see Section 5.8.6); and

- the namespace declarations are those defined in the root element of the stylesheet.

The XPath function namespace is implicitly defined as default, thus the fn namespace prefix is not required.

5.3   Template Rules

A typical template rule has the following syntax:

```
<xsl:template match="...">
  ...
</xsl:template>
```

A template rule **matches** a part of the input document and **constructs** a part of the output document.

The `match` attribute contains a *pattern* and the content of the `template` instruction is a *sequence constructor* (both explained below). A collection of template rules is evaluated in a context as follows:

- the subset of template rules whose patterns *match* the context node is identified;

- if more than one template rule remains, then the most *specific* one is selected; and

- the result is obtained by evaluating the sequence constructor of the selected template rule in the given context (and this evaluation may involve further pattern matching and evaluation recursively).

The *built-in* template rules explained in Section 5.6 ensure that some template rule is always found when performing the pattern matching.

The overall behavior of an XSLT stylesheet and the notion of specificity is clearly inspired by CSS stylesheets (see Section 1.5). For CSS, the precise definition of specificity is complicated but can be summarized as 'the most complicated selector wins'. Similarly, the definition of specificity for XSLT can be summarized as 'the most complicated pattern wins'. Technically, the specificity is decided by a *priority*, which is a number that by default is computed as a function of the syntax of the pattern.

5.3.1   Patterns and Matching

An XSLT *pattern* is simply a restricted version of an XPath 2.0 expression. They are defined (somewhat obscurely) as a syntactic subset of the abbreviated syntax (see Section 3.4). In brief, a pattern must satisfy these requirements:

- it is a union of path expressions (perhaps only one);

- each path expression contains a number of steps separated by `/` or `//`; and

- each step may only use the `child` or `attribute` axis (and only in the abbreviated syntax).

A **pattern** is a restricted **XPath** **expression**.

Node tests and predicates may use the general syntax. Note that the `descendant-or-self` axis is available in a restricted form, since `//` is an abbreviation of `/descendant-or-self::node()/`.

A pattern *matches* a given node if it is possible to evaluate it in a context in which *some* node in the source document is the context node and the resulting sequence contains the given node.

This rather implicit definition is actually a clever means of expressing that patterns should be read backward, similarly to CSS selectors. For example, the XSLT pattern

```
rcp:recipe/rcp:ingredient//rcp:preparation
```

matches those `preparation` elements that appear anywhere below an `ingredient` in a `recipe`. For further illustration, we consider the following source document:

```
<students n="1">
    <student id="100026" n="2">
        <name n="3">Joe Average</name>
        <age n="4">21</age>
        <major n="5">Biology</major>
        <results n="6">
          <result course="Math 101" grade="C-" n="7"/>
          <result course="Biology 101" grade="C+" n="8"/>
          <result course="Statistics 101" grade="D" n="9"/>
        </results>
    </student>
    <student id="100078" n="10">
        <name n="11">Jack Doe</name>
        <age n="12">18</age>
        <major n="13">Physics</major>
        <major n="14">XML Science</major>
        <results n="15">
          <result course="Math 101" grade="A" n="16"/>
          <result course="XML 101" grade="A-" n="17"/>
          <result course="Physics 101" grade="B+" n="18"/>
          <result course="XML 102" grade="A" n="19"/>
        </results>
    </student>
</students>
```

Note that all element nodes have been given a unique n attribute, which is only used for identification in the examples below. We now list several examples of nodes that are matched by patterns and indicate the context node from which the evaluation of the pattern should correspondingly start. The pattern

```
students
```

matches the node 1 (since evaluating the pattern starting from the document root results in the single node 1 and starting anywhere else yields the empty set of nodes). The pattern

```
student
```

matches both of the nodes 2 and 10 (in both cases starting evaluation from the root element 1). Similarly, the pattern

```
students/student
```

matches both of the nodes 2 and 10 (starting evaluation from the document root). The pattern

```
@grade
```

matches all `grade` attribute nodes (starting evaluation from the corresponding `result` nodes), but the pattern

```
student//@grade[. eq "B+"]
```

only matches the `grade` attribute node below the node 18 (starting from the node 10). The pattern

```
student[@id="100078"]/age
```

matches the node 12 (starting from the node 1). Finally, the pattern

```
result[ancestor::student/@id="100026"][@grade="D"]
```

matches only the node 9 (starting from the node 6).

In practical use, XSLT patterns are quite simple. In an analysis of 200,000 lines of XSLT code written by hundreds of different authors, we found the following distribution of patterns:

QName	62%
QName/*QName*	7%
QName[@*QName*="..."]	6%
QName/.../*QName*	6%
/	3%
QName[...]	3%
*	3%
QName|...|*QName*	2%
text()	1%
other	7%

Thus, by far the most common pattern is just a single QName matching exactly the element nodes with that name, which is also how the tiny XSLT stylesheet for business cards is written.

5.3.2 Names, Modes, and Priorities

A `template` may have other attributes besides `match`.

The `name` attribute is used to provide a name for explicit references allowing templates to be called like functions (see Section 5.4.8). If the `name` attribute is present, the `match` attribute may be absent.

The `mode` attribute, which is only allowed if the `match` attribute is present, is used to restrict the template rules that are candidates for matching a given node (see Section 5.4.5). A mode is either a QName or the token `#default` (which is also the default mode of a template). The value of the `mode` attribute is either a space separated sequence of modes or the token `#all` which is interpreted as a list of all possible modes.

The `priority` attribute, which is only allowed if the `match` attribute is present, assigns an explicit priority value to the template rule.

5.4 Sequence Constructors

The body of a template rule constructs a sequence of items that are *atomic values* or *nodes*, just like XPath expressions (see Section 3.5.1).

5.4.1 Element and Attribute Constructors

The simplest kind of sequence constructor is a *literal* sequence of character data nodes and element nodes that do not belong to the XSLT namespace. These simply evaluate to themselves. As a small example, the following stylesheet will generate a constant HTML document, regardless of the source document:

```
<xsl:stylesheet version="2.0"
                xmlns:xsl="http://www.w3.org/1999/XSL/Transform"
                xmlns="http://www.w3.org/1999/xhtml">

   <xsl:template match="/">
      <html>
        <head>
          <title>Hello World</title>
        </head>
        <body bgcolor="green">
          <b>Hello World</b>
        </body>
      </html>
   </xsl:template>

</xsl:stylesheet>
```

Whitespace is stripped from literal elements.

It is also possible to generate elements and attributes using explicit *constructors*, with which the above example looks as follows:

```
<xsl:stylesheet version="2.0"
                xmlns:xsl="http://www.w3.org/1999/XSL/Transform"
                xmlns="http://www.w3.org/1999/xhtml">

   <xsl:template match="/">
      <xsl:element name="html">
```

```
            <xsl:element name="head">
              <xsl:element name="title">
                Hello World
              </xsl:element>
            </xsl:element>
            <xsl:element name="body">
              <xsl:attribute name="bgcolor" select="'green'"/>
              <xsl:element name="b">
                Hello World
              </xsl:element>
            </xsl:element>
          </xsl:element>
        </xsl:template>

    </xsl:stylesheet>
```

The `select` attribute of the `attribute` element is an XPath 2.0 expression that is evaluated in the current context and whose resulting sequence value is transformed into a string as follows:

- the sequence is atomized (see Section 3.5.1); and

- the resulting strings are concatenated, separated by single space characters.

A different separating string may be chosen using the `separator` attribute. Note that in the above example we write

```
select="'green'"
```

to produce the constant attribute value `green`, since the seemingly reasonable variant

```
select="green"
```

contains a path expression that attempts to select all child nodes named `green` of the current context node. In general, attribute values may be computed, as in the following example that inherits its background color from the source document:

```
<xsl:stylesheet version="2.0"
                xmlns:xsl="http://www.w3.org/1999/XSL/Transform"
                xmlns="http://www.w3.org/1999/xhtml">

  <xsl:template match="/">
    <xsl:element name="html">
      <xsl:element name="head">
        <xsl:element name="title">
          Hello World
        </xsl:element>
```

```
        </xsl:element>
        <xsl:element name="body">
          <xsl:attribute name="bgcolor" select="//@bgcolor"/>
          <xsl:element name="b">
            Hello World
          </xsl:element>
        </xsl:element>
      </xsl:element>
    </xsl:template>

</xsl:stylesheet>
```

A literal element constructor may actually have a non-constant attribute value, since a substring of the form

```
{...}
```

is replaced by the atomized value of the XPath expression that it is assumed to enclose. Thus, the above example may also be written as:

```
<xsl:stylesheet version="2.0"
                xmlns:xsl="http://www.w3.org/1999/XSL/Transform"
                xmlns="http://www.w3.org/1999/xhtml">

    <xsl:template match="/">
       <html>
         <head>
           <title>Hello World</title>
         </head>
         <body bgcolor="{//@bgcolor}">
           <b>Hello World</b>
         </body>
       </html>
    </xsl:template>

</xsl:stylesheet>
```

It is also possible to generate a namespace declaration using the namespace element, whose name attribute must be an NCName corresponding to the namespace prefix and whose select attribute computes the namespace string as described for the attribute element above. It is rarely necessary to use this instruction, since all constructed element nodes automatically contain all relevant namespace declarations. However, if the generated output uses namespaces in a non-standard manner, then namespace declarations must be inserted explicitly. An example of non-standard use of namespaces is the presence of namespace prefixes in attribute values in XML Schema and other languages.

Literal elements and explicit constructors may be mixed arbitrarily. In general, their contents are specified by general sequence constructors.

If a collection of attributes is used several times, it may be useful to declare it as an *attribute set*:

```
<xsl:attribute-set name="mytable">
  <xsl:attribute name="border" select="'1'"/>
  <xsl:attribute name="cellspacing" select="'5'"/>
  <xsl:attribute name="cellpadding" select="'5'"/>
</xsl:attribute-set>
```

This set of attributes may then be used as follows:

```
<table xsl:use-attribute-sets="mytable">
  ...
</table>
```

The `use-attribute-sets` attribute may be used in both literal elements, explicit constructors, and `copy` instructions. Attribute values may be overridden by inner occurrences of the `attribute` instruction.

5.4.2 Text Constructors

Apart from literals, character data may be constructed in two ways. The `text` instruction may be wrapped around literal character data to preserve whitespace. The `value-of` instruction generates character data from an XPath expression in a `select` attribute, similarly to the `attribute` instruction explained above. Thus, for example, the sequence constructor

```
<xsl:text>2+2 = </xsl:text><xsl:value-of select="2+2"/>
```

generates the output

```
2+2 = 4
```

Without the use of the `text` instruction, the output would be

```
2+2 =4
```

If the `select` expression generates a sequence of length greater than one, then the textual versions of the items are concatenated, separated by a single space character (the separator may be changed using a `separator` attribute).

5.4.3 Other Constructors

It is also possible to construct processing instructions and comments in the target document, as illustrated by the stylesheet

```
<xsl:stylesheet version="2.0"
                xmlns:xsl="http://www.w3.org/1999/XSL/Transform"
                xmlns="http://www.w3.org/1999/xhtml">

   <xsl:template match="/">
       <xsl:processing-instruction name="xml-stylesheet">
         type="text/css" href="mystyle.css"
       </xsl:processing-instruction>
       <html>
         <xsl:comment select="'We will make the background green'"/>
         <head>
           <title>Hello World</title>
         </head>
         <body bgcolor="green">
           <b>Hello World</b>
         </body>
       </html>
   </xsl:template>

</xsl:stylesheet>
```

whose output is

```
<?xml-stylesheet type="text/css" href="mystyle.css"?>
<html>
  <!-- We will make the background green -->
  <head>
    <title>Hello World</title>
  </head>
  <body bgcolor="green">
    <b>Hello World</b>
  </body>
</html>
```

5.4.4 Copying Nodes

The `copy-of` instruction creates a deep copy of the trees rooted by the element nodes specified by a `select` attribute. This, of course, only makes sense if the input language is (a subset of) the output language. The `copy` instruction creates a shallow copy of the context node, excluding attributes. A typical use of these constructs is the following template rule which transforms any XHTML list by making the top-most bullets square:

```
<xsl:template match="ol|ul">
  <xsl:copy>
    <xsl:attribute name="style"
                   select="'list-style-type: square;'"/>
    <xsl:copy-of select="*"/>
  </xsl:copy>
</xsl:template>
```

The `sequence` instruction seems to be equivalent to `copy-of` (the current specification is unclear about this). While `copy-of` is supposed to copy just nodes from the source tree, `sequence` may construct arbitrary sequences containing also atomic values. However, they are described the same in the specification and they appear to be identical in implementations.

5.4.5   Recursive Application

The `apply-templates` instruction recursively applies the entire stylesheet to the nodes that are specified by the `select` attribute, concatenating their result sequences. The default value of the `select` attribute is

```
child::node()
```

The business card example in Section 5.1 contains a typical use of `apply-templates`. Another simple example is the following, which generates summaries of grades for students:

```
<xsl:stylesheet version="2.0"
                xmlns:xsl="http://www.w3.org/1999/XSL/Transform">

  <xsl:template match="students">
    <summary>
      <xsl:apply-templates select="student"/>
    </summary>
  </xsl:template>

  <xsl:template match="student">
    <grades>
      <xsl:attribute name="id" select="@id"/>
      <xsl:apply-templates select=".//@grade"/>
    </grades>
  </xsl:template>

  <xsl:template match="@grade">
    <grade>
```

```
          <xsl:value-of select="."/>
        </grade>
      </xsl:template>

  </xsl:stylesheet>
```

The output of this transformation is:

```
<summary>
  <grades id="100026">
    <grade>C-</grade>
    <grade>C+</grade>
    <grade>D</grade>
  </grades>
  <grades id="100078">
    <grade>A</grade>
    <grade>A-</grade>
    <grade>B+</grade>
    <grade>A</grade>
  </grades>
</summary>
```

The following XSLT stylesheets works like an identity transformation (similarly to the `copy-of` instruction):

```
<xsl:stylesheet version="2.0"
                xmlns:xsl="http://www.w3.org/1999/XSL/Transform">

  <xsl:template match="/|@*|node()">
    <xsl:copy>
      <xsl:apply-templates select="@*|node()"/>
    </xsl:copy>
  </xsl:template>

</xsl:stylesheet>
```

An `apply-templates` instruction may use a `mode` attribute to only consider those templates rules that have a corresponding `mode` attribute (see Section 5.3.2). This restriction may be used to process the same set of nodes several times with different results. As an example, the XSLT stylesheet

```
<xsl:stylesheet version="2.0"
                xmlns:xsl="http://www.w3.org/1999/XSL/Transform">

  <xsl:template match="students">
    <summary>
      <xsl:apply-templates mode="names" select="student"/>
```

```
        <xsl:apply-templates mode="grades" select="student"/>
      </summary>
    </xsl:template>

    <xsl:template mode="names" match="student">
      <name>
        <xsl:attribute name="id" select="@id"/>
        <xsl:value-of select="name"/>
      </name>
    </xsl:template>

    <xsl:template mode="grades" match="student">
      <grades>
        <xsl:attribute name="id" select="@id"/>
        <xsl:apply-templates select=".//@grade"/>
      </grades>
    </xsl:template>

    <xsl:template match="@grade">
      <grade>
        <xsl:value-of select="."/>
      </grade>
    </xsl:template>

  </xsl:stylesheet>
```

starts by listing the names of students and then lists their grades:

```
<summary>
  <name id="100026">Joe Average</name>
  <name id="100078">Jack Doe</name>
  <grades id="100026">
    <grade>C-</grade>
    <grade>C+</grade>
    <grade>D</grade>
  </grades>
  <grades id="100078">
    <grade>A</grade>
    <grade>A-</grade>
    <grade>B+</grade>
    <grade>A</grade>
  </grades>
</summary>
```

Notice how the student elements are processed in two different ways. The special token #current denotes the mode with which the current template rule itself was invoked.

The value of the `select` attribute may be arbitrarily complex, but another study of our sample of 200,000 lines of XSLT stylesheets indicates that they are usually quite simple:

apply-templates is a central instruction in XSLT.

default	31%
QName	30%
QName / *QName* / *QName*	11%
*	7%
QName | *QName* | *QName*	4%
`text()`	2%
QName [. . .]	2%
/ *QName* / *QName* / *QName*	1%
other	12%

5.4.6 Repetitions

The `for-each` instruction computes the sequence specified by its `select` attribute and computes for each of these the sequence constructor in its body with that sequence item as context item, concatenating the results. This construction is analogous to `for` expressions in XPath (see Section 3.5.12).

The following example has the same effect as the first stylesheet presented in Section 5.4.5:

```
<xsl:stylesheet version="2.0"
                xmlns:xsl="http://www.w3.org/1999/XSL/Transform">

  <xsl:template match="students">
    <summary>
      <xsl:apply-templates select="student"/>
    </summary>
  </xsl:template>

  <xsl:template match="student">
    <grades>
      <xsl:attribute name="id" select="@id"/>
      <xsl:for-each select=".//@grade">
        <grade>
          <xsl:value-of select="."/>
        </grade>
      </xsl:for-each>
    </grades>
  </xsl:template>

</xsl:stylesheet>
```

5.4.7 Conditionals

The if instruction returns the result of the sequence constructor in its body, if the XPath expression in its test attribute evaluates to true as described in Section 3.5.10. Otherwise, it returns an empty sequence. This construction is analogous to if expressions in XPath (see Section 3.5.13). A simple example is the following stylesheet, which only lists passing grades:

```
<xsl:stylesheet version="2.0"
                xmlns:xsl="http://www.w3.org/1999/XSL/Transform">

   <xsl:template match="students">
     <summary>
       <xsl:apply-templates select="student"/>
     </summary>
   </xsl:template>

   <xsl:template match="student">
     <grades>
       <xsl:attribute name="id" select="@id"/>
       <xsl:for-each select=".//@grade">
         <xsl:if test=". ne 'F'">
           <grade>
             <xsl:value-of select="."/>
           </grade>
         </xsl:if>
       </xsl:for-each>
     </grades>
   </xsl:template>

</xsl:stylesheet>
```

The choose instruction is a conditional which allows several different branches that are tried in order. An example is the following stylesheet which decides the preferred contact information from a business card:

```
<xsl:stylesheet version="2.0"
                xmlns:xsl="http://www.w3.org/1999/XSL/Transform">
                xmlns:b="http://businesscard.org"

   <xsl:template match="b:card">
      <contact>
        <xsl:choose>
          <xsl:when test="b:email">
            <xsl:value-of select="b:email"/>
          </xsl:when>
```

```
              <xsl:when test="b:phone">
                <xsl:value-of select="b:phone"/>
              </xsl:when>
              <xsl:otherwise>
                No information available
              </xsl:otherwise>
            </xsl:choose>
          </contact>
        </xsl:template>

    </xsl:stylesheet>
```

5.4.8 Template Invocation

If a template rule has a name attribute (see Section 5.3.2), then it may be called directly on the current context, bypassing the pattern matching mechanism. This mechanism can be useful for structuring and modularizing a stylesheet. A variation of the students example uses this feature:

```
<xsl:stylesheet version="2.0"
                xmlns:xsl="http://www.w3.org/1999/XSL/Transform">

    <xsl:template match="students">
      <summary>
        <xsl:apply-templates select="student"/>
      </summary>
    </xsl:template>

    <xsl:template match="student">
      <grades>
        <xsl:attribute name="id" select="@id"/>
        <xsl:for-each select=".//@grade">
          <xsl:call-template name="listgrade"/>
        </xsl:for-each>
      </grades>
    </xsl:template>

    <xsl:template name="listgrade">
      <grade>
        <xsl:value-of select="."/>
      </grade>
    </xsl:template>

    </xsl:stylesheet>
```

For each grade attribute, we explicitly call a template generating a corresponding grade element.

5.5   Variables and Parameters

Variables and
parameters
allow
information to
be shared
between
template rules.

The `variable` instruction declares a (read-only) variable. The value is either assigned through an XPath expression in a `select` attribute or through a sequence constructor in its body. The scope of a variable declaration is the remainder of the content sequence in which it occurs. Variable declarations may also occur at the level of template rules, in which case they are globally visible.

Template rules invoked through `apply-templates` or `call-template` may be passed parameters. A formal parameter is declared inside the `template` using a `param` instruction, which may also supply a default value, either through an XPath expression in a `select` attribute or through a sequence constructor in its body. The default for the default value is the empty string. The actual parameter is supplied through a similar `with-param` instruction inside the `apply-templates` or `call-template` instruction. If a formal parameter does not have a corresponding actual parameter, then the default value is used instead.

An example using both variables and parameters shows how XSLT may be used as an ordinary, if somewhat cumbersome, programming language:

```
<xsl:stylesheet version="2.0"
                xmlns:xsl="http://www.w3.org/1999/XSL/Transform">

  <xsl:template name="fib">
    <xsl:param name="n"/>
    <xsl:choose>
      <xsl:when test="$n le 1">
        <xsl:value-of select="1"/>
      </xsl:when>
      <xsl:otherwise>
        <xsl:variable name="f1">
          <xsl:call-template name="fib">
            <xsl:with-param name="n" select="$n -1"/>
          </xsl:call-template>
        </xsl:variable>
        <xsl:variable name="f2">
          <xsl:call-template name="fib">
            <xsl:with-param name="n" select="$n -2"/>
          </xsl:call-template>
        </xsl:variable>
        <xsl:value-of select="$f1+$f2"/>
      </xsl:otherwise>
    </xsl:choose>
  </xsl:template>

  <xsl:template match="/">
    <xsl:call-template name="fib">
      <xsl:with-param name="n" select="10"/>
```

```
    </xsl:call-template>
  </xsl:template>

</xsl:stylesheet>
```

Recall that the extra space between $n and the minus operator is required to have the expression parsed correctly (see Section 3.5.4).

Parameters may also be declared at the level of template rules, in which case they are globally visible. The corresponding actual parameters will then be supplied externally when the XSLT tool is invoked (see Section 7.3.5).

Both the `param` and `with-param` instructions may be given a `tunnel` attribute with value `yes`, which has the effect of implicitly passing the parameter through all intermediate template invocations (similarly to dynamically scoped variables in some programming languages).

5.6 Built-In Template Rules

If no available pattern matches a given context node, then a *built-in* template rule is applied as default. The document root is handled by the rule

```
<xsl:template match="/">
  <xsl:apply-templates/>
</xsl:template>
```

which, in fact, has been used in all of our previous examples. Text and attribute nodes are handled by this rule, which just copies their values:

```
<xsl:template match="text()|@*" mode="#all">
  <xsl:value-of select="."/>
</xsl:template>
```

Processing instruction nodes and comment nodes are effectively ignored by the following rule:

```
<xsl:template match="processing-instruction()|comment()"
              mode="#all"/>
```

A general invocation, such as

```
<xsl:apply-templates select="foo" mode="bar">
  <xsl:with-param name="baz" select="42"/>
</xsl:apply-template>
```

is – if no explicit rule applies – handled by an implicit rule that is created on the fly:

```
<xsl:template match="foo" mode="#all">
  <xsl:param name="baz"/>
```

```
    <xsl:apply-templates mode="#current">
      <xsl:with-param name="baz" select="$baz"/>
    </xsl:apply-templates>
  </xsl:template>
```

This rule accepts the selected element in all modes, receives the baz parameter, and invokes the stylesheet on all child nodes with the current mode and while passing on the baz parameter. Built-in rules have lower priority than all others.

5.7   Simple Traversals

In a frequent pattern for using XSLT, the transformation performs a simple top-down recursive traversal of the input tree. When the input language is the same as the output language, a stylesheet for an application may be short and appealing. Continuing the example from Section 5.4.4, we write a stylesheet that works on XHTML documents and simultaneously

- makes all bullets square;

- replaces i tags with em tags;

- replaces b tags with strong tags; and

- changes all character data to upper case.

It looks as follows:

```
<xsl:stylesheet version="2.0"
                xmlns="http://www.w3.org/1999/xhtml"
                xmlns:xsl="http://www.w3.org/1999/XSL/Transform">

  <xsl:template match="@*|*">
    <xsl:copy>
      <xsl:apply-templates select="@*|node()"/>
    </xsl:copy>
  </xsl:template>

  <xsl:template match="ol|ul">
    <xsl:copy>
      <xsl:attribute name="style"
                     select="'list-style-type: square;'"/>
      <xsl:apply-templates select="@*|node()"/>
    </xsl:copy>
  </xsl:template>

  <xsl:template match="i">
    <em>
      <xsl:apply-templates select="@*|node()"/>
```

```
      </em>
    </xsl:template>

    <xsl:template match="b">
      <strong>
        <xsl:apply-templates select="@*|node()"/>
      </strong>
    </xsl:template>

    <xsl:template match="text()">
      <xsl:value-of select="upper-case(.)"/>
    </xsl:template>

  </xsl:stylesheet>
```

Note how the priority mechanism of templates rules ensures that the specific rules are chosen for the ol, ul, i, and b tags, while a common template rule copies all other elements.

5.8 Advanced Features

The above instructions are sufficient for many simple XSLT applications. In this section we present features that allow more advanced control of the generated output.

5.8.1 Grouping

The for-each-group instruction allows elements in a sequence to be *grouped* according to a *key*. As an example, we could group ingredients according to the name of the recipe in which they are used.

The sequence to be grouped is specified in a select attribute, and the key is specified as an XPath expression in a group-by attribute. The for-each-group constructor is evaluated as follows:

- the expression in the select attribute is evaluated, resulting in a *population* sequence;

- for each item in the population, the group-by expression is evaluated with the corresponding context item;

- the resulting values are compared using the eq operator to yield a set of unique *grouping keys*;

- the sequence constructor in the body of the for-each-group instruction is evaluated for each of those grouping keys; and

- the final result is obtained by concatenating those sequences.

When evaluating the body of `for-each-group`, two special functions are available:

- `current-grouping-key()` returns the current grouping key; and

- `current-group()` returns the sequence of items with that given key.

Also, the `position()` function now refers to the position of the current key in the sequence of all keys.

Continuing the above motivating example, the following stylesheet will list all ingredients by name along with the number of recipes in which they are used:

```
<xsl:stylesheet version="2.0"
                xmlns:rcp="http://www.brics.dk/ixwt/recipes"
                xmlns:xsl="http://www.w3.org/1999/XSL/Transform">

   <xsl:template match="rcp:collection">
      <uses>
        <xsl:for-each-group select="//rcp:ingredient"
                            group-by="@name">
          <use name="{current-grouping-key()}"
               count="{count(current-group())}"/>
        </xsl:for-each-group>
      </uses>
   </xsl:template>

</xsl:stylesheet>
```

This stylesheet produces the following output:

```
<uses>
   <use name="beef cube steak" count="1"/>
   <use name="onion, sliced into thin rings" count="1"/>
   <use name="green bell pepper, sliced in rings" count="1"/>
   <use name="Italian seasoned bread crumbs" count="1"/>
   <use name="grated Parmesan cheese" count="1"/>
   <use name="olive oil" count="2"/>
   <use name="spaghetti sauce" count="1"/>
   <use name="shredded mozzarella cheese" count="1"/>
   <use name="angel hair pasta" count="1"/>
   <use name="minced garlic" count="3"/>
   ...
</uses>
```

5.8.2 Sorting

The `apply-templates`, `for-each`, and `for-each-group` instructions process sequences generated by XPath expressions supplied in the `select` attributes. Such sequences may be *sorted* before they are processed, using `sort` instructions that appear at the beginning of the contents. The `sort` instructions specify keys for sorting using a `select` attribute. The first `sort` occurrence gives the primary key, the second gives the secondary key, and so on. The comparison relation on each key may be specified through a number of optional attributes. The most important are the `order` attribute (which has value `ascending` or `descending`), the `case-order` attribute (which has value `upper-first` or `lower-first`), and the `data-type` attribute (which has value `text` or `number`). The default setting is `ascending`, `lower-first`, and `text`.

As an example, consider the following stylesheet which sorts students first by age (older first) and then alphabetically by name:

```
<xsl:stylesheet version="2.0"
                xmlns:xsl="http://www.w3.org/1999/XSL/Transform">

  <xsl:template match="students">
    <enrolled>
      <xsl:apply-templates select="student">
        <xsl:sort select="age" data-type="number"
                  order="descending"/>
        <xsl:sort select="name"/>
      </xsl:apply-templates>
    </enrolled>
  </xsl:template>

  <xsl:template match="student">
    <student name="{name}" age="{age}"/>
  </xsl:template>

</xsl:stylesheet>
```

For our tiny example document, the result is:

```
<enrolled>
  <student name="Joe Average" age="21"/>
  <student name="Jack Doe" age="18"/>
</enrolled>
```

It is also possible to sort an existing sequence using the `perform-sort` instruction. Thus, the above example could also be written as follows:

```
<xsl:stylesheet version="2.0"
                xmlns:xsl="http://www.w3.org/1999/XSL/Transform">

  <xsl:template match="students">
    <enrolled>
      <xsl:perform-sort>
        <xsl:sort select="age" data-type="number"
                  order="descending"/>
```

```
        <xsl:sort select="name"/>
        <xsl:apply-templates select="student"/>
      </xsl:perform-sort>
    </enrolled>
  </xsl:template>

  <xsl:template match="student">
    <student name="{name}" age="{age}"/>
  </xsl:template>

</xsl:stylesheet>
```

In this version, we first compute the result of

```
<xsl:apply-templates select="student"/>
```

(in document order) and subsequently sort the resulting sequence.

5.8.3 Numbering

XSLT supports an elaborate scheme for creating numberings. This scheme is a document-centric concept that is mainly useful for generating documents with chapters, sections, and numbered list items. In its simplest version, the number instruction computes a sequence of integers through an XPath expression given in a value attribute and generates a presentation of those integers using a format attribute. The sequence of integers may also be computed by counting occurrences of elements specified by a pattern in a count attribute. Numerous other attributes allows many variations and fancy layout of the generated numbers. A simple example is the following, which provides hierarchical level numbers for ingredients in the recipe collection:

```
<xsl:stylesheet version="2.0"
                xmlns:rcp="http://www.brics.dk/ixwt/recipes"
                xmlns:xsl="http://www.w3.org/1999/XSL/Transform">

  <xsl:template match="rcp:ingredient">
    <rcp:ingredient>
      <xsl:apply-templates select="@*|*"/>
      <xsl:attribute name="level">
        <xsl:number level="multiple" count="rcp:ingredient"/>
      </xsl:attribute>
    </rcp:ingredient>
  </xsl:template>

  <xsl:template match="@*">
    <xsl:copy/>
  </xsl:template>
```

```
<xsl:template match="*">
  <xsl:copy><xsl:apply-templates/></xsl:copy>
</xsl:template>

</xsl:stylesheet>
```

Each `ingredient` element is now extended with an appropriate `level` attribute; for example, 'mushroom juices' in Cailles en Sarcophages has level `2.3.2`. Note also that this stylesheet exploits the fact that the first template rule has higher priority than the third.

5.8.4 Keys

XSLT contains a collection of features that allows cross-references to be defined in an XML document.

The `key` instruction defines a map from *key values* to nodes. The name of the map is given by a `name` attribute and the nodes that are targets of the map are given by a `match` attribute whose value is a pattern (see Section 5.3.1). The `use` attribute contains an XPath expression that for each matched node is evaluated to produce the key value that maps to that node. Since key values are not required to be unique, a given key value may map to several nodes.

The `key` function (not to confuse with the `key` instruction) accepts as arguments the name of a key map and a key value, and it returns the sequence of corresponding nodes (without duplicates and in document order).

A typical use of keys also involves the function `generate-id`, which generates a unique string value for a given node.

An example is the following stylesheet, which generates an ordered list of all recipe title and for each indicates the numbers of the related recipes (with links to their titles):

```
<xsl:stylesheet version="2.0"
    xmlns="http://www.w3.org/1999/xhtml"
    xmlns:rcp="http://www.brics.dk/ixwt/recipes"
    xmlns:xsl="http://www.w3.org/1999/XSL/Transform">

  <xsl:key name="rel" match="rcp:recipe" use="@id"/>

  <xsl:template match="rcp:collection">
    <html>
      <head>
        <title>Relationship Graph</title>
      </head>
      <body>
        <ol>
          <xsl:apply-templates select="rcp:recipe"/>
        </ol>
      </body>
    </html>
  </xsl:template>
```

```
<xsl:template match="rcp:recipe">
  <li>
    <a name="{generate-id(.)}"/>
    <xsl:value-of select="rcp:title"/>
    <br/>
    Related to:
    <xsl:apply-templates select="rcp:related"/>
  </li>
</xsl:template>

<xsl:template match="rcp:related">
  <a href="#{generate-id(key('rel',@ref))}">
    <xsl:for-each select="key('rel',@ref)">
      <xsl:number/>
    </xsl:for-each>
  </a>
  <xsl:if test="position() lt last()">
    <xsl:text>, </xsl:text>
  </xsl:if>
</xsl:template>

</xsl:stylesheet>
```

Here, the `rel` key maps from recipes `id` values to the corresponding nodes. For our tiny recipe collection (with only one `related` element), the output looks as follows:

```
<html xmlns="http://www.w3.org/1999/xhtml">
  <head>
    <title>Relationship Graph</title>
  </head>
  <body>
    <ol>
      <li>
        <a name="d1e6"/>Beef Parmesan with Garlic Angel
        Hair Pasta<br/>
        Related to: <a href="#d1e129">3</a>
      </li>
      <li>
        <a name="d1e61"/>Ricotta Pie<br/>
        Related to:
      </li>
      <li>
        <a name="d1e129"/>Linguine Pescadoro<br/>
        Related to:
      </li>
      <li><a name="d1e197"/>Zuppa Inglese<br/>
        Related to:
      </li>
```

```
        <li><a name="d1e251"/>Cailles en Sarcophages<br/>
          Related to:
        </li>
      </ol>
    </body>
  </html>
```

5.8.5   Analyzing Strings

The `analyze-string` instruction is used to iterate through various components of a string.
Consider the example with integer lists from Section 4.4.2:

```
<integerlist> 7 42 87 </integerlist>
```

We want to transform this document into the following more explicit format:

```
<integerlist>
  <int>7</int>
  <int>42</int>
  <int>87</int>
</integerlist>
```

The necessary stylesheet looks as follows:

```
<xsl:stylesheet version="2.0"
                xmlns:xsl="http://www.w3.org/1999/XSL/Transform">

  <xsl:template match="integerlist">
    <integerlist>
      <xsl:analyze-string select="." regex="[0-9]+">
        <xsl:matching-substring>
          <int><xsl:value-of select="."/></int>
        </xsl:matching-substring>
      </xsl:analyze-string>
    </integerlist>
  </xsl:template>

</xsl:stylesheet>
```

The selected string is partitioned into matching and non-matching substrings that are it-
eratively processed by either `matching-substring` or `non-matching-substring` instructions. An example using both these instructions is the following that replaces newline
characters in a string by `br` elements:

```
<xsl:analyze-string select="..." regex="\n">
  <xsl:non-matching-substring>
    <xsl:value-of select="."/>
  </xsl:non-matching-substring>
```

```
<xsl:matching-substring>
  <br/>
</xsl:matching-substring>
</xsl:analyze-string>
```

5.8.6 Functions

To allow reuse and modularization, computations on sequence values may be defined as functions. The `function` element is named using a `name` attribute and parameters are declared using `param` instructions (see Section 5.5). The name of a function must be a QName. Once a function has been defined, it can be called from within XPath expressions.

Thus, an alternative implementation of the stylesheet generating Fibonacci numbers (see Section 5.5) is the following:

```
<xsl:stylesheet version="2.0"
        xmlns:xsl="http://www.w3.org/1999/XSL/Transform">

  <xsl:function name="fib">
    <xsl:param name="n"/>
    <xsl:value-of select="if ($n le 1)
                          then 1
                          else fib($n -1)+fib($n -2)"/>
  </xsl:function>

  <xsl:template match="/">
    <xsl:value-of select="fib(10)"/>
  </xsl:template>

</xsl:stylesheet>
```

5.8.7 Sequence Types

XPath 2.0 and XQuery 1.0 defines a notion of *sequence types* that define particular kinds of sequence values (see Section 6.7.1). These types may also be used for type annotations on `template`, `function`, `variable`, `param`, and `with-param` instructions. In all cases, the computed sequence value is *matched* against the sequence type (see Section 6.7.3, which may cause a runtime type error. As an example, the following is a stylesheet with valid type annotations:

```
<xsl:stylesheet version="2.0"
        xmlns:xsl="http://www.w3.org/1999/XSL/Transform"
        xmlns:rcp="http://www.brics.dk/ixwt/recipes"
        xmlns:xs="http://www.w3.org/2001/XMLSchema"
        xmlns="http://www.w3.org/1999/xhtml">

  <xsl:function name="captitle" as="xs:string">
    <xsl:param name="r" as="element(rcp:recipe)"/>
```

```
      <xsl:value-of select="upper-case($r/rcp:title/text())"/>
    </xsl:function>

    <xsl:template match="rcp:collection" as="element()">
      <html>
        <head><title>Recipe Titles</title></head>
        <body>
          <xsl:apply-templates select="//rcp:recipe"/>
        </body>
      </html>
    </xsl:template>

    <xsl:template match="rcp:recipe" as="item()+">
      <xsl:value-of select="captitle(.)"/>
      <br/>
    </xsl:template>

</xsl:stylesheet>
```

5.8.8 Multiple Documents

So far, we have viewed XSLT as transforming a single source document into a single target document. However, XSLT may, in fact, work with multiple documents.

For input documents, the doc function from XPath (see Section 3.5.11) may be used to read additional information from arbitrary XML documents. An example is the following stylesheet, which extracts the subset of recipes that are not present in the recipe collection dislikes.xml:

```
<xsl:stylesheet version="2.0"
                xmlns:rcp="http://www.brics.dk/ixwt/recipes"
                xmlns:xsl="http://www.w3.org/1999/XSL/Transform">

    <xsl:template match="rcp:collection">
        <rcp:collection>
            <rcp:title>Selected Recipes</rcp:title>
            <xsl:apply-templates select="rcp:recipe"/>
        </rcp:collection>
    </xsl:template>

    <xsl:template match="rcp:recipe">
      <xsl:variable name="t" select="rcp:title/text()"/>
      <xsl:if test="not(doc('dislikes.xml')//
                        rcp:recipe[rcp:title eq $t])">
        <xsl:copy-of select="."/>
      </xsl:if>
    </xsl:template>

</xsl:stylesheet>
```

Note that the `doc` function is called without a namespace prefix, since XSLT uses a default function namespace.

For output documents, the `result-document` may direct the output to different files, specified by the `href` attribute. The specification allows a general URI, but the implementation may of course impose further restrictions. As an example, consider a stylesheet that generates two files: `names.html` with a list of students and `grades.html` with their grades. Furthermore, each student has a link to the corresponding grades. It looks as follows:

```
<xsl:stylesheet version="2.0"
                xmlns="http://www.w3.org/1999/xhtml"
                xmlns:xsl="http://www.w3.org/1999/XSL/Transform">

  <xsl:template match="students">
    <xsl:result-document href="names.html">
      <html>
        <head><title>Students</title></head>
        <body>
          <xsl:apply-templates select="student" mode="name"/>
        </body>
      </html>
    </xsl:result-document>
    <xsl:result-document href="grades.html">
      <html>
        <head><title>Grades</title></head>
        <body>
          <xsl:apply-templates select="student" mode="grade"/>
        </body>
      </html>
    </xsl:result-document>
  </xsl:template>

  <xsl:template match="student" mode="name">
    <a href="grades.html#{@id}"><xsl:value-of select="name"/></a>
    <br/>
  </xsl:template>

  <xsl:template match="student" mode="grade">
    <a name="{@id}"/>
    <xsl:value-of select="name"/>
    <ul>
      <xsl:apply-templates select="results/result"/>
    </ul>
  </xsl:template>

  <xsl:template match="result">
    <li>
      <xsl:value-of select="@course"/>:
```

```
        <xsl:text> </xsl:text>
        <xsl:value-of select="@grade"/>
      </li>
    </xsl:template>

  </xsl:stylesheet>
```

The generated `names.html` file contains

```
<html xmlns="http://www.w3.org/1999/xhtml">
  <head><title>Students</title></head>
  <body>
    <a href="grades.html#100026">Joe Average</a>
    <br/>
    <a href="grades.html#100078">Jack Doe</a>
    <br/>
  </body>
</html>
```

and the `grades.html` file contains the following:

```
<html xmlns="http://www.w3.org/1999/xhtml">
  <head><title>Grades</title></head>
  <body>
    <a name="100026"/>Joe Average
    <ul>
      <li>Math 101: C-</li>
      <li>Biology 101: C+</li>
      <li>Statistics 101: D</li>
    </ul>
    <a name="100078"/>Jack Doe
    <ul>
      <li>Math 101: A</li>
      <li>XML 101: A-</li>
      <li>Physics 101: B+</li>
      <li>XML 102: A</li>
    </ul>
  </body>
</html>
```

5.8.9 Include and Import

A large stylesheet may be divided into modules that are included to form the complete document. Modularization is, of course, also useful for reusing parts of a stylesheet for several applications.

XSLT supports two different instructions for such purposes: `include` and `import`. Both elements are only allowed immediately below the `stylesheet` root element, and `import` instructions must appear before other top-level declarations.

The `include` instruction has a mandatory `href` attribute that contains the URL of another XSLT stylesheet. Its effect is textually to replace the `include` instruction with the *contents* of the indicated stylesheet. Inclusion may be performed to an arbitrary depth, but it is, of course, an error if a cycle arises.

The `import` instruction is a variation of `include` that allows the templates in the imported stylesheet to be *overridden*. This overriding is achieved by modifying the priority mechanism, such that the templates in the main file always have higher priority than the imported ones. In the case of nested applications of `import` instructions, the result coincides with ordinary scope rules of nested declarations in programming languages. In contrast, when using `include`, conflicts between templates are resolved by the usual specificity mechanism.

The two variations have different strengths. The low-level `include` mechanism is useful for relegating parts of a large stylesheet to a separate document, with a guarantee that the semantics is preserved. The `import` mechanism is useful for designing a stylesheet as a combination and extension of existing stylesheets.

Clearly, `include` and `import` may have a different semantics. Consider an XSLT stylesheet in a file `negative.xsl` whose contents is:

```
<xsl:stylesheet version="2.0"
                xmlns:xsl="http://www.w3.org/1999/XSL/Transform">

  <xsl:template match="howabout">
    <answer>
      I don't like <xsl:value-of select="text()"/>
    </answer>
  </xsl:template>

</xsl:stylesheet>
```

We now consider the following stylesheet:

```
<xsl:stylesheet version="2.0"
                xmlns:xsl-"http://www.w3.org/1999/XSL/Transform">

  <xsl:include href="negative.xsl"/>

  <xsl:template match="*">
    <answer>
      I'm crazy for <xsl:value-of select="text()"/>
    </answer>
  </xsl:template>

</xsl:stylesheet>
```

Applied to the XML document

```
<howabout>Zuppa Inglese</howabout>
```

the output is

```
<answer>I don't like Zuppa Inglese</answer>
```

In contrast, the following stylesheet where `include` has been replaced by `import`

```
<xsl:stylesheet version="2.0"
                xmlns:xsl="http://www.w3.org/1999/XSL/Transform">

  <xsl:import href="negative.xsl"/>

  <xsl:template match="howabout">
    <answer>
      I'm crazy for <xsl:value-of select="text()"/>
    </answer>
  </xsl:template>

</xsl:stylesheet>
```

generates the output

```
<answer>I'm crazy for Zuppa Inglese</answer>
```

A hierarchy of nested `import` declarations is similar to a class hierarchy in object-oriented programming, where templates may be overridden like methods. XSLT also supports an analog of the `super` meta-object, which in Java is used to invoke overridden version of methods. The `apply-imports` instruction invokes the stylesheet again on the current context node, but considers only those templates that occur in imported stylesheets.

Assume the stylesheet for business cards from Section 5.1 resides in a file called `business_card.xsl`. Consider now the following stylesheet:

```
<xsl:stylesheet version="2.0"
                xmlns:xsl="http://www.w3.org/1999/XSL/Transform"
                xmlns:b="http://businesscard.org"
                xmlns="http://www.w3.org/1999/xhtml">

  <xsl:import href="business_card.xsl"/>

  <xsl:template match="b:name|b:title|b:email|b:phone">
    <b><xsl:apply-imports/></b>
  </xsl:template>

</xsl:stylesheet>
```

In this new version of the stylesheet, the business card information is written in boldface.

Careful use of the `include` and `import` instructions may greatly help in structuring large stylesheets. For example, the styleheets for the DocBook project (an XML language for defining publications for print) are written in 181 XSLT documents connected by 40 `import` instructions and 299 `include` instructions.

5.8.10 Generating XSLT Output

There seems to be a curious limitation in the design of XSLT: how can we generate an XSLT stylesheet as the result of a transformation? The problem is that the XSLT namespace is used to distinguish instructions from literal elements, but this convention breaks down just in this case.

XSLT enables a solution through the `namespace-alias` instruction which may appear as a declaration just below `stylesheet`. It specifies that a namespace indicated by a `result-prefix` attribute in the resulting document should be replaced by a namespace indicated by a `stylesheet-prefix` attribute. If one of these is the default namespace, then the token `#default` is used.

As an example, consider the task of translating business cards into foreign languages. Each translation may be specified by an XML document such as

```
<translate language="Danish">
  <card>kort</card>
  <name>navn</name>
  <title>titel</title>
  <email>email</email>
  <phone>telefon</phone>
  <logo>logo</logo>
</translate>
```

or

```
<translate language="French">
  <card>carte</card>
  <name>nom</name>
  <title>titre</title>
  <email>courriel</email>
  <phone>telephone</phone>
  <logo>logo</logo>
</translate>
```

Based on such documents, we would like to generate stylesheets that perform the actual translation of business cards. This translation is accomplished by the following stylesheet:

```
<xsl:stylesheet version="2.0"
                xmlns:xsl="http://www.w3.org/1999/XSL/Transform"
                xmlns:b="http://businesscard.org"
                xmlns:myxsl="foo">
```

```
    <xsl:namespace-alias stylesheet-prefix="myxsl"
                         result-prefix="xsl"/>

    <xsl:template match="translate">
        <myxsl:stylesheet version="2.0">
            <xsl:namespace name=""
                select="concat('http://businesscard.org/',@language)"/>
            <myxsl:template match="b:card">
                <myxsl:element name="{card}">
                    <myxsl:apply-templates/>
                </myxsl:element>
            </myxsl:template>
            <myxsl:template match="b:name">
                <myxsl:element name="{name}">
                    <myxsl:value-of select="."/>
                </myxsl:element>
            </myxsl:template>
            <myxsl:template match="b:title">
                <myxsl:element name="{title}">
                    <myxsl:value-of select="."/>
                </myxsl:element>
            </myxsl:template>
            <myxsl:template match="b:email">
                <myxsl:element name="{email}">
                    <myxsl:value-of select="."/>
                </myxsl:element>
            </myxsl:template>
            <myxsl:template match="b:phone">
                <myxsl:element name="{phone}">
                    <myxsl:value-of select="."/>
                </myxsl:element>
            </myxsl:template>
            <myxsl:template match="b:logo">
                <myxsl:element name="{logo}">
                    <myxsl:attribute name="uri" select="@uri"/>
                </myxsl:element>
            </myxsl:template>
        </myxsl:stylesheet>
    </xsl:template>

</xsl:stylesheet>
```

Given the French document as input, this stylesheet generates the output

```
<xsl:stylesheet version="2.0"
  xmlns:xsl="http://www.w3.org/1999/XSL/Transform"
  xmlns:b="http://businesscard.org"
  xmlns="http://businesscard.org/French">
  <xsl:template match="b:card">
```

```
        <xsl:element name="carte">
          <xsl:apply-templates/>
        </xsl:element>
      </xsl:template>
      <xsl:template match="b:name">
        <xsl:element name="nom">
          <xsl:value-of select="."/>
        </xsl:element>
      </xsl:template>
      <xsl:template match="b:title">
        <xsl:element name="titre">
          <xsl:value-of select="."/>
        </xsl:element>
      </xsl:template>
      <xsl:template match="b:email">
        <xsl:element name="courriel">
          <xsl:value-of select="."/>
        </xsl:element>
      </xsl:template>
      <xsl:template match="b:phone">
        <xsl:element name="telephone">
          <xsl:value-of select="."/>
        </xsl:element>
      </xsl:template>
      <xsl:template match="b:logo">
        <xsl:element name="logo">
          <xsl:attribute name="uri" select="@uri"/>
        </xsl:element>
      </xsl:template>
    </xsl:stylesheet>
```

which in turn transforms the document

```
<card xmlns="http://businesscard.org">
  <name>John Doe</name>
  <title>CEO, Widget Inc.</title>
  <email>john.doe@widget.inc</email>
  <phone>(202) 555-1414</phone>
  <logo uri="widget.gif"/>
</card>
```

into the corresponding French version

```
<carte xmlns="http://businesscard.org/French">
  <nom>John Doe</nom>
  <titre>CEO, Widget Inc.</titre>
  <courriel>john.doe@widget.inc</courriel>
  <telephone>(202) 555-1414</telephone>
  <logo uri="widget.gif"/>
</carte>
```

Note that the aliased namespace with prefix `myxsl` can be bound to any harmless namespace string (in this case `foo`).

5.9 XSLT 1.0 Restrictions

XSLT 1.0 has many restrictions compared to XSLT 2.0. First of all, it is restricted to use XPath 1.0 (see Section 3.5.16), which may, in fact, change the semantics of some patterns. Furthermore, XSLT 1.0 does not support `for-each-group`, `sequence`, `function`, or `result-document`. Also, there are differences in the default priorities of template rules and various restrictions in the generality of operators.

A major restriction of XSLT 1.0 is the absence of general sequence values. Instead, templates generate values of type *result tree fragment* which can only be output and not subjected to further computations. Consequently, XSLT 1.0 is not Turing complete on XML trees and XSLT 1.0 stylesheets are often constructed to be executed in sequence as a workaround.

As a concrete example, consider an XSLT 1.0 stylesheet that transforms a sequence of numbers into XHTML. It is possible to output the numbers in sorted order, and it is possible to color them alternately red and blue. However, it is not possible to construct a single XSLT 1.0 stylesheet that *both* sorts the numbers *and* colors them alternately red and blue. Assume that the input document is of the following form:

```
<integerlist>
  <int>15</int>
  <int>12</int>
  <int>17</int>
  <int>25</int>
  <int>18</int>
  <int>17</int>
  <int>23</int>
</integerlist>
```

A solution is XSLT 2.0 is straightforward:

```
<xsl:stylesheet version="2.0"
                xmlns="http://www.w3.org/1999/xhtml"
                xmlns:xsl="http://www.w3.org/1999/XSL/Transform">

  <xsl:template match="integerlist">
    <html>
      <head>
        <title>Integers</title>
      </head>
      <body>
        <xsl:variable name="sorted">
```

```
          <xsl:for-each select="int">
            <xsl:sort select="." data-type="number"/>
            <xsl:copy-of select="."/>
          </xsl:for-each>
        </xsl:variable>
        <xsl:apply-templates select="$sorted"/>
      </body>
    </html>
  </xsl:template>

  <xsl:template match="int">
    <li>
      <font>
        <xsl:attribute name="color"
          select="if (position() mod 2 = 0)
                     then 'blue' else 'red'"/>
        <xsl:value-of select="text()"/>
      </font>
    </li>
  </xsl:template>
</xsl:stylesheet>
```

In XSLT 1.0, the variable `$sorted` is of type result tree fragment, which cannot be subjected to further processing. A solution in XSLT 1.0 will require that two stylesheets are applied in sequence. The first stylesheet takes care of the sorting:

```
<xsl:stylesheet version="1.0"
                xmlns:xsl="http://www.w3.org/1999/XSL/Transform">

  <xsl:template match="integerlist">
    <xsl:copy>
      <xsl:apply-templates>
        <xsl:sort select="." data-type="number"/>
      </xsl:apply-templates>
    </xsl:copy>
  </xsl:template>

  <xsl:template match="int">
    <xsl:copy-of select="."/>
  </xsl:template>

</xsl:stylesheet>
```

The second stylesheets performs the transformation into XHTML:

```
<xsl:stylesheet version="1.0"
                xmlns="http://www.w3.org/1999/xhtml"
                xmlns:xsl="http://www.w3.org/1999/XSL/Transform">
```

```
<xsl:template match="integerlist">
  <html>
    <head>
      <title>Integers</title>
    </head>
    <body>
      <xsl:apply-templates/>
    </body>
  </html>
</xsl:template>

<xsl:template match="int[position() mod 2 = 0]">
  <li>
    <font color="blue">
      <xsl:value-of select="text()"/>
    </font>
  </li>
</xsl:template>

<xsl:template match="int[position() mod 2 = 1]">
  <li>
    <font color="red">
      <xsl:value-of select="text()"/>
    </font>
  </li>
</xsl:template>

</xsl:stylesheet>
```

Note that the absence of an `if` construction in XPath 1.0 is handled by using two different `match` expressions. Clearly, XSLT 2.0 is a more mature language than XSLT 1.0.

5.10   Stylesheets for Recipe Collections

As a larger example, we consider stylesheets for the familiar recipe collection. The first example generates an XHTML presentation of the collection, suitable for viewing in browsers:

```
<xsl:stylesheet version="2.0"
                xmlns="http://www.w3.org/1999/xhtml"
                xmlns:rcp="http://www.brics.dk/ixwt/recipes"
                xmlns:xsl="http://www.w3.org/1999/XSL/Transform">

  <xsl:template match="rcp:collection">
    <html>
      <head>
```

```
        <title><xsl:value-of select="rcp:description"/></title>
        <link href="style.css" rel="stylesheet" type="text/css"/>
      </head>
      <body>
        <table border="1">
          <xsl:apply-templates select="rcp:recipe"/>
        </table>
      </body>
    </html>
  </xsl:template>

  <xsl:template match="rcp:recipe">
    <tr>
      <td>
        <h1><xsl:value-of select="rcp:title"/></h1>
        <i><xsl:value-of select="rcp:date"/></i>
        <ul><xsl:apply-templates select="rcp:ingredient"/></ul>
        <xsl:apply-templates select="rcp:preparation"/>
        <xsl:apply-templates select="rcp:comment"/>
        <xsl:apply-templates select="rcp:nutrition"/>
      </td>
    </tr>
  </xsl:template>

  <xsl:template match="rcp:ingredient">
    <xsl:choose>
      <xsl:when test="@amount">
        <li>
          <xsl:if test="@amount!='*'">
            <xsl:value-of select="@amount"/>
            <xsl:text> </xsl:text>
            <xsl:if test="@unit">
              <xsl:value-of select="@unit"/>
              <xsl:if test="number(@amount)>1">
                <xsl:text>s</xsl:text>
              </xsl:if>
              <xsl:text> of </xsl:text>
            </xsl:if>
          </xsl:if>
          <xsl:text> </xsl:text>
          <xsl:value-of select="@name"/>
        </li>
      </xsl:when>
      <xsl:otherwise>
        <li><xsl:value-of select="@name"/></li>
        <ul><xsl:apply-templates select="rcp:ingredient"/></ul>
        <xsl:apply-templates select="rcp:preparation"/>
      </xsl:otherwise>
```

```
      </xsl:choose>
    </xsl:template>

    <xsl:template match="rcp:preparation">
      <ol><xsl:apply-templates select="rcp:step"/></ol>
    </xsl:template>

    <xsl:template match="rcp:step">
      <li><xsl:value-of select="text()|node()"/></li>
    </xsl:template>

    <xsl:template match="rcp:comment">
      <ul>
        <li type="square"><xsl:value-of select="text()|node()"/></li>
      </ul>
    </xsl:template>

    <xsl:template match="rcp:nutrition">
      <table border="2">
        <tr>
          <th>Calories</th><th>Fat</th>
                          <th>Carbohydrates</th><th>Protein</th>
          <xsl:if test="@alcohol">
            <th>Alcohol</th>
          </xsl:if>
        </tr>
        <tr>
          <td align="right"><xsl:value-of select="@calories"/></td>
          <td align="right"><xsl:value-of select="@fat"/></td>
          <td align="right"><xsl:value-of select="@carbohydrates"/></td>
          <td align="right"><xsl:value-of select="@protein"/></td>
          <xsl:if test="@alcohol">
            <td align="right"><xsl:value-of select="@alcohol"/></td>
          </xsl:if>
        </tr>
      </table>
    </xsl:template>

</xsl:stylesheet>
```

As an example, the recipe for Zuppa Inglese is presented in a browser as shown in Figure 5.1.
There are several interesting observations about this stylesheet:

- the generated XHTML document uses a CSS stylesheet as well, which makes perfect
  sense since issues about HTML styling are still best described in a separate document;

- the template for ingredient is recursive, since composite ingredients contain other
  ingredients;

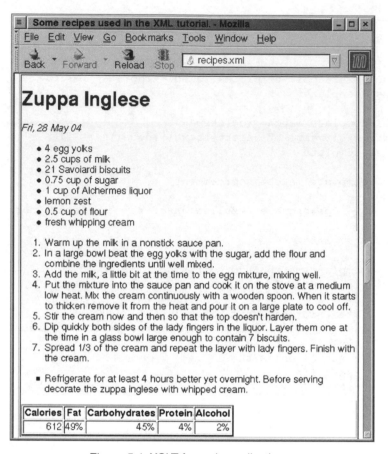

Figure 5.1 XSLT for recipe collections.

- great care is taken to denote simple ingredients in a natural language style; and

- nutrition tables only contain a column for alcohol if this constituent is used in the recipe.

An obvious requirement is that the output is always a valid XHTML document. This requirement can, of course, be validated for each concrete output document, but we would like to obtain a static guarantee that this property holds. More generally, given schemas for the source and target language, we want to decide if valid documents are always transformed into valid documents. This question is, however, undecidable since XSLT is a Turing complete language. Approximative tools may be constructed, but, in general, this correctness property must be proven by hand using invariant techniques.

We may also use XSLT to create different *views* of our data. For example, the recipe collection may be transformed into a nutrition table by the following stylesheet:

```
<xsl:stylesheet version="2.0"
                xmlns:rcp="http://www.brics.dk/ixwt/recipes"
                xmlns:xsl="http://www.w3.org/1999/XSL/Transform">

  <xsl:template match="rcp:collection">
    <nutrition>
      <xsl:apply-templates select="rcp:recipe"/>
    </nutrition>
  </xsl:template>

  <xsl:template match="rcp:recipe">
    <dish name="{rcp:title/text()}"
          calories="{rcp:nutrition/@calories}"
          fat="{rcp:nutrition/@fat}"
          carbohydrates="{rcp:nutrition/@carbohydrates}"
          protein="{rcp:nutrition/@protein}"
          alcohol="{if (rcp:nutrition/@alcohol)
                    then rcp:nutrition/@alcohol else '0%'}"/>
  </xsl:template>

</xsl:stylesheet>
```

The output looks as follows:

```
<nutrition>
  <dish name="Beef Parmesan with Garlic Angel Hair Pasta"
        calories="1167"
        fat="23%" carbohydrates="45%" protein="32%" alcohol="0%"/>
  <dish name="Ricotta Pie"
        calories="349"
        fat="18%" carbohydrates="64%" protein="18%" alcohol="0%"/>
  <dish name="Linguine Pescadoro"
        calories="532"
        fat="12%" carbohydrates="59%" protein="29%" alcohol="0%"/>
  <dish name="Zuppa Inglese"
        calories="612"
        fat="49%" carbohydrates="45%" protein="4%" alcohol="2%"/>
  <dish name="Cailles en Sarcophages"
        calories="8892"
        fat="33%" carbohydrates="28%" protein="39%" alcohol="0%"/>
</nutrition>
```

These kinds of data may then be transformed into XHTML using another stylesheet:

```
<xsl:stylesheet version="2.0"
                xmlns="http://www.w3.org/1999/xhtml"
                xmlns:xsl="http://www.w3.org/1999/XSL/Transform">

  <xsl:template match="nutrition">
    <html>
```

```
  <head>
    <title>Nutrition Table</title>
  </head>
  <body>
    <table border="1">
      <tr>
        <th>Dish</th>
        <th>Calories</th>
        <th>Fat</th>
        <th>Carbohydrates</th>
        <th>Protein</th>
      </tr>
      <xsl:apply-templates select="dish"/>
    </table>
  </body>
</html>
  </xsl:template>

<xsl:template match="dish">
  <tr>
    <td><xsl:value-of select="@name"/></td>
    <td align="right"><xsl:value-of select="@calories"/></td>
    <td align="right"><xsl:value-of select="@fat"/></td>
    <td align="right"><xsl:value-of select="@carbohydrates"/></td>
    <td align="right"><xsl:value-of select="@protein"/></td>
  </tr>
</xsl:template>

</xsl:stylesheet>
```

This stylesheet finally generates the output shown in Figure 5.2 when viewed in a browser.

Dish	Calories	Fat	Carbohydrates	Protein
Beef Parmesan with Garlic Angel Hair Pasta	1167	23%	45%	32%
Ricotta Pie	349	18%	64%	18%
Linguine Pescadoro	532	12%	59%	29%
Zuppa Inglese	612	49%	45%	4%
Cailles en Sarcophages	8892	33%	28%	39%

Figure 5.2 XSLT for nutrition tables.

5.11 XSL-FO

XSL-FO is a target language for presenting document-centric XML.

XSLT is designed in combination with XSL-FO, which is just a particular target language reflecting the document-centric origins of the XSL project.

XSL-FO (Formatting Objects) is a language for specifying printed text. Unlike the original HTML language, XSL-FO is entirely oriented toward the physical layout, much like the well-known PDF format.

Contrary to the original ambitions, XSL-FO is not used for publishing data on the Web. Browsers still only provide native support for XHTML and this will likely not change for some time. Eventually, if browsers render XSL-FO directly, then XHTML is relegated to being just another XML language that is translated into XSL-FO by an XSLT stylesheet.

In the general publishing industry, however, XSL-FO is being used intensely as a common intermediate format. Translators from XSL-FO to PDF, PostScript, PCL, SVG, and many other formats are abundantly available.

The XSL-FO language is huge and will not be covered in any detail here. Instead, we will show a small example by generating XSL-FO output for business cards. This generation is accomplished by the following stylesheet:

```
<xsl:stylesheet version="2.0"
                xmlns:xsl="http://www.w3.org/1999/XSL/Transform"
                xmlns:b="http://businesscard.org"
                xmlns:fo="http://www.w3.org/1999/XSL/Format">

  <xsl:template match="b:card">
    <fo:root>
      <fo:layout-master-set>
        <fo:simple-page-master master-name="simple"
                               page-height="5.5cm"
                               page-width="8.6cm"
                               margin-top="0.4cm"
                               margin-bottom="0.4cm"
                               margin-left="0.4cm"
                               margin-right="0.4cm">
          <fo:region-body/>
        </fo:simple-page-master>
      </fo:layout-master-set>
      <fo:page-sequence master-reference="simple">
        <fo:flow flow-name="xsl-region-body">
          <fo:table>
            <fo:table-column column-width="5cm"/>
            <fo:table-column column-width="0.3cm"/>
            <fo:table-column column-width="2.5cm"/>
            <fo:table-body>
              <fo:table-row>
                <fo:table-cell>
                  <fo:block font-size="18pt"
                            font-family="sans-serif"
                            line-height="20pt"
                            background-color="#A0D0FF"
                            padding-top="3pt">
                    <xsl:value-of select="b:name"/>
                  </fo:block>
```

```
            <fo:block font-size="14pt"
                      font-family="sans-serif"
                      line-height="16pt"
                      padding-top="7pt">
              <xsl:value-of select="b:title"/>
            </fo:block>
            <fo:block font-size="12pt"
                      font-family="Courier"
                      line-height="16pt"
                      padding-top="7pt">
              <xsl:value-of select="b:email"/>
            </fo:block>
            <xsl:if test="b:phone">
              <fo:block font-size="14pt"
                        font-family="sans-serif"
                        line-height="16pt"
                        padding-top="7pt">
                <xsl:value-of select="b:phone"/>
              </fo:block>
            </xsl:if>
          </fo:table-cell>
          <fo:table-cell/>
          <fo:table-cell>
            <xsl:if test="b:logo">
              <fo:block>
                <fo:external-graphic src="url({b:logo/@uri})"
                                     content-width="2.5cm"/>
              </fo:block>
            </xsl:if>
          </fo:table-cell>
        </fo:table-row>
      </fo:table-body>
    </fo:table>
   </fo:flow>
  </fo:page-sequence>
 </fo:root>
</xsl:template>

</xsl:stylesheet>
```

With this translation, the example business card is rendered as follows:

5.12   Chapter Summary

The XSL technology is derived from CSS to provide stylesheets for presentations of XML data. CSS selectors are generalized into XSLT and CSS properties are generalized into XSL-FO.

The most interesting part is XSLT, which is a declarative language for programming transformations between XML languages. The central features are pattern matching and computation of sequences. XSLT relies on XPath for selecting nodes to process, pattern matching, and computation of boolean condition and string values.

The XSL-FO language is used for specifying layout of text for presentations of document-centric XML data.

5.13   Further Reading

XSLT is described in many books, but the specification [48], which is available online, is a good place to study the details of the language. The Saxon implementation (see the online resources) is a reference implementation with ample documentation that supports all XSLT 2.0 features.

As for XPath, theoretical aspects of XSLT (mostly 1.0, though) have been investigated in research papers. Formal models and expressiveness of a fragment of XSLT are considered in [7]. A formal semantics of pattern matching is given in [83]. The paper [49] proves that even XSLT 1.0 is Turing complete. Some results on static analysis and type checking of XSLT programs are presented in the papers [80, 30, 62].

5.14   Online Resources

http://www.w3.org/TR/xslt20/
  The XSLT 2.0 working draft specification.

http://saxon.sourceforge.net/
  The Saxon open source XSLT 2.0 processor.

http://www.w3.org/TR/xsl/
  The XSL-FO 1.0 specification.

http://xml.apache.org/fop/
  The Apache XSL-FO processor.

5.15   Exercises

The main lessons to be learned from these exercises are:

- the concepts of template and pattern;

- use of sequence constructors; and
- familiarity with stylesheet programming.

Exercise 5.1 Which of the following XPath expressions are legal patterns?

(a) `child::foo[//bar]`
(b) `/foo//bar/@baz`
(c) `parent::foo/@bar`
(d) `foo[parent::bar]/@baz`

Exercise 5.2 Rewrite the element constructors in the stylesheet *EX*/`elements.xsl` into explicit form.

TIP

XSLT stylesheets may be syntax checked by checking their validity against the XML Schema description of XSLT (see Section 5.2).

Exercise 5.3 Create a new stylesheet for the recipes by changing the XHTML markup to obtain a different look.

TIP

XSLT processing may be performed by most browsers, but beware that they generally only support XSLT 1.0. The Saxon tool implements all XSLT 2.0 features.

Exercise 5.4 Write stylesheets that perform the following transformations on arbitrary XML documents:

(a) Delete all attributes.
(b) Change all character data into upper case.
(c) Add the comment `<!-- foo -->` to the beginning of the contents of every element named `foo`.

Exercise 5.5 Make explicit the built-in template rules in *EX*/`builtin.xsl`.

Exercise 5.6 Use grouping to determine which units are used in the recipe collection, and for each unit which ingredients they are used to measure. The output should look as in *EX*/`units.xml`.

Exercise 5.7 Change the stylesheet for recipe collections to list the recipes in the following order:

- first consider the nesting depth of `ingredient` elements;
- second consider the total number of `ingredient` elements; and
- third consider the number of calories.

Exercise 5.8 Consider your solution to Exercise 2.2. Write a stylesheet transforming driving directions into XHTML.

Exercise 5.9 Extend the stylesheet for recipes in the following three steps:

(a) Make the document begin with a list of the titles of all recipes.
(b) Make the list sorted alphabetically.
(c) Make each title in the list link to the place in the document where the full recipe appears.

Exercise 5.10 Write a stylesheet that outputs `Version 1.0` when executed by an XSLT 1.0 processor, but outputs `Version 2.0` when executed by an XSLT 2.0 processor.

Exercise 5.11 The *LIX value* of a text is defined to be the average length of sentences plus the percentage of words with 7 or more letters. Write a stylesheet that uses the `analyze-string` mechanism to compute the LIX value of the text in an XHTML document.

QUERYING XML DOCUMENTS WITH XQUERY

6

Objectives

In this chapter, you will learn:

- How XML generalizes relational databases
- The XQuery language
- How XML may be supported in relational databases

6.1   Querying XML Documents

An ambitious application of XML documents aims at generalizing the traditional relational model of databases. The actual generalization is fairly straightforward, as we shall see. The main challenge lies in extending the query language correspondingly, thus inventing an XML analog of the popular SQL query language.

XML documents naturally generalize database relations. **XQuery** is the corresponding generalization of SQL.

There are several reasons why a merger of XML and databases is attractive. For XML developers, the creation of XML languages is akin to data modeling in databases, only with fewer constraints on the data format. Thus, there is an immediate desire to extract information directly from these richer models. In the database community, there has been a long quest for a richer data model to replace the plain relational tables, but little consensus has been reached. Some of the earlier suggestions have been *hierarchical databases*, *object-oriented databases*, and *multi-dimensional databases* that all seek in different ways to extend the relational data model. XML is a tempting alternative, since we have previously seen that XML may describe both data-oriented and document-oriented information (see Section 2.5). Thus, it directly offers a richer data model that includes many aspects of the previous proposals; however, XML comes with a ready-made consensus. Another strategic advantage for the database community is that if XML is the future of the World Wide Web and XML becomes the future of databases, then in the future the World Wide Web will simply become one gigantic database.

6.1.1   From Relations to Trees

XML queries are easily motivated by observing that XML documents generalize relational tables in a surprisingly obvious manner (readers unfamiliar with databases may safely skip this section). A few pictures should be sufficient to get the point across. A table could typically look as follows:

people(firstname,lastname,age)

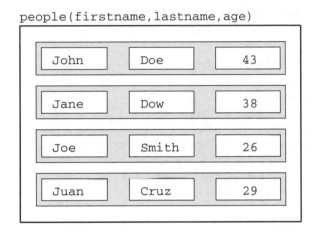

Here, we have a table with four *records*, each containing three *fields*, corresponding to first names, last names, and ages of some people. Relational database tables are often drawn like this, but we may, in fact, just as well draw them as trees:

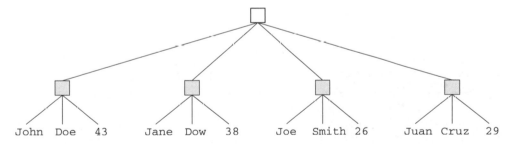

In this version, the table itself corresponds to the root of the tree, the records correspond to the nodes in the layer just below, and the fields are present as the leaves of the tree. Clearly, this representation is an embedding of the table view: we can translate a table into a tree and back again without loss of information.

The potential generalization of XML documents is now immediate: relational tables correspond to *some* trees, while XML documents correspond to *all* trees. In fact, we can quite precisely characterize those trees that correspond to tables:

- they have height two (meaning they have three layers of nodes);

- the root has an unbounded number of child nodes; and

- all nodes in the second layer (the records) have a fixed number of child nodes (corresponding to the fields).

Note that the reverse embedding is not immediately possible for several reasons:

- not all trees satisfy the above characterization; and

- trees are *ordered*, while both rows and columns of tables may be permuted without changing the meaning of the data.

Why then, do we want to use general trees? As we are now familiar with XML technology, the answer may seem obvious, but from a database point of view, we are about to perform an interesting generalization.

Consider again the example of *student records*, where we store information about the student id, name, age, major, and exam results of students. These first four data fit well into the relational model, since they just become four fields in a record. However, the number of exam results is not fixed, which requires a less intuitive structure. Things are further complicated by the possibility of double majors. A typical relational representation of such data would involve a number of tables:

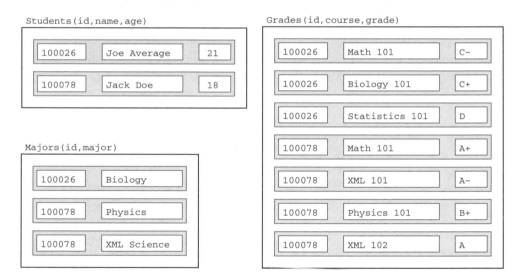

If student records correspond to XML documents, we achieve a more natural data model, collecting all information locally in one document (as we saw in Section 5.3.1):

```
<students>
   <student id="100026">
      <name>Joe Average</name>
      <age>21</age>
      <major>Biology</major>
```

```
                <results>
                  <result course="Math 101" grade="C-"/>
                  <result course="Biology 101" grade="C+"/>
                  <result course="Statistics 101" grade="D"/>
                </results>
            </student>
            <student id="100078">
                <name>Jack Doe</name>
                <age>18</age>
                <major>Physics</major>
                <major>XML Science</major>
                <results>
                  <result course="Math 101" grade="A"/>
                  <result course="XML 101" grade="A-"/>
                  <result course="Physics 101" grade="B+"/>
                  <result course="XML 102" grade="A"/>
                </rcsults>
            </student>
        </students>
```

Of course, this document is just one possible model. Note that XML schemas are named
after database schemas since they are meant to be generalizations. For the above example,
the database schema looks as follows in SQL:

```
CREATE TABLE Students (
  id INTEGER NOT NULL,
  name CHAR(30),
  age SMALLINT NOT NULL,
  PRIMARY KEY (id)
);

CREATE TABLE Grades (
  id INTEGER NOT NULL,
  course CHAR(30) NOT NULL,
  grade CHAR(2) NOT NULL
);
ALTER TABLE Grades FOREIGN KEY (id) REFERENCES Students;

CREATE TABLE Majors (
  id INTEGER NOT NULL,
  major CHAR(30) NOT NULL
);
ALTER TABLE Majors FOREIGN KEY (id) REFERENCES Students;
```

The following is an XML Schema definition of the corresponding XML version:

```
<xsd:schema xmlns:xsd="http://www.w3.org/2001/XMLSchema"
            elementFormDefault="qualified">
```

```
<xsd:element name="students">
  <xsd:complexType>
    <xsd:sequence>
      <xsd:element name="student"
                   minOccurs="0" maxOccurs="unbounded">
        <xsd:complexType>
          <xsd:sequence>
            <xsd:element name="name" type="xsd:string"/>
            <xsd:element name="age" type="xsd:integer"/>
            <xsd:element name="major" type="xsd:string"
                         maxOccurs="unbounded"/>
            <xsd:element name="results">
              <xsd:complexType>
                <xsd:sequence>
                  <xsd:element name="result"
                               minOccurs="0" maxOccurs="unbounded">
                    <xsd:complexType>
                      <xsd:attribute name="course"
                                     type="xsd:string"/>
                      <xsd:attribute name="grade"
                                     type="Grade"/>
                    </xsd:complexType>
                  </xsd:element>
                </xsd:sequence>
              </xsd:complexType>
            </xsd:element>
          </xsd:sequence>
          <xsd:attribute name="id" type="xsd:string" use="required"/>
        </xsd:complexType>
      </xsd:element>
    </xsd:sequence>
  </xsd:complexType>
  <xsd:key name="student-id">
    <xsd:selector xpath="student"/>
    <xsd:field xpath="@id"/>
  </xsd:key>
</xsd:element>

<xsd:simpleType name="Grade">
  <xsd:restriction base="xsd:string">
    <xsd:enumeration value="A"/>
    <xsd:enumeration value="A-"/>
    <xsd:enumeration value="B+"/>
    <xsd:enumeration value="B"/>
    <xsd:enumeration value="B-"/>
    <xsd:enumeration value="C+"/>
    <xsd:enumeration value="C"/>
    <xsd:enumeration value="C-"/>
    <xsd:enumeration value="D+"/>
```

```
        <xsd:enumeration value="D"/>
        <xsd:enumeration value="D-"/>
        <xsd:enumeration value="F"/>
      </xsd:restriction>
    </xsd:simpleType>
  </xsd:schema>
```

While certain similarities are obvious, the XML Schema version is seen to be more expressive (and verbose).

6.1.2 Usage Scenarios

It is quite easy to envision usage scenarios for a hypothetical query language on general XML documents. These relate to the rough classification of XML languages that we discussed in Section 2.5.

For *data-oriented* languages, like the above XML representation of student records, we wish to carry over the kinds of queries that we performed in the original relational model. Thus, we need to be able to transform data into new XML representations, and to integrate data from multiple heterogeneous data sources.

For *document-oriented* languages, queries could be used to retrieve parts of documents, to provide dynamic indexes, to perform context-sensitive searching, and to generate new documents as combinations of existing documents. In fact, these tasks have long been studied in the area called *information retrieval*, dating back to the 1960s. The need for intelligent manipulation of vast amounts of ordinary documents is made clear by the success of search engines, which presently do not employ anything as advanced as a full query language, but basically just uses string matching.

For *protocols* and *programming* languages, examples are less natural, but queries could be used to automatically generate documentation, similarly to the Javadoc tool.

For *hybrid* languages, the situation is even more intriguing. These are documents of which parts are data-oriented and other parts are human-readable and less structured. The archetypical example is a hospital record for a patient. It contains some highly structured data, like prescriptions for medication, billing information, blood pressure measurements, and such. Other data is much less structured, like notes from doctors and nurses or background interviews. An interesting query might span both of these: *find those patients who experienced a sudden rise in blood pressure following a certain post-operative medication and where the GP has previously noted that the patient probably drinks too much.*

Once the idea of performing XML queries has been suggested, ideas for possible applications are easy to come by.

6.2   The XQuery Design

The XQuery language has been designed with very specific goals in mind. The working group identified several technical requirements, of which the most important were that the language

- must be able to *transform* and *create* XML trees and make it possible to *combine* information from multiple documents;

- must be *declarative*;

- must be *namespace aware*;

- must be *coordinated* with XML Schema and support *simple* and *complex* datatypes; and

- must have at least one *XML syntax* and at least one *human-readable syntax*.

Underlying most of these requirements is a desire to maintain the flavor of SQL and generalize its expressive power to XML documents.

XQuery is designed to **generalize** SQL, as XML generalizes database tables.

Note that XQuery, unlike XSLT, will not only have an XML syntax. In fact, XQuery is supposed to be programmed in a syntax that is similar to that of SQL. This choice is partly a practical consideration, since XML syntax is rather verbose and can be hard to read, and to a large extent a tactical consideration, since the transition from SQL to XQuery will then be vastly simpler for database programmers. A similar choice has been made for the schema language RELAX NG, which also offers a non-XML syntax as an alternative (see Section 4.6.5).

Also note that XQuery is tied to the XML Schema language – other schemas languages are not considered here.

The development of XQuery followed a number of independent research projects that each made attempts to solve the fundamental problem of generalizing SQL to arbitrary XML trees. The most important examples were XML-QL, YATL, Lorel, and Quilt, whose proponents are strongly represented in the XQuery working group. While these languages turned out very different and looked nothing alike with respect to syntax, it became apparent that they describe very similar computational models. This situation seems to indicate that the design of a generalized query language could be more canonical than perhaps previously suspected.

6.2.1 Relationship to XPath

All the early prototypes of query languages contained mechanisms for pointing at sets or sequences of nodes in XML trees. This observation was influential in identifying the need for the XPath language. Furthermore, it has been the driving force behind the design of XPath 2.0.

The XQuery 1.0 language is designed to be a strict superset of the XPath 2.0 language. That is, every XPath 2.0 expression is directly an XQuery 1.0 expression (a query). We have already seen that many XPath expressions feel like queries, in that they extract fairly complicated information from XML documents. In fact, the only thing that XQuery needs beyond the expressive power of XPath is the ability to *join* information from different sources and to *generate* new XML fragments. Also, XQuery introduces *user-defined* functions and thus permits arbitrary computations. (In contrast, XPath allows *implementation-defined* functions, where specific implementations may extend the function library.)

6.2.2   Relationship to XSLT

XQuery and XSLT seem to share many ambitions, as they both are domain-specific languages for combining and transforming XML data from multiple sources. They are vastly different in design, partly for historical reasons. While XQuery is designed from scratch with inspiration from SQL, XSLT is an intellectual descendant of CSS (see Section 1.5) and has developed for a long time. Technically, they actually have different fortes. XSLT is exceedingly good for defining complicated recursive traversals and transformations to arbitrary depths of XML documents, where XQuery must use explicit recursion of user-defined functions. Conversely, XQuery has more the flavor of a database programming language and allows simple solutions for simple problems, where XSLT may be more verbose.

It is argued that XSLT is soon deprecated and should be replaced by XQuery. Apart from the huge amount of legacy code to consider, XSLT is, however, still the simplest choice for many applications. Also, XSLT already has several very efficient implementations, while the general design of XQuery seems to pose more of a challenge. Thus, both languages will most likely be around for a while yet.

When raw expressive power is considered, XQuery and XSLT are surprisingly evenly matched, as shown in Section 6.6. However, while the languages may emulate each other, they each display a lack of elegance when doing so – emphasizing that domain-specific syntax is a valuable asset.

6.3   The Prolog

Like XPath expressions, XQuery expressions are evaluated relatively to a *context*, which is explicitly provided by a *prolog* defining several different aspects.

Some declarations specify various parameters for the XQuery processor. The `version` declaration defines the chosen version of the XQuery language:

```
xquery version "1.0";
```

At the time of writing, this is the only version that exists.

The `boundary-space` declaration decides whether boundary whitespace in element constructors (see Section 6.4.3) is preserved or stripped. The two simple possibilities are

```
declare boundary-space preserve;
```

and

```
declare boundary-space strip;
```

The following declaration defines default namespaces for unprefixed XML elements (see Section 6.4.3):

```
declare default element namespace URI;
```

Namespaces for unprefixed function names are declared similarly:

```
declare default function namespace URI;
```

Since it is always possible to syntactically distinguish functions from elements in XQuery expressions, it makes sense to employ two default namespaces. This overloading would of course not be possible if XQuery used an XML syntax. The declaration

```
declare namespace prefix = URI;
```

declares the given URI as a namespace with the given prefix (see Section 2.6). Having multiple declarations of the same namespace prefix is an error, and no namespace prefix can be called xmlns. The following declarations are implicitly defined in any XQuery implementation:

```
declare namespace xml =
    "http://www.w3.org/XML/1998/namespace";
declare namespace xs =
    "http://www.w3.org/2001/XMLSchema";
declare namespace xsi =
    "http://www.w3.org/2001/XMLSchema-instance";
declare namespace fn =
    "http://www.w3.org/2005/04/xpath-functions";
declare namespace xdt =
    "http://www.w3.org/2005/04/xpath-datatypes";
```

Of these, only the xml prefix cannot be redefined. The declaration

```
import schema at URI;
```

imports the schema (written in XML Schema) that is located at URI. The variation

```
import schema namespace prefix = URI₁ at URI₂;
```

imports the schema that is located at URI_2 and specifies a prefix for its namespace URI_1. The declaration

```
declare variable $name := exp;
```

declares a new variable with the given name (a QName) and the result of the given expression as initial value. Only the part of the prolog that precedes this declaration can be used when evaluating the expression or defining any namespace prefix in the name.

Function declarations are explained in Section 6.5. All the functions mentioned in Section 3.5.11 are implicitly defined with the appropriate signatures.

6.4 Expressions

XQuery 1.0 is an extension of XPath 2.0. This means that any XPath expression is also an XQuery expression, which makes sense since we already noticed that such expressions could be used to extract information from XML documents. XQuery furthermore extends XPath with the ability to operate on arbitrary datatypes defined in XML Schema (see Section 6.4.2), to construct new XML fragments (see Section 6.4.3), and to join information from different XML documents (see Section 6.4.3).

XQuery 1.0 imposes one restriction compared to XPath 2.0, since only the axes `child`, `descendant`, `parent`, `attribute`, `self`, and `descendant-or-self` are required to be implemented (presumably to enable *streaming* implementations, see Section 7.6).

Values in XQuery are similar to those for XPath 2.0: sequences of nodes and atomic values. However, for XQuery we consider more atomic values, as explained in Section 6.4.2.

6.4.1 XPath Expressions

XPath expressions are required to be evaluated in a static context (see Section 3.2.1), which must be provided by the invoking application. The XQuery prolog contains all the required information, except for the initial context node, position, and size. Since an XQuery expression does not work on a single XML document, these values are chosen to be initially undefined. Instead, the `fn:doc()` function and path expressions are used to define the current context node, position, and size. Accessing an undefined value by an XPath expression causes a runtime error.

> XQuery expressions extend XPath expressions with operations for **constructing** and **joining** XML data.

6.4.2 Datatype Expressions

In Chapter 3 on XPath we only considered a simple collection of atomic values, consisting of integers, booleans, decimals, floats, doubles, and strings. However, both XPath 2.0 and XQuery 1.0 allow all simple types defined in imported schemas (see Section 4.4.2) to be used as atomic values.

These values are denoted using constructor functions that correspond to the type names. A constructor function accepts a single Unicode string as argument and constructs the corresponding value of the given type, yielding a runtime error if the string is not a value of the type. In particular, the primitive simple values shown in Section 4.4.2 are constructed as follows (where `xs` is as defined in Section 6.3):

```
xs:string("XML is fun")
xs:boolean("true")
xs:decimal("3.1415")
xs:float("6.02214199E23")
xs:double("42E970")
xs:duration("P1Y2M3DT10H30M")
```

```
xs:dateTime("2004-09-26T16:29:00-05:00")
xs:time("16:29:00-05:00")
xs:date("2004-09-26")
xs:gYearMonth("2004-09")
xs:gYear("2004")
xs:gMonthDay("--09-26")
xs:gDay("--26")
xs:gMonth("--09")
xs:hexBinary("48656c6c6f0a")
xs:base64Binary("SGVsbG8K")
xs:anyURI("http://www.brics.dk/ixwt/")
xs:QName("rcp:recipe")
```

Corresponding to these types of atomic values, numerous functions and operators are defined as documented in

```
http://www.w3.org/TR/xpath-functions/
```

It is also possible to construct atomic values corresponding to simple types in imported schemas. For example, the following expression is legal:

```
import schema namespace rcp = "http://www.brics.dk/ixwt/recipes"
    at "http://www.brics.dk/ixwt/examples/recipes.xsd";
rcp:percentage("55%")
```

Functions operating on user-defined atomic types can be defined as explained in Section 6.5.

6.4.3   XML Expressions

XQuery expressions may compute new XML nodes, which is a major extension compared to the XPath subset. Specifically, expressions may denote nodes of the following kinds: element, attribute, character data, comment, and processing instruction. Each time such an expression is evaluated, it dynamically creates a new node with a unique node identity. (Technically speaking, XQuery is not a *purely* functional language, since expressions thus have side-effects!) Element constructors may be either *direct* or *computed*.

Direct element constructors use the standard XML syntax. Thus, the expression

```
<p><hr/>mushroom</p>
```

evaluates to an XML fragment with a p root element whose contents are an empty hr element and the character data mushroom. The fact that nodes are created with unique identity is seen from the expression

```
<banana/> is <banana/>
```

which evaluates to false (the operator is is defined in Section 3.5.9). The namespaces of nodes are given by the prolog, either through declared namespace prefixes or through the

---

declared default namespace (see Section 6.3). It is also possible to use the standard XML namespace declarations (see Section 2.6). Thus, the expressions

```
declare default element namespace "http://businesscard.org";
<card>
  <name>John Doe</name>
  <title>CEO, Widget Inc.</title>
  <email>john.doe@widget.inc</email>
  <phone>(202) 555-1414</phone>
  <logo uri="widget.gif"/>
</card>
```

and

```
declare namespace b = "http://businesscard.org";
<b:card>
  <b:name>John Doe</b:name>
  <b:title>CEO, Widget Inc.</b:title>
  <b:email>john.doe@widget.inc</b:email>
  <b:phone>(202) 555-1414</b:phone>
  <b:logo uri="widget.gif"/>
</b:card>
```

and

```
<card xmlns="http://businesscard.org">
  <name>John Doe</name>
  <title>CEO, Widget Inc.</title>
  <email>john.doe@widget.inc</email>
  <phone>(202) 555-1414</phone>
  <logo uri="widget.gif"/>
</card>
```

all have the same effect (if ignoring the choice of prefixes).

Often, XML expressions are not constant as in the above examples. Instead, the constructors are used to create wrappers around other computed contents. Such computation is made possible through the syntax for *enclosed* expressions:

```
{ exp }
```

These may occur in the contents of an element constructor. This syntax, of course, means that the character { now has a special significance and must itself be represented as

```
"&#123;"
```

using the XML-style character entities. An enclosed expression is evaluated and the resulting sequence is converted into XML contents by transforming each item as follows:

- maximal adjacent sequences of atomic values are converted into a single character data node whose content is the string obtained by converting each atomic value to a string using the `xs:string` function (described in Section 6.4.2) and separating these strings with single space characters; and

- each node is converted into a copy of the subtree that it roots, such that every constituent node has a new, unique node identity.

(This is admittedly quite complicated!) If the `boundary-space` declaration has value `strip` (see Section 6.3), then each string obtained from atomic values is stripped of boundary whitespace, and if the resulting character data string consists only of whitespace, then no node is created. As an example, the following expressions

```
<numbers>1 2 3 4 5</numbers>

<numbers>{1, 2, 3, 4, 5}</numbers>

<numbers>{1, "2", 3, 4, 5}</numbers>

<numbers>{1 to 5}</numbers>

<numbers>1 {1+1} {" "} {"3"} {" "} {4 to 5}</numbers>
```

will all create an element named `numbers` whose contents is a single character data node with value `1 2 3 4 5` provided that `boundary-space` is set to `strip`.

Enclosed expressions are also allowed inside attribute values. For example, the expression

```
<note value="2+2 is {2+2}"/>
```

has the same effect as the constant

```
<note value="2+2 is 4"/>
```

In general, the enclosed expression evaluates to a sequence of items which is converted to a string as follows:

- if the sequence is empty, then the result is the empty string;

- otherwise, the sequence is first atomized (see Section 3.5.1);

- each atomic value is then converted to a string using the `xs:string` function; and

- the resulting strings are concatenated, separated by a single space character.

An alternative syntax allows both element and attribute names to be computed as well. First, the syntax can be made more explicit. The constant expression

```
<card xmlns="http://businesscard.org">
  <name>John Doe</name>
  <title>CEO, Widget Inc.</title>
  <email>john.doe@widget.inc</email>
  <phone>(202) 555-1414</phone>
  <logo uri="widget.gif"/>
</card>
```

may instead be written as follows:

```
element card {
  namespace { "http://businesscard.org" },
  element name { text { "John Doe" } },
  element title { text { "CEO, Widget Inc." } } ,
  element email { text { "john.doe@widget.inc" } },
  element phone { text { "(202) 555-1414" } },
  element logo {
    attribute uri { "widget.gif" }
  }
}
```

In the next step of generalization, the qualified names for elements and attributes may be replaced by enclosed expressions evaluating to equivalent strings:

```
element { "card" } {
  namespace { "http://businesscard.org" },
  element { "name" } { text { "John Doe" } },
  element { "title" } { text { "CEO, Widget Inc." } },
  element { "email" } { text { "john.doe@widget.inc" } },
  element { "phone" } { text { "(202) 555-1414" } },
  element { "logo" } {
    attribute { "uri" } { "widget.gif" }
  }
}
```

In particular, these names may then be computed by non-constant expressions. Suppose that we want to generate bilingual business cards, using markup in either Danish or English, governed by a global variable $lang. The code could then look as follows:

```
element { if ($lang="Danish") then "kort" else "card" } {
  namespace { "http://businesscard.org" },
  element { if ($lang="Danish") then "navn" else "name" }
    { text { "John Doe" } },
```

```
element { if ($lang="Danish") then "titel" else "title" }
  { text { "CEO, Widget Inc." } },
element { "email" }
  { text { "john.doe@widget.inc" } },
element {if ($lang="Danish") then "telefon" else "phone" }
  { text { "(202) 456-1414" } },
element { "logo" } {
  attribute { "uri" } { "widget.gif" }
}
}
```

In Danish mode, this expression would produce the following result:

```
<kort xmlns="http://businesscard.org">
  <navn>John Doe</navn>
  <titel>CEO, Widget Inc.</titel>
  <email>john.doe@widget.inc</email>
  <telefon>(202) 555-1414</telefon>
  <logo uri="widget.gif"></logo>
</kort>
```

6.4.4 FLWOR Expressions

The full generality of a database query language is obtained through the introduction of the
FLWOR expression (pronounced *flower*) which allows information to be restructured and
joined. It generalizes the `for` expression from XPath.

For
Let
Where
Order
Return

A FLWOR expression generally uses a mixture of `for` and `let` clauses to generate a
sequence of ordered tuples of variable bindings, one binding for each clause. This sequence
is then filtered by a boolean expression in a `where` clause. The remaining sequence is then
ordered according to an `order` clause. For each tuple of bindings in the given order, an
expression in a `return` clause is then evaluated, each resulting in a sequence. The final
result is the concatenation of those sequences.

As a simple example, consider the student records from Section 6.1.1. The following
query finds the names of students with double majors:

```
for $s in fn:doc("students.xml")//student
let $m := $s/major
where fn:count($m) ge 2
order by $s/@id
return <double>
         { $s/name/text() }
       </double>
```

The `for` clause iterates through the `student` elements in the XML document. Each occurrence results in a binding of the `$s` variable to that element node. The `let` clause finds

for each such binding the sequence of `major` elements it contains and then creates a single binding of that sequence to the `$m` variable. We have now created binding tuples of the form (`$s, $m`). The sequence of such tuples is now filtered by the `where` clause which only retains those tuples in which the sequence bound to `$m` has length at least 2. The `order` clause orders the remaining sequence of tuples by the `id` attribute of the element bound to `$s`. Finally, a sequence of `double` elements containing the names of students is created as the result of the entire FLWOR expression.

If we wanted the expression to produce an XML document as output, rather than merely a sequence of nodes, then we could wrap the entire FLWOR expression in an XML constructor to ensure that a singleton sequence containing a complete XML tree is constructed:

```
<doubles>
  { for $s in fn:doc("students.xml")//student
    let $m := $s/major
    where fn:count($m) ge 2
    order by $s/@id
    return <double>
              { $s/name/text() }
           </double>
  }
</doubles>
```

For the tiny example document from Section 6.1.1, the result is as follows:

```
<doubles>
  <double>
     Jack Doe
  </double>
</doubles>
```

To illustrate the differences between `for` and `let` bindings, we consider four different variations of a FLWOR expression. The version

```
for $x in (1, 2)
let $y := ("a", "b", "c")
return ($x, $y)
```

generates the output

```
1, a, b, c, 2, a, b, c
```

The variation

```
let $x := (1, 2)
for $y in ("a", "b", "c")
return ($x, $y)
```

generates the output

```
1, 2, a, 1, 2, b, 1, 2, c
```

The variation

```
for $x in (1, 2)
for $y in ("a", "b", "c")
return ($x, $y)
```

generates the output

```
1, a, 1, b, 1, c, 2, a, 2, b, 2, c
```

Finally, the variation

```
let $x := (1, 2)
let $y := ("a", "b", "c")
return ($x, $y)
```

generates the output

```
1, 2, a, b, c
```

Each `for` or `let` clause may refer to variables that are bound in earlier clauses, enabling classical join operations between XML documents. As a simple example, consider the following XML document, `fridge.xml`, describing the contents of a refrigerator:

```
<fridge>
  <stuff>eggs</stuff>
  <stuff>olive oil</stuff>
  <stuff>ketchup</stuff>
  <stuff>unrecognizable moldy thing</stuff>
</fridge>
```

In preparation for making dinner, we now want to compute the subset of recipes that use at least *some* of the ingredients in our refrigerator:

```
declare namespace rcp = "http://www.brics.dk/ixwt/recipes";
for $r in
  fn:doc("http://www.brics.dk/ixwt/recipes/recipes.xml")//rcp:recipe
for $i in $r//rcp:ingredient/@name
for $s in fn:doc("fridge.xml")//stuff[text()=$i]
return fn:distinct-values($r/rcp:title/text())
```

Here, we first declare the appropriate namespace prefix `rcp`. The three `for` clauses generate binding tuples of the form (`$r`, `$i`, `$s`), where `$r` is a `recipe` with an `ingredient` `$i` and `$s` is some `stuff` in the fridge with the same name as `$i`. For each such tuple it is relevant to output the `title` text of `$r`. To avoid duplicates we then apply the `fn:distinct-values` function to get the final result:

```
"Beef Parmesan with Garlic Angel Hair Pasta",
"Ricotta Pie",
"Linguine Pescadoro"
```

As another example, we could turn the recipe collection inside out and produce an XML document that for each ingredient lists the recipes in which it is used:

```
declare namespace rcp = "http://www.brics.dk/ixwt/recipes";
<ingredients>
  { for $i in
      distinct-values(fn:doc("recipes.xml")//rcp:ingredient/@name)
    return <ingredient name="{$i}">
              { for $r in fn:doc("recipes.xml")//rcp:recipe
                where $r//rcp:ingredient[@name=$i]
                return <title>$r/rcp:title/text()</title>
              }
           </ingredient>
  }
</ingredients>
```

(For brevity, we here assume that the recipe collection resides in a local file.) The outer `for` clause generates an `ingredient` element for each distinct `name`. The inner `for` clause generates the list of recipe titles corresponding to recipes that use the given ingredient. The output looks like this:

```
<ingredients>
  <ingredient name="beef cube steak">
    <title>Beef Parmesan with Garlic Angel Hair Pasta</title>
  </ingredient>
  <ingredient name="onion, sliced into thin rings">
    <title>Beef Parmesan with Garlic Angel Hair Pasta</title>
  </ingredient>
  <ingredient name="butter">
    <title>Beef Parmesan with Garlic Angel Hair Pasta</title>
    <title>Cailles en Sarcophages</title>
  </ingredient>
  ...
</ingredients>
```

Suppose that we in the above example want ingredients ordered by name and recipes ordered by title. We could then modify the expression as follows:

```
declare namespace rcp = "http://www.brics.dk/ixwt/recipes";
<ingredients>
  { for $i in
      distinct-values(fn:doc("recipes.xml")//rcp:ingredient/@name)
    order by $i
    return <ingredient name="{$i}">
              { for $r in fn:doc("recipes.xml")//rcp:recipe
                where $r//rcp:ingredient[@name=$i]
                order by $r/rcp:title/text()
                return <title>$r/rcp:title/text()</title>
              }
           </ingredient>
  }
</ingredients>
```

The `order` clause may be quite involved, allowing descending or ascending orders, and specifying several ordering specifications that define a lexicographic order. To show the full generality, consider the task of listing students in order of academic merits. To evaluate these merits, we first consider the number of 'A' grades received. In case of a tie, we then consider the number of majors pursued. In case of another tie, we consider the age, where younger is better. This ordering is expressed by the following expression:

```
for $s in document("students.xml")//student
order by
  fn:count($s/results/result[fn:contains(@grade,"A")]) descending,
  fn:count($s/major) descending,
  xs:integer($s/age/text()) ascending
return $s/name/text()
```

Note that we cast the age to an integer to obtain the desired sorting criterion; without this cast, the values would be compared lexicographically as strings.

As mentioned earlier, many expressions produce sequences that are in document order, like `union`, `except`, and all path expressions. FLWOR expressions by default produce sequences that are in the natural order specified by the `for` clauses. XQuery contains the construction

unordered { *exp* }

which computes the value of *exp* but makes the order of the resulting sequence depend on the implementation. This construction is just meant for optimizations, allowing the XQuery engine to pick an efficient ordering strategy.

6.5   Defining Functions

XQuery allows the definition of ordinary *functions*, much like in XSLT. These are declared in the prolog (see Section 6.3) using the syntax

```
declare function name ( $x₁, $x₂, ..., $xₖ ) { exp } ;
```

where the function name is a QName and $k \geq 0$. Inside *exp*, the variables x_i are visible. Function calls correspondingly have the syntax

```
name ( exp₁, exp₂, ..., expₖ )
```

and, as expected, the values of the actual arguments are bound to formal arguments, the body of the function is evaluated, and the result is the value of the function call.

Functions may be convenient, as illustrated by the following example which computes grade point averages of students:

```
declare function grade($g) {
  if ($g="A") then 4.0 else if ($g="A-") then 3.7
  else if ($g="B+") then 3.3 else if ($g="B")  then 3.0
  else if ($g="B-") then 2.7 else if ($g="C+") then 2.3
  else if ($g="C")  then 2.0 else if ($g="C-") then 1.7
  else if ($g="D+") then 1.3 else if ($g="D")  then 1.0
  else if ($g="D-") then 0.7 else 0
};

declare function gpa($s) {
  fn:avg(for $g in $s/results/result/@grade return grade($g))
};

<gpas>
  { for $s in fn:doc("students.xml")//student
    return <gpa id="{$s/@id}" gpa="{gpa($s)}"/>
  }
</gpas>
```

For the tiny document from Section 6.1.1, the result is as follows:

```
<gpas>
  <gpa id="100026" gpa="1.666666666666666667"></gpa>
  <gpa id="100078" gpa="3.75"></gpa>
</gpas>
```

Functions may also, however, be used to extend the expressive power of XQuery. While XPath expressions may be used to probe deeply into XML documents, the FLWOR expressions by themselves can only generate output with bounded tree height. Thus, certain transformations are only possible with the use of recursive functions. As a simple example, consider the following recursive function which generates an XML tree of a given height:

```
declare function gen($n) {
  if ($n eq 0) then <bar/>
  else <foo>{ gen($n -1), gen($n -1) }</foo>
};
```

Dually, the following function computes the height of a given XML tree (which is 8 for the recipe collection):

```
declare function height($x) {
  if (fn:empty($x/*)) then 1
  else fn:max(for $y in $x/* return height($y))+1
};
```

A more unusual example of recursion produces an outline of the recipe collection that looks as follows for a single recipe:

```
Cailles en Sarcophages
  pastry
    chilled unsalted butter
    flour
    salt
    ice water
  filling
    baked chicken
      marinated chicken
        small chickens, cut up
        Herbes de Provence
        dry white wine
        orange juice
        minced garlic
        truffle oil
      stock
        chicken wings, giblets, and kidney
        onions, peeled
        carrots, peeled and cut lengthwise
        celery, cut lengthwise
        bay leaf
        small bunch parsley
        whole peppercorns
        salt
    sauteed mushrooms
      white button mushrooms
      butter
```

```
          dry white wine
          minced garlic
          minced shallots
        sauce
          chicken juices
          mushroom juices
          sherry
          flour
          butter
      package phyllo dough
      egg whites, lightly beaten
```

The code for this example is special, since it generates plain text as its output.

```
declare namespace rcp = "http://www.brics.dk/ixwt/recipes";

declare function ingredients($i,$p) {
  fn:string-join(
    for $j in $i/rcp:ingredient
    return fn:string-join(
      ($p,$j/@name,"&#x0A;",
      ingredients($j,fn:concat($p,"  "))),
      ""),
    "")
};

declare function recipes($r) {
  fn:concat($r/rcp:title/text(),"&#x0A;",
            ingredients($r,"  "))
};

fn:string-join(
  for $r in fn:doc("http://www.brics.dk/ixwt/recipes/recipes.xml")
            //rcp:recipe[5]
  return recipes($r),
  ""
)
```

Note that the use of XML-style Unicode character references (like
 for the newline character) is permitted inside string literals, even though XQuery is not an XML language.

6.6   XQuery versus XSLT ★

We present some examples demonstrating how XQuery and XSLT may emulate each other. This study is mainly a theoretical exercise in comparing their expressiveness. Each language

XQuery and XSLT may **emulate** each other but are designed for different tasks.

should be used for the applications where they excel: XSLT for stylesheet-like transformation of document-centric XML, and XQuery for query-like transformations of data-centric XML.

6.6.1   Emulating XSLT in XQuery

XQuery has the same expressive power as XSLT and may in theory replace it completely, but it is often simpler to express certain XML transformations in XSLT since its support for pattern matching and recursive traversals may be cumbersome to emulate in XQuery. Recall the small stylesheet for business cards from Section 5.1:

```
<xsl:stylesheet version="2.0"
    xmlns:xsl="http://www.w3.org/1999/XSL/Transform"
    xmlns:b="http://businesscard.org"
    xmlns="http://www.w3.org/1999/xhtml">

  <xsl:template match="b:card">
    <html>
      <head>
        <title><xsl:value-of select="b:name/text()"/></title>
      </head>
      <body bgcolor="#ffffff">
        <table border="3">
          <tr>
            <td>
              <xsl:apply-templates select="b:name"/><br/>
              <xsl:apply-templates select="b:title"/><p/>
              <tt><xsl:apply-templates select="b:email"/></tt><br/>
              <xsl:if test="b:phone">
                Phone: <xsl:apply-templates select="b:phone"/><br/>
              </xsl:if>
            </td>
            <td>
              <xsl:if test="b:logo">
                <img src="{b:logo/@uri}"/>
              </xsl:if>
            </td>
          </tr>
        </table>
      </body>
    </html>
  </xsl:template>

  <xsl:template match="b:name|b:title|b:email|b:phone">
    <xsl:value-of select="text()"/>
  </xsl:template>

</xsl:stylesheet>
```

This stylesheet can be transformed quite systematically into an equivalent XQuery version, by translating each template rule into a function that accepts as argument the current node that has been selected. The body of this function then returns the template contents, making explicit calls in place of `apply-templates`. For the business card example, the resulting expression looks as follows:

```
declare namespace b = "http://businesscard.org";

declare function t-card($x) {
  <html>
    <head>
      <title> { $x/b:name/text() } </title>
    </head>
    <body bgcolor="#ffffff">
      <table border="3">
        <tr>
          <td>
            { t-name($x/b:name) }
            { t-title($x/b:title) }
            <tt>{ t-email($x/b:email) }</tt><br/>
            { if ($x/b:phone)
              then (text{ "Phone:" },
                    t-phone($x/b:phone),
                    element br {()})
              else ()
            }
          </td>
          <td>
            { if ($x/b:logo)
              then element img { attribute src { $x/b:logo/@uri } }
              else ()
            }
          </td>
        </tr>
      </table>
    </body>
  </html>
};

declare function t-name($x)  { $x/text() };
declare function t-title($x) { $x/text() };
declare function t-email($x) { $x/text() };
declare function t-phone($x) { $x/text() };

t-card(fn:doc("card.xml")/b:card)
```

This expression is probably not as legible as the XSLT version, and if pattern matching or recursive traversals are used in a more advanced manner, then the behavior becomes much more difficult to capture since the complete pattern matching algorithm must then be encoded in XQuery.

6.6.2   Emulating XQuery in XSLT

XQuery expressions can also be expressed in XSLT, even if the result is often more verbose (partly because of the XML syntax).

Consider the following simple XQuery expression, which lists the titles of all recipes:

```
declare namespace rcp = "http://www.brics.dk/ixwt/recipes";
<titles>
  { for $t in fn:doc("recipes.xml")//rcp:title
    return $t
  }
</titles>
```

An equivalent XSLT stylesheet is the following:

```
<xsl:stylesheet version="2.0"
    xmlns:xsl="http://www.w3.org/1999/XSL/Transform"
    xmlns:rcp="http://www.brics.dk/ixwt/recipes">

  <xsl:template match="/">
    <titles>
      <xsl:for-each select="doc('recipes.xml')//rcp:title">
        <xsl:copy-of select="."/>
      </xsl:for-each>
    </titles>
  </xsl:template>

</xsl:stylesheet>
```

This stylesheet ignores its source document and instead uses the document function to access the recipe collection. The outermost template just matches the document root node to initiate the transformation.

As another example, consider the following XQuery expression which finds the recipes that use flour and returns their titles in a special format:

```
declare namespace rcp = "http://www.brics.dk/ixwt/recipes";
<floury>
  { for $r in
      fn:doc("recipes.xml")//
      rcp:recipe[.//rcp:ingredient[@name="flour"]]
    return <dish>{$r/rcp:title/text()}</dish>
  }
</floury>
```

The output of this query is:

```
<floury>
  <dish>Ricotta Pie</dish>
  <dish>Zuppa Inglese</dish>
  <dish>Cailles en Sarcophages</dish>
</floury>
```

The following is an equivalent XSLT stylesheet:

```
<xsl:stylesheet version="2.0"
    xmlns:xsl="http://www.w3.org/1999/XSL/Transform"
    xmlns:rcp="http://www.brics.dk/ixwt/recipes">

  <xsl:template match="/">
    <floury>
      <xsl:for-each
          select="doc('recipes.xml')//
                       rcp:recipe[.//rcp:ingredient[@name='flour']]">
        <dish>
          <xsl:value-of select="./rcp:title/text()"/>
        </dish>
      </xsl:for-each>
    </floury>
  </xsl:template>

</xsl:stylesheet>
```

Again, we notice the similarity of the structures of the two versions.

Next, recall the XQuery expression from Section 6.4.4, which joins the recipe collection with the contents of a refrigerator:

```
declare namespace rcp = "http://www.brics.dk/ixwt/recipes";
for $r in fn:doc("recipes.xml")//rcp:recipe
for $i in $r//rcp:ingredient/@name
for $s in fn:doc("fridge.xml")//stuff[text()=$i]
return $r/rcp:title/text()
```

An equivalent XSLT stylesheet is the following:

```
<xsl:stylesheet version="2.0"
    xmlns:xsl="http://www.w3.org/1999/XSL/Transform"
    xmlns:rcp="http://www.brics.dk/ixwt/recipes">

  <xsl:template match="/">
    <xsl:for-each select="doc('recipes.xml')//rcp:recipe">
      <xsl:variable name="r" select="."/>
      <xsl:for-each select=".//rcp:ingredient/@name">
        <xsl:variable name="i" select="."/>
        <xsl:for-each select="doc('fridge.xml')//stuff[text()=$i]">
```

```
            <xsl:value-of select="$r/rcp:title/text()"/>
          </xsl:for-each>
        </xsl:for-each>
      </xsl:for-each>
    </xsl:template>

</xsl:stylesheet>
```

Note how the XSLT variable mechanism is used to provide names for the iterants. This approach works for translating arbitrary FLWOR expressions.

Finally, consider the XQuery expression for listing students in order of academic merits:

```
for $s in document("students.xml")//student
order by
  fn:count($s/results/result[fn:contains(@grade,"A")]) descending,
  fn:count($s/major) descending,
  xs:integer($s/age/text()) ascending
return $s/name/text()
```

An equivalent XSLT stylesheet is the following:

```
<xsl:stylesheet version="2.0"
    xmlns:xsl="http://www.w3.org/1999/XSL/Transform"
    xmlns:rcp="http://www.brics.dk/ixwt/recipes">

  <xsl:template match="/">
    <xsl:for-each select="doc('students.xml')//student">
      <xsl:sort select=
                "count(./results/result[contains(@grade,'A')])"
                order="descending"/>
      <xsl:sort select="count(./major)" order="descending"/>
      <xsl:sort select="xs:integer(./age/text())"
                order="ascending"/>
      <xsl:value-of select="./name/text()"/>
    </xsl:for-each>
  </xsl:template>

</xsl:stylesheet>
```

We see that beneath the surface syntax, XSLT and XQuery are quite similar – in part because they are both built around the already quite expressive XPath language.

6.7   The Type System ★

From a programming language point of view, XQuery can be characterized as follows:

- it is *functional* (but not *purely* functional, since node creation expressions have side-effects as explained in Section 6.4.3);

- it is *first-order*, since functions are not themselves values; and

- is is *typed*, since expressions may be type checked.

This section describes the type system of XQuery and its use in programming. Normally, type systems for first-order functional languages are quite simple and undramatic. However, XQuery has an unusually rich collection of datatypes and must interface with XML Schema which further complicates matters.

6.7.1   Sequence Types

Types in XQuery describe the possible values: sequences of nodes and atomic values. Type expressions are generated by the following grammar:

```
SequenceType  →   empty-sequence() | ItemType | ItemType Occurs
Occurs        →   ? | * | +
ItemType      →   item() | SimpleType | NodeType
NodeType      →   node()
                | element()
                | element(QName)
                | element(QName, ComplexType)
                | element(*, ComplexType)
                | schema-element(QName)
                | attribute()
                | attribute(QName)
                | attribute(QName, SimpleType)
                | attribute(*, SimpleType)
                | schema-attribute(QName)
                | text()
                | comment()
                | processing-instruction()
```

Here, a *SimpleType* is as described in Section 6.4.2 and a *ComplexType* is similarly a complex type mentioned in one of the imported schemas (see Section 6.3). The `empty-sequence()` type describes only the empty sequence; `item()` describes any single atomic value or node; the `element`, `schema-element`, `attribute`, and `schema-attribute` types describes various sets of element and attribute nodes; `text()` describes a character data node; `comment()` describes a comment node; and `processing-instruction()` describes a processing instruction node – the exact definitions are given in Section 6.7.3. The use of ?, *, and + is, of course, a restricted form of regular expressions (see Section 4.2). An example of a type generated by this grammar is

```
schema-element(rcp:ingredient)+
```

which describes non-empty sequences of (validated) `ingredient` elements from the recipe collection.

6.7.2   Validation and Dynamic Types

The `fn:doc` function returns an XML tree that is not validated. Thus, the schema types of nodes and atomic values are unknown to the XQuery engine. It is possible, however, to request that an XML tree is validated. The expression

validate { *exp* }

validates the XML tree rooted by the node that results from evaluating *exp*. This validation requires that the XQuery prolog imports a schema (see Section 6.3) for the root element. Specifically, the `validate` expression returns a new XML tree which is a copy of the original in which defaults have been inserted and whitespace normalization has been performed (see Section 4.4.9). Additionally, every node and atomic value has been given a *dynamic type* corresponding to the validation. Note that no XML nodes created within XQuery will have associated type information, unless the `validate` construction is explicitly used.

Technically, the element nodes and atomic values of unvalidated XML are given the types `xdt:untyped` and `xdt:untypedAtomic`. In this case, atomization is performed as described in Section 3.5.1 and every atomic value is converted into a string. For validated XML, however, XQuery performs *typed atomization*, in which atomic values are converted into instances of the datatypes corresponding to their dynamic types (see Section 6.4.2). For example, the expression

```
fn:doc("recipes.xml")//
rcp:recipe[rcp:title="Ricotta Pie"]/rcp:nutrition/@protein
```

yields an instance of the datatype `xs:string`, whereas the expression

```
validate{fn:doc("recipes.xml")}//
rcp:recipe[rcp:title="Ricotta Pie"]/rcp:nutrition/@protein
```

yields an instance of the datatype `rcp:percentage`. The impact of validation on query optimization is not yet fully understood.

6.7.3   Type Matching

XQuery types describe sets of values. Thus, given a sequence value, which has been assigned a dynamic type as above, we may ask whether or not it is described by a given sequence type. This property, called *type matching*, is defined as follows:

- `empty-sequence()` matches only the empty sequence;

- `ItemType` matches a singleton sequence whose item is matched by the `ItemType`;

- `ItemType?` matches the empty sequence or a singleton sequence whose item is matched by `ItemType`;

- `ItemType*` matches any sequence in which all items are matched by `ItemType`;

- `ItemType+` matches any non-empty sequence in which all items are matched by `ItemType?`;

- `item()` matches any single item (atomic value or node);

- `SimpleType` matches any item whose type is (derived from) the given type;

- `node()` matches any node;

- `element()` matches any element node;

- `element(QName)` matches any element node with the given name;

- `element(QName, ComplexType)` matches any element node with the given name and whose type is (derived from) the given type;

- `element(*, ComplexType)` matches any element node whose type is (derived from) the given type;

- `schema-element(QName)` matches any element node with the given name and with the type associated to that name;

- `attribute()` matches any attribute node;

- `attribute(QName)` matches any attribute node with the given name;

- `attribute(QName, SimpleType)` matches any attribute node with the given name and whose type is (derived from) the given type;

- `attribute(*, ComplexType)` matches any attribute node whose type is (derived from) the given type;

- `schema-attribute(QName)` matches any attribute node with the given name and with the type associated to that name;

- `text()` matches any text node;

- `comment()` matches any comment node; and

- `processing-instruction()` matches any processing instruction node.

In the above, the notion of *derived from* refers to extensions, restrictions, and substitution groups as explained in Section 4.4.8. Note that the sequence type

```
item()*
```

matches any sequence value. XQuery may test the matching relationship at runtime, as the boolean expression

exp **instance of** *SequenceType*

decides if the result of *exp* is matched by *SequenceType*. The concepts of sequence types and matching can then be illustrated by the following expressions, which all evaluate to true:

```
2 instance of xs:integer

2 instance of item()

2 instance of xs:integer?

() instance of empty-sequence()

() instance of xs:integer?

() instance of xs:integer*

(1,2,3,4) instance of xs:integer*

(1,2,3,4) instance of xs:integer+

<foo/> instance of item()

<foo/> instance of node()

<foo/> instance of element()

<foo/> instance of element(foo)

<foo bar="baz"/> instance of element(foo)

<foo bar="baz"/>/@bar instance of attribute()

<foo bar="baz"/>/@bar instance of attribute(bar)

fn:doc("recipes.xml")//rcp:ingredient instance of element()+

fn:doc("recipes.xml")//rcp:ingredient
instance of element(rcp:ingredient)+

fn:doc("recipes.xml")//rcp:ingredient
instance of schema-element(rcp:ingredient)+

fn:doc("recipes.xml")//rcp:step/text() instance of text()*

validate {fn:doc("recipes.xml")}//@protein
instance of attribute(*,rcp:percentage)+
```

6.7.4   Type Annotations and Type Errors

Sequence types may also be used to provide annotations for variables in `for` and `let` expressions, function arguments, and function results. The syntax for such annotations is

as *SequenceType*

which applies to variable declarations, function arguments, and function results. If no type annotations are provided, the type is by default

```
item()*
```

which does not impose any constraints on the allowed values. Thus, the function

```
declare function grade($g) {
  if ($g="A") then 4.0 else if ($g="A-") then 3.7
  else if ($g="B+") then 3.3 else if ($g="B")  then 3.0
  else if ($g="B-") then 2.7 else if ($g="C+") then 2.3
  else if ($g="C")  then 2.0 else if ($g="C-") then 1.7
  else if ($g="D+") then 1.3 else if ($g="D")  then 1.0
  else it ($g="D-") then 0.7 else 0
};
```

has the default type annotations

```
declare function grade($g as item()*) as item()* {
  if ($g="A") then 4.0 else if ($g="A-") then 3.7
  else if ($g="B+") then 3.3 else if ($g="B")  then 3.0
  else if ($g="B-") then 2.7 else if ($g="C+") then 2.3
  else if ($g="C")  then 2.0 else if ($g="C-") then 1.7
  else if ($g="D+") then 1.3 else if ($g="D")  then 1.0
  else if ($g="D-") then 0.7 else 0
};
```

which, by adding explicit type annotations, could be sharpened into

```
declare function grade($g as xs:string) as xs:decimal {
  if ($g="A") then 4.0 else if ($g="A-") then 3.7
  else if ($g="B+") then 3.3 else if ($g="B")  then 3.0
  else if ($g="B-") then 2.7 else if ($g="C+") then 2.3
  else if ($g="C")  then 2.0 else if ($g="C-") then 1.7
  else if ($g="D+") then 1.3 else if ($g="D")  then 1.0
  else if ($g="D-") then 0.7 else 0
};
```

Similarly, the following function has precise type annotations:

```
declare function grades($s as element(students))
        as attribute(grade)* {
  $s/student/results/result/@grade
};
```

Type annotations are checked during runtime, thus a runtime type error is provoked when

- an actual argument value does not match the declared type;
- a function result value does not match the declared type; or
- a value assigned to a variable does not match the declared type.

All built-in functions and operators may be viewed as functions with appropriate signatures, such as

```
fn:contains($x as xs:string?, $y as xs:string?) as xs:boolean
```

and

```
op:union($x as node()*, $y as node()*) as node()*
```

Thus, many runtime errors (excluding things like division by zero) are uniformly described as type errors in the above sense. Note that op is a fake namespace prefix that is used in the XQuery specification to describe operators as functions.

6.7.5   Static Type Checking

Dynamic types catch errors at runtime, **static** types catch errors at compile time.

XQuery implementations may support a *type checking* analysis that at compile time decides if a type error may occur at runtime. This is a potentially useful feature that is well-known from other languages, such as Java, but it has not been tested in practice for XQuery yet.

The property in question is naturally undecidable (as for Java), so the analysis must be approximative and is usually *conservative*, meaning that if an XQuery expression is permitted by the static type checker, then type errors are guaranteed not to occur at runtime. Note that not all runtime errors are characterized as type errors; for example, division by zero and errors from treat as (see below) will not be caught by a static type checker.

XQuery specifies an analysis algorithm but allows specific implementations to be less approximative. The analysis uses *type inference*, which computes a type for every subexpression of a query.

Sequence types are not expressive enough to describe these types with any reasonable precision. Instead, the type inference algorithm uses a richer language of types to describe sets of intermediate values with greater accuracy. A general type looks as follows (slightly simplified):

```
Type         →    empty
                  | none
                  | SimpleType
                  | element QName
                  | element QName of type Type
                  | attribute QName
                  | attribute QName of type Type
                  | text
                  | comment
                  | processing-instruction
                  | TypeName
                  | Type Occurs
                  | Type | Type
                  | Type , Type
                  | Type & Type
SimpleType   →    QName
Occurs       →    ? | * | +
```

The additional expressive power comes from the type none, which describes the empty set of values, and the three type operators, which have the following meaning:

- $Type_1$ | $Type_2$ describes the union of the sequences described by $Type_1$ and $Type_2$;

- $Type_1$, $Type_2$ describes the concatenation of the sequences described by $Type_1$ and $Type_2$; and

- $Type_1$ & $Type_2$ describes all interleavings (see Section 4.6.1) of the sequences described by $Type_1$ and $Type_2$.

The *TypeName* refers to a named definition of another type describing the contents of the element or attribute. As a major extension, types are allowed to be defined using mutually recursive type equations (with limitations similar to those for RELAX NG patterns, see Section 4.6.1). Thus, the extended types can describe XML trees. For example, the type

```
type Genealogy = element person of (
                    attribute name of xs:string,
                    (element mother of Genealogy)?,
                    (element father of Genealogy)?
                 )
```

describes simple family trees, such as the following:

```
<person name="Jack Doe">
  <mother>
    <person name="Jane Dow"/>
```

```
    </mother>
    <father>
      <person name="John Doe>
        <father>
          <person name="Zacharias Doe/>
        </father>
      </person>
    </father>
  </person>
```

The extended types are so expressive that they can capture the essential meaning of XML Schema types. They are similar to RELAX NG grammars (see Section 4.6) and they are directly inspired by the type system of the XDuce language (see Section 7.7.1). XQuery supports a translation from XML Schema into extended types that, however, does not handle features such as

- facets on simple types;

- attribute and element normalization; and

- keys and references.

While the set of XML trees accepted by the extended type is close to the set of those expressible by XML Schema, the two sets are technically incomparable. However, the parts of XML Schema that deal with the structure of elements and their contents are soundly captured by extended types.

For the type inference algorithm, all information about XML trees is then represented by extended types. As an example, the schema for recipes (see Section 4.4.11) is represented as follows:

```
type Collection = element rcp:collection of (Description, Recipe*)
type Description = element rcp:description of text
type Recipe = element rcp:recipe of (
                 element rcp:title of text,
                 element rcp:date of text,
                 Ingredient*,
                 Preparation,
                 (element comment of text)?,
                 Nutrition,
                 Related*
              )
type Ingredient = element rcp:ingredient of (
                    attribute name of xs:string,
                    (attribute amount of xs:string)?,
                    (attribute unit of xs:string)?,
                    Ingredient*,
                    Preparation
                  )
```

```
type Preparation = element rcp:preparation of (element step of text)*
type Nutrition   = element rcp:nutrition of (
                     attribute calories of rcp:nonNegativeDecimal,
                     attribute protein of rcp:percentage,
                     attribute carbohydrates of rcp:percentage,
                     attribute fat of rcp:percentage,
                     (attribute alcohol of rcp:percentage)?
                   )
type Related = element rcp:related of (
                 attribute ref of xs:string,
                 text
               )
```

Note that facets restrictions on simple types are ignored.

The type inference algorithm works by recursively traversing the parse tree of an XQuery expression and assigning an extended type to each subexpression. The computation of inferred types is rather complicated and will not be described here.

Once these *static types* have been computed, it is a simple matter to test if they will cause type errors in the sense of Section 6.7.4. Being conservative, the type checker will certainly reject some expressions that do not cause actual type errors during runtime. The static type checking in XQuery is unsupported by most implementations and its practical precision is as yet untested.

If a particular expression is unfairly rejected by the static type checker, then a possibility is to use the construction

exp **treat as** *SequenceType*

which instructs the type checker to use the *SequenceType* as the static type of the expression (like casts in Java). A runtime error will then occur if the resulting value turns out not to be matched by the given type. Similarly, XQuery support functions such as fn:exactly-one, which causes a runtime error unless its argument is a sequence of length one – and allows the static type checker to assume that the resulting type is a singleton sequence.

Note that the type inference algorithm is not strong enough to provide static guarantees about the overall behavior of an XQuery expression. Consider for example a query that transforms recipe collections into XHTML documents, each described by their respective schemas. Since the translation from XML Schema to extended types is not complete, the type inference algorithm will not be able to guarantee that the possible output documents are valid according to the XML Schema description of XHTML. Even so, many programming errors will be caught early by a static type checker.

6.8   XQueryX

The XQuery language designers have chosen to use an SQL-like syntax. However, the original W3C XQuery design requirements also demand that an XML syntax is provided.

This requirement has resulted in the XQueryX language, which is simply a straightforward XML representation of XQuery syntax trees. The main use will supposedly be for supplying a default parser for XQuery and a data format for storing and optimizing queries. The XQueryX syntax is voluminous, as evidenced by the tiny query

```
for $t in fn:doc("recipes.xml")/rcp:collection/rcp:recipe/rcp:title
return $t
```

which in XQueryX is represented as the following document:

```
<xqx:module
     xmlns:xqx="http://www.w3.org/2003/12/XQueryX"
     xmlns:xsi="http://www.w3.org/2001/XMLSchema-instance"
     xsi:schemaLocation="http://www.w3.org/2003/12/XQueryX
                         xqueryx.xsd">
  <xqx:mainModule>
    <xqx:queryBody>
      <xqx:expr xsi:type="xqx:flwrExpr">
          <xqx:forClause>
            <xqx:forClauseItem>
              <xqx:typedVariableBinding>
                <xqx:varName>t</xqx:varName>
              </xqx:typedVariableBinding>
              <xqx:forExpr>
                <xqx:expr xsi:type="xqx:pathExpr">
                  <xqx:expr xsi:type="xqx:functionCallExpr">
                    <xqx:functionName>doc</xqx:functionName>
                    <xqx:parameters>
                      <xqx:expr xsi:type="xqx:stringConstantExpr">
                        <xqx:value>recipes.xml</xqx:value>
                      </xqx:expr>
                    </xqx:parameters>
                  </xqx:expr>
                  <xqx:stepExpr>
                    <xqx:xpathAxis>child</xqx:xpathAxis>
                    <xqx:elementTest>
                      <xqx:nodeName>
                        <xqx:QName>rcp:collection</xqx:QName>
                      </xqx:nodeName>
                    </xqx:elementTest>
                  </xqx:stepExpr>
                  <xqx:stepExpr>
                    <xqx:xpathAxis>child</xqx:xpathAxis>
                    <xqx:elementTest>
                      <xqx:nodeName>
                        <xqx:QName>rcp:recipe</xqx:QName>
                      </xqx:nodeName>
                    </xqx:elementTest>
```

```
              </xqx:stepExpr>
              <xqx:stepExpr>
                <xqx:xpathAxis>child</xqx:xpathAxis>
                <xqx:elementTest>
                  <xqx:nodeName>
                    <xqx:QName>rcp:title</xqx:QName>
                  </xqx:nodeName>
                </xqx:elementTest>
              </xqx:stepExpr>
            </xqx:expr>
          </xqx:forExpr>
        </xqx:forClauseItem>
      </xqx:forClause>
      <xqx:returnClause>
        <xqx:expr xsi:type="xqx:variable">
          <xqx:name>t</xqx:name>
        </xqx:expr>
      </xqx:returnClause>
    </xqx:expr>
  </xqx:elementContent>
    </xqx:expr>
  </xqx:queryBody>
  </xqx:mainModule>
</xqx:module>
```

Evidently, this syntax is not intended to be written nor read by humans.

6.9   XML Databases

The term *XML database* may be interpreted in many different ways. Most commercial database products claim to support XML in some manner, but the variations are significant.

Existing relational database technology has been developed for more than 40 years and has achieved impressive results in areas such as optimization, security, concurrency, transactions, indexing, and recovery. In contrast, current implementations of native XQuery engines do not scale to large commercial applications, but they are lightweight and easy to extend with new XML features. For the foreseeable future, hybrid implementations must try to achieve the best of both worlds.

> For large applications, XML must be **integrated** into relational databases.

6.9.1   XML Publishing

In the simplest level of XML support, the relational database merely publishes XML views of relational data. Suppose our database contains the three relations Students, Majors, and `Grades` shown in Section 6.1.1. An automatic XML view of the `Students` relation could look like

```
<Students>
  <record id="100026" name="Joe Average" age="21"/>
  <record id="100078" name="Jack Doe" age="18"/>
</Students>
```

or using a different strategy:

```
<Students>
  <record>
    <id>100026</id>
    <name>Joe Average</name>
    <age>21</age>
  </record>
  <record>
    <id>100078</id>
    <name>Jack Doe</name>
    <age>18</age>
  </record>
</Students>
```

Most database systems support some way of dumping existing relational data in some (possibly user-defined) XML format. This approach, however, still employs the relational data model and leaves no room for the real power of XQuery.

The SQL/XML language is an extension of SQL that allows construction of XML data as the results of SQL queries. Thus, the above publishing strategies (and many more) can be expressed as queries in SQL/XML. For example, the first strategy is implemented by the SQL/XML query

```
xmlelement(name, "Students",
   SELECT xmlelement(name, "record",
                       xmlattributes(s.id, s.name, s.age))
   FROM Students
)
```

and the second strategy by this one:

```
xmlelement(name, "Students",
   SELECT xmlelement(name, "record", xmlforest(s.id, s.name, s.age))
   FROM Students
)
```

6.9.2 XML Shredding

A more ambitious approach is to store general XML documents in a relational database, where they may benefit from the existing database technology. This process is called *XML shredding* and can be done in different manners. We will present a simple construction:

- each element type is represented by a relation;
- each element node is assigned a unique key in document order;
- each element node contains the key of its parent;
- the possible attributes are represented as fields, where absent attributes have the `null` value; and
- content consisting of a single character data node is inlined as a field.

Using this particular algorithm, which obviously requires knowledge of the schema for the XML language in question, the recipe collection is represented as follows:

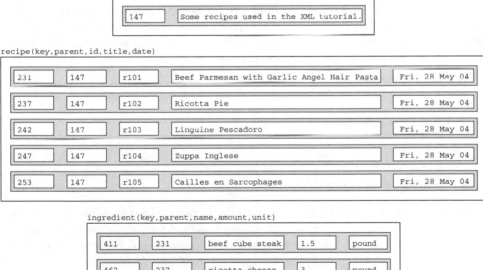

```
collection(key,description)
```

| 147 | Some recipes used in the XML tutorial. |

```
recipe(key,parent,id,title,date)
```

231	147	r101	Beef Parmesan with Garlic Angel Hair Pasta	Fri, 28 May 04
237	147	r102	Ricotta Pie	Fri, 28 May 04
242	147	r103	Linguine Pescadoro	Fri, 28 May 04
247	147	r104	Zuppa Inglese	Fri, 28 May 04
253	147	r105	Cailles en Sarcophages	Fri, 28 May 04

```
ingredient(key,parent,name,amount,unit)
```

411	231	beef cube steak	1.5	pound
462	237	ricotta cheese	3	pound
535	247	egg yolks	4	null
612	253	pastry	null	null
789	612	flour	3	cup

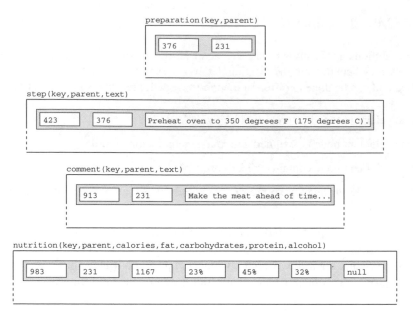

preparation(key,parent)

376   231

step(key,parent,text)

423   376   Preheat oven to 350 degrees F (175 degrees C).

comment(key,parent,text)

913   231   Make the meat ahead of time...

nutrition(key,parent,calories,fat,carbohydrates,protein,alcohol)

983   231   1167   23%   45%   32%   null

Clearly, any XML document can be faithfully represented in this manner and take advantage of the existing database implementation. However, queries must now be phrased in ordinary SQL rather than XQuery, but it turns out that an automatic translation is possible for any query. For example, the simple XQuery expression

```
//rcp:ingredient[@name="butter"]/@amount
```

is translated into the following SQL query:

```
SELECT ingredient.amount
FROM ingredient
WHERE ingredient.name="butter"
```

In the above shredding algorithm, we encoded the document order using the key attributes (*global* ordering). However, this simple strategy makes it difficult to evaluate predicates based on the position() function. As a remedy, we may add a field that explicitly stores the position of an element among its siblings (*local* ordering). In any case, translations of queries into SQL become much more complex for general XQuery expressions. As a further complication, the shredding algorithm and the translation algorithm influence each other and must be correlated to obtain high performance.

There is, in fact, a spectrum of possibilities. The approach shown above represents one extreme where all XML data is shredded. Another option is shredding that retains *fine* XML fragments, observing that it is not always necessary or practical to shred every bit of XML. Instead, small irregular XML fragments may be stored as character data in records (VARCHAR). A typical case would be XHTML help texts, where the shredding would be simplified and the subsequent performance improved by not considering the several dozen element types in XHTML. An alternative is shredding with *coarse* XML fragments, where larger XML fragments are stored as external character data (CLOB). In both cases, such XML fragments could be directly queried using native XQuery engines.

It is certainly possible that relational databases in time will be replaced by industrial strength native XML databases, but this development requires new advances in the underlying implementation technologies. As the shredding strategies discussed here indicate, there seems to be no silver bullet to the problem of storing XML data in relational databases while permitting efficient queries.

6.10   Full-Text Searching

XQuery is currently being extended with constructions for full-text searching. These features are relevant for document-oriented or hybrid languages, where character data nodes are used extensively for weakly structured information. The research area of *information retrieval* has for decades studied how to query text documents, and XQuery Full-Text applies these results to broaden the scope of XQuery.

XQuery is extended in two manners: a new class of boolean ftcontains expressions is added, and the FLWOR expression is extended with a score clause.

The left-hand argument of an ftcontains expression is a sequence expression that must return a sequence of element nodes. The text to be searched consists of the character data nodes appearing anywhere below these nodes. This character data is then tokenized into *words*, *sentences*, and *paragraphs*, providing the context for the evaluation of a full-text search.

The right-hand argument of an ftcontains expression is a specification written in a domain-specific language for expressing text search criteria. This sublanguage has it own (non-XML) syntax, and is not really related to the rest of XQuery. It includes boolean combinations of substring matching modified by weights, distances, and scoping (with respect to sentences and paragraphs). In addition, the searches may during matching ignore cases and diacritics, perform stemming of words, and perform thesaurus lookups.

As a simple example, the following full-text query looks for recipes whose preparation (probably) involves chopping onions:

```
for $r in fn:doc("recipes.xml")//rcp:recipe
where $r//rcp:preparation ftcontains
    ("chop" with stemming
            with default thesaurus ) &&
    ("onion" || "onions")
    distance at most 5 words
    case insensitive
return $r
```

This search criterion matches such different phrases as

- chop the onions
- start chopping that tasty onion

- the onions must be finely chopped

- slice and dice your onion

assuming that dice is a synonym for chop in the default thesaurus.

Each match is given a *score*, which is a value between 0 and 1. These scores can be accessed using the novel score clause in FLWOR expressions. A typical use is the following, where we want to rank the recipes according to how likely they are to involve chopping onions:

```
for $r in fn:doc("recipes.xml")//rcp:recipe
score $s as $r//rcp:preparation ftcontains
    ("chop" with stemming
            with default thesaurus ) &&
    (("onion" weight 0.8) || "onions")
    distance at most 5 words
    case insensitive
where $s > 0
order by $s descending
return $r
```

Note that we have influenced the computed scores by adding a slightly lower weight to the single-onion case.

6.11 Chapter Summary

XML trees generalize relational tables in a natural manner. XQuery is the corresponding generalization of SQL, which is obtained by extending XPath 2.0 with a richer notion of datatypes (inherited from XML Schema), XML constructors, and the FLWOR expressions that allow joins through nested iterations.

XQuery has the same expressive power as XSLT, but the two languages specialize in expressing different kinds of tasks. XQuery excels at query-like transformations of data-centric XML and XSLT at stylesheet-like transformations of document-centric XML.

XQuery has a type system which allows it to exploit the extra information available in validated XML. A static type checking algorithm may enable XQuery implementations to catch many type errors before they occur at runtime.

We have briefly studied the relationship between XQuery and relational databases, and we have seen how XQuery may be extended to support full-text searches.

6.12 Further Reading

XQuery is being developed by W3C [10]. The book [16] provides a detailed presentation of the XQuery language, its type system, and the relationship to databases. The book [18] contains detailed discussions of native XML databases and XML-enabled relational database systems. There are also numerous research papers on these issues; see for example [28, 33, 34]. The relation between XQuery and XSLT is examined in the papers [37, 55].

Unlike SQL, XQuery does not yet support updates, but the requirements for this functionality have been published as a W3C working draft [17]. The paper [32] considers also other future developments of XQuery. The tool Galax, which is a popular reference implementation of XQuery, is described in the paper [31] (see also the online resources below). A Java API for XQuery, XQJ, is under development; see [59].

6.13   Online Resources

`http://www.w3.org/TR/xquery/`
The XQuery 1.0 working draft specification.

`http://www.w3.org/TR/xquery-use-cases`
A collection of XQuery 1.0 use cases.

`http://www.w3.org/TR/xquery-semantics/`
The formal semantics of XQuery 1.0, which explains the type checking algorithm.

`http://www.w3.org/TR/xpath-functions`
The collection of available functions in XPath 2.0 and XQuery 1.0.

`http://www.galaxquery.org/`
The Galax reference implementation of XQuery 1.0 (also includes a variant with full-text searching).

`http://www.w3.org/XML/Query`
The W3C main page on XQuery, with lots of other resources.

`http://sqlx.org/`
The SQL/XML project.

`http://www.w3.org/TR/xquery-full-text/`
The XQuery 1.0 Full-Text working draft specification.

`http://www.rpbourret.com/xml/XMLDBLinks.htm`
An extensive collection of links to material on XML and databases.

6.14   Exercises

The main lessons to be learned from these exercises are:

- expressing (typed) queries in XQuery; and
- representing XML documents in relational databases.

Exercise 6.1 Rewrite the constant expression in *EX*/constant.xq to use explicit element and attribute constructors.

Exercise 6.2 Write queries computing the following results for the recipe collection:

   (a)   For each recipe, the total number of simple ingredients.
   (b)   The titles of recipes with ingredients nested to a depth of at least 2.
   (c)   The recipes that use more butter than olive oil.

TIP

Use the Galax tool to execute XQuery expressions.

Exercise 6.3 Consider your solution to Exercise 2.11. Write a query that finds the longest straight part of the journey.

Exercise 6.4 Consider the collection of business cards in *EX*/cardlist.xml and the list of domain names in *EX*/domains.xml. Write an expression that selects the subset of business cards whose email addresses use only the given domains.

Exercise 6.5 A generic *genealogy* tree looks as described in *EX*/genealogy.xml. Write a (recursive) function mkgen(n) that generates a genealogy tree of height n.

Exercise 6.6 Consider the XSLT stylesheet *EX*/xslt2xquery.xsl. Write a query that has the same effect.

Exercise 6.7 Translate the query in *EX*/xquery2xslt.xq into an equivalent XSLT stylesheet.

Exercise 6.8 For each of the following sequence types, write an expression whose value is matched:

   (a)   `attribute(*,xs:integer)+`
   (b)   `element(foo)`
   (c)   `empty-sequence()?`
   (d)   `element()?*+`

Exercise 6.9 Consider the function in *EX*/untyped.xq. Add type annotations that are as sharp as possible.

Exercise 6.10 Discuss different approaches to representing *EX*/shreddable.xml in relational databases. For each approach, consider how to evaluate the following queries:

   (a)   `//fruit[@taste="sweet"]`
   (b)   `//dessert[.//fruit]`
   (c)   `//fruit[not(ancestor::dessert)]`

7 XML PROGRAMMING

Objectives

In this chapter, you will learn:

- How XML data may be manipulated from general-purpose programming languages using DOM and JDOM
- How data binding is used for mapping from schemas to programming languages
- How streaming with SAX or STX may be useful for handling large documents
- How XML may be integrated into novel programming languages

7.1 Programming with XML Documents

The preceding chapters have presented domain-specific languages for performing computations on XML:

- the schema languages are used for applications that validate and normalize XML data;
- the XSLT language is used for applications that transform document-centric XML; and
- the XQuery language is used for applications that transform data-centric XML.

All of these languages further use the XPath language for computing sequences of nodes in XML trees. However, many computations on XML cannot be handled using such languages. Examples are tools that are specific to the application domain of the given XML language (like a 3D rotating molecule visualizer for the Chemical Markup Language) or a novel generic tool (like a processor for the next domain-specific language for XML).

Thus, at some stage we will need to write programs that operate on XML documents using a general-purpose programming language. Since an XML file is simply represented as a sequence of Unicode characters, this is, in principle, possible in any ordinary programming language, like Java or C++. However, XML is a nontrivial data format and higher-level primitives could be a significant help. In fact, for writing a program manipulating XML documents, we need primitives for the following tasks:

- *parsing* XML documents into XML trees;

- *navigating* through XML trees;

- *manipulating* XML trees; and

- *serializing* XML trees as textual XML documents.

The following sections consider various approaches to providing support for this problem.

We first consider DOM and JDOM, which provide general APIs for representing arbitrary XML documents as internal data structures. Next, we look at data binding, exemplified by JAXB, which translates from XML Schema to Java class models and hides most details from the programmer. We then consider streaming approaches, which is essential for processing large XML documents that cannot be represented in memory. The SAX framework provides a general API for streaming XML, while STX is a domain-specific language for writing streaming versions of XSLT transformations. We conclude by looking at type-safe XML programming, where XML schemas are integrated into the programming language and the compilers guarantee validity of the generated XML documents. XDuce exemplifies this for functional languages, while XACT is a type-safe extension of Java.

7.2   The DOM API

A basic solution to supporting XML programming is to provide an internal data structure that represents XML trees. One example of such a data structure is the *DOM (Document Object Model)* from W3C, which is a *language neutral* API for manipulating XML trees.

DOM is an API for XML that is **common** to several languages.

This project has grown out of the popular DOM for ECMAScript (JavaScript), which provides an API for accessing the document being rendered by a browser. The W3C DOM is still meant to be used for this situation, so it also covers features like event handling and CSS stylesheets, which we will not consider here. From an XML point of view, the relevant features are the basic tree model and support for XPath, DTD, and XML Schema. DOM is designed to be a vehicle for implementing all kinds of XML applications.

The language neutrality of W3C DOM is realized by writing the API in the *OMG Interface Definition Language*, which is a generic formalism for specifying interfaces of object-oriented implementations. Any programming language offering an implementation of the DOM must then supply a *language binding*, which translates these interfaces into native syntax. The W3C DOM specification contains normative language bindings for Java and ECMAScript.

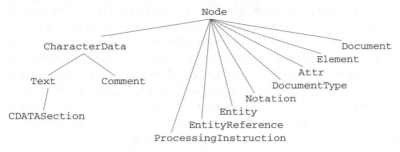

Figure 7.1 Interfaces in DOM.

Any data structure representing XML trees must decide upon a level of *abstraction*. A natural choice seems to be the XPath data model (see Section 2.3) that we have used so far. However, the DOM has chosen a less abstract model, in which also entity references, notations, and CDATA sections are explicitly represented in the data structure. This model is a reasonable choice, since it also supports applications like XML editors that must preserve such details.

In object-oriented terms, DOM specifies an interface Node that encapsulates the common behavior of all XML nodes. It is specialized in a number of derived interfaces shown in Figure 7.1. These correspond to the well-known concepts introduced in Section 2.3 and Section 4.3.1. The Text, CDATASection, and Comment interfaces are also derived from a common interface CharacterData, which supports simple string operations.

XML trees are then built from such nodes, but clearly a number of constraints must be satisfied (or else runtime errors occur):

- the root must be a Document node;

- the children of a Document node must be among ProcessingInstruction, Comment, Element (at most one), and DocumentType (at most one);

- the children of an Element node must be among Element, ProcessingInstruction, Comment, Text, CDATASection, and EntityReference;

- the children of an Attr node are Text or EntityReference;

- the children of an EntityReference node are among Element, ProcessingInstruction, Comment, Text, CDATASection, and EntityReference;

- the children of an Entity node are among Element, ProcessingInstruction, Comment, Text, CDATASection, and EntityReference;

- all other nodes have no children.

Some explanation is required here: An Attr node is not considered to be a child of the Element node to which it belongs, and neither is the Element node a parent of the Attr node (this choice differs from the prevailing XPath data model, see Section 2.3). An EntityReference node has children corresponding to its expansion, if the corresponding Entity is known.

Given such trees, DOM allows various kinds of navigation through XML trees: The parent is accessed using the `parentNode` method, and the siblings through `previousSibling` and `nextSibling` methods. The children may either be accessed through the `firstChild` method (followed by invocations of the `nextSibling` method) or through the `childNodes` method which returns a `NodeList` interface that allows random access to nodes using indices. For `Element` nodes, attributes are accessed by name using the `getAttributeNode` method or through the `attributes` method which returns a `NamedNodeMap` interface that extracts all attributes at once. Individual properties of nodes may be inspected, including names and namespace declarations. Similarly, DOM supports several methods for manipulating XML trees: Nodes and attributes may be normalized, inserted, replaced, and deleted.

This data structure is called *DOM Level 3 Core*, which is a W3C recommendation. More advanced operations are available in separate specifications. *DOM Level 3 Load and Save*, which is also a W3C recommendation, allows DOM structures to be parsed from input streams and serialized to output streams. *DOM Level 3 Validation*, again a W3C recommendation, allows DTD and XML Schema validation of XML trees represented as DOM structures. *DOM Level 3 XPath*, which is currently a W3C working group note, allows the application of XPath 1.0 expressions to DOM structures.

In the W3C tradition, DOM is a huge and general specification containing dozens of interfaces supporting close to 200 methods. Each language binding is a further specification, providing translations of these interfaces and methods into a host language. For example, the `Text` interface is in Java represented as the following declaration:

```
package org.w3c.dom;

public interface Text extends CharacterData {
  public Text splitText(int offset) throws DOMException;
  public boolean isElementContentWhitespace();
  public String getWholeText();
  public Text replaceWholeText(String content)
    throws DOMException;
}
```

The situation is less elegant for ECMAScript, which has no proper notion of interfaces, classes, or inheritance. An interface is instead represented as a concrete object that is described using prose:

```
Objects that implement the Text interface:
  Objects that implement the Text interface have all properties
  and functions of the CharacterData interface as well as the
  properties and functions defined below.
    Properties of objects that implement the Text interface:
      isElementContentWhitespace
        This read-only property is a Boolean.
      wholeText
        This read-only property is a String.
    Functions of objects that implement the Text interface:
```

```
splitText(offset)
   This function returns an object that implements Text.
   The offset parameter is a Number.
   This function can raise an object
   that implements DOMException.
replaceWholeText(content)
   This function returns an object
   that implements the Text interface.
   The content parameter is a String.
   This function can raise an object
   that implements DOMException.
```

Clearly, however, expertise in DOM programming may to a large extent be carried between different host languages as essentially the same methods are available. This portability is the advantage of a language neutral approach.

The Online Resources section at the end of this chapter has a reference to the details of the DOM API.

7.3   The JDOM API

The W3C DOM is designed to be as general as possible and to be available in potentially all implementation languages. As always, such generality comes with a price: The language bindings necessitate that the OMG IDL definitions only use features that are common to *all* object-oriented languages.

The *JDOM* project instead applies an 80/20 principle where 80 percent of the applications are readily supported in Java and the remaining 20 percent requires case-by-case solutions. Thus, JDOM sacrifices some generality to offer better support for the common applications.

7.3.1   Embracing Java

For a seasoned Java programmer, it may be tempting to integrate a DOM data structure into the Java language, exploiting special features and obtaining the familiar look and feel of the Java APIs. The JDOM project has done exactly this and is a popular alternative to W3C DOM. There are several advantages to embracing the Java syntax and semantics:

> JDOM is an API for XML that is **specific** to Java.

- collections of elements and attributes are represented using the `java.util.List` interface and traversed using `Iterator` objects (rather than using the `NodeList` class in DOM);

- Java language features are used to describe the data model as a class hierarchy;

- the implementation may be optimized for Java performance (though the current JDOM implementation is not tuned); and

- the API can be learned without the additional complexity of a language binding specification.

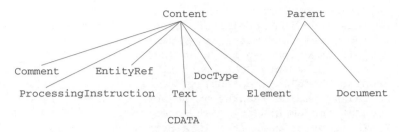

Figure 7.2 The essential classes and interfaces in JDOM.

JDOM is not supported by the W3C but, like RELAX NG, it shows how programmers may ultimately vote with their feet.

7.3.2 Data Model

We provide here a brief overview of JDOM – as usual, consult the online resources for further details. The JDOM data model uses both abstract classes and interfaces. The abstract class `Content` contains the common behavior for those nodes that may appear as content of other nodes. These correspond to the classes `Comment`, `DocType`, `Element`, `EntityRef`, `ProcessingInstruction`, and `Text`. The remaining kinds of nodes are `Attribute` and `Document`. The `Parent` interface describes the common behavior of those nodes that may have contents, and it is implemented by `Document` and `Element`. The `Text` class has a subclass `CDATA` describing those character data nodes that are represented as CDATA sections. The relationship is illustrated in Figure 7.2.

The basic navigation allows various methods for accessing contents from a parent. A child node at a specific position may be obtained, or all child nodes may be retrieved in a list (possibly filtered using boolean combinations of tests for names and node kinds). Attributes may similarly be selected individually by name or together in a list. It is also possible to access all descendants through an iterator. Finally, content nodes may navigate to their parent.

The basic manipulations of XML trees allow adding, replacing, and removing contents and attributes. Also, a child node may be detached from its parent. XML trees in JDOM are mutable, so operations may have side-effects. Elements may be cloned to create copies of the subtrees they root. Text nodes may be modified and normalized (see Section 4.5.5). New nodes are created using ordinary constructor methods of the appropriate classes. The tree structure is carefully maintained: attempting to add a node as child of two different parents or introducing a cycle will cause an exception to be thrown. (With the current implementation, inserting a single element takes time proportional to the number of ancestors because of this check!)

As an example, the following Java method will compute the height of the subtree rooted by its argument (assumed not to be null):

```
int xmlHeight(Element e) {
  List contents = e.getContent();
  Iterator i = contents.iterator();
  int max = 0;
```

```
    while (i.hasNext()) {
      Object c = i.next();
      int h;
      if (c instanceof Element)
        h = xmlHeight((Element)c);
      else
        h = 1;
      if (h>max)
        max = h;
    }
    return max+1;
  }
```

The method performs a recursive traversal of the XML tree, updating the current height and maintaining the global maximum. Note that casts are required, due to the generic nature of the Iterator class (Java 5 integration is not discussed yet). Another example is a method that modifies a RecipeML document by doubling the amount of sugar used in every recipe:

```
static void doubleSugar(Document d)
  throws DataConversionException {
  Namespace rcp =
    Namespace.getNamespace("http://www.brics.dk/ixwt/recipes");
  Filter f = new ElementFilter("ingredient", rcp);
  Iterator i = d.getDescendants(f);
  while (i.hasNext()) {
    Element e = (Element)i.next();
    if (e.getAttributeValue("name").equals("sugar")) {
      double amount = e.getAttribute("amount").getDoubleValue();
      e.setAttribute("amount", new Double(2*amount).toString());
    }
  }
}
```

Here, the use of ElementFilter determines the subset of elements that are visited by the getDescendants method, namely those with the name ingredient. For each such element we update the amount attribute if the name attribute has value sugar.

Next, we present an example with a method that emphasizes the quality of homemade recipes by transforming butter from a simple to a composite ingredient:

```
void makeButter(Element e) throws DataConversionException {
  Namespace rcp =
    Namespace.getNamespace("http://www.brics.dk/ixwt/recipes");
  ListIterator i = e.getChildren().listIterator();
  while (i.hasNext()) {
    Element c = (Element)i.next();
    if (c.getName().equals("ingredient") &&
        c.getAttributeValue("name").equals("butter")) {
      Element butter = new Element("ingredient", rcp);
```

```
      butter.setAttribute("name", "butter");
      Element salt = new Element("ingredient", rcp);
      salt.setAttribute("name", "salt");
      salt.setAttribute("amount", "*");
      butter.addContent(salt);
      Element cream = new Element("ingredient", rcp);
      cream.setAttribute("name", "cream");
      cream.setAttribute("unit", c.getAttributeValue("unit"));
      double amount = c.getAttribute("amount").getDoubleValue();
      cream.setAttribute("amount", new Double(2*amount).toString());
      butter.addContent(cream);
      Element preparation = new Element("preparation", rcp);
      Element churn = new Element("step", rcp);
      churn.addContent("Add salt and churn until the cream turns
         to butter.");
      preparation.addContent(churn);
      butter.addContent(preparation);
      i.set(butter);
    } else
      makeButter(c);
  }
}
```

The argument is assumed to be a recipe element in which all ingredient elements named butter are assumed to be simple and subsequently are laboriously replaced with corresponding composite ingredient elements, such that elements like

```
<ingredient name="butter" amount="0.25" unit="cup"/>
```

are turned into a more elaborate version (note that twice the amount of cream must be used):

```
<ingredient name="butter">
  <ingredient name="salt" amount="*" />
  <ingredient name="cream" unit="cup" amount="0.5" />
  <preparation>
    <step>
      Add salt and churn until the cream turns to butter.
    </step>
  </preparation>
</ingredient>
```

Finally, we program in two different ways a method that computes the concatenation of two recipe collections. The first method performs a *destructive* concatenation that physically moves the recipe nodes from the document d2 to the document d1:

```
static void concat(Document d1, Document d2) {
  Namespace rcp =
    Namespace.getNamespace("http://www.brics.dk/ixwt/recipes");
  Element r1 = d1.getRootElement();
```

```
    Element r2 = d2.getRootElement();
    Iterator i = r2.getChildren("recipe", rcp).iterator();
    ArrayList a = new ArrayList();
    while (i.hasNext()) {
      Element e = (Element)i.next();
      a.add(e);
    }
    i = a.iterator();
    while (i.hasNext())
      ((Element)i.next()).detach();
    r1.addContent(a);
  }
```

There are two important points to notice here. First, the `recipe` nodes must be *detached* before they are added to `d1`, as they would otherwise have two parents, which is disallowed by JDOM. Second, the `detach` method could not be invoked inside the first loop, since that would cause a `ConcurrentModificationException` from the underlying collection class. The other version of the `concat` method is not destructive, since it *clones* the `recipe` nodes before they are added to `d1`:

```
static void concat(Document d1, Document d2) {
  Namespace rcp =
    Namespace.getNamespace("http://www.brics.dk/ixwt/recipes");
  Element r1 = d1.getRootElement();
  Element r2 = d2.getRootElement();
  Iterator i = r2.getChildren("recipe", rcp).iterator();
  while (i.hasNext()) {
    Element e = (Element)i.next();
    r1.addContent(e.clone());
  }
}
```

Applications like these seem rather low-level when compared to XSLT or XQuery versions. However, the point is that JDOM is used from a general-purpose programming language that allows more general applications than the domain-specific languages (see Section 7.3.6 for an example).

7.3.3   Parsing, Validation, and Serializing

The JDOM system does not provide an XML parser by itself. Instead, it interfaces with existing parsers, either DOM parsers or SAX parsers (see Section 7.5). The default is the JAXP SAX parser (JAXP is a bundle from Sun containing Java implementations of XML parsing, validation, and transformation), but several other parsers may be selected.

By default, validation is not performed by the parser, but this option may be chosen. The parser may validate against both DTD and XML Schema. Validation errors result in exceptions being thrown. It is only possible to validate during parsing: an XML tree in memory cannot be validated (unlike for DOM).

A `Document` object may conversely be output in several formats: as a DOM tree, as a stream of SAX events (see Section 7.5.2), or as a stream of Unicode characters corresponding to its serialization.

As an example, the following complete application will read a recipe collection from the file `recipes.xml`, modify the `description` element, and output the resulting collection to the `System.out` stream:

```java
import java.io.*;
import org.jdom.*;
import org.jdom.input.*;
import org.jdom.output.*;

public class ChangeDescription {
  public static void main(String[] args) {
    try {
      SAXBuilder b = new SAXBuilder();
      Document d = b.build(new File("recipes.xml"));
      Namespace rcp =
        Namespace.getNamespace("http://www.brics.dk/ixwt/recipes");
      d.getRootElement()
       .getChild("description", rcp)
       .setText("Cool recipes!");
      XMLOutputter outputter = new XMLOutputter();
      outputter.output(d, System.out);
    } catch (Exception e) {
      System.err.println(e);
    }
  }
}
```

Since the parser generates exceptions in case the input is not well-formed XML, we can easily build a simple well-formedness checker:

```java
import java.io.*;
import org.jdom.*;
import org.jdom.input.*;

public class CheckWellformed {
  public static void main(String[] args) {
    try {
      SAXBuilder b = new SAXBuilder();
      String msg = "Document is well-formed XML!";
      try {
        Document d = b.build(new File(args[0]));
      } catch (JDOMParseException e) {
        msg = e.getMessage();
      }
```

```
      System.out.println(msg);
    } catch (Exception e) {
      System.err.println(e);
    }
  }
}
```

If the document specified on the command line is well-formed, the message `Document is well-formed XML!` is output. The following variant additionally performs DTD validation:

```
import java.io.*;
import org.jdom.*;
import org.jdom.input.*;

public class ValidateDTD {
  public static void main(String[] args) {
    try {
      SAXBuilder b = new SAXBuilder();
      b.setValidation(true);
      String msg = "No errors!";
      try {
        Document d = b.build(new File(args[0]));
      } catch (JDOMParseException e) {
        msg = e.getMessage();
      }
      System.out.println(msg);
    } catch (Exception c) {
      System.err.println(e);
    }
  }
}
```

The JAXP parser can also validate against XML Schema descriptions, referenced from the XML document as shown in Section 4.4.1. The change from DTD to XML Schema requires an extra setting:

```
import java.io.*;
import org.jdom.*;
import org.jdom.input.*;

public class ValidateXMLSchema {
  public static void main(String[] args) {
    try {
      SAXBuilder b = new SAXBuilder();
      b.setValidation(true);
      b.setProperty(
        "http://java.sun.com/xml/jaxp/properties/schemaLanguage",
        "http://www.w3.org/2001/XMLSchema");
      String msg = "No errors!";
```

```
        try {
          Document d = b.build(new File(args[0]));
        } catch (JDOMParseException e) {
          msg = e.getMessage();
        }
        System.out.println(msg);
      } catch (Exception e) {
        System.err.println(e);
      }
    }
  }
```

As the property name indicates, this feature is specific to JAXP. The following variant validates an XML document against an XML Schema description that is given on the command line (even if the document itself specifies another using the `xsi:schemaLocation` attribute). This option allows the programmer to decide which XML language the application will be prepared to accept, which is often more useful:

```
import java.io.*;
import org.jdom.*;
import org.jdom.input.*;

public class ValidateExternalXMLSchema {
  public static void main(String[] args) {
    try {
      SAXBuilder b = new SAXBuilder();
      b.setValidation(true);
      b.setProperty(
        "http://java.sun.com/xml/jaxp/properties/schemaLanguage",
        "http://www.w3.org/2001/XMLSchema");
      b.setProperty(
        "http://java.sun.com/xml/jaxp/properties/schemaSource",
        args[1]);
      String msg = "No errors!";
      try {
        Document d = b.build(new File(args[0]));
        if (!d.getRootElement().getNamespaceURI().equals(args[2]))
          msg = "Wrong namespace of root element!";
      } catch (JDOMParseException e) {
        msg = e.getLineNumber()+":"+e.getColumnNumber()+" "+
              e.getMessage();
      }
      System.out.println(msg);
    } catch (Exception e) {
      System.err.println(e);
    }
  }
}
```

The schema source property overrides the `xsi:schemaLocation` attribute, but only if the given schema has the same target namespace. For this reason, this program requires the expected target namespace of the schema to be given as the third argument and performs an extra check.

7.3.4 XPath Evaluation

JDOM has built-in support for evaluation of XPath expressions, but currently only for XPath 1.0. The following example shows an alternative (but presumably less efficient) implementation of the `DoubleSugar` method that finds the relevant nodes using XPath instead of filters:

```
void doubleSugar(Document d) throws JDOMException {
  XPath p = XPath.newInstance("//rcp:ingredient[@name='sugar']");
  p.addNamespace("rcp", "http://www.brics.dk/ixwt/recipes");
  Iterator i = p.selectNodes(d).iterator();
  while (i.hasNext()) {
    Element e = (Element)i.next();
    if (e.getAttributeValue("name").equals("sugar")) {
      double amount = e.gctAttribute("amount").getDoubleValue();
      e.setAttribute("amount", new Double(2*amount).toString());
    }
  }
}
```

7.3.5 XSLT Transformation

It is equally straightforward to perform XSLT transformation from JDOM using, for example, the Saxon tool. The following example is a general tool for performing XSLT transformations from the command line:

```
import java.io.*;
import org.jdom.*;
import org.jdom.transform.*;
import org.jdom.input.*;
import org.jdom.output.*;

public class ApplyXSLT {
  public static void main(String[] args) {
    try {
      System.setProperty("javax.xml.transform.TransformerFactory",
                "net.sf.saxon.TransformerFactoryImpl");
      SAXBuilder b = new SAXBuilder();
      Document d = b.build(new File(args[0]));
      XSLTransformer t = new XSLTransformer(args[1]);
      Document h = t.transform(d);
      XMLOutputter outputter = new XMLOutputter();
```

```
        outputter.output(h, System.out);
      } catch (Exception e) {
        System.err.println(e);
      }
    }
  }
```

This tool is invoked as follows:

```
java ApplyXSLT foo.xml bar.xsl
```

The `setProperty` method is used for specifying the XSLT implementation. Note that XSLT transformations are performed in memory, unlike validation that in JDOM only can take place during parsing.

Unfortunately, the `XSLTransformer` cannot accept stylesheet parameters (see Section 5.5). For some reason this feature requires that we fall back to the lower-level `Transformer` class. The following example runs a stylesheet on an XML document with a single parameter and value, all specified in the command line:

```
import java.io.*;
import org.jdom.*;
import org.jdom.transform.*;
import org.jdom.input.*;
import org.jdom.output.*;
import javax.xml.transform.*;
import javax.xml.transform.stream.*;

public class ParamXSLT {
  public static void main(String[] args) {
    try {
      SAXBuilder b = new SAXBuilder();
      Document d = b.build(new File(args[0]));
      Transformer t =
        TransformerFactory
          .newInstance()
          .newTransformer(new StreamSource(new File(args[1])));
      JDOMSource in = new JDOMSource(d);
      JDOMResult out = new JDOMResult();
      t.setParameter(args[2], args[3]);
      t.transform(in, out);
      Document h = out.getDocument();
      XMLOutputter outputter = new XMLOutputter();
      outputter.output(h, System.out);
    } catch (Exception e) {
      System.err.println(e);
    }
  }
}
```

This tool is invoked as follows:

```
java ParamXSLT foo.xml bar.xsl param value
```

7.3.6   A Business Card Editor

JDOM is often used to develop tools that are specific to a given application domain. As a case in point, we consider again the XML language for business cards. If a large collection of business cards were to be maintained, then a graphical editor would be useful. There are many general XML editors, but we want to have an editor that is tailor made to business cards. A screenshot of the editor we want looks as follows:

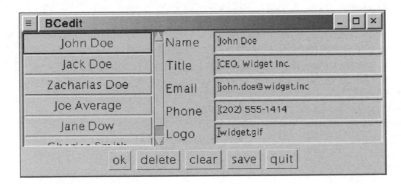

We will look in detail at the code for this simple application, which clearly cannot be realized by, say, XSLT or XQuery. First, the required packages for both JDOM and the standard AWT libraries must be imported:

```
import java.awt.*;
import java.awt.event.*;
import java.io.*;
import java.util.*;
import org.jdom.*;
import org.jdom.input.*;
import org.jdom.output.*;
```

During the editing process, it is inconvenient to work directly on a JDOM representation. Instead, we model a business card by a simple Card class:

```
class Card {
  public String name, title, email, phone, logo;

  public Card(String name, String title, String email,
              String phone, String logo) {
    this.name = name;
```

```
        this.title = title;
        this.email = email;
        this.phone = phone;
        this.logo = logo;
    }
  }
```

The application declares the required GUI elements, a `cardvector` that stores the current business cards, and an index of the current card being considered:

```
public class BCedit extends Frame implements ActionListener {
  // declare the user interface
  Button ok = new Button("ok");
  Button delete = new Button("delete");
  Button clear = new Button("clear");
  Button save = new Button("save");
  Button quit = new Button("quit");
  TextField name = new TextField(20);
  TextField title = new TextField(20);
  TextField email = new TextField(20);
  TextField phone = new TextField(20);
  TextField logo = new TextField(20);
  Panel cardpanel = new Panel(new GridLayout(0, 1));

  String cardfile;
  Vector cardvector;
  int current = -1;
  Namespace b = Namespace.getNamespace("http://businesscard.org");
```

The `main` method just creates an instance of the application:

```
public static void main(String[] args) { new BCedit(args[0]); }
```

We need a method to translate from JDOM to the internal representation:

```
Vector doc2vector(Document d) {
  Vector v = new Vector();
  Iterator i = d.getRootElement()
                 .getChildren("card", b).iterator();
  while (i.hasNext()) {
    Element e = (Element)i.next();
    String phone = e.getChildText("phone", b);
    if (phone==null)
      phone = "";
    Element logo = e.getChild("logo", b);
    String uri;
    if (logo==null)
      uri = "";
```

```
       else
         uri = logo.getAttributeValue("uri");
       Card c = new Card(e.getChildText("name", b),
                         e.getChildText("title", b),
                         e.getChildText("email", b),
                         phone,
                         uri);
       v.add(c);
     }
     return v;
   }
```

This method iterates through the card elements and for each constructs a corresponding Card object.

Similarly, we need a method to translate from the internal representation to JDOM:

```
Document vector2doc() {
  Element cardlist = new Element("cardlist", b);
  for (int i=0; i<cardvector.size(); i++) {
    Card c = (Card)cardvector.elementAt(i);
    if (c!=null) {
      Element card = new Element("card", b);
      Element name = new Element("name", b);
      name.addContent(c.name);
      card.addContent(name);
      Element title = new Element("title", b);
      title.addContent(c.title);
      card.addContent(title);
      Element email = new Element("email", b);
      email.addContent(c.email);
      card.addContent(email);
      if (!c.phone.equals("")) {
        Element phone = new Element("phone", b);
        phone.addContent(c.phone);
        card.addContent(phone);
      }
      if (!c.logo.equals("")) {
        Element logo = new Element("logo", b);
        logo.setAttribute("uri", c.logo);
        card.addContent(logo);
      }
      cardlist.addContent(card);
    }
  }
  return new Document(cardlist);
}
```

In this case we traverse the vector of Card objects and build corresponding card elements. We skip null entries as they correspond to deleted cards.

The following method is used to add buttons for the current cards to the user interface:

```
void addCards() {
  cardpanel.removeAll();
  for (int i=0; i<cardvector.size(); i++) {
    Card c = (Card)cardvector.elementAt(i);
    if (c!=null) {
      Button b = new Button(c.name);
      b.setActionCommand(String.valueOf(i));
      b.addActionListener(this);
      cardpanel.add(b);
    }
  }
  pack();
}
```

The main application reads in the XML file and sets up the user interface:

```
public BCedit(String cardfile) {
  super("BCedit");
  this.cardfile = cardfile;
  try {
    SAXBuilder b = new SAXBuilder();
    b.setValidation(true);
    b.setProperty(
      "http://java.sun.com/xml/jaxp/properties/schemaLanguage",
      "http://www.w3.org/2001/XMLSchema");
    b.setProperty(
      "http://java.sun.com/xml/jaxp/properties/schemaSource",
      "business_card_list1.xsd");
    Document d = b.build(new File(cardfile));
    if (!d.getRootElement().getNamespaceURI()
          .equals("http://businesscard.org"))
      throw new JDOMException("Wrong namespace of root element!");
    cardvector = doc2vector(d);
  } catch (Exception e) {
    System.err.println(e);
    System.exit(-1);
  }
  // initialize the user interface
  setLayout(new BorderLayout());
  ScrollPane s = new ScrollPane();
  s.setSize(200, 0);
  s.add(cardpanel);
  add(s,BorderLayout.WEST);
  Panel l = new Panel(new GridLayout(5, 1));
  l.add(new Label("Name"));
  l.add(new Label("Title"));
```

```
    l.add(new Label("Email"));
    l.add(new Label("Phone"));
    l.add(new Label("Logo"));
    add(l,BorderLayout.CENTER);
    Panel f = new Panel(new GridLayout(5, 1));
    f.add(name);
    f.add(title);
    f.add(email);
    f.add(phone);
    f.add(logo);
    add(f,BorderLayout.EAST);
    Panel p = new Panel();
    ok.addActionListener(this);
    p.add(ok);
    delete.addActionListener(this);
    p.add(delete);
    clear.addActionListener(this);
    p.add(clear);
    save.addActionListener(this);
    p.add(save);
    quit.addActionListener(this);
    p.add(quit);
    add(p,BorderLayout.SOUTH);
    addCards();
    show();
  }
```

Finally, the event handler reacts appropriately to the user commands:

```
public void actionPerformed(ActionEvent event) {
    Card c;
    String command = event.getActionCommand();
    if (command.equals("ok")) {
      c = new Card(name.getText(),
                   title.getText(),
                   email.getText(),
                   phone.getText(),
                   logo.getText());
      if (current==-1)
        cardvector.add(c);
      else
        cardvector.setElementAt(c, current);
      addCards();
    } else if (command.equals("delete")) {
      if (current!=-1) {
        cardvector.setElementAt(null, current);
        current = -1;
        addCards();
      }
```

```
    } else if (command.equals("clear")) {
      current = -1;
      name.setText("");
      title.setText("");
      email.setText("");
      phone.setText("");
      logo.setText("");
    } else if (command.equals("save")) {
      try {
        new XMLOutputter().output(vector2doc(),
                                 new FileOutputStream(cardfile));
      } catch (Exception e) {
        System.err.println(e);
      }
    } else if (command.equals("quit")) {
      System.exit(0);
    } else {
      current = Integer.parseInt(command);
      c = (Card)cardvector.elementAt(current);
      name.setText(c.name);
      title.setText(c.title);
      email.setText(c.email);
      phone.setText(c.phone);
      logo.setText(c.logo);
    }
  }
}
```

Note that the doc2vector method exploits the fact that its input has been validated according to the schema for business card lists: the name, title, and email elements are assumed to be present in every card element, since they are mandatory in the schema for business cards. Similarly, the uri attribute is known to exist in the logo element. Thus, the assumption of validity may simplify the development of applications. Without validation of the input, invalid data could result in null pointer errors.

The complete source code for the example is available from the companion Web site.

7.4   XML Data Binding

Looking at the example in Section 7.3.6, we realize that the methods doc2vector and vector2doc are tedious to write and seem to cry out for automatic generation. Obviously, many applications will similarly need to perform transformations between elements and objects, which is supported by various tools for *XML data binding* that map schemas into specific declarations and generate the corresponding code.

7.4.1 Binding Compilers

A tool for automatic binding must *compile* a schema written in DTD or XML Schema into a collection of classes (assuming Java is the target language). This process may be performed in many different ways, and there are several dozen different tools available. Each binding compiler must make some fundamental design decisions.

First, which schemas are supported? Generally, the choices are DTD or XML Schema, with RELAX NG at a distant third. Binding compilers rarely support all of XML Schema, often missing out on features like mixed content, wildcards, and keys.

Second, is the binding fixed or customizable? All tools support a default binding that often tries to avoid clumsy constructions. Still, programmers may want to influence the binding and decide on the choices of collection classes and naming conventions. A downside of customization is that the process is no longer automatic and thus becomes a source of errors.

Third, does *roundtripping* preserve information? All binding compilers generate code for *unmarshalling* (parsing) and *marshalling* (serialization). A roundtrip consisting of an unmarshalling followed by a marshalling may lose some information, typically comments, processing instructions, entities, and schema locations. For some applications, such loss of information may be a practical problem.

Fourth, what is the support for validation? All tools enable validation during unmarshalling. Most tools allow validation of a full XML tree in memory, but few are able dynamically to validate local modifications of an XML tree.

Finally, are the generated classes implemented by some generic framework? Most use ad hoc implementations, but the generated classes could, in fact, be instances of DOM or JDOM that are simply accessed through specific interfaces. In general, ad hoc classes will allow more efficient runtime operations.

XML data binding **embed** XML data into programming languages based on **schemas**.

7.4.2 The JAXB Framework

JAXB (Java Architecture for XML Binding) is a popular XML data binding framework. It supports most of XML Schema, excluding wildcards, notations, redefinitions, keys, and substitution groups. The binding is customizable, which is expressed either in a separate file or by extending the schema written in XML Schema with annotation elements belonging to a JAXB namespace. Roundtripping is almost complete, except that CDATA sections are transformed into ordinary character data. Validation is supported during unmarshalling or on demand (for a full document) during execution. The JAXB specification only describes the interfaces to the generated classes and allows implementations to use different frameworks for the concrete representations.

7.4.3 A Business Card Editor using JAXB

We now modify the program in Section 7.3.6 to make use of the JAXB tool. Recall that a collection of business cards is described by the following schema written in XML Schema (see Section 4.4.4):

```
<schema xmlns="http://www.w3.org/2001/XMLSchema"
        xmlns:b="http://businesscard.org"
        targetNamespace="http://businesscard.org"
        elementFormDefault="qualified">

<element name="cardlist" type="b:cardlist_type"/>
<element name="card" type="b:card_type"/>
<element name="name" type="string"/>
<element name="email" type="string"/>
<element name="phone" type="string"/>
<element name="logo" type="b:logo_type"/>

<attribute name="uri" type="anyURI"/>

<complexType name="cardlist_type">
  <sequence>
    <element name="title" type="b:cardlist_title_type"
             minOccurs="0"/>
    <element ref="b:card" minOccurs="0" maxOccurs="unbounded"/>
  </sequence>
</complexType>

<complexType name="cardlist_title_type" mixed="true">
  <sequence>
    <any namespace="http://www.w3.org/1999/xhtml"
         minOccurs="0" maxOccurs="unbounded"
         processContents="lax"/>
  </sequence>
</complexType>

<complexType name="card_type">
  <sequence>
    <element ref="b:name"/>
    <element name="title" type="string"/>
    <element ref="b:email"/>
    <element ref="b:phone" minOccurs="0"/>
    <element ref="b:logo" minOccurs="0"/>
  </sequence>
</complexType>

<complexType name="logo_type">
  <attribute ref="b:uri" use="required"/>
</complexType>
</schema>
```

The JAXB binding compiler correspondingly generates a package `org.businesscard`
containing the following classes and interfaces (the latter written here in italics):

- *Cardlist*, *CardlistType*, CardlistImpl, CardlistTypeImpl;

- *CardlistTitle*, *CardlistTitleType*, CardlistTitleImpl, CardlistTitleTypeImpl;

- *Card*, *CardType*, CardImpl, CardTypeImpl;

- *Name*, NameImpl;

- *Email*, EmailImpl;

- *Phone*, PhoneImpl;

- *Logo*, *LogoType*, LogoImpl, LogoTypeImpl; and

- ObjectFactory.

Note that the title element is not represented as a class, since it is declared as a local element. Otherwise, the structure is fairly simple. A card element is described by the Card interface, its content by the CardType interface, and these are implemented by the CardImpl and CardTypeImpl classes. The use of interfaces is required to allow different implementations of the JAXB tree models to coexist. The ObjectFactory class is used to generate objects corresponding to the various elements. The CardType interface looks as follows:

```
public interface CardType {
   java.lang.String getEmail();
   void setEmail(java.lang.String value);

   org.businesscard.LogoType getLogo();
   void setLogo(org.businesscard.LogoType value);

   java.lang.String getTitle();
   void setTitle(java.lang.String value);

   java.lang.String getName();
   void setName(java.lang.String value);

   java.lang.String getPhone();
   void setPhone(java.lang.String value);
}
```

The applied binding corresponds to the JAXB default, which for this example provides an appealing API for our business cards. We can use it to create a new and simpler implementation of the editor. First, we need to import a different set of packages:

```
import java.awt.*;
import java.awt.event.*;
import java.io.*;
import java.util.*;
import javax.xml.bind.JAXBContext;
```

```
import javax.xml.bind.JAXBException;
import javax.xml.bind.Unmarshaller;
import javax.xml.bind.Marshaller;
```

In particular, we must use the package containing the binding classes:

```
import org.businesscard.*;
```

Much of the global state looks as before:

```
public class BCedit2 extends Frame implements ActionListener {
  // declare the user interface
  ...
```

However, the collection of business cards is now stored in the classes defined by the binding, and some JAXB specific objects must be declared:

```
java.util.List cardlist;
Cardlist cl;
int current = -1;
JAXBContext jc;
ObjectFactory objFactory = new ObjectFactory();
```

As before, the `main` method creates an instance of the application:

```
public static void main(String[] args) { new BCedit2(args[0]); }
```

The `addCards` method now uses the `cardlist` object:

```
void addCards() {
  cardpanel.removeAll();
  Iterator i = cardlist.iterator();
  int j = 0;
  while (i.hasNext()) {
    Card c = (Card)i.next();
    Button b = new Button(c.getName());
    b.setActionCommand(String.valueOf(j++));
    b.addActionListener(this);
    cardpanel.add(b);
  }
  pack();
}
```

The main differences are caused by the JAXB binding compiler choosing to use the `List` interface instead of the `Vector` class.

The main application is as before, except that it uses automatic unmarshalling to read the business card document:

```
public BCedit2(String cardfile) {
  super("BCedit2");
  this.cardfile = cardfile;
```

```
    try {
      jc = JAXBContext.newInstance("org.businesscard");
      Unmarshaller u = jc.createUnmarshaller();
      cl = (Cardlist)u.unmarshal(new FileInputStream(cardfile));
      cardlist = cl.getCard();
    } catch (Exception e) {
      System.err.println(e);
      System.exit(-1);
    }
    // initialize the user interface
    ...
}
```

Finally, the event handler also uses the binding classes and automatic marshalling:

```
public void actionPerformed(ActionEvent event) {
    Card c = null;
    String command = event.getActionCommand();
    if (command.equals("ok")) {
      try {
        c = objFactory.createCard();
        c.setName(name.getText());
        c.setTitle(title.getText());
        c.setEmail(email.getText());
        c.setPhone(phone.getText());
        Logo l = objFactory.createLogo();
        l.setUri(logo.getText());
        c.setLogo(l);
      } catch (Exception e) {
        System.err.println(e);
      }
      if (current==-1)
        cardlist.add(c);
      else
        cardlist.set(current, c);
      addCards();
    } else if (command.equals("delete")) {
      if (current!=-1) {
        cardlist.remove(current);
        current = -1;
        addCards();
      }
    } else if (command.equals("clear")) {
      current = -1;
      name.setText("");
      title.setText("");
      email.setText("");
      phone.setText("");
      logo.setText("");
```

```
        } else if (command.equals("save")) {
          try {
            Marshaller m = jc.createMarshaller();
            m.marshal(cl,new FileOutputStream(cardfile));
          } catch (Exception e) {
            System.err.println(e);
          }
        } else if (command.equals("quit")) {
          System.exit(0);
        } else {
          current = Integer.parseInt(command);
          c = (Card)cardlist.get(current);
          name.setText(c.getName());
          title.setText(c.getTitle());
          email.setText(c.getEmail());
          phone.setText(c.getPhone());
          LogoType lt = c.getLogo();
          if (lt!=null)
            logo.setText(lt.getUri());
          else
            logo.setText("");
        }
      }
    }
```

In all, the application has shrunk from 214 lines to 153, mainly due to the absence of the doc2vector and vector2doc methods. Many of the changes in the new implementation are caused by the different representation of cards and card lists. For larger applications using several or more complicated schemas, JAXB and similar data binding tools significantly ease the programming and eliminates entire sources of errors.

7.5   The SAX API

Technologies like DOM, JDOM, and JAXB provide data structures for representing XML documents in memory. This strategy is clearly a problem if the XML document in question is of size, say 100GB, that cannot fit into memory.

Streaming may handle **large** XML documents without storing everything in memory.

7.5.1   Streaming XML

For very large documents, it is only possible to perform *streaming* of the document, which means that it must be processed during a single scan (or in some cases a few scans) of the file without at any point having the whole document in memory. Streaming is well known from other technologies working on large data: movies are often streamed across the Internet rather than being downloaded as a whole, and many Unix file commands are able to operate on streams of characters.

It is easy to stream a file, simply by reading it character by character. In principle, XML documents could be processed in the same manner, but clearly every application would need to start by reconstructing (parts of) the corresponding XML tree. Thus, a general framework for streaming XML is needed and it is provided by *SAX (Simple API for XML)*, which is another non-W3C project that has solved an important problem.

7.5.2   Parsing Events

The key to program streaming applications is to view the XML document as a stream of *events*, rather than as a stream of characters. The events correspond to the syntactic features that are encountered while reading through the document file, such as:

- the document starts;

- a start tag is encountered;

- an end tag is encountered;

- a namespace declaration is seen;

- some whitespace is seen;

- character data is encountered; or

- the document ends.

The SAX tool observes these events while reading the XML document and reacts by calling corresponding methods that are specified by the programmer (this is known as a *callback* technique). The programmer must then supply the corresponding actions to be taken when these events occur. This is easily done through the DefaultHandler class, which provides empty implementations of all possible event handlers. The relevant methods may then be overridden in a subclass, an instance of which is supplied to the SAX parser.

To illustrate the available events, we consider the following definition of a subclass which traces all occurring events:

```
import java.io.*;
import org.xml.sax.*;
import org.xml.sax.helpers.*;

public class Trace extends DefaultHandler {
  int indent = 0;

  void printIndent() {
    for (int i=0; i<indent; i++)
      System.out.print("-");
  }
```

```java
    public void startDocument() {
      System.out.println("start document");
      indent++;
    }

    public void endDocument() {
      indent--;
      System.out.println("end document");
    }

    public void startElement(String uri, String localName,
                             String qName, Attributes atts) {
      printIndent();
      System.out.println("start element: "+qName);
      indent++;
    }

    public void endElement(String uri, String localName, String qName) {
      indent--;
      printIndent();
      System.out.println("end element: "+qName);
    }

    public void ignorableWhitespace(char[] ch, int start, int length) {
      printIndent();
      System.out.println("whitespace, length "+length);
    }

    public void processingInstruction(String target, String data) {
      printIndent();
      System.out.println("processing instruction: "+target);
    }

    public void characters(char[] ch, int start, int length) {
      printIndent();
      System.out.println("character data, length "+length);
    }

    public static void main(String[] args) {
      try {
        Trace tracer = new Trace();
        XMLReader reader = XMLReaderFactory.createXMLReader();
        reader.setContentHandler(tracer);
        reader.parse(args[0]);
      } catch (Exception e) {
        System.err.println(e);
      }
    }
  }
```

Applied to the recipe collection, it generates the following output (abbreviated):

```
start document
-start element: rcp:collection
--character data, length 3
--start element: rcp:description
---character data, length 44
---character data, length 3
--end element: rcp:description
--character data, length 3
--start element: rcp:recipe
---character data, length 5
---start element: rcp:title
----character data, length 42
...
---start element: rcp:nutrition
---end element: rcp:nutrition
---character data, length 3
--end element: rcp:recipe
--character data, length 1
-end element: rcp:collection
end document
```

An XMLReader is dependent on an implementation of a SAX driver. The Java system property org.xml.sax.driver may be used to specify an available implementation.

7.5.3   SAX Applications

The following example provides a streaming version of the program computing the height of an XML document (see Section 7.3.2):

```
import java.io.*;
import org.xml.sax.*;
import org.xml.sax.helpers.*;

public class Height extends DefaultHandler {
  int h = -1;
  int max = 0;

  public void startElement(String uri, String localName,
                           String qName, Attributes atts) {
    h++;
    if (h>max)
      max = h;
  }
```

```
    public void endElement(String uri, String localName,
                           String qName) {
      h--;
    }

    public void characters(char[] ch, int start, int length) {
      if (h+1>max)
        max = h+1;
    }

    public static void main(String[] args) {
      try {
        Height handler = new Height();
        XMLReader reader = XMLReaderFactory.createXMLReader();
        reader.setContentHandler(handler);
        reader.parse(args[0]);
        System.out.println(handler.max);
      } catch (Exception e) {
        System.err.println(e);
      }
    }
}
```

Note that this version is less intuitive, since it is programmed in a stack-like style rather than in a recursive style, which is typical of streaming applications.

The advantage of streaming may be seen by comparing the performances of the two versions of the height computations. With an XML document of size 18MB the JDOM version causes a `java.lang.OutOfMemoryError`, while the SAX version happily processes a 1GB file in less than a minute (all on a standard PC).

The SAX and JDOM approaches clearly have the same expressive power. The SAX events correspond to a recursive preorder traversal of the JDOM tree, and a SAX event handler may choose to construct a JDOM tree as exemplified by the following (non-validating) business card parser:

```
import java.io.*;
import java.util.*;
import org.jdom.*;
import org.jdom.output.*;
import org.xml.sax.*;
import org.xml.sax.helpers.*;

public class BCparse extends DefaultHandler {
  Vector contents = new Vector();
  Document doc = null;
  Element card = null;
  Element field = null;
  Namespace b = Namespace.getNamespace("http://businesscard.org");
```

```java
    public void startElement(String uri, String localName,
                             String qName, Attributes atts) {
      if (localName.equals("card"))
        card = new Element("card", b);
      else if (localName.equals("name"))
        field = new Element("name", b);
      else if (localName.equals("title"))
        field = new Element("title", b);
      else if (localName.equals("email"))
        field = new Element("email", b);
      else if (localName.equals("phone"))
        field = new Element("phone", b);
      else if (localName.equals("logo")) {
        field = new Element("logo", b);
        field.setAttribute("uri", atts.getValue("", "uri"));
      }
    }

    public void endElement(String uri, String localName, String qName) {
      if (localName.equals("card"))
        contents.add(card);
      else if (localName.equals("cardlist")) {
        Element cardlist = new Element("cardlist", b);
        cardlist.setContent(contents);
        doc = new Document(cardlist);
      } else {
        card.addContent(field);
        field = null;
      }
    }

    public void characters(char[] ch, int start, int length) {
      if (field!=null)
        field.addContent(new String(ch, start, length));
    }

    public static void main(String[] args) {
      try {
        BCparse handler = new BCparse();
        XMLReader reader = XMLReaderFactory.createXMLReader();
        reader.setContentHandler(handler);
        reader.parse(args[0]);
        XMLOutputter outputter = new XMLOutputter();
        outputter.output(handler.doc, System.out);
      } catch (Exception e) {
        System.err.println(e);
      }
    }
  }
```

JDOM's SAXBuilder class works in much the same manner, but for arbitrary XML structures with unbounded depth it is necessary to maintain a stack of lists of content nodes.

So far, our SAX applications have performed fairly localized actions. However, an event handler may store information about the part of the XML tree that it has seen at a given time. The limit case is, of course, a complete construction of the tree, but, in general, the relevant information may be much smaller. Consider XHTML documents, for which we want to check three properties that happen *not* to be covered by the W3C validator (see Section 1.6):

- that all form `input` tags are inside `form` tags;

- that all `form` tags have distinct `name` attributes; and

- that `form` tags are not nested.

Using SAX, we implement a handler that stores exactly the required amount of contextual information:

```
import java.io.*;
import java.util.*;
import org.xml.sax.*;
import org.xml.sax.helpers.*;

public class CheckForms extends DefaultHandler {
  int formheight = 0;
  HashSet formnames = new HashSet();
  Locator locator;

  public void setDocumentLocator(Locator locator) {
    this.locator = locator;
  }

  void report(String s) {
    System.out.print(locator.getLineNumber());
    System.out.print(":");
    System.out.print(locator.getColumnNumber());
    System.out.println(" ---"+s);
  }

  public void startElement(String uri, String localName,
                           String qName, Attributes atts) {
    if (uri.equals("http://www.w3.org/1999/xhtml")) {
      if (localName.equals("form")) {
        if (formheight>0)
          report("nested forms");
        String name = atts.getValue("", "name");
        if (formnames.contains(name))
          report("duplicate form name");
        else
          formnames.add(name);
        formheight++;
```

```
        } else if (localName.equals("input") ||
                   localName.equals("select") ||
                   localName.equals("textarea"))
          if (formheight==0)
            report("form field outside form");
    }
  }

  public void endElement(String uri, String localName,
                         String qName) {
    if (uri.equals("http://www.w3.org/1999/xhtml"))
      if (localName.equals("form"))
        formheight--;
  }

  public static void main(String[] args) {
    try {
      CheckForms handler = new CheckForms();
      XMLReader reader = XMLReaderFactory.createXMLReader();
      reader.setContentHandler(handler);
      reader.parse(args[0]);
    } catch (Exception e) {
      System.err.println(e);
    }
  }
}
```

The Locator class is used to locate the line and column numbers of SAX events in the input file.

In the above example, we only investigate the part of the document that has been visited so far, particularly the ancestors. Generalizing this technique, it is clear that also a significant subset of XPath can be evaluated efficiently using streaming. We look further into this issue in Section 7.6.

7.5.4 SAX Filters

A useful property of Unix file commands is the ability to connect them using *pipes*, providing a composition of streaming applications. SAX supports a similar technique through the concept of *filters*, which are event handlers that may act upon the various events and (possibly) send them on to a *parent* handler.

An easy way to use this feature is to create subclasses of the helper class XMLFilterImpl, which implements a filter that just passes on all parsing events. The event handling methods may then be overridden with specific implementations, and the event is passed on by invoking the same method in the super object.

The following example applies three filters to an XML document. The first removes all processing instructions, the second adds an id attribute with a unique value to all elements, and the third computes the total length of character data:

```
import java.io.*;
import org.xml.sax.*;
import org.xml.sax.helpers.*;

class PIFilter extends XMLFilterImpl {
  public void processingInstruction(String target, String data)
      throws SAXException {}
}

class IDFilter extends XMLFilterImpl {
  int id = 0;
  public void startElement(String uri, String localName,
                           String qName, Attributes atts)
      throws SAXException {
    AttributesImpl idatts = new AttributesImpl(atts);
    idatts.addAttribute("", "id", "id", "ID",
                        new Integer(id++).toString());
    super.startElement(uri, localName, qName, idatts);
  }
}

class CountFilter extends XMLFilterImpl {
  public int count = 0;
  public void characters(char[] ch, int start, int length)
      throws SAXException {
    count = count+length;
    super.characters(ch, start, length);
  }
}

public class FilterTest {
  public static void main(String[] args) {
    try {
      XMLReader reader = XMLReaderFactory.createXMLReader();
      PIFilter pi = new PIFilter();
      pi.setParent(reader);
      IDFilter id = new IDFilter();
      id.setParent(pi);
      CountFilter count = new CountFilter();
      count.setParent(id);
      count.parse(args[0]);
      System.out.println(count.count);
    } catch (Exception e) {
      System.err.println(e);
    }
  }
}
```

The PIFilter is applied first, then IDFilter, and finally CountFilter.

Note that there is no guarantee that the events passed on by a filter actually correspond to those obtained by parsing a well-formed XML document – this is a source of tricky errors when programming with filters.

7.5.5 Streaming with XmlPull

SAX is sometimes described as a *push* framework, since the parser has the initiative and the programmer must react to events as they are produced. In contrast, XML streaming may also be performed in a *pull* framework, where the next event is explicitly requested by the programmer.

The *XmlPull* system provides an API for a pull parser, which we use to illustrate this concept. Consider the earlier SAX application that checks requirements of XHTML forms (see Section 7.5.3). In a pull version, this code looks as follows:

```java
import java.io.*;
import java.util.*;
import org.xmlpull.v1.*;

public class CheckForms2 {
  static void report(XmlPullParser xpp, String s) {
    System.out.print(xpp.getLineNumber());
    System.out.print(":");
    System.out.print(xpp.getColumnNumber());
    System.out.println(" ---"+s);
  }

  public static void main (String args[])
    throws XmlPullParserException, IOException {
    XmlPullParserFactory factory = XmlPullParserFactory.newInstance();
    factory.setNamespaceAware(true);
    factory.setFeature(XmlPullParser.FEATURE_PROCESS_NAMESPACES, true);

    XmlPullParser xpp = factory.newPullParser();

    int formheight = 0;
    HashSet formnames = new HashSet();

    xpp.setInput(new FileReader(args[0]));
    int eventType = xpp.getEventType();
    while (eventType!=XmlPullParser.END_DOCUMENT) {
      if (eventType==XmlPullParser.START_TAG) {
        if (xpp.getNamespace().equals("http://www.w3.org/1999/xhtml")
            && xpp.getName().equals("form")) {
          if (formheight>0)
            report(xpp,"nested forms");
          String name = xpp.getAttributeValue("","name");
```

```
        if (formnames.contains(name))
          report(xpp,"duplicate form name");
        else
          formnames.add(name);
        formheight++;
      } else if (xpp.getName().equals("input") ||
                 xpp.getName().equals("select") ||
                 xpp.getName().equals("textarea"))
        if (formheight==0)
          report(xpp,"form field outside form");
    }
    else if (eventType==XmlPullParser.END_TAG) {
      if (xpp.getNamespace().equals("http://www.w3.org/1999/xhtml")
          && xpp.getName().equals("form"))
        formheight--;
    }
    eventType = xpp.next();
  }
}
}
```

This program is really not that different from the SAX version. In general, the advantages of
pull parsing are claimed to be a smaller memory footprint and a more direct programming
style. On the downside, pipelining in the form of filter chains is not available (in a language
like Java that does not support higher-order functions).

7.6   Streaming Transformations with STX ★

The examples in Section 7.5.3 show that a broad spectrum of applications may be executed
in streaming mode. Clearly, not all applications have this property: Unless the required contextual information has almost constant size, an application is not viable for huge documents.

The `CheckForms` example seems to indicate that certain XPath expressions can be evaluated in streaming mode and several research projects have identified various such subsets.
Path expressions are generally restricted to the `child` and `descendant` axes, but other axes
may sometimes be included without too much contextual information.

STX is a
variation of
XSLT suitable
for **streaming**.

It is perhaps more surprising that even a large subset of XSLT may be evaluated in
streaming mode. This fact is best illustrated by studying the language *STX (Streaming
Transformations for XML)*.

STX is quite similar to XSLT and supports many of the same features and functionalities.
In fact, the following elements exist in both languages with much the same semantics:
`template`, `copy`, `value-of`, `if`, `else`, `choose`, `when`, `otherwise`, `text`, `element`,
`attribute`, `variable`, `param`, and `with-param`. Also, most of the XSLT functions (see
Section 3.5.11) are available in STX.

The differences between STX and XSLT reflect the necessary limitations in control flow to enable streaming. Also, since many streaming applications accumulate information during processing, STX supports *mutable* variables.

7.6.1   STXPath

STX uses a subset of XPath 2.0 which is called *STXPath*. Syntactically, STXPath expressions form a subset of XPath 2.0 expressions, and they similarly evaluate to sequences of nodes and atomic values. However, the semantics of STXPath expressions differs considerably from that of XPath expressions.

A streaming application does not have access to all axes. The parts of the document that have not yet been read are obviously unavailable, but it is also impractical to store everything that has been read. STXPath is only able to examine the *ancestor stack*, which consists of the sequence of nodes from the root to the current context node. The term *stack* is used, since this sequence behaves like a stack data structure during the streaming process.

Thus, the result of an STXPath path expression is defined to be the result of the corresponding XPath path expression, but restricted to the set of nodes contained in the ancestor stack. The resulting sequence is always sorted in document order. Note that the STXPath semantics may produce different results than the XPath semantics; for example, on the XML document

```
<A>
  <B/>
  <C><D/></C>
</A>
```

with the element named D as context node, the expression

```
count(//B)
```

outputs 0 with the STXPath semantics, but 1 with the XPath semantics.

The syntactic restrictions on STXPath expressions require the use of abbreviated syntax (see Section 3.4) and otherwise eliminate the now useless `following` and `preceding` axes. STXPath also adds two node tests: `cdata()` and `doctype()`, which accept CDATA sections and DOCTYPE declarations, respectively.

7.6.2   Transformations and Templates

An STX document, called a *transformation sheet*, contains a `transform` root element that encloses a set of `template` rules.

Each `template` has a `match` attribute whose value is a *pattern*. An STX pattern is similar to an XSLT pattern (see Section 5.3.1).

The content is a sequence expression, again similar to XSLT (see Section 5.4), but fewer constructs are available. In particular, the apply-templates construct is not allowed. Instead, STX offers the process-children, process-siblings, and process-self instructions.

The process-children construct invokes the STX transformation sheet on the sequence of child nodes. Only a single occurrence of this element is allowed in a template, and this restriction is sufficient to make the transformation equivalent to a SAX streaming application.

Consider the following simple example:

```
<stx:transform xmlns:stx="http://stx.sourceforge.net/2002/ns"
               version="1.0"
               xmlns:rcp="http://www.brics.dk/ixwt/recipes">

  <stx:template match="rcp:collection">
    <comments>
      <stx:process-children/>
    </comments>
  </stx:template>

  <stx:template match="rcp:comment">
    <comment><stx:value-of select="."/></comment>
  </stx:template>

</stx:transform>
```

This transformation extracts comments from a recipe collection. A default template invokes process-children on all nodes that are not explicitly matched. The above STX transformation is equivalent to the following SAX filter:

```
import java.io.*;
import java.util.*;
import org.xml.sax.*;
import org.xml.sax.helpers.*;

public class ExtractComments extends XMLFilterImpl {
  bool chars = true;

  public void startElement(String uri, String localName,
                           String qName, Attributes atts) {
    if (uri.equals("http://www.brics.dk/ixwt/recipes")) {
      if (localName.equals("collection"))
        System.out.print("<comments>");
      if (localName.equals("comment")) {
        System.out.print("<comment>");
        chars = true;
      }
    }
  }
```

```
public void characters(char[] ch, int start, int length){
    if (chars)
        System.out.print(new String(ch, start, length));
}

public void endElement(String uri, String localName, String qName) {
    if (uri.equals("http://www.brics.dk/ixwt/recipes")) {
        if (localName.equals("collection"))
            System.out.print("</comments>");
        if (localName.equals("comment")) {
            System.out.print("</comment>");
            chars = false;
        }
    }
}
}
```

STX has some obvious advantages. First, the domain-specific syntax greatly simplifies the programming task. Second, unlike the SAX version, the STX transformation is guaranteed to produce only well-formed XML output.

The following tiny example illustrates how the ancestor stack changes during the streaming process:

```
<stx:transform xmlns:stx="http://stx.sourceforge.net/2002/ns"
               version="1.0">

  <stx:template match="*">
     <stx:message select="concat(count(//*),' ',local-name())"/>
    <stx:process-children/>
  </stx:template>

</stx:transform>
```

The message element outputs the value of the select attribute to a different output stream. On the document

```
<A>
  <B/>
  <B><C/></B>
  <A/>
  <B><A><C/></A></B>
</A>
```

the output is

```
1 A
2 B
2 B
```

```
3 C
2 A
2 B
3 A
4 C
```

which clearly shows the stack behavior, by listing for each encountered element its name and the height of the ancestor stack.

The `process-siblings` construct deviates from the plain recursive traversal, while still allowing streaming. Each node is still only processed once. Several `process-siblings` elements may appear, and each can be limited with a `while` or `until` attribute, whose value is a pattern. A vital restriction applies: no `process-children` element may follow a `process-siblings` element. The use of `process-siblings` is illustrated by the following tiny example:

```
<stx:transform xmlns:stx="http://stx.sourceforge.net/2002/ns"
               version="1.0">

  <stx:template match="*">
    <stx:copy>
      <stx:process-children/>
      <stx:process-siblings/>
    </stx:copy>
  </stx:template>

</stx:transform>
```

This transformation sheet transforms the XML document

```
<a>
  <b><c/></b>
  <d><e/></d>
</a>
```

into the following version where the d sibling of the b node is processed before the processing of the b node is completed:

```
<a>
  <b>
    <c/>
    <d><e/></d>
  </b>
</a>
```

Notice that the sequence of start tags is unchanged in the two documents. This transformation is harder to express as a SAX filter, since it is necessary to maintain an explicit stack of undischarged end tags.

The `process-self` instruction allows the current node to be processed again with a different template (the current template is ignored when pattern matching is performed again).

7.6.3 Variables

Variables in STX are declared similarly to those in XSLT, but they differ in being mutable. This mutability is relevant for STX, since many streaming applications accumulate information about the source document. For example, the following transformation sheet finds the maximum `ingredient` nesting depth of a recipe collection:

```
<stx:transform xmlns:stx="http://stx.sourceforge.net/2002/ns"
                version="1.0"
                xmlns:rcp="http://www.brics.dk/ixwt/recipes">
  <stx:variable name="depth" select="0"/>
  <stx:variable name="maxdepth" select="0"/>

  <stx:template match="rcp:collection">
     <stx:process-children/>
     <maxdepth><stx:value-of select="$maxdepth"/></maxdepth>
  </stx:template>

  <stx:template match="rcp:ingredient">
    <stx:assign name="depth" select="$depth + 1"/>
    <stx:if test="$depth > $maxdepth">
      <stx:assign name="maxdepth" select="$depth"/>
    </stx:if>
    <stx:process-children/>
    <stx:assign name="depth" select="$depth - 1"/>
  </stx:template>

</stx:transform>
```

We here use `assign` instructions to update the variables. Note that this transformation sheet exploits the default `template` rules. For our example recipe collection the output is

```
<maxdepth>4</maxdepth>
```

A similar example is an STX version of the SAX application `CheckForms` from Section 7.5.3:

```
<stx:transform xmlns:stx="http://stx.sourceforge.net/2002/ns"
                version="1.0"
                xmlns:xhtml="http://www.w3.org/1999/xhtml">
  <stx:variable name="formheight" select="0"/>
  <stx:variable name="formnames" select="'#'"/>

  <stx:template match="xhtml:form">
    <stx:if test="$formheight&gt;0">
      <stx:message select="'nested forms'"/>
    </stx:if>
```

```
              <stx:if test="contains($formnames,concat('#',@name,'#'))">
                <stx:message select="'duplicate form name'"/>
              </stx:if>
              <stx:assign name="formheight" select="$formheight + 1"/>
              <stx:assign name="formnames"
                          select="concat($formnames,@name,'#')"/>
              <stx:process-children/>
              <stx:assign name="formheight" select="$formheight - 1"/>
            </stx:template>

            <stx:template match="xhtml:input|xhtml:select|xhtml:textarea">
              <stx:if test="$formheight=0">
                <stx:message select="'form field outside form'"/>
              </stx:if>
              <stx:process-children/>
            </stx:template>

          </stx:transform>
```

This example closely simulates the behavior of the SAX version. Note how we creatively encode a map using the string variable `formnames` (exploiting that QNames cannot contain the character #).

7.6.4 Groups

STX has a notion of *group* that serves two purposes: first, it replaces the concept of *mode* from XSLT (see Section 5.3.2); second, it defines the scope of variables.

The `group` element surrounds a collection of top-level STX elements and provides a `name` attribute. The `process-children`, `process-siblings`, `process-self` elements accept an optional `group` attribute, which identifies the relevant group of `template` elements.

Groups are central to a programming technique that is often necessary (for an example see Section 7.6.6). Consider the following sketchy source document:

```
<person>
  <email/><email/><email/>
  <phone/><phone/>
</person>
```

We wish to write a transformation sheet that produces the following target document, where the `email` elements have been grouped:

```
<person>
  <emails>
    <email/><email/><email/>
  </emails>
  <phone/><phone/>
</person>
```

At first, this transformation seems difficult since we apparently need to process the child nodes of `person` in two rounds (first to select the `email` nodes and then to select the `phone` nodes), but only a single invocation of `process-children` is allowed. However, the following transformation sheet does the trick:

```
<?xml version="1.0"?>
<stx:transform xmlns:stx="http://stx.sourceforge.net/2002/ns"
               version="1.0"
               strip-space="yes">
  <stx:template match="person">
     <person><stx:process-children/></person>
  </stx:template>

  <stx:template match="email">
    <emails><stx:process-self group="foo"/></emails>
  </stx:template>

  <stx:group name="foo">
    <stx:template match="email">
      <email/>
      <stx:process-siblings while="email" group="foo"/>
    </stx:template>
  </stx:group>

  <stx:template match="phone">
    <phone/>
  </stx:template>
</stx:transform>
```

As the children of the `person` element are being processed, the first `email` element is processed by the top-level template, which produces the enclosing `emails` elements and then transfers control to the template in the `foo` group that processes all the `email` elements. The `while` attribute contains a pattern that limits the extent of the `process-siblings` instruction.

7.6.5 Limitations of Streaming

Many XSLT applications can be written as streaming versions in STX, but there are some clear limitations. Since the output of an STX transformation sheet is produced linearly during the processing, significant rearrangements are not possible. An extreme case is the following XSLT stylesheet, which performs a mirror reflection of its source argument:

```
<xsl:stylesheet version="2.0"
                xmlns:xsl="http://www.w3.org/1999/XSL/Transform">

  <xsl:template name="mirror" match="/|@*|node()">
    <xsl:copy>
      <xsl:apply-templates select="@*"/>
```

```
            <xsl:apply-templates select="reverse(node())"/>
        </xsl:copy>
    </xsl:template>

</xsl:stylesheet>
```

Less drastic rearrangements will also be impossible to perform in streaming mode, but if only a small amount of data must be shifted, then variables are an option. STX does support a concept of *buffers*, which allow rearrangements but with severe penalties to the streaming performance.

7.6.6 STX for Recipes

The following STX transformation sheet behaves exactly like the XSLT stylesheet from Section 5.10, except that it processes its source document in streaming mode. This difference has two consequences. On the negative side, though it appears quite similar to the XSLT version, it contains some tricky programming that requires insight into the streaming paradigm. On the positive side, while the XSLT version throws a `java.lang.OutOfMemoryError` exception on a recipe collection of 18MB, the STX versions processes a 1.2GB recipe collection in less than 8 minutes (all on a standard PC).

```
<stx:transform xmlns:stx="http://stx.sourceforge.net/2002/ns"
               version="1.0"
               xmlns:rcp="http://www.brics.dk/ixwt/recipes"
               xmlns="http://www.w3.org/1999/xhtml"
               strip-space="yes">

  <stx:template match="rcp:collection">
    <html>
      <stx:process-children/>
    </html>
  </stx:template>

  <stx:template match="rcp:description">
    <head>
      <title><stx:value-of select="."/></title>
      <link href="style.css" rel="stylesheet" type="text/css"/>
    </head>
  </stx:template>

  <stx:template match="rcp:recipe">
    <body>
      <table border="1">
        <stx:process-self group="outer"/>
      </table>
    </body>
  </stx:template>
```

```
<stx:group name="outer">
  <stx:template match="rcp:description">
    <tr>
      <td><stx:value-of select="."/></td>
    </tr>
  </stx:template>

  <stx:template match="rcp:recipe">
    <tr>
      <td>
        <stx:process-children/>
      </td>
    </tr>
  </stx:template>

  <stx:template match="rcp:title">
    <h1><stx:value-of select="."/></h1>
  </stx:template>

  <stx:template match="rcp:date">
    <i><stx:value-of select="."/></i>
  </stx:template>

  <stx:template match="rcp:ingredient" >
    <ul><stx:process-self group="inner"/></ul>
  </stx:template>

  <stx:template match="rcp:preparation">
    <ol><stx:process-children/></ol>
  </stx:template>

  <stx:template match="rcp:step">
    <li><stx:value-of select="."/></li>
  </stx:template>

  <stx:template match="rcp:comment">
    <ul>
      <li type="square"><stx:value-of select="."/></li>
    </ul>
  </stx:template>

  <stx:template match="rcp:nutrition">
    <table border="2">
      <tr>
        <th>Calories</th><th>Fat</th>
        <th>Carbohydrates</th><th>Protein</th>
        <stx:if test="@alcohol">
          <th>Alcohol</th>
        </stx:if>
      </tr>
```

```
            <tr>
              <td align="right"><stx:value-of
                                 select="@calories"/></td>
              <td align="right"><stx:value-of
                                 select="@fat"/></td>
              <td align="right"><stx:value-of
                                 select="@carbohydrates"/></td>
              <td align="right"><stx:value-of
                                 select="@protein"/></td>
              <stx:if test="@alcohol">
                <td align="right"><stx:value-of
                                   select="@alcohol"/></td>
              </stx:if>
            </tr>
          </table>
        </stx:template>
      </stx:group>

      <stx:group name="inner">
        <stx:template match="rcp:ingredient">
          <stx:choose>
            <stx:when test="@amount">
              <li>
                <stx:if test="@amount!='*'">
                  <stx:value-of select="@amount"/>
                  <stx:text> </stx:text>
                  <stx:if test="@unit">
                    <stx:value-of select="@unit"/>
                    <stx:if test="number(@amount)>number(1)">
                      <stx:text>s</stx:text>
                    </stx:if>
                    <stx:text> of </stx:text>
                  </stx:if>
                </stx:if>
                <stx:text> </stx:text>
                <stx:value-of select="@name"/>
              </li>
            </stx:when>
            <stx:otherwise>
              <li><stx:value-of select="@name"/></li>
              <stx:process-children group="outer"/>
            </stx:otherwise>
          </stx:choose>
          <stx:process-siblings while="rcp:ingredient"
                                group="inner"/>
        </stx:template>
      </stx:group>
    </stx:transform>
```

To a large extent, this transformation sheet is a literal translation of the stylesheet from Section 5.10. The main challenge is that we twice must use the trick from Section 7.6.4: first for wrapping the recipes in a `table` element, and second for wrapping the ingredients in a `ul` element.

7.7 Type-Safe XML Programming Languages

We have already seen a number of ways of integrating XML into programming languages:

- the SAX approach, where the programmer implements methods that react on parsing events;

- the DOM/JDOM approach, where the programmer uses a data structure for general XML trees; and

- the JAXB approach, where the programmer uses a data structure for specific XML trees.

The approaches offer a lot of conveniences, but no compile time guarantees about validity of the constructed XML documents (and SAX does not even guarantee well-formedness).

The development of *type-safe* XML programming languages is an active research area. Type safety in this context is concerned with validity of computed XML and avoidance of navigation errors. We shall briefly look at two example languages, both of which are research prototypes and thus not industrial strength implementations.

Programming languages may provide **guarantees** *by using XML schemas as* **types**.

7.7.1 XDuce

XDuce is a first-order functional language in which XML trees are native values. The types are *regular expression types*, which are generalized DTD schemas similar to those used for static type checking in XQuery (see Section 6.7.5). In fact, the type system of XQuery is modeled after that of XDuce.

Function arguments and return values are explicitly typed. XDuce supports a notion of *pattern matching* (known from other functional languages) for deconstructing XML values. Type inference is performed for the variables bound by such patterns.

Applications are type checked at compile time, which ensures that both XML navigation and generation is safe. An example will illustrate this point. First, the recipe collection is described using XDuce types as follows:

```
namespace rcp = "http://www.brics.dk/ixwt/recipes"

type Collection = rcp:collection[Description,Recipe*]
type Description = rcp:description[String]
type Recipe = rcp:recipe[@id[String]?,
```

```
                                    Title,
                                    Date,
                                    Ingredient*,
                                    Preparation,
                                    Comment?,
                                    Nutrition,
                                    Related*]
     type Title = rcp:title[String]
     type Date = rcp:date[String]
     type Ingredient = rcp:ingredient[@name[String],
                                      @amount[String]?,
                                      @unit[String]?,
                                      (Ingredient*,Preparation)?]
     type Preparation = rcp:preparation[Step*]
     type Step = rcp:step[String]
     type Comment = rcp:comment[String]
     type Nutrition = rcp:nutrition[@calories[String],
                                    @carbohydrates[String],
                                    @fat[String],
                                    @protein[String],
                                    @alcohol[String]?]
     type Related = rcp:related[@ref[String],String]
```

These mutually recursive type equations describe in a straightforward manner the possible contents and attributes of the given elements. Note that these types capture exactly the same properties as the DTD schema for recipes (see Section 4.3.6). However, XDuce types are actually as expressive as RELAX NG (if ignoring datatypes for attribute values and character data), so we could have chosen a more expressive type (see Section 4.6.3). The recipe collection is parsed and validated as follows:

```
let val collection = validate load_xml("recipes.xml") with Collection
```

The following XDuce types describe nutrition tables (see Section 5.10):

```
     type NutritionTable = nutrition[Dish*]
     Type Dish = dish[@name[String],
                      @calories[String],
                      @fat[String],
                      @carbohydrates[String],
                      @protein[String],
                      @alcohol[String]]
```

We can now write functions that extract nutrition tables from recipe collections:

```
     fun extractCollection(val c as Collection) : NutritionTable =
       match c with
         rcp:collection[Description, val rs]
           -> nutrition[extractRecipes(rs)]
```

```
fun extractRecipes(val rs as Recipe*) : Dish* =
  match rs with
    rcp:recipe[@..,
                rcp:title[val t],
                Date,
                Ingredient*,
                Preparation,
                Comment?,
                val n as Nutrition,
                Related*], val rest
      -> extractNutrition(t,n), extractRecipes(rest)
  | () -> ()

fun extractNutrition(val t as String, val n as Nutrition) : Dish =
  match n with
    rcp:nutrition[@calories[val calories],
                  @carbohydrates[val carbohydrates],
                  @fat[val fat],
                  @protein[val protein],
                  @alcohol[val alcohol]]
      -> dish[@name[t],
              @calories[calories],
              @carbohydrates[carbohydrates],
              @fat[fat],
              @protein[protein],
              @alcohol[alcohol]]
  | rcp:nutrition[@calories[val calories],
                  @carbohydrates[val carbohydrates],
                  @fat[val fat],
                  @protein[val protein]]
      -> dish[@name[t],
              @calories[calories],
              @carbohydrates[carbohydrates],
              @fat[fat],
              @protein[protein],
              @alcohol["0%"]]
```

Notice how the pattern matching mechanism (match ... with ...) is used to de-construct the recipe collection. In the extractRecipes function we use two patterns: the first accepts non-empty lists and the other empty lists. For the case of a non-empty list, we furthermore deconstruct the first recipe element into the components that we need: the title element (written as an inline type) and the nutrition element (written using the Nutrition type). The function extractNutrition uses two patterns to determine if the optional alcohol attribute is present. The transformation is invoked as follows:

```
let val _ = print(extractCollection(collection))
```

The XDuce type checker now conservatively determines that:

- every function returns a value that validates according to the return type;
- every function argument validates according to the declared type of the called function;
- every `match` has an exhaustive collection of patterns; and
- every pattern matches some values.

Clearly, such guarantees may eliminate many potential errors.

7.7.2 XACT

XACT has a different approach to type-safe XML programming and provides a framework for programming with XML trees in Java. In some sense, this framework is similar to JDOM; however, XACT differs in some important areas:

- it is based on immutable XML *templates*, which are sequences of XML trees containing named *gaps*;
- XML documents are constructed from the templates by *plugging* strings or other templates into the gaps;
- it allows *syntactic sugar* for template constants;
- XML is navigated using XPath; and
- a special analyzer can at compile time decide conservatively if an XML expression will validate according to a given schema.

The following tiny XACT program transforms a business card document into an XHTML phone list:

```
import dk.brics.xact.*;
import java.io.*;

public class PhoneList {
  public static void main(String[] args) throws XactException {
    String[] map = {"c", "http://businesscard.org",
                    "h", "http://www.w3.org/1999/xhtml"};
    XML.setNamespaceMap(map);

    XML wrapper = [[<h:html>
                     <h:head>
                       <h:title><[TITLE]></h:title>
                     </h:head>
                     <h:body>
                       <h:h1><[TITLE]></h:h1>
                       <[MAIN]>
```

```
                </h:body>
              </h:html>]];

   XML cardlist = XML.get("file:cards.xml",
                          "file:businesscards.dtd",
                          "http://businesscard.org");
   XML x = wrapper.plug("TITLE", "My Phone List")
                  .plug("MAIN", [[<h:ul><[CARDS]></h:ul>]]);

   XMLIterator i = cardlist.select("//c:card[c:phone]").iterator();
   while (i.hasNext()) {
     XML card = i.next();
     x = x.plug("CARDS",
                [[<h:li>
                    <h:b><{card.select("c:name/text()")}></h:b>,
                    phone: <{card.select("c:phone/text()")}>
                  </h:li>
                  <[CARDS]>]]);
   }
   System.out.println(x);
 }
}
```

The `wrapper` template contains the boilerplate part of an XHTML page. The `cards.xml` file is parsed and validated against its DTD schema. The variable x is then assigned a copy of the wrapper in which the two occurrences of the TITLE gap are plugged with an appropriate text, and the MAIN gap is plugged with the outline of an unnumbered list. An XMLIterator is used to iterate through the contents elements of the XML template containing those business cards that have phone numbers, and each of these cards is plugged into the list. Finally, the resulting XHTML document is printed on the output stream.

The XML class has the following central methods:

- `constant(s)` builds a template constant from the string s;

- `x.plug(g,y)` constructs a template as a copy of x in which all gaps named g have been replaced by a copy of the string or template y;

- `x.select(p)` returns a template containing the targets of the XPath expression p evaluated on x;

- `x.gapify(p,g)` (not appearing in the example) constructs a template in which the targets of the XPath expression p evaluated on x have been replaced by gaps named g;

- `get(u,d,n)` parses a template from the URL u and validates (at runtime) with DTD d and namespace n; and

- `x.analyze(d,n)` has no effect at runtime but instructs the static analyzer to verify that the value of x is always valid according to the DTD d and namespace n.

Several other variations of these functionalities are available. The XMLIterator class works like iterators from collection classes in Java, except that the next method returns object of class XML (rather than of class Object). The [[...]] notation for XML constants is desugared into calls of the constant method. Gaps of the form <{...}> (*code gaps*) are desugared into ordinary gaps followed by plug operations whose arguments correspond to the contained code.

To further illustrate the use of XACT, we program a transformation on recipe collections that *flattens* nested ingredients. For example, the following recipe seems excessively structured:

```
<rcp:recipe id="117">
  <rcp:title>Fried Eggs with Bacon</rcp:title>
  <rcp:date>Fri, 10 Nov 2004</rcp:date>
  <rcp:ingredient name="fried eggs">
    <rcp:ingredient name="egg" amount="2"/>
    <rcp:preparation>
       <rcp:step>Break the eggs into a bowl.</rcp:step>
       <rcp:step>Fry until ready.</rcp:step>
    </rcp:preparation>
  </rcp:ingredient>
  <rcp:ingredient name="bacon" amount="3" unit="strip"/>
  <rcp:preparation>
    <rcp:step>Fry the bacon until crispy.</rcp:step>
    <rcp:step>Serve with the eggs.</rcp:step>
  </rcp:preparation>
  <rcp:nutrition calories="517"
                 fat="64%" carbohydrates="0%" protein="0%"/>
</rcp:recipe>
```

It could be flattened into the following version:

```
<rcp:recipe id="117">
  <rcp:title>Fried Eggs with Bacon</rcp:title>
  <rcp:date>Fri, 10 Nov 2004</rcp:date>
  <rcp:ingredient name="egg" amount="2"/>
  <rcp:ingredient name="bacon" amount="3" unit="strip"/>
  <rcp:preparation>
    <rcp:step>Break the eggs into a bowl.</rcp:step>
    <rcp:step>Fry until ready.</rcp:step>
    <rcp:step>Fry the bacon until crispy.</rcp:step>
    <rcp:step>Serve with the eggs.</rcp:step>
  </rcp:preparation>
  <rcp:nutrition calories="517"
                 fat="64%" carbohydrates="0%" protein="36%"/>
</rcp:recipe>
```

That is, the nested ingredients and their steps for preparation are moved to the outermost level. This transformation is achieved with the following XACT program:

```
import dk.brics.xact.*;

public class Flatten {
  static final String rcp = "http://www.brics.dk/ixwt/recipes";
  static final String[] map = { "rcp", rcp };

  static { XML.setNamespaceMap(map); }

  public static void main(String[] args) throws XactException {
    XML collection = XML.get("file:recipes.xml",
                             "file:recipes.dtd", rcp);
    XML recipes = collection.select("//rcp:recipe");
    XML result = [[<rcp:collection>
                     <{collection.select("rcp:description")}>
                     <[MORE]>
                   </rcp:collection>]];
    XMLIterator i = recipes.iterator();
    while (i.hasNext()) {
      XML r = i.next();
      result = result.plug("MORE",
        [[<rcp:recipe>
            <{r.select("rcp:title|rcp:date")}>
            <{r.select("//rcp:ingredient[@amount]")}>
            <rcp:preparation>
              <{r.select("//rcp:step")}>
            </rcp:preparation>
            <{r.select("rcp:comment|rcp:nutrition|rcp:related")}>
          </rcp:recipe>
          <[MORE]>]]);
    }
    result.analyze("file:recipes.dtd", rcp);
    System.out.println(result);
  }
}
```

The recipe collection is parsed and validated, and the recipes are extracted. A template for the result is then created with a copy of the original description element and a gap for the flattened recipes. For each original recipe, the flattened version is constructed by copying the title and date elements, extracting all simple ingredient and step elements, and copying the comment, nutrition, and related elements. Finally, the result is analyzed to ensure that the program will always generate valid output.

Let us now introduce an error in the above program by changing the occurrence of the recipe element into an ingredient element:

```
<rcp:ingredient>
  <{r.select("rcp:title|rcp:date")}>
  <{r.select("//rcp:ingredient[@amount]")}>
  <rcp:preparation>
```

```
           <{r.select("//rcp:step")}>
         </rcp:preparation>
         <{r.select("rcp:comment|rcp:nutrition|rcp:related")}>
       </rcp:ingredient>
```

This change will clearly cause the running program to generate invalid recipe data, and the compile time analyzer immediately detects this potential error:

```
*** Invalid XML at line 31
 sub-element 'rcp:ingredient' of element 'rcp:collection'
   not declared
 required attribute 'name' missing in element 'rcp:ingredient'
 sub-element 'rcp:title' of element 'rcp:ingredient'
   not declared
 sub-element 'rcp:related' of element 'rcp:ingredient'
   not declared
 sub-element 'rcp:nutrition' of element 'rcp:ingredient'
   not declared
 sub-element 'rcp:date' of element 'rcp:ingredient' not declared
```

Note that XACT programs, unlike XDuce programs, do not require any type annotations, except for the specification of DTD schemas for `get` and `analyze`. This choice allows a natural Java-like programming style and, importantly, does not require intermediate XML values to be valid according to any given schema.

7.8   Chapter Summary

There are many occasions to write programs that operate on XML data. Domain-specific languages, like XSLT and XQuery, may cover many applications, but general-purpose programming is essential. Frameworks like DOM and JDOM simply provide a generic data structure for representing and manipulating XML trees. XML data binding, as exemplified by JAXB, provides schema specific data structures for XML trees belonging to a particular language. Streaming techniques, like SAX and STX, handle the situation where huge XML documents must be processed but do not fit into memory. As a final twist, type-safe XML programming languages solve similar programming tasks as DOM/JDOM, but provide compile time guarantees about the validity of the computed XML results. XDuce is such a language in the functional tradition, and XACT is based on Java.

7.9   Further Reading

Details of the presented technologies are best obtained from the specifications available through the online resources. Two alternative frameworks for DOM-style APIs for XML in

Java are DOM4J and XOM (see the online resources). Publications about the XDuce project include the papers [47, 46]. The XACT project is documented in [51, 50]. A survey of typed XML transformation languages is available in [62].

7.10   Online Resources

`http://www.w3.org/DOM/`
The W3C DOM Level 3 specifications (several documents).

`http://www.jdom.org/`
The JDOM project.

`http://www.dom4j.org/`
The DOM4J project.

`http://www.cafeconleche.org/XOM/`
The XOM project.

`http://java.sun.com/xml/jaxp/`
Sun's JAXP documentation and download.

`http://java.sun.com/xml/jaxb/`
Sun's JAXB documentation and download.

`http://jaxb.dev.java.net/`
The JAXB Reference Implementation Project.

`http://www.saxproject.org/`
The SAX project.

`http://www.xmlpull.org/`
The XmlPull project.

`http://stx.sourceforge.net/`
The STX project.

`http://xduce.sourceforge.net/`
The XDuce project.

`http://www.brics.dk/Xact/`
The XACT project.

7.11   Exercises

The main lessons to be learned from these exercises are:

- using JDOM and JAXB to write XML applications in Java;
- writing streaming applications using SAX and STX; and
- using typed XML transformation languages.

Exercise 7.1 Write a Java/JDOM program that combines two recipe collections (and removes doublets).

Exercise 7.2 Write a Java/JDOM program that has the same effect as the XSLT transformation for business cards (see Section 5.1).

TIP

The javadoc documentations for the various frameworks are indispensable when developing applications.

Exercise 7.3 Use JAXB to write a Java application that reads XML documents describing small computations, such as *EX*/while.xml, and computes their results. Use the XML Schema description *EX*/while.xsd.

Exercise 7.4 Write a Java/SAX parser that reads the recipe collection and finds those ingredients that use the largest and the smallest volume, respectively. Use the following conversions: 1 cup = 240ml, 1 tablespoon = 15ml, 1 teaspoon = 5 ml.

Exercise 7.5 Extend the business card editor (see Section 7.3.6) with a load button that allows the user to specify an XML document whose contents are added to the current collection.

Exercise 7.6 Consider the task of counting the number of input elements in XHTML documents. Make an implementation in both JDOM and SAX. How large input documents can each of the two handle? How do their running times compare?

Exercise 7.7 Implement a SAX version of the solution to Exercise 7.1. How much data must be stored during processing?

Exercise 7.8 Implement SAX filters for each of the following tasks:

(a) Change all character data to upper case.
(b) Delete all entity references.
(c) Rename all elements with local name foo to bar.

Create an implementation that chains them together. Run it on *EX*/filter.xml.

Exercise 7.9 Write an XmlPull version of your solution to Exercise 7.4.

Exercise 7.10 Consider the XSLT stylesheets *EX*/stx1.xsl and *EX*/stx2.xsl. Try to write equivalent STX transformation sheets for both of them.

Exercise 7.11 Consider the XDuce application *EX*/buggy.q. Use the XDuce compiler to find all type errors and then correct them.

Exercise 7.12 Consider the XACT application *EX*/Buggy.xact. Use the XACT compiler to find all type errors and then correct them.

PART II
WEB TECHNOLOGIES

THE HTTP PROTOCOL

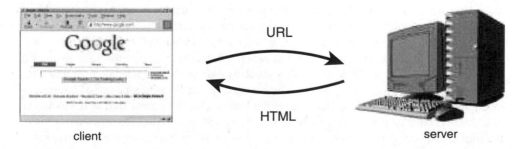

8

Objectives

In this chapter, you will learn:

- How the HTTP protocol works
- The SSL security extension from a programmer's point of view
- How to write servers and clients in Java

8.1   The Internet and HTTP

HTTP, *HyperText Transfer Protocol*, is one of the cornerstones of the infrastructure of the Web. It prescribes how machines on the Web can exchange HTML and XML documents, form field values, and other data. HTTP uses a *client–server* model where communication follows a simple *request–response* pattern. That is, a client, typically a Web browser, takes the initiative to request some resource identified by a URL, for example an HTML document, from a server. (In this and the following chapters, we often mean 'HTML or XHTML' when we write 'HTML'.) Provided that the request is accepted, the server responds by returning the resource:

HTTP is the main communication protocol of the Web.

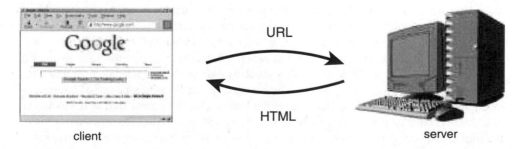

client   server

Note that this approach is unlike other communication patterns, most notably *peer-to-peer* (P2P) networks where nodes act as both clients and servers and any node can initiate interaction.

Originally, the resources being communicated on the Web were mostly static documents, such as reports, manuals, and home pages, residing in the file system of the Web server. However, since then, the applications have gradually shifted towards dynamically generated contents. Instead of merely dishing out files from the disk, modern Web servers increasingly generate their response by executing specialized programs that are developed using frameworks such as Java servlets and JSP (see Chapters 9 and 10). Typically, the HTML documents being transmitted contain forms (see Section 1.4), which allow data to be sent also from the client to the server. Such *interactive Web services* can provide up-to-date and tailor-made information, since the replies are generated at the time of the request and based on user input and the current state of the data on the server.

To understand in more detail how HTTP works, we first need to look briefly at its foundation: the underlying network protocols of the Internet. These are organized in a number of layers:

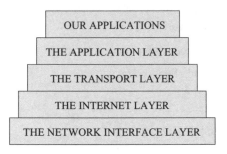

(This is, in fact, a simplified view with a level of abstraction that suffices for our needs; the commonly used OSI model operates with seven layers instead.)

The bottom layer – the *network interface layer* – is the hardware that handles the actual transportation of individual bits from one physical location to another, using Ethernet, smoke signals, or whatever.

IP is a low-level protocol for unreliable communication of small data packets.

On the *Internet layer* we find the Internet Protocol (IP). It introduces the notions of *IP addresses* and *datagrams*. IP addresses (also called *IP numbers*) are used for identifying machines on the network. For example, the IP address 165.193.130.107 belongs to the main Web server of Pearson Education. The Internet Assigned Numbers Authority (IANA) manages the allocation of IP addresses in various sized blocks to organizations. A datagram is a packet of data of limited size (up to 65,535 bytes, but only 1500 bytes on Ethernet networks). The Internet Protocol tells how to send individual datagrams from one machine to another machine, identified by an IP address. This involves *routing* though intermediate machines on the network. We will not explain the deeper structure of IP addresses nor of the routing mechanisms, however, we note that one particularly useful IP address during development is 127.0.0.1, which always refers to the current machine, also called the *localhost*. IP is an *unreliable* protocol: datagrams may be lost (if a router crashes, for example), they may arrive in a different order than they were sent (if the datagrams are sent through different paths to the destination), and they may even be duplicated.

The *transport layer* contains TCP, the Transmission Control Protocol. It adds a number of useful features: conceptually, data is transmitted in a *stream* of unbounded size. TCP takes care of cutting such a stream into IP datagrams and reassembling them when they are received. *Reliability* is ensured by retransmitting lost datagrams, reordering the datagrams appropriately when they are received, and throwing away duplicates. We say that TCP is *connection-oriented*: to use TCP, one sets up a *connection* between the two machines involved. Once the connection is established, both parties can send and receive data (this ability is also called *full-duplex*) until the connection is terminated.

The two end points of a TCP connection are called *sockets*. To allow one machine to be involved in many TCP connections simultaneously, it is necessary to know not just the IP address of the machine but also the *port* that has been bound to each socket on that machine. A port is a number between 0 and 65535. Those in the range 0–1023 are called *well known ports* and are assigned to server applications that are executed by privileged processes (the root user on UNIX and variants). For example, port 80 is reserved for HTTP communication, ports 20 and 21 are for FTP servers, port 25 is for SMTP servers, and 443 is for HTTPS. (FTP, SMTP, and HTTPS are mentioned further below.) The range 1024–49151 contains the *registered ports*, which are allocated through IANA to avoid vendor conflicts. For example, port 8080 is reserved as an alternative to port 80 for running a Web server using ordinary user privileges. The remaining ports are called *dynamic and/or private ports* and can be used freely by any client or server program. It is perfectly acceptable to set up a Web server listening for requests on port 50042, for example, even though port 80 is more common. Browsers obtain ports for their TCP sockets arbitrarily among the unused non-well-known ports, chosen by the operating system. Since a TCP connection is characterized by a 4-tuple consisting of the IP addresses and port numbers of the end points, it is possible for each port on a machine to be involved in many concurrent connections. This capability is useful for building multi-threaded servers that handle multiple connections concurrently. We will see in Section 8.4 how to directly access the TCP layer from Java, bypassing HTTP.

An alternative to TCP in the transport layer is UDP (User Datagram Protocol) which basically just makes IP communication available to upper-level processes. That is, it is unreliable and datagram-oriented, but in return, it is faster than TCP. UDP is used for video and voice transmission where speed is essential and occasional losses are acceptable. These applications often exploit a multicasting mechanism in IP for delivering information to multiple destinations simultaneously. UDP is also used as the foundation for higher-level protocols such as DNS, which is described below.

The layers described so far constitute the basic infrastructure of the Internet. The specifications for the TCP/IP suite are from 1981, but the ideas originate from the late 1960s when ARPANET, a wide-area network created by the United States Defense Advanced Research Project Agency, was initially designed. Most of the Internet traffic today uses what is called Version 4 of the IP protocol, also known as IPv4, which after more than 20 years of service is beginning to have problems. In particular, there is a growing shortage of IP addresses, even though IPv4 theoretically permits up to four billion addresses. IPv6, the next generation IP protocol, solves this problem and also adds many other improvements in the areas of routing and network configuration.

TCP provides reliable bidirectional streaming data connections between client and server programs.

HTTP belongs in the *application layer*. The layer has this confusing name for historical reasons – it contains *applications* of the transport layer; our own applications usually build on top of HTTP. Similarly, the name *Internet layer* is confusing since 'Internet' colloquially refers to the entire protocol stack, including hardware and applications.

HTTP requests and responses are transmitted using TCP. We go into further detail of HTTP in the following sections. First, Sections 8.1.1 and 8.1.2 describe the formats of requests and responses, Section 8.1.3 shows how form field input is transferred, and in Section 8.1.4 we discuss HTTP support for authentication of clients. There are two main versions of HTTP: HTTP/1.0 and HTTP/1.1. The Web is gradually shifting towards using HTTP/1.1, which provides better support for caching, bandwidth optimization, error notification, security, and content negotiation. We will look into some of these issues later in the chapter.

Other protocols on the application layer include FTP (File Transfer Protocol), which was popular for transferring files on networks before HTTP was invented and dates back to 1973 (long before TCP/IP was invented); SMTP (Simple Mail Transfer Protocol), which is the standard protocol for the exchange of email; and DNS (Domain Name System), which defines the structure of *domain names* and services that govern their association with IP addresses, for example, that `www.pearsoned.com` is associated with IP address 165.193.130.107.

The use of domain names and DNS has several benefits. First, domain names are resistant to moving services from one machine to another on the network. Second, one domain name may be associated with multiple IP addresses, which permits easy replication of servers for decreasing workload and improving fault tolerance. Third, one IP address may be associated with multiple domain names to permit one machine to host many domains (this is called *virtual hosting*). And finally, domain names are more easily remembered by humans than IP addresses.

In this chapter, we will mainly look at the transport layer (TCP connections), the application layer (HTTP), and, of course, the actual applications that we can build on top.

One important issue is missing in this description: none of the protocols that we have mentioned so far guarantee confidentiality and integrity of the communication, nor authentication of the server. These security aspects are the topic of Section 8.3, which describes the SSL protocol from an application programmer's perspective.

8.1.1 Requests

As discussed in Section 1.3, a URI identifies a network resource. It is presumably well known to most Web surfers that URIs often have the following form:

```
http://host:port/path?query
```

A typical example is

```
http://www.google.com/search?q=An+Introduction+to+XML+and
                             +Web+Technologies
```

This form of URIs uses the scheme `http`, which identifies the HTTP protocol. The host field, `www.google.com` in the example above, is a domain name, which has been registered via DNS. IP addresses may be used instead of domain names. The port field is omitted in this example, but for the `http` scheme, port 80 is the default. Together, the host field and the port field identify the Web server program to process our request. The path field, here just the string `search`, is typically a path in the server's file system where the resource is stored, or it may locate a program that is able to generate the appropriate response. Generally, the server decides the interpretation of this field. The query field, if present, contains arguments to the program that processes the request. We will see below how such arguments are encoded. As described in Section 1.3, a URI reference may additionally contain a fragment identifier.

An **HTTP request** is a message being sent from the client to the server using TCP.

An HTTP request from a client to a server is simply sent using TCP. As an example, entering the above URI in a browser will cause a TCP connection to be established with the designated IP address (determined from the host name using DNS) and TCP port (80 in this example). A message like the following will then be sent from the browser to the server:

```
GET /search?q=An+Introduction+to+XML+and+Web+Technologies HTTP/1.1
Host: www.google.com
User-Agent: Mozilla/5.0 (X11; U; Linux i686; en-US; rv:1.7.2)
    Gecko/20040803
Accept: text/xml,application/xml,application/xhtml+xml,
    text/html;q=0.9,text/plain;q=0.8,image/png,*/*;q=0.5
Accept-Language: da,en-us;q=0.8,en;q=0.5,sw;q=0.3
Accept-Encoding: gzip,deflate
Accept-Charset: ISO-8859-1,utf-8;q=0.7,*;q=0.7
Keep-Alive: 300
Connection: keep-alive
Referer: http://www.google.com/
```

(The two indented lines indicate line breaks that have been inserted to make the example fit the page.) An HTTP request always begins with a *request line*:

```
GET /search?q=An+Introduction+to+XML+and+Web+Technologies HTTP/1.1
```

This particular request uses the GET method (explained below), asking the server to send the resource `/search?q=An+Introduction+to+XML+and+Web+Technologies`, using version 1.1 of the HTTP protocol. The remaining lines in the message are *header lines*, each having the form

```
field: value
```

Both HTTP/1.0 and HTTP/1.1 follow this form, the main difference being that HTTP/1.1, which we focus on, supports an extended set of header fields. We will in the following go through the essential fields that are related to requests.

`Host:` The value of this field is the domain name (and the port number, if not using the default) of the server that the request is intended for, in this case `www.google.com`. This field is necessary for virtual hosting (as mentioned earlier) where one machine is host for several domain names, since the domain name system is independent of the TCP connection that has been established between the client machine and the server machine. The field is optional in HTTP/1.0 but mandatory in all requests that use HTTP/1.1.

User-Agent: This field contains information about the user agent (typically a browser or a search robot) originating the request. This information is intended for statistical purposes and for tailoring responses to avoid particular user agent limitations. The value in the example tells us that the request originates from a Mozilla 1.7.2 browser running on a Linux i686 architecture with X11, with strong security (indicated by the U) and using the Gecko layout engine version 20040803 – or at least, that is what the user agent claims. The format is determined by the user agent developer.

Referer: This field (sadly misspelled in the original HTTP specification) allows the client to specify the URI of the resource from which the request URI was obtained, which can be useful for tracking user behavior. For example, if an HTML page contains an img image link, then the request for the image will contain a Referer field set to the URI of the HTML page.

A number of fields pertain to describing client capabilities, characteristics, and preferences. One use of these fields is for *content negotiation*. This is a mechanism that allows servers to supply the user with the best available information. For example, in a request, the client may inform the server that English documents are preferred, so if a requested document on the server exists in multiple languages, like English and Swahili, the most useful version can be chosen by the server.

Accept: The Accept field can be used to specify *media types* that are acceptable as a response. These are also called *MIME types* – this stands for *Multipurpose Internet Mail Extensions*, although nowadays being used for much more than email communication. They describe various aspects of data formats, that is, the kind of data that eventually is represented as bits and bytes. Common media types include the following:

text/plain: a generic type for plain unformatted text.

text/html: describes HTML documents (not XHTML).

text/xml: describes XML documents.

application/xml: describes XML documents – as the previous type, but preferable for application data rather than human readable data. (The distinction is admittedly a bit blurry.)

application/xhtml+xml: the recommended type to associate with XHTML documents. (The previous two may also be used.)

multipart/form-data: used for transmission of HTML-like form field values (see Section 8.1.3).

application/octet-stream: represents arbitrary binary data, often also used for binary data that does not fit into other established categories.

image/jpeg: describes JPEG images.

A long list of media types is registered at IANA.

The `Accept` field in the example shows that the client is willing to receive XML, XHTML, and HTML documents, and also plain text and PNG images:

```
Accept: text/xml,application/xml,application/xhtml+xml,
    text/html;q=0.9,text/plain;q=0.8,image/png,*/*;q=0.5
```

In addition, the field contains `*/*`, which represents all media types, meaning that whatever the server might send, the client will accept it and do its best. The `q` parameters indicate a relative quality factor on a scale from 0 to 1 (with 1 as default) of the preceding media type. The value 0 means 'not acceptable'. The example can then be interpreted as: 'I prefer XML and XHTML documents and PNG images but if the server judges that the quality of such data will be at most 90% compared to an HTML version (or if an XML/XHTML/PNG version is not available at all), then send me the HTML version; similarly, if a plain text version is the best available after an 80% mark-down in quality I'll prefer that one; and finally, an arbitrary other type is acceptable if nothing else fits'. In particular, this header line tells us that the client prefers XHTML over HTML and PNG over GIF.

`Accept-Language`: This field is similar to `Accept` but describes the natural languages being preferred instead of the media types. Consider again the example:

```
Accept-Language: da,en-us;q=0.8,en;q=0.5,sw;q=0.3
```

This header line means that Danish is preferred, next comes US English, then other dialects of English, and finally Swahili. Any other language is also implicitly acceptable, but with the lowest precedence. All this can be configured in most browsers by the user.

`Accept-Encoding`: This field specifies the accepted *content codings*, which are usually data compression techniques. The client in our example accepts data that has been compressed with *gzip* or *deflate*:

```
Accept-Encoding: gzip,deflate
```

The server is then allowed to compress its response using one of these techniques for saving network bandwidth. Quality factors may be specified, as above.

`Accept-Charset`: This field can be used to specify the accepted character sets for the response.

```
Accept-Charset: ISO-8859-1,utf-8;q=0.7,*;q=0.7
```

This particular header line means that the ISO-8859-1 character encoding (see Section 1.8) is preferred. (Since both `utf-8` and `*` have quality factor 0.7 and the latter matches any code, the part containing `utf-8` is in fact redundant.)

The fields `Keep-Alive` and `Connection` that occur in the example request are explained in Section 8.1.5.

The example uses, as mentioned, the GET method, which is one particular kind of request. This method simply instructs the server to return the specified resource. Another commonly used request method is the POST method, which is intended for more complex requests that involve submitting data to the server, for example large form field values, in conjunction with the request URI. As we shall see in Section 8.1.3, both GET and POST actually permit data to be uploaded to the server, and the differences are, in fact, quite subtle.

Several other request methods are possible, although less widely used. The most interesting are the following: *HEAD* works as GET but only the header of the response is returned, not the body; *PUT* is in a sense the opposite of GET – it uploads a resource to be made available at a given URI; and *DELETE* deletes the designated resource. Practical use of the latter two naturally requires some sort of access control (see Section 8.1.4). Still, neither PUT nor DELETE are used much in practice. Instead, POST requests are commonly used for achieving a similar functionality.

8.1.2   Responses

The response from the server to the client is sent using the same TCP connection as the request (recall that TCP connections are bidirectional). It consists of a *header* and a *body*. The first line in the header is a *status line* indicating the overall result of the attempt to satisfy the request, and the lines that follow are header lines, which we describe below. The response body (not to confuse with the `body` element in the example below), which is separated from the header by a single empty line, contains the resource that has been requested, provided that the request could be satisfied.

As an example, requesting the URI

```
http://www.brics.dk/index.html
```

might give us the following response from the server (abbreviated with '. . .'):

```
HTTP/1.1 200 OK
Date: Fri, 17 Sep 2009 07:59:01 GMT
Server: Apache/2.0.50 (Unix) mod_perl/1.99_10 Perl/v5.8.4
    mod_ssl/2.0.50 OpenSSL/0.9.7d DAV/2 PHP/4.3.8 mod_bigwig/2.1-3
Last-Modified: Tue, 24 Feb 2009 08:32:26 GMT
ETag: "ec002-afa-fd67ba80"
Accept-Ranges: bytes
Content-Length: 2810
Content-Type: text/html

<!DOCTYPE HTML PUBLIC "-//W3C//DTD HTML 4.01 Transitional//EN">
<html>
<head>
<meta http-equiv="Content-Type"
      content="text/html; charset=ISO-8859-1">
```

```
<title>BRICS - Basic Research in Computer Science</title>
</head>
<body>
...
</body>
</html>
```

(As before, the line breaks at the indented lines do not appear in the actual data.) Here, the status line is

```
HTTP/1.1 200 OK
```

This line tells us that the response is using HTTP/1.1 and that the status code for the request is *200 OK*, meaning that the request has succeeded and that the requested resource follows. Note that it is possible that the client request is using HTTP/1.0 but the server replies in HTTP/1.1 – but fortunately, HTTP/1.0 is designed to be forward compatible and tolerant to deviations from the specification, for example, by ignoring header fields that are not understood.

Status codes are grouped into five classes, according to the first digit:

1xx: *Informational.* Indicate a provisional response. (This class is not commonly used.)

2xx: *Success.* The request was successfully received, understood, and accepted. Common status codes in this group are:

200 OK: The request has succeeded and the requested resource follows, as in the example above.

206 Partial Content: This code is related to *range requests* (see Section 8.1.5).

3xx: *Redirection.* Further action must be taken by the client in order to complete the request.

301 Moved Permanently: The requested resource has been assigned a new permanent URI and any future references to this resource should use the returned URI (specified with the `Location` header field; see below). When receiving this message, browsers will automatically issue a second request for the new URI.

304 Not Modified: This code is related to *conditional requests* (see Section 8.1.5).

307 Temporary Redirect: The requested resource resides temporarily under a different URI. Unlike code 301, the client should not update any bookmarks since the new URI might change in later requests. (Temporary Redirect was numbered 302 in HTTP/1.0 but was changed to avoid confusion about the rules for automatic redirection.)

4xx: *Client Error.* The request contains syntax errors or cannot be fulfilled for other reasons caused by the client.

400 Bad Request: The request could not be understood by the server due to malformed syntax.

401 Unauthorized: This code is related to *user authorization* (see Section 8.1.4).

403 Forbidden: The server understood the request, but is refusing to fulfill it. The reason might be given in the response body. Often it results from improper file or directory permissions on the server.

404 Not Found: Even novice Web surfers presumably know this code. It indicates that the server has not found anything matching the request (often due to a mistyped URI in the browser), or that the server does not wish to reveal exactly why the request has been refused.

406 Not Acceptable: The server is unable to fulfill the request, given the `Accept`, `Accept-Language`, `Accept-Encoding`, and `Accept-Charset` header lines specified in the request.

415 Unsupported Media Type: The server cannot fulfill the request because it uses media types that are not supported.

5xx: *Server Error.* The server failed to fulfill an apparently valid request.

500 Internal Server Error: Indicates a serious error in the server. Details about the error might be available in the server log.

501 Not Implemented: The functionality required to handle the request has not been implemented.

503 Service Unavailable: The server is currently unable to handle the request, typically due to overloading or maintenance.

In the case of unsuccessful requests, an explanatory message, usually an HTML document, is returned in the body of the response message. For the full list of status codes, see the HTTP specification.

Let us now examine the most common header lines in an HTTP response. In the example, the header tells us, among other information, that the response contains a 2,810 byte HTML document.

`Date`: This field shows the date and time at which the message was sent, which is relevant for caching purposes.

`Server`: The `Server` field contains information about the server software. In the example,

```
Server: Apache/2.0.50 (Unix) mod_perl/1.99_10 Perl/v5.8.4
    mod_ssl/2.0.50 OpenSSL/0.9.7d DAV/2 PHP/4.3.8 mod_bigwig/2.1-3
```

the server identifies itself as an Apache server version 2.0.50 configured with a number of modules, such as `mod_perl` (for Perl scripts) and `mod_ssl` (for SSL).

`ETag`: This field is used in cache management (see Section 8.1.5). Although it looks cryptic, it is usually just a simple digest of the resource being returned, based on, for example, the file size and last modification time.

Content-Length: The value of this field is the number of bytes in the message body that follows the header.

Content-Type: This field can be used to describe the media type of the resource being returned. In the example, the resource is an HTML document:

```
Content-Type: text/html
```

This media type should naturally be among those allowed by the Accept request header field described in the previous section, if that field is present.

Content-Encoding: The Content-Encoding field shows if the data is compressed, for example with gzip, or some other coding has been applied. See also the description of the Accept-Encoding request header field in the previous section. (This field and the next two do not occur in the example shown above.)

Transfer-Encoding: If present, the value of this field is usually chunked meaning that the response body has been split into a series of *chunks*. This feature can be useful in conjunction with persistent connections (see Section 8.1.5) for large HTML pages that are dynamically generated top-down in chunks where the length of the entire content is not known in advance, such that each chunk can be delivered and presented to the user as soon as possible.

Location: This header field is used together with status codes *301 Moved Permanently*, *307 Temporary Redirect*, and others, for specifying the new URI.

The header fields Last-Modified and Accept-Ranges, which both appear in the example, are explained in Section 8.1.5 along with other advanced features of HTTP.

8.1.3 HTML Forms

In the HTML Survivor's Guide (see Section 1.4), we explained the HTML fill-out form mechanism from the HTML author's and user's perspective. We are now in a position to understand what happens under the hood.

Consider the following HTML fragment:

```
<h3>The Poll Service</h3>
<form action="http://freewig.brics.dk/users/laudrup/soccer.jsp"
      method="post">
Who wins the World Cup 2006?
<select name="bet">
<option value="br">Brazil!</option>
<option selected value="dk">Denmark!</option>
<option value="other country">someone else?</option>
</select><br>
Please enter your email address: <input type="text" name="email"><br>
<input type="submit" name="send" value="Go!">
</form>
```

Note that the HTML code contains one `form` element with an `action` attribute and a `method` attribute, in addition to three form fields: a selection menu named `bet`, a text field named `email`, and a submit button named `send`.

A browser might render this HTML fragment as follows, after the user has filled out the form and is ready to submit it to the server:

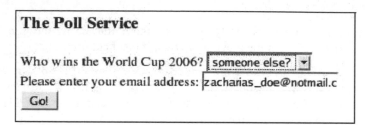

When the submit button is clicked, the browser collects the form field values as a list of name–value pairs:

Name	Value
bet	other country
email	zacharias_doe@notmail.com
send	Go!

This list is then encoded into a *query string* according to the media type chosen by an `enctype` attribute of the `form` element. By default, the media type `application/x-www-form-urlencoded` (also called *URL encoding*) is used, which results in the following for our example:

```
bet=other+country&email=zacharias_doe%40notmail.com&send=Go%21
```

The fields are listed in the order they appear in the HTML document with an ampersand (`&`) between each field and an equals symbol (`=`) between each name and the corresponding value. Names and values are encoded by replacing each space character by a plus symbol (`+`) and each non-alphanumeric character (except the following symbols: `$-_.+!*'(),`) by `%NN`, where *NN* is the ASCII code of the character in hexadecimal form. Line breaks are encoded as `%0d%0a`. This media type should not be used with non-ASCII symbols, however, this restriction is often ignored; most browsers choose to represent such symbols according to the declared character set encoding of the source document (for example using `Content-Type: text/html; charset=UTF-8`). An alternative media type, `multipart/form-data`, is described later in this section.

Now, what happens from here on depends on whether the `method` attribute of the `form` element has the value `get` or `post`, corresponding to the two main request methods of HTTP:

GET: With the GET request method, the query string is incorporated into the request URI as indicated in Section 8.1.1. In our HTML form example, this method results in the following URI (without the line break):

```
http://freewig.brics.dk/freewig.brics.dk/users/laudrup/soccer.jsp?
bet=other+country&email=zacharias_doe%40notmail.com&send=Go%21
```

That is, the following request line will appear in the HTTP request (again, all on a single line):

```
GET /users/laudrup/soccer.jsp?bet=other+country&email=
zacharias_doe%40notmail.com&send=Go%21 HTTP/1.1
```

POST: With the POST request method, the query string will instead be placed in the *body* of the HTTP request, which then may look as follows:

```
POST /users/laudrup/soccer.jsp HTTP/1.1
Host: freewig.brics.dk
Content-Type: application/x-www-form-urlencoded
Content-Length: 62

bet=other+country&email=zacharias_doe%40notmail.com&send=Go%21
```

As in HTTP responses, the request body is separated from the header by an empty line.

Why the need for two different methods? Although they seem to provide the same functionality there are several technical differences:

> The **GET** request method is mainly intended for retrieving data; **POST** is intended for operations that have side-effects on the server.

- GET requests should be *safe* to the client meaning that the client cannot be held accountable for any side-effects that are generated by retrieving the requested resource. (This is admittedly a rather vague definition.) Moreover, GET requests should also be *idempotent*, meaning that the side-effects of a number of identical GET requests are the same as for a single request. POST requests do not have these restrictions. Clicking 'Reload' on a page that results from a POST request causes browsers to pop up a window warning the user that this might repeat the action that the form has carried out; such a warning is not necessary for GET requests.

- Responses to GET requests are cachable unless otherwise specified in the response header; for POST requests it is the opposite: these are by default *not* cachable. (However, most browsers treat GET requests of URIs with non-empty query strings as non-cachable regardless of this, just to be on the safe side.) We discuss caching further in Section 8.1.5.

- Clicking on an HTML link results in a GET request. The URI in such a link may contain a query string. With forms, both GET and POST are possible, as described above, and GET is the default.

- Some browsers and servers unfortunately limit the length of URLs (2048 bytes in Internet Explorer), which makes the GET method impractical for large input field values.

- For GET requests, the only possible media type for the query string is `application/ x-www-form-urlencoded`.

- Servers usually log request URIs, but not the request bodies. Sensitive information, such as passwords, should therefore always be submitted using POST.

Uploading files with forms requires a different media type encoding, `multipart/form- data` (and therefore only works with the POST method). This media type is also more suitable for submission of non-ASCII data. The body of such a request consists of a sequence of parts corresponding to the sequence of form fields, where each part contains a *content- disposition header* and the field value. This header describes the field name, the content type and character set of the value, its transfer encoding, and, in the case of a file upload field, also the file name.

8.1.4 Authentication

Many Web applications restrict access to authorized users only. There are various techniques for achieving this, the simplest of which are the following:

- *IP-address-based:* The server only permits access from certain IP addresses (or do- main names).

- *Form-based:* The first page being shown to the user contains an ordinary form with a name field and a password field (where the latter is often an input field with `type="password"`).

- *HTTP Basic:* This is a simple challenge–response mechanism that is built into the HTTP protocol; we explain it below in detail.

- *HTTP Digest:* This is a complex variant of HTTP Basic authentication ensuring that passwords are always transmitted in encrypted form.

These authentication techniques work only in one direction: none of them helps the client authenticate the server. Also, none of the techniques helps ensuring confidentiality and integrity of the communication. We return to these issues in Section 8.3.

HTTP Basic authentication works as follows. When the client first requests the resource, the server responds with a *401 Unauthorized* message:

```
HTTP/1.1 401 Authorization Required
WWW-Authenticate: Basic realm="The Doe Family Site"
Content-Length: 476
Content-Type: text/html; charset=iso-8859-1
```

```
<!DOCTYPE HTML PUBLIC "-//IETF//DTD HTML 2.0//EN">
<html><head>
<title>401 Authorization Required</title>
</head><body>
<h1>Authorization Required</h1>
<p>This server could not verify that you are authorized to access
the document requested. Either you supplied the wrong credentials
(such as, bad password), or your browser doesn't understand how
to supply the credentials required.</p>
<hr />
<address>Apache/2.0.50 (Unix) at www.brics.dk Port 80</address>
</body></html>
```

(The status line should have been HTTP/1.1 401 Unauthorized, but this is what the Apache 2.0.50 server generates – except for certain irrelevant headers that are not shown here.) The header line

```
WWW-Authenticate: Basic realm="The Doe Family Site"
```

describes how the server wants the authentication to take place. The word Basic means that the server is asking the user to authenticate himself using the HTTP Basic authentication mechanism. (The HTTP Digest mechanism instead uses the word Digest, not surprisingly.) The value of realm is the name of the part of the server that this authentication applies to.

The browser then pops up a familiar-looking window requesting the user to enter a username and password (this information is also called the *challenge*):

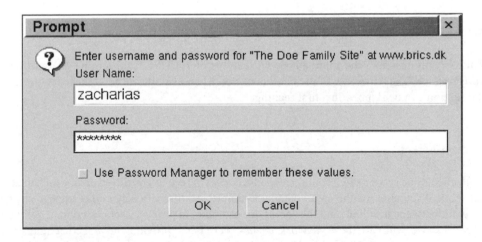

If the user clicks 'Cancel', the message placed in the body of the HTTP response, in this case an HTML document, is shown to the user. If instead the user enters a name and a password and then clicks 'OK', a second interaction takes place: the client responds to the challenge by repeating the original request but adding an extra HTTP header line (the *response* to the challenge):

```
Authorization: Basic emFjaGFyaWFzOmFwcGxlcGllCg==
```

The text following `Basic` is the *base64* encoding of the string `username:password`. Base64 is a simple encoding scheme whereby binary data can be converted to printable ASCII characters. Although the result looks cryptic there is no encryption involved – anyone can decode the string to obtain the original data, which is the reason why this mechanism is usually combined with SSL encryption (see Section 8.3). The point in using base64 here is mainly that the printable ASCII characters are legal in HTTP headers, unlike the possible original characters.

The server then decodes the username and password and checks them with its access restrictions. If the values are not accepted, the *401 Unauthorized* message is returned again. Otherwise, the server can begin processing the actual request.

In subsequent interactions with that server, the browser can send the `Authorization` header immediately, without any user involvement. This is, of course, convenient to the user, but it is also potentially insecure if the browser is shared by many people. There is unfortunately no way the server can tell the client to forget the username/password that the user has entered in order to log out of the restricted area.

We will not describe the details of HTTP Digest. It is not widely used since SSL, perhaps combined with HTTP Basic, provides stronger security guarantees.

Compared with form-based authentication, HTTP authentication has the benefit of being supported by most servers, so it is easy to use for the Web application programmer. The form-based approach provides more flexibility but also requires more work by the programmer.

8.1.5   Other Advanced Features

This section describes the more advanced features of HTTP/1.1, all aiming at improving performance. The remainder of the book does not depend significantly on these features, so the section can be skipped in a first reading.

Cache Control

Cache control, range requests, and **persistent connections** improve HTTP performance.

Both clients and servers often contain response *caches* of recently retrieved data, which makes subsequent requests for the same data superfluous. Additional caches may appear on the network between the client and the server, for example, in proxy servers or content delivery networks; we will call these *network caches*. HTTP/1.1 provides advanced features for controlling caches, which can significantly improve performance by removing redundancy. These features are controlled by the `Cache-Control` header field. This field is relevant both in responses (when the server needs to control the client and network caches) and in requests (when the client needs to control the server and network caches). Some of the possibilities are explained in the following:

`no-store`: This value instructs caches not to keep a copy of the message under any conditions.

`no-cache`: This value instructs caches to never return a cached version of the message without a successful revalidation with the origin server. That is, the server must confirm that the cached version is still valid before it can be used.

`public`: When this value is used in a response header, it indicates that the response may be cached.

`private`: This value indicates that the response message is intended for a single user and may not be cached by a shared cache (in particular, a network cache).

`max-age`: This value can be used in responses to specify expiration of the accompanying data. For example, `max-age=42` means that the response is stale 42 seconds after being sent. Alternatively, the absolute date and time of expiration can be specified using the `Expires` header field.

`must-revalidate`: Unless this value occurs in a response, caches are in some conditions allowed to ignore the server specified expiration time and return stale data (for example, if the server is not responding).

As a nontrivial example, the following header line occurring in an HTTP response means that the data may be cached, but only for one hour, and the server should confirm all uses of the cached version if possible:

```
Cache-Control: public, no-cache, max-age=3600
```

In order to be able to determine whether a resource has changed, responses contain either a `Last-Modified` header field, which shows the time and date of the last modification, or an `ETag` header field, whose value is unique for the present version of the resource. The response shown in Section 8.1.2 contains both these fields, for example. A cached response with a `Last-Modified` header field can be validated by sending a *conditional* request to the server using the header field `If-Modified-Since`, asking if the resource has been modified since the given time. If not, the server responds with the *304 Not Modified* status code; otherwise, the newest version is returned. Similarly, the `ETag` value can be used together with the `If-None-Match` header field to validate the cached version.

For dynamically generated contents, it is particularly useful to be able to disable caching. Since not all browsers have implemented these cache-control features correctly, a reasonably safe way of disable caching of HTTP responses is to include the following header lines:

```
Cache-Control: no-store, no-cache, must-revalidate
Expires: Thu, 01 Jan 1970 00:00:00 GMT
Pragma: no-cache
```

The header fields `Expires` and `Pragma` are defined in HTTP/1.0, which does not support `Cache-Control`.

Of course, there are no guarantees that servers and clients implement the protocol properly. For example, do not base your business on the assumption that specifying `no-store` ensures that there will be made no copies of your messages.

Range Requests

With the `Range` header field, the client can request partial content rather than the entire resource. This can be useful for efficient recovery from partially failed transfers. As an example, the request header line

```
Range: bytes=100-200,300-
```

means that only the bytes from 100 to 200 and from 300 until end of the resource are requested. If the server supports range requests (it is an optional feature in HTTP/1.1), it will return the requested ranges together with the *206 Partial Content* status code; otherwise, the `Range` header field is simply ignored.

Persistent Connections

In early versions of HTTP, every single request was sent on a separate TCP connection that was closed when the response had been received. However, establishing a TCP connection takes a relatively long time, and requesting an HTML document is usually immediately followed by a number of requests to the same server for images and stylesheets that are necessary to render the document in a browser.

The notion of *persistent connections* in HTTP/1.1 avoids this overhead to a large extent by enabling the client and server to perform multiple request–response interactions on the same TCP connection. After a request has been processed, the server keeps the connection open for a number of seconds in anticipation of receiving further requests. Note that in order to be able to determine the boundary of each message, it is now vital that, for example, the otherwise optional `Content-Length` header field is used.

An additional benefit of the persistent connection mechanism is that it paves the way for another – and very substantial – performance improvement known as *pipelining*. This is a technique that allows the client to send multiple (idempotent) HTTP requests on a persistent connection without waiting for each response. It also allows multiple requests (or responses) to be transmitted using fewer TCP/IP packets.

With HTTP/1.1, persistent connections are by default in use. The header line

```
Connection: close
```

can be used in either requests or responses to cleanly terminate the connection after the present interaction is completed.

Some older versions of HTTP have preliminary support for persistent connections, which must be explicitly enabled to be used. This is the reason for the two lines

```
Keep-Alive: 300
Connection: keep-alive
```

in the example in Section 8.1.1, which mean that the connection should be kept alive for up to 300 seconds.

Although there are numerous HTTP request methods, status codes, header fields, etc. that we have not covered, we have by now seen all commonly used features in sufficient detail to be able to build advanced Web applications.

8.1.6   Limitations of HTTP

As with the other technologies covered by this book, it is important to be aware of what HTTP has been designed to achieve, in order to understand its limitations.

- HTTP is designed for client–server communication that follows the request–response pattern. This simple model is a major key to its success. However, it is not a silver bullet that solves all problems related to Internet communication – in particular, there exist more suitable protocols for other communication patterns and applications, such as streaming video, publish/subscribe systems, and P2P.

- By adhering cleanly to the request–response pattern, HTTP is a *stateless* protocol. A common pattern in Web communication is that a client repeatedly interacts with the same server, for example, logs in to an online shop, puts products into a shopping cart, enters address and payment information, and finally logs out. Seen at the HTTP level, this is just a sequence of independent request–response interactions that happen to be between the same client and server. Persistent connections are not the solution since their duration is usually limited. The *state* of the overall communication pattern, for example, the contents of the shopping cart, must be managed at a level above HTTP.

- TCP/IP, and thereby also HTTP, are by themselves inherently insecure protocols. It is easy to set up network sniffers that can read and make sense of the contents of TCP/IP packets. Also, the nodes on the network between the client and the server can maliciously be made to modify the packets being transmitted or pretend being the other end of the connection (also called spoofing). Clearly, this situation is unacceptable for modern Web applications.

In the following two sections we look into solutions to the problems of statelessness and insecurity.

8.2 Sessions

A *session* is a sequence of related interactions between a client and a server. As described in the previous section, such sessions are common in Web applications, but since HTTP is stateless, session state must be managed at a higher level.

Conceptually, a session can be viewed as a thread of execution managed by the server:

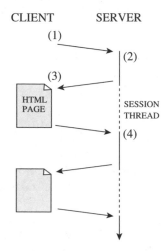

Here, (1) the client initiates a session thread by contacting the server. The server (2) then executes some code to produce the reply, typically an HTML page (3), which contains forms or links. While the session thread on the server is waiting, the client then fills out the forms and clicks on a submit button or a link causing the session thread to be reactivated (4) – and so on, until the client logs out (or stops responding, in which case the session thread will time out at some point). A concrete implementation is, of course, not required to represent each session as one physical thread or process since that may be too costly; we return to this issue in Sections 9.2.5 and 9.6.

The *state* of the service can generally be divided into three categories:

- *Shared state*, also called global data, is shared between all sessions and usually resides in a database on the server.

- *Session state*, also called local data, is private to a particular session thread. For instance, the contents of the shopping cart from the example mentioned earlier belongs in this category. It also includes information such as the 'program pointer' of the thread, for example, whether or not the client has logged in yet, whether or not an order has been placed, and so on.

- *Transient state* contains data that is only used for a single interaction, such as intermediate results from computations.

The session state is the tricky part here. There is a variety of techniques for managing session state in order to implement sessions on top of HTTP, as described in the following.

URL Rewriting

The technique of *URL rewriting* typically tracks a session identifier in the URLs that correspond to forms and links in the HTML page being shown to the user. Consider, for example, a page containing the URL

```
http://www.widget.inc/buy
```

occurring in the `action` attribute of a `form` element or in the `href` attribute of an `a` element whose activation corresponds to continuing the session. This URL could be rewritten by the server to

```
http://www.widget.inc/buy;21A9A8089C305319C679820D0B3B58D7
```

When the client requests this URL, the server can disassemble it and determine the actual resource (`www.widget.inc/buy`) and the identity of the relevant session (`21A9A...`), which then can be mapped to the relevant session state stored on the server. Note that a semicolon (`;`) is used here to separate the two parts – in particular, it is *not* a question mark (`?`) since that would interfere with the query string for GET requests. Also, to make session hijacking difficult, the session identifier is chosen as long string that is practically impossible to guess by others.

A variant of this scheme tracks the entire session state in the URLs rather than storing it on the server. However, that only works for small data sizes because of the length limitation of URLs mentioned earlier. Also, it means that the user can always use the 'back' button in the browser to step back to an earlier session state and continue from there – this can be useful for some kinds of services (like simple 'shopping cart' applications) but unacceptable for others (such as games that are played against the server).

Another variant of the URL rewriting scheme is the *session URL* technique where the same URL is used for the entire duration of the session, and this URL at all times points to the newest HTML page that has been shown to the user. Different URLs are then used for distinguishing between requests for the newest HTML page and requests for continuing the session. In the latter case, the response from the server is a redirection (307 Temporary Redirect) to the HTML page, which ensures that the URL of the HTML page appears in the address bar and the history buffer in the browser. This technique avoids the well-known problem where a user clicks the 'back' button to get to an earlier page without being aware of the fact that its contents may be obsolete. Instead, clicking the 'back' button simply brings the user to the page where the session was initiated. Also, this technique makes it possible to use the browser's bookmark mechanism to 'suspend' a session and later resume it; that is not possible with the classical URL rewriting mechanism if the HTTP POST method is being used since that would require a repetition of the request for continuing the session. The downside of the session URL technique is that it requires the server to store the newest

HTML page for each session and that it introduces an overhead for redirecting the client to its HTML page in each interaction. An implementation of the technique exists as part of the JWIG system (see Section 9.6).

Hidden Form Fields

The technique of *hidden form fields* places either a session identifier or the entire session state in hidden form fields, that is, input fields with `type="hidden"`, which are not displayed in the browser but are automatically submitted along with other fields that may occur. An example is the following form with a hidden field:

```
<form action="http://www.widget.inc/buy" method="POST">
  <input type="hidden" name="sessionid"
         value="21A9A8089C305319C679820D0B3B58D7">
  ...
</form>
```

One advantage compared to the URL rewriting technique is that there is no limit on the size of the data being placed in hidden fields – provided that only the HTTP POST method is being used for interacting with the server as discussed earlier. However, this technique obviously only works with forms, not with links (unless one hacks up some JavaScript code that reacts on certain events and simulates a POST request). A problem with both the URL rewriting technique and the hidden form field technique is that the HTML pages must be tailor-made for each user – even if the remaining contents are to be shared for all users.

Cookies

Cookies are small data packages that are stored on the clients (usually browsers) but mainly managed by the servers. This mechanism can be used to track session state, but also to track user identity independently of sessions. Unlike the other approaches described above, cookies are controlled via HTTP header fields – without modifying the HTML pages. Although the mechanism is actually not a part of the HTTP/1.1 specification, all modern browsers support cookies.

A server can send a cookie along with an ordinary HTTP response using the header field `Set-Cookie` as in the following example header line:

```
Set-Cookie: sessionid=21A9A8089C305319C679820D0B3B58D7; path=/
```

The client will then store this cookie. In subsequent requests to the same server, the cookie data will be sent along with the HTTP request header:

```
Cookie: sessionid=21A9A8089C305319C679820D0B3B58D7
```

This particular cookie stores the session identity, much like with the previously mentioned approaches. In some applications, the entire session state is stored in cookies.

Although multiple 'standards' exist, the value of the `Set-Cookie` header field is usually comprised of the following parts:

name=value: This part contains the name and value of the cookie, which is the data being returned to the server in later requests.

expires=time: This part specifies the lifetime of the cookie, for example as `Mon, 02-05-2005 21:37:45 GMT`. After this time, the cookie can be deleted at the client. By default, the cookie is deleted when the browser exits. Persistent cookies are stored in a file, usually named `cookies.txt`.

domain=pattern: This part specifies the domain names of servers that the cookie can be returned to. For example, the pattern `.widget.inc` (notice the leading dot) matches all domain names that end in `.widget.inc`, for example `www.widget.inc` and `payment.widget.inc`. Thereby, cookies can be returned to other servers than the one it originates from (however, to prevent flooding the network with cookies, short patterns like `.com` or `.co.uk` are forbidden). If this part is omitted, the cookie will only be returned to the originating server.

path=path: By specifying this part, the cookie will only be returned together with URLs whose path component begins with *path*. For example, if *path* is `/business/shop`, then the cookie will be sent together with a request URL whose path component is `/business/shop/buy` (provided that the cookie has not expired yet and the domain name matches properly, of course), but not if the path component is `/catalog/view`.

secure: A cookie marked as `secure` will only be sent over SSL connections (see Section 8.3).

If a client retrieves a cookie whose path and name match those of an existing one, the new one overwrites the old one. This can be used to remove a cookie on the client by sending an already expired cookie with the same path and name.

One `Set-Cookie` response header line may specify multiple cookies. Also, multiple cookies may be returned with a single `Cookie` request header line if more than one stored cookie has a matching domain and path. However, there are limitations on the sizes of the cookies and on the number of cookies that a client can be expected to store: max 4KB per cookie, max 20 cookies per domain name, and max 300 cookies in total. Clients are always free to ignore incoming cookies or remove stored cookies if these limits are reached.

One limitation of tracking sessions using cookies is that these cookies are stored somewhere by the browser and they cannot easily be moved to another person's browser. This makes it practically impossible for one user that starts a session to let another user take over. Another problem is that cookies are shared for all windows in the user's browser, so it is not possible with this technique to run several sessions simultaneously from the same browser. (This problem also applies to session management based on SSL sessions as described later.)

It has been argued that the cookie mechanism can impose a threat to privacy. The servers may learn too much about the user's behavior on the Web, and for browsers that are shared by many people, cookies can be inadvertently shared with other people. Acknowledging these concerns, cookie support may be disabled by the user in most browsers. Additionally, the server never knows when cookies disappear on the client because a limit has been reached. Since the cookie mechanism thus cannot be fully trusted to work on the client side, some amount of defensive programming is required to make Web applications robust if using cookies. One common approach – although not an ideal one – is to switch between URL rewriting and cookie-based session management based on the client's capabilities. (This switching is, for example, done by Java servlets as described in Chapter 9.)

8.3 SSL and TLS

As mentioned earlier, the HTTP protocol by itself is insecure, which is problematic for users of an open system like the Internet. We would like four properties of our communication:

- *confidentiality* – that information being transmitted between the client and the server cannot be eavesdropped by third parties;

- *integrity* – that the information cannot be altered during transmission without the receiver becoming aware of it;

- *authenticity* – that the receiver is able to identify the sender and vice versa; and

- *non-repudiation* – that the sender cannot deny having sent a message, and the receiver cannot deny having received it (provided that the transmission is successful, of course).

Secure Sockets Layer (SSL) provides a widely used solution that guarantees the first three of these properties – although, in typical use only the servers are authenticated, not the clients. The fourth property is not guaranteed by SSL, and for this reason, digital signatures are sometimes applied on top.

Although the technology described in this section is mostly used under the name SSL, which was introduced by the Netscape Corporation, the most recent standard is known as *TLS* – the *Transport Layer Security* protocol, which is being developed by the Internet Engineering Task Force (IETF).

SSL is an extra network layer that can be inserted between the application layer (HTTP) and the transport layer (TCP). Seen from the application level, one may use *HTTPS*, a secure version of HTTP based on SSL. In URLs, HTTPS is recognized by the scheme `https` (see Section 1.3).

SSL provides **confidentiality, integrity,** and **authenticity**.
When a client contacts a server using HTTPS, an *SSL session* is established and may be used for two-way communication involving multiple connections between the two. (Note that this notion of sessions is different from the one discussed in Section 8.2 – however, SSL sessions can be used as yet another mechanism for implementing HTTP sessions.) First, a secure channel between the client and the server is set up using a (slow) public-key encryption handshake technique where a cipher suite (a collection of crypto algorithms) is negotiated,

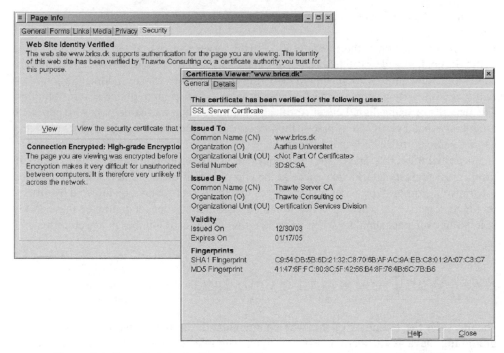

Figure 8.1 Security information about the current page as shown by Mozilla.

the server is authenticated to the client (and in some cases also the other way around), and a secret session key is created. Subsequently, communication is performed using a (fast) symmetric encryption technique. All this works using modern cryptography and digital certificate techniques, whose details most Web application programmers fortunately need not be aware of. One thing to note, however, is that SSL merely sets up a secure channel between the two parties where the digital certificates are only used for the initial hand-shake, not for the actual communication of data. (This is the reason why SSL does not ensure non-repudiation.)

It is also valuable to know the basic terminology of public-key cryptography: each user has a pair of related keys. The *private* key must be kept secret as it is used for making digital signatures and decrypting data sent to the key owner. The other, called the *public key*, is made public and can be widely distributed. This key is used for checking signatures and for encrypting data to the key owner. A *certificate* is information that associates the identity of the user, such as name and address, to the public key.

When browsing on an HTTPS connection, information about the authentication and encryption can be examined, as shown in Figure 8.1.

A typical use of server authentication is for electronic commerce where the client needs to be certain of the server's identity before credit card numbers or other sensitive information can safely be submitted. For the server authentication to work, the server must have a digital certificate originating from some authority that the client trusts. Browsers come with a built-in list of authorities (including companies like VeriSign and thawte) that are trusted by default.

The other direction, authorizing the client to the server with digital certificates, is possible with SSL but less widely used. Recall from Section 8.1.4 that there are various techniques for achieving client authorization without involving cryptography. Mostly, adding the confidentiality and integrity guarantees that SSL can provide is sufficient to obtain secure solutions. The benefits of using digital client certificates compared to a username/password approach are mainly that a certificate is practically impossible to guess and that the client can safely use the same certificate for many services.

As a final note, SSL and related techniques, of course, only provide security to a certain limit: most security attacks take place at the end points of the communication, not during the transmission. SSL provides no guarantees that the servers cannot be infected by viruses that read sensitive information being stored on disk; neither does it guarantee that nobody is looking over your shoulder when you enter your credit card number in a Web form.

8.4   Web Programming with Java

Java makes it easy to program with TCP/IP, HTTP, and SSL.

Having seen the essentials of the Web communication protocols, we now move to programming. Java is for many reasons a highly suitable framework for Web (and XML) programming:

- it is platform independent (using bytecode interpretation and a well-defined language semantics);

- it has a safe runtime model (for example, with array bound checks, automatic garbage collection, and bytecode verification);

- it has good support for multi-threading and concurrency control, which is useful for development of both servers and clients;

- its sandboxing security mechanism makes it easier to safely execute non-trusted code (the permission class `SocketPermission` is particularly relevant here);

- it natively supports Unicode;

- it supports data migration (serialization) and dynamic class loading; and

- it comes with a suite of powerful libraries for network programming (in addition to the XML libraries we have seen in Chapter 7).

If this is not convincing, try comparing the list with the features of other languages, for example, C, Perl, Visual Basic, or PHP. The C# language has been designed to compete with Java and is also becoming suitable for Web programming.

We will show how the standard Java libraries can be used to perform TCP, HTTP, and SSL communication. For a very brief overview, the most relevant functionality is found in the following packages:

java.net: contains classes for implementing basic TCP/IP and HTTP applications;

java.nio.channels: contains support for TCP with non-blocking I/O and efficient buffering, among other features; and

javax.net.ssl: contains support for SSL.

8.4.1 TCP/IP in Java

Accessing TCP/IP from Java is straightforward. The main functionality is in the following classes:

java.net.InetAddress: represents an IP address (either IPv4 or IPv6), and has methods for performing DNS lookups (see Section 8.1);

java.net.Socket: represents a TCP socket (see Section 8.1); and

java.net.ServerSocket: represents a *server socket*, which is capable of waiting for requests from clients.

Note that a 'server socket' is technically not a 'socket': when a client connects to a server socket, a TCP connection is made, and a (normal) socket is created for each end point. (The terminology is a bit confusing here.)

The following program performs a DNS lookup to find the IP numbers that are associated with a given domain name:

```java
import java.net.*;

public class DomainName2IPNumbers {
  public static void main(String[] args) {
    try {
      InetAddress[] a = InetAddress.getAllByName(args[0]);
      for (int i = 0; i<a.length; i++)
        System.out.println(a[i].getHostAddress());
    } catch (UnknownHostException e) {
      System.out.println("Unknown host!");
    }
  }
}
```

As an example, running

```
java DomainName2IPNumbers www.google.com
```

yields the output

```
66.102.9.104
66.102.9.99
```

The next example program finds the domain name and IP number of the machine on which it is executed:

```java
import java.net.*;

public class MyAddress {
  public static void main(String[] args) {
    try {
      InetAddress a = InetAddress.getLocalHost();
      System.out.println("domain name: "+a.getHostName());
      System.out.println("IP address:  "+a.getHostAddress());
    } catch (UnknownHostException e) {
      System.out.println("Help! I don't know who I am!");
    }
  }
}
```

Running this program gives the following result on our machine:

```
domain name: gorm.daimi.au.dk
IP address:  130.225.16.12
```

Next, we show how to set up a simple TCP connection between a server and a client. The server creates a server socket that listens on the port given on the command line. It then enters an infinite loop doing the following: when a connection with a client is established, it reads some input from the client (terminated with a 0 byte), sends back the message 'Simon says:' plus the input received, and closes the connection:

```java
import java.net.*;
import java.io.*;

public class SimpleServer {
  public static void main(String[] args) {
    try {
      ServerSocket ss = new ServerSocket(Integer.parseInt(args[0]));

      while (true) {
        Socket con = ss.accept();

        InputStreamReader in =
          new InputStreamReader(con.getInputStream());
        StringBuffer msg = new StringBuffer();
```

```
            int c;
            while ((c = in.read())!=0) // we use 0 as end-of-message marker
              msg.append((char)c);

            PrintWriter out = new PrintWriter(con.getOutputStream());
            out.print("Simon says: "+msg);
            out.flush();

            con.close();
          }
      } catch (IOException e) {
        System.err.println(e);
      }
    }
  }
```

(Using proper buffering would certainly be more efficient than reading one character at a time, but we will keep it simple here and focus on the networking facilities. Also, all uses of `PrintWriter` or `PrintStream` ought to check errors with the `checkError` method.) The client tries to connect to the server and port given on the command line, then sends some output to the server, and finally receives some input which is printed on the screen:

```
import java.net.*;
import java.io.*;

public class SimpleClient {
  public static void main(String[] args) {
    try {
      Socket con = new Socket(args[0], Integer.parseInt(args[1]));

      PrintStream out = new PrintStream(con.getOutputStream());
      out.print(args[2]);
      out.write(0); // mark end of message
      out.flush();

      InputStreamReader in =
        new InputStreamReader(con.getInputStream());
      int c;
      while ((c = in.read())!=-1)
        System.out.print((char)c);

      con.close();
    } catch (IOException e) {
      System.err.println(e);
    }
  }
}
```

(The `read` method returns -1 when end-of-stream is reached.) We first start the server, for example on port 1234:

```
java SimpleServer 1234
```

Then, we start a client:

```
java SimpleClient localhost 1234 "Hello World"
```

The output from the client is now the following:

```
Simon says: Hello World
```

As explained earlier, TCP/IP permits any combination of messages in either direction while the connection is open. In the communication pattern exhibited by these particular example programs, the client first sends a message to the server, and then the server responds with a message in the other direction, which is exactly the request–response pattern that HTTP follows. In Section 8.5, we extend the `SimpleServer` program to become a simple but functioning Web server.

Non-Blocking I/O

The support for TCP/IP in Java as explained above works well as long as the applications do not use many concurrent connections. The reason is that operations are *blocking*. For example, a `read` operation blocks until data is available (in particular, end-of-stream is only returned when the connection is closed). This blocking means that each connection needs its own thread, and having many threads can seriously affect performance and complexity of the code.

For this reason, the *NIO* (New I/O) packages were introduced in Java 1.4. With NIO, a thread can be made to wait for an event on many sockets simultaneously using a *selector* mechanism, as illustrated below. Alternatively, it may poll a socket for events without blocking. An additional feature is the *buffer* abstraction, which improves efficiency compared to using streams (and should not be confused with buffered streams).

The following program runs a single thread that listens on multiple ports (as specified on the command line). Whenever a client connects to one of the ports, this program behaves essentially as the `SimpleServer` above (so we can use the `SimpleClient` program as a client).

```java
import java.util.*;
import java.net.*;
import java.nio.*;
import java.nio.channels.*;
import java.io.*;

public class NonblockingServer {
  public static void main(String[] args) {
```

```
try {
  // set up server sockets for the given ports
  ServerSocketChannel[] ss = new ServerSocketChannel[args.length];
  Selector sel = Selector.open();
  for (int i=0; i<args.length; i++) {
      int port = Integer.parseInt(args[i]);
      ss[i] = ServerSocketChannel.open();
      ss[i].configureBlocking(false);
      ss[i].socket().bind(new InetSocketAddress(port));
      ss[i].register(sel, SelectionKey.OP_ACCEPT);
  }

  ByteBuffer buf = ByteBuffer.allocateDirect(1024);
  while (true) {
    // wait for a client to connect
    sel.select();

    // process each connection
    Iterator j = sel.selectedKeys().iterator();
    while (j.hasNext()) {
      SelectionKey k = (SelectionKey)j.next();
      j.remove();
      if (k.isAcceptable()) {

        // establish connection
        ServerSocketChannel s = (ServerSocketChannel)k.channel();
        SocketChannel c = s.accept();
        c.configureBlocking(false);

        try {
          // read input
          Selector readsel = Selector.open();
          c.register(readsel, SelectionKey.OP_READ);
          StringBuffer msg = new StringBuffer();
          boolean eos = false;
          while (!eos) {
            buf.clear();
            readsel.select(); // wait for a chunk of input
            c.read(buf);

            int p = buf.position();
            if (p>0 && buf.get(p-1)==0) {
              eos = true; // we have reached the terminating 0
              buf.position(p-1);
            }

            buf.flip();
            byte[] bb = new byte[buf.remaining()];
```

```
            buf.get(bb);
            msg.append(new String(bb));
        }

        // write output
        Selector writesel = Selector.open();
        c.register(writesel, SelectionKey.OP_WRITE);
        buf.clear();
        buf.put((new String("Rumors at port "+
                              c.socket().getLocalPort()+
                            ": "+msg))
                  .getBytes());
        buf.flip();
        while (buf.remaining()>0) {
          writesel.select(); // wait for client to be ready
          c.write(buf);
        }
        c.socket().shutdownOutput();

      } catch (Exception e) { // presumably lost connection
        continue;
      }
      c.close();
    }
      }
    }
  } catch (IOException e) {
    System.err.println(e);
  }
  }
}
```

The program prepares a number of server sockets and then enters an infinite loop processing one request at a time. Compared to the `SimpleServer` program, we here use `ServerSocketChannel` and `SocketChannel` instead of `ServerSocket` and `Socket`, respectively, we use `Selector` objects to wait for the clients (`OP_ACCEPT` for accepting connections, `OP_READ` for reading, and `OP_WRITE` for writing), and we use a `ByteBuffer` for reading and writing.

Obviously, this server program quickly becomes more involved than the simple version shown earlier. The online javadoc documentation for `java.nio` is a good place to study these features further.

8.4.2   HTTP in Java

There are two ways of building HTTP applications using the standard Java libraries. One way is to manually implement HTTP support on top of TCP/IP. In the previous section we saw that it is quite straightforward to communicate using TCP/IP, and as we have seen in

Section 8.1, the core of HTTP is a reasonably simple application of TCP/IP. The other way is to use the more high-level features of the Java libraries. In this section, we shall explore both approaches.

The following program sends a request to the Google server and extracts the result. This is done by manually constructing an HTTP request and parsing the necessary parts of the response:

```java
import java.net.*;
import java.io.*;

public class ImFeelingLucky {
  public static void main(String[] args) {
    try {
      Socket con = new Socket("www.google.com", 80);

      String req = "/search?"+
        "q="+URLEncoder.encode(args[0], "UTF8")+"&"+
        "btnI="+URLEncoder.encode("I'm Feeling Lucky", "UTF8");

      BufferedWriter out =
        new BufferedWriter
              (new OutputStreamWriter(con.getOutputStream(), "UTF8"));
      out.write("GET "+req+" HTTP/1.1\r\n");
      out.write("Host: www.google.com\r\n");
      out.write("User-Agent: IXWT\r\n\r\n");
      out.flush();

      BufferedReader in =
        new BufferedReader
              (new InputStreamReader(con.getInputStream()));
      String line;
      System.out.print("The prophet spoke thus: ");
      while ((line = in.readLine()) != null) {
        if (line.startsWith("Location:")) {
          System.out.println("Direct your browser to "+
                              line.substring(9).trim()+
                    " and you shall find great happiness in life.");
          break;
        } else if (line.trim().length()==0) {
          System.out.println("I am sorry - my crystal ball is blank.");
          break;
        }
      }
      con.close();
    } catch (IOException e) {
      System.err.println(e);
    }
  }
}
```

This program exploits the fact that the 'I'm Feeling Lucky' feature of the Google search engine accepts GET requests of a specific format and that the reply always contains a `Location` header line (see Section 8.1.2) if the search is successful. The format of the request was obtained by studying the HTML source for the front page of www.google.com. (Please read `http://www.google.com/terms_of_service.html` before running this program.)

The class `HttpURLConnection` and the related classes in the `java.net` package make it easier to create the HTTP requests and to parse the responses. As an example, the `ImFeelingLucky` program can be written more elegantly using these features:

```java
import java.net.*;
import java.io.*;

public class ImFeelingLucky2 {
  public static void main(String[] args) {
    try {
      String req = "http://www.google.com/search?"+
        "q="+URLEncoder.encode(args[0], "UTF8")+"&"+
        "btnI="+URLEncoder.encode("I'm Feeling Lucky", "UTF8");

      HttpURLConnection con =
        (HttpURLConnection) (new URL(req)).openConnection();

      con.setRequestProperty("User-Agent", "IXWT");
      con.setInstanceFollowRedirects(false);

      String loc = con.getHeaderField("Location");

      System.out.print("The prophet spoke thus: ");
      if (loc!=null)
        System.out.println("Direct your browser to "+loc+
                  " and you shall find great happiness in life.");
      else
        System.out.println
                  ("I am sorry - my crystal ball is blank.");

    } catch (IOException e) {
      System.err.println(e);
    }
  }
}
```

A central class here is the URL class, which not surprisingly represents the concept of URLs. As in the example above, we can construct a URL object and obtain a URLConnection using the `openConnection` method. URLConnection is an abstract class representing a potential TCP connection to the resource specified by the URL. For URLs using the `http` scheme, an instance of `HttpURLConnection` is created. (A few schemes have built-in support – others can be supported by specifying a new `URLStreamHandler`.) The methods `setRequestProperty` and `setInstanceFollowRedirects` are explained below.

The following methods in `HttpURLConnection` (some are inherited from `URL-Connection`), together with some convenience methods, control the HTTP requests and responses (here shown in the typically used order):

`setRequestMethod`: sets the request method, usually `GET` (the default) or `POST`;

`setRequestProperty`: sets a name–value property of the request (see the example above);

`setDoInput`: should be set to true (which is the default) if we plan to read input from the connection;

`setDoOutput`: should be set to true if we plan to write output to the connection, typically for POST requests (and this option is set to false by default);

`connect`: establishes the TCP connection – this method is rarely necessary to invoke explicitly since the connection will be established automatically at the first attempt to write the request body or read the response;

`getOutputStream`: gives an output stream for the request body of POST requests;

`getResponseCode`: returns the response code, for example `200` for 'OK' (see Section 8.1.2);

`getHeaderField`: returns a field from the response header; and

`getInputStream`: gives an input stream for reading the response body.

Note that the terminology is slightly unusual here: request header lines are called *properties* (and a *header field* only refers to the response). The methods involving the response will block until the response is ready.

In addition to these basic features, the `HttpURLConnection` class provides some additional functionality that deserves to be mentioned:

- By default, HTTP redirects (see Section 8.1.2) are followed automatically. This feature can be disabled with `setInstanceFollowRedirects` as in the example above.

- By default, responses are cached by the implementation of `HttpURLConnection` if permitted by the protocol (see Section 8.1.5). This can be disabled with the `setUseCaches` method.

- If enabled by the `setAllowUserInteraction` method, authentication can be handled conveniently using the `Authenticator` class (see the javadoc for details).

- With the `getContent` method, the resource being returned from the server can be automatically converted into a Java object of an appropriate type based on its media type. A *content handler* is a piece of code that performs the translation, and a *content handler factory* defines the mapping from media types to content handlers. (Again, see the javadoc for details.)

The class `HttpURLConnection` does not have special support for features that are specific to HTTP/1.1. If those features are needed, they can be controlled manually using the `setRequestProperty` and `getHeaderField` methods.

8.4.3   SSL in Java (JSSE)

Communication through SSL is also supported by Java in the form of Java Secure Socket Extension (JSSE), located in the package `javax.net.ssl`. Although the technical details of the cryptographic protocols are hidden from the programmer, it is still necessary to manage keys and certificates. To illustrate how JSSE works, we will develop a secure version of the `SimpleServer` and `SimpleClient` programs shown in Section 8.4.1. JSSE is divided into an interface and an implementation provider in order to ensure implementation independence and interoperability. In the program examples shown below, we focus on the common features provided by the interface; the *SunJSSE* implementation provider, which is a part of Sun's JDK, supports a wide range of cryptographic algorithms (in particular in J2SE 5) and is usually sufficient.

First, we change the server program to use SSL by using a `SSLServerSocket` and a `SSLSocket` instead of a `ServerSocket` and a `Socket`, respectively:

```
import java.net.*;
import java.io.*;
import javax.net.ssl.*;

public class SecureSimpleServer {
  public static void main(String[] args) {
    try {
      SSLServerSocketFactory sf =
        (SSLServerSocketFactory)SSLServerSocketFactory.getDefault();
      SSLServerSocket ss =
        (SSLServerSocket)sf.
          createServerSocket(Integer.parseInt(args[0]));

      while (true) {
        SSLSocket con = (SSLSocket)ss.accept();

        InputStreamReader in =
          new InputStreamReader(con.getInputStream());
        StringBuffer msg = new StringBuffer();
        int c;
        while ((c = in.read())!=0) // use 0 as end-of-message
          msg.append((char)c);

        PrintWriter out = new PrintWriter(con.getOutputStream());
        out.print("Simon says: "+msg);
        out.flush();
```

```
        con.close();
      }
    } catch (IOException e) {
      System.err.println(e);
    }
  }
}
```

and similarly for the client:

```
import javax.net.ssl.*;

public class SecureSimpleClient {
  public static void main(String[] args) {
    try {
      SSLSocketFactory sf =
        (SSLSocketFactory)SSLSocketFactory.getDefault();
      SSLSocket con =
        (SSLSocket)sf.createSocket(args[0],
                                    Integer.parseInt(args[1]));

      PrintStream out = new PrintStream(con.getOutputStream());
      out.print(args[2]);
      out.write(0); // mark end of message
      out.flush();

      InputStreamReader in =
        new InputStreamReader(con.getInputStream());
      StringBuffer buf = new StringBuffer();
      int c;
      while ((c = in.read())!=-1)
        System.out.print((char)c);

      con.close();
    } catch (IOException e) {
      System.err.println(e);
    }
  }
}
```

To make this program run, we need a server certificate (called an *X.509* certificate). That can be obtained by performing the following steps:

1. First use the tool `keytool` to create a new *key store* (here a file named `serverkey. jks`) and generate a key pair and a self-signed certificate (here named `widgetorg`,

using the RSA algorithm, and valid for 7 days):

```
keytool -genkey -alias widgetorg -keyalg RSA -validity 7
        -keystore serverkey.jks
Enter keystore password:  ToPsEcReT
What is your first and last name?
  [Unknown]:  www.widget.inc
What is the name of your organizational unit?
  [Unknown]:  Web Division
What is the name of your organization?
  [Unknown]:  Widget Inc.
What is the name of your City or Locality?
  [Unknown]:  Punxsutawney
What is the name of your State or Province?
  [Unknown]:  Pennsylvania
What is the two-letter country code for this unit?
  [Unknown]:  US
Is CN=www.widget.inc, OU=Web Division, O=Widget Inc.,
L=Punxsutawney, ST=Pennsylvania, C=US correct?
  [no]:  yes

Enter key password for <widgetorg>
        (RETURN if same as keystore password):
```

(The parts written in boldface are written by the user.) When constructing certificates for Web sites, the 'first and last name' is set to the domain name of the server. This key store must be kept secret as it contains the server's private key.

2. The next step is to have a certificate authority (one that our future clients hopefully trust) sign that the information we entered above is correct (typically based on off-line authentication):

```
keytool -certreq -alias widgetorg -keystore serverkey.jks
        -keyalg RSA -file widgetorg.csr
Enter keystore password:  ToPsEcReT
```

This instruction generates a *certificate signing request* (`widgetorg.csr`), which we then send to the certificate authority, who (after having received an exorbitant fee) returns a signed certificate (or technically, a chain of certificates) authenticating the server's public key.

3. Before inserting the signed certificate, we need to import the certificate authority's own certificate (here stored in a file named `ca.cer`, obtained from the authority's Web site):

```
keytool -import -alias root -keystore serverkey.jks
        -trustcacerts -file ca.cer
Enter keystore password:  ToPsEcReT
Certificate was added to keystore
```

The `-trustcacerts` option means that we choose to trust the preregistered certificates that come with the Java tools. If we are obtaining the signed certificate from an authority that is already trusted, this step can be skipped.

4. Finally, we replace the self-signed certificate in the key store with the one signed by the certificate authority (here named `widgetorg.cer`):

```
keytool -import -alias widgetorg -keystore serverkey.jks
        -file widgetorg.cer
Enter keystore password:  ToPsEcReT
Certificate was added to keystore
```

We can now run our `SecureSimpleServer` as follows:

```
java -Djavax.net.ssl.keyStore=serverkey.jks
     -Djavax.net.ssl.keyStorePassword=ToPsEcReT
     SecureSimpleServer 8443
```

The properties could also be set from the program using the method `System.setProperty`.

As an alternative to paying an established certificate authority to sign the server's certificate we can run the client program with a homemade *trust store*, a key store containing certificates that we trust. This can be done as follows (typically as an alternative to steps 2–4 above):

5. We export the self-signed certificate (to a file named `widgetorgself.cer`):

```
keytool -export -keystore serverkey.jks -alias widgetorg
        -file widgetorgself.cer
Enter keystore password:  ToPsEcReT
Certificate stored in file <widgetorgself.cer>
```

6. Then we construct the trust store (named `truststore.jks`):

```
keytool -import -alias widgetorg -file widgetorgself.cer
        -keystore truststore.jks
Enter keystore password:  HuShHuSh
Owner: CN=www.widget.inc, OU=Web Division, O=Widget Inc.,
  L=Punxsutawney, ST=Pennsylvania, C=US
Issuer: CN=www.widget.inc, OU=Web Division, O=Widget Inc.,
  L=Punxsutawney, ST=Pennsylvania, C=US
Serial number: 41b85a6c
Valid from: Thu Dec 09 15:00:12 CET 2009
      until: Thu Dec 16 15:00:12 CET 2009
Certificate fingerprints:
 MD5:  6D:D6:8E:92:F5:AA:24:E7:1C:2C:0D:0B:59:3E:59:EC
 SHA1: 11:4E:2B:6B:41:50:7C:D7:7D:CA:9A:32:47:F5:A0:E3:...
Trust this certificate? [no]:  yes
Certificate was added to keystore
```

Here we have to explicitly state that we trust the certificate, because it has not been issued by a trusted authority.

Step 6 can also be carried out separately if the server certificate was signed by an authority that the client does not already trust (in which case we use `ca.cer` from step 3 in place of `widgetorgself.cer`).

We can now run our `SecureSimpleClient` using the new trust store:

```
java -Djavax.net.ssl.trustStore=truststore.jks
     -Djavax.net.ssl.trustStorePassword=HuShHuSh
     SecureSimpleClient localhost 8443 "Hello World"
```

Some interesting information about the SSL connection can be obtained by inserting the following snippet in addition to also importing `java.security.cert.*`:

```
SSLSession ses = con.getSession();
System.out.println("Cipher suite: "+ses.getCipherSuite());
System.out.println("Protocol: "+ses.getProtocol());
Certificate[] cert = ses.getPeerCertificates();
  for (int i=0; i<cert.length; i++) {
    System.out.println("Server certificate type: "+
                          cert[i].getType());
    if (cert[i] instanceof X509Certificate) {
      X509Certificate c = (X509Certificate)cert[i];
      System.out.println("  Subject: "+c.getSubjectDN());
      System.out.println("  Issuer: "+c.getIssuerDN());
    }
  }
}
```

With this extension, the output from `SecureSimpleClient` could contain the following (abbreviated with '...'):

```
Cipher suite: SSL_RSA_WITH_RC4_128_MD5
Protocol: TLSv1
Server certificate type: X.509
  Subject: CN=www.widget.inc, OU=Web Division, O=Widget Inc.,
      L=Punxsutawney, ST=Pennsylvania, C=US
  Issuer: OU=www.verisign.com/CPS Incorp.by Ref. LIABILITY LTD...
Server certificate type: X.509
  Subject: OU=www.verisign.com/CPS Incorp.by Ref. LIABILITY LTD...
  Issuer: OU=Class 3 Public Primary Certification Authority, ...
```

We see that the TLS protocol is being used and that the server is identified by our 'Widget Inc.' certificate, which has been issued by VeriSign.

Certificate management is central when developing programs that communicate through SSL.

The `HttpsURLConnection` class in `javax.net.ssl` extends `HttpURLConnection` (see Section 8.4.2) with support for HTTPS-specific features. For details, see the javadoc.

A new feature in Java 5 is the class `SSLEngine`, which provides non-blocking I/O support (see Section 8.4.1) for SSL. An advanced example is presented in the JSSE Reference Guide (see the Further Reading section for this chapter).

And finally, other security components are naturally also available in the Java platform: the *Java Cryptography Extension (JCE)* provides fine-grained cryptographic services, and the *Java Authentication and Authorization Service (JAAS)* provides high-level support for – as the name implies – authentication and authorization for running code.

8.5   A Web Server in 145 Lines of Code

We now present the source code for a simple but functioning Web server, written using Java's TCP/IP libraries (see Section 8.4.1).

The first part of the program reads a port number (where the server will listen for requests) and a directory (which will be the root for files being served) from the command line, and starts a `FileServer`:

```
import java.net.*;
import java.io.*;
import java.util.*;

public class FileServer {
  int port;
  String wwwhome;

  Socket con;
  BufferedReader in;
  OutputStream out;
  PrintStream pout;

  FileServer(int port, String wwwhome) {
    this.port = port;
    this.wwwhome = wwwhome;
  }

  public static void main(String[] args) {
    if (args.length!=2) {
      System.out.println("Usage: java FileServer <port> <wwwhome>");
      System.exit(-1);
    }
    int port = Integer.parseInt(args[0]);
    String wwwhome = args[1];
    FileServer fs = new FileServer(port, wwwhome);
    fs.run();
  }
```

The `run` method creates a `ServerSocket` and then enters an infinite loop of processing requests:

```
void run() {
  ServerSocket ss = null;
  try {
    ss = new ServerSocket(port);
```

```
    } catch (IOException e) {
      System.err.println("Could not start server: "+e);
      System.exit(-1);
    }
    System.out.println("FileServer accepting connections on port "+
                       port);

    while (true) {
      try {
        con = ss.accept();
        in = new BufferedReader
                   (new InputStreamReader(con.getInputStream()));
        out = new BufferedOutputStream(con.getOutputStream());
        pout = new PrintStream(out);

        String request = in.readLine();
        con.shutdownInput(); // ignore the rest
        log(con, request);

        processRequest(request);

        pout.flush();
      } catch (IOException e) {
        System.err.println(e);
      }
      try {
        if (con!=null)
          con.close();
      } catch (IOException e) {
        System.err.println(e);
      }
    }
  }
```

The `processRequest` method parses the request line. Requests for file paths that contain `/.` or end with `~` result in `403 Forbidden` responses (the former restriction implies that only files below the `wwwhome` directory can be accessed). Requests for directories return the `index.html` file; however, directory requests are redirected (with a `301 Moved Permanently` response) if not ending in a `/` to ensure that subsequent relative URL requests behave correctly. If an existing file is requested, it is returned with a `200 OK` response:

```
void processRequest(String request) throws IOException {
  if (!request.startsWith("GET") || request.length()<14 ||
      !(request.endsWith("HTTP/1.0") ||
        request.endsWith("HTTP/1.1")) ||
      request.charAt(4)!='/') {
    errorReport(pout, con, "400", "Bad Request",
                "Your browser sent a request that "+
                "this server could not understand.");
```

```
      } else {
        String req = request.substring(4, request.length()-9).trim();
        if (req.indexOf("/.")!=-1 || req.endsWith("~")) {
          errorReport(pout, con, "403", "Forbidden",
                          "You don't have permission to access "+
                          "the requested URL.");
        } else {
          String path = wwwhome+"/"+req;
          File f = new File(path);
          if (f.isDirectory() && !path.endsWith("/")) {
            pout.print("HTTP/1.0 301 Moved Permanently\r\n"+
                          "Location: http://"+
                          con.getLocalAddress().getHostAddress()+":"+
                          con.getLocalPort()+req+"/\r\n\r\n");
          log(con, "301 Moved Permanently");
          } else {
            if (f.isDirectory()) {
              path = path+"index.html";
              f = new File(path);
            }
            try {
              InputStream file = new FileInputStream(f);
              String contenttype =
                URLConnection.guessContentTypeFromName(path);
              pout.print("HTTP/1.0 200 OK\r\n");
              if (contenttype!=null)
                pout.print("Content-Type: "+contenttype+"\r\n");
              pout.print("Date: "+new Date()+"\r\n"+
                          "Server: IXWT FileServer 1.0\r\n\r\n");
              sendFile(file, out); // send raw file
              log(con, "200 OK");
            } catch (FileNotFoundException e) {
              errorReport(pout, con, "404", "Not Found",
                          "The requested URL was not found "+
                          "on this server.");
            }
          }
        }
      }
    }
  }
}
```

Finally, we have a few auxiliary methods for logging, sending error reports, and sending files:

```
void log(Socket con, String msg) {
  System.err.println(new Date()+" ["+
                      con.getInetAddress().getHostAddress()+
                      ":"+con.getPort()+"] "+msg);
}
```

```
void errorReport(PrintStream pout, Socket con,
                 String code, String title, String msg) {
  pout.print(
    "HTTP/1.0 "+code+" "+title+"\r\n"+
    "\r\n"+
    "<!DOCTYPE HTML PUBLIC \"-//IETF//DTD HTML 2.0//EN\">\r\n"+
    "<TITLE>"+code+" "+title+"</TITLE>\r\n"+
    "</HEAD><BODY>\r\n"+
    "<H1>"+title+"</H1>\r\n"+msg+"<P>\r\n"+
    "<HR><ADDRESS>IXWT FileServer 1.0 at "+
    con.getLocalAddress().getHostName()+
    " Port "+con.getLocalPort()+"</ADDRESS>\r\n"+
    "</BODY></HTML>\r\n");
  log(con, code+" "+title);
}

void sendFile(InputStream file, OutputStream out)
    throws IOException {
  byte[] buffer = new byte[1000];
  while (file.available()>0)
    out.write(buffer, 0, file.read(buffer));
}
}
```

As usual, the complete program can also be obtained from the companion Web site. Try compiling and running the program (using some directory containing HTML files as wwwhome), and use an ordinary browser as client. You will see that this short program suffices for ordinary browsing.

This simple `FileServer` program can be viewed as a foundation for building a fully-fledged Web server. Following the explanation of the technologies presented in the previous sections in this chapter, it is possible (and quite fun!) to add, for example, the following functionality:

- client authentication (see Section 8.1.4);

- content negotiation (see Section 8.1.1);

- persistent connections (see Section 8.1.5);

- support for range requests (see Section 8.1.5); and

- SSL (see Section 8.3).

Additionally, fault tolerance and efficiency can be improved using NIO buffers and multi-threading.

One thing missing here is the ability to plug in code to handle form input and provide dynamically generated response. However, with Java's class loading capabilities this is straightforward. We simply extend the request parser of our Web server to recognize requests for executing programs, and then dynamically load the appropriate class files and let them generate the response. In fact, this is exactly what the Java servlet technology is all about, as explained in the next chapter.

8.6   Chapter Summary

In this chapter we have looked into the main communication protocols of the Web, with the focus on HTTP. We have seen that HTTP is a reasonably simple layer on top of TCP/IP, and that SSL can be inserted in between to provide certain security guarantees.

The Java standard libraries contain support for programming with each of these protocols. We have seen how to set up TCP connections to communicate between machines on the Internet (using the `java.net` package), how to implement HTTP support either manually using TCP sockets or at a higher abstraction level (using the `HttpURLConnection` class), and finally, how to program servers and clients that communicate through SSL (using the `javax.net.ssl` package).

Among main players in this area are IETF (the Internet Engineering Task Force), which is responsible for the development of IP, TCP, and TLS along with numerous other Internet protocols, and W3C, which has developed HTTP as part of the World Wide Web architecture. Having reached its goals with HTTP/1.1, W3C has closed their HTTP activity.

8.7   Further Reading

For the main specifications, see the online resources below. The HTTP/1.1 specification is published through IETF [35]. The original HTTP (called version 0.9) is described by Tim Berners-Lee [5]. A readable description of the differences between HTTP/1.0 and HTTP/1.1 can be found in the article [53]. The newest version of the cookie extension is specified in IETF RFC 2965 [54]. *REST* (Representational State Transfer) is the name of the architectural style for distributed systems that has guided the development of the HTTP and URI standards. An overview of REST is given in the article [36].

The underlying protocols, TCP, IPv4, and the newer IPv6 are also developed by IETF; see [70, 69, 27]. The TLS protocol, which succeeds SSL, is specified in the document [29]. All documents by IETF can be obtained from their Web site.

To learn about the inner workings of TCP/IP, we recommend the book [25]. A useful book about SSL and the related technologies is [73]. There are lots of good books dedicated to network programming with Java, however, the essential information is available online (see below).

8.8   Online Resources

`http://www.w3.org/Protocols/rfc2616/rfc2616.html`
    The HTTP/1.1 specification.

```
http://www.ietf.org/
```
Web site of IETF, The Internet Engineering Task Force. Contains *Internet-Drafts* (working documents) and *RFC*s ('Request for Comments', including standards-related specifications).

```
http://www.iana.org/
```
Web site of IANA, The Internet Corporation for Assigned Names and Numbers. The list of registered MIME media types is at `http://www.iana.org/assignments/media-types/`.

```
http://java.sun.com/j2se/1.5.0/docs/api/
```
The javadoc API specification for J2SE 5, including the `java.net`, `java.nio.channels`, and `javax.net.ssl` packages.

```
http://java.sun.com/j2se/1.5.0/docs/guide/net/
```
Documentation of the networking features in Java.

```
http://java.sun.com/j2se/1.5.0/docs/guide/security/
jsse/JSSERefGuide.html
```
Reference guide to JSSE.

8.9   Exercises

The main lessons to be learned from these exercises are:

- how HTTP works; and
- how to program HTTP servers and clients using Java.

Exercise 8.1 Give examples of when the GET method is more appropriate than POST, and vice versa.

Exercise 8.2 Explain how the POST method can be used as an alternative to PUT and DELETE.

Exercise 8.3 Modify the `SimpleClient` program (see Section 8.4.1) to become a `DownloadClient`, which given a host, a port, and a file name on the command line performs a GET request to download the file and stores it locally. (Use a TCP connection manually; do not use `URLConnection` for this exercise.)

Exercise 8.4 Continuing Exercise 8.3, extend your `DownloadClient` such that it:

(a)   understands '301 Moved Permanently' responses by automatically following the redirection,
(b)   becomes capable of performing HTTP Basic authentication, and
(c)   if the file has been partly downloaded already but a failure occurred before it finished, uses a range request to retrieve only the remaining part.

Exercise 8.5 The following programs can be useful for experimenting with HTTP servers and clients:

(a)   Write a program, `TestServer`, that repeatedly listens for a TCP connection on a given port and processes every connection as follows:
- the request (assumed to be an HTTP request) is printed to the screen; and, in parallel;
- all input from the keyboard is sent as response until a line 'DONE' is entered, at which time the connection is closed.

(b) Write a program, `TestClient`, that
  - connects to a given host and port;
  - sends all input from the keyboard until a line 'DONE' is entered; and, in parallel,
  - prints the response on the screen, terminating when the connection is closed by the server.

You can try running both programs at the same time, making them communicate with each other. You can also run the `TestServer` program using an ordinary browser as client, and you can run the `TestClient` program with a real Web server at the other end.

TIP

If you are using Internet Explorer, make sure that the option 'friendly HTTP error messages' is disabled in the configuration. (Otherwise, HTTP error messages from servers will not be shown.)

Exercise 8.6 Extend the `FileServer` program from Section 8.5 as suggested on page 386.

Exercise 8.7 The service `http://www.brics.dk/ixwt/wordcount` can be used to count the number of words in a file that is POSTed on input. Write a Java program that accepts a file name from the command line and uses this service to report the number of words it contains. Sometimes the service is inordinately slow, so write your Java program to instead report 'connection timed out' if the service does not respond within 30 seconds.

TIP

A powerful alternative to `HttpURLConnection` is the Jakarta Commons HttpClient; see `http://jakarta.apache.org/commons/httpclient/`.

Exercise 8.8 Discuss the problems that may arise if some of the four security properties mentioned in Section 8.3 (confidentiality, integrity, authenticity, and non-repudiation) are not satisfied, for example for electronic commerce applications.

PROGRAMMING WEB APPLICATIONS WITH SERVLETS

9

Objectives

In this chapter, you will learn:

- How to program Web applications using servlets

- Advanced concepts, such as listeners, filters, and request dispatchers

- Running servlets using the Tomcat server

9.1 Writing Web Applications

In the previous chapter, we saw how to construct a simple Web server using the TCP/IP functionality of the Java framework. We noticed an essential thing missing: the ability to generate responses *dynamically* by code that has been plugged in, rather than just returning static files from the file system. This is exactly what servlets are about. The servlet framework contains a Java-based API for programming Web applications. A *servlet* is a program written for this API. Although there are several implementations, servlets are to a large extent implementation independent, even when it comes to deployment of the applications.

Before going into the details of the servlet API, we will first briefly explain the basic concepts of general Web applications.

A *Web server* is a program that responds to HTTP requests. In modern Web servers, the responses can be generated by *Web applications*, which contain programs that are plugged into the server. One server typically runs many concurrent *threads* (or processes) of each application, where each thread handles one HTTP request or one client. The threads can communicate by various means, even across applications.

Additionally, as explained in Section 8.2, the series of request–response interactions with a particular client form a *session*. We have described three kinds of state: *shared* state (accessible by all sessions), *session* state (private to one session but may span multiple

A **servlet** is a program in a Web server, written using the servlet API.

interactions), and *transient* state (only lives during the construction of a single response). The shared state can be further divided into *application* state, which is private to one Web application, and *server* state, which is shared for all applications. State management in servlets is described in Sections 9.2.4 and 9.2.5.

Many Web servers allow applications to be inserted, updated, or removed while running. We discuss the deployment and configuration of servlets in Section 9.3.1.

Development of Web applications generally involves different tasks: management of persistent state, construction of HTML pages, and controlling how the user's interactions are connected with the persistent state and HTML pages. Following the *Model–View–Controller* pattern, this may be reflected by dividing the code correspondingly, which can lead to more manageable systems. We describe it further in Section 10.3.

9.2 The Servlet API

Programming with the servlet API follows the request–response pattern from HTTP. The following tiny program reacts on GET requests and responds with a dynamically generated HTML page:

```java
import java.io.*;
import javax.servlet.*;
import javax.servlet.http.*;

public class HelloWorld extends HttpServlet {
  public void doGet(HttpServletRequest request,
                    HttpServletResponse response)
      throws IOException, ServletException {
    response.setContentType("text/html");
    PrintWriter out = response.getWriter();
    out.println("<html><head><title>Servlet Example</title></head>"+
                "<body><h1>Hello World!</h1>"+
                "This page was last updated: "+new java.util.Date()+
                "</body></html>");
  }
}
```

In Section 9.3.2, we show how to run servlets with the Tomcat server. The result may look as follows in the client's browser:

Hello World!

This page was last updated: Fri Dec 24 19:38:23 CET 2004

The servlet API is comprised of two packages: `javax.servlet` and `javax.servlet.http`, the latter containing all functionality specific to HTTP. As in the example, a servlet is (typically) a subclass of `HttpServlet`. The method `doGet` is invoked when a GET request to the right path is made. This method has two arguments: a `HttpServletRequest` object, which holds various information about the request (being ignored here), and a `HttpServletResponse` object, which is used for generating the response to the client.

9.2.1 The Life Cycle of Servlets

A Web application may consist of a collection of servlets and other resources, such as auxiliary class or jar files, static HTML documents, CSS stylesheets, and GIF images. (We explain how to wrap up and configure a Web application for deployment in Section 9.3.1.) When the Web application is deployed into the Web server, one instance of each servlet is created per servlet declaration (however, see the discussion about *distributable applications* in Section 9.2.4) and the `init` method is invoked on each instance. This method can be used for initialization routines, such as connecting to a database. Using a separate class loader for each Web application, one server is able to run several Web applications in parallel without risking interference (however, see Section 9.2.4).

Now the application is ready to handle requests. A GET or POST request causes the `doGet` method or the `doPost` method, respectively, to be invoked. Variables declared in these methods correspond to transient state. The server typically runs many threads concurrently, each handling one request, and it is the programmer's responsibility to ensure thread safety. (Java's `synchronized` blocks and the `wait`/`notify` methods are indispensable for concurrency control.) Another useful method one may implement is `getLastModified`, which can be used to improve caching (see Section 8.1.5) by setting the time of last modification of the resource denoted by the given request.

If the server is terminated cleanly, the `destroy` method is invoked on each servlet object. This method is typically used to disconnect from databases and the like. (Of course, it is not invoked in case of, for example, a power failure.)

With the notion of *listeners* (described in Section 9.4.1), these life cycle events can also trigger execution of code located elsewhere, which can be used to improve the source code structure.

In addition to the main methods mentioned above, servlets should additionally implement the `getServletInfo` method, which returns a short string describing the servlet, such as author, version, and copyright. This string may then used by server administration programs in overviews of installed applications.

The methods mentioned above are ones that are typically implemented by the servlet programmer (although dummy defaults are available). Other methods are available to the programmer, the two most important being the `getInitParameter` method, which is used to obtain information about the deployment configuration (see Section 9.3.1) and the `log` method for writing messages to the server log file.

The following extension of the `HelloWorld` servlet illustrates some of these mechanisms:

```
import java.io.*;
import javax.servlet.*;
import javax.servlet.http.*;
```

```
public class HelloWorld2 extends HttpServlet {
  public String getServletInfo() {
    return "servlet example, by Møller & Schwartzbach";
  }

  public void init() {
    log("initializing");
  }

  public void doGet(HttpServletRequest request,
                    HttpServletResponse response)
      throws IOException, ServletException {
    log("a thread is entering doGet");
    response.setContentType("text/html");
    PrintWriter out = response.getWriter();
    out.println("<html><head><title>Servlet Example</title></head>"+
                "<body><h1>Hello World!</h1>"+
                "This page was last updated: "+new java.util.Date()+
                "</body></html>");
    log("a thread is leaving doGet");
  }

  public void doPost(HttpServletRequest request,
                     HttpServletResponse response)
      throws IOException, ServletException {
    response.sendError(response.SC_METHOD_NOT_ALLOWED,
                       "¿Que? - No habla POST!");
  }

  public void destroy() {
    log("shutting down");
  }
}
```

(The sendError method is explained in Section 9.2.3.) Deploying this servlet, issuing a few requests, and then shutting down may result in the following log entries (using Tomcat):

```
2005-10-25 12:41:21 StandardContext[/IXWT]HelloWorld2:
  initializing
2005-10-25 12:41:25 StandardContext[/IXWT]HelloWorld2:
  a thread is entering doGet
2005-10-25 12:41:25 StandardContext[/IXWT]HelloWorld2:
  a thread is leaving doGet
2005-10-25 12:41:34 StandardContext[/IXWT]HelloWorld2:
  a thread is entering doGet
2005-10-25 12:41:34 StandardContext[/IXWT]HelloWorld2:
  a thread is entering doGet
2005-10-25 12:41:34 StandardContext[/IXWT]HelloWorld2:
  a thread is leaving doGet
```

```
2005-10-25 12:41:34 StandardContext[/IXWT]HelloWorld2:
  a thread is leaving doGet
2005-10-25 12:42:47 StandardContext[/IXWT]HelloWorld2:
  shutting down
```

Notice that in this run, two GET requests are being processed in parallel.

9.2.2   Requests

The `HttpServletRequest` parameter of `doGet` and `doPost` contains information about the incoming request (see Section 8.1.1). Numerous methods are available, but the most important are the following:

> `getHeader`: returns the value of the specified header name as a string (some convenience methods are available for parsing the values as integers or dates);

> `getParameter`: returns the properly decoded value of a given form field as a string (variants of this method can be used in case of multiple fields with the same name);

> `getInputStream`: returns an input stream for accessing the raw HTTP request body (for obvious reasons, don't mix this method with `getParameter`); and

> `getRemoteHost`, `getRemoteAddr`, and `getRemotePort`: return information about the client end of the TCP connection.

Other useful request methods are mentioned in the following sections. For the full list, see the online javadoc (the URL can be found in the online resources for the chapter).

*Servlets build on the request–response model of **HTTP**.* The `getParameter` method particularly shows how the servlet API provides a higher level of abstraction compared to manipulating HTTP messages manually as described in Chapter 8. Recall that form fields are represented differently for GET and POST requests and the latter furthermore may use different encodings. The `getParameter` method hides all these technical details and parses the request for us.

The following servlet shows some of these methods in use:

```
import java.io.*;
import javax.servlet.*;
import javax.servlet.http.*;

public class Requests extends HttpServlet {
  public void doGet(HttpServletRequest request,
                    HttpServletResponse response)
    throws IOException, ServletException {
    response.setContentType("text/html");
    PrintWriter out = response.getWriter();
    out.println("<html><head><title>Requests</title></head><body>");
    out.println("<h1>Hello, visitor from "+
                request.getRemoteHost()+"</h1>");
```

```java
    String useragent = request.getHeader("User-Agent");
    if (useragent!=null)
      out.println("You seem to be using "+useragent+"<p>");
    String name = request.getParameter("name");
    if (name==null)
      out.println("No <tt>name</tt> field was given!");
    else
      out.println("The value of the <tt>name</tt> field is: <tt>" +
                  htmlEscape(name) + "</tt>");
    out.println("</body></html>");
  }

  public void doPost(HttpServletRequest request,
                     HttpServletResponse response)
    throws IOException, ServletException {
    doGet(request, response);
  }

  private String htmlEscape(String s) {
    StringBuffer b = new StringBuffer();
    for (int i = 0; i<s.length(); i++) {
      char c = s.charAt(i);
      switch (c) {
      case '<': b.append("&lt;"); break;
      case '>': b.append("&gt;"); break;
      case '"': b.append("&quot;"); break;
      case '\'': b.append("&apos;"); break;
      case '&': b.append("&amp;"); break;
      default: b.append(c);
      }
    }
    return b.toString();
  }
}
```

Running this servlet might give the following response:

Hello, visitor from britney.widget.inc

You seem to be using Mozilla/5.0 (X11; U; Linux i686; en-US; rv:1.5) Gecko/20031007

The value of the name field is: John Doe

Notice that POST requests are in this example simply redirected to the doGet handler. That works fine, even with form fields, but one should generally respect the different intentions of GET and POST as noted in Section 8.1.3.

Another thing to note in this example is the use of the little `htmlEscape` method, which converts the characters that have a special meaning in HTML to their equivalent entity references. A common omission in Web applications is to allow data entered by users to end up unescaped in HTML documents.

Since it is easy to fake HTTP requests (see, for example, the `ImFeelingLucky` program in Section 8.4.2), one should never trust that expected form fields or request header fields are always present – make sure to check that the result from, for instance, `getParameter` is not null. Furthermore, it is common in Web applications that also the HTML page containing the form is dynamically generated by a servlet. Even disregarding cheating or faulty clients, it is generally difficult to ensure statically that the form fields being expected by one servlet always appear in the HTML page that has been generated by a different servlet. We return to this issue in Section 9.6.

9.2.3   Responses

The `HttpServletResponse` parameter of `doGet` and `doPost` is used to construct the outgoing response (see Section 8.1.2) as seen in the examples in the previous sections.

The main methods available in `HttpServletResponse` are:

`setStatus`: sets the response status code, default is 200 (see Section 8.1.2);

`addHeader` and `setHeader`: adds or overwrites header fields (some convenience methods are available for setting integer and date values);

`getOutputStream`: returns an output stream for writing the response body (often the `getWriter` method is used instead – it simply wraps the output stream into a `PrintWriter`, which can be used for sending characters rather than bytes);

`setContentType`: controls the content type and character encoding: it both sets the `Content-Type` header and the character encoding for the `PrintWriter` obtained from `getWriter`;

`sendError` and `sendRedirect`: convenience methods for easy construction of error responses (with some given status code) or temporary redirects (status code 307);

One should naturally always finish the header before starting to send the response body. Output is usually buffered by the server; to force a partial response body to be sent, use the `flushBuffer` method. Also, as noted in Section 8.4.1, uses of `PrintWriter` (as obtained from `getWriter`) ought to check errors regularly with the `checkError` method.

In the examples in the previous sections, we have seen simple but typical uses of `HttpServletResponse`, so let us now show an example that connects servlets, XML, JDOM, and XSLT and is also relevant for Web services (see Chapter 11). This example uses JDOM (see Section 7.3) to construct a business card XML document containing an XSLT stylesheet reference (see Section 5.1) and sends it to the client:

```
import java.io.*;
import java.util.*;
```

```
import javax.servlet.*;
import javax.servlet.http.*;
import org.jdom.*;
import org.jdom.output.*;

public class BusinessCardServlet extends HttpServlet {
  public void doGet(HttpServletRequest request,
                    HttpServletResponse response)
    throws IOException, ServletException {
    response.setContentType("text/xml;charset=UTF-8");
    long expires = new Date().getTime() + 1000*60*60*24; // now + 1 day
    response.addDateHeader("Expires", expires);
    XMLOutputter outputter = new XMLOutputter();
    outputter.output(getBusinessCard(), response.getOutputStream());
  }

  Document getBusinessCard() {
    Namespace ns = Namespace.getNamespace("http://businesscard.org");
    Element card =
      (new Element("card", ns))
      .addContent((new Element("name", ns))
                  .setText("John Doe"))
      .addContent((new Element("title", ns))
                  .setText("CEO, Widget Inc."))
      .addContent((new Element("email", ns))
                  .setText("john.doe@widget.inc"))
      .addContent((new Element("phone", ns))
                  .setText("(202) 555-1414"))
      .addContent((new Element("logo", ns))
                  .setAttribute("uri", "widget.gif"));
    Map m = new HashMap();
    m.put("type", "text/xsl");
    m.put("href", "business_card.xsl");
    return (new Document())
      .addContent(new ProcessingInstruction("xml-stylesheet", m))
      .addContent(card);
  }
}
```

We here rely on the browser for performing the XSLT transformation into XHTML. The result looks as on page 190. Also notice that we set the Expires header field (see Section 8.1.5) to the current time plus one day. In this example, we just return a constant XML document; a more realistic servlet would, of course, construct the document from information in a database.

A general problem when developing large-scale Web applications purely with servlets is that the business logic and the construction of HTML pages tends to become mixed together in the program code. It is necessary to be able to separate the concerns of programmers and HTML designers, since these are often different people with different skills. Combining servlets and JSP using the Model–View–Controller pattern as explained in Section 10.3 to some degree alleviates this problem.

9.2.4 Servlet Contexts and Shared State

A `ServletContext` object holds information about the context of a given servlet. One such object exists per Web application (except for distributable applications as explained below). This object is available via the `getServletContext` method in the servlet class.

One of the basic methods in `ServletContext` is `getServerInfo`, which returns general information about the server, such as this:

```
Apache Tomcat/5.0.30
```

Every Web application, which may consist of multiple servlets and other resources as noted earlier, is associated with a unique *context path*. This is used as the first part of the path-part (see Section 1.3) of URIs denoting these resources. The context path is determined by the deployment configuration (see Section 9.3.1). The configuration may also set initialization parameters, which can be read with the `getInitParameter` method.

The `getRealPath` method is useful for converting a path of some resource, relative to the current context path, into the corresponding absolute directory path. Additionally, a number of methods are available in the `HttpServletRequest` class for accessing various parts of the request URI. In particular the methods `getContextPath` and `getServletPath` are useful when constructing response HTML pages containing links back to the Web application. (See the javadoc for further explanation of these methods.)

The `ServletContext` object can also be used to store shared state (as defined in Section 9.1):

> **The `ServletContext` object holds general information about the Web application.**

`setAttribute`: binds an object to an *attribute name*, which is a string that follows the same convention as Java package names.

`getAttribute`: returns the object bound to a given attribute name.

Normal field variables in the servlet class can also be used, but keep in mind that one instance is created of each servlet per servlet declaration in the Web application. (We explain what a servlet declaration is in Section 9.3.1.) A benefit of using the context attribute mechanism to store shared state is that it is integrated with the *listener* mechanism that we describe in Section 9.4.1. Still, it is important to note that neither of these approaches for storing shared data will survive a server crash. For mission critical data, one should always use a proper database, for instance via Java's JDBC API or J2EE entity beans.

With the context attribute mechanism together with the `getContext` method, which gives access to the `ServletContext` object of another Web application on the same server, it is straightforward to communicate data across applications that run on the same server. There are some limits to this sharing, though: it may be forbidden by the server configuration

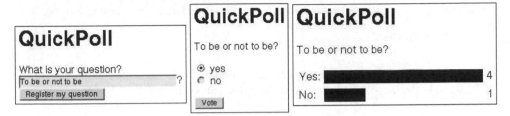

Figure 9.1 Screen shots from the polling service.

(for safety, this is even the default for Tomcat), and furthermore, since each application has its own class loader, classes in one application cannot see those in another application. For sharing classes between applications, servlet implementations also provide a common directory where such classes can be placed, and these are then loaded by an additional shared class loader.

A Web application may be configured as being *distributable*, meaning that the server may run it in multiple JVMs simultaneously, typically on different machines, to improve performance. Not surprisingly, each JVM then has its own instances of each servlet class for each Web application. However, it also means that each JVM in this case has its own `ServletContext` object for each Web application.

A Polling Service

Let us illustrate the essential features described above by making a small polling service. This is a Web application consisting of five resources:

- a static HTML page named `QuickPollQuestion.html` containing a form for entering the poll question;

- a servlet named `QuickPollSetup` for receiving the form data;

- a servlet named `QuickPollAsk` for making an HTML page containing the question and a form where either 'yes' or 'no' can be selected;

- a servlet named `QuickPollVote` for receiving a vote; and

- a servlet named `QuickPollResults` for showing the results.

Some screen shots from the running application are shown in Figure 9.1. For simplicity, we store all shared state in context attributes. First, the file `QuickPollQuestion.html`:

```
<html><head><title>QuickPoll</title></head><body>
<h1>QuickPoll</h1>
<form method=post action=setup>
What is your question?<br>
<input name=question type=text size=40>?<br>
```

```
<input type=submit name=submit value="Register my question">
</form>
</body></html>
```

The deployment configuration (explained in Section 9.3.1) defines the mapping from the URI setup to the QuickPollSetup servlet, which looks as follows:

```
import java.io.*;
import javax.servlet.*;
import javax.servlet.http.*;

public class QuickPollSetup extends HttpServlet {
  public void doPost(HttpServletRequest request,
                     HttpServletResponse response)
      throws IOException, ServletException {
    String q = request.getParameter("question");
    ServletContext c = getServletContext();
    c.setAttribute("question", q);
    c.setAttribute("yes", new Integer(0));
    c.setAttribute("no", new Integer(0));
    response.setContentType("text/html");
    PrintWriter out = response.getWriter();
    out.print("<html><head><title>QuickPoll</title></head><body>"+
              "<h1>QuickPoll</h1>"+
              "Your question has been registered. "+
              "Let the vote begin!"+
              "</body></html>");
  }
}
```

We use three context attributes, question, yes, and no, to store the question and the number of 'yes' and 'no' votes.

The QuickPollAsk servlet is made as follows:

```
import java.io.*;
import javax.servlet.*;
import javax.servlet.http.*;

public class QuickPollAsk extends HttpServlet {
  public void doGet(HttpServletRequest request,
                    HttpServletResponse response)
      throws IOException, ServletException {
    response.setContentType("text/html");
    PrintWriter out = response.getWriter();
    out.print("<html><head><title>QuickPoll</title></head><body>"+
              "<h1>QuickPoll</h1>"+
              "<form method=post action=vote>");
```

```
      String question =
         (String)getServletContext().getAttribute("question");
      out.print(question+"?<p>");
      out.print("<input name=vote type=radio value=yes> yes<br>"+
                "<input name=vote type=radio value=no> no<p>"+
                "<input type=submit name=submit value=Vote>"+
                "</form>"+
                "</body></html>");
  }
}
```

We here simply read the `question` context attribute and build the HTML page. Notice that we have to downcast the question string since the return type of `getAttribute` is `Object`.

The `QuickPollVote` servlet:

```
import java.io.*;
import javax.servlet.*;
import javax.servlet.http.*;

public class QuickPollVote extends HttpServlet {
  public void doPost(HttpServletRequest request,
                     HttpServletResponse response)
      throws IOException, ServletException {
    String vote = request.getParameter("vote");
    ServletContext c = getServletContext();
    if (vote.equals("yes")) {
      int yes = ((Integer)c.getAttribute("yes")).intValue();
      yes++;
      c.setAttribute("yes", new Integer(yes));
    } else if (vote.equals("no")) {
      int no = ((Integer)c.getAttribute("no")).intValue();
      no++;
      c.setAttribute("no", new Integer(no));
    }
    PrintWriter out = response.getWriter();
    response.setContentType("text/html");
    out.print("<html><head><title>QuickPoll</title></head><body>"+
              "<h1>QuickPoll</h1>"+
              "Thank you for your vote!"+
              "</body></html>");
  }
}
```

Finally, the `QuickPollResults` servlet:

```
import java.io.*;
import javax.servlet.*;
import javax.servlet.http.*;
```

```
public class QuickPollResults extends HttpServlet {
  public void doGet(HttpServletRequest request,
                    HttpServletResponse response)
      throws IOException, ServletException {
    ServletContext c = getServletContext();
    String question = (String)c.getAttribute("question");
    int yes = ((Integer)c.getAttribute("yes")).intValue();
    int no = ((Integer)c.getAttribute("no")).intValue();
    int total = yes+no;
    response.setContentType("text/html");
    response.setDateHeader("Expires", 0);
    response.setHeader("Cache-Control",
                        "no-store, no-cache, must-revalidate");
    response.setHeader("Pragma", "no-cache");
    PrintWriter out = response.getWriter();
    out.print("<html><head><title>QuickPoll</title></head><body>"+
               "<h1>QuickPoll</h1>");
    if (total==0)
      out.print("No votes yet...");
    else {
      out.print(
        question + "?<p>"+
        "<table border=0>"+
        "<tr><td>Yes:<td>"+drawBar(300*yes/total)+"<td>"+yes+
        "<tr><td>No:<td>"+drawBar(300*no/total)+"<td>"+no+
        "</table>");

    }
    out.print("</body></html>");
  }

  String drawBar(int length) {
    return "<table><tr><td bgcolor=black height=20 width="+
            length+"></table>";
  }
}
```

We here set the response headers to disable caching as explained in Section 8.1.5. The drawBar method constructs a black box of the given width.

Notice that we choose some servlets to react on GET requests while others use POST: we use POST in the cases where executing the servlet has a side-effect, as required by the specification (see Section 8.1.3).

Still, this Web application has some notable flaws:

* Everybody has access to the QuickPollSetup servlet – we ought to use some kind of authentication to restrict the access (see Section 9.4.4).

- We tacitly assume that the question being entered does not contain special HTML characters like <, or else the output may not be valid HTML. The solution to this problem is shown in Section 9.2.2.

- A runtime exception occurs if the servlets are executed in an unindented order (and by default, such exceptions end up being shown in the user's browser and in the server's log file). For example, the `QuickPollVote` servlet assumes that `Integer` objects have been stored earlier in the `yes`/`no` context attributes.

- The `getParameter` method returns null if the right form field data is not present, and several of the servlets lack checks for null values. This means that a malicious or buggy client may cause null pointer exceptions in the server code.

- Race conditions are possible: the increments of the `yes` and `no` attributes in the `QuickPollVote` servlet are not synchronized, which may lead to votes not being counted.

- And finally, we ought to store the shared state in, for example, a database to improve robustness as discussed earlier.

Each of these problems is a typical pitfall when programming servlets. We look into the solutions in an exercise.

Another thing to note in this example is the redundancy in the HTML generation: All HTML pages, including the static one, contain the same wrapper (`<html>...</html>`). A good programming style would be to factor this part out to avoid the redundancy, for example, moving it to a separate class. Another approach would be to combine the resources into fewer servlet classes, perhaps just one, and then branch according to the available form field data or configuration parameters. Yet another approach is to use JSP for the HTML generation, as explained in the next chapter.

9.2.5 Sessions

We have now seen that execution of servlets closely follows the request–response pattern of HTTP. As discussed in Section 8.2 there are various ways of managing sessions and client state. The servlet API provides a convenient abstraction of the techniques based on URL rewriting, cookies, or SSL sessions (see Section 8.3), or perhaps even on combinations of these to improve robustness.

An `HttpSession` object encapsulates information related to a session while hiding the details of the implementation techniques being used. The `getSession` method in `HttpServletRequest` returns the current `HttpSession` object. If the session has been inactive for a certain time interval (as determined, for example, by the `setMaxInactiveInterval` method) or the `invalidate` method is invoked, the session can no longer be used.

Since the session management may be using the URL rewriting technique, all URLs that are emitted to the response HTML page and correspond to continuing the session must

HttpSession hides the technical details of implementing sessions on top of HTTP.

contain the appropriate session ID (see Section 8.2). Such URLs should always be passed through the `encodeURL` method of the `HttpServletResponse` object, which takes care of adding this session ID if necessary.

In the same way the `ServletContext` object can be used to store shared state, the `HttpSession` object can be used to store session state, that is, state that is local to one user but shared across many interactions. This state is accessed via the `setAttribute` and `getAttribute` methods in the `HttpSession` objects. Unlike `ServletContext` objects, `HttpSession` objects in a Web application that is configured as distributable (see Section 9.3.1) are shared for all JVMs running the application. This requires all objects stored in session attributes to be serializable (that is, implement the `Serializable` interface).

The following example servlet implements the core of the ubiquitous online shopping cart Web application using `HttpSession`:

```java
import java.io.*;
import java.util.*;
import javax.servlet.*;
import javax.servlet.http.*;

public class ShoppingCart extends HttpServlet {
  public void doGet(HttpServletRequest request,
                    HttpServletResponse response)
     throws IOException, ServletException {
    doPost(request, response);
  }

  public void doPost(HttpServletRequest request,
                     HttpServletResponse response)
     throws IOException, ServletException {
    response.setContentType("text/html");
    PrintWriter out = response.getWriter();
    out.println("<html><head><title>Widget Inc.</title></head><body>"+
               "<h1>Widget Inc. Online Shopping</h1>");

    HttpSession session = request.getSession();
    Map cart;
    if (session.isNew()) {
      cart = new TreeMap();
      session.setAttribute("cart", cart);
    } else
      cart = (Map)session.getAttribute("cart");

    if (request.getMethod().equals("POST")) {
      String item = request.getParameter("item");
      String amount = request.getParameter("amount");
      if (item!=null)
        try {
          addToCart(cart, item, Integer.parseInt(amount));
```

```
      } catch (Exception e) {
        response.sendError(response.SC_BAD_REQUEST,
                          "malformed request");
      }
   }


   String url = request.getRequestURI();
   out.println(
     "<form method=post action=\""+response.encodeURL(url)+"\">"+
     "Item: <input type=text name=item size=20>"+
     "Amount: <input type=text name=amount size=5>"+
     "<input type=submit name=submit value=\"Add to shopping cart\">"+
     "</form><p>");


   if (cart.isEmpty())
     out.println("Your shopping cart is empty.");
   else {
     out.println("Your shopping cart now contains:<p>"+
                 "<table border=1><tr><th>Item<th>Amount");
     Iterator i = cart.entrySet().iterator();
     while (i.hasNext()) {
       Map.Entry me = (Map.Entry)i.next();
       out.println("<tr><td>"+me.getKey()+
                   "<td align=right>"+me.getValue());
     }
     out.println("</table><p>");

     out.println(
       "<form method=post action=\""+response.encodeURL("buy")+"\">"+
       "<input type=submit name=submit"+
       " value=\"Proceed to cashier\">"+
       "</form>");
   }

   out.println("</body></html>");
  }


  void addToCart(Map cart, String item, int amount) {
    if (amount<0)
      return;
    Integer a = (Integer)cart.get(item);
    if (a==null)
      a = new Integer(0);
    cart.put(item, new Integer(a.intValue()+amount));
  }
}
```

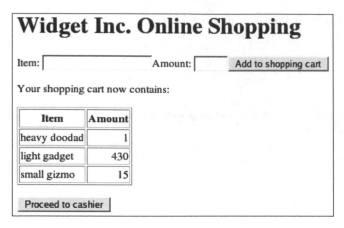

Figure 9.2 The widget shopping service.

The essential part of this servlet is the use of the `getSession`, `getAttribute`, and `setAttribute` methods: we use a session attribute named `cart` to store the contents of the shopping cart. The contents are represented as a `TreeMap` that maps from item names to amounts. The `addToCart` method simply adds the specified items to the cart map.

This servlet is used both for showing the current contents of the shopping cart and for adding more items. Notice that it reacts on both GET and POST requests. The former is appropriate for showing the shopping cart contents, whereas the latter is the right one for adding more items (see Section 8.1.3). Also notice that we return a 400 Bad Request message if reading the `amount` field fails (in case of a malicious or faulty client). Finally, we remember to pass the URLs through the `encodeURL` method as explained above. The code for the `buy` servlet, which is activated when clicking 'Proceed to cashier', is not shown here. After a few interactions, the user might see the HTML page shown in Figure 9.2.

Due to the `HttpSession` mechanism, the programmer usually does not have to think about cookies. However, if one wants to use cookies for other purposes than session management (for example, for storing user preferences or tracking which banner ads have been exposed to the user), then the `addCookie` method of `HttpServletResponse` and the `getCookies` method of `HttpServletRequest` can be used as a convenient alternative to manually accessing the relevant HTTP header fields.

The example above additionally illustrates a general problem with managing sessions in servlets (this is related to the discussion in the last part of Section 9.2.2 about receiving form field data): the control-flow through a session is not explicit in the program code. That is, it is often far from obvious how a generated HTML page is connected with the servlet that is activated when the user continues the session. This can make it difficult to develop Web applications that involve complex session flows.

9.3 Running Web Applications

We now look into the issues of wrapping up, configuring, and running Web applications.

9.3.1 Web Applications and Deployment

With servlets, Web applications are portable. Regardless of the server implementation, files are organized in a common directory structure and accessed via URIs in a standardized way. The directory structure is as follows for a Web application with the hypothetical context path `myapp`:

- `myapp/` and all subdirectories except `WEB-INF`: contain static resources, such as HTML files, images, and stylesheets, and also JSP files (see Chapter 10);

- `myapp/WEB-INF/`: contains the deployment descriptor (described below);

- `myapp/WEB-INF/classes/`: contains all servlet class files and also auxiliary class files used by the servlets;

- `myapp/WEB-INF/lib/`: contains additional jar files (which are automatically included by the application class loader);

The class files must be placed in subdirectories that match their package names, as usual in Java. For example, a servlet class file `MyServlet.class` in a package `inc.widget` is placed in `myapp/WEB-INF/classes/inc/widget/`.

An entire Web application can be bundled in a single file called a Web Archive (or WAR) file, having extension `.war`, using the `jar` tool.

Deployment Descriptors

All Web applications contain a *deployment descriptor*, which is an XML file named `web.xml`. This file contains the configuration of the application, including

- the mapping from URI paths to application resources;

- initialization parameters (see Section 9.2.1);

- error handling;

- security constraints and client authentication; and

- registration of *listeners* and *filters* (two advanced features described in Sections 9.4.1 and 9.4.2).

Deployment descriptors specify configuration properties in a declarative manner, separately from the servlet code, which makes it easy to adjust a Web application to its surroundings in the server.

As a small example, the following deployment descriptor can be used for the `HelloWorld` servlet from Section 9.2:

```
<web-app xmlns="http://java.sun.com/xml/ns/j2ee" version="2.4">
  <display-name>A Small Web Application</display-name>
```

```
<servlet>
  <servlet-name>MyFirstServlet</servlet-name>
  <servlet-class>HelloWorld</servlet-class>
</servlet>
<servlet-mapping>
  <servlet-name>MyFirstServlet</servlet-name>
  <url-pattern>/hello/*</url-pattern>
</servlet-mapping>
</web-app>
```

The (optional) `display-name` element contains a short name for the application. Generally, one `web-app` can contain several `servlet` and `servlet-mapping` elements. A `servlet` element, called a *servlet declaration*, associates a name to a (fully qualified) servlet class. One servlet class may be used in multiple servlet declarations in the same application, and each servlet declaration results in one instance of the class (for each JVM, in case of a distributed application). A `servlet-mapping` element associates a URI pattern to a servlet name. This pattern should be interpreted relative to the context path, for example `myapp`, if the application is stored in the `myapp` directory. In this example, any URI that points to the right server and where the path part begins with `myapp/hello/` will cause the `HelloWorld` servlet to be executed.

Also notice the namespace declaration that identifies the deployment descriptor language. An XML Schema description (see Section 4.4) of the deployment descriptor language is available at

```
http://java.sun.com/xml/ns/j2ee/web-app_2_4.xsd
```

Deployment descriptors contain Web application configuration, separately from the servlet code.

In earlier versions of the servlet framework, deployment descriptors did not use namespaces and were described with DTD instead of XML Schema.

There are two kinds of initialization parameters: context parameters and servlet parameters. The former kind applies to the whole application and is accessed via the `getInitParameter` method of the `ServletContext` object; the latter is specific to individual servlet declarations and can be accessed via the `getInitParameter` method of the `HttpServlet` object. (Notice that both methods are named `getInitParameter`.) This distinction between the two kinds is mainly relevant when declaring multiple instances of the same servlet.

We could add a couple of initialization parameters to the example as follows:

```
<web-app xmlns="http://java.sun.com/xml/ns/j2ee" version="2.4">
  <display-name>A Small Web Application</display-name>
  <context-param>
    <param-name>admin</param-name>
    <param-value>john.doe@widget.inc</param-value>
  </context-param>
  <servlet>
    <servlet-name>MyFirstServlet</servlet-name>
    <servlet-class>HelloWorld</servlet-class>
```

```
      <init-param>
        <param-name>verbose</param-name>
        <param-value>true</param-value>
      </init-param>
    </servlet>
    <servlet-mapping>
      <servlet-name>MyFirstServlet</servlet-name>
      <url-pattern>/hello/*</url-pattern>
    </servlet-mapping>
  </web-app>
```

We have here inserted a context parameter named admin and a servlet parameter named verbose.

In Section 9.2.4, we mentioned distributable applications. An application is declared as distributable by placing the following element in the contents of web-app:

```
<distributable/>
```

This declaration indicates that the application has been programmed appropriately to run on a distributed server. (The presence of this element does *not* guarantee that the application actually works on a distributed server – it only shows the programmer's intentions.)

The error-page element defines a mapping from exceptions or HTTP error codes to resources that are returned if errors occur:

```
<web-app ...>
  ...
  <error-page>
    <error-code>404</error-code>
    <location>/not_found.html</location>
  </error-page>
  <error-page>
    <exception-type>
      inc.widget.NotImplementedException
    </exception-type>
    <location>/error</location>
  </error-page>
  ...
</web-app>
```

The location URLs are always relative to the current Web application root. In this example, 404 Not Found errors cause the not_found.html page to be shown, and if a servlet throws an inc.widget.NotImplementedException and does not catch it, then the error resource (which might be a servlet declared elsewhere) is invoked. This error mapping feature makes it easy to produce specialized error messages as an alternative to the default ones made by the server.

Other interesting configuration elements are described in later sections.

9.3.2 Running Servlets with Tomcat

A popular implementation of the servlet framework is the open source Apache Jakarta Tomcat server (in short just Tomcat), which is the official reference implementation of the servlet framework and also of JSP. (Colloquially, being a 'reference implementation' means that any behavior by Tomcat not covered by the servlet specification is a feature, not a bug.) In this section, we give a crash course in getting Tomcat up and running. Unlike all other sections in this chapter, the information in this section is specific to the Tomcat server.

First, download and extract the Tomcat binaries (see the online resources for this chapter). Among the files and directories are:

`common/lib/servlet-api.jar`: the main jar file needed for compiling servlets;

`bin/`: contains scripts for starting and stopping the server;

`conf/`: contains server configuration files (see below); and

`webapps/`: the root for all Web application directories.

Tomcat is the reference implementation of the servlet framework.

By default, Tomcat uses port 8080 for HTTP traffic. This can be changed in `conf/server.xml`. To configure SSL support, this file is also the one to edit. We can use our homemade server certificate (see Section 8.4.3) and port 8443 for HTTPS traffic by inserting the following (assuming that `serverkey.jks` is located in the directory `/home/jdoe`):

```
<Connector port="8443" scheme="https" secure="true"
           keystoreFile="/home/jdoe/serverkey.jks"
           keystorePass="ToPsEcReT"/>
```

We look more into SSL in Section 9.4.4.

Tomcat comes with a useful application called *manager*, which makes it easy to deploy and update individual applications in a running server. To make the manager work, it is necessary to add a user with role `manager` to the file `conf/tomcat-users.xml`, for example:

```
<role rolename="manager"/>
<user username="jdoe" password="qwerty" roles="manager"/>
```

(We discuss user roles in Section 9.4.4.) We can then start the server using the appropriate script, as mentioned above. To add a new Web application, we copy it (using the directory layout explained in Section 9.3.1) to a directory, for example `webapps/myapp` (corresponding to the context path `myapp`). Assuming we have a browser running on the same machine, we can now request the following URL to instruct the manager to activate the application:

```
http://localhost:8080/manager/start?path=/myapp
```

We will then be requested to enter username and password, in this case `jdoe` and `qwerty`. The application should now be ready to handle requests. In case we later update class files or jar files, we can inform the manager as follows:

```
http://localhost:8080/manager/reload?path=/myapp
```

What we have seen in this section is sufficient to get the examples shown in the chapter up and running. Tomcat is highly configurable and additionally contains a wide range of advanced features, such as load balancing and integration with the powerful Apache httpd server. For the full documentation, see the Tomcat Web site.

9.4 Advanced Features

In the previous sections, we have seen the basic features of servlets. We now turn to the more advanced topics (which may be skipped in a first reading).

9.4.1 Listeners

A *listener* is an event handler that the server invokes when certain events occur, for example, when the Web application is initialized or shut down, a session is created or times out, or a context attribute has been updated. In design pattern terms, this is also called the *observer pattern*, in which an observer (in this case, the listener) is notified when an event occurs in the subject (the server). The overall benefit of using this pattern as opposed to inserting the event handler code explicitly at all places where the events may occur is that a lower degree of coupling between the subject and the observer is obtained, and that tends to provide more manageable code.

The typical uses of listeners include

- application-wide initialization routines;

- managing dependencies between data stored in context or session attributes, such that whenever one attribute is changed, others that depend on it are automatically updated; and

- monitoring the running application, for example, measuring the current number of active sessions.

There are different kinds of listeners, each corresponding to an interface and a group of events. Some of them are:

`ServletContextListener`: the Web application is being initialized or shut down;

`ServletRequestListener`: a request handler is starting or finishing;

`HttpSessionListener`: a session is created or invalidated;

`ServletContextAttributeListener`: a context attribute has been added, removed, or replaced;

`HttpSessionAttributeListener`: a session attribute has been added, removed, or replaced.

(For the full list, see the javadoc.) To use a listener, one simply implements the appropriate interface and registers the listener in the deployment descriptor.

As an example, the following listener monitors the current and maximum number of active sessions, for example for the `ShoppingCart` application:

```
import javax.servlet.*;
import javax.servlet.http.*;

public class SessionMonitor
    implements HttpSessionListener, ServletContextListener {
  private int active = 0, max = 0;

  public void contextInitialized(ServletContextEvent sce) {
    store(sce.getServletContext());
  }

  public void contextDestroyed(ServletContextEvent sce) {}

  public void sessionCreated(HttpSessionEvent se) {
    active++;
    if (active>max)
      max = active;
    store(se.getSession().getServletContext());
  }

  public void sessionDestroyed(HttpSessionEvent se) {
    active--;
    store(se.getSession().getServletContext());
  }

  private void store(ServletContext c) {
    c.setAttribute("sessions_active", new Integer(active));
    c.setAttribute("sessions_max", new Integer(max));
  }
}
```

A **listener** is notified when certain events occur in the observed objects.

The counters are made visible to the rest of the application using context attributes. This class implements both `HttpSessionListener` and `ServletContextListener` such that it is notified when the application starts (to initialize the context attributes) and when a session is created or invalidated. The listener is registered in the deployment descriptor as follows:

```
<web-app ...>
  ...
  <listener>
    <listener-class>SessionMonitor</listener-class>
  </listener>
  ...
</web-app>
```

To make the counters visible, we write a small servlet that shows their values:

```
import java.io.*;
import javax.servlet.*;
import javax.servlet.http.*;

public class GetSessionStat extends HttpServlet {
  public void doGet(HttpServletRequest request,
                    HttpServletResponse response)
      throws IOException, ServletException {
    ServletContext c = getServletContext();
    int active =
      ((Integer)c.getAttribute("sessions_active")).intValue();
    int max = ((Integer)c.getAttribute("sessions_max")).intValue();
    response.setContentType("text/html");
    response.setDateHeader("Expires", 0);
    PrintWriter out = response.getWriter();
    out.println("<html><head><title>Widget Inc.</title></head><body>"+
                "<h1>Session Statistics</h1>"+
                "Current number of active sessions: "+active+"<br>"+
                "Maximum number of active sessions: "+max+
                "</body></html>");
  }
}
```

This servlet simply reads the context attributes that have been set by the listener (and disables caching of the response). Notice that the use of the listener allows us to solve the task without any modification of the ShoppingCart code.

9.4.2 Filters

A *filter* is some code that is executed before or after the servlets to inspect or modify the requests or responses. There are many uses of filters, including

- security, in particular authentication (see Section 9.4.4);

- data conversion, for example performing XSLT transformations (see Section 7.3.5) or changing image formats in combination with content negotiation (see Section 8.1.1);

- data compression (see Section 8.1.2);

- auditing; and

- specialized caching.

Filters are associated to the servlets declaratively using the deployment descriptor. As with listeners, this design can provide more manageable programs compared with explicitly inserting the code in all relevant servlets. A request URL that matches both a filter and a servlet will first cause the filter to be executed. The filter can then access the request data, set up *wrappers* for modifying the request or response as explained below, and then either invoke the servlet, redirect the request, or generate the response itself. In case multiple filters match, these are executed in a chain with the servlet in the end. Filters can also be applied to requests for static resources, such as XML files or images, not just to servlets.

Technically, a filter is a class that implements the `Filter` interface that contains a method `doFilter`. This method has three arguments: a request object, a response object, and a *filter chain* object. The latter is used for invoking the next filter or resource in the chain. The interface has two additional methods, `init` and `destroy`, which are executed by the server when the filter object is initialized or shut down, much like the methods of the same names in `HttpServlet` (see Section 9.2.1).

As an example, the following filter counts and logs all incoming requests and outgoing responses and the number of milliseconds that the processing takes:

```
import java.io.*;
import javax.servlet.*;
import javax.servlet.http.*;

public class LoggingFilter implements Filter {
  ServletContext context;
  int counter;

  public void init(FilterConfig c) throws ServletException {
    context = c.getServletContext();
  }

  public void destroy() {}

  public void doFilter(ServletRequest request,
                       ServletResponse response,
                       FilterChain chain)
      throws IOException, ServletException {
    String uri = ((HttpServletRequest)request).getRequestURI();
    int n = ++counter;
    context.log("starting processing request #"+n+" ("+uri+")");
```

```
        long t1 = System.currentTimeMillis();
        chain.doFilter(request, response);
        long t2 = System.currentTimeMillis();
        context.log("done processing request #"+n+", "+(t2-t1)+" ms");
    }
}
```

This filter simply writes to the log before and after invoking the next filter or resource in the chain. The server log is obtained through the FilterConfig object given to the init method. One additional thing to note here is that the types of the request and response objects are *not* HttpServletRequest and HttpServletResponse but instead superclasses of these that contain the non-HTTP specific information. However, if the only servlets we write are HTTP servlets, which is usually the case, then it is safe to downcast as in the example.

To register this filter for all request URLs to the application, we add the following to the deployment descriptor:

```
<web-app ...>
  ...
  <filter>
    <filter-name>My Logging Filter</filter-name>
    <filter-class>LoggingFilter</filter-class>
  </filter>

  <filter-mapping>
    <filter-name>My Logging Filter</filter-name>
    <url-pattern>/*</url-pattern>
  </filter-mapping>
  ...
</web-app>
```

In case of multiple filters, the order of the filter declarations determines the order of execution.

As indicated by the LoggingFilter example, servlet filters do not necessarily filtrate anything. The name 'filter' is perhaps more appropriate when the doFilter method is *not* always invoked, for example when performing access control.

Wrappers

To be able to modify the request or response by a filter, we cannot just make changes to the request and response objects before or after calling the next filter or resource in the chain, because both the request and the response are read and written in a streaming fashion. Instead, they can be wrapped-in such that filter code is executed whenever code further down the chain reads from the request or writes to the response. In design pattern terms, this is also called the *wrapper pattern*.

The class `HttpServletRequestWrapper` implements the `HttpServletRequest` interface, which extends `ServletRequest`. This means that we can pass an instance of `HttpServletRequestWrapper` to the `doFilter` method of the filter chain for wrapping in the request. Similarly, an instance of the class `HttpServletResponseWrapper` can be used for wrapping in the response.

As an example, we can use a response wrapper to construct a filter that performs server-side XSLT transformation (see Section 7.3.5) on the response, unless the `User-Agent` field of the request indicates that the client is able to do the work. Recall from Chapter 7 that XSLT transformations are generally performed in memory, so we have to sacrifice the streaming of the response and instead collect it in a buffer, which we then apply the XSLT transformation on.

Filters and **wrappers** can – separately from the main servlet code – inspect and modify requests and responses.

The following filter solves the task, but under some assumptions to keep things simple: the XML document must be generated by a servlet using the `getWriter` method of the response object (not using `getOutputStream`, which we for simplicity do not wrap in here), the generated XML document must begin with a single processing instruction that contains the URL of the XSLT stylesheet (see Section 5.1), and the stylesheet must generate XHTML:

```java
import java.io.*;
import java.util.*;
import javax.servlet.*;
import javax.servlet.http.*;
import org.jdom.*;
import org.jdom.transform.*;
import org.jdom.input.*;
import org.jdom.output.*;

public class XSLTFilter implements Filter {
  ServletContext context;

  public void init(FilterConfig c) throws ServletException {
    context = c.getServletContext();
  }

  public void destroy() {}

  public void doFilter(ServletRequest request,
                       ServletResponse response,
                       FilterChain chain)
    throws IOException, ServletException {
    HttpServletRequest hreq = (HttpServletRequest)request;
    HttpServletResponse hresp = (HttpServletResponse)response;
    boolean client_capable =
      checkXSLTSupport(hreq.getHeader("User-Agent"));
    ServletResponse res;
    if (client_capable)
      res = response;
```

```
      else
        res = new BufferingResponseWrapper(hresp);
      chain.doFilter(request, res);
      if (!client_capable) {
        try {
          hresp.setContentType("application/xhtml+xml");
          transform(((BufferingResponseWrapper)res).getReader(),
                    response.getWriter());
        } catch (Throwable e) {
          context.log("XSLT transformation error", e);
          hresp.sendError(500, "XSLT transformation error");
        }
      }
    }

  boolean checkXSLTSupport(String user_agent) {
    if (user_agent==null)
      return false;
    return
      user_agent.indexOf("MSIE 5.5")!=-1 ||
      user_agent.indexOf("MSIE 6")!=-1 ||
      user_agent.indexOf("Gecko")!=-1;
  }

  void transform(Reader in, Writer out)
      throws JDOMException, IOException {
    System.setProperty("javax.xml.transform.TransformerFactory",
                "net.sf.saxon.TransformerFactoryImpl");
    SAXBuilder b = new SAXBuilder();
    Document d = b.build(in);
    List pi = d.getContent(new org.jdom.filter.ContentFilter
                            (org.jdom.filter.ContentFilter.PI));
    String xsl = ((ProcessingInstruction)(pi.get(0)))
                .getPseudoAttributeValue("href");
    XSLTransformer t = new XSLTransformer(xsl);
    Document h = t.transform(d);
    (new XMLOutputter()).output(h, out);
  }
}

class BufferingResponseWrapper extends HttpServletResponseWrapper {
  CharArrayWriter buffer;
  PrintWriter writer;

  public BufferingResponseWrapper(HttpServletResponse res) {
    super(res);
    buffer = new CharArrayWriter();
    writer = new PrintWriter(buffer);
  }
```

```
    public PrintWriter getWriter() {
      return writer;
    }

    Reader getReader() {
      return new CharArrayReader(buffer.toCharArray());
    }
  }
```

Notice how the `BufferingResponseWrapper` class constructs a `CharArrayWriter` for accumulating the response and that it wraps in the `getWriter` method for the servlet. The `getReader` method is used for subsequently reading the generated XML document. The check for XSLT support in the browser is determined from the `User-Agent` field using an incomplete but simple list of characteristics. The `transform` method performs the actual XSLT transformation along the lines of the example in Section 7.3.5. Since the program uses JDOM and Saxon, we must remember to install jar files for these packages in the `WEB-INF/lib/` directory as explained in Section 9.3.1.

9.4.3 Request Dispatchers

To enhance modularity of the application code, it can sometimes be convenient for a servlet to be able to forward the request to another resource, for example based on available form input or client authentication. The `RequestDispatcher` class provides such functionality as the following code snippet shows:

```
RequestDispatcher disp = context.getRequestDispatcher("/shop/buy");
disp.forward(req, resp);
```

Request dispatchers are often used in the Model–View–Controller pattern together with JSP pages.

We here assume that the variable `context` holds a `ServletContext` object (see Section 9.2.4), and `req` and `resp` are a request object and a response object, respectively (see Section 9.2). These lines will forward the processing to the resource `buy` in the Web application `shop`. (A `RequestDispatcher` object can also be obtained from the request object, in which case the URI will be relative to the URI of the calling servlet.) Forwarding is widely used in combination with JSP pages, which we return to in Section 10.3.

An obvious alternative to using the `forward` mechanism is the `sendRedirect` method described in Section 9.2.3. One difference is that `forward` is handled without involving the client, however, it only permits redirection to resources on the same server. Additionally, with `forward`, the caller servlet can pass information to the callee by adding new attributes to the request using a `setAttribute`/`getAttribute` mechanism similar to the ones for `ServletContext` and `HttpSession`. The server automatically sets a number of attributes that provide information about the original request, for example its URI (see the specification for details). And finally, `forward` can be combined with request and response wrappers (see Section 9.4.2).

A variant of `forward` is the `include` method, which allows one servlet to invoke another resource, typically a servlet or a JSP page, for producing a part of the response but not necessarily all of it.

9.4.4 Security

The servlet framework provides support for building secure applications using client authentication (see Section 8.1.4) and SSL (see Section 8.3). This support comes in two parts: (1) a mechanism where security constraints can be specified declaratively in the deployment descriptor, and (2) some extra methods in the `HttpServletRequest` class.

A central concept is that of a *realm*, which is a collection of usernames and passwords that identify users of the Web application (not to confuse with the 'realms' used in HTTP authentication). Each username is additionally associated with a set of *roles*. A role is a logical group, for example, `administrator` or `student`, that has certain privileges.

The roles that are used in the application must be declared in the deployment descriptor:

```
<web-app ...>
  ...
  <security-role>
    <role-name>administrator</role-name>
    <role-name>teacher</role-name>
    <role-name>student</role-name>
  </security-role>
  ...
</web-app>
```

Management of realms is unfortunately entirely implementation specific. With the Tomcat server, realms are typically managed via JDBC or JAAS. However, for simple applications, a static XML document, `conf/tomcat-users.xml`, can be used as mentioned in Section 9.3.2.

Declarative Security Constraints

Declarative security constraints make it possible to specify authentication and SSL requirements in the deployment descriptor, without modifying the actual servlet code. Of course, it is also possible to implement, for example, HTTP Basic authentication manually since the servlet API does provide full access to the HTTP headers, but that would require a lot of tedious programming. Also, having separated the security constraints from the servlet code makes it easier to ensure that all servlets are properly protected and to perform changes in the security policy.

The following is an example of a security constraint, expressed as a `security-constraint` element appearing in the deployment descriptor:

```
<web-app ...>
  ...
  <security-constraint>
    <web-resource-collection>
      <web-resource-name>Restricted Area</web-resource-name>
      <url-pattern>/restricted/*</url-pattern>
```

```
      <http-method>GET</http-method>
      <http-method>POST</http-method>
    </web-resource-collection>
    <auth-constraint>
      <role-name>administrator</role-name>
      <role-name>teacher</role-name>
    </auth-constraint>
    <user-data-constraint>
      <transport-guarantee>CONFIDENTIAL</transport-guarantee>
    </user-data-constraint>
  </security-constraint>
  ...
</web-app>
```

The `web-resource-collection` part identifies the resources that the security constraint applies to (however, security constraints do *not* apply to forwarding or inclusion with request dispatchers). In this example, the constraint applies to all GET and POST requests matching the pattern `/restricted/*`. (If no `http-method` were specified, the constraint would apply to all request methods.) Only users that are associated with one of the roles listed in the `auth-constraint` element have access. A `*` matches any role name. Finally, the presence of CONFIDENTIAL ensures that access is only permitted through a secure connection, which in practice means SSL.

Users are authenticated either with forms, HTTP Basic, HTTP Digest, or SSL client certificates (although the latter two are not available in all implementations). The mechanism is chosen by the `login-config` element in the deployment descriptor. For HTTP Basic, this may look as follows:

```
<web-app ...>
  ...
  <login-config>
    <auth-method>BASIC</auth-method>
    <realm-name>Administration</realm-name>
  </login-config>
</web-app>
```

The value of `realm-name` will appear in the login windows. A Web application can have at most one `login-config` element, and its scope is the whole application.

When a user tries to access a page protected by HTTP Basic authentication, the server will follow the protocol explained in Section 8.1.4 behind the scenes. Recall that this protocol ensures that subsequent interactions from the same browser will authenticate without involving the user any further (until the browser is restarted).

Form-based authentication requires us to specify URIs (relative to the application root) of resources for the login page and the error page:

```
<web-app ...>
  ...
  <login-config>
```

```
    <auth-method>FORM</auth-method>
    <form-login-config>
       <form-login-page>/login</form-login-page>
       <form-error-page>/login-error.html</form-error-page>
    </form-login-config>
  </login-config>
</web-app>
```

The login page, which might be a static HTML document or generated by a servlet, must contain a form that uses the POST method, a specific action attribute, and specific names for the username/password fields such that the server can recognize the values being submitted:

```
<form method="POST" action="j_security_check">
  User name: <input type="text" name="j_username"> <br>
  Password: <input type="password" name="j_password"> <br>
  <input type="submit" name="login" value="Login">
</form>
```

To avoid involving the user in the authentication in every subsequent interaction, the server will in the form-based approach cache information about the user in the session object. However, since the form-based approach does not fit well with the URL rewriting technique (see Section 8.2), the specification mentions a notable limitation: 'form based login should be used only when sessions are being maintained by cookies or by SSL session information'. This limitation can be quite annoying since the browsers generally cannot be trusted to support cookies as discussed in Section 8.2, and requiring SSL for all interactions may be too costly.

Programmatic Support

The declarative security constraints are powerful but often not sufficient. Sometimes, it is necessary in the servlet code to be able to, for example, read the username or the SSL client certificate. Such information is available in the request object (see Section 9.2.2):

getRemoteUser(): returns the username of the user making the request, or null if the user has not been authenticated;

isUserInRole(String role): determines if the user belongs to the given role;

isSecure(): determines if the request was made using a secure channel, that is, using SSL;

getAuthType(): returns the authentication scheme being used.

If SSL client authentication is in use, some special attributes are set in the request object. For instance, getAttribute("javax.servlet.request.X509Certificate") returns an object of type java.security.cert.X509Certificate containing the X.509 certificate of the user.

These request methods can be combined with filters (see Section 9.4.2) to implement flexible security policies.

To allow the servlet code to be written independently of the actual role names being declared in the deployment descriptor, a mapping can be defined by `security-role-ref` elements:

```
<web-app ...>
  ...
  <servlet>
    ...
    <security-role-ref>
      <role-name>VIP</role-name>
      <role-link>administrator</role-link>
    </security-role-ref>
  </servlet>
  ...
</web-app>
```

Here, the servlet code may refer to the role `VIP` as an alias for `administrator`. This mapping may be useful if the servlet shares username/password information with other servlets or Web applications on the server.

9.5   Limitations of Servlets

In summary, compared with the simple Web server shown in Section 8.5, the servlet framework adds a number of useful features including:

- multi-threading;

- declarative configuration (deployment descriptors), in particular defining the mapping from request URI to resources on the server;

- request parsing, including decoding form field data;

- shared state (servlet contexts);

- session management (as an abstraction of the techniques discussed in Section 8.2);

- advanced code structuring mechanisms (listeners, filters, and wrappers); and

- support for client authentication (as an abstraction of the techniques from Section 8.1.4) and SSL (based on what we saw in Section 8.4.3).

Still, one may argue that some general problems remain. First, the dynamic construction of HTML documents is still low-level: fragments of textual HTML are written to an output stream, eventually forming a complete HTML document. There are no compile time guarantees that the result is valid according to some schema, or even well-formed. For nontrivial programs it can be exceedingly difficult to avoid this kind of bug.

Second, as discussed in Section 9.2.3, it difficult to separate the concerns of programmers and HTML designers. We return to this issue in the next chapter.

Third, although the servlet framework does make it easier to manage sessions compared to manually using the techniques from Section 8.2, the control-flow through a session involving different servlets can be difficult to follow for the programmer. The connection between the code that generates an HTML document with a form and the code that subsequently handles the form field data is often not obvious, as noted in Section 9.2.5. Moreover, the way session state is managed via the `setAttribute`/`getAttribute` mechanism is vulnerable. Since the session control-flow is not always clear, the programmer must be careful about assuming that certain attributes have or have not been set in an earlier interaction. Also, as we have seen it is necessary to downcast all results from `getAttribute`, which is an additional source of errors that are not detected statically.

9.6   Web Applications with JWIG ★

JWIG is a research project whose goal has been to alleviate some of the limitations of servlets and related frameworks, in particular regarding management of sessions. The current implementation of JWIG builds on top of the servlet framework, adding the ability to program sessions as Java threads directly reflecting the illustration in Section 8.2. When a client has initiated a session thread, interactions between the thread and the client take place like remote procedure calls (RPC) but with the roles reversed: the thread running on the server sends an XHTML page with a form to the client and sleeps until the client submits the response. Thereby, the control flow of the session becomes explicit in the code. This means that session state can simply be defined by fields and method variables in the thread code (without using `setAttribute`/`getAttribute`). Moreover, interactions with the client can be made even in deeply nested method invocations; execution simply resumes after the call to the client when the response has been submitted. Of course, having a thread for each session incurs a memory overhead compared to using traditional servlets, but for many applications the benefits outweigh this overhead.

JWIG is closely related to the XACT project (see Section 7.7.2): JWIG programs typically use XACT code for dynamic construction of XHTML pages. This combination makes it possible, based on static analysis, to provide compile time guarantees of two desirable properties:

> JWIG adds **session threads** to servlets and supports **static checking** of output validity and form field consistency.

- that only valid XHTML is ever produced; and

- that form field data being read using `getParameter` always matches the fields that appear in the corresponding XHTML page.

The former property is checked using the XACT analyzer; the latter requires a separate analysis, which exploits the explicit control flow and the template-based construction of XHTML pages.

For tracking clients, JWIG uses the URL rewriting technique, and optionally the session URL variant as described in Section 8.2.

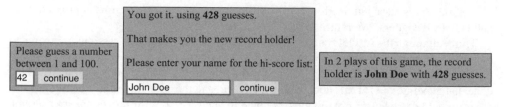

Figure 9.3 The guessing game in action.

As an example, we can write a small guessing game application where the user is asked to guess a number between 1 and 100. Some screen shots from the running application are shown in Figure 9.3. The main part of the code is the following session thread. When executed, it first requests the user to guess a number. It then enters a loop telling the user whether the right number is lower or higher. When the right number is hit, the hi-score list is updated if there is a new record, and finally, a closing message is sent.

```
import java.io.*;
import java.util.*;
import javax.servlet.*;
import javax.servlet.http.*;
import org.jwig.*;
import dk.brics.xact.*;

public class GuessingGamePlay extends SessionThread {
  public XML main() throws IOException, ServletException {
    XML wrapper = XML.loadConstant("GuessingGameWrapper.xml");
    XML form = [[
      <form>
        <input name="guess" type="text" size="2" maxlength="2"/>
        <input type="submit" name="continue" value="continue"/>
      </form>
    ]];

    ServletContext c = getServletContext();
    Integer plays = (Integer)c.getAttribute("plays");
    if (plays==null)
      plays = newInteger(1);
    else
      plays = new Integer(plays.intValue()+1);
    c.setAttribute("plays", plays);
    int number = (new Random()).nextInt(100)+1;

    show(wrapper.plug("BODY",
      [[Please guess a number between 1 and 100: <{form}>]]));
    int guesses = 1;
    boolean done = false;
```

```
    while (!done) {
      int guess = Integer.parseInt(getParameter("guess"));
      if (guess==number)
        done = true;
      else {
        show(wrapper.plug("BODY", [[
          That is not correct. Try a
          <b><{(guess>number)?"lower":"higher"}></b> number:
          <{form}>
        ]]));
        guesses++;
      }
    }

    XML msg = [[You got it, using <b><{guesses}></b> guesses.]];
    XML thanks = [[Thank you for playing this exciting game!]];
    XML res;
    if (guesses<getCurrentRecord()) {
      show(wrapper.plug("BODY", [[
        <{msg}><p/>
        That makes you the new record holder!<p/>
        Please enter your name for the hi-score list:
        <form>
          <input name="name" type-"text" size="20"/>
          <input type="submit" name="continue" value="continue"/>
        </form>
      ]]));
      synchronized(c) {
        if (guesses<getCurrentRecord()) {
          c.setAttribute("holder", getParameter("name"));
          c.setAttribute("record", new Integer(guesses));
        }
      }
      res = wrapper.plug("BODY", thanks);
    } else
      res = wrapper.plug("BODY", [[<{msg}><p/><{thanks}>]]);
    return res;
  }

  int getCurrentRecord() {
    Integer record = (Integer)c.getAttribute("record");
    if (record!=null)
      return record.intValue();
    else
      return Integer.MAX_VALUE; // no players yet
  }
}
```

The special syntax [[...]] and <{...}> was introduced in Section 7.7.2. Each show statement sends an XHTML document to the client and awaits a response. The return statement sends the final document and terminates the session. XACT XML templates are used for constructing the XHTML pages. The action attributes in the form elements are inserted automatically to ensure that the thread resumes execution when the client submits the response. Notice that we use a synchronized block to avoid a race condition at the update of the servlet context attributes.

The GuessingGameWrapper.xml template looks as follows:

```
<html>
<head><title>The Guessing Game</title></head>
<body bgcolor="aqua"><[BODY]></body>
</html>
```

The following servlet produces the hi-score page:

```
import java.io.*;
import javax.servlet.*;
import javax.servlet.http.*;
import org.jwig.*;
import dk.brics.xact.*;

public class GuessingGameHiscore extends HttpServlet {
  public void doGet() throws IOException, ServletException {
    ServletContext c = getServletContext();
    Integer plays = (Integer)c.getAttribute("plays");
    String holder = (String)c.getAttribute("holder");
    Integer record = (Integer)c.getAttribute("record");
    XML body;
    if (record!=null)
      body = [[In <{plays.toString()}> plays of this game,
              the record holder is <b><{holder}></b> with
              <b><{record.toString()}></b> guesses.]];
    else
      body = [[No players yet.]];
    XML.loadConstant("GuessingGameWrapper.xml")
      .plug("BODY", body).output(response.getWriter());
  }
}
```

Notice that this servlet also uses XACT and reuses the GuessingGameWrapper.xml template.

Running the static program analyses on this application tells us that the client always receives valid XHTML and that the calls to getParameter always return a non-null value. Both properties increase the confidence that the application behaves as desired.

We leave it as an exercise to program a similar application entirely with servlets.

9.7   Chapter Summary

This chapter has shown how the servlet framework makes it possible to program Web servers using Java. The framework is closely tied with the request–response pattern of the HTTP protocol. Compared to programming with the more low-level TCP/IP and HTTP support in the standard Java libraries, the servlet API adds many useful features, including parsing of form data, session management, and declarative configuration.

We have briefly mentioned the Tomcat server, which is a reference implementation and freely available, making it a popular choice.

In addition, we have seen some more advanced features of servlets that are particularly useful for development of large scale Web applications: listeners, filters, wrappers, request dispatchers, and security mechanisms.

Finally, we have touched upon the research project JWIG that aims to alleviate some of the limitations of servlets, mostly related to session management.

9.8   Further Reading

The best places to look for more information about servlets are the specification [75], the online API documentation, and the Web site for Tomcat (see URLs below). An early version of JWIG was presented in the article [20].

9.9   Online Resources

`http://jakarta.apache.org/tomcat/tomcat-5.5-doc/servletapi/`
   The javadoc for the Servlet 2.4 API.

`http://java.sun.com/products/servlet/`
   Sun's home page for servlets.

`http://jakarta.apache.org/tomcat/`
   The Apache Jakarta Tomcat server.

`http://www.jwig.org/`
   Web site for the JWIG project.

9.10   Exercises

The main lessons to be learned from these exercises are:

- using the servlet API; and
- applications of advanced features.

Exercise 9.1 Write a servlet that accepts GET and POST requests and outputs as much information about a given request as can be obtained through the `HttpServletRequest` object.

> **TIP**
>
> For detailed instructions on how to set up a Tomcat server on Windows or Linux, see `http://www.brics.dk/ixwt/tomcat/`.

Exercise 9.2 Consider the servlet in *EX*/`Scopes.java`. Can you use it to distinguish between the behavior of data saved in the `ServletContext` object, the `HttpSession` object, and in local variables?

Exercise 9.3 Fix the following flaws with the polling service from Section 9.2.4.

(a) Use HTTP Basic authentication to restrict access to the `QuickPollSetup` servlet.
(b) Make sure special characters in the user's input are escaped properly (for example, < is converted to `&lt;`).
(c) Insert some checks in the code to make sure that the control flow is correct. For example, `QuickPollVote` should not be executed unless `QuickPollSetup` has been executed first.
(d) Synchronize the increments of the `yes` and `no` attributes in `QuickPollVote`.

Exercise 9.4 Extend the polling service to use cookies such that users are prevented from voting twice.

Exercise 9.5 The file *EX*/`students.xml` contains information about students and their grades. Write a servlet `Lookup` that on a GET request accepts a single parameter named `id` and returns all information about the corresponding student.

Exercise 9.6 Write a *guest book* servlet that has the following behavior:

- It stores a list of *entries*, each consisting of some text and a name.
- When invoked with a GET request, it shows the list of entries together with a form where the user can fill in a new entry.
- When invoked with a POST request and appropriate form fields, it adds a new entry to the list and produces the same reply as with GET requests.

Exercise 9.7 Implement a pure servlet version of the guessing game (see Section 9.6). Compare the resulting code with the version using XACT and JWIG.

Exercise 9.8 Write a class named `BigBrother` that implements all listener interfaces (see Section 9.4.1) and logs the events as they occur. Try it out with the polling service.

Exercise 9.9 Write a filter class (see Section 9.4.2) named `GateKeeper` that prevents access from all clients except those that appear on a positive list of IP addresses. Rejected clients instead receive an appropriate message. Try it out with the polling service.

Exercise 9.10 Modify the `XSLTFilter` class (see Section 9.4.2) to apply the stylesheet *EX*/`xml2text.xsl` if the resulting response is of type `text/xml` and the client's browser is the text-based Lynx tool (whose `User-Agent` value always starts with `Lynx`).

Exercise 9.11 Implement a JWIG version of your guest book servlet from Exercise 9.6.

PROGRAMMING WEB APPLICATIONS WITH JSP

10

Objectives

In this chapter, you will learn:

- How to program Web applications using JSP

- How to extend the JSP syntax using tag libraries

- The interplay with servlets and the Model–View–Controller pattern

10.1 The JSP Framework

The servlet technology makes heavy use of the Java language and requires a certain sophistication of its programmers. Other Web application frameworks, such as ASP and PHP, are based on scripting languages and view Web applications as conglomerates of *active* pages, that is, HTML documents with embedded fragments of script code that are executed on the server. For many simple applications, this framework is more accessible. For larger and more complex applications, however, the weaknesses of scripting languages (in particular, the lack of static type checking) become apparent.

JavaServer Pages (JSP) is an extra layer of syntax that is built on top of the servlet technology to make it appear more like ASP and PHP. However, JSP pages are systematically translated into servlets that are then compiled using a standard Java compiler. Thus, the full power of the Java libraries and the security of static type checking are maintained.

As a simple example, we consider the following JSP page that maintains a hit counter and prints the current server time:

> JSP views a Web service as a collection of **active pages**.

```
<% response.addDateHeader("Expires", 0); %>
<html>
  <head><title>JSP</title></head>
  <body>
    <h1>Hello World!</h1>
```

```
<%! int hits = 0; %>
You are visitor number
<% synchronized(this) { out.println(++hits); } %>
since the last time the service was restarted.
<p>
This page was last updated:
<%= new java.util.Date().toLocaleString() %>
  </body>
</html>
```

The output from this page looks as follows:

> # Hello World!
>
> You are visitor number 43 since the last time the service was restarted.
>
> This page was last updated: 28-02-2005 13:56:49

The JSP page is clearly an HTML document with embedded Java code, in which the variable out implicitly is declared to hold the current output stream. This section will in detail explain the syntax of JSP pages and how they are translated into ordinary servlets.

Ideally, JSP authoring should be as simple as HTML authoring, but the use of the synchronized construction and the reference to java.util.Date actually indicates that a full understanding of Java is required. In Section 10.2, we study the notion of *tag libraries* that are used to capture common application paradigms and make them accessible to more casual script authors.

The JSP framework is not inherently bound to the HTML language. In fact, a JSP page may just as well generate arbitrary XML output.

As explained in Section 9.3.1, JSP pages are deployed simply by placing their files below the application directory. Compilation and further deployment of the generated class files is performed automatically by the server implementation.

10.1.1 Templates

A JSP page is written as a *template*, which is a text file containing snippets of Java code and JSP specific *directives*. The Java code may appear as either *expressions*, *statements*, or *declarations*.

Several variables are implicitly declared to be available inside the Java code. Some of these are familiar from the servlet world, reflecting the fact that a JSP page is eventually translated into a servlet:

```
HttpServletRequest request;
HttpServletResponse response;
HttpSession session;
ServletContext application;
ServletConfig config;
```

Others are specific to the particular implementation of JSP pages. The output stream is declared as follows:

```
JspWriter out;
```

The `JspWriter` class differs from the `PrintWriter` class used by servlets only in its use of exceptions and its support of buffering (we also encountered these issues with `PrintWriter` in Section 8.4.1). A `PrintWriter` does nothing if a `print` method fails, whereas a `JspWriter` throws a `java.io.IOException`. Also, a `PrintWriter` outputs its characters immediately, while a `JspWriter` may buffer them first. As explained in Section 10.1.6, the constant parts of a JSP page are also output to the `JspWriter` stream. The variable

```
PageContext pageContext;
```

is used to supply extra functionality on top of that available in the servlet implementation. For example, it adds an extra layer of `setAttribute` and `getAttribute` methods that works similarly to those of the `ServletRequest`, `HttpSession`, and `ServletContext` classes. In fact, we now have a hierarchy containing four layers of scopes for storing and retrieving attributes, which are called, respectively,

- the *page* scope;
- the *request* scope;
- the *session* scope; and
- the *application* scope.

Variables in the page scope correspond to local variables in the servlet thread, but they may now be accessed in a manner similar to the other three scopes. The `PageContext` class contains a method `findAttribute`, which searches for a named attribute through all four scopes, considering first *page*, then *request*, then *session*, and finally *application*. `PageContext` is a subclass of the more general `JspContext` class which is used in both JSP pages and JSP tag files (see Section 10.2).

10.1.2 Expressions

Java expressions are embedded in JSP pages using the special syntax

```
<%= expression %>
```

As a simple example, the following JSP page adds two numbers that are provided as parameters (which typically result from form fields; see Section 9.2.2):

```
<html>
  <head><title>Addition</title></head>
  <body>
    The sum of <%= request.getParameter("x") %>
    and <%= request.getParameter("y") %> is
```

```
<%= Integer.parseInt(request.getParameter("x")) +
    Integer.parseInt(request.getParameter("y")) %>
  </body>
</html>
```

If one of the parameters is missing or is not a number, then the evaluation of the expression will, of course, throw an exception (see Section 10.1.5).

10.1.3   Statements

Java statements are embedded in JSP pages using the special syntax

```
<% statement %>
```

The execution of a statement must have side-effects to be noticeable, for example, by changing the state of some variables or by printing to the output stream. As a simple example, the following JSP page prints the numbers from zero to a given parameter:

```
<html>
  <head><title>Numbers</title></head>
  <body>
    <ul>
      <% int n = Integer.parseInt(request.getParameter("n"));
         for (int i=0; i<n; i++)
           out.println("<li>"+i+"</li>"); %>
    </ul>
  </body>
</html>
```

10.1.4   Declarations

Java declarations are embedded in JSP pages using the special syntax

```
<%! declaration %>
```

Java statements may, of course, also contain variable declarations, as in the example above, where both the variables n and i are declared. Proper declarations, however, appear in the generated servlet class and may thus contain both class fields and methods. Thus, the addition example could be written instead as follows:

```
<%! int add(String x, String y) {
      return Integer.parseInt(x)+Integer.parseInt(y);
    } %>
<html>
  <head><title>Addition</title></head>
```

```
<body>
   The sum of <%= request.getParameter("x") %>
   and <%= request.getParameter("y") %> is
   <%= add(request.getParameter("x"),request.getParameter("y")) %>
 </body>
</html>
```

There is a significant difference between placing variable declarations in statement fragments or declaration fragments. Consider again this example:

```
<% response.addDateHeader("Expires", 0); %>
<html>
  <head><title>JSP</title></head>
  <body>
    <h1>Hello World!</h1>
    <%! int hits = 0; %>
    You are visitor number
    <% synchronized(this) { out.println(++hits); } %>
    since the last time the service was restarted.
    <p>
    This page was last updated:
    <%= new java.util.Date().toLocaleString() %>
  </body>
</html>
```

In its present form, `hits` is declared as a field of the servlet class, and the initialization is thus performed only once when the corresponding object is created. If we omitted the ! character and instead wrote

```
<% int hits = 0; %>
```

then `hits` would become a local variable that is initialized for every interaction, which means that every visitor will always be assigned number 1.

10.1.5 Directives

JSP directives appear in the special syntax

```
<%@ directive %>
```

and are used to supply parameters to the JSP processor.

The `include` directive allows raw file inclusion during processing. Thus, if the file `header.jsp` contains

```
<html>
  <head><title><%= title %></title></head>
  <body>
```

---

and the file `footer.jsp` contains

```
  </body>
</html>
```

then the addition example may also be written as follows:

```
<%! String title = "Addition"; %>
<%@ include file="header.jsp" %>
  The sum of <%= request.getParameter("x") %>
  and <%= request.getParameter("y") %> is
  <%= Integer.parseInt(request.getParameter("x")) +
      Integer.parseInt(request.getParameter("y")) %>
<%@ include file="footer.jsp" %>
```

Note how the variable `title` is used to pass a parameter into the included file.

The `taglib` directive is used in connection with tag libraries, as discussed in Section 10.2. Finally, the `page` directive includes a whole family of different settings defined by additional attributes including the following:

`buffer="size"`: Sets the size of the buffer for the output stream.

`autoFlush="boolean"`: Decides if the buffer should be automatically flushed (the default is true).

`contentType="type"`: Sets the media type (see Section 8.1.1) for the generated output (the default is `text/html`).

`pageEncoding="encoding"`: Sets the character encoding for the generated output (the default is `ISO-8859-1`).

`info="string"`: An arbitrary string that identifies the page and which may later be recovered using the method `getServletInfo()` of the servlet object.

`errorPage="path"`: Indicates another JSP page that should be invoked in case an uncaught exception is thrown.

`isErrorPage="boolean"`: Decides if the current page is an error page. In practical terms, this just means that a variable `exception` is available and contains the thrown exception.

`import="package"`: Specifies an additional Java package that is imported in the generated class.

The interplay between a page and its error page is shown in the following example. Consider first the following JSP page:

```
<%@ page errorPage="error.jsp" %>
<html>
  <head><title>Division</title></head>
```

```
  <body>
    <% int n = Integer.parseInt(request.getParameter("n")); %>
    <% int m = Integer.parseInt(request.getParameter("m")); %>
    <%= n %>/<%= m %> equals <%= n/m %>
  </body>
</html>
```

The page `error.jsp` is then appropriately defined as follows:

```
<%@ page isErrorPage="true" %>
<html>
  <head><title>Error</title></head>
  <body>
    Something bad happened:
    <%= exception.getMessage() %>
  </body>
</html>
```

If the first page is processed for example with the parameter m having value zero, then an exception will be thrown and control is passed to the error page.

10.1.6   Translation into Servlets

JSP pages are just syntactic sugar, since they are translated by the JSP processor into ordinary servlet code. As an example, consider again the following simple JSP page:

```
<% response.addDateHeader("Expires", 0); %>
<html>
  <head><title>JSP</title></head>
  <body>
    <h1>Hello World!</h1>
    <%! int hits = 0; %>
    You are visitor number
    <% synchronized(this) { out.println(++hits); } %>
    since the last time the service was restarted.
    <p>
    This page was last updated:
    <%= new java.util.Date().toLocaleString() %>
  </body>
</html>
```

It is (using Tomcat in this case) translated into the following, where the parts we have contributed are highlighted:

```
package org.apache.jsp;

import javax.servlet.*;
import javax.servlet.http.*;
import javax.servlet.jsp.*;
```

```
public final class hello_jsp
  extends org.apache.jasper.runtime.HttpJspBase
  implements org.apache.jasper.runtime.JspSourceDependent {

  int hits = 0;
  private static java.util.Vector _jspx_dependants;

  public java.util.List getDependants() {
    return _jspx_dependants;
  }

  public void _jspService(HttpServletRequest request,
                          HttpServletResponse response)
    throws java.io.IOException, ServletException {

    JspFactory _jspxFactory = null;
    PageContext pageContext = null;
    HttpSession session = null;
    ServletContext application = null;
    ServletConfig config = null;
    JspWriter out = null;
    Object page = this;
    JspWriter _jspx_out = null;
    PageContext _jspx_page_context = null;

    try {
      _jspxFactory = JspFactory.getDefaultFactory();
      response.setContentType("text/html");
      pageContext = _jspxFactory.getPageContext(
                      this, request, response,
                      null, true, 8192, true);
      _jspx_page_context = pageContext;
      application = pageContext.getServletContext();
      config = pageContext.getServletConfig();
      session = pageContext.getSession();
      out = pageContext.getOut();
      _jspx_out = out;
      response.addDateHeader("Expires", 0);
      out.write("\n");
      out.write("<html><head><title>JSP</title></head>\n");
      out.write("<body><h1>Hello World!</h1>\n");
      out.write("\n");
      out.write("You are visitor number ");
      synchronized(this) { out.println(++hits); }
      out.write("\n");
      out.write("since the last time the service was restarted.\n");
      out.write("<p>\n");
      out.write("This page was last updated: ");
      out.print(new java.util.Date().toLocaleString());
```

```
      out.write("\n");
      out.write("</body></html>\n");
    } catch (Throwable t) {
      if (!(t instanceof SkipPageException)) {
        out = _jspx_out;
        if (out != null && out.getBufferSize() != 0)
          out.clearBuffer();
        if (_jspx_page_context != null)
          _jspx_page_context.handlePageException(t);
      }
    } finally {
      if (_jspxFactory != null)
        _jspxFactory.releasePageContext(_jspx_page_context);
    }
  }
}
```

The translation contains a large amount of boilerplate code, but the overall structure is clear: the `HttpJspBase` class is a subclass of the `Servlet` class that adds the special JSP functionality. Statements are merely inserted into the generated Java code, expressions are wrapped in a call to `out.print(...)`, and HTML markup is wrapped in calls to `out.write(...)`. Note that the declaration of `hits` is placed as a field in the class.

The translation takes place at the lexical level, as neither the HTML markup nor the Java code is parsed. Thus, the following is a perfectly legal JSP page:

```
<% if (Math.random()<0.5) { %>
  Have a <b>nice day!
<% } else { %>
  Have a <b>lousy day!
<% } %>
</b>
```

Here, none of the statement fragments contain syntactically correct Java code, but the complete translation becomes legal:

```
if (Math.random()<0.5) {
    out.write("\n");
    out.write("  Have a <b>nice day!\n");
} else {
    out.write("\n");
    out.write("  Have a <b>lousy day!\n");
}
out.write("</b>\n");
```

Consequently, syntax errors in JSP pages are caught rather late. If the generated Java code contains errors, then these are only detected when the page is processed and compiled, and the error messages are often reported in terms of the generated servlet code, not the JSP source code.

If the special JSP syntax should appear as part of the template text, then it may be escaped by writing <\% in place of <%. Comments may be inserted using the syntax

```
<%-- this is a comment --%>
```

An unfortunate side-effect of the translation is that whitespace between JSP instructions is generated as part of the output. This effect means that the JSP page

```
<%@ page contentType="text/plain" %>
<%@ page info="A Tiny Test" %>
This is a tiny test
```

generates the output

```
This is a tiny test
```

which includes two blank lines at the top. To avoid such output, it is customary to make use of strange rewritings, such as

```
<%@ page contentType="text/plain"
%><%@ page info="A Tiny Test"
%>This is a tiny test
```

or

```
<%@ page contentType="text/plain" %><%--
--%><%@ page info="A Tiny Test" %><%--
--%>This is a tiny test
```

In both these variations, no blank lines will appear in the output.

10.1.7 XML Version of JSP

As we have seen, the JSP processor performs a lexical translation of JSP pages. Thus, no real syntactic requirements are enforced. As an alternative, JSP pages may be written in XML syntax, in which case they are called JSP *documents*. Adhering to the XML framework enables validation and also makes JSP documents amenable to manipulation by XML tools.

This feature will simply be illustrated by an example. Consider the following ordinary JSP page:

```
<% response.addDateHeader("Expires", 0); %>
<html>
```

```
<head><title>JSP Color</title></head>
<body bgcolor=<%= request.getParameter("color") %>>
  <h1>Hello World!</h1>
  <%! int hits = 0; %>
  You are visitor number
  <% synchronized(this) { out.println(++hits); } %>
  since the last time the service was restarted.
  <p>
  This page was last updated:
  <%= new java.util.Date().toLocaleString() %>
</body>
</html>
```

This page is clearly not an XML document, for two reasons:

- it uses HTML syntax, not XHTML syntax; and

- the occurrences of `<%...%>` break well-formedness.

The equivalent JSP document looks as follows:

```
<jsp:root xmlns:jsp="http://java.sun.com/JSP/Page" version="2.0"
        xmlns="http://http://www.w3.org/1999/xhtml">
  <jsp:directive.page contentType="text/html"/>
  <jsp:scriptlet>
    response.addDateHeader("Expires", 0);
  </jsp:scriptlet>
  <html>
    <head><title>JSP</title></head>
    <jsp:element name="body">
      <jsp:attribute name="bgcolor">
        <jsp:expression>
          request.getParameter("color")
        </jsp:expression>
      </jsp:attribute>
      <h1>Hello World!</h1>
      <jsp:declaration>
        int hits = 0;
      </jsp:declaration>
      You are visitor number
      <jsp:scriptlet>
        synchronized(this) { out.println(++hits); }
      </jsp:scriptlet>
      since the last time the service was restarted.
      <p/>
      This page was last updated:
      <jsp:expression>
        new java.util.Date().toLocaleString()
```

```
    </jsp:expression>
  </jsp:element>
 </html>
</jsp:root>
```

A schema for the XML version of JSP currently seems unavailable. Note, however, that validation of a JSP document is still only a weak guarantee against syntax errors. A schema would clearly not capture the syntactic restrictions on the embedded Java fragments, and it would not help in statically validating the generated output.

10.1.8 The Expression Language

In addition to fragments of code, JSP supports its own *expression language* which will allow more applications to be written without knowledge of Java syntax. Anywhere inside template text or attribute values of markup, the JSP processor will recognize the special syntax

```
${ expression }
```

which is then replaced with the string obtained by evaluating this expression.

The expression language is a typical scripting language, vaguely like JavaScript. It supports strings, booleans, and a range of numerical types, along with the usual arithmetic, logical, and comparison operators (see the JSP specification for these details). References to named variables are resolved using the findAttribute method described in Section 10.1.1.

Certain operations on objects are also supported. For example, the expression

```
${gadget.weight}
```

is translated into the Java expression

```
pageContext.findAttribute("gadget").getWeight()
```

A number of *implicit objects* are defined, which provides access to parts of the state of the page. These include param which is a map of the request parameters, pageContext that references the corresponding object, and cookie which is a map corresponding to the getCookies method discussed in Section 9.2.5.

Using the expression language, the earlier addition example may alternatively be written as follows, where we also allow the background color of the response to be determined by a request parameter:

```
<html>
  <head><title>Addition</title></head>
  <body bgcolor="${param.color}">
    The sum of ${param.x} and ${param.y} is ${param.x+param.y}
  </body>
</html>
```

The expression language is more succinct than the corresponding Java code and does not require knowledge of the Java language. On the other hand, we now have two different manners of expressing the same computations.

10.1.9   A JSP Shopping Cart

Consider again the shopping cart example from Section 9.2.5, which is written as a single servlet. We may as well write it as a JSP page, which corresponds to 'turning it inside out' with respect to HTML fragments and Java code. The result looks as follows:

```
<%@ page import="java.util.*" %>
<html>
  <head>
    <title>Widget Inc.</title>
  </head>
  <body>
    <h1>Widget Inc. Online Shopping</h1>
    <% Map cart;
       if (session.isNew()) {
         cart = new TreeMap();
         session.setAttribute("cart", cart);
       } else
         cart = (Map)session.getAttribute("cart");
       if (request.getMethod().equals("POST")) {
         String item = request.getParameter("item");
         String amount = request.getParameter("amount");
         if (item!=null)
         try {
           addToCart(cart, item, Integer.parseInt(amount));
         } catch (Exception e) {
           response.sendError(response.SC_BAD_REQUEST,
                              "malformed request");
         }
       }
       String url = request.getRequestURI();
    %>
    <form method=post action="<%= response.encodeURL(url) %>">
      Item: <input type=text name=item size=20>
      Amount: <input type=text name=amount size=5>
      <input type=submit name=submit value="Add to shopping cart">
    </form>
    <p>
    <% if (cart.isEmpty()) { %>
      Your shopping cart is empty.
    <% } else { %>
      Your shopping cart now contains:<p>
      <table border=1><tr><th>Item<th>Amount
```

```
      <% Iterator i = cart.entrySet().iterator();
          while (i.hasNext()) {
            Map.Entry me = (Map.Entry)i.next();
      %>
            <tr><td><%= me.getKey() %>
            <td align=right><%= me.getValue() %>
      <% }%>
      </table><p>
      <form method=post
            action="<%= response.encodeURL("buy") %>">
        <input type=submit name=submit
              value="Proceed to cashier">
      </form>
    <% }%>
  </body>
</html>

<%! void addToCart(Map cart, String item, int amount) {
      if (amount<0)
        return;
      Integer a = (Integer)cart.get(item);
      if (a==null)
        a = new Integer(0);
      cart.put(item, new Integer(a.intValue()+amount));
    }
%>
```

The structure of the generated HTML page is now more clearly presented (and highlighted above). Conversely, the Java code now appears more fragmented.

10.2   Tags

JSP has been introduced to make Web application development available to people who are not expert Java programmers. However, the above examples show that Java features may creep into JSP pages anyway, and the end result thus becomes an unsatisfactory mixture of code and markup. An approach to avoiding this trap is to extend the JSP notation with *tags*, which capture common programming patterns in an accessible syntax.

10.2.1   Tag Files

A *tag file* is a variation of a JSP page that defines an abstraction as a new tag. This mechanism was introduced in JSP 2.0. Compared to JSP pages, tag files allow several new features described below. Another difference is that tag files use the more restricted implicit object

```
JspContext jspContext;
```

in place of the pageContext object (the PageContext class is a subclass of JspContext and they share most of their functionality).

As a simple example, consider the HTML wrappers that we have used in most of our examples, and that we in Section 10.1.5 tried to make parameterized as follows:

```
<%! String title = "Addition"; %>
<%@ include file="header.jsp" %>
  The sum of <%= request.getParameter("x") %>
  and <%= request.getParameter("y") %> is
  <%= Integer.parseInt(request.getParameter("x")) +
      Integer.parseInt(request.getParameter("y")) %>
<%@ include file="footer.jsp" %>
```

This approach is clearly insufficient and inelegant, as the solution is pieced together from several unrelated parts. Instead, we may define the entire wrapper in the following tag file (called wrap.tag, notice that these files are recognized by the extension .tag):

```
<%@ tag %>
<%@ attribute name="title" required="true" %>
<html>
  <head><title>${title}</title></head>
  <body>
    <jsp:doBody/>
  </body>
</html>
```

The first line identifies the file as being a JSP tag definition rather than an ordinary JSP template. The title parameter is now declared to be a required attribute of this tag (the default is for attributes to be optional), and the jsp:doBody instruction indicates where the contents of the tag should be inserted.

The new tag is used as follows:

```
<%@ taglib prefix="foo" tagdir="/WEB-INF/tags" %>
<foo:wrap title="Addition">
  The sum of ${param.x} and ${param.y} is ${param.x+param.y}
</foo:wrap>
```

The file wrap.tag is here assumed to reside in the directory /WEB-INF/tags that is associated with the foo prefix (heavily inspired by XML namespaces).

Clearly, this approach provides a better structure and a more pleasant syntax than the approach using include.

There are many other features available for defining tags. The jsp:doBody instruction without attributes will copy the body to the output stream, but the variation

```
<jsp:doBody var="name"/>
```

copies the value of the body to the given variable for later use. An example is the following tag file `image.tag` that provides an alternative syntax for images:

```
<%@ tag %>
<jsp:doBody var="src"/>
<img src="http://www.brics.dk/ixwt/images/${src}"/>
```

This tag may now be invoked as follows:

```
<%@ taglib prefix="foo" tagdir="/WEB-INF/tags" %>
<foo:image>widget.jpg</foo:image>
```

It is also possible for the caller to read variables defined by the callee. This is a useful feature, as illustrated by the following tag file named `date.tag`:

```
<%@ tag import="java.util.*" %>
<%@ variable name-given="date" %>
<%@ variable name-given="month" %>
<%@ variable name-given="year" %>
<% Calendar cal = new GregorianCalendar();
   int date = cal.get(Calendar.DATE);
   int month = cal.get(Calendar.MONTH)+1;
   int year = cal.get(Calendar.YEAR);
   jspContext.setAttribute("date", String.valueOf(date));
   jspContext.setAttribute("month", String.valueOf(month));
   jspContext.setAttribute("year", String.valueOf(year));
%>
<jsp:doBody/>
```

Inside the `date` tag, the variables `date`, `month`, and `year` are now available:

```
<%@ taglib prefix="foo" tagdir="/WEB-INF/tags" %>
<foo:date>
  In the US today is
  ${month}/${date}/${year},
  but in Europe it is
  ${date}/${month}/${year}.
</foo:date>
```

10.2.2 Tags for Quick Polls

JSP tags may be used to encode domain-specific languages on top of Java. Consider as an example the polling service from Section 9.2.4. The code is clearly a mixture of HTML design and Java programming, but it would be better to separate these two roles. The programmer should be able to develop the business logic without assumptions about the layout, and the designer should be able to develop the layout with only the minimally required assumptions about the programming.

The following code is written to support such a clean separation. The layout of a polling service is written as follows (with copious use of tags):

```
<%@ taglib prefix="poll" tagdir="/WEB-INF/tags/poll" %>
<poll:quickpoll title="Quickies" duration="3600">
  <poll:setup>
    The question has been set to "${question}".
  </poll:setup>
  <poll:ask>
    ${question}?
    <select name="vote">
      <option value="yes">yes
      <option value="no">no
    </select>
    <input type="submit" value="vote">
  </poll:ask>
  <poll:vote>
    You have voted ${vote}.
  </poll:vote>
  <poll:results>
    In favor: ${yes}<br>
    Against: ${no}<br>
    Total: ${total}
  </poll:results>
  <poll:timeout>
    Sorry, the polls have closed.
  </poll:timeout>
</poll:quickpoll>
```

The `quickpoll` tag surrounds the entire definition and accepts the attribute `title` (which supplies the titles for the generated HTML pages) and the novel attribute `duration` (which specifies in seconds how long the polls will be open). An optional `sheet` attribute (not used in this example) specifies a CSS stylesheet to be applied. If the service is installed at

```
http://www.quickpolls.foo/poll
```

then its sessions are invoked as follows:

```
http://www.quickpolls.foo/poll?question=...
http://www.quickpolls.foo/poll?ask
http://www.quickpolls.foo/poll?results
```

The `setup` tag provides the reply page when a new question has been set and the polls open, and the variable `question` may be used to refer to the text of the given question. The `ask` tag provides the page that collects the vote and must supply an input field named `vote` with value yes or no. The vote tag provides the reply page when a vote has been given, and it may use the vote variable. The results tag defines the page giving the (preliminary) results of the vote using the variables yes, no, and total. Finally, the timeout tag gives the page to be shown when the polls have closed.

The code for the above tags is fairly simple. The whole service is encoded (through JSP) as a single servlet that unravels the control flow of the business logic. The quickpoll.tag file looks as follows (with literal HTML fragments emphasized):

```
<%@ attribute name="title" required="true" %>
<%@ attribute name="duration" required="true" %>
<%@ attribute name="sheet" %>
<% response.addDateHeader("Expires", 0);
   application.setAttribute("duration",
                            jspContext.findAttribute("duration"));
%>
<html>
  <head>
    <title>${title}</title>
<%  if (jspContext.findAttribute("sheet")!=null) { %>
    <link rel="stylesheet" href="${sheet}" type="text/css">
<%  } %>
  </head>
  <body>
    <jsp:doBody/>
  </body>
</html>
```

Note that the duration attribute must be copied into the ServletContext object to be available for the other tag files. The setup.tag file is programmed as follows:

```
<%@ tag import="java.util.Date" %>
<%@ variable name-given="question" %>
<% String question = request.getParameter("question");
   if (question!=null) {
     jspContext.setAttribute("question", question);
     application.setAttribute("question", question);
     application.setAttribute("yes", new Integer(0));
     application.setAttribute("no", new Integer(0));
     int duration =
       Integer.parseInt
         ((String)application.getAttribute("duration"));
     long stop = new Date().getTime()+(1000*duration);
     application.setAttribute("stop", String.valueOf(stop));
     application.removeAttribute("timeout");
%>
     <jsp:doBody/>
<% } %>
```

The `stop` variable contains the future time when the polls must close (after which, only the contents of the `timeout` tag is shown). The `ask.tag` file has the following contents:

```
<%@ tag import="java.util.Date" %>
<%@ variable name-given="question" %>
<% if (request.getParameter("ask")!=null) {
      long stop =
        Long.parseLong((String)application.getAttribute("stop"));
      if (new Date().getTime()>stop)
        application.setAttribute("timeout", "");
      else {
        jspContext.setAttribute("question",
                                 application.getAttribute("question"));
%>
      <form
        method="post"
        action="<%= response.encodeURL(request.getRequestURI()) %>">
      <jsp:doBody/>
      </form>
<%   }
    } %>
```

Note how the `action` attribute of the HTML form is computed to invoke the URL of the main generated servlet. The `vote.tag` file looks as follows:

```
<%@ variable name-given="vote" %>
<% String vote = request.getParameter("vote");
    if (vote!=null) {
      jspContext.setAttribute("vote", vote);
      if (vote.equals("yes")) {
        int yes = ((Integer)application.getAttribute("yes")).intValue();
        application.setAttribute("yes", new Integer(yes+1));
      } else {
        int no = ((Integer)application.getAttribute("no")).intValue();
        application.setAttribute("no", new Integer(no+1));
      }
%>
      <jsp:doBody/>
<% } %>
```

The `results.tag` file has the following contents:

```
<%@ variable name-given="yes" %>
<%@ variable name-given="no" %>
<%@ variable name-given="total" %>
<% if (request.getParameter("results")!=null) {
```

```
      int yes = ((Integer)application.getAttribute("yes"))
               .intValue();
      int no = ((Integer)application.getAttribute("no"))
               .intValue();
      jspContext.setAttribute("yes", String.valueOf(yes));
      jspContext.setAttribute("no", String.valueOf(no));
      jspContext.setAttribute("total", String.valueOf(yes+no));
%>
      <jsp:doBody/>
<% } %>
```

Finally, the `timeout.tag` file is programmed as follows:

```
<% if (request.getParameter("ask")!=null &&
       application.getAttribute("timeout")!=null) {
%>
      <jsp:doBody/>
<% } %>
```

Given this framework, the designer may produce a more appealing layout – without involving the programmer. This new version of the polling service may look as follows:

```
<%@ taglib prefix="poll" tagdir="/WEB-INF/tags/poll" %>
<poll:quickpoll title="Quick Poll"
                duration="3600"
                sheet="http://www.quickpolls.foo/fancy.css">
  <poll:setup>
    The question has been set to "${question}".
  </poll:setup>
  <poll:ask>
      <center>
        ${question}?
      </center>
      <button type="submit" name="vote" value="yes">
        <img src="http://www.quickpolls.foo/yes.gif">
      </button>
      <button type="submit" name="vote" value="no">
        <img src="http://www.quickpolls.foo/no.gif">
      </button>
  </poll:ask>
  <poll:vote>
    You have voted ${vote}.
  </poll:vote>
  <poll:results>
      <table border="0">
        <tr>
          <td>Yes:</td>
          <td>
```

```
          <table>
            <tr>
              <td bgcolor=black height=20
                  width="${(300*yes)/total}">
            </tr>
          </table>
        </td>
        <td>${yes}</td>
      </tr>
      <tr>
        <td>No:</td>
          <table>
            <tr>
              <td bgcolor=black height=20
                  width="${(300*no)/total}">
            </tr>
          </table>
        <td>${no}</td>
      </tr>
    </table>
  </poll:results>
  <poll:timeout>
      Sorry, the polls have closed.
  </poll:timeout>
</poll:quickpoll>
```

If the old version of the polling service worked, then so will this new one that simply uses more fancy graphics. There is, of course, an *implicit contract* between the designer and the programmer:

- the specification must have an outermost quickpoll tag whose contents are in sequence a question, ask, vote, results, and timeout tag;

- the programmer will provide the variables question, vote, yes, no, and total;

- the designer must send an input field named vote from the ask session.

This contract is not enforced in any way, which is a weakness of this approach.

10.2.3   Tag Libraries and JSTL

Similarly to our collection of polling tags, numerous *tag libraries* are freely available. They cover programming patterns for such diverse application domains as text pagination, dates and times, database queries, regular expressions, HTML scraping, bar charts, cookies, email, WML, JPEG images, and much more. Such libraries serve two purposes. First, they empower Web authors without real programming skills, who may now apply more advanced concepts in their productions. Second, they provide a convenient shorthand and modularization for programmers.

JSTL is a **tag library** that is part of the JSP specification.

A particular set of tags has been collected into the *JSP Standard Tag Library (JSTL)*, which is distributed along with the JSP framework. It covers the following areas:

- assigning to variables;

- writing to the output stream;

- catching exceptions;

- conditionals;

- iterations;

- URL construction;

- string formatting;

- SQL queries; and

- XML manipulation.

In all, JSTL defines a programming language that for many typical applications is presented as a lightweight alternative to Java.

As an example of the use of JSTL, we consider the following two JSP pages. One reads the recipe collection and asks the client through an HTML form to select some recipes, and another returns a collection containing that subset of recipes. The first JSP page resides in a file called select.jsp and looks as follows:

```
<%@ taglib uri="http://java.sun.com/jsp/jstl/core" prefix="c"%>
<%@ taglib uri="http://java.sun.com/jsp/jstl/xml" prefix="x"%>
<c:import url="http://www.brics.dk/ixwt/examples/recipes.xml"
          var="xml"/>
<x:parse xml="${xml}" var="recipes" scope="session"/>
<html>
  <head><title>Select Some Recipes</title></head>
  <body>
    <form method="post" action="show.jsp">
      <x:forEach select="$recipes//*[local-name()='recipe']">
        <c:set var="id">
          <x:out select="@id"/>
        </c:set>
        <input type="checkbox" name="selected" value="${id}"/>
        <x:out select="*[local-name()='title']/text()"/>
        <br/>
      </x:forEach>
      <input type="submit" value="Select"/>
    </form>
  </body>
</html>
```

Note that the `recipes` variable containing the parsed recipe collection is given scope `session`, which ensures that it is also available in the JSP page handling the next part of the interaction. The second JSP page resides in a file called `show.jsp` and looks as follows:

```
<%@ taglib uri="http://java.sun.com/jsp/jstl/core" prefix="c"%>
<%@ taglib uri="http://java.sun.com/jsp/jstl/xml" prefix="x"%>
<html>
 <head><title>Nutrition Overview</title></head>
 <body>
  <table border="1">
   <tr>
    <td>Title</td>
    <td>Calories</td>
    <td>Fat</td>
    <td>Carbohydrates</td>
    <td>Protein</td>
    <td>Alcohol</td>
   </tr>
   <x:forEach select="$recipes//*[local-name()='recipe']">
   <c:forEach var="id" items="${paramValues.selected}">
    <x:if select="self::node()[@id=$id]">
     <tr>
      <td>
       <x:out select=".//*[local-name()='title']"/>
      </td>
      <td align="right">
       <x:out select=".//*[local-name()='nutrition']/@calories"/>
      </td>
      <td align="right">
       <x:out select=".//*[local-name()='nutrition']/@fat"/>
      </td>
      <td align="right">
       <x:out select=".//*[local-name()='nutrition']/@carbohydrates"/>
      </td>
      <td align="right">
       <x:out select=".//*[local-name()='nutrition']/@protein"/>
      </td>
      <td align="right">
       <x:out select=".//*[local-name()='nutrition']/@alcohol"/>
       <x:if select="not(.//*[local-name()='nutrition']/@alcohol)">
        0%
       </x:if>
      </td>
     </tr>
    </x:if>
   </c:forEach>
```

```
        </x:forEach>
      </table>
    </body>
  </html>
```

The above JSP code looks nothing like Java but more like a new dialect of XSLT. Notice, however, that we could not write a corresponding application in pure XSLT, since the interaction with the client across the Web is not within its application domain.

Note that the XPath expressions applied look somewhat odd. This is because the JSTL library in version 1.1 does not support XML namespaces correctly, so we must resort to testing only the local names of elements.

Using this service, the client is first confronted with a Web form that looks as follows:

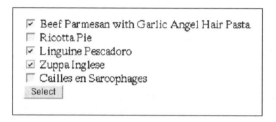

When this form is submitted, the service responds with the following information:

Title	Calories	Fat	Carbohydrates	Protein	Alcohol
Beef Parmesan with Garlic Angel Hair Pasta	1167	23%	45%	32%	0%
Linguine Pescadoro	532	12%	59%	29%	0%
Zuppa Inglese	612	49%	45%	4%	2%

It should now also be clear how the shopping cart example from Section 10.1.9 can be written in a more elegant manner. With an appropriate tag library for the application domain of shopping carts, it could simply look as follows:

```
<%@ taglib prefix="s" tagdir="/WEB-INF/tags/shopping" %>
<%@ taglib prefix="u" tagdir="/WEB-INF/tags/urls" %>
<html>
  <head>
    <title>Widget Inc.</title>
  </head>
  <body>
    <h1>Widget Inc. Online Shopping</h1>
    <s:cart>
      <s:add item="${param.item}" amount="${param.amount}"/>
      <u:url target="##self">
        <form method=post action="${url}">
          Item: <input type=text name=item size=20>
          Amount: <input type=text name=amount size=5>
```

```
          <input type=submit name=submit value="Add to shopping cart">
        </form>
    </u:url>
    <p>
    <s:process>
      <s:empty>Your shopping cart is empty.</s:empty>
      <s:nonempty>
        Your shopping cart now contains:<p>
        <table border=1><tr><th>Item<th>Amount
        <s:loop>
          <tr><td>${item}<td>${amount}
        </s:loop>
        </table><p>
        <u:url target="buy">
          <form method=post action="${url}">
            <input type=submit name=submit
                   value="Proceed to cashier">
          </form>
        </u:url>
      </s:nonempty>
    </s:process>
  </s:cart>
  </body>
</html>
```

We leave the implementation of this tag library as an exercise to the reader.

10.2.4 Limitations of Tags

Tag files and libraries play an important role in the architecture of applications building on the servlet and JSP framework. They allow for the design and implementation of a multitude of tiny domain-specific languages for many different application domains. To some extent, this high-level syntax also makes Web service programming accessible to a wider range of developers.

A potential drawback of this approach is that the plentitude of tag libraries will create a Babylonian confusion, where JSP pages look nothing like each other and certainly nothing like the Java code that forms their common base.

The actual implementation of tags also seem rather brittle (which is often the cases for such macro systems). Consider, for example, the following simple tag definition (that resides in a file called square.tag) for computing the square of a given number:

```
<%@ taglib uri="http://java.sun.com/jsp/jstl/core" prefix="c"%>
<%@ variable name-given="n2" %>
<%@ attribute name="n" required="true" %>
<c:set var="n2" value="${n*n}"/>
<jsp:doBody/>
```

The following JSP page (called `test.jsp`) then applies the tag:

```
<%@ taglib prefix="foo" tagdir="/WEB-INF/tags" %>
<foo:square n="87">
  The result is ${n2}.
</foo:square>
```

We now introduce various errors in these programs and observe how they are reported to the programmer. In each case, the error message is read from the stack trace of a runtime exception.

- If we misspell the URI for the JSTL library, we get a sensible error message:

  ```
  The absolute uri: http://java.sn.com/jsp/jstl/core cannot
  be resolved in either web.xml or the jar files deployed with
  this application
  ```

- If we misspell the path (`/WEB-INF/tags`) to the `square` tag, the application runs without error messages, but fails to output a number.

- If we fail to declare the attribute n, we get a somewhat sensible error message:

  ```
  Attribute n invalid for tag square according to TLD
  ```

- If we fail to declare the variable n2 or misspell its name, the application runs without error messages, but fails to output a number.

- If we mistakenly supply the string `forty-two` as the attribute n to the `square` tag, then we get the following error message and stack trace (slightly abbreviated):

  ```
  JspException: An exception occurred
    trying to convert String "forty-two" to type "java.lang.Long"
  PageContextImpl.doHandlePageException(PageContextImpl.java:842)
  PageContextImpl.handlePageException(PageContextImpl.java:779)
  test_jsp._jspService(test_jsp.java:61)
  HttpJspBase.service(HttpJspBase.java:94)
  HttpServlet.service(HttpServlet.java:802)
  JspServletWrapper.service(JspServletWrapper.java:324)
  JspServlet.serviceJspFile(JspServlet.java:292)
  JspServlet.service(JspServlet.java:236)
  HttpServlet.service(HttpServlet.java:802)
  ```

  This output all refers to the translated Java code, which makes it hard to figure out which part of the `test.jsp` file is causing the error.

It is evident that debugging of programs that use tag libraries poses an extra challenge for developers. The JSP specification requires that implementations provide better diagnostic tools, like mapping line numbers in the generated servlet files back into the original line numbers.

10.3   The Model–View–Controller Pattern

So far, we have seen Web applications as collections of JSP pages (or servlets) that the client navigates between. This design is also known as the *Model 1* approach. For larger applications, this architecture is too ad hoc. Instead, it is recommended to use the *Model 2* approach, which is an instance of the *Model–View–Controller* design pattern (MVC) that dates back to graphical user interface applications in the early Smalltalk-80 system.

The MVC pattern distributes an application into three main parts: *model*, *view*, and *controller*. The model encapsulates the data and accompanying operations (the *business logic*), and is typically programmed as general Java classes, perhaps with an underlying database. The view is typically a collection of JSP pages that interact with the model to present various data to the client. The controller is written as a single servlet that handles all interactions with the client, updates the model, and selects appropriate views as responses. This pattern is often illustrated by the following general picture (where arrows indicate method invocations):

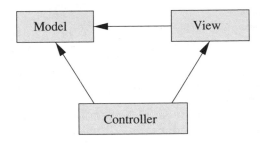

To demonstrate these concepts, we will look at different implementations of a simple business card server: The client may enter a search string, which is matched against a collection of business cards. The hits are displayed to the client, which may then view the details of a selected card. We assume that the current collection of business cards is simply stored in an XML file.

10.3.1   A Model 1 Business Card Server

In this version, we think about the sequence of pages that a client will encounter. First, we construct a (constant) page search_card.jsp that asks the client for a pattern string:

```
<html>
  <head>
    <title>Search For Business Cards</title>
```

```
    </head>
    <body>
      <form method="GET" action="select_card.jsp">
        Enter a search string: <input type="text" name="pattern">
        <p>
        <input type="submit" value="Go">
      </form>
    </body>
  </html>
```

Second, we present using a page select_card.jsp the list of names that match the given
pattern:

```
<%@ taglib uri="http://java.sun.com/jsp/jstl/core" prefix="c"%>
<%@ taglib uri="http://java.sun.com/jsp/jstl/xml" prefix="x"%>
<c:import url="cardlist.xml" var="xml"/>
<x:parse xml="${xml}" var="cardlist" scope="session"/>
<html>
  <head>
    <title>Select A Card</title>
  </head>
  <body>
    <ul>
      <c:set var="pattern" value="${param.pattern}"/>
      <x:forEach varStatus="i"
                 select="$cardlist//*[local-name()='card']">
        <x:if select="*[contains(.,$pattern)]">
          <li>
          <a href="display_card.jsp?i=${i.index}">
            <x:out select="*[local-name()='name']/text()"/>
          </a>
        </x:if>
      </x:forEach>
    </ul>
  </body>
</html>
```

Finally, the selected card is presented by the page display_card.jsp:

```
<%@ taglib uri="http://java.sun.com/jsp/jstl/core" prefix="c"%>
<%@ taglib uri="http://java.sun.com/jsp/jstl/xml" prefix="x"%>
<html>
  <head>
    <title>The Requested Business Card</title>
  </head>
```

```
<body>
  <x:forEach varStatus="i"
             select="$cardlist//*[local-name()='card']">
    <c:if test="${param.i==i.index}">
      <table border="3">
        <tr>
          <td>
            <x:out select="*[local-name()='name']"/><br/>
            <x:out select="*[local-name()='title']"/><br/>
            <tt><x:out select="*[local-name()='email']"/></tt><br/>
            <x:if select="*[local-name()='phone']">
              Phone: <x:out select="*[local-name()='phone']"/><br/>
            </x:if>
          </td>
          <td>
            <x:if select="*[local-name()='logo']">
              <c:set var="uri">
                <x:out select="*[local-name()='logo']/@uri"/>
              </c:set>
              <img src="${uri}"/>
            </x:if>
          </td>
        </tr>
      </table>
    </c:if>
  </x:forEach>
</body>
</html>
```

When searching for the business card of John Doe, the client may encounter these three pages:

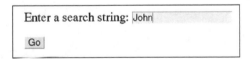

On the surface, this is a reasonable and straightforward implementation. However, if we think in terms of larger and more complex applications, it becomes a liability that the semantics and the presentation are intertwined. Specifically, the following issues work against modularity and flexibility:

- the schema of the XML document must be known by both the `select_card.jsp` and `display_card.jsp` pages;

- the semantics of the search operation is hardwired into the `select_card.jsp` page;

- the designs of the pages cannot be developed in isolation; and

- the representation of the XML data cannot be changed in isolation.

10.3.2   A Model 2 Business Card Server

We now apply the MVC pattern to our architecture. First, we create the *model* encapsulating the data representation and the business logic:

```java
import java.io.*;
import java.util.*;
import org.jdom.*;
import org.jdom.input.*;

public class Model {
  static Document cardlist;
  static Namespace b =
          Namespace.getNamespace("http://businesscard.org");
  String pattern;
  ArrayList cards = new ArrayList();
  int selected;

  static {
    try {
      cardlist = new SAXBuilder().build(new File("cardlist.xml"));
    } catch (Exception e) {
      cardlist = new Document(new Element("cardlist", b));
    }
  }

  public Model() {}

  public void setPattern(String s) {
    pattern = s;
  }

  public List getMatches() {
    Iterator i = cardlist.getRootElement()
                         .getChildren("card", b).iterator();
    ArrayList matches = new ArrayList();
    while (i.hasNext()) {
      Element card = (Element)i.next();
      String name = card.getChildText("name", b);
```

```
      if (name.indexOf(pattern)!=-1) {
        cards.add(card);
        matches.add(name);
      }
    }
    return matches;
  }

  public void setSelected(int i) {
    selected = i;
  }

  String cs(String s) {
    if (s==null)
      return "";
    return s;
  }

  public String getName() {
    return cs(((Element)cards.get(selected))
          .getChildText("name", b));
  }

  public String getTitle() {
    return cs(((Element)cards.get(selected))
          .getChildText("title", b));
  }

  public String getEmail() {
    return cs(((Element)cards.get(selected))
          .getChildText("email", b));
  }

  public String getPhone() {
    return cs(((Element)cards.get(selected))
          .getChildText("phone", b));
  }

  public String getUri() {
    Element logo = ((Element)cards.get(selected))
                .getChild("logo", b);
    if (logo==null)
      return "";
    return logo.getAttributeValue("uri");
  }
}
```

This class encapsulates the entire data representation and the domain-specific operations that we perform:

- setting the search pattern using the `setPattern` method;

- getting the corresponding matches using the `getMatches` method;

- setting the index of the selected match using the `setSelected` method; and

- get the details of the selected match using methods such as `getName` and `getTitle`.

In isolation from the remaining parts of the application, we are now free to

- change the representation of the business card collection from an XML document to a relational database; and

- redefine the semantics of the pattern match operation to consider the title as well as the name.

The `Model` class is an example of a *JavaBean*: a class (with an empty constructor) that encapsulates an application state and provides access to components using methods such as `getMatches` and `setSelected`.

The *views* correspond to the three JSP pages from the Model 1 version, but now they only perform computations and decisions that consider the presentation of data. The `search_card2.jsp` page looks as follows:

```
<html>
  <head>
    <title>Search For Business Cards</title>
  </head>
  <body>
    <form method="GET" action="select.do">
      Enter a search string: <input type="text" name="pattern">
      <p>
      <input type="submit" value="Go">
    </form>
  </body>
</html>
```

Note that control is passed to `select.do` as explained below. The `select_card2.jsp` page looks as follows:

```
<%@ taglib uri="http://java.sun.com/jsp/jstl/core" prefix="c"%>
<html>
  <head>
    <title>Select A Card</title>
  </head>
  <body>
    <ul>
      <c:forEach varStatus="i" items="${model.matches}"
                 var="match">
        <li>
```

```
        <a href="display.do?i=${i.index}">
          ${match}
        </a>
      </c:forEach>
    </ul>
  </body>
</html>
```

Notice how we benefit from the JavaBean conventions, since the expression
`model.matches` is translated into the Java expression

```
pageContext.findAttribute("model").getMatches()
```

Also, since `getMatches` returns an object of a collection class, we may use the `forEach` tag from JSTL.

Finally, the `display_card2.jsp` page looks as follows:

```
<%@ taglib uri="http://java.sun.com/jsp/jstl/core" prefix="c"%>
<html>
  <head>
    <title>The Requested Information</title>
  </head>
  <body>
    <table border="3">
      <tr>
        <td>
          ${model.name}<br/>
          ${model.title}<br/>
          <tt>${model.email}</tt><br/>
          <c:if test='${model.phone != ""}'>
            Phone: ${model.phone}<br/>
          </c:if>
        </td>
        <td>
          <c:if test='${model.uri != ""}'>
            <img src="${model.uri}"/>
          </c:if>
        </td>
      </tr>
    </table>
  </body>
</html>
```

Again, the JavaBean conventions help to make this page more legible.

The three view pages may be developed independently from the rest of the application, based on an implicit *contract* between the programmer and the Web designer. The essence of such a contract is that the programmer must provide certain values, such as `model.matches`, while the designer must provide certain input fields, such as `pattern`.

The interaction with the client is performed by a *controller* servlet. In line with the Model 2 traditions, we use the convention that all requests with extension `.do` are routed to the controller. This routing is obtained by adding the following lines to the `web.xml` deployment descriptor:

```
<servlet>
  <servlet-name>Controller</servlet-name>
  <servlet-class>Controller</servlet-class>
</servlet>
<servlet-mapping>
  <servlet-name>Controller</servlet-name>
  <url-pattern>*.do</url-pattern>
</servlet-mapping>
```

The `Controller` class itself looks as follows:

```
import java.io.*;
import javax.servlet.*;
import javax.servlet.http.*;

public class Controller extends HttpServlet {
  public void doGet(HttpServletRequest request,
                    HttpServletResponse response)
      throws IOException, ServletException {
    HttpSession session = request.getSession();
    String command = request.getServletPath();
    Model model;
    if (command.equals("/search.do")) {
      model = new Model();
      session.setAttribute("model", model);
      getServletContext()
        .getRequestDispatcher("/search_card2.jsp")
        .forward(request, response);
    } else if (command.equals("/select.do")) {
      model = (Model)session.getAttribute("model");
      model.setPattern(request.getParameter("pattern"));
      session.setAttribute("matches", model.getMatches());
      getServletContext()
        .getRequestDispatcher("/select_card2.jsp")
        .forward(request, response);
    } else if (command.equals("/display.do")) {
      model = (Model)session.getAttribute("model");
      model.setSelected(Integer.parseInt(request.getParameter("i")));
      getServletContext()
        .getRequestDispatcher("/display_card2.jsp")
        .forward(request, response);
    }
  }
}
```

The controller determines the command that it must execute by testing the value of the `getServletPath` method. It then calls the corresponding methods in the model and forwards control to the appropriate view (as described in Section 9.4.3). This simple implementation does not handle possible errors, like missing form fields, in a robust manner.

The general picture of the Model–View–Controller pattern may for our application be specialized to the following sequence diagram, showing the overall behavior of our Web application:

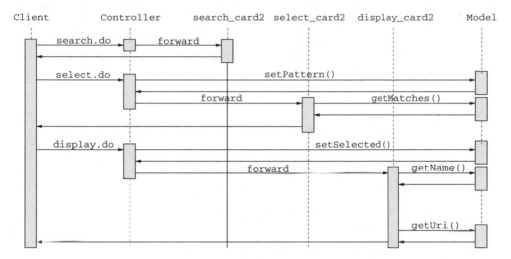

This diagram shows how the control is passed among the different components. A session with a client corresponds to a complete traversal through the diagram, starting with the `search.do` string being passed to the controller, and terminating with the result being passed from `display_card2`.

For larger Web applications, the Model 2 architecture is clearly superior. There are numerous Java frameworks that help to enforce the standards outlined in our example. A popular example is Apache Struts, which provides an extensive collection of tag libraries that simplify the programming of controllers and views.

*The MVC pattern provides **high cohesion** and **low coupling** to Web applications.*

10.4   Chapter Summary

JSP is a solid alternative to plain Java programming. JSP pages are XML-like documents that contain fragments of Java code, and they are processed into servlets through a simple lexical translation.

Using tag files and libraries, common programming patterns may be expressed in an XML-like syntax and entire domain-specific languages may be designed and implemented on top of Java.

The main weakness of JSP is the difficulty of debugging elaborate layers of syntax that are eventually desugared into unobvious Java code. Error messages may appear at all levels of the translation and are not always presented in terms of the high-level primitives.

The MVC pattern may be used to structure larger Web applications, providing a separation of independent parts of the implementation.

10.5 Further Reading

The official specifications of JSP and JSTL are quite readable documents and are the best places for obtaining further details [76, 77]. The MVC pattern as instantiated by Model 2 for Web applications is presented in the online description of core J2EE patterns. The paper [12] discusses formalizations of contracts between designers and programmers in the context of the JWIG framework.

10.6 Online Resources

http://java.sun.com/products/jsp/
Sun's homepage for JSP.

http://java.sun.com/products/jsp/jstl/
The JSTL specification and API.

http://java.sun.com/blueprints/corej2eepatterns/
Sun's collection of design patterns for Web programming.

http://struts.apache.org/
The Apache Struts framework.

10.7 Exercises

The main lessons to be learned from these exercises are:

- writing JSP templates;
- defining and using tags; and
- designing applications with the MVC pattern.

Exercise 10.1 Consider a Web application where people are paired together to play chess matches. Classify each of the following data as belonging to the page, request, session, or application scope:

(a) The ranking of the best players.
(b) The list of ongoing matches.
(c) The names of two opponents engaged in a match.
(d) The position of the pieces on a board.
(e) The number of moves played so far.
(f) The current move.

Exercise 10.2 Add an appropriate error page to the page *EX*/errorprone.jsp.

Exercise 10.3 Write a JSP version of the servlet *EX*/TicTacToe.java.

Exercise 10.4 Implement the following extensions to the Quick Poll framework (see Section 10.2.2):

(a) Allow the ask tag to have access to the yes, no, and total variables.

(b) Provide default implementations of the contents of the setup, ask, vote, and results tags that take effect if they are left out.

TIP

When using JSP in Tomcat, add the directive

```
<\%@ page isELIgnored="false" \%>
```

to make sure that tags and expressions are recognized correctly.

Exercise 10.5 Rewrite the page *EX*/usejstl.jsp to use plain Java code rather than JSTL tags.

Exercise 10.6 Implement the tags cart, add, process, empty, nonempty, loop, and url that make the shopping cart example work (see Section 10.2).

Exercise 10.7 Extend the shopping cart framework from Exercise 10.6 with the following features:

(a) A check that amount is really a number.

(b) An attribute capacity on the cart tag that limits the number of different products the cart may contain.

(c) A tag full that specifies the message to be given when the cart runs full.

Exercise 10.8 Introduce some tags to simplify the programming of your solution to Exercise 10.3.

Exercise 10.9 Answer the following questions about the JSTL libraries:

(a) What is the difference between c:out and x:out?

(b) What is c:catch used for?

(c) How are XSLT transformations performed?

(d) How may the fmt:* tags be used?

Exercise 10.10 Consider the Web application that in the Model 1 architecture is realized by the three pages *EX*/hello.jsp, *EX*/howareyou.jsp, and *EX*/goodbye.jsp. Write an alternative implementation that follows the Model 2 architecture.

WEB SERVICES

Objectives

In this chapter, you will learn:

- The SOAP protocol for exchanging XML messages on a network
- The WSDL language for describing interfaces of Web services
- The UDDI system for managing registries of Web services

11.1 Distributed Systems and Web Services

As discussed in the beginning of this book, the first generation of Web technology focused on communication of HTML documents and form data. XML then emerged as a more suitable format than HTML for representing general structured data and for machine-to-machine interaction. Together, the XML data representation format and the HTTP communication protocol provide a powerful foundation for building *Web services*. There are many definitions of what the term 'Web service' covers – we will view it in the broad meaning of software that makes services available on a network using technologies such as XML and HTTP.

Web services support **service-oriented architectures**, using in particular XML and HTTP.

The main vision of Web services is that they support *service-oriented architectures*, that is, development of large scale applications from distributed collections of smaller loosely coupled service providers. As an example of a Web service, imagine that our hypothetical company Widget Inc. wants to make it easy for other companies to obtain information about its inventory and prices, and enable them to buy widgets. This could be achieved with a Web service that makes a few operations available: one for inquiring whether a given product is in stock and obtaining its current price, and another for placing an order by supplying a customer ID, a product number, and an amount. Such a Web service would then act as a component of the company's inventory control system.

Compared to other frameworks for developing distributed systems, such as CORBA, DCOM, or Java/RMI, there is conceptually only little novelty in Web services. The main selling point of the Web service model is that it builds on XML and HTTP, which are platform neutral, widely accepted and utilized, and come with a range of useful technologies as we have seen in the previous chapters.

At first, the idea of Web services sounds simple. We already know how to represent information with XML and how to write programs that communicate using HTTP. What more could we possibly want? In fact, we want several things, the most important being the following:

- Message passing frameworks must account for the possibility of things going wrong. Of course, building on, for example, TCP does solve many of the potential problems related to communication, but errors may still occur at the application level. Messages may be ill-formatted or servers may be down, and loosely connected applications must be able to handle such situations. XML and HTTP do not help ensuring *fault tolerance* at the application level, so we need new mechanisms.

- Even on the application level, messages do not always pass directly from the sender to the receiver. It can be useful to insert *intermediaries* on the message path for monitoring, routing, or transforming the messages. More specific examples include encrypting or decrypting the message contents, performing access control, load balancing, and application level auditing. This calls for a notion of extensibility where the actual messages can be augmented with appropriate metadata.

- In Section 7.4, we saw ways of mapping programming language values into XML data and back. This mapping is naturally relevant for distributed systems, in particular the many that follow the RPC (Remote Procedure Call) pattern where services are viewed as collections of remote procedures that can be invoked while passing arguments and receiving return values. Web services need to incorporate a general mechanism to support such uses.

- A service exposes a set of operations that are made available to other services. We need a common way of formally describing this *interface*: which operations are provided, which arguments they expect, and perhaps also how the operations are correlated.

- To enable the organization of Web services to be flexible, we need a common way of *locating* services that can solve a given task. This may be achieved through registries where service users can find the relevant service providers.

As we have seen before in this book, whenever common problems are identified it can be beneficial to develop common solutions in the form of new languages or protocols. To address these specific problems, the technologies SOAP, WSDL, and UDDI have been invented. In the following sections, we shall look into each of them. First, however, we will consider a simple example of a Web service that uses plain XML and HTTP, based on what we have already seen in the previous chapters.

11.1.1   A Recipe Server with XML and HTTP

Consider the following scenario. We want to develop a *recipe server* that allows clients to perform various operations on a recipe collection (see Section 2.7) in an RPC style:

getRecipes: returns the list of recipes stored on the server;

lockRecipe: obtains a *lock* on a given recipe ID, or fails if someone else already has that lock;

writeRecipe: uploads a recipe to the server – if one already exists with the same ID, then a valid lock must also be exhibited and the old recipe is overwritten; and

unlockRecipe: releases the given lock.

The lock mechanism avoids concurrent modifications of a recipe and illustrates a typical case of correlation between operations.

The recipes being transmitted are represented using XML as described in Section 2.7 (and we assume that every recipe element has an id attribute). Note that this requirement does not enforce a particular representation within the server; the service programmer may use any internal representation that he finds suitable, or perhaps even store the data in a database on another server.

We choose to implement this server as follows. The server listens for HTTP POST requests on a port. The body of the request is an XML document that contains the name of an operation and an encoding of the arguments, as in this example:

```
POST /personal/jdoe/recipeserver HTTP/1.0
Host: www.widget.inc
Content-Type: text/xml
Content-length: 5714

<?xml version="1.0"?>
<call xmlns="http://www.brics.dk/ixwt/xmlrpc"
      xmlns:rcp="http://www.brics.dk/ixwt/recipes">
  <operation>writeRecipe</operation>
  <arg>4DHX5ZV3D871AQ09</arg>
  <arg>
    <rcp:recipe id="r105">
      <rcp:title>Cailles en Sarcophages</rcp:title>
      <rcp:date>Tue, 26 Sep 06</rcp:date>
      ...
    </rcp:recipe>
  </arg>
</call>
```

This requests the server to perform the writeRecipe operation with the given arguments: a lock (a hard to guess string), which has been obtained earlier using lockRecipe, and the recipe to be written to the collection. Notice that we use XML namespaces to identify the various parts of the XML document in the request body.

Similarly, the body of the response is an XML document containing the return value. For example, the result of a `lockRecipe` operation might be the following:

```
HTTP/1.1 200 OK
Date: Tue, 26 Sep 2006 22:29:08 GMT+1
Content-Type: text/xml
Content-Length: 101

<?xml version="1.0"?>
<return xmlns="http://www.brics.dk/ixwt/xmlrpc">
  4DHX5ZV3D871AQ09
</return>
```

This particular operation succeeded in locking the given recipe and returns a lock in the response body. In case the locking failed, we could choose to return the empty string, for example.

Based on what we already know about programming HTTP in Java (see Section 8.4) or using Servlets (see Chapter 9), it is straightforward to implement such a server, and we leave it as an exercise.

As soon as we start writing many services, we obviously need precise conventions about the representation of requests and responses rather than inventing ad hoc rules for every new service. The choices we have made in this small example are, in fact, close to those made in *XML-RPC* – a simple RPC protocol based on XML and HTTP. However, XML-RPC is in some respects too simple: for example, it only supports a few predefined argument types, not even including general XML (which we need in this example). Alternatively, we could use the more advanced protocol SOAP, which we describe in Section 11.3. Much of the discussion of pros and cons of the various protocols boils down to one issue: how many details should be standardized as opposed to being left to ad hoc solutions. Standardizing too much implies dense specifications, whereas standardizing too little may damage system interoperability.

> Web service developers must find a balance between **ad hoc solutions** and use of **standards**.

At a more abstract level, the RPC model, which we use in this example, focuses on software components (concretely, request URIs point to code in the example), whereas the Web architecture (see the note on REST in Section 8.6) is more leaning towards data-oriented resources. Some REST advocates argue that the latter model to a large degree is responsible for the success of the Web and should also be used as the foundation for Web service protocols, but at this point there are no standards of this kind.

11.2   Web Service Standards

To accommodate the need for conventions about the many aspects of Web service communication, a range of protocols has been suggested in the last years, and the development is

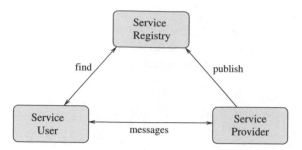

Figure 11.1 Components of a service-oriented architecture.

far from stable at this point. We will now discuss what are commonly believed to be the essential technologies (although they are not particularly simple):

- *SOAP* is a protocol for exchanging XML documents, typically but not necessarily using HTTP;

- *WSDL* is an interface description language for Web services; and

- *UDDI* is a system for making clients and servers find each other.

Not surprisingly, all three use an XML notation. The following sections go into more detail of each of them. Figure 11.1 illustrates their use in a service-oriented architecture. A *service user* (also called a *client*) is a network component that uses a service made available by a *service provider* through an exchange of messages. The interface of the service is formalized using WSDL. A *service registry* (also called a *broker*) is a metaservice that, using UDDI, allows the service providers to publish their services and the service users to find appropriate services. All communication between the components is performed using SOAP.

The basic Web service standards are **SOAP**, **WSDL**, and **UDDI**.

In this chapter, we focus on the three technologies mentioned above. However, these are just the beginning: there already exists a chaotic swarm of specifications aiming to standardize additional layers of aspects of Web service communication. Most of these specifications are commonly referred to as 'WS-*' as their names begin with 'Web Services'. Many are working drafts whose development is driven more by a desire to standardize than dire need, and ad hoc solutions often suffice for getting the concrete work done. It is *not* necessary to be an expert in WS-* to be able to build Web services; however, if getting into building many and complex Web services, then learning more about these advanced specifications may help to avoid reinventing the wheel.

As a small taster, the WS-* specifications deal with the following issues – among numerous others – in most cases building on SOAP and often with connections to WSDL:

- *WS-Addressing* provides transport-neutral mechanisms (that is, independent of HTTP, in particular) to address Web services;

- *WS-ReliableMessaging* provides transport-neutral reliable communication;

- *WS-Security* and *WS-Policy* provide standardized ways of talking about security mechanisms, requirements, and capabilities, and obtaining agreement about which protocols to use;

- *WS-Resource* is a framework for managing stateful resources (actually, this single framework consists of six individual specifications, *WS-ResourceProperties*, *WS-ResourceLifetime*, *WS-ServiceGroup*, *WS-BaseFaults*, *WS-Notification*, and *WS-RenewableReference*, which incurs a quite steep learning curve);

- *WS-Choreography*, in particular *WS-CDL*, the *Web Services Choreography Description Language*, provides description of linkages and usage patterns between Web services, including sequences and conditions in which messages are exchanged (which goes beyond the scope of WSDL);

- *WS-BPEL* (Web Services Business Process Execution Language, formerly known as *BPEL4WS*), which largely overlaps with WS-Choreography (but developed by a different organization, not surprisingly); and

- *WS-Coordination* and *WS-AtomicTransaction* provide standardization of coordination of activities and transaction processing, and *WS-CAF*, the *Web Services Composite Application Framework*, is a competing initiative.

Hopefully, a more solid range of standards will in the next few years emerge from the current chaos.

11.3 SOAP

Development of SOAP originally started as as an attempt to standardize RPC-like communication using XML and HTTP along the lines indicated by the example in Section 11.1.1, but the specification has since swollen considerably. The resulting standard is a mix of many things: in particular, RPC is just one possible communication pattern supported by SOAP, and HTTP is just one possible transport protocol for SOAP messages. It is designed to address several of the issues we raised in Section 11.1: fault management, application-level intermediaries, and RPC interactions.

The name *SOAP* was originally an acronym for Simple Object Access Protocol, but, acknowledging the fact that at some point in the development calling it *simple* or *object oriented* could not be justified anymore, SOAP is now just a name and not an acronym.

11.3.1 The Processing Model

A SOAP message is an XML document having the following structure, called an *envelope*:

```
<Envelope xmlns="http://www.w3.org/2003/05/soap-envelope">
  <Header>...</Header>
  <Body>...</Body>
</Envelope>
```

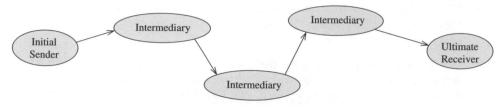

Figure 11.2 The path of a SOAP message involving three intermediaries.

The contents of the `Body` element, called the *body* of the message, contains the main information to be transmitted from the sender to the receiver. The contents of `Header`, which is optional, are subelements called the *header blocks* of the message. These contain meta-information (that is, information about the main information) and are typically used for

- naming an encryption mechanism being used for the data in the body;

- access control information, such as a ticket that authorizes some operation;

- routing information, for example for load balancing on a server;

- auditing information being collected on the way to the receivers; or

- other kinds of data extensions that for some reason do not fit into the message body, for example because some potential recipient requires the body to be valid according to some fixed and more restrictive schema.

Since there is often no clear division between information and meta-information, there are no formal rules about what data belongs in the body and what should be placed in headers.

The main strengths of SOAP are support for **intermediaries**, **fault** management, and **RPC** interactions.

We distinguish between the *initial sender* of a message, the *ultimate receiver* for which the message is targeted, and *intermediaries* which act in between the two end points. Each intermediary inspects the message (especially the header, usually), then perhaps modifies it, and finally passes it on to the next node on the path. Figure 11.2 illustrates the path of a SOAP message involving three intermediaries.

A complete SOAP message might look as follows:

```
<env:Envelope xmlns:env="http://www.w3.org/2003/05/soap-envelope"
              xmlns:w="http://www.widget.inc/shop"
              xmlns:n="http://notaries.example.org">
  <env:Header>
    <w:ticket>54B42CF401A</w:ticket>
    <n:token>
       <n:value>32158546</n:value>
       <n:issuer>http://notarypublic.example.com</n:issuer>
    </n:token>
  </env:Header>
  <env:Body>
    <w:buy>
       <w:product>light gadget</w:product>
```

```
      <w:amount>430</w:amount>
    </w:buy>
  </env:Body>
</env:Envelope>
```

This particular message contains a request for buying 430 light gadgets, using a hypothetical widget shopping XML language. (In this example we do *not* use the SOAP RPC and SOAP encoding conventions described later in the chapter.) The header here contains a 'ticket', a kind of session identifier that might be used by intermediaries within Widget Inc. to authenticate the sender and route the message to the right server machine. The `token` header block belonging to the namespace `http://notaries.example.org` contains a 'token' that has been generated by a third-party notarization intermediary for ensuring non-repudiation of the message.

The header blocks may contain some special attributes belonging to the namespace `http://www.w3.org/2003/05/soap-envelope` (declared with prefix `env` in the following):

`role`: specifies who should handle the header block. The value is a URI (much like a namespace URI). If the receiver (an intermediary or the ultimate receiver) assumes this 'role' – we say that the header block is *targeted* at this receiver – then it will act appropriately on the header block and otherwise ignore it. Different roles may, for example, be used for intermediaries that perform encryption, routing, or auditing. In addition, three special URIs are predefined:

> `http://www.w3.org/2003/05/soap-envelope/role/`**next**: indicates that the header block is targeted for the next node on the message path (this is for example used for message tracing);

> `http://www.w3.org/2003/05/soap-envelope/role/`**ultimateReceiver**: means that the header block is targeted only for the ultimate receiver (and this is the default value); and

> `http://www.w3.org/2003/05/soap-envelope/role/`**none**: means that the header block should be interpreted as an extension of the data in the message body and not as a normal part of the header. The typical use is for maintaining compatibility with older systems that may not allow extensions of the message bodies.

`mustUnderstand`: with the value `true` means that the receiver must be able to understand the header block if the role matches, or else a fault must be generated. (We discuss faults in the next section.) It is important for extensibility to be able to distinguish between header blocks that are essential for correct processing (an example is a header block that describes a compression algorithm that has been used for the data in the body) and ones that are not (for instance, header blocks used for logging). A receiver performs no actual processing of a message until it has been determined that all header blocks that are targeted at this receiver and marked `env:mustUnderstand="true"` are, in fact, understood.

`relay`: By default, an intermediary receiver removes all header blocks that are targeted for that receiver, even if the header block is not understood. That can be changed by specifying `env:relay="true"`, which means that the header block should be left unchanged if it is not understood. (If the header block *is* understood, then the intermediary may of course determine to reinsert it as part of the processing before passing on the message, and if `env:mustUnderstand="true"` is set then the `relay` attribute is irrelevant.)

`encodingStyle`: this attribute can be used for specifying how the information in the header block has been encoded in XML; we return to the issue of encodings in Section 11.3.3.

As an example, the following SOAP message contains two header blocks:

```
<env:Envelope xmlns:env="http://www.w3.org/2003/05/soap-envelope"
              xmlns:c="http://encodings.example.org"
              xmlns:r="http://routings.example.org">
  <env:Header>
    <c:encoding env:role="http://encodings.example.org/decoder"
                env:mustUnderstand="true">
      gzip+base64
    </c:encoding>
    <r:route env:relay="true"
             env:role=
             "http://www.w3.org/2003/05/soap-envelope/role/next">
      <r:node>130.225.16.12</r:node>
      <r:node>10.11.40.201</r:node>
    </r:route>
  </env:Header>
  <env:Body>
    H4sICACI/0EAA3EA80jNycnXUSjPL8pJUeQCABinVXsOAAAA
  </env:Body>
</env:Envelope>
```

The first header block describes the encoding of the body (here gzip followed by base64). This information is relevant for receivers that perform decoding, which is specified using the `role` attribute. The `mustUnderstand` attribute specifies that such receivers *must* be able to process the header, that is, perform the decoding, before passing on the message. The second header block contains message tracing information. This information is relevant for all receivers on the path, but the message can succeed even if they are unable to process this header block – and in that case, the header block is relayed, that is, left unchanged, as specified by the `relay` attribute.

11.3.2 Faults

In loosely connected distributed systems, many things can go wrong: invalid data may be transmitted, servers may be unavailable, and so on. SOAP provides a uniform way to indicate such errors. A SOAP *fault* is a SOAP message as the following:

```
<env:Envelope xmlns:env="http://www.w3.org/2003/05/soap-envelope"
              xmlns:w="http://www.widget.inc/shop">
  <env:Body>
    <env:Fault>
      <env:Code>
        <env:Value>env:Sender</env:Value>
        <env:Subcode>
          <env:Value>w:InvalidBuyRequest</env:Value>
        </env:Subcode>
      </env:Code>
      <env:Reason>
        <env:Text xml:lang="en">
          The value of 'amount' is invalid!
        </env:Text>
        <env:Text xml:lang="da">
          Værdien af 'amount' er ugyldig!
        </env:Text>
      </env:Reason>
    </env:Fault>
  </env:Body>
</env:Envelope>
```

The `Fault` element from the SOAP envelope namespace indicates to the receiver that something has gone wrong, typically with the processing of an earlier message originating from the receiver of this fault message. The `Value` element inside `Code` specifies the overall kind of error:

`Sender`: means that the error was caused by the sender of the earlier message (who is typically the receiver of the fault message) – this is reminiscent of the 4*xx* status codes in HTTP (see Section 8.1.2);

`Receiver`: means that the error was caused by the receiver of the earlier message (who is typically the sender of the fault message) – this is reminiscent of the 5*xx* status codes in HTTP;

`MustUnderstand`: indicates that a header block that was marked as 'must understand' (see Section 11.3.1) was *not* understood;

`VersionMismatch`: is generated if a SOAP envelope uses a namespace that its receiver does not understand (notice that the SOAP namespace URI specifies the version of SOAP being used); and

`DataEncodingUnknown`: is generated if a header block or the body uses a data encoding that is not understood (we describe data encodings in Section 11.3.3).

Note that the text in `Value` is a QName, qualified by the SOAP envelope namespace. (Using namespace prefixes in character data is technically not a part of XML Namespaces – this is similar to the use of prefixes in attribute values in, for example, XML Schema; see Section 4.4.5). Further details of the error are given in the `Subcode` element. Here, we also use a QName, but this time qualified by a namespace that is specific to the application. Finally, a human readable explanation is given in the `Reason` element, which contains a number of `Text` elements, each with a mandatory `xml:lang` attribute (see Section 2.4) describing the natural language being used.

In addition to the information shown in the example above, a fault message may optionally contain a `Detail` element specifying extra information about the cause, a `Node` element containing a URI of the receiver that detected the error, and a `Role` element describing the role it played. Further information may be specified in the header, in particular for `MustUnderstand` faults.

11.3.3 Data Representation and RPC

SOAP contains a simple data encoding scheme, called *SOAP encoding*, for representing general object graphs in XML. This encoding is particularly useful for performing RPC interactions (although alternative encoding schemes may also be used in SOAP messages). The SOAP encoding somewhat resembles the XML data binding techniques discussed in Section 7.4, however, the approach discussed here is not tied to any particular programming language.

SOAP encoding provides an XML serialization of data graphs.

In the SOAP data model, data is organized as a directed labeled graph. This provides a uniform abstraction of the heap structures that appear in typical programming languages. A graph node then corresponds to an object or a primitive value, and an edge corresponds to a field pointing from one object to another or to a value. For example, the graph shown in Figure 11.3 represents eight objects and values having pointers to each other. Nodes with outgoing edges represent *compound* values, and those without correspond to *simple* values

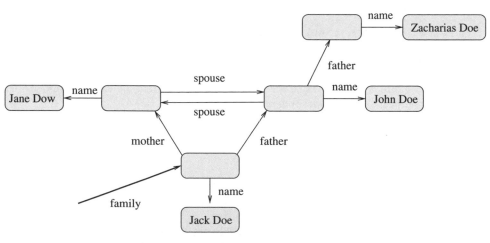

Figure 11.3 An object graph.

given by their label. A node cannot have multiple outgoing edges with the same label. A SOAP encoding of this graph, starting from the `family` edge, looks as follows:

```
<family xmlns:env="http://www.w3.org/2003/05/soap-envelope"
        xmlns:enc="http://www.w3.org/2003/05/soap-encoding"
        env:encodingStyle="http://www.w3.org/2003/05/soap-encoding"
        xmlns="http://www.widget.inc/encoding">
  <name>Jack Doe</name>
  <father enc:id="1">
    <name>John Doe</name>
    <father>
      <name>Zacharias Doe</name>
    </father>
    <spouse enc:ref="2"/>
  </father>
  <mother enc:id="2">
    <name>Jane Dow</name>
    <spouse enc:ref="1"/>
  </mother>
</family>
```

(Notice that SOAP encoding is identified by the URI `http://www.w3.org/2003/05/soap-encoding`.) This representation is obtained by a traversal of the graph. Edges become elements (edge labels are generally QNames), compound values correspond to sequences of elements, and simple values become character data. As long as the graph has a tree structure, this technique fits smoothly into the XML tree model. However, when there are nodes with multiple incoming edges – as in the example – we need a little more: the ID/IDREF mechanism (see Section 4.3.3). Each element that represents a node with multiple incoming edges has an `enc:id` attribute with a unique value, and the second time that node is encountered during the encoding, an empty element with a `enc:ref` attribute is produced, pointing to the right element. This representation is obviously not canonical as it depends on the traversal order.

A feature not illustrated above is representation of multidimensional arrays. For example, an unbounded array of arrays of size two containing the values

$$((56°10'N, 10°13'E), (51°29'N, 0°0'W), (37°37'N, 122°23'W))$$

may be encoded as follows using SOAP encoding:

```
<coordinates xmlns:enc="http://www.w3.org/2003/05/soap-encoding"
             enc:arraySize="* 2">
  <value>56°10'N</value>
  <value>10°13'E</value>
  <value>51°29'N</value>
  <value>0°0'W</value>
  <value>37°37'N</value>
  <value>122°23'W</value>
</coordinates>
```

(The names of the elements containing the entries are irrelevant.) To make it clear whether an element represents a simple value, a compound structure, or an array, we may add an attribute named enc:nodeType with the value simple, struct, or array, respectively. Moreover, it is common to annotate elements with type information using XML Schema types via the xsi:type mechanism (see Section 4.4).

It is important to note that SOAP encoding is designed for the object graph model. This is clearly a very general model that is closely related to heap structures in typical programming languages. Still, it does not fit well with all kinds of data, a notable example being data that is already XML. We encounter an example below.

Remote Procedure Calls

SOAP encoding is a natural foundation for communication using the Remote Procedure Call (RPC) pattern. One procedure call then corresponds to two SOAP messages: first, one from the caller to the callee containing the procedure name and the arguments; second, one in the opposite direction containing the return values or fault data. In each direction, the data is represented as a compound structure as illustrated in Figure 11.4. The SOAP encoding of the resulting structure is transmitted in the body of a SOAP envelope.

The procedure name becomes the name of the outermost element in the call message, and the (unordered) list of arguments are placed within this element. The name of the outermost element in the return message is irrelevant. The return message may contain multiple return values. One of them may be a distinguished 'result' value; this one is identified by placing the element result from the namespace http://www.w3.org/2003/05/soap-rpc among the return value elements, containing the name of the result value element. (This allows distinction between *out* parameters and the procedure return value.)

To illustrate the SOAP RPC conventions, let us see how the writeRecipe operation from the example in Section 11.1.1 looks when using SOAP. Recall that this operation takes two arguments: a lock which is a string, and a recipe which is an XML tree. Since we regard the latter as already encoded in XML, we do not use SOAP encoding for this part. Instead, we encode this part by a trivial 'literal XML' encoding style. A commonly used URI for this encoding is http://xml.apache.org/xml-soap/literalxml. (Notice that this URI is defined by Apache, not W3C!) An RPC call for the writeRecipe operation may then

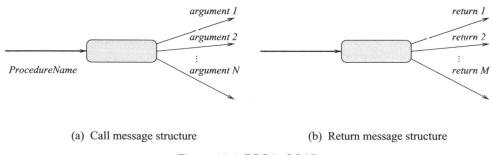

(a) Call message structure   (b) Return message structure

Figure 11.4 RPC in SOAP.

look as follows (abbreviated with '...'):

```
<env:Envelope xmlns:env="http://www.w3.org/2003/05/soap-envelope"
              xmlns:rs="http://www.brics.dk/ixwt/recipeserver"
              xmlns:rcp="http://www.brics.dk/ixwt/recipes">
  <env:Body>
    <rs:writeRecipe
        env:encodingStyle=
          "http://www.w3.org/2003/05/soap-encoding">
      <rs:lock>4DHX5ZV3D871AQ09</rs:lock>
      <rs:recipe
        env:encodingStyle=
          "http://xml.apache.org/xml-soap/literalxml">
        <rcp:recipe id="r105">
          <rcp:title>Cailles en Sarcophages</rcp:title>
          <rcp:date>Tue, 26 Sep 06</rcp:date>
          ...
        </rcp:recipe>
      </rs:recipe>
    </rs:writeRecipe>
  </env:Body>
</env:Envelope>
```

Notice that two different encodings are in use: SOAP encoding for the main part of the body, and literal XML encoding for the recipe argument. In the case that no faults occur, the return message is quite simple since the return type of `writeRecipe` is void:

```
<cnv:Envelope xmlns:env="http://www.w3.org/2003/05/soap-envelope"
              xmlns:rs="http://www.brics.dk/ixwt/recipeserver">
  <env:Body>
    <rs:writeRecipeResponse
        env:encodingStyle=
          "http://www.w3.org/2003/05/soap-encoding"/>
  </env:Body>
</env:Envelope>
```

We do not need headers in this simple RPC example.

Is is important to know that the SOAP processing model can be used without the SOAP RPC conventions: some services use SOAP messages in other communication patterns than RPC, and some use an RPC style with SOAP messages but with other conventions than those prescribed by SOAP RPC. (Yes, this may be confusing.)

11.3.4   Protocol Binding

SOAP messages may be transmitted using various underlying protocols. Most common is naturally HTTP, although the SOAP framework is open to bindings with other protocols, such as SMTP (the email protocol). The different hops on the path from the initial sender of a

SOAP message to the ultimate receiver may generally involve different protocol bindings. In this section we focus on the HTTP binding. The RPC call message maps naturally to an HTTP request, and the corresponding RPC return message maps naturally to the HTTP response.

The HTTP binding supports two message exchange patterns:

- the *request–response* pattern, which is the one used for RPC; and

- the *SOAP response* pattern, in which only the response is a SOAP message (and the request is made by other means).

SOAP
messages may
be transmitted
by various
protocols,
including
HTTP.

The former corresponds to the HTTP POST method, whereas the latter can be used only with GET. However, recall from Chapter 8 that GET is appropriate for operations that only retrieve data. Although the HTTP binding in SOAP does support the GET method, the RPC part of the current version of SOAP only works with POST (since it does not specify a standard encoding of RPC calls into request URIs). This means that ad hoc solutions are required if one wants to use RPC with GET.

As an example using the HTTP binding, the response from the writeRecipe operation shown in the previous section looks as follows in an HTTP response message:

```
HTTP/1.1 200 OK
Content-Type: application/soap+xml; charset="utf-8"
Content-Length: 273

<env:Envelope xmlns:env="http://www.w3.org/2003/05/soap-envelope"
              xmlns:rs="http://www.brics.dk/ixwt/recipeserver">
  <env:Body>
    <rs:writeRecipeResponse
        env:encodingStyle=
          "http://www.w3.org/2003/05/soap-encoding"/>
  </env:Body>
</env:Envelope>
```

The HTTP status code reflects the overall result of the processing; for example, if the response is a fault message with the code Receiver then the HTTP status code is in the 5*xx* range. As the example indicates, a special media type is allocated for SOAP messages: application/soap+xml. It is important that HTTP requests include a header line

```
Accept: application/soap+xml
```

to indicate that a SOAP response is acceptable.

11.4   WSDL

WSDL, *Web Services Description Language* is, as the name implies, an interface description language for Web services. That is, a WSDL description of a Web service contains the necessary information required to write clients of the Web service:

- What functionality is provided? In other words, which operations are provided and what are the types of their arguments and return values?

- How should the service be accessed, that is, how is data encoded and which communication protocols are used?

- Where on the Web is the service located?

Having formally described the interface moreover makes it possible to automatically generate stubs for the client code and skeletons for the server code, which may accelerate the programming of both sides.

We note that the version of WSDL that we describe in this section is 2.0, which at the time of writing is a W3C working draft (see Section 1.9). Further changes should be expected but the overall picture will most likely remain as explained here.

WSDL is an XML language. The general structure of a typical WSDL description is as follows:

A WSDL description of a Web service describes its **functionality**, **data encodings**, **communication protocols**, and **location**.

```
<description xmlns="http://www.w3.org/2004/08/wsdl"
             targetNamespace="..." ...>
  <types>
    <!-- XML Schema description of types being used in messages -->
    ...
  </types>

  <interface name="...">
    <!-- list of operations and their input and output -->
    ...
  </interface>

  <binding name="..." interface="..." type="...">
    <!-- message encodings and communication protocols -->
    ...
  </binding>

  <service name="..." interface="...">
    <!-- combination of an interface, a binding,
         and a service location -->
    ...
  </service>
</description>
```

The `targetNamespace` attribute provides a name to the description, similar to the attribute of the same name in XML Schema. The `types` part contains schema definitions of types that are used by the operations. Usually, the XML Schema language is used here, however, the specification also shows how to use RELAX NG as an alternative. The `types` element typically contains an embedded schema or a number of XML Schema `import` instructions. Each `interface` part describes a named collection of operations; each `binding` part specifies the message encodings and communication protocols used for a given interface; and each `service` part combines an interface, a binding, and a service location to describe a complete service. Each of these parts is described in more detail in the following. An XML Schema description of the syntax of the main part of WSDL is available at

```
http://www.w3.org/2004/08/wsdl/
```

Example

The following complete WSDL document describes the interface of a recipe server as the one in Section 11.1.1 but using the SOAP protocol:

```
<description xmlns="http://www.w3.org/2004/08/wsdl"
             targetNamespace=
               "http://www.brics.dk/ixwt/recipes/wsdl"
             xmlns:x=
               "http://www.brics.dk/ixwt/recipes/wsdl">
  <types>
    <xs:schema
        xmlns:xs="http://www.w3.org/2001/XMLSchema"
        targetNamespace=
          "http://www.brics.dk/ixwt/recipes/wsdl/types"
        xmlns:t=
          "http://www.brics.dk/ixwt/recipes/wsdl/types">

      <xs:import namespace="http://www.brics.dk/ixwt/recipes"
                 schemaLocation="recipes.xsd"/>

      <xs:element name="lock">
        <xs:simpleType>
          <xs:restriction base="xs:string">
            <xs:length value="16"/>
          </xs:restriction>
        </xs:simpleType>
      </xs:element>

      <xs:element name="lockError" type="xs:string"/>

      <xs:element name="getRecipes">
        <xs:complexType><xs:sequence/></xs:complexType>
      </xs:element>

      <xs:element name="lockRecipe">
        <xs:complexType>
```

```
            <xs:sequence>
              <xs:element name="id" type="xs:NMTOKEN"/>
            </xs:sequence>
          </xs:complexType>
        </xs:element>

        <xs:element name="lockRecipeResponse">
          <xs:complexType>
            <xs:sequence>
              <xs:element ref="t:lock"/>
            </xs:sequence>
          </xs:complexType>
        </xs:element>

        <xs:element name="writeRecipe">
          <xs:complexType>
            <xs:sequence>
              <xs:element ref="t:recipe"/>
              <xs:element ref="t:lock"/>
            </xs:sequence>
          </xs:complexType>
        </xs:element>

        <xs:element name="unlockRecipe">
          <xs:complexType>
            <xs:sequence>
              <xs:element ref="t:lock"/>
            </xs:sequence>
          </xs:complexType>
        </xs:element>

    </xs:schema>
  </types>

  <interface name="recipeserverInterface"
             xmlns:t="http://www.brics.dk/ixwt/recipes/wsdl/types"
             styleDefault="http://www.w3.org/2004/03/wsdl/style/rpc">

    <fault name="lockFault" element="t:lockError"/>

    <operation name="getRecipesOperation"
               pattern="http://www.w3.org/2004/03/wsdl/in-out">
      <input messageLabel="In" element="t:getRecipes"/>
      <output messageLabel="Out" element="t:collection"/>
    </operation>

    <operation name="lockRecipeOperation"
               pattern="http://www.w3.org/2004/03/wsdl/in-out">
      <input messageLabel="In" element="t:lockRecipe"/>
```

```
      <output messageLabel="Out" element="t:lockRecipeResponse"/>
      <outfault ref="x:lockFault" messageLabel="Out"/>
    </operation>

    <operation name="writeRecipeOperation"
              pattern=
                "http://www.w3.org/2004/03/wsdl/robust-in-only">
      <input messageLabel="In" element="t:writeRecipe"/>
      <outfault ref="x:lockFault"/>
    </operation>

    <operation name="unlockRecipeOperation"
              pattern="http://www.w3.org/2004/03/wsdl/in-only">
      <input messageLabel="In" element="t:lock"/>
    </operation>

  </interface>

  <binding name="recipeserverSOAPBinding"
          interface="x:recipeserverInterface"
          type="http://www.w3.org/2004/08/wsdl/soap12"
          xmlns:ws="http://www.w3.org/2004/08/wsdl/soap12"
          ws:protocol=
            "http://www.w3.org/2003/05/soap/bindings/HTTP"
          ws:mepDefault=
            "http://www.w3.org/2003/05/soap/mep/request-response"
          xmlns:soap="http://www.w3.org/2003/05/soap-envelope">
    <fault ref="x:lockFault" ws:code="soap:Sender"/>
  </binding>

  <service name="recipeserver" interface="x:recipeserverInterface">
    <endpoint name="recipeserverEndpoint"
          binding=
            "x:recipeserverSOAPBinding"
          address=
            "http://www.widget.inc/personal/jdoe/recipeserver"/>
  </service>
</description>
```

The following sections show how to read such a description. To put it briefly: this particular WSDL description tells us that there is a Web service at the URI http://www.widget.inc/personal/jdoe/recipeserver; it understands the RPC-style operations getRecipes, lockRecipe, writeRecipe, and unlockRecipe; the communication uses SOAP with the SOAP HTTP binding; certain faults may occur; and input and output values are required to be valid according the given schema definitions.

Most elements may additionally contain a documentation element that contains additional information about the Web service, typically informal human readable documentation. Larger WSDL descriptions can be split into multiple files using import and include instructions like in XML Schema (see Section 4.4.7). Moreover, to support reuse of descriptions, interfaces can be defined as extensions of existing interfaces (similar to extension of interfaces in Java).

11.4.1 Interface Descriptions

An *operation* is a collection of logically related messages that follow a certain pattern. WSDL specifies eight such patterns, each being identified by a URI. The following explanations are seen from the service provider's point of view:

In-Only (`http://www.w3.org/2004/08/wsdl/in-only`): one message is received;

Robust In-Only (`http://www.w3.org/2004/08/wsdl/robust-in-only`): as the previous, but a fault may be triggered in response;

In-Out (`http://www.w3.org/2004/08/wsdl/in-out`): one message is received followed by one message being returned, and the latter may be a fault message;

In-Optional-Out (`http://www.w3.org/2004/08/wsdl/in-opt-out`): as the previous, but the response is optional;

Out-Only (`http://www.w3.org/2004/08/wsdl/out-only`): one message is sent;

Robust Out-Only (`http://www.w3.org/2004/08/wsdl/robust-out-only`): as the previous, but a fault may be triggered in response;

Out-In (`http://www.w3.org/2004/08/wsdl/out-in`): one message is sent followed by one message being received, and the latter may be a fault message; and

Out-Optional-In (`http://www.w3.org/2004/08/wsdl/out-opt-in`): as the previous, but the response is optional.

Not surprisingly, by far the most used pattern is In-Out as it corresponds to a general RPC interaction (and In-Only and Robust In-Only can be viewed as specialized versions of In-Out). The converse, Out-In, may be used when the service provider is the initiator, although that is less common. The In-Only and Out-Only patterns and the robust versions can be used as a foundation for asynchronous communication or as primitives for more complex interactions. The usefulness of the two patterns involving optional messages is more debatable.

Clearly, the list of possible patterns has been developed in an attempt to achieve optimal generality from an abstract point of view. However, when mapping to the concrete transport layer, for example HTTP, many details are unspecified, which leads to non-interoperable implementations. Yet again, the In-Out pattern corresponding to RPC interactions works well, and it is sufficient for typical Web services.

An operation involves a number of message parts, each being labeled according to its role in the message exchange pattern of the operation. For instance, the operation getRecipes from our example follows the In-Out pattern, which requires description of one input message and one output message (although the input is trivial):

```
<operation name="getRecipesOperation"
           pattern="http://www.w3.org/2004/03/wsdl/in-out">
  <input messageLabel="In" element="t:getRecipes"/>
  <output messageLabel="Out" element="t:collection"/>
</operation>
```

The predefined message exchange patterns all involve at most one input and output, which are always labeled `In` and `Out`, respectively. Faults being used in `outfault` as shown in the example on page 482 and the related `infault` (which may be used with Out-In and the related patterns) must be declared separately in the interface:

```
<fault name="..."
       element="..."/>
```

This declaration simply associates an element definition from the `types` part to the given fault name.

An `operation` element may have a `style` attribute specifying that the message schema conforms to certain rules. One such style is *RPC-style*, which is expressed as the value `http://www.w3.org/2004/08/wsdl/style/rpc`. Using this style imposes a number of constraints that reflect the RPC communication pattern, including the following:

- the types of input and output must describe sequences of elements (not involving the `choice` construct from XML Schema, for example); and

- the wrapper element in the body of the request message has the name of the operation.

This style can only be used with the In-Out, In-Only, and Robust In-Only patterns. Other styles are only meaningful for particular bindings (for example, *URI-style* and *multipart-style* for HTTP binding). A default style may be specified by the `styleDefault` attribute in the `interface` element (as in the example on page 482).

11.4.2 Binding Descriptions

A *binding* specifies which encodings and protocols to use for a given interface. WSDL comes with predefined bindings for SOAP and HTTP. In light of the discussions of protocol bindings for SOAP in Section 11.3.4, this may seem like déjà vu. Certainly, there is an unfortunate overlap that is caused by the design methodology of making the specifications modular and extensible in an attempt to accommodate all imaginable usage scenarios: one can use WSDL with SOAP using SOAP HTTP binding, or WSDL without SOAP using the WSDL HTTP binding. Confusion is inevitable.

WSDL supports description of services that use **SOAP** or **raw HTTP**.

In WSDL, the choice of binding is selected with the `type` attribute of the `binding` element, as illustrated in the previously shown WSDL document. Additional binding-specific information may be given for each operation.

The SOAP Binding

The SOAP binding is identified by the URI

```
http://www.w3.org/2004/08/wsdl/soap12
```

Using this binding means that messages relevant to the interface are exchanged using the SOAP processing model as explained in Section 11.3.1. This URI also acts as a namespace for information relevant to the binding. The underlying protocol, usually HTTP as explained in Section 11.3.4, is selected by setting the `protocol` attribute from this namespace to the following value:

```
http://www.w3.org/2003/05/soap/bindings/HTTP/
```

The example shown on page 482 contains a binding for SOAP using the SOAP HTTP binding underneath. The `ws:mepDefault` attribute on the `binding` element declares the default message exchange pattern as request–response using its URI (see Section 11.3.4). We could write that more explicitly using an `operation` description for each operation:

```
<binding name="recipeserverSOAPBinding"
         interface="x:recipeserverInterface"
         type="http://www.w3.org/2004/08/wsdl/soap12"
         xmlns:ws="http://www.w3.org/2004/08/wsdl/soap12"
         ws:protocol="http://www.w3.org/2003/05/soap/bindings/HTTP"
         xmlns:soap="http://www.w3.org/2003/05/soap-envelope">

  <operation ref="x:getRecipesOperation"
    ws:mep=
      "http://www.w3.org/2003/05/soap/mep/request-response"/>

  <operation ref="x:lockRecipeOperation"
    ws:mep=
      "http://www.w3.org/2003/05/soap/mep/request-response"/>

  <operation ref="x:writeRecipeOperation"
    ws:mep=
      "http://www.w3.org/2003/05/soap/mep/request-response"/>

  <operation ref="x:unlockRecipeOperation"
    ws:mep=
      "http://www.w3.org/2003/05/soap/mep/request-response"/>

  <fault ref="x:lockFault" ws:code="soap:Sender"/>
</binding>
```

Here, each operation is explicitly characterized by its SOAP message exchange pattern, and the single fault type is characterized by a SOAP fault code (see Section 11.3.2). As explained earlier, the SOAP HTTP binding only supports two message exchange patterns:

request–response and SOAP response. The WSDL patterns In-Out, In-Only, and Robust In-Only map naturally to request–response. Unfortunately, it is unclear from the current WSDL specification how the remaining message exchange patterns from WSDL work with SOAP.

Other properties of the SOAP binding that are relevant when using HTTP as underlying protocol – for example, the use of HTTP authentication – can be specified in the same way as for the WSDL HTTP binding described below.

The HTTP Binding

Not all Web services use SOAP. If the advanced features, such as intermediaries or the SOAP encoding are not needed for a particular service – and this is often the case – then the complex machinery involved in using SOAP may outweigh the benefits. Also, for simpler services, the fault mechanism in SOAP provides nothing new compared to using HTTP directly, since HTTP already has a system for status codes. To accommodate such services, WSDL also support a 'raw' HTTP binding that bypasses SOAP. This binding allows a closer connection to HTTP, which makes it fit more elegantly with the REST architectural style mentioned in Section 8.6. The HTTP binding is identified by the URI

```
http://www.w3.org/2004/08/wsdl/http
```

This binding is only defined for the patterns In-Out, In-Only, and Robust In-Only. Each of them fits naturally to an HTTP request–response interaction.

In the `binding` part of the WSDL document, each `operation` may have various attributes that are qualified by the HTTP binding namespace URI:

`method`: specifies the HTTP method (`GET`, `POST`, `PUT`, or `DELETE`) being used for the operation;

`inputSerialization`, `outputSerialization`, `faultSerialization`: specify media types for the input, output, and faults, respectively (usually `application/xml`, `application/x-www-form-urlencoded`, or `multipart/form-data` are used here); and

`location`: specifies a relative URI for the operation (relative to a URI given in the service description part described in the next section).

Unlike the HTTP binding in SOAP, the WSDL HTTP binding does support the use of GET (and also PUT and DELETE) even with operations that take arguments. This is achieved by allowing the `location` attribute to be a *template*. For example, an operation `search` that takes one argument named `q` could be specified by

```
<operation ref="x:search"
           xmlns:wh="http://www.w3.org/2004/08/wsdl/http"
           wh:method="GET"
           wh:location="search-engine/find/{q}"/>
```

Using this method requires the `inputSerialization` to be set to `application/x-www-form-urlencoded` (which is conveniently the default input serialization for GET), that is, the actual argument is URL encoded in the request URI in place of `{q}`.

Each `fault` may in the binding be associated with a HTTP status code, as in this example (where we assume that the fault has been declared in the interface description):

```
<fault ref="x:ServiceUnavailable"
       wh:code="503"/>
```

Finally, services that employ HTTP authentication may specify the type (`basic` or `digest`) and a realm name in the service description. For details, see the WSDL specification.

11.4.3 Service Descriptions

The `service` component of the WSDL document is in most cases quite simple: it connects an interface, a binding, and a service location:

```
<service name="recipeserver" interface="x:recipeserverInterface">
  <endpoint name="recipeserverEndpoint"
    binding="x:recipeserverSOAPBinding"
    address="http://www.widget.inc/personal/jdoe/recipeserver"/>
</service>
```

This particular service combines the interface and binding defined earlier and specifies the URI where the service is located.

Together, this information tells us what we need to be able to write clients of the service. Sometimes, it is not sufficient, though: a formalized interface description only covers certain aspects of a service, and there may be additional requirements that go beyond the expressiveness of WSDL. A couple of examples from our recipe service: we cannot in WSDL formalize the requirements that it is illegal to invoke `unlockRecipe` repeatedly with the same argument and that the lock passed to `writeRecipe` is obtained from an earlier invocation of `lockRecipe`. These limitations motivate the need for more advanced languages (such as WS-CDL or WS-BPEL) for formalizing complex aspects of Web service interfaces.

11.5 UDDI

UDDI, *Universal Description, Discovery, and Integration*, is a mechanism for *registering* and *discovering* Web services. UDDI may be used through browsers, but the full vision of service-oriented architectures implies that also Web services should use UDDI to find other Web services that they need to support their functionality. UDDI has grown from the equivalent of a simple yellow pages directory to a framework for brokering collaboration between Web services.

UDDI allows Web services to be **registered** and **discovered**.

For the applications we have considered so far, an external Web service would typically be discovered manually by the programmer and be hardwired into the application. This is known as *static* discovery. UDDI also targets *dynamic* discovery, where the application itself at runtime finds a required Web service selected on the basis of, for example, price, availability, or efficiency.

Static discovery has the advantage of human intelligence to determine functionality and to evaluate to what extent a service provider should be trusted. Thus, *public* UDDI registries may be used for this purpose. In contrast, dynamic discovery can only succeed with *private* UDDI registries, where the semantics and validity of entries are guaranteed by trusted organizations.

UDDI has as yet few applications, compared to the more widespread use of SOAP and WSDL, and most available case studies only consider static discovery. Thus, to some extent, UDDI seems to be a solution in search of a problem.

11.5.1 Descriptions

Web services are described in UDDI through a hierarchy of five levels:

publisherAssertion: describes the relationship between a collection of businesses, for example, that one is a subsidiary of another;

businessEntity: describes a concrete business with its contact information and a unique UDDI key;

businessService: describes a particular Web service that a business may provide, with an informal description, a unique UDDI key, and key references that capture various formal aspects;

bindingTemplate: describes how to invoke a given Web service, with a physical address and a reference to a tModel; and

tModel: describes the technical details for invoking a given Web service, typically in the form of a reference to a WSDL specification.

The UDDI language uses several levels of key/reference indirections to ensure generality and modularity.

To illustrate these concepts, we provide UDDI descriptions of the recipe service described in Section 11.4. The Widget Inc. business is described in a single XML document as follows:

```
<businessEntity xmlns="urn:uddi-org:api_v3"
                businessKey="uddi:7398388-7F63-73K3-H314-763272DA7G41">
  <name>Widget Inc.</name>
  <description>The Widget People</description>
  <contacts>
    <contact useType="Chief Executive Officer">
      <description>CEO of Widget Inc.</description>
      <personName>John Doe</personName>
      <phone useType="CEO">(202) 555-1414</phone>
      <email useType="CEO">john.doe@widget.inc</email>
```

```
      </contact>
    </contacts>

  <businessServices>
    <businessService
        serviceKey="uddi:9X65542-8JE7-8732-U893-8272634H7362"
        businessKey="uddi:7398388-7F63-73K3-H314-763272DA7G41">
      <name>Doe Personal Recipe Server</name>
      <description>John Doe's personal recipe service</description>
      <bindingTemplates>
        <bindingTemplate
            bindingKey="uddi:8H62363-K725-3345-73V5-823763FS7265"
            serviceKey="uddi:9X65542-8JE7-8732-U893-8272634H7362">
          <accessPoint URLType="http">
            http://www.widget.inc/personal/jdoe/recipeserver
          </accessPoint>
          <tModelInstanceDetails>
            <tModelInstanceInfo
              tModelKey="uddi:5241HY7-6252-KN72-7291-3126HJ8237A2"/>
          </tModelInstanceDetails>
        </bindingTemplate>
      </bindingTemplates>
    </businessService>
  </businessServices>
</businessEntity>
```

This describes first the Widget Inc. business and then the recipe service that it offers. The technical details about the service are relegated to a separate document, which looks as follows:

```
<tModel xmlns="urn:uddi-org:api_v3"
        tModelKey="uddi:5241HY7-6252-KN72-7291-3126HJ8237A2">
  <name>Doe Personal Recipe Server</name>
  <description>John Doe's personal recipe service</description>
  <overviewDoc>
    <overviewURL>
      http://www.widget.inc/personal/jdoe/recipes.wsdl
    </overviewURL>
  </overviewDoc>
  <categoryBag>
    <keyedReference
        keyName="uddi-org:types"
        keyValue="wsdlSpec"
        tModelKey="uddi:C1ACF26D-9672-4404-9D70-39B756E62AB4"/>
    <keyedReference
        keyName="IAAWG"
        keyValue="WDG18762"
        tModelKey="uddi:82761UHS-442P-1712-KL82-8272HSH76519"/>
  </categoryBag>
</tModel>
```

By itself, a `tModel` does not have to say much, but when the service is described using WSDL, then the UDDI organization proposes that this information is encoded as shown above. The `overviewDoc` element is optional and is meant as a kind of comment, but it is in this case used to carry the URL of the WSDL document. The `categoryBag` element is generally meant to encode semantic information about the given service, and the above choice of attributes for the first `keyedReference` element is by convention taken to mean that the `overviewURL` contains a link to a WSDL specification. The second `keyedReference` element states that the service is registered with the *International Association for the Advancement of Web Gastronomy*, where John Doe's recipe server has member id `WDG18762`.

By itself, the UDDI formalism seems rather vague and redundant. However, sensible use of categories will enable semantic searches for relevant services, and the conventions for encoding WSDL specifications will facilitate access to them.

11.5.2 Discovery

A UDDI registry is a Web service that accepts operations to save and delete businesses, services, and bindings. To find a particular service, a client may issue a request whose body looks as follows:

```
<find_service xmlns="urn:uddi-org:api_v3">
  <categoryBag>
    <keyedReference
        keyName="IAAWG"
        keyValue="%"
        tModelKey="uddi:82761UHS-442P-1712-KL82-8272HSH76519"/>
  </categoryBag>
</find_service>
```

This request searches for all Web services that are registered with IAAWG (since `%` is a wildcard). The response from a UDDI registry could then be the following:

```
<serviceList xmlns="urn:uddi-org:api_v3">
  <serviceInfos>
    <serviceInfo
        businessKey="uddi:7398388-7F63-73K3-H314-763272DA7G41"
        serviceKey="uddi:9X65542-8JE7-8732-U893-8272634H7362">
      <name>Doe Personal Recipe Server</name>
    </serviceInfo>
    <serviceInfo
        businessKey="uddi:82736H57-HA32-P581-0021-8373H6S73443"
        serviceKey="uddi:7252OX72-K23J-4X44-7W23-K82737292527">
      <name>Average Recipes on The Web</name>
    </serviceInfo>
  </serviceInfos>
</serviceList>
```

Further queries may then provide the WSDL specifications of these services.

11.6   Chapter Summary

The vision of Web services is that software systems should be able to interoperate based on XML and Web protocols. In this chapter we have encountered various protocols for exchanging messages and describing and locating services. A recurring theme is the balance between ad hoc solutions and standardization: in one extreme, one simply writes code that exchanges XML data using the HTTP protocol; in the other, one uses SOAP, WSDL, UDDI, and the entire WS-* stack whenever appropriate. The ad hoc approach may lead to simpler solutions for less complex Web services but may involve reinventing the wheel when developing multiple and more complex services. On the other hand, the standards-compliance approach requires deep knowledge of numerous specifications.

SOAP provides a uniform processing model of XML data involving intermediaries, fault management, encoding of object graphs, and RPC conventions – all independent of concrete transport protocols, in principle, but usually building on HTTP. Moreover, SOAP is the foundation for the WS-* specifications.

Still, the benefits of using SOAP have been debated intensely. A prototypical discussion is about whether or not the SOAP-based API for Google's Web service is better than their ad hoc HTTP API [71]. This particular Web service does not exploit intermediaries or SOAP encoding, for example, and the support for SOAP has been described as pure buzzword compliance. Many experts state that the HTTP interface is easier to use. A similar situation occurs for Amazon's Web service. In defense of SOAP, there are some general points worth noticing: First, a SOAP API is more scalable in the sense that if a later version would involve, for example, some sort of intermediaries, then the strength of SOAP becomes evident. Second, as discussed in Chapter 2 on XML, simply *agreeing* on using some protocol or notation is a major step in obtaining interoperability of systems, even if the technology is not perfectly designed.

WSDL is an interface description language for Web services. A WSDL description of a Web service shows which operations are provided, the types of their arguments and return values, bindings to encoding and communication protocols that the service requires, and the location of the service. This information is necessary for writing clients to the service. We have in this chapter described a draft of WSDL 2.0; most implementations currently support only version 1.1.

WSDL supports a range of message exchange patterns. The most widely used is In-Out, which corresponds to the request–response pattern and RPC interactions. The existing binding descriptions support SOAP and raw HTTP, although others are possible.

UDDI is a framework for providing descriptions of Web services and performing semantic searches. Its practical value relies on the quality of the categorizations and classifications provided by the supporting organizations.

SOAP, WSDL, WS-Addressing, and WS-Choreography are developed by W3C, and UDDI, WS-ReliableMessaging, WS-BPEL, WS-Resource, and WS-Security are OASIS standards (or have been submitted for standardization). An organization named *WS-I, The Web Service Interoperability Organization*, has been formed to join efforts in promoting development of Web service standards. The world of Web services is still new, and many of the specifications are working drafts. The core Web service technologies, which we have focused on in this chapter, are stabilizing, whereas much of the WS-* stack is at the time of writing a jumble of competing initiatives.

11.7   Further Reading

The SOAP 1.2 specification has two main parts, which are both W3C recommendations. Part 1 describes the core messaging framework [40], and Part 2 describes the SOAP encoding and RPC conventions [41].

The WSDL 2.0 specification consists of three main parts: Part 1 contains the core language [19], Part 2 describes message exchange patterns [42], and Part 3 describes the SOAP and HTTP bindings [43].

A popular implementation of SOAP and related technologies is Apache Axis, which can be used together with Tomcat to build Web services and clients. Axis handles SOAP envelopes and also supports construction of code stubs and skeletons from WSDL descriptions. The Axis documentation is a good place to start when you begin writing your own Web services.

To learn the details of UDDI, see the UDDI 3.0 specification [24]. For an overview of the WS-* architecture we recommend the book [85].

11.8   Online Resources

http://www.w3.org/TR/soap/
   W3C's SOAP specifications.

http://www.w3.org/2002/ws/desc/
   W3C's WSDL specifications.

http://www.uddi.org
   Web site for UDDI.

http://www.xmlrpc.com/
   Web site for XML-RPC.

http://www.google.com/apis/
   Google's Web service.

http://webservices.amazon.com/
   Amazon's Web service.

http://www.ws-i.org/
   Web site for WS-I, The Web Service Interoperability Organization.

http://www.oasis-open.org/
   OASIS's Web site, with links to their Web service committees.

http://ws.apache.org/axis/
   Apache Axis, an implementation of SOAP.

11.9   Exercises

The main lessons to be learned from these exercises are:

- how to take advantage of the main Web service standards; and
- familiarity with SOAP messages and WSDL descriptions.

Exercise 11.1 We want to implement the following chess-playing system using SOAP, WSDL, and UDDI. An *chess engine* is a service that is capable of playing chess against human opponents. It may simultaneously be engaged in multiple games. A *chess broker* is a service that performs load balancing of a collection of chess engines. That is, when a new player arrives, the chess broker is responsible for finding an available chess engine. Moreover, the identities of the chess engines must not be revealed to the players, so all communication goes through the broker. A *chess frontend* is an interactive service that allows human players to use the system.

(a) During a play, the broker may be viewed as an *intermediary* between a frontend and an engine. Give an example of a SOAP message from a chess frontend to the chess broker corresponding to a move in a game.
(b) Explain how UDDI may be used for managing registries of chess engines.
(c) Describe the chess engine and chess broker services using WSDL.

Exercise 11.2 Implement the recipe server described in Section 11.1.1 using Servlets.

Exercise 11.3 Continuing Exercise 11.2, implement the SOAP variant of the recipe server as described on page 482. (You can either implement the necessary SOAP manipulations directly using, for example, JDOM, or you can use a tool such as Axis.)

Exercise 11.4 Explain the meaning of the SOAP messages `EX/soap1.xml`, `EX/soap2.xml`, and `EX/soap3.xml`.

Exercise 11.5 Construct a SOAP encoding of the object graph illustrated at `EX/soapbubbles.gif`.

Exercise 11.6 Consider the WSDL description `EX/warehouse.wsdl`.

(a) Which operations are described?
(b) Give an example of a SOAP message corresponding to a request to the `inventory` operation.
(c) Extend the description with an operation `status` that given a `shelf` argument returns a `product` list.

TIP

You can find publicly accessible Web services on `http://www.xmethods.com/`.

Exercise 11.7 Which functionality is provided by Google's Web service? How is this described using WSDL?

Exercise 11.8 Which data is available through Amazon's Web service? Discuss pros and cons of the SOAP- and REST-based access methods that are provided.

A COMPLETE APPLICATION

12

Objectives

In this chapter, you will learn:

- How various tools can be applied in a concrete project
- How the different XML and Web technologies play together

12.1   The Web of Jokes

By now, we have obtained a toolbox full of XML and Web technologies. In this chapter we will apply these tools to implement a solution for a concrete project. Not all technologies will be used in this simple application, so part of the exercise is to select the appropriate ones. We aim for simplicity, not production quality; variations and extensions are considered in Section 12.7, Section 12.8, and in the exercises.

Our application will create the infrastructure for a worldwide network of servers and clients authoring, publishing, and reading *jokes*.

Jokes will be represented in a specially designed XML language, with appropriate markup for representing their structure. The language will be formally described using XML Schema.

The Web of Jokes consists of **servers**, **clients**, and a **metaserver**.

A *joke server* is a Web service that acts as a repository for jokes. Through appropriate operations, clients may submit and retrieve jokes (possibly restricted to certain categories). All joke servers may be registered in a global *joke metaserver* to make their services available worldwide.

A *joke client* is a Web application that offers an interface to human clients through a browser. It allows jokes to be authored and submitted to a local joke server, and makes all jokes in the servers that are known by the metaserver available for reading. From the point of view of the human clients, the joke client is itself a server that is accessed using a browser.

The network may be illustrated as follows:

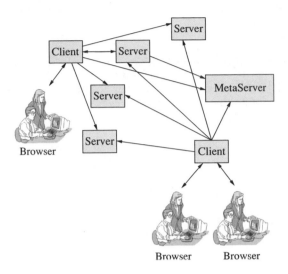

The subject of jokes in this chapter is, of course, only incidental, but the overall picture of browsers, clients, servers, and metaservers is a pattern for many applications of XML and Web technologies.

12.2 The Joke Language

As discussed in Chapter 2, to design an XML language for representing collections of jokes, we must first analyze the structure of a joke. We view the main data of a joke to consist of:

- a possibly empty sequence of *setups*; and
- a single *punchline* (hopefully funny).

A joke also has some useful metadata:

- a *category*;
- a unique *id*;
- a *date*;
- a *title*; and
- an optional *author*.

12.2.1 Representing Jokes

Given this analysis of jokes, we can define the appropriate markup. Two classical jokes are then represented as follows:

```
<jml:collection xmlns:jml="http://www.brics.dk/ixwt/jokes">
  <jml:joke id="183736363" category="animals">
    <jml:title>Two Cows in a Field</jml:title>
    <jml:date>2005-02-15</jml:date>
    <jml:author>John Doe</jml:author>
    <jml:setup>
      Two cows are standing in a field eating grass.
    </jml:setup>
    <jml:setup>
      The first cow says: "Moooo"!
    </jml:setup>
    <jml:punchline>
      The second cow replies: "Hey, I was just gonna say that"!
    </jml:punchline>
  </jml:joke>
  <jml:joke id="827272622" category="animals">
    <jml:title>Mad Cows</jml:title>
    <jml:date>2004-12-14</jml:date>
    <jml:setup>
      Two cows are talking.
    </jml:setup>
    <jml:setup>
      The first cow: "Hey, did you hear about that mad cow disease?"
    </jml:setup>
    <jml:setup>
      The second cow: "Yeah, but I'm not worried about it."
    </jml:setup>
    <jml:setup>
      The first cow: "Why not?"
    </jml:setup>
    <jml:punchline>
      The second cow: "I'm a duck."
    </jml:punchline>
  </jml:joke>
</jml:collection>
```

12.2.2 XML Schema for Jokes

Using the XML Schema language presented in Chapter 4, the joke language may be represented by the following XML Schema specification:

```
<schema xmlns="http://www.w3.org/2001/XMLSchema"
        xmlns:jml="http://www.brics.dk/ixwt/jokes"
        targetNamespace="http://www.brics.dk/ixwt/jokes"
        elementFormDefault="qualified">

  <element name="collection">
    <complexType>
      <sequence>
        <element ref="jml:joke" minOccurs="0" maxOccurs="unbounded"/>
      </sequence>
    </complexType>
    <unique name="joke-id-uniqueness">
      <selector xpath=".//jml:joke"/>
      <field xpath="@id"/>
    </unique>
  </element>

  <element name="joke">
    <complexType>
      <sequence>
        <element name="title" type="string"/>
        <element name="date" type="date"/>
        <element name="author" type="string" minOccurs="0"/>
        <element name="setup" type="string"
                 minOccurs="0" maxOccurs="unbounded"/>
        <element name="punchline" type="string"/>
      </sequence>
      <attribute name="id" type="unsignedLong" use="required"/>
      <attribute name="category" type="string" use="required"/>
    </complexType>
  </element>

</schema>
```

In this specification, we have made some choices:

- the id attributes of jokes must be unique (this requirement actually extends to all jokes in the network, but the schema can, of course, only enforce this for a single document);

- the date element is of the XML Schema simple type date;

- an id attribute is of the XML Schema simple type unsignedLong; and

- the setup and punchline elements are not formatted.

12.2.3 XSLT for Jokes

As presented in Chapter 5, we may wish to create an XSLT stylesheet for rendering a collection of jokes in XHTML. A simple solution looks as follows:

```
<xsl:stylesheet version="2.0"
      xmlns="http://www.w3.org/1999/xhtml"
      xmlns:jml="http://www.brics.dk/ixwt/jokes"
      xmlns:xsl="http://www.w3.org/1999/XSL/Transform">
  <xsl:template match="jml:collection">
    <html>
      <head>
        <title>Jokes</title>
        <link href="style.css" rel="stylesheet" type="text/css"/>
      </head>
      <body>
        <hr/>
        <ul>
          <xsl:apply-templates select="jml:joke" mode="summary"/>
        </ul>
        <xsl:apply-templates select="jml:joke" mode="full"/>
        <hr/>
      </body>
    </html>
  </xsl:template>

  <xsl:template match="jml:joke" mode="summary">
    <li><a href="#{@id}"><xsl:value-of select="jml:title"/></a></li>
  </xsl:template>

  <xsl:template match="jml:joke" mode="full">
    <hr/>
    <h3><a name="{@id}"><xsl:value-of select="jml:title"/></a></h3>
    <i>
      <xsl:value-of select="jml:author"/>
      (<xsl:value-of select="jml:date"/>)
    </i>
    <ul>
      <xsl:apply-templates select="jml:setup"/>
      <xsl:apply-templates select="jml:punchline"/>
    </ul>
  </xsl:template>

  <xsl:template match="jml:setup|jml:punchline">
    <li><xsl:value-of select="."/></li>
  </xsl:template>

</xsl:stylesheet>
```

This stylesheet first generates a summary of the joke titles with links to the individual jokes, which are then written quite plainly. The XSLT stylesheet refers to a CSS stylesheet which defines the layout of the generated XHTML documents, as discussed in Chapter 1. It looks as follows:

```
body {
  font-family: sans-serif;
  color: black;
  background: white;
  margin-left: 4%;
  margin-right: 3%;
}
h1, h2 {
  text-align: center;
  margin-top: 1pt;
  margin-bottom: 1pt;
}
h1 {
  color: #888;
  font: 50px/50px "Impact", sans-serif;
}
h2 {
  color: #008;
  font: bold 35px/35px "Verdana", sans-serif;
}
h3 {
  color: #800;
  font-size: 15pt;
  margin-left: -2%;
}
hr {
  margin-left: -2%;
  margin-right: -1%;
}
a:link {
  color: #c00;
}
a:visited {
  color: #800;
}
a:active {
  color: #f00;
}
```

With these definitions, the previous collection of cow jokes is rendered as follows:

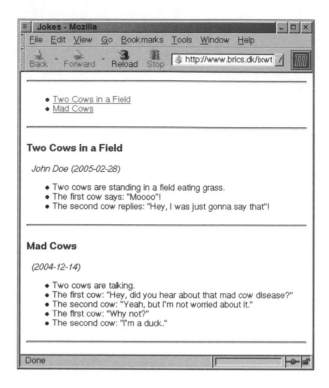

12.3 The Joke Server

A joke server is a repository for a (growing) collection of jokes. For our purposes, this data is simply stored in a JDOM tree which is occasionally backed up on the disk. A JDBC database would, of course, be a more robust and efficient choice, in which case the XML document could be stored as discussed in Section 6.9.

The components of our implementation of the joke server are listed in Figure 12.1.

```
Jokes.java: a class that manages the current joke collection

List.java: a servlet that lists the known joke categories

categories.xsl: an XSLT stylesheet that extracts categories from a joke collection

Retrieve.java: a servlet that retrieves the known jokes of a given category

retrieve.xsl: an XSLT stylesheet that selects jokes of a given category

Submit.java: a servlet for submitting another joke to the server

jokes.xsd: a schema for the XML language representing jokes
```

Figure 12.1 Components of the joke *server* implementation.

12.3.1 State

The state of a joke server is quite simple, being just a single joke document. Updates to this document should naturally be synchronized to avoid loss of data.

12.3.2 Operations

The joke server supports three kinds of operations, all implemented through XML over HTTP (as discussed in Chapter 11). First, it is possible to request the *list* of categories that occur in a collection of jokes. The answer is returned in a simple XML document:

```
<categories xmlns="http://www.brics.dk/ixwt/categories">
  <category>animals</category>
  <category>lawyers</category>
  <category>blondes</category>
  <category>XML Schema</category>
</categories>
```

Second, a client may *retrieve* all jokes belonging to a given category. Third, a client may *submit* a joke document which is then added to the current collection. When submitting, the XML document containing the jokes is placed in the body part of an HTTP POST request.

For this simple application, the above informal description is sufficient. A larger project would, of course, document the interface using WSDL (as discussed in Section 11.4).

12.3.3 Implementation

We implement each operation as a servlet. We want to apply the MVC pattern (as discussed in Section 10.3), so we first need a class `Jokes` to manage the XML document containing the current joke collection:

```
import java.io.*;
import org.jdom.*;
import org.jdom.input.*;
import org.jdom.output.*;
import javax.servlet.*;

public class Jokes {
  static Namespace jml =
    Namespace.getNamespace("http://www.brics.dk/ixwt/jokes");

  ServletContext context;
  String jokeFile;
  Document jokes;

  public Jokes(ServletContext context)
      throws JDOMException, IOException {
    this.context = context;
```

```
      jokes = (Document)context.getAttribute("jokes");
      jokeFile = context.getInitParameter("JokeFile");
      if (jokes==null) {
        try {
          jokes = new SAXBuilder().build(new File(jokeFile));
        } catch (Exception e) {
          jokes = new Document(new Element("collection", jml));
        }
        context.setAttribute("jokes", jokes);
      }
    }

    public Document getJokes() {
      return jokes;
    }

    public void addJokes(Document more)
        throws JDOMException, IOException {
      synchronized(context) {
        jokes.getRootElement()
             .addContent(more.getRootElement().removeContent());
        new XMLOutputter()
             .output(jokes, new FileOutputStream(new File(jokeFile)));
      }
    }
  }
```

The collection of jokes is backed up on the file system in the location specified by the `jokeFile` string. A copy of the corresponding JDOM tree is stored in the current `ServletContext` object as an attribute named `jokes`. When jokes are added to the collection, the `addJokes` method enforces a critical region by synchronizing on the current `Servlet Context` object (of which only one exists for the entire Web application) and the copy on the file system is updated.

The `List` operation is implemented as a simple servlet that employs an XSLT stylesheet to perform the actual transformation (as discussed in Section 7.3.5). This servlet looks as follows:

```
import java.io.*;
import org.jdom.*;
import org.jdom.output.*;
import org.jdom.transform.*;
import javax.servlet.*;
import javax.servlet.http.*;

public class List extends HttpServlet {
  public void doGet(HttpServletRequest request,
                    HttpServletResponse response)
      throws IOException, ServletException {
```

```
        try {
          response.setContentType("text/xml");
          Document doc = new Jokes(getServletContext()).getJokes();
          String xslt =
            getServletContext().getInitParameter("CategoriesXSLT");
          XSLTransformer t = new XSLTransformer(xslt);
          new XMLOutputter().output(t.transform(doc),
                                    response.getWriter());
        } catch (Exception e) {
          response.sendError(500, "Internal error");
        }
      }
    }
  }
```

To simplify the code, we perform only a rudimentary error handling; in Section 12.7, we discuss how to make the application more robust. Above, the location of the following XSLT stylesheet is obtained through an initialization parameter from the deployment descriptor:

```
<xsl:stylesheet version="2.0"
    xmlns="http://www.brics.dk/ixwt/categories"
    xmlns:jml="http://www.brics.dk/ixwt/jokes"
    xmlns:xsl="http://www.w3.org/1999/XSL/Transform">

  <xsl:template match="jml:collection">
    <categories>
      <xsl:for-each-group select="jml:joke" group-by="@category">
        <category>
          <xsl:value-of select="current-grouping-key()"/>
        </category>
      </xsl:for-each-group>
    </categories>
  </xsl:template>

</xsl:stylesheet>
```

This stylesheet is rather straightforward and uses the for-each-group construction to remove duplicate categories. However, since the current version of JAXP only supports XSLT 1.0 (and thus not for-each-group), we may have to use a more contorted and inefficient stylesheet:

```
<xsl:stylesheet version="1.0"
    xmlns="http://www.brics.dk/ixwt/categories"
    xmlns:jml="http://www.brics.dk/ixwt/jokes"
    xmlns:xsl="http://www.w3.org/1999/XSL/Transform">

  <xsl:template match="jml:collection">
    <categories>
```

```
        <xsl:apply-templates select=
            "jml:joke[not(@category=following::jml:joke/@category)]"/>
      </categories>
    </xsl:template>

    <xsl:template match="jml:joke">
      <category>
        <xsl:value-of select="@category"/>
      </category>
    </xsl:template>

</xsl:stylesheet>
```

The Retrieve operation is implemented in a similar manner. It accepts a parameter category, which contains the desired category:

```
import java.io.*;
import org.jdom.*;
import org.jdom.input.*;
import org.jdom.output.*;
import org.jdom.transform.*;
import javax.servlet.*;
import javax.servlet.http.*;
import javax.xml.transform.*;
import javax.xml.transform.stream.*;

public class Retrieve extends HttpServlet {
  public void doGet(HttpServletRequest request,
                    HttpServletResponse response)
      throws IOException, ServletException {
    try {
      response.setContentType("text/xml");
      Document doc = new Jokes(getServletContext()).getJokes();
      Transformer t =
        TransformerFactory.newInstance()
          .newTransformer(new StreamSource(new File(
            getServletContext().getInitParameter("RetrieveXSLT"))));
      JDOMSource in = new JDOMSource(doc);
      JDOMResult out = new JDOMResult();
      t.setParameter("category", request.getParameter("category"));
      t.transform(in, out);
      new XMLOutputter().output(out.getDocument(),
                                response.getWriter());
    } catch (Exception e) {
      response.sendError(500, "Internal error");
    }
  }
}
```

The associated XSLT stylesheet looks as follows:

```
<xsl:stylesheet version="2.0"
    xmlns="http://www.brics.dk/ixwt/categories"
    xmlns:jml="http://www.brics.dk/ixwt/jokes"
    xmlns:xsl="http://www.w3.org/1999/XSL/Transform">

  <xsl:param name="category"/>

  <xsl:template match="jml:collection">
    <xsl:copy>
      <xsl:apply-templates select="jml:joke[@category=$category]"/>
    </xsl:copy>
  </xsl:template>

  <xsl:template match="/|@*|node()">
    <xsl:copy>
      <xsl:apply-templates select="@*|node()"/>
    </xsl:copy>
  </xsl:template>
</xsl:stylesheet>
```

It produces a copy of the XML document, except that only jokes with the desired category attribute are considered. We could, of course, also have used JDOM to implement the same functionality.

The Submit operation is implemented as a servlet that must be invoked using the POST method (as discussed in Section 8.1.1):

```
import java.io.*;
import org.jdom.*;
import org.jdom.input.*;
import javax.servlet.*;
import javax.servlet.http.*;

public class Submit extends HttpServlet {
  static Namespace jml =
    Namespace.getNamespace("http://www.brics.dk/ixwt/jokes");

  public void doPost(HttpServletRequest request,
                     HttpServletResponse response)
      throws IOException, ServletException {
    PrintWriter out = response.getWriter();
    SAXBuilder b = new SAXBuilder();
    b.setValidation(true);
    b.setProperty(
      "http://java.sun.com/xml/jaxp/properties/schemaLanguage",
      "http://www.w3.org/2001/XMLSchema");
```

```
   b.setProperty(
     "http://java.sun.com/xml/jaxp/properties/schemaSource",
     getServletContext().getInitParameter("JokesXSD"));
   try {
     Document doc = b.build(request.getInputStream());
     if (!doc.getRootElement().getNamespaceURI().equals(jml))
       response.sendError(400, "Wrong namespace of root element!");
     else
       new Jokes(getServletContext()).addJokes(doc);
   } catch (Exception e) {
     response.sendError(500, "Internal error");
   }
 }
}
```

Notice that we perform a validation against the XML Schema specification (see Section 7.3.3) to ensure that only valid jokes are added to the repository.

12.4   The Joke Metaserver

The metaserver exists to allow the servers to be registered and discovered. It also generates unique IDs for consumption of the joke clients. The components of our implementation are listed in Figure 12.2. In an exercise, we examine using UDDI as an alternative.

12.4.1   State

Since a joke client needs access to the two operations List and Retrieve for each joke server, we represent a collection of joke servers as illustrated by the following example:

```
<servers xmlns="http://www.brics.dk/ixwt/servers">
  <server>
    <list>http://example.org/ixwt-jokeserver/list</list>
    <retrieve>http://example.org/ixwt-jokeserver/retrieve</retrieve>
  </server>
```

Servers.java: a class that manages the collection of servers

Register.java: a servlet that registers a new server

register.html: an HTML page for registering a new server

Discover.java: a servlet that returns information about all registered servers

Unique.java: a servlet that returns a unique integer (for creating IDs)

Figure 12.2 Components of the joke *metaserver* implementation.

```
<server>
  <list>http://www.widget.inc/funny/do_list</list>
  <retrieve>http://www.widget.inc/funny/do_retrieve</retrieve>
</server>
</servers>
```

Note that the above servers presumably reside on different physical servers that each use appropriate deployment descriptors to interpret the respective operation URLs (as discussed in Section 9.3).

12.4.2 Operations

The metaserver is fairly similar to a joke server. It has an operation `Register` for adding a new joke server, and an operation `Discover` for obtaining the full list of registered joke servers. The `Unique` operation returns an integer that may be used as a unique ID.

12.4.3 Implementation

We first implement a wrapper class for storing the XML document containing the list of servers:

```
import java.io.*;
import org.jdom.*;
import org.jdom.input.*;
import org.jdom.output.*;
import javax.servlet.*;

public class Servers {
  String serverFile;
  static Namespace sml =
    Namespace.getNamespace("http://www.brics.dk/ixwt/servers");
  ServletContext context;
  Document servers;

  public Servers(ServletContext context)
      throws JDOMException, IOException {
    this.context = context;
    serverFile = context.getInitParameter("ServerFile");
    servers = (Document)context.getAttribute("servers");
    if (servers==null) {
      try {
        servers = new SAXBuilder().build(new File(serverFile));
      } catch (Exception e) {
        servers = new Document(new Element("servers", sml));
      }
```

```
      context.setAttribute("servers", servers);
    }
  }

  public Document getServers() {
    return servers;
  }

  public void addServer(String l, String r)
      throws JDOMException, IOException {
    Element server = new Element("server", sml);
    Element list = new Element("list", sml);
    Element retrieve = new Element("retrieve", sml);
    list.addContent(l);
    retrieve.addContent(r);
    server.addContent(list).addContent(retrieve);
    synchronized(context) {
      servers.getRootElement().addContent(server);
      new XMLOutputter()
        .output(servers,
                new FileOutputStream(new File(serverFile)));
    }
  }
}
```

The `Register` operation is implemented as a servlet that accepts two parameters corresponding to the URIs of joke server operations:

```
import java.io.*;
import org.jdom.*;
import javax.servlet.*;
import javax.servlet.http.*;

public class Register extends HttpServlet {
  public void doGet(HttpServletRequest request,
                    HttpServletResponse response)
      throws IOException, ServletException {
    response.setContentType("text/html");
    PrintWriter out = response.getWriter();
    String list = request.getParameter("list");
    String retrieve = request.getParameter("retrieve");
    out.println("<html>");
    out.println("<head><title>Joke MetaServer</title></head>");
    out.println("<body>");
    try {
      new Servers(getServletContext()).addServer(list, retrieve);
      out.println("Joke Server successfully registered.");
    } catch (Exception e) {
```

```
         out.println("Joke Server failed to register.");
      }
      out.println("</body>");
      out.println("</html>");
   }
 }
```

This operation may be invoked through a URL such as

```
  http://www.brics.dk:8080/ixwt-jokes/Register?list=foo&retrieve=bar
```

or using the following HTML form, `register.html`:

```
<html>
  <head>
    <title>Joke MetaServer</title>
    <link href="style.css" rel="stylesheet" type="text/css"/>
  </head>
  <body>
    <form method="GET" action="Register">
      <table border="0">
        <tr>
          <td>List:</td>
          <td><input type="text" name="list" size="40"/></td>
        </tr>
        <tr>
          <td>Retrieve:</td>
          <td><input type="text" name="retrieve" size="40"/></td>
        </tr>
      </table>
      <input type="submit" value="Register"/>
    </form>
  </body>
</html>
```

A person wishing to register a joke server is then met with the following HTML form:

The `Discover` operation is just a tiny servlet that returns the XML document containing the registered joke servers:

```
import java.io.*;
import org.jdom.*;
```

```
import org.jdom.output.*;
import javax.servlet.*;
import javax.servlet.http.*;

public class Discover extends HttpServlet {
  public void doGet(HttpServletRequest request,
                    HttpServletResponse response)
      throws IOException, ServletException {
    try {
      response.setContentType("text/xml");
      Document doc = new Servers(getServletContext()).getServers();
      new XMLOutputter().output(doc, response.getWriter());
    } catch (Exception e) {
      response.sendError(500, "Internal error");
    }
  }
}
```

Finally, the Unique operation is a servlet that returns a random number:

```
import java.io.*;
import javax.servlet.*;
import javax.servlet.http.*;
import java.util.*;

public class Unique extends HttpServlet {
  public void doGet(HttpServletRequest request,
                    HttpServletResponse response)
      throws IOException, ServletException {
    response.setContentType("text/xml");
    long x = Math.abs(new Random().nextLong());
    response.getWriter().println("<id>"+x+"</id>");
  }
}
```

Strictly speaking, random numbers are not guaranteed to be unique, but with the given range this technique is a safe and common solution.

12.5   The Joke Client

A joke client interacts with people around the world, who wish to read and write jokes. Thus, it is a client to a joke server but a server from the point of view of a human client using a browser. It works as an interface both to a local joke server and to the global joke metaserver.

When reading jokes, the joke client contacts all joke servers known to the joke metaserver, and their combined list of categories is collected. The user then selects a category from the

```
Read.java: a servlet that allows human clients to read jokes

choose.jsp: a JSP page that gives a choice of joke categories

Show.java: a servlet that presents jokes of the chosen category

Write.java: a servlet that allows human clients to write jokes

collect.jsp: a JSP page that collects metadata for a new joke

Compose.java: a servlet that collects data for a new joke

contents.jsp: a JSP page for writing a part of a joke

thanks.jsp: a JSP page for acknowledging a new joke

main.html: an HTML page for accessing The Web of Jokes
```

Figure 12.3 Components of the joke *client* implementation.

combined list and all jokes of that category are collected from all (relevant) joke servers and presented.

When writing jokes, the joke client allows the user to choose a category from the existing ones or to invent a new category. The data for the joke is entered, a unique ID is retrieved from the metaserver, and the joke is submitted into the local joke server.

The components of our implementation are listed in Figure 12.3.

12.5.1   State

A joke client does not need any global state, since it relies on the joke servers and the joke metaserver.

12.5.2   Operations

A joke client has two operations, Read and Write. Each of these may, of course, involve multiple interactions with the user.

12.5.3   Implementation

A plain, unadorned implementation of a joke client is fairly simple to implement. First, the Read operation is implemented as a servlet that works a controller in the MVC pattern (see Section 10.3):

```
import java.io.*;
import java.util.*;
import org.jdom.*;
import org.jdom.filter.*;
import org.jdom.input.*;
```

```
import javax.servlet.*;
import javax.servlet.http.*;
import java.net.*;

public class Read extends HttpServlet {
  static Namespace cml =
    Namespace.getNamespace("http://www.brics.dk/ixwt/category");
  static Namespace sml =
    Namespace.getNamespace("http://www.brics.dk/ixwt/servers");

  public void doGet(HttpServletRequest request,
                    HttpServletResponse response)
      throws IOException, ServletException {
    try {
      ServletContext context = getServletContext();
      HashSet categories = new HashSet();
      SAXBuilder b = new SAXBuilder();
      Element servers =
        b.build(new URL(context.getInitParameter("DiscoverURL")))
          .getRootElement();
      Iterator i =
        servers.getDescendants(new ElementFilter("list", sml));
      while (i.hasNext()) {
        Element s = (Element)i.next();
        try {
          Element c = b.build(new URL(s.getText()))
                        .getRootElement();
          Iterator j = c.getChildren().iterator();
          while (j.hasNext())
            categories.add(((Element)j.next()).getText());
        } catch (Exception e) {}
      }
      request.setAttribute("categories", categories);
      RequestDispatcher dispatcher =
        context.getRequestDispatcher("/choose.jsp");
      dispatcher.forward(request, response);
    } catch (Exception e) {
      response.sendError(500, "Internal error");
    }
  }
}
```

First, the Discover servlet of the metaserver is invoked to obtain the list of known joke servers. Each of these is then queried to obtain the total list of available joke categories. The Read servlet then passes control to the following JSP page called choose.jsp which generates the appropriate view:

```
<%@ taglib uri="http://java.sun.com/jstl/core" prefix="c"%>
<html>
```

```
  <head>
    <title>Joke Client</title>
    <link href="style.css" rel="stylesheet" type="text/css"/>
  </head>
  <body>
    <form method="GET" action="show">
      Please select the desired category:
      <select name="category">
        <c:forEach var="category" items="${categories}">
          <option>${category}</option>
        </c:forEach>
      </select>
      <br/>
      <input type="submit" value="Select"/>
    </form>
  </body>
</html>
```

This page generates output looking as follows:

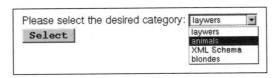

This is mostly a static HTML page, except that the category options are dynamically generated. Note that we use the forEach tag from JSTL to iterate through the categories set.

When the user submits the form data, the final interaction is handled by a Show servlet:

```
import java.io.*;
import java.util.*;
import org.jdom.*;
import org.jdom.input.*;
import org.jdom.output.*;
import javax.servlet.*;
import javax.servlet.http.*;
import java.net.*;

public class Show extends HttpServlet {
  static Namespace jml =
    Namespace.getNamespace("http://www.brics.dk/ixwt/jokes");
  static Namespace cml =
    Namespace.getNamespace("http://www.brics.dk/ixwt/category");
  static Namespace sml =
    Namespace.getNamespace("http://www.brics.dk/ixwt/servers");
```

```
      public void doGet(HttpServletRequest request,
                        HttpServletResponse response)
         throws IOException, ServletException {
      try {
        Element jokes = new Element("collection", jml);
        response.setContentType("text/xml");
        ServletContext context = getServletContext();
        SAXBuilder b = new SAXBuilder();
        Element servers =
          b.build(new URL(context.getInitParameter("DiscoverURL")))
            .getRootElement();
        String category = request.getParameter("category");
        Iterator i = servers.getChildren().iterator();
        while (i.hasNext()) {
          Element s = (Element)i.next();
          try {
            URL r = new URL(s.getChildText("retrieve", sml)+
                            URLEncoder.encode("?category="+category));
            Element j = b.build(r).getRootElement();
            jokes = jokes.addContent(j.removeContent());
          } catch (Exception e) {}
        }
        Document doc = new Document();
        Map m = new HashMap();
        m.put("type", "text/xsl");
        m.put("href", "jokes.xsl");
        doc.addContent(new ProcessingInstruction("xml-stylesheet", m))
          .addContent(jokes);
        new XMLOutputter().output(doc, response.getWriter());
      } catch (Exception e) {
        response.sendError(500, "Internal Error");
      }
    }
  }
}
```

This servlet queries all the known servers to obtain the joint collection of jokes of the
chosen category. This XML document is then instrumented with the XSLT stylesheet from
Section 12.2.3, which is evaluated on the client side (server side evaluation could have been
performed as discussed in Section 9.4.2).

The Write operation is initially handled by the following servlet, which is quite similar
to the Read servlet:

```
import java.io.*;
import java.util.*;
import org.jdom.*;
import org.jdom.filter.*;
import org.jdom.input.*;
import javax.servlet.*;
```

```java
import javax.servlet.http.*;
import java.net.*;

public class Write extends HttpServlet {
  static Namespace cml =
    Namespace.getNamespace("http://www.brics.dk/ixwt/category");
  static Namespace sml =
    Namespace.getNamespace("http://www.brics.dk/ixwt/servers");

  public void doGet(HttpServletRequest request,
                    HttpServletResponse response)
      throws IOException, ServletException {
    try {
      HashSet categories = new HashSet();
      ServletContext context = getServletContext();
      SAXBuilder b = new SAXBuilder();
      Element servers =
        b.build(new URL(context.getInitParameter("DiscoverURL")))
          .getRootElement();
      Iterator i =
        servers.getDescendants(new ElementFilter("list", sml));
      while (i.hasNext()) {
        Element s = (Element)i.next();
        try {
          Element c = b.build(new URL(s.getText())).getRootElement();
          Iterator j = c.getChildren().iterator();
          while (j.hasNext())
            categories.add(((Element)j.next()).getText());
        } catch (Exception e) {}
      }
      request.setAttribute("categories", categories);
      RequestDispatcher dispatcher =
        context.getRequestDispatcher("/collect.jsp");
      dispatcher.forward(request, response);
    } catch (Exception e) {
    response.sendError(500, "Internal Error");
    }
  }
}
```

The JSP page `collect.jsp` collects metadata about the new joke from the user (except the current date):

```jsp
<%@ taglib uri="http://java.sun.com/jstl/core" prefix="c"%>
<html>
  <head>
    <title>Joke Client</title>
```

```
        <link href="style.css" rel="stylesheet" type="text/css"/>
    </head>
    <body>
      <form method="POST" action="Compose">
        <table border="0">
          <tr>
            <td>Please select the desired category:</td>
            <td>
              <select name="category">
                <c:forEach var="category" items="${categories}">
                  <option>${category}</option>
                </c:forEach>
              </select>
            </td>
          </tr>
          <tr>
            <td>Or define a new category:</td>
            <td><input type="text" name="newcat" size="40"/>
          </tr>
          <tr>
            <td>Author:</td>
            <td><input type="text" name="author" size="40"/>
          </tr>
          <tr>
            <td>Title:</td>
            <td><input type="text" name="title" size="40"/>
          </tr>
          <tr>
            <td><input type="submit" value="Continue"/></td>
          </tr>
      </form>
    </body>
</html>
```

The generated page looks as follows:

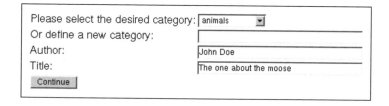

The submitted data is then transferred to the Compose servlet, which collects the setups and the punchline for the joke. Each part is collected by the contents.jsp page, which invokes Compose again, until all parts of the joke have been collected.

```java
import java.io.*;
import java.util.*;
import org.jdom.*;
import org.jdom.input.*;
import org.jdom.output.*;
import javax.servlet.*;
import javax.servlet.http.*;
import java.net.*;

public class Compose extends HttpServlet {
  static Namespace jml =
    Namespace.getNamespace("http://www.brics.dk/ixwt/jokes");

  String pad2(int i) {
    if (i<10)
      return "0"+i;
    else
      return String.valueOf(i);
  }

  public void doGet(HttpServletRequest request,
                    HttpServletResponse response)
      throws IOException, ServletException {
    try {
      response.setContentType("text/html");
      HttpSession session = request.getSession(true);
      ServletContext context = getServletContext();
      String part = request.getParameter("part");
      Element joke;
      if (part==null) {
        String category = request.getParameter("category");
        String newcat = request.getParameter("newcat");
        if (!newcat.equals(""))
          category = newcat;
        String title = request.getParameter("title");
        String author = request.getParameter("author");
        SAXBuilder b = new SAXBuilder();
        String id =
          b.build(new URL(context.getInitParameter("UniqueURL")))
            .getRootElement().getText();
        Calendar calendar = new GregorianCalendar();
        String date = calendar.get(Calendar.YEAR)+"-"+
                      pad2(calendar.get(Calendar.MONTH))+"-"+
                      pad2(calendar.get(Calendar.DATE));
        joke = new Element("joke", jml)
                 .setAttribute("id", id)
                 .setAttribute("category", category)
                 .addContent(new Element("title", jml)
                                 .setText(title))
```

```
                    .addContent(new Element("date", jml)
                                .setText(date))
                    .addContent(new Element("author", jml)
                                .setText(author));
          session.setAttribute("joke", joke);
        } else {
          joke = (Element)session.getAttribute("joke");
          String contents = request.getParameter("contents");
          Element e;
          if (part.equals("setup"))
            e = new Element("setup", jml).setText(contents);
          else
            e = new Element("punchline", jml).setText(contents);
          joke.addContent(e);
        }
        if (part==null || part.equals("setup")) {
          RequestDispatcher dispatcher =
            context.getRequestDispatcher("/contents.jsp");
          dispatcher.forward(request, response);
        } else {
          URL url = new URL(context.getInitParameter("SubmitURL"));
          HttpURLConnection connection =
            (HttpURLConnection)url.openConnection();
          connection.setRequestMethod("POST");
          connection.setDoOutput(true);
          OutputStream outs = connection.getOutputStream();
          Document doc = new Document(new Element("collection", jml)
                            .addContent(joke));
          new XMLOutputter().output(doc, outs);
          outs.close();
          if (connection.getResponseCode()!=200)
            throw new ServletException("Submit failed");
          RequestDispatcher dispatcher =
            getServletContext().getRequestDispatcher("/thanks.jsp");
          dispatcher.forward(request, response);
        }
      } catch (Exception e) {
        response.sendError(500, "Internal error");
      }
    }
  }
}
```

Note that we use POST to comply with the safety requirement mentioned in Section 8.1.3. The contents.jsp page looks as follows:

```
<html>
  <head>
    <title>Joke Client</title>
```

```
      <link href="style.css" rel="stylesheet" type="text/css"/>
  </head>
  <body>
    <form method="GET" action="Compose">
      <input type="radio" name="part" value="setup" checked="checked"/>
        Setup
      <input type="radio" name="part" value="punchline"/>
        Punchline
      <p/>
      <textarea name="contents" cols="40" rows="20"></textarea>
      <p/>
      <input type="submit" value="Continue"/>
    </form>
  </body>
</html>
```

One of the generated pages looks as follows:

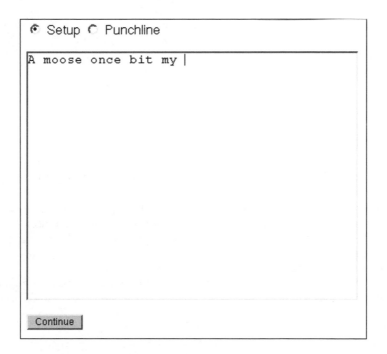

The final acknowledgement to the user is provided by the JSP page `thanks.jsp`:

```
<html>
  <head>
    <title>Joke Client</title>
```

```
      <link href="style.css" rel="stylesheet" type="text/css"/>
    </head>
    <body>
      Thank you!
    </body>
  </html>
```

As a front page to the joke client, we may use an HTML document such as the following:

```
<html>
  <head>
    <title>The Web of Jokes</title>
    <link href="style.css" rel="stylesheet" type="text/css"/>
  </head>
  <body>
    <h1>The Web of Jokes</h1>
    <form method="GET" action="Read">
      <input type="submit" value="Read a joke"/>
    </form>
    <form method="GET" action="Write">
      <input type="submit" value="Write a joke"/>
    </form>
  </body>
</html>
```

12.6   Deployment

The deployment of the metaserver is defined by the following web.xml file:

```
<web-app xmlns="http://java.sun.com/xml/ns/j2ee" version="2.4">
  <display-name>Web of Jokes: MetaServer</display-name>

  <context-param>
    <param-name>ServerFile</param-name>
    <param-value>/users/jdoe/jokes/servers.xml</param-value>
  </context-param>

  <servlet>
    <servlet-name>Register</servlet-name>
    <servlet-class>Register</servlet-class>
  </servlet>

  <servlet-mapping>
    <servlet-name>Register</servlet-name>
    <url-pattern>/Register</url-pattern>
  </servlet-mapping>
```

```
  <servlet>
    <servlet-name>Discover</servlet-name>
    <servlet-class>Discover</servlet-class>
  </servlet>

  <servlet-mapping>
    <servlet-name>Discover</servlet-name>
    <url-pattern>/Discover</url-pattern>
  </servlet-mapping>

  <servlet>
    <servlet-name>Unique</servlet-name>
    <servlet-class>Unique</servlet-class>
  </servlet>

  <servlet-mapping>
    <servlet-name>Unique</servlet-name>
    <url-pattern>/Unique</url-pattern>
  </servlet-mapping>
</web-app>
```

The deployment of the server is defined by the following web.xml file:

```
<web-app xmlns="http://java.sun.com/xml/ns/j2ee" version="2.4">
  <display-name>Web of Jokes: Server</display-name>

  <context-param>
    <param-name>JokeFile</param-name>
    <param-value>/users/jdoe/jokes/jokes.xml</param-value>
  </context-param>

  <context-param>
    <param-name>JokesXSD</param-name>
    <param-value>/users/jdoe/jokes/jokes.xsd</param-value>
  </context-param>

  <context-param>
    <param-name>RetrieveXSLT</param-name>
    <param-value>/users/jdoe/jokes/retrieve.xsl</param-value>
  </context-param>

  <context-param>
    <param-name>CategoriesXSLT</param-name>
    <param-value>/users/jdoe/jokes/categories.xsl</param-value>
  </context-param>

  <servlet>
    <servlet-name>List</servlet-name>
```

```
      <servlet-class>List</servlet-class>
   </servlet>

   <servlet-mapping>
      <servlet-name>List</servlet-name>
      <url-pattern>/List</url-pattern>
   </servlet-mapping>

   <servlet>
      <servlet-name>Retrieve</servlet-name>
      <servlet-class>Retrieve</servlet-class>
   </servlet>

   <servlet-mapping>
      <servlet-name>Retrieve</servlet-name>
      <url-pattern>/Retrieve</url-pattern>
   </servlet-mapping>

   <servlet>
      <servlet-name>Submit</servlet-name>
      <servlet-class>Submit</servlet-class>
   </servlet>

   <servlet-mapping>
      <servlet-name>Submit</servlet-name>
      <url-pattern>/Submit</url-pattern>
   </servlet-mapping>
</web-app>
```

The deployment of the server is defined by the following `web.xml` file:

```
<web-app xmlns="http://java.sun.com/xml/ns/j2ee" version="2.4">
   <display-name>Web of Jokes: Client</display-name>

   <context-param>
      <param-name>SubmitURL</param-name>
      <param-value>
         http://www.brics.dk:8080/ixwt-jokes/Submit
      </param-value>
   </context-param>

   <context-param>
      <param-name>UniqueURL</param-name>
      <param-value>
         http://www.brics.dk:8080/ixwt-jokes/Unique
      </param-value>
   </context-param>
```

```xml
<context-param>
  <param-name>DiscoverURL</param-name>
  <param-value>
    http://www.brics.dk:8080/ixwt-jokes/Discover
  </param-value>
</context-param>

<servlet>
  <servlet-name>Read</servlet-name>
  <servlet-class>Read</servlet-class>
</servlet>

<servlet-mapping>
  <servlet-name>Read</servlet-name>
  <url-pattern>/Read</url-pattern>
</servlet-mapping>

<servlet>
  <servlet-name>Show</servlet-name>
  <servlet-class>Show</servlet-class>
</servlet>

<servlet-mapping>
  <servlet-name>Show</servlet-name>
  <url-pattern>/Show</url-pattern>
</servlet-mapping>

<servlet>
  <servlet-name>Write</servlet-name>
  <servlet-class>Write</servlet-class>
</servlet>

<servlet-mapping>
  <servlet-name>Write</servlet-name>
  <url-pattern>/Write</url-pattern>
</servlet-mapping>

<servlet>
  <servlet-name>Compose</servlet-name>
  <servlet-class>Compose</servlet-class>
</servlet>

<servlet-mapping>
  <servlet-name>Compose</servlet-name>
  <url-pattern>/Compose</url-pattern>
</servlet-mapping>
</web-app>
```

12.7   Robustness

In the above implementation, we have used a casual approach to handling exceptions that may occur to simplify the presentation of the code. To obtain a robust production quality, we should make conscious choice about all possible exceptions.

As an example, consider again the `List` servlet which we have implemented as follows:

```
public class List extends HttpServlet {
  public void doGet(HttpServletRequest request,
                    HttpServletResponse response)
      throws IOException, ServletException {
    try {
      response.setContentType("text/xml");
      Document doc = new Jokes(getServletContext()).getJokes();
      String xslt =
        getServletContext().getInitParameter("CategoriesXSLT");
      XSLTransformer t = new XSLTransformer(xslt);
      new XMLOutputter().output(t.transform(doc),
                                      response.getWriter());
    } catch (Exception e) {
      response.sendError(500, "Internal error");
    }
  }
}
```

A more robust version will properly catch all exceptions and write to the log:

```
public class List extends HttpServlet {
  public void doGet(HttpServletRequest request,
                    HttpServletResponse response) {
    try {
      response.setContentType("text/xml");
      Document doc = null;
      try {
        doc = new Jokes(getServletContext()).getJokes();
      } catch (IOException e) {
        throw new ServletException("Unable to get jokes "+
                                      e.getMessage());
      } catch (JDOMException e) {
        throw new ServletException("Unable to create new document "+
                                      e.getMessage());
      }
      XSLTransformer t = null;
      try {
        String xslt =
          getServletContext().getInitParameter("CategoriesXSLT");
        t = new XSLTransformer(xslt);
```

```
      } catch (XSLTransformException e) {
        throw new ServletException("Failed to create XSLT "+
                                   e.getMessage());
      }
      Writer out = null;
      try {
        out = response.getWriter();
      } catch (IOException e) {
        throw new ServletException("Unable to create writer "+
                                   e.getMessage());
      }
      try {
        new XMLOutputter().output(t.transform(doc), out);
      } catch (XSLTransformException e) {
        throw new ServletException(
             "Failed to perform XSL Transformation "+e.getMessage());
      } catch (IOException e) {
        throw new ServletException("Failed to output document "+
                                   e.getMessage());
      }
    } catch (ServletException e) {
      log(e.getMessage);
      response.sendError(500, "Internal error");
    }
  }
}
```

Other general robustness issues regarding servlets were discussed in Section 9.2.4.

12.8 Reflections

The application we have presented covers many of the aspects we have presented in this book, but is, of course, too tiny to justify some of the larger frameworks, as mentioned below.

We create several new XML languages to represent our data, following a conceptual analysis of the application domain. We then use XML Schema to provide formal documentation of this language and associate an XSLT stylesheet to perform a translation into XHTML. XSLT is also used to perform simple queries on the data (XQuery or JDOM could be used alternatively).

We create a server to function as a repository of data, by implementing a servlet for each required operation. Communication with this server is performed using XML over HTTP (SOAP could have been used instead). The JDOM framework is used for internal manipulations of XML data, and XML Schema is used for server side validation of the input documents (JAXB could have been used for this).

We use a metaserver to provide discovery of available servers, which must be manually registered (UDDI could play this part).

A multitude of clients may be implemented. They can exploit the network of servers, as long as they obey a simple protocol (which ideally could be defined using WSDL). We provide a particularly simple server, which is implemented as a collaboration of servlets and JSP pages using JSTL and server side XSLT stylesheets (we could here have used a more formal MVC framework such as Struts). Also, other servers could define more fancy HTML pages instead of the rather drab look we have implemented.

12.9 Exercises

The main lessons to be learned from these exercises are:

- how to refine the current implementation of The Web of Jokes; and
- choosing the right XML and Web technologies for a given task.

Exercise 12.1 Extend the joke language to allow HTML-like markup in the main data, corresponding to the tags b, i, and br. Make the necessary changes throughout the project.

Exercise 12.2 Modify the joke client to obtain a more fancy layout of the generated pages.

Exercise 12.3 The current implementation of the joke client assumes that servers always respond.

(a) Identify the places in the code where this assumption is made.
(b) Use nonblocking I/O (see Section 8.4.1) to remedy this situation.

Exercise 12.4 Discuss for each component of the implementation how alternative technologies could be used. For example,

- JDOM instead of XSLT in the List servlet;
- JAXB instead of JDOM in the Jokes class;
- SOAP instead of raw XML over HTTP for the communication;
- WSDL for formalizing the interface of the server; or
- UDDI instead of the metaserver.

BIBLIOGRAPHY

[1] Murray Altheim, Frank Boumphrey, Sam Dooley, Shane McCarron, Sebastian Schnitzenbaumer, and Ted Wugofski. Modularization of XHTML, April 2001. W3C Recommendation. `http://www.w3.org/TR/xhtml-modularization/`.

[2] Murray Altheim and Shane McCarron. XHTML 1.1 – module-based XHTML, May 2001. W3C Recommendation. `http://www.w3.org/TR/xhtml11/`.

[3] Michael Benedikt, Wenfei Fan, and Gabriel M. Kuper. Structural properties of XPath fragments. In *Proc. 9th International Conference on Database Theory, ICDT '03*, volume 2572 of *LNCS*, pages 79–95. Springer-Verlag, 2003.

[4] Anders Berglund, Scott Boag, Don Chamberlin, Mary F. Fernández, Michael Kay, Jonathan Robie, and Jérôme Siméon. XML Path Language (XPath) 2.0, April 2005. W3C Working Draft. `http://www.w3.org/TR/xpath20/`.

[5] Tim Berners-Lee. The original HTTP as defined in 1991. `http://www.w3.org/Protocols/HTTP/AsImplemented.html`.

[6] Tim Berners-Lee. *Weaving the Web*. Harper-Collins, 1999.

[7] Geert Jan Bex, Sebastian Maneth, and Frank Neven. A formal model for an expressive fragment of XSLT. *Information Systems*, 27(1):21–39, 2002.

[8] Geert Jan Bex, Frank Neven, and Jan Van den Bussche. DTDs versus XML schema: A practical study. In *Proc. 7th International Workshop on the Web and Databases, WebDB '04*, pages 79–84, June 2004.

[9] Paul V. Biron and Ashok Malhotra. XML Schema part 2: Datatypes second edition, October 2004. W3C Recommendation. `http://www.w3.org/TR/xmlschema-2/`.

[10] Scott Boag, Don Chamberlin, Mary F. Fernández, Daniela Florescu, Jonathan Robie, and Jérôme Siméon. XQuery 1.0: An XML Query Language, April 2005. W3C Working Draft. `http://www.w3.org/TR/xquery/`.

[11] Bert Bos, Tantek Çelik, Ian Hickson, and Håkon Wium Lie. Cascading Style Sheets, level 2 revision 1, February 2004. W3C Candidate Recommendation. `http://www.w3.org/TR/CSS21`.

[12] Henning Böttger, Anders Møller, and Michael I. Schwartzbach. Contracts for cooperation between Web service programmers and HTML designers. *Journal of Web Engineering*, 2006.

[13] Tim Bray, Dave Hollander, Andrew Layman, and Richard Tobin. Namespaces in XML 1.1, February 2004. W3C Recommendation. `http://www.w3.org/TR/xml-names11`.

[14] Tim Bray, Jean Paoli, C. M. Sperberg-McQueen, Eve Maler, and François Yergeau. Extensible Markup Language (XML) 1.0 (third edition), February 2004. W3C Recommendation. `http://www.w3.org/TR/REC-xml`.

[15] Tim Bray, Jean Paoli, C. M. Sperberg-McQueen, Eve Maler, François Yergeau, and John Cowan. Extensible Markup Language (XML) 1.1, February 2004. W3C Recommendation. `http://www.w3.org/TR/xml11/`.

[16] Don Chamberlin, Denise Draper, Mary Fernández, Michael Kay, Jonathan Robie, Michael Rys, Jérôme Siméon, Jim Tivy, and Philip Wadler. *XQuery by The Experts*. Addison Wesley, 2004.

[17] Don Chamberlin and Jonathan Robie. XQuery Update Facility Requirements, February 2005. W3C Working Draft `http://www.w3.org/TR/2005/WD-xquery-update-requirements-20050211/`.

[18] Akmal B. Chaudhri, Awais Rashid, and Roberto Zicari. *ML Data Management: Native XML and XML-Enabled Database Systems*. Addison Wesley, 2003.

[19] Roberto Chinnici, Martin Gudgin, Jean-Jacques Moreau, Jeffrey Schlimmer, and Sanjiva Weerawarana. Web services description language (WSDL) version 2.0 part 1: Core language, August 2004. W3C Working Draft. `http://www.w3.org/TR/wsdl20`.

[20] Aske Simon Christensen, Anders Møller, and Michael I. Schwartzbach. Extending Java for high-level Web service construction. *ACM Transactions on Programming Languages and Systems*, 25(6):814–875, November 2003.

[21] James Clark. Comparison of SGML and XML, December 1997. W3C Note. `http://www.w3.org/TR/NOTE-sgml-xml.html`.

[22] James Clark. An algorithm for RELAX NG validation, February 2002. `http://www.thaiopensource.com/relaxng/derivative.html`.

[23] James Clark and Makoto Murata. RELAX NG specification, December 2001. OASIS. `http://www.oasis-open.org/committees/relax-ng/spec-20011203.html`.

[24] Luc Clement, Andrew Hately, Claus von Riegen, and Tony Rogers. UDDI Version 3.0.2, October 2004. OASIS. `http://uddi.org/pubs/uddi_v3.htm`.

[25] Douglas E. Comer. *Internetworking with TCP/IP*. Prentice-Hall, fourth edition, 2000.

[26] John Cowan and Richard Tobin. XML information set, February 2004. W3C Recommendation. `http://www.w3.org/TR/xml-infoset/`.

[27] Steve Deering and Robert Hinden. Internet Protocol, version 6 (IPv6), December 1998. IETF RFC 2460.

[28] David DeHaan, David Toman, Mariano P. Consens, and M. Tamer Özsu. A comprehensive XQuery to SQL translation using dynamic interval encoding. In *Proc. International Conference on Management of Data, SIGMOD '03*, pages 623–634. ACM, June 2003.

[29] Tim Dierks and Christopher Allen. The TLS protocol, version 1.0, January 1999. IETF RFC 2246.

[30] Ce Dong and James Bailey. Static analysis of XSLT programs. In *Proc. 15th Australasian Database Conference, ADC '04*, pages 151–160, January 2004.

[31] Mary F. Fernández. Implementing XQuery 1.0: The story of Galax. In *Proc.*

Datenbanksysteme für Business, Technologie und Web, BTW '05, LNI, pages 30–47, March 2005.

[32] Mary F. Fernández and Jérôme Siméon. Growing XQuery. In *Proc. 17th European Conference on Object-Oriented Programming, ECOOP '03*, volume 3363 of *LNCS*, pages 405–430. Springer-Verlag, July 2003.

[33] Mary F. Fernández, Yana Kadiyska, Dan Suciu, Atsuyuki Morishima, and Wang Chiew Tan. SilkRoute: A framework for publishing relational data in XML. *ACM Transactions on Database Systems*, 27(4):438–493, 2002.

[34] Mary F. Fernández, Lucian Popa, and Dan Suciu. A structure-based approach to querying semi-structured data. In *Proc. 6th International Workshop on Database Programming Languages, DBPL '97*, volume 1369 of *LNCS*, pages 136–159. Springer-Verlag, 1997.

[35] Roy T. Fielding, Jim Gettys, Jeffrey C. Mogul, Henrik Frystyk Nielsen, Larry Masinter, Paul J. Leach, and Tim Berners-Lee. Hypertext Transfer Protocol – HTTP/1.1, June 1999. IETF RFC 2616.

[36] Roy T. Fielding and Richard N. Taylor. Principled design of the modern Web architecture. *ACM Transactions on Internet Technology*, 2(2):115–150, 2002.

[37] Achille Fokoue, Kristoffer Rose, Jérôme Siméon, and Lionel Villard. Compiling XSLT 2.0 into XQuery 1.0. In *Proc. 14th International World Wide Web Conference, WWW '05*. W3C, May 2005.

[38] Georg Gottlob, Christoph Koch, and Reinhard Pichler. XPath processing in a nutshell. *SIGMOD Record*, 32(1):12–19, 2003.

[39] Georg Gottlob, Christoph Koch, and Reinhard Pichler. XPath query evaluation: Improving time and space efficiency. In *Proc. 19th International Conference on Data Engineering, ICDE '03*, pages 379–390. IEEE Computer Society, 2003.

[40] Martin Gudgin, Marc Hadley, Noah Mendelsohn, Jean-Jacques Moreau, and Henrik Frystyk Nielsen. SOAP version 1.2 part 1: Messaging framework, June 2003. W3C Recommendation. `http://www.w3.org/TR/soap12-part1/`.

[41] Martin Gudgin, Marc Hadley, Noah Mendelsohn, Jean-Jacques Moreau, and Henrik Frystyk Nielsen. SOAP version 1.2 part 2: Adjuncts, June 2003. W3C Recommendation. `http://www.w3.org/TR/soap12-part2/`.

[42] Martin Gudgin, Amy Lewis, and Jeffrey Schlimmer. Web services description language (WSDL) version 2.0 part 2: Predefined extensions, August 2004. W3C Working Draft. `http://www.w3.org/TR/wsdl20-extensions`.

[43] Hugo Haas, Philippe Le Hégaret, Jean-Jacques Moreau, David Orchard, Jeffrey Schlimmer, and Sanjiva Weerawarana. Web services description language (WSDL) version 2.0 part 3: Bindings, August 2004. W3C Working Draft. `http://www.w3.org/TR/wsdl20-bindings`.

[44] Jan Hidders. Satisfiability of XPath expressions. In *Proc. 9th International Workshop on Database Programming Languages, DBPL '03*, volume 2921 of *LNCS*, pages 21–36. Springer-Verlag, 2003.

[45] John E. Hopcroft and Jeffrey D. Ullman. *Introduction to Automata Theory, Languages and Computation*. Addison-Wesley, April 1979.

[46] Haruo Hosoya and Benjamin C. Pierce. XDuce: A statically typed XML processing language. *ACM Transactions on Internet Technology*, 3(2), 2003.

[47] Haruo Hosoya, Jerome Vouillon, and Benjamin C. Pierce. Regular expression types for XML. *ACM Transactions on Programming Languages and Systems*, 2004.

[48] Michael Kay. XSL Transformations (XSLT) Version 2.0, April 2005. W3C Working Draft. `http://www.w3.org/TR/xslt20/`.

[49] Stephan Kepser. A simple proof of the Turing-completeness of XSLT and XQuery. Extreme Markup Languages 2004.

[50] Christian Kirkegaard, Aske Simon Christensen, and Anders Møller. A runtime system for XML transformations in Java. In *Proc. Second International XML Database Symposium, XSym '04*, volume 3186 of *LNCS*. Springer-Verlag, August 2004.

[51] Christian Kirkegaard, Anders Møller, and Michael I. Schwartzbach. Static analysis of XML transformations in Java. *IEEE Transactions on Software Engineering*, 30(3):181–192, March 2004.

[52] Nils Klarlund, Anders Møller, and Michael I. Schwartzbach. The DSD schema language. *Automated Software Engineering*, 9(3):285–319, 2002. Kluwer.

[53] Balachander Krishnamurthy, Jeffrey C. Mogul, and David M. Kristol. Key differences between HTTP/1.0 and HTTP/1.1. *Computer Networks*, 31(11–16):1737–1751, May 1999.

[54] David M. Kristol and Lou Montulli. HTTP state management mechanism, October 2000. IETF RFC 2965.

[55] Stephan Lechner, Günter Preuner, and Michael Schrefl. Translating XQuery into XSLT. In *ER 2001 Workshops*, volume 2465 of *LNCS*, pages 239–252. Springer-Verlag, November 2002.

[56] Hartmut Liefke and Dan Suciu. XMill: An efficient compressor for XML data. *ACM SIGMOD Record*, 29(2):153–164, June 2000.

[57] Ashok Malhotra and Murray Maloney. XML Schema requirements, February 1999. W3C Note. `http://www.w3.org/TR/NOTE-xml-schema-req`.

[58] Jonathan Marsh. XML Base, June 2001. W3C Recommendation. `http://www.w3.org/TR/xmlbase/`.

[59] Jan-Eike Michels. XQuery API for Java (XQJ) 1.0 specification, May 2004. Available from `http://www.jcp.org/en/jsr/detail?id=225`.

[60] Gerome Miklau and Dan Suciu. Containment and equivalence for a fragment of XPath. *J. ACM*, 51(1):2–45, 2004.

[61] Anders Møller. Document Structure Description 2.0, December 2002. BRICS, Department of Computer Science, University of Aarhus, Notes Series NS-02-7. Available from `http://www.brics.dk/DSD/`.

[62] Anders Møller and Michael I. Schwartzbach. The design space of type checkers for XML transformation languages. In *Proc. Tenth International Conference on Database Theory, ICDT '05*, volume 3363 of *LNCS*, pages 17–36. Springer-Verlag, January 2005.

[63] Makoto Murata. Hedge automata: a formal model for XML schemata. Technical report, Fuji Xerox Information Systems, 1999.

[64] Makoto Murata, Dongwon Lee, and Murali Mani. Taxonomy of XML schema languages using formal language theory. In *Proc. Extreme Markup Languages*, August 2001.

[65] Peter Murray-Rust and Henry S. Rzepa. Chemical Markup Language. A position paper, April 2001. `http://www.xml-cml.org/`.

[66] Frank Neven. Automata, logic, and XML. In *Proc. 16th International Workshop on Computer Science Logic, CSL '02*, volume 2471 of *Lecture Notes in Computer Science*, pages 2–26. Springer, September 2002.

[67] Frank Neven and Thomas Schwentick. XPath containment in the presence of disjunction, DTDs, and variables. In *Proc. 9th International Conference on Database Theory, ICDT '03*, volume 2572 of *LNCS*, pages 315–329. Springer-Verlag, 2003.

[68] Steven Pemberton et al. XHTML 1.0: The Extensible HyperText Markup Language, January 2000. W3C Recommendation. `http://www.w3.org/TR/xhtml1`.

[69] Jon Postel et al. Internet Protocol, September 1981. IETF RFC 791.

[70] Jon Postel et al. Transmission Control Protocol, September 1981. IETF RFC 793.

[71] Paul Prescod. Questioning the Google API, April 2002. `http://www.prescod.net/rest/googleapi/`.

[72] Dave Raggett, Arnaud Le Hors, and Ian Jacobs. HTML 4.01 specification, December 1999. W3C Recommendation. `http://www.w3.org/TR/html4/`.

[73] Eric Rescorla. *SSL and TLS: Designing and Building Secure Systems*. Addison-Wesley, 2000.

[74] Jérôme Siméon and Philip Wadler. The essence of XML. In *Proc. 30th ACM SIGPLAN-SIGACT Symposium on Principles of Programming Languages, POPL '03*, pages 1–13. ACM, 2003.

[75] Sun Microsystems. Java Servlet Specification, Version 2.4, 2003. Available from `http://java.sun.com/products/servlet/`.

[76] Sun Microsystems. JavaServer Pages Specification, Version 2.0, 2003. Available from `http://java.sun.com/products/jsp/`.

[77] Sun Microsystems. JavaServer Pages Standard Tag Library, Version 1.1, 2003. Available from `http://java.sun.com/products/jsp/jstl/`.

[78] The Unicode Consortium. *The Unicode Standard, Version 4.0*. Addison Wesley, 2003. `http://www.unicode.org/`.

[79] Henry S. Thompson, David Beech, Murray Maloney, and Noah Mendelsohn. XML Schema part 1: Structures second edition, October 2004. W3C Recommendation. `http://www.w3.org/TR/xmlschema-1/`.

[80] Akihiko Tozawa. Towards static type checking for XSLT. In *Proc. ACM Symposium on Document Engineering, DocEng '01*, November 2001.

[81] UN/CEFACT and OASIS. ebXML. `http://www.ebxml.org/`.

[82] Eric van der Vlist. *RELAX NG*. O'Reilly, December 2003. Available online at `http://books.xmlschemata.org/relaxng/`.

[83] Philip Wadler. A formal semantics of patterns in XSLT and XPath. *Markup Languages: Theory and Practice*, 2(2):183–202, 2000.

[84] Philip Wadler. Two semantics of XPath, January 2000. Available from `http://homepages.inf.ed.ac.uk/wadler/topics/xml.html`.

[85] Sanjiva Weerawarana, Francisco Curbera, Frank Leymann, Tony Storey, and Donald F. Ferguson. *Web Services Platform Architecture: SOAP, WSDL, WS-Policy, WS-Addressing, WS-BPEL, WS-Reliable Messaging and More*. Prentice-Hall, 2005.

[86] Wireless Application Protocol Forum. Wireless Markup Language, version 2.0, September 2001. Available from `http://www.openmobilealliance.org/tech/affiliates/wap/wapindex.html`.

INDEX

candidate recommendation, 28

cascading, 18

CDATA
  node, 40
  section, 42

`CDATA`, 102, 290

`CDATASection`, 287

certificate, 367, 379

`char`, 27

character, 25
  data, 41, 64, 396
  encoding, 26, 27
  reference, 42

`CharacterData`, 287

child, 35, 62

`choice`, 125, 170, 171, 175

`choose`, 206

client, 343

CML, 46

code point, 25

code unit, 26

coercion, 65, 74, 78

`Comment`, 287, 290

comment, 42, 64, 97, 99
  node, 37

`comment`, 201

commutativity, 66

comparison
  general, 76
  node, 76
  value, 75

`complexContent`, 131

`complexType`, 125

complex type, 114, 125
  extension, 131
  restriction, 132

compression, 44, 349, 353

conditional section, 108

confidentiality, 366

connection, 345
  persistent, 360

conservative, 334

`Content`, 290

`Content-Encoding`, 353

`Content-Length`, 353, 360

`Content-Type`, 353

content model, 98, 124, 166

content negotiation, 348

contents, 35, 41, 98

context, 17, 61, 193, 247
  item expression, 74
  node, 59, 61

  path, 398
  sensitivity, 112, 137, 157

controller, 455

`Cookie`, 364

cookie, 364, 406

`copy`, 201

`copy-of`, 201

CORBA, 467

CSS, 6, 16, 189, 501
  limitations, 189

data
  binding, 304
  model, 37
  oriented, 45, 100, 245

`data`, 174

database, 240, 277

datagram, 344

datatype, 70, 112, 114, 119, 174, 249

`Date`, 352

DCOM, 467

decimal, 70

declaration, 115, 163, 247, 430, 432

`declare`, 163

default
  attribute, 105, 149, 166
  content, 149, 166

`define`, 173

DELETE, 350

deployment descriptor, 407, 522

descendant, 36, 62

detach, 293

directive, 430, 433

discovery, 489, 492

distributable, 399

DNS, 345, 346

`doc`, 219

`DocType`, 290

`Document`, 287, 290

document, 9, 35
  ordering, 39
  oriented, 45, 100, 245

`documentation`, 142

`DocumentType`, 287

document type
  declaration, 96
  node, 40

Document Type Definition, *see* DTD

DOM, 286, 314

domain name, 346

double, 70

DSD2, 159

DTD, 4, 43, 96